NAMING YOUR LITTLE ALL-STAR

BABY NAMES FROM THE WORLD'S GREATEST ATHLETES

SCOTT RUBIN

AUTHOR OF *NAMING YOUR LITTLE GEEK*

Published by Familius LLC, www.familius.com
PO Box 1130, Sanger, CA 93657

Familius books are available at special discounts for bulk purchases, whether for sales promotions or for family or corporate use. For more information, contact Familius Sales at orders@familius.com.

Vector illustrations and cover photo sourced from Vecteezy.com

No artificial intelligence was used in the writing or production of this book.

Library of Congress Control Number: 2025943763

Print ISBN 9781641709637
Ebook ISBN 9798893960884

Printed in China

Edited by Peg Sandkam and Gretchen Picklesimer Kinney
Cover design by Carlos Mireles-Guerrero
Book design by Maggie Wickes and Brooke Jorden

10 9 8 7 6 5 4 3 2 1

First Edition

MIX
Paper
FSC FSC® C188448

Dedication

For my champions Chris, Benjamin, and Maximilian.
Your love continues to drive my creativity.

–S.R.

Disclaimer

An important note on gender: For organizational purposes, this book is divided up into "boys'" and "girls'" names based on the athletes and competitors who have had them. Further, in providing humorous advice for naming your children, I talk about sons and daughters specifically, comparing how they might turn out like the historical examples I've researched. I also make note when unisex names have been used for both male and female athletes. All of that being said, there's no such thing as a gendered name in English, and any name can be given to (or used by) boy, girl, trans person, or non-binary person.

INTRODUCTION

Choosing a name for a child is like the ultimate overtime—you want to hit a home run and not fumble the ball in the end zone. This book can help you do just that! *Naming Your Little All-Star* is one part baby-naming book and one part sports almanac, with over one thousand entries that discuss names, the athletes who have had them, and advice on how those names might shape a kid's future (for entertainment purposes only, of course). My goal is to provide parents (as well as anyone looking for names) with a fun, thematic resource, just like my first book *Naming Your Little Geek*. And you don't have to be a sports fan to learn about names and inspirational figures!

I tried to include as many athletes and sports/events as possible; hopefully you find your favorites alongside athletics and people you've never heard of. This book focuses on people who have achieved greatness and whom we can look up to—I have purposefully left out confirmed cheaters, violent criminals, and the like. The process was a case-by-case basis and your opinion on certain individuals may vary, and, of course, there's no way to know what trouble any athletes might have gotten into since the book was written.

Every name entry comes with one or more references to athletes, sportspeople, record setters, etc. The reference includes the person's name (which may be in a different first name/last name format according to language), their sport/event and any specialty, country of origin or country they've represented, and the impactful years they competed or achieved greatness. If the athlete competed in a team sport, the reference will also include the team with which they played the longest and/or won the most.

Like the stats on a rookie baseball card, the information in this book for *current* athletes is a snapshot in time, up to date only until the manuscript was completed.

Lastly, I highly encourage you to use this book as a jumping-off point for learning about different sports and events around the world!

A

BOYS

AARON

Sometimes translated as "exalted" or "strong," Aaron is a name that famously appears in the Bible with Moses's priestly brother. Strength is definitely an asset for athletes named Aaron, ranging from the X Games-medalist skateboarder Aaron "Papa Jaws" Homoki to the New Zealand All Blacks' halfback Aaron Smith, the most-capped scrum half ever on that team! Probably the most famous Aaron in sports is the longtime quarterback for the Green Bay Packers, Aaron Rodgers. Consistently ranked among the top NFL quarterbacks ever, Rodgers has a long list of records and awards, and was MVP when the Packers won Super Bowl XLV in 2010.

Give your kid an inner strength to succeed with the name Aaron and he'll go far, whether that's on the field or on a set of wheels.

Aaron "Papa Jaws" Homoki, Skateboarding, USA, 2011–current

Aaron Rodgers, Football (Quarterback), Green Bay Packers, USA, 2005–current

Aaron Smith, Rugby (Halfback), Highlanders, New Zealand, 2008–current

ABDALLAH/ABDOLLAH

An Arabic phrase meaning "servant of Allah" is the basis for a family of names including Abdallah and Abdollah, all of which have achieved impressive international athletic successes. Iranian freestyle wrestler Abdollah Movahed took home an Olympic gold medal, five world championships, and two Asian Games gold medals; and Egyptian volleyball setter Abdallah Abdalsalam has a massive trophy collection including thirteen Egyptian Volleyball League championships, twelve Egyptian Volleyball Cups, eight African Clubs Championships, six Arab Clubs Championships, an Italian Volleyball League championship, Coppa Italia, a Lebanese Volleyball League championship, six gold medals and a silver from African Championships, and numerous best server and MVP awards!

Consider one of these names for your son and teach him about volleyball, wresting, and table tennis; he may reach his own huge successes in one of those.

Abdallah Abdalsalam Ahmed Bekhit, Volleyball (Setter), Egypt, 2001–current

Abdollah Movahed, Freestyle Wrestling, Iran, 1959–1972

ABDELATIF/ABDULLATIF

Abdelatif and Abdullatif may be names that mean "servant of the gentle" in Arabic, but in athletics, their bearers are aggressive and powerful! Abdullatif "Latif" Alhmili of Saudi Arabia is a professional esports fighting games competitor who won the 2009 Evo *Guilty Gear XX Accent Core Plus* championship, while Palestinian soccer center back Abdelatif Bahdari has racked up wins, including a pair of Jordan Premier League championships, the Jordan FA Cup twice, a Jordan FA Shield, the Jordan Super Cup twice, a West Bank Premier League championship, the AFC Challenge Cup, and the Bangabandhu Gold Cup.

Encourage your son named Abdelatif or Abdullatif to play video games and soccer with his friends; you never know where inspiration will strike, and he can succeed in any sport or event he chooses.

Abdullatif "Latif" Alhmili, Esports (Fighting Games), Saudi Arabia, 2008–current

Abdelatif Bahdari, Soccer (Center Back), Al-Wehdat Sport Club, Palestine, 2001–current

ABDULRASHID

If you're looking for a classical, respectful name that can inspire strength and power in a child, consider Abdulrashid, which comes from the Arabic epithet Abd al-Rashid or Abd ar-Rashid, meaning "servant of the rightly guided." The name is world famous in freestyle wrestling thanks to one man known as the "Russian Tank," Abdulrashid Sadulaev, who has won two Olympic gold medals, five world championships, an individual World Cup gold medal, two gold medals at Golden Grand Prix Ivan Yarygin events, and many, many more to be considered the greatest of his generation!

Abdulrashid "The Russian Tank" Sadulaev, Freestyle Wrestling, Russia, 2012–current

ADAM

A very down-to-earth name, Adam appears in the Book of Genesis and is Hebrew for "human." Three former competitors on the world stage named Adam were anything but, seemingly superhuman in their respective accomplishments. Football kicker Adam Vinatieri set numerous records for points, field goals, and Super Bowl wins, earning three Pro Bowl appearances, four Super Bowl championships, and more. Cricketer Adam Gilchrist set records and consistently ranks among the highest-rated wicketkeeper/batsman of all time, while his emotional outbursts and penchant for "walking" have set him apart and earned him fans as well. Adam Malysz, meanwhile, is one of the most winningest ski jumpers ever with titles and medals in World Cups, Winter Olympics, and World Championships. And after retiring from that sport, he even became a successful rally driver!

Let an Adam in your family fly high, hit hard, and drive fast.

Adam Gilchrist, Cricket (Wicketkeeper/Batsman), Western Australian Men's Cricket Team, Australia, 1996–2008

Adam Malysz, Ski Jumping, Poland, 1995–2011

Adam Vinatieri, Football (Kicker), New England Patriots, USA, 1996–2019

A.J.

Do you want your child to go fast, especially if you like names starting with "A" and "J"? Then consider a combo set with the nickname A.J.! You can put pretty much any such names together, and we see athletes called A.J. with *Anthony, Allan*, and *Adam* combined with *James, Joseph*, and *Joshua*. These include speed kings like champion race car drivers A.J. Allmendinger and A.J. Foyt, no-hitter pitcher A.J. Burnett, and Great Britain's most successful luger A.J. Rosen.

Anthony James "A.J." Allmendinger, Auto Racing (NASCAR), USA, 2001–current

Allan James "A.J." Burnett, Baseball (Pitcher), New York Yankees, USA, 1999–2015

Anthony Joseph "A.J." Foyt Jr., Auto Racing (United States Automobile Club), USA, 1953–1996

Adam Joseph "A.J." Rosen, Luge, USA/England, 2003–2021

AL

Like *A.J.*, Al is a nickname for a variety of longer names, including *Albert*, *Alfred*, and *Aloysius*. Multiple Als appear in a few different sports, notably baseball, with outfielders Al Kaline and Al Simmons, who both started their careers in the 1950s, and auto racing with father and son multiple-Indianapolis 500-winners Al Unser Junior and Senior (specializing in IndyCar and Champ Car, respectively). Lastly, we can't forget Olympian discus thrower Al Oerter, the first athlete to capture the gold medal in the same event in four consecutive games!

Al is a great nickname for any "Al-" name and can guide your son to the winner's podium.

Albert "Al" Kaline, Baseball (Outfield), Detroit Tigers, USA, 1953–1974

Alfred "Al" Oerter, Track & Field (Discus), USA, 1956–1980

Aloysius "Al" Simmons, Baseball (Outfield), Philadelphia Athletics, USA, 1924–1944

Alfred "Al" Unser Jr., Auto Racing (IndyCar), USA, 1982–2007

Alfred "Al" Unser Sr., Auto Racing (Champ Car), USA, 1965–1993

ALAIN/ALAN/ALLEN

The name Alan (along with its many variants, including Alain and Allen) goes back to Old English and Brittany in the eleventh century, though its original meaning is uncertain. We see athletes with these names excelling around the world and in many different disciplines, from Alan Page and Alan Trammell playing football for the Minnesota Vikings in the 1960s and baseball for the Detroit Tigers in the '70s, respectively; to Formula 1's French star Alain Prost; Newcastle United soccer striker Alan Shearer; and Allen Iverson, one of the all-time basketball greats.

Pick your favorite version of the name Alan for a kid who can do whatever he puts his mind to.

Allen Iverson, Basketball (Shooting Guard/Point Guard), Philadelphia 76ers, USA, 1996–2011

Alan Page, Football (Defensive Tackle), Minnesota Vikings, USA, 1967–1981

Alain Prost, Auto Racing (Formula 1), France, 1980–1993

Alan Shearer, Soccer (Striker), Newcastle United Football Club, England, 1988–2000

Alan Trammell, Baseball (Shortstop), Detroit Tigers, USA, 1977–1996

ALBERT/ALBERTO

Albert and its popular variant Alberto are classic names, coming to us from a Germanic root for "noble" or "bright." They may not appear on "most popular names" lists these days, but check out some of the highly talented sports stars that could inspire a comeback! There's Italian Formula 1 legend Alberto Ascari, Cuban champion endurance runner Alberto Juantorena, Italian alpine skiing world champion Alberto Tomba, Russian luger Albert Demchenko, and slugger Albert Pujols, who won two World Series championships with the Cardinals.

Alberto Ascari, Auto Racing (Formula 1), Italy, 1950–1955

Albert Demchenko, Luge, Russia, 1992–2014

Alberto Juantorena, Track & Field (Sprinting), Cuba, 1975–1984

Albert Pujols, Baseball (First Baseman), St. Louis Cardinals, Dominican Republic, 2001–current

Alberto Tomba, Alpine Skiing, Italy, 1985–1998

ALEKSANDR/ALEX/ALEXANDER

One of the most heroic of all names dates back all the way to the ancient world, with Alexander coming from Ancient Greek meaning "protector of men." And you don't have to look to Alexander the Great to see people with this name achieving incredible accomplishments; just check out the long list of highly successful athletes, winners, champions, and record breakers from around the world named Alexander, Alex, and variants like Aleksandar, Aleksandr, and Alexandr. The USSR and Russia have produced tons of Aleksandrs who have reached international heights, notably Aleksandr Dityatin, who won a then-record eight medals at the 1980 Summer Olympics; Aleksandr Popov, who is called the greatest sprint swimmer in history; gold-medalist skeleton rider Aleksandr Tretyakov; and fencer Alexandr Romankov, whose medal count ranks him among the top foilists of the modern age. The USSR's wrestling dominance in the second half of the twentieth century was anchored by Aleksandr Medved, Aleksandr Ivanitsky, and Aleksandr Karelin, the latter two ranking among the top wrestlers of all time. Also on "best of" lists are ice hockey left wing legend Alexander Ovechkin and baseball's star slugger Alexander "A-Rod" Rodriguez!

An Alex or Alexander in your family may not necessarily be a protector of men, but you can expect him to excel in his chosen sport, hobby, or career and make a name for himself among his contemporaries and experts.

Aleksandr Dityatin, Artistic Gymnastics, USSR, 1976–1980

Aleksandr Ivanitsky, Freestyle Wrestling, USSR, 1962–1966

Aleksandr Karelin, Greco-Roman Wrestling, USSR, 1987–2000

Aleksandr Medved, Freestyle Wrestling, USSR, 1962–1972

Alexander Ovechkin, Ice Hockey (Left Wing), Washington Capitals, USSR, 2001–current

Aleksandr Popov, Swimming (Sprinter), USSR/Russia, 1979–2005

Alexander "Alex" (A-Rod), Rodriguez, Baseball (Shortstop/Third Baseman), New York Yankees, USA, 1994–2016

Alexandr Romankov, Fencing (Foil), USSR, 1974–1989

Aleksandr Tretyakov, Skeleton, Russia, 2004–current

ALEKSEI/ALEXEI/ALEXEY

The name Aleksei (with many alternate spellings including Alexei, Aleksey, and others) comes from Ancient Greek meaning "defender" and appears most often in Russia and surrounding countries. As we'd expect then, the most famous and popular athletes with this name come mainly from that part of the world. Among these have been Russian gymnast Alexei Nemov (twelve Olympic medals and multiple world and European championships), Belarusian freestyle skier Aleksei Grishin (gold medal at both Olympics and World Championships), Russian canoe pioneer Alexey Korovashkov (more than a dozen gold medals at European and World Championships), and Russian para-alpine skier Alexey Bugaev (multiple golds at Paralympic Games and IPC Alpine Skiing World Championships).

Alexeys are great wherever they appear, so feel free to celebrate your son with the name whether your family comes from Eastern Europe or not.

Alexey Bugaev, Para-Alpine Skiing, Russia, 2013–2018

Aleksei Grishin, Freestyle Skiing, Belarus, 1999–2014

Alexey Korovashkov, Canoeing, Russia, 2011–2017

Alexei Nemov, Artistic Gymnastics, Russia, 1996–2004

ANDERSON

As you might expect, Anderson comes from a classic patronymic meaning "son of Andrew (or Ander)." The name *Andrew* comes from an Ancient Greek root for "man" or "manly," and it doesn't get much more manly than a world-class MMA fighter and boxer like Anderson "The Spider" Silva. The Brazilian-American started learning martial arts as a child, and racked up quite a collection of black belt ranks in Muay Thai, Brazilian Jiu-Jitsu, and Taekwondo. Silva is credited with thirty-four wins in his forty-six MMA fights, and he held the UFC Middleweight Championship for a record 2,457 days with sixteen victories during that time!

You can name your son Anderson if your name is *Andrew* to go with an old-school tradition, or if you want to give him a fighter's spirit to dominate his opponents in or out of the ring.

Anderson "The Spider" Silva, MMA (Middleweight/Heavyweight), Brazil, 1997–current

ANDRE/ANDRÉ/ANDREI/ANDRÉS

Originally a French/Portuguese version of *Andrew* that developed via the Greek name *Andreas*, Andre has multiple different forms around the world, like Andrei and Andres, and appears with or without the accent. And wow, is there a variety of sports and events with athletes of these names! Just some of these include track and field (Canadian Olympic gold-medalist sprinter Andre De Grasse), bobsled (Germany's André Lange, who holds the most international wins ever in the sport), skiing (Swedish slalom gold-medalist André Myhrer), cricket (West Indies Andre Russell, who regularly tops the rankings of T20 cricketers), weightlifting (Belarusian Olympics and World Championships gold-medalist Andrei Aramnau), and soccer (top-ranked midfielder Andrés Iniesta of Barcelona). And one Andre stands out as a pinnacle in his sport: Andre Agassi, international tennis star and philanthropist.

Give an Andre (or André, Andrei, Andres) in your family the chance to try all different kinds of sports and athletics; he'll find one he really loves.

Andre Agassi, Tennis, USA, 1986–2006

Andrei Aramnau, Weightlifting, Belarus, 2007–2019

Andre De Grasse, Track & Field (Sprinting), Canada, 2015–current

Andrés Iniesta, Soccer (Central Midfielder), Fútbol Club Barcelona, Spain, 2002–current

André Lange, Bobsled, Germany, 2000–2010

André Myhrer, Skiing, Sweden, 2003–2020

Andre Russell, Cricket (All-Rounder), Kolkata Knight Riders, Jamaica, 2011–current

ANDREAS

If you've read the previous entry and assumed Andreas has a similar origin to *Andre*, you'd be right! In this case, the name comes directly from the Ancient Greek word for "man" and is in the same overall family as *Andrew* and similar names. Andreas is traditionally popular in specific parts of Europe, with major athletes following that natural distribution. First up is javelin throwing with Norway's Andreas Thorkildsen, who scored gold medals at Olympic Games, World Championships, European Championships, and the Continental Cup. On the snow and ice in the 2000s were Germany's ski jumper Andreas Wellinger, winning World Championship and Olympic gold, and Austrian luge phenom Andreas Linger, who racked up seven golds at various championship events. Competing indoors is Denmark's esports champ Andreas "Xyp9x" Højsleth playing *Counter-Strike: Global Offensive*.

You don't have to be from Europe to name a kid Andreas, but if you do, he may very well gravitate toward the javelin, winter sports, or video games.

See *Niki* for Andreas Nikolaus "Niki" Lauda.

Andreas "Xyp9x" Højsleth, Esports (*Counter-Strike: Global Offensive*), Denmark, 2011–current

Andreas Linger, Luge, Austria, 2000–2014

Andreas Thorkildsen, Track & Field (Javelin), Norway, 2000–2016

Andreas Wellinger, Ski Jumping, Germany, 2012–current

ANDREW

If you're looking for a classically "manly" name for a kid who's likely to pick up a sport using a ball, Andrew could be a good match for you. Coming to us all the way from the Ancient Greek word for "man," Andrew is hugely popular around the world and in many sports. And while there are some superstars in things like rowing (multiple gold medal–winning Andrew Hodge), the majority of Andrews play on fields or courts like and Andrew "Freddie" Flintoff, who reached the pinnacle of cricket in all of its different versions (ODI, Test, and Twenty20). Majorly significant Andrews have appeared in baseball (top-ranked pitcher in the Negro leagues and hall of famer Andrew "Rube" Foster and slugger Andrew McCutchen), basketball (Australian NBA champ with the Golden State Warriors Andrew Bogut, as well as Andrew Bynum, who won two championships with the Los Angeles Lakers), and rugby (megastars of Australia and New Zealand, respectively, halfback Andrew Johns and first five-eighth Andrew Mehrtens, both consistently ranked among the top players in their positions).

Andrew Bogut, Basketball (Center), Golden State Warriors, USA, 2005–2020

Andrew Bynum, Basketball (Center), Los Angeles Lakers, USA, 2005–2014

Andrew "Freddie" Flintoff, Cricket (All-Rounder), Lancashire County Cricket Club, England, 1998–2009

Andrew "Rube" Foster, Baseball (Pitcher), Chicago American Giants, USA, 1902–1914

Andrew Hodge, Rowing, England, 2002–2016

Andrew Johns, Rugby (Halfback/Hooker), Newcastle Knights, Australia, 1993–2005

Andrew McCutchen, Baseball (Outfielder), Pittsburgh Pirates, USA, 2009–current

Andrew Mehrtens, Rugby (First Five-Eighth), Canterbury, New Zealand, 1995–2013

ANDY

Andrew is a great name on its own, but some just embody a different spirit and become decidedly Andys. Andy can also be a nickname for other "A" names, like *Andreas*. As with Andrew, Andy shows up all over the place and in a lot of different events, though there is a different theme here. There are one-off all-stars like British European Touring Car Championship champ Andy Priaulx; and Andy Macdonald, who holds the record for most X Games medals in vert skateboarding, including eight golds. Interestingly, we see Andys tending toward a couple different fields, with several in combat sports: in 1893, Andy Bowen participated in the world's longest boxing match against Jack Burke, and Andy Hug not only is ranked as one of the greatest heavyweight kickboxers in history but also won multiple gold medals in karate tournaments and championships around the world. Where Andys really shine, though, is on the tennis court. Israel's Andy Ram won three Grand Slam doubles events, while USA's Andy Roddick and Great Britain's Andy Murray both hit the height of the sport with a world top ranking!

Andy is a great name on its own or as a short form, and if you use it for your child, make sure to start him on tennis or martial arts early.

Andy Bowen, Boxing (Lightweight), USA, 1887–1894

Andreas "Andy" Hug, Karate/Kickboxing, Switzerland, 1977–2000

Andy Macdonald, Skateboarding, USA, 1994–2017

Andrew "Andy" Murray, Tennis, Scotland, 2005–current

Andrew "Andy" Priaulx, Auto Racing (FIA Touring Car), Guernsey, 1998–current

Andreas "Andy" Ram, Tennis, Israel, 1998–2014

Andrew "Andy" Roddick, Tennis, USA, 2000–2012

ANTHONY

A patrician name descended from the Roman Antonii family name by way of *Antonius*, Anthony is best known in athletics from two big men in American professional sports. NFL Hall of Famer Anthony Muñoz ranks among the top offensive lineman of all time, having played thirteen seasons for the Cincinnati Bengals in the '80s and early '90s. More recently, Anthony Davis started his NBA career with the New Orleans Hornets before moving to the Los Angeles Lakers and immediately winning a championship. Both athletes also have a long list of awards and other accolades for their high level of play.

Keep up the tradition of noble and powerful Anthonys with the name in your family.

Anthony Davis Jr., Basketball (Power Forward/Center), New Orleans Hornets, USA, 2012–current

Michael "Anthony" Muñoz, Football (Offensive Tackle), Cincinnati Bengals, USA, 1980–1993

APOLO

Not to be confused with the Greek god Apollo, Apolo Ohno has the most medals at Winter Olympics of any American competitor, with two golds, two silvers, and four bronzes in speed skating events. Ohno, whose first name is said to be a combination of Greek words to mean "look out" and "here he comes," started his athletic career very early, competing in swimming and roller skating at age six. From there he found speed skating and never looked back.

You, too, can give a kid the gift of speed and prowess with the name Apolo (or the more commonly known *Apollo* from Greek mythology).

Apolo Anton Ohno, Speed Skating, USA, 1996–2010

ARNOLD

Originating in Old Germanic root words for "eagle" and "power" or "brightness," the name Arnold was first recorded in Francia in the seventh century, gaining popularity in medieval Germany between the eighth and eleventh centuries, and maintaining regular usage in German, Dutch, and English today. The early twentieth century saw some pretty impressive Arnolds, like Finnish speed skater Arnold "Clas" Thunberg, who won the most medals at the first two Winter Olympics, and Estonian weightlifter Arnold Luhaäär, who medaled in 1928 and 1936.

For most, however, there are two people that come to mind when you hear the name Arnold. Arnold Schwarzenegger began lifting weights in Austria in his teens, going on to win Mr. Universe and Mr. Olympia titles before a massive acting career and even a stint as governor of California. Finally, golf would not be the game it is today without Arnold Palmer. With a career spanning five decades, Palmer ranks fifth on the PGA Tour's all-time winners list, and his charisma, looks, and character helped drive golf's popularity among the public.

I can't guarantee your son named Arnold will become a legendary champion, gold medalist, or even bodybuilder/actor/politician, but he'll be your high-flying eagle no matter what.

Arnold Luhaäär, Weightlifting, Estonia, 1928–1938

Arnold Palmer, Golf, USA, 1954–2006

Arnold Schwarzenegger, Bodybuilding, Austria, 1968–1980

Arnold "Clas" Thunberg, Speed Skating, Finland, 1920–1932

AROLDIS

Bearing a rare Spanish-Caribbean name (that may have come from a root word for "temperamental"), Aroldis Chapman has made a big mark on the game of baseball. Ranked among the greatest relief pitchers, he has played in seven All-Star games, has won a World Series championship, was named American League Reliever of the Year, became a member of the 300 save club, and set the record for the fastest pitch in history at 105.8 miles per hour!

If you're looking for a unique name for your son that will set him apart as a reliable teammate who will always help finish the job, then consider Aroldis.

Albertin Aroldis Chapman de la Cruz, Baseball (Relief Pitcher), New York Yankees, USA, 2010–current

ARTHUR/ARTUR

As popular as it is, the Welsh Arthur is a name with uncertain origins. Various sources have been proposed (including the popular theory that it means "bear-like"), but it's well known that it became famous with the legendary King Arthur of Camelot. There are also several variants and related names, most notably Artur that has become popular in Eastern Europe. They may not be knights, but prominent Arthurs and Arturs in real life have succeeded at wrestling (Artur Aleksanyan, who won gold medals for Armenia across Olympic Games, World Championships, European Championships, and more), figure skating (two-time Olympic gold-medalist Artur Dmitriev, who has competed for the USSR, Unified Team, and Russia), and soccer (one of the best players of all time, Brazil's Arthur "Zico" Coimbra). Arguably none of these have had as much impact on their sport as Arthur Ashe did on tennis (he won three Grand Slam titles), in addition to his activism for equality, philanthropy, and legacy of raising awareness of HIV and AIDS.

Unleash an Arthur (or Artur) upon the world and he'll definitely make his mark.

Artur Aleksanyan, Greco-Roman Wrestling, Armenia, 2011–current

Arthur "Zico" Antunes Coimbra, Soccer (Attacking Midfielder), Clube de Regatas do Flamengo, Brazil, 1971–1994

Arthur Ashe, Tennis, USA, 1969–1980

Artur Dimitriev, Figure Skating, Russia, 1975–1999

GIRLS

ABBY/ABBYE

While *Abigail* has a somewhat demure history as King David's wife in the Book of Samuel and a meaning of "my father's joy" in Hebrew, athletes known as Abby or Abbye are known for their strength and toughness. Professional strongwoman Abbye "Pudgy" Stockton was a pioneer in women's bodybuilding. She co-organized an early women's weightlifting competition in 1947 and won the Miss Physical Culture Venus event in 1948. More recently, Abby Wambach began her stellar soccer career winning the NCAA Division I Women's Soccer Championship with the Florida Gators before playing professionally and on the international stage. Known for her diving headers, she's racked up record-setting goals and earned gold medals at both the FIFA World Cup and Olympic Games.

I can't promise a girl called Abby (or Abbye) in your family will be a famous athlete, but if she takes after these role models, she'll be strong with a hard head.

Abbye "Pudgy" Stockton, Bodybuilding, USA, 1948

Mary Abigail "Abby" Wambach, Soccer (Forward), Washington Freedom, USA, 2001–2015

ADELINE

From a Germanic root for "noble" or "nobility" by way of the French *Adele*, the name Adeline sounds old-fashioned—but it's ready for a comeback with an impressive wrestler leading the way! Freestyle wrestler and Colorado native Adeline Gray has won six world championships to date, along with medals in the Olympics, Pan American Games, and Pan American Championships while representing the United States of America all over the world.

Adeline Gray, Freestyle Wrestling, USA, 2011–current

AGNES

Seen as somewhat old-fashioned in the United States these days, the name Agnes still maintains a level of popularity around the world. Its origins extend back to Ancient Greek meaning "chaste," though it later became associated with a Latin word for "lamb." The name has also spawned various alternate forms, most notably the accented Hungarian *Ágnes*.

Interestingly, athletes with this name seem to be drawn to the water. Hungarian water polo driver Ágnes Valkai helped her team win the world championship in 2005, overlapping the career of swimmer Ágnes Kovács (a fellow Hungarian), whose mighty breaststroke powered her to Olympic gold and bronze medals and two golds and a bronze from World Championships. They both swam in the footsteps of Agnes Beckwith of England, who began setting records when she swam five miles across the River Thames in 1875 when she was only fourteen years old!

Of course, an Agnes (or Ágnes) is in no way restricted to just those events. On the contrary, a girl with this name could find that her talents take her in all sorts of interesting directions, such as basketball like guard Agnes Webb, who won the 1953 World Championship with the very first USA women's team; table tennis like German Agnes Simon, who won a set of medals at World Championships in the 1950s; curling like Swedish Olympic gold-, silver-, and bronze-medalist Agnes Knochenhauer; long-distance running like Kenyan three-time World

Cross Country Championships-winner Agnes Tirop; or artistic gymnastics like Hungarian ten-time Olympic medal-winner (five of them gold) and world champion Ágnes Keleti.

Agnes Beckwith, Swimming (Endurance Racing), England, 1875–1885

Ágnes Keleti, Artistic Gymnastics, Hungary, 1937–1958

Agnes Knochenhauer, Curling (Second), Sweden, 2011–current

Ágnes Kovács, Swimming (Breaststroke), Hungary, 1996–2007

Agnes Simon, Table Tennis, Germany, 1953–1976

Agnes Tirop, Long-Distance Running, Kenya, 2012–2021

Ágnes Valkai, Water Polo (Driver), Hungary, 2004–2006

Agnes Webb, Basketball (Guard), Nashville Business College, USA, 1953

AI

Depending on which characters are used to write it, "love," "affection," and "indigo" are just a few ways the Japanese name Ai can be translated, and so a girl that you give this name to will be loving, like the color indigo, and possibly excel at sports like swimming, golf, judo, or tennis! In this way she could take after luminaries like Olympic gold-medalist freestyle swimmer Ai Shibata; golfer Ai Miyazato, who won twenty-five professional events and reached the rank of number one in the world; two-time world champion and World Masters gold-medalist judoka Ai Shishime, who took home sixteen medals from International Judo Federation Grand Slam events and five from Grand Prix; and former tennis doubles number one Ai Sugiyama, who won thirty-eight titles and four Grand Slams.

Ai Miyazato, Golf, Japan, 2004–2017

Ai Shibata, Swimming (Freestyle), Japan, 2004–2008

Ai Shishime, Judo, Japan, 2013–current

Ai Sugiyama, Tennis, Japan, 1992–2009

AILEEN/EILEEN

Irish has given us the dual names Aileen and Eileen, possibly stemming from an Old Germanic source and the name *Avila* or from a variant of the name *Helen*. Fair warning, sometimes these names bring with them a love of going fast, so one in your family may be your little speed demon if she takes after pioneering British Grand Prix race driver Eileen Ellison, who won the Duchess of York women's race at Brooklands in 1932, or Scottish visually impaired cyclist Aileen McGlynn, who has won three gold medals, three silvers, and a bronze in track cycling at Paralympic Games along with five golds, six silvers, and two bronzes at Para-Cycling World Track Championships! Alternatively, she may have great accuracy and coordination like Dutch World Masters darts champion Aileen de Graaf; a love of water and diving into it like Aileen Riggin, who won Olympic gold and silver on the 3-meter springboard in the 1920s; or trekking across the slopes like Chinese/American freestyle skier Eileen Gu (Gu Ailing), who has collected two gold medals apiece at the Olympics, World Championships, and X Games, as well as a silver, a bronze, and a bronze respectively.

Aileen de Graaf, Darts, Netherlands, 2011–current

Eileen Ellison, Auto Racing (Grand Prix), England, 1928–1940

Eileen Gu (Gu Ailing), Freestyle Skiing, USA/China, 2018–current

Aileen McGlynn, Para-Cycling, Scotland, 2004–current

Aileen Riggin, Diving/Swimming (Backstroke), USA, 1920–1925

ALENA

The name Alena has various sources and meanings. It appears as a shortened form of *Magdelena* or *Helena*, a derivation of *Alexandra* or *Jelena*, and more. In the sporting world, Alenas come from Belarus with expertise in equestrian events (Alena Tseliapushkina competed at two Olympic Games) and canoeing (Alena Nazdrova has multiple gold medals in sprint canoe at European and World Championships).

Your daughter may not take up horseback riding or canoeing just because you name her Alena, but chances are good she'll like the outdoors and racing with her friends.

Alena Nazdrova, Sprint Canoeing, Belarus, 2016–current

Alena Tseliapushkina, Equestrian (Eventing), Belarus, 2005–2014

ALEX/ALEXANDRA

Alexandra is a popular feminine version of the name *Alexander*, which comes from Ancient Greek for "protector of men." Athletes with this name, and the unisex short form Alex, don't require men for their accomplishments, making it on their own in cool events like equestrian dressage (Norway's Alexandra Andresen), skeleton (Great Britain's Alex Coomber), handball (Brazil's multi-gold medalist Alexandra do Nascimento), and fencing (USSR's legendary foilist Alexandra Zabelina, who won a dozen gold medals at Olympic Games and World Fencing Championships).

Present a young Alex or Alexandra in your family with lots of options and she'll find a path to success, whether it's by riding horses, racing, playing ball games, learning the way of the sword, or by forging her own path.

Alexandra Andresen, Equestrian (Dressage), Norway, 2016–current

Alexandra "Alex" Coomber, Skeleton, England, 1999–2002

Alexandra do Nascimento, Handball (Right Wing), Brazil, 2003–current

Alexandra Zabelina, Fencing (Foil), USSR, 1956–1971

ALEXIS

Alexis (from Ancient Greek meaning "defender") belongs to the same family of names as *Alexander* and *Alexei*. There are currently two American athletes born with this name operating at the pinnacles of their disciplines. Alexis "Lexi" Thompson began her professional golf career in 2010 at age fifteen and has racked up eleven wins on the LPGA Tour. On the asphalt, Alexis Sablone tears it up as a professional skateboarder; with half a dozen X Games medals under her belt, she is ranked twelfth in the world as of this writing.

Make sure to offer your young Alexis (or Lexi) a golf club or skateboard and see how far she can go!

Alexis Sablone, Skateboarding, USA, 2018–current

Alexis "Lexi" Thompson, Golf, USA, 2010–current

ALICE/ALICIA

The names Alice and Alicia can both trace their roots back to Germanic words for "heathland" and "noble." There have been three pretty exemplary athletes with these names. Most recently, Alicia Sacramone achieved an impressive medal count competing in gymnastics events around the world, with a silver at the 2008 Olympics and four golds at World Championships. Alice Coachman started her track and field career in high school in the late 1930s and quickly became a high jump phenom. Coachman went to the London Olympics in 1948 and secured the gold; in doing so, she became the first black woman to win the top medal at an Olympic Games. And then there's Alice Marble. She was a championship tennis player in the 1930s, but that's just the start. She also campaigned to achieve desegregation in American tennis, leading to Althea Gibson's inclusion in the 1950 US National Championships!

Let these inspirational ladies be role models for a young Alice or Alicia in your family.

Alice Coachman, Track & Field (High Jump), USA, 1948–1952

Alice Marble, Tennis, USA, 1933–1940

Alicia Sacramone, Artistic Gymnastics, USA, 2002-2012

ALISON/ALLISON/ALLYSON

From a Medieval French nickname for *Alice* comes the family of Allison names. With some fun variants, like Alison and Allyson, there's a phenomenal athlete with each one in very different fields. Wheelchair fencer Alison Yu collected an impressive medal count in the Paralympic Games from 2004 to 2016, including seven golds, and Allison Pineau has gold medals for handball in Olympics Games, European Championships, and World Championships. Sprinter Allyson Felix is one of the most decorated track and field stars today, with over twenty wins in international competitions!

Whichever version of the name Allison you choose, giving it to a daughter will ensure she's on a path toward great success.

Allyson Felix, Track & Field (Sprinting), USA, 2003–current

Allison Pineau, Handball (Center Back), France, 2007–current

Alison Yu, Wheelchair Fencing (Épée/Foil), Hong Kong, 2004–2016

AMANDA

The name Amanda may come from the Latin verb "to love," but Amandas in the ring are pure fighters. Puerto Rican Amanda Serrano is a champion boxer with world titles who has made successful inroads into MMA, while UFC veteran Amanda Nunes is a reigning champion in two weight classes and consistently ranked among the best and fiercest women's MMA competitors of all time. Amandas aren't limited to combat sports; Canadian baseball player Amanda Asay scored medals with her team at the Pan American Games and the Women's Baseball World Cup before entering the crucial science of forest ecology.

Name your child Amanda and introduce her to martial arts and science early!

Amanda Asay, Baseball (First Base), Canada, 2006–2018

Amanda "The Lioness" Nunes, MMA (Bantamweight/Featherweight), Brazil, 2008–current

Amanda Serrano, Boxing/MMA (Flyweight/Bantamweight/Featherweight/Lightweight/Welterweight), Puerto Rico, 2009–current

AMBER

Amber is a classic name and comes from the word for the fossilized tree resin that has been made into jewelry and other decorations for thousands of years. Ambers in sports tend to move fast, like Australian wheelchair basketball forward Amber Merritt, who has won medals in Paralympic Games and Women's World Championships, and Canadian NASCAR racer Amber Balcaen, who has multiple wins in the All-American Series.

Just try to keep up with an Amber in your family!

Amber Balcaen, Auto Racing (NASCAR), Canada, 2014–current

Amber Merritt, Wheelchair Basketball (Forward), Australia, 2011–2015

AMÉLIE

Originally a French form of the old Germanic name *Amalia* (from a root meaning "work" or "activity"), Amélie has spread around the world and appears both with and without the accent. Famous athletes with these names have, of course, put a ton of work into their activities, like Canadian Amélie Goulet-Nadon, whose brief short-track speed skating career saw her medal in both Olympic Games and World Championships. Probably the most famous is French tennis star Amélie Mauresmo. A member of the International Tennis Hall of Fame, Mauresmo was a dominant force on the court, winning two Grand Slam singles titles and holding the world number one spot for five weeks!

Whatever an Amélie in your family decides is her passion, she will approach it with hard work and dedication that'll make you proud.

Amélie Goulet-Nadon, Speed Skating, Canada, 2002–2003

Amélie Mauresmo, Tennis, France, 1993–2009

AMY

Another "lovely" name, Amy comes from the same Latin word (*amare*) as *Amanda*. There are Amys winning championships in many different fields, making this a great name for any child destined for a full life and sporting accomplishments. Americans with this name include World Golf Hall of Famer Amy Alcott, who has five major championships under her belt; gold medalist gymnast and member of the 1996 Olympics "Magnificent Seven" team Amy Chow; soccer forward Amy Rodriguez, who was on the world champion team in 2015; and swimmer Amy Van Dyken, who won multiple gold medals at Pan American Games, Pan Pacific Championships, World Championships, and Olympic Games!

Amy Alcott, Golf, USA, 1975–1991

Amy Chow, Artistic Gymnastics, USA, 1990–2001

Amy Rodriguez, Soccer (Forward), Utah Royals, USA, 2005–current

Amy Van Dyken, Swimming (Butterfly/Freestyle), USA, 1996–2000

ANA/ANNA

An ancient name that appears in Roman literature, Anna is a Latin variation of a Greek name that descends from the Hebrew *Hannah* (root meaning "favor" or "grace"). The name, along with its shorter Ana version, shows up all over the globe and, subsequently, in all types of athletes and sports stars.

In winter events, speed skater Anna "Anni" Friesinger-Postma won nearly twenty gold medals for Germany in Olympic Games, World Allround Championships, World Sprint Championships, and World Single Distance Championships; Sweden's Anna Le Moine brought home gold in curling from the Olympic Games and World Championships; and paraplegic para-alpine skier Anna Schaffelhuber of Germany has won multiple IPC Alpine Skiing World Championships and Paralympic Games (including five golds at the 2014 event) over her decade-long career. Australian freestyle skier Anna Segal won slopestyle gold and two bronzes at Freestyle World Ski Championships and a medal of each color at the X Games, and Russian figure skater Anna Shcherbakova's growing medal and trophy collection includes Olympic gold, a World Championship, and a World Team Trophy championship!

In other events, Anas and Annas have excelled on their own, like Russian esports champion Anna "Ant1ka" Ananikova, who blows away the competition in *Counter-Strike: Global Offensive* tournaments; Greek pistol markswoman Anna Korakaki, who has won Olympic gold and World Championship gold; Swedish golfer Anna Nordqvist, who has won thirteen professional events and three majors; and French four-time world champion freestyle wrestler Anna Gomis.

Anas and Annas who have competed and won with partners and teams include Russian tennis doubles player Anna Kournikova, who reached the world number one spot and won sixteen titles and a Grand Slam; New Zealand rugby first five-eighth Anna Richards, who helped the Black Ferns to victory in four Rugby World Cups; and Cuban volleyball middle blocker Ana Fernández, who won three Olympic gold medals, two world championships, two World Cups, and more.

Lastly, there are a few sports and events that seem particularly suited to athletes with these names! The 1928 Olympic gold-medalist artistic gymnastics team from Netherlands included not one but two of them (Anna "Ans" Dresden-Polak and Anna "Annie" van der Vegt). In track and field events, Russian high jumper Anna Chicherova was an Olympic gold-medalist and world champion, and fans of sprint canoeing have cheered on Australian three-time world champion Anna Wood and Hungarian Olympic gold-medalist and four-time world champion Anna Kárász. Finally, the world of cycling has seen the exploits of Anna van der Breggen of the Netherlands, whose long list of wins and achievements include general classification at the Giro d'Italia Femminile four times, an Olympic gold medal and two bronzes, and three golds and six silvers at World Championships.

Instill your child with grace and a winning spirit with the name Anna and let her loose on the world to find her favorite sport or event!

Anna "Ant1ka" Ananikova, Esports (*Counter-Strike: Global Offensive*), Russia, 2015–current

Anna Chicherova, Track & Field (High Jump), Russia, 2011

Anna "Ans" Dresden-Polak, Artistic Gymnastics, Netherlands, 1928

Ana Fernández, Volleyball (Middle Blocker), Cuba, 1992–2004

Anna "Anni" Friesinger-Postma, Speed Skating, Germany, 1998–2010

Anna Gomis, Freestyle Wrestling, France, 1993–2010

Anna Kárász, Sprint Canoeing, Hungary, 2011–current

Anna Korakaki, Sport Shooting (Pistol), Greece, 2010–current

Anna Kournikova, Tennis, Russia, 1995–2003

Anna Le Moine, Curling (Lead), Sweden, 2005–2010

Anna Nordqvist, Golf, Sweden, 2008–current

Anna Richards, Rugby (First Five-Eighth), New Zealand Women's National Rugby Union Team, New Zealand, 1986–2010

Anna Schaffelhuber, Para-Alpine Skiing, Germany, 2010–current

Anna Segal, Freestyle Skiing, Australia, 2003–2014

Anna Shcherbakova, Figure Skating, Russia, 2007–current

Anna van der Breggen, Road Cycling, Netherlands, 2009-2021

Anna "Annie" van der Vegt, Artistic Gymnastics, Netherlands, 1928

Anna Wood, Sprint Canoeing, Australia, 1983–2001

ANASTASIA/ANASTASIYA

You don't have to be Russian to appreciate the name Anastasia (or its variant Anastasiya), though that's where all of the most famous competitors with that name come from.

While it's most popular in Eastern Europe, Anastasia comes from a Greek word meaning "resurrection." Among its bearers have been five-time Olympic gold-medalist in synchronized swimming Anastasia Davydova; professional *Counter-Strike: Global Offensive* player Anastasiya "Nast1a" Evdokina; and Anastasiya Kuzmina, who won multiple gold medals in biathlon at Olympics and World Championships for Slovakia.

Anastasia Davydova, Synchronized Swimming, Russia, 2001–2012

Anastasiya "Nast1a" Evdokina, Esports (*Counter-Strike: Global Offensive*), Russia, 2014–current

Anastasiya Kuzmina, Biathlon, Russia, 2006–2019

ANDREA/ANDREEA

In the same family as *Andrew*, *Andre*, and others, Andrea comes from an Ancient Greek word for "manly" or "virtue." And as with those, the name Andrea (and its variants) shows up around the world and has a slew of cool sports role models. These range from Germans Andrea Ehrig-Mitscherlich, who dominated long distance speed skating in the 1980s, and biathlon champ Andrea Henkel, who both have gold medals at Olympics Games and World Championships, to Romanian multiple gold-winning gymnast Andreea Răducan.

Andrea Ehrig-Mitscherlich, Speed Skating, Germany, 1976–1988

Andrea Henkel, Biathlon, Germany, 1995–2014

Andreea Răducan, Artistic Gymnastics, Romania, 1998–2002

ANGEL/ANGELA/ANGELIKI

Names and words based on "angel" stretch back to an Ancient Greek word for "messenger," as in a messenger of God. This has led to lots of different name forms that have been given to both boys and girls, though here we're going to look at a few ladies named Angel, Angela, and Angeliki. This trio includes champions on land, sea, and ice with basketball's WNBA star and gold medalist Angel McCoughtry, Greek world champion water skier Angeliki Andriopoulou, and Angela Ruggiero, who ranked number one in the NCAA for ice hockey and won medals at the Olympics with the USA team four Games in a row!

If you like the "messenger" and angelic aspects of these names, there are lots of versions of Angel/Angela out there.

Angeliki Andriopoulou, Water Skiing, Greece, 1988–2015

Angel McCoughtry, Basketball (Small Forward/Shooting Guard), Atlanta Dream, USA, 2009–current

Angela Ruggiero, Ice Hockey (Defense), Boston Blades, USA, 1996–2011

ANITA

If you like the classical origins of *Anna* or *Anne* but are looking for something different—especially if you're a fan of swimming, handball, skiing, or throwing things—consider the name Anita for your child. Anitas appear in many different fields with world-class athletes. However, there are some sports in which more champion Anitas tend; Hungary's handball elite include World Championship-medalists Anita Görbicz and Anita Kulcsár; Great Britain's Anita Lonsbrough and USA's Anita Nall have won Olympic gold in swimming events; skiing Olympians have included Norway's Anita Moen and Austria's Anita Wachter; and when it comes to hurling heavy objects, some of the best have been Hungarian shot putter Anita Márton and Poland's Anita Włodarczyk, who is consistently ranked as the best women's hammer thrower of all time!

Anita Görbicz, Handball (Center Back/Left Wing), Hungary, 1997–current

Anita Kulcsár, Handball (Line Player), Hungary, 1995–2005

Anita Lonsbrough, Swimming (Breaststroke), England, 1958–1962

Anita Márton, Track & Field (Shot Put), Hungary, 2009–current

Anita Moen, Cross-Country Skiing, Norway, 1992–2002

Nadia "Anita" Nall, Swimming (Breaststroke), USA, 1992–2000

Anita Wachter, Alpine Ski Racing, Austria, 1985–2001

Anita Włodarczyk, Track & Field (Hammer Throw), Poland, 2016

ANJA/ANYA

The distinctly European Anja and Anya can come from the same roots as *Anna*, though there are a couple of other possible derivations in Kurdish, Hungarian, and Berber specifically. If you're thinking of naming a child Anja or Anya, look no further for cool role models than Danish handball gold medalist Anja Andersen; foilist Anja Fichtel, who won golds at Olympic Games and World Fencing Championships for Germany; champion alpine skier Anja Pärson of Sweden; and German bobsled gold medalist Anja Schneiderheinze-Stöckel.

Anja Andersen, Handball (Back), Denmark, 1986–1999

Anja Fichtel, Fencing (Foil), Germany, 1986–1996

Anja Pärson, Alpine Skiing, Sweden, 1998–2012

Anja Schneiderheinze-Stöckel, Bobsled, Germany, 2001-2016

ANN/ANNE

From the same Hebrew root for "favor" or "grace" as *Anna*, Anne and its alternate Ann are also popular around the world and appear in all sorts of interesting places. American boxer Ann Wolfe won twenty-four out of her twenty-six fights and held three world titles simultaneously, Ann Trason's ultramarathon appearances set twenty world records and solidified her place among the best-ever ultrarunners, and International Waterski & Wakeboard Federation Hall of Famer Ann Procter of Australia won multiple championships during her career. Anne Donovan won gold medals for the United States in basketball at the 1984 and 1988 Olympic Games; on the ice and snow, American Anne Henning made a huge splash winning gold in 500-meter speed skating at the 1972 Olympic games at only sixteen years old; Anne Heggtveit was the first Canadian to win Olympic skiing gold (slalom) in 1960; and French Anne Floriet won gold in the 12.5 kilometer biathlon at the 2006 Paralympic Games.

The world belongs to an Anne (or Ann) in your family!

Anne Donovan, Basketball (Center), Chanson V-Magic, USA, 1984–1988

Anne Floriet, Skiing, France, 1998–2006

Anne Heggtveit, Alpine Skiing, Canada, 1954–1960

Anne Henning, Speed Skating, USA, 1972

Ann Procter, Water Skiing, Australia, 2001–2011

Ann Trason, Ultramarathon, USA, 1985–2003

Ann Wolfe, Boxing (Middleweight/Heavyweight), USA, 1998–2006

ANNIKA

"Grace" is something Annikas have in abundance, and it's just natural because that's exactly the meaning of the root of the biblical Hebrew name *Channah/Hannah* from which it comes. Graceful Annikas from the United States and Europe have become winners and champions in unique fields and sports, from bobsleigh (like German two-time world champion Annika Drazek) to biking (like Danish mountain bike racing world champion and five-time mountain bike marathon world champion Annika Langvad). The most famous person with this name in sports is one of the greatest golfers of all time, Annika Sörenstam! The Swedish athlete won a record ninety-seven professional events, a record ten LPGA majors, a record eight Player of the Year awards, and more. Sörenstam reached the lofty career grand slam in 2003 with at least one win at all four major championships, was the only woman to shoot fifty-nine in competition, in 2003 became the first woman to play in the PGA since 1945, was inducted into the World Golf Hall of Fame, and, despite being retired since 2008, is still the winningest LPGA player with over $22 million.

Name your daughter Annika and get her out on the links, though she'll be headstrong enough to figure out the perfect sport for her.

Annika Drazek, Bobsleigh, Germany, 2014–current

Annika Langvad, Mountain Biking, Denmark, 2011–current

Annika Sörenstam, Golf, Sweden, 1992–2008

ARIANA/ARIANNA

Another interesting family of names with various sources is that covering Ariana and Arianna. Those names can descend from an ancient term for Aryans, the people of Persia/Iran; a Latinized form of the Greek *Ariadne*; or even a Welsh word for "silver."

Where have women with these names made a name for themselves? Ariana Kukors set a world record during her swimming career and collected medals at Pan Pacific and World Championships, Italian champion fencer Arianna Errigo has won one of each Olympic medal and eight World Championships golds, and Arianna Fontana is an eight-time Italian Olympic medalist short track speed skater.

How high can an Ariana, Arianna, or similar in your family reach?

Arianna Errigo, Fencing (Foil/Sabre), Italy, 2009–current

Arianna Fontana, Speed Skating, Italy, 2006–current

Ariana Kukors, Swimming (Breaststroke/Freestyle/Medley), USA, 2006–2011

ASHLEY

The unisex name Ashley comes from a place name with Old English roots meaning "ash tree clearing." Multiple Ashleys have succeeded in several different athletic events, but they're certainly not locked into specific sports. They can really do anything, as proven by two-time world champion sprinter and World Relay Championship-winner Ashley Spencer; deaf four-time AMA Motocross champion Ashley Fiolek; and Ashley Kidd, whose status as one of the greatest wake surfers of all time is proven by her six world championships.

Competitors who have exemplified the grace and agility Ashleys are capable of include gymnasts like balance beam world champion Ashley Postell. The fastest Ashleys in the water have been Olympic freestyle gold medalist Ashley Whitney and long-distance swimmer Ashley Twichell, who has won a pair of each color medals from World Championships, while on the soccer field, Canadian Women's Player of the Year fullback/midfielder Ashley Lawrence's trophy and medal count includes an Olympic gold, a Division 1 Féminine championship, the Coupe de France twice, the Four Nations Tournament, and more.

Last but not least are the fastest Ashleys in the world, two legendary pioneers in auto racing. Ashley Force Hood (of the famed Force racing family) won three Top Alcohol Dragster races and two Funny Car events while achieving numerous firsts for women, including leading the NHRA Funny Car point standings, winning at Indianapolis, and winning in two different classes. Meanwhile, Ashley Freiberg won twenty-five races and two championships in Formula Mazda and became the first woman to win a Skip Barber Racing championship and the first woman to win races in IMSA GT3 Cup Challenge and Continental Tire SportsCar Challenge!

An Ashley in your family may enjoy hanging out in forest clearings, but she's more likely to be active and competitive, possibly preferring swimming, soccer, gymnastics, or tearing down the track behind the wheel.

- **Ashley Fiolek**, Motocross, USA, 2008–2012
- **Ashley Force Hood**, Auto Racing (NHRA), USA, 2004–2011
- **Ashley Freiberg**, Auto Racing (IMSA SportsCar Championship), USA, 2013–current
- **Ashley Kidd**, Wakesurfing, USA, 2010–current
- **Ashley Lawrence**, Soccer (Full-Back/Midfielder), Paris Saint-Germain Féminine, Canada, 2013–current
- **Ashley Postell**, Artistic Gymnastics, USA, 1997–2004
- **Ashley Spencer**, Track & Field (Sprinting/Hurdling), USA, 2012–2017
- **Ashley Twichell**, Swimming (Long-Distance), USA, 2011–current
- **Ashley Whitney**, Swimming (Freestyle), USA, 1996–1999

B

BOYS

BABE

See *Georg/George/Georges* for George Herman "Babe" Ruth.

BARRY

There are several distinct origins for the name Barry, including old Gaelic and Irish words for "fair-haired" or the more martial "sharp" or "spear." Barry can also be a short form or nickname for a variety of "B" names, including *Bartholomew*, *Barnabus*, and even *Barack*.

In the wide world of sports, the name Barry is inextricably tied to all-time greats in baseball and football. Top-ranked running back Barry Sanders absolutely dominated the NFL during his ten-year stint with the Detroit Lions, while America's pastime has several great Barrys, like World Series champ and twelve-time All-Star Barry Larkin of the Cincinnati Reds and Barry Bonds, who racked up fourteen All-Star appearances and multiple records, including most career home runs.

Give your kid the name (or nickname) Barry and he'll probably like playing catch with you.

- **Barry Bonds**, Baseball (Left Fielder), San Francisco Giants, USA, 1986–2007
- **Barry Larkin**, Baseball (Shortstop), Cincinnati Reds, USA, 1986–2004
- **Barry Sanders**, Football (Running Back), Detroit Lions, USA, 1989–1998

BEAU

All babies are cute, but you can hedge your bets on having a particularly good-looking son, and one who could excel in America's pastime or water sports, by naming him Beau. A French name meaning "handsome," Beau has seen success on the baseball field with MLB right fielder Beau Bell, who was selected as an All-Star in 1937, and on the water with Olympic gold and bronze medal-winning men's eight rower Beau Hoopman.

- **Roy Chester "Beau" Bell**, Baseball (Right Fielder), St. Louis Browns, USA, 1935–1941
- **Beau Hoopman**, Rowing, USA, 2001–2008

BEN/BENJAMIN

Biblical Hebrew gives us the name Benjamin, originally the son of Jacob and progenitor of the Tribe of Benjamin. The name itself is based on Hebrew for "son of the right hand,"

and in modern times is often shortened to Ben or given various nicknames like *Benny* and *Benjy*.

Athletic Benjamins and Bens run the full gamut, with Olympic and World Championship gold medalists on the water in swimming (USA's Ben Wildman-Tobriner), as well as on the ice in dancing (Ben Agosto), snowboarding (Benjamin Karl), and skiing (Benjamin Raich). There's also golfer Ben Hogan with the fourth-most PGA Tour wins of all time, Olympic gold-medalist and four-time MLB All-Star pitcher Ben Sheets, and probably the most famous athlete on this list, two-time Super Bowl champion Ben Roethlisberger, who has a long catalogue of career highlights and awards from his many years with the Pittsburgh Steelers.

Benjamin is a fantastic name, and any child you give it to will do you proud.

- **Benjamin "Ben" Agosto**, Ice Dancing, USA, 1989–2010
- **William "Ben" Hogan**, Golf, USA, 1930–1971
- **Benjamin Karl**, Snowboarding, Austria, 2009–current
- **Benjamin Raich**, Ski Racing, Austria, 1996–2015
- **Benjamin "Ben" Roethlisberger**, Football (Quarterback), Pittsburgh Steelers, USA, 2004–current
- **Ben Sheets**, Baseball (Pitcher), Milwaukee Brewers, USA, 2001–2012
- **Benjamin "Ben" Wildman-Tobriner**, Swimming (Freestyle), USA, 2007–2008

BERNARD/BERNIE

Not all Bernards and Bernies are like bears, though their names descend from West Germanic roots for "bear" and "brave" or "hardy." Where have Bernards and Bernies shown their courage? Five-time All-Star Bernie Williams won four World Series with the Yankees, Bernard Hinault won five Tour de France General Classifications as part of his 147 career victories in cycling, two-time NLF Pro Bowler Bernie Kosar won the XXVIII Super Bowl with the Dallas Cowboys, and Bernard Lagat has multiple world championships and records in middle- and long-distance running!

Meanwhile, ranked among the best ice hockey players of all time are slapshot innovator Bernie "Boom Boom" Geoffrion, who was on Stanley Cup-winning teams six times, and two-time Stanley Cup-winner Bernie Parent, who's considered by many to be one of the best goaltenders ever.

Will a little Bernard or Bernie in your family go on to great success in ice hockey or other sports? Possibly, but whatever he gets into, he'll tackle it like a bear.

- **Joseph Bernard "Bernie" (Boom Boom) Geoffrion**, Ice Hockey (Right Wing), Montreal Canadiens, Canada, 1950–1968
- **Bernard Hinault**, Road Cycling, France, 1975–1986
- **Bernard "Bernie" Kosar**, Football (Quarterback), Cleveland Browns, USA, 1985–1996
- **Bernard Lagat**, Track & Field (Middle-Distance Running), Kenya/USA, 1998–current
- **Bernard "Bernie" Parent**, Ice Hockey (Goaltender), Philadelphia Flyers, Canada, 1965–1979
- **Bernabé "Bernie" Williams**, Baseball (Center Fielder), New York Yankees, Puerto Rico, 1991–2006

BILL

The ever-popular *William* has lots of nicknames, including the short and sturdy Bill. There are tons of famous Bills out there, with a scattering across many different disciplines and interesting concentrations.

The fastest Bills include thirteen-time NHRA drag race-winner "Grumpy" Bill Jenkins and

NASCAR legend Bill Elliott, who won forty-four races and the 1988 championship in the Winston Cup Series, while the strongest have been five-time Mr. Universe-winning bodybuilder Bill Pearl and "strongest man who ever lived" Bill Kazmaier, who won the World's Strongest Man contest three times, a World Muscle Power Championship, and more.

The hardwood floors of the NBA have witnessed Hall of Famers in New York Knicks All-Star small forward, two-time NBA champion, and Olympic gold-medalist Bill Bradley; two-time All-Star center and two-time NBA champion Bill Walton; and Boston Celtics twelve-time All-Star center, eleven-time NBA champion, and Olympic gold-medalist Bill Russell, who was named All-Star Game MVP, led the league in rebounding four times, and was given the NBA Lifetime Achievement Award.

Football fans have cheered on Minnesota Vikings four-time Pro Bowl fullback and 1969 NFL champion Bill Brown, and Chicago Bears eight-time Pro Bowl middle linebacker, 1963 NFL champion, and Hall of Famer Bill George.

And then America's pastime has featured a huge number of Hall of Famer Bills, like Pittsburgh Pirates ten-time All-Star second baseman and two-time World Series champion Bill Mazeroski, who won eight Gold Glove awards; and New York Yankees eleven-time All-Star catcher and seven-time World Series champion Bill Dickey.

Whether it's in a team sport like baseball, football, or basketball; strength athletics; auto racing; or anything else, a boy named Bill in your family will be a skilled and fair competitor who will do you proud.

- **William "Bill" Bradley**, Basketball (Shooting Guard/Small Forward), New York Knicks, USA, 1965–1977
- **William "Bill" Brown**, Football (Fullback), Minnesota Vikings, USA, 1961–1974
- **William "Bill" Dickey**, Baseball (Catcher), New York Yankees, USA, 1928–1946
- **William "Bill" Elliott**, Auto Racing (NASCAR), USA, 1976–2018
- **William "Bill" George**, Football (Middle Linebacker), Chicago Bears, USA, 1952–1966
- **William "Bill" Jenkins**, Auto Racing (NHRA), USA, 1965–1975
- **William "Bill" Kazmaier**, Powerlifting/Strength Athletics, USA, 1978–1992
- **William "Bill" Mazeroski**, Baseball (Second Baseman), Pittsburgh Pirates, USA, 1956–1972
- **William "Bill" Pearl**, Bodybuilding, USA, 1953–1974
- **William "Bill" Russell**, Basketball (Center), Boston Celtics, USA, 1956–1969
- **William "Bill" Walton III**, Basketball (Center), Portland Trail Blazers, USA, 1974–1988

BILLY

While *Bill*s have a wide range of appearances with a preponderance in basketball and baseball, Billy is a bit of a different story. Considered at once more relaxed while also having more of a "bad boy" image than *Bill*, Billy appears in a similarly wide range of sports and events with a particular focus in baseball and football.

On the links, Billy Burke's career (winning seventeen professional events, including the 1931 US Open) overlapped with that of Billy Casper, whose seventy-two wins include three major championships, rank him seventh of all time on the PGA Tour list (with fifty-one wins), and earned him induction into the World Golf Hall of Fame.

America's pastime has seen stars like six-time All-Star left fielder and Hall of Famer Billy Williams, who was National League Rookie of the Year in 1961 and batting champion in 1972; and seven-time All-Star pitcher Billy Wagner, who was the 1999 National League Rolaids Relief Man Award recipient and threw a combined no-hitter in 2003. And lastly there are the football Billys with three-time Pro Bowlers like halfback Billy Ray Barnes and wide receiver/return specialist Billy "White Shoes" Johnson.

You don't have to be a bad boy (or play team sports) to rock the name Billy, so give it to your next kid and he'll go far in whatever he likes to do!

- **Billy Ray Barnes**, Football (Halfback), Philadelphia Eagles, USA, 1957–1966
- **William "Billy" Burke**, Golf, USA, 1928–1962
- **William "Billy" Casper Jr.**, Golf, USA, 1954–1989
- **William "Billy White Shoes" Johnson**, Football (Wide Receiver/Return Specialist), Houston Oilers, USA, 1974–1988
- **William "Billy" Wagner**, Baseball (Pitcher), Houston Astros, USA, 1995–2010
- **Billy Williams**, Baseball (Left Fielder), Chicago Cubs, USA, 1959–1976

BJORN

Are you looking for a fierce name that could inspire a child to greatness on skis or the tennis court? Then maybe Bjorn is for you! From a Germanic root for "bear," the name Bjorn has lots of versions with different characters depending on the language of origin, as well as variants like *Beorn*.

Athletes with these names are predominantly from Western Europe and tend to focus on sports on the water or snow, with German World Championship gold-medalist canoer Björn Bach; Norwegian cross-country skier Bjørn Dæhlie, who has dozens of Olympic Games and World Championship medals; Nordic combined skier Björn Kircheisen, who won a World Championship gold representing Germany; and Olympic two-time gold-medalist cross-country skier Björn Lind of Sweden. The most famous athlete with this name is tennis legend Björn Borg, who is ranked among the top tennis players ever with his seventy-seven singles titles and eleven Grand Slam titles.

- **Björn Bach**, Canoeing, Germany, 1997–2006
- **Björn Borg**, Tennis, Sweden, 1973–1984
- **Bjørn Dæhlie**, Cross-Country Skiing, Norway, 1989–1999
- **Björn Kircheisen**, Nordic Combined Skiing, Germany, 2003–2018
- **Björn Lind**, Cross-Country Skiing, Sweden, 2000–2010

BO

With an origin in Old Norse meaning "to live," Bo is one of the shortest names around and can serve as a nickname, a diminutive of names like *Bowie*, or a name all on its own. When it comes to athletes with this name, team sports are the name of the game. You can see this in everything from rowing (with Bo Vestergaard of Denmark, who won two gold medals, four silvers, and a bronze at World Rowing Championships) to baseball (with Toronto Blue Jays two-time All-Star shortstop Bo Bichette, who led the American League in hits twice).

Some Bos are truly multitalented, like Bo Jackson, who is the first and only American dual-sport All-Star as an NFL Pro Bowl running back and an MLB All-Star outfielder!

A boy you name Bo will be a quintessential team player on and off the field, eager to strive side by side with his friends and teammates. Introduce him to as many sports and events as possible so he can find his favorite . . . or maybe even *favorites*.

- **Bo Bichette**, Baseball (Shortstop), Toronto Blue Jays, USA, 2019–current
- **Vincent "Bo" Jackson**, Football (Running Back)/Baseball (Outfielder/Designated Hitter), Los Angeles Raiders/Kansas City Royals, USA, 1986–1994
- **Bo Vestergaard**, Rowing, Denmark, 1988–1995

BOB

A sturdy, down-to-earth name, Bob can be a given name on its own or a nickname of *Robert* or *Bobby*. We'll look at those names as well, but here we're looking at people who are through and through Bobs, and there are a lot of them! They range across all of the major sports and beyond, with examples in ice hockey (four-time NHL All-Star and five-time Stanley Cup–winner Bob Gainey), skateboarding (Brazilian fourteen-time X Games gold-medalist Bob Burnquist), water skiing (world record-setter Hall of Fame inductee Bob LaPoint, who has fifteen major championship wins), and track and field (two-time decathlon champ and Olympic gold-medalist Bob Mathias and high jumper Bob Beamon, who is best known for crushing the world record at the time by nearly two feet).

Bobs in the United States have congregated in this country's most popular sports. Starting with basketball, we have five-time All-Star power forward/center and two-time champ Bob McAdoo, eight-time All-Star center Bob Lanier, eleven-time All-Star power forward/center and champ Bob Pettit, and point guard Bob Cousy, who has a staggering thirteen All-Star appearances and six championships. Highly successful Bobs on the gridiron have included Baltimore Colts five-time Pro Bowler and two-time NFL champion tackle Bob Vogel, offensive tackle Bob Brown (who has six Pro Bowl appearances), Miami Dolphins six-time Pro Bowler and two-time Super Bowl champion quarterback Bob Griese, and Dallas Cowboys legendary defensive tackle Bob Lilly (who racked up eleven Pro Bowl appearances and a Super Bowl win).

Finally, you can't talk about Bobs without looking at the range of them in America's favorite pastime. Among the best of the best are Cleveland Indians seven-time All-Star and World Series champ pitcher Bob Lemon; eight-time All-Star batter and outfielder Bob Johnson; Cleveland Indians Hall of Fame pitcher Bob Feller, who has eight All-Star appearances and a World Series win; and Bob Gibson, who pitched for the St. Louis Cardinals on his way to nine All-Star appearances and two World Series championships!

Clearly Bob is a winning name, so give it to your little slugger!

Robert "Bob" Beamon, Track & Field (Long Jump), USA, 1967–1968

Robert "Bob" Brown, Football (Offensive Tackle), Philadelphia Eagles, USA, 1964–1973

Robert "Bob" Burnquist, Skateboarding, Brazil, 1992–current

Robert "Bob" Cousy, Basketball (Point Guard), Boston Celtics, USA, 1950–1970

Robert "Bob" Feller, Baseball (Pitcher), Cleveland Indians, USA, 1936–1956

Robert "Bob" Gainey, Ice Hockey (Left Wing), Montreal Canadiens, Canada, 1973–1989

Robert "Bob" Gibson, Baseball (Pitcher), St. Louis Cardinals, USA, 1959–1975

Robert "Bob" Griese, Football (Quarterback), Miami Dolphins, USA, 1967–1980

Robert "Bob" Johnson, Baseball (Left Fielder), Philadelphia Athletics, 1933–1945

Robert "Bob" Lanier Jr., Basketball (Center), Detroit Pistons, USA, 1970–1984

Robert "Bob" LaPoint, Water Skiing, USA, 1975–1987

Robert "Bob" Lemon, Baseball (Pitcher), Cleveland Indians, USA, 1941–1958

Robert "Bob" Lilly, Football (Defensive Tackle), Dallas Cowboys, USA, 1961–1974

Robert "Bob" Mathias, Track & Field (Decathlon), USA, 1948–1952

Robert "Bob" McAdoo, Basketball (Power Forward/Center), Los Angeles Lakers, USA, 1972–1992

Robert "Bob" Pettit Jr., Basketball (Power Forward/Center), Milwaukee Hawks, USA, 1954–1965

Robert "Bob" Vogel, Football (Tackle), Baltimore Colts, USA, 1963–1972

BOBBY

Like *Bob*, the unisex name Bobby is typically (but not always) a nickname for *Robert*, though it can also stand on its own or serve as a nickname for other names. Also like *Bob*, there are Bobbys all over the place in sports and athletics! Can we see a theme among them; are there more bad boy Bobbys than their more strait-laced *Bob* brothers?

Several men with this name have reached the pinnacle in auto racing, burning rubber and getting checkered flags in IndyCar (Hall of Famer Bobby Unser with multiple championships and the fourth-most wins ever) and NASCAR (Cup Series champions Bobby Labonte with twenty-one wins, Bobby Isaac with thirty-seven, and Bobby Allison with eighty-four).

Other Bobbys have triumphed in freestyle skiing (multiple X Games gold-medalist Bobby Brown), with even more focused in a few sports. Great American football players include four-time Pro Bowl halfback/flanker Bobby Mitchell; quarterback and placekicker Bobby Layne, who has six Pro Bowl appearances and three NFL championships; and Bobby Wagner, who has already racked up seven Pro Bowl appearances and a Super Bowl championship as a middle linebacker for the Seattle Seahawks. On the soccer front, the England National Football Team has featured multiple superstar Bobbys like two members of the 1966 FIFA World Cup-winning team (record-breaking goal-scorer Charlton and Moore, one of the greatest defenders ever in the sport).

Just like *Bob*, Bobbys have certainly made a name for themselves in baseball. These have included six-time All-Star second baseman Bobby Grich; six-time All-Star and World Series champ slugger Bobby Bonilla; second baseman Bobby Richardson, who has eight All-Star appearances and three World Series wins with the New York Yankees; and nine-time All-Star second baseman for the Boston Red Sox Bobby Doerr!

- **Robert "Bobby" Allison**, Auto Racing (NASCAR), USA, 1961–1988
- **Roberto "Bobby" Bonilla**, Baseball (Third Baseman/Right Fielder), Pittsburgh Pirates, USA, 1986–2001
- **Bobby Brown**, Skiing, USA, 2008–2016
- **Robert "Bobby" Charlton**, Soccer (Attacking Midfielder/Forward), Manchester United Football Club, England, 1956–1980
- **Robert "Bobby" Doerr**, Baseball (Second Baseman), Boston Red Sox, USA, 1937–1951
- **Robert "Bobby" Grich**, Baseball (Second Baseman), California Angels, USA, 1970–1986
- **Robert "Bobby" Isaac**, Auto Racing (NASCAR), USA, 1961–1976
- **Robert "Bobby" Labonte**, Auto Racing (NASCAR), USA, 1982–current
- **Robert "Bobby" Layne**, Football (Quarterback), Detroit Lions, USA, 1948–1962
- **Robert "Bobby" Mitchell**, Football (Halfback/Flanker), Washington Redskins, USA, 1958–1968
- **Robert "Bobby" Moore**, Soccer (Defender), West Ham United Football Club, England, 1958–1983
- **Robert "Bobby" Richardson**, Baseball (Second Baseman), New York Yankees, USA, 1955–1966
- **Robert "Bobby" Unser**, Auto Racing (IndyCar), USA, 1955–1982
- **Bobby Joseph Wagner**, Football (Middle Linebacker), Seattle Seahawks, USA, 2012–current

BODE

The name Bode, which comes from an Old Saxon root meaning "command" or "order," can inspire a boy in your family to great success in winter sports, though you should help him manage his expectations and stresses so he can enjoy himself without being overly concerned about victory. American alpine ski racer Bode Miller won a gold medal, three silvers, and two bronzes at Olympic Games; four golds and a silver at World Championships; and a monumental thirty-three golds, twenty-nine silvers, and seventeen bronzes at World Cup events, along with two overall titles and six discipline titles.

Samuel Bode Miller, Alpine Skiing, USA, 1997-2017

BORIS

You don't have to have Eastern European roots to use the name Boris in your family, though it couldn't hurt. This noble name comes from the ancient Turkic language Bulgar; some think it comes from a root word for "wolf" or possibly "short" or "fight." Nowadays, Boris remains popular mainly in countries around Russia, and it's sometimes used as a short form of other names like *Borislav*.

Where have athletes named Boris excelled? Boris Alexandrov was a member of the Soviet Union's Olympic gold medal-winning ice hockey team in 1976; Germany's tennis star Boris Becker won six Grand Slam titles and an Olympic gold medal while reaching the highest ranking in the world; American Boris Said has had a huge auto racing career with ten wins in the Rolex Sports Car Series and a Rolex Sports Car Series GT championship; not one but two Boris Gurevichs won Olympic gold in wrestling for the USSR (in 1952 and 1968, respectively); and Soviet gymnast Boris Shakhlin won nearly twenty gold medals in Olympic Games, World Championships, and European Championships.

Boris Alexandrov, Ice Hockey (Right Wing), Torpedo Hockey Club, USSR, 1972–1996

Boris Becker, Tennis, Germany, 1984–1999

Boris Gurevich, Greco-Roman Wrestling, USSR, 1950–1963

Boris Gurevich, Freestyle Wrestling, USSR, 1961–1969

Boris Said III, Auto Racing (Rolex Sports Car Series), USA, 1995–current

Boris Shakhlin, Artistic Gymnastics, USSR, 1954–1967

BRAD/BRADLEY

Bradley is an example of a place name originally connected to a specific geographic feature; in this case, Bradley comes from an Old English place name meaning "broad wood" or "broad meadow." The four-letter version Brad can be short for the "broad" full name, or stand on its own (there are lots of "just" Brads out there).

Athletic Brads and Bradleys have included rugby union lock Brad Thorn, who was the first to win a World Cup, a Super Rugby title, and the Heineken Cup; top ten Australian cricketer Brad Hogg; and cycling Olympic gold-medalists Bradley McGee of Australia and Tour de France–winner Bradley Wiggins of Great Britain. Here in the US, quarterback Brad Johnson had two Pro-Bowl appearances and a Super Bowl win.

Brads and Bradleys have a lot of potential, and the names are highly recommended even if you don't live in the woods or a meadow.

George Bradley "Brad" Hogg, Cricket (Bowling All-Rounder), Western Australia Cricket Team, Australia, 1993-2015

James Bradley "Brad" Johnson, Football (Quarterback), Tampa Bay Buccaneers, USA, 1992-2008

Bradley McGee, Track Cycling, Australia, 1997-2012

Bradley "Brad" Thorn, Rugby (Second-Row/Prop), Brisbane Broncos Rugby League Football Club Ltd., New Zealand, 1994-2016

Bradley Wiggins, Road/Track Cycling, England, 2001-2016

BRADY

If you're looking for a "B" name for a high-spirited boy who may be a solid anchor for his team, or who may enjoy baseball, ice hockey, skiing, or archery, then look no further than Brady! Brady comes from an old Irish surname (and possibly an older root word meaning "roguish"). In North American professional sports, Brady has the unique distinction of receiving three All-Star selections apiece in baseball and ice hockey with Baltimore Orioles outfielder Brady Anderson and Ottawa Senators left wing Brady Tkachuk, respectively. Meanwhile, on international stages, Canadian freestyle skier Brady Leman has won ski cross gold at the Winter Olympics and gold and bronze at the X Games, and record-setting former world number one recurve archer Brady Ellison has collected two medals of each color at World Championships; two golds and two bronzes at World Indoor Championships; six golds, three silvers, and two bronzes at World Cup events; and four golds, a silver, and a bronze at World Field Championships.

Brady Anderson, Baseball (Outfielder), Baltimore Orioles, USA, 1988–2002

Brady Ellison, Archery, USA, 2007–current

Brady Leman, Freestyle Skiing, Canada, 2010–current

Braeden "Brady" Tkachuk, Ice Hockey (Left Wing), Ottawa Senators, USA, 2018–current

BRANDEN/BRANDON/BRENDON

The primary origin of the name Brandon (and its variants Branden and Brendon) is humble, coming from an Old English place name meaning "hill covered with gorse," though it can also be connected to an Irish name meaning "prince."

Basketball fans have cheered on NBA three-time All-Star shooting guard Brandon Roy and Canadian wheelchair basketball Paralympic gold-medalist Brandon Wagner. On the ice, Canadian left wing Brendan Shanahan cemented his place among the greatest ice hockey players ever with a world championship win, an Olympic gold medal, eight All-Star selections, three Stanley Cup wins, and multiple records! On four wheels, Brendon Hartley of New Zealand has racked up twenty-one wins and four championships in the FIA World Endurance Championship series and three 24 Hours of Le Mans wins.

A trio of Brandons are celebrated three-time MLB All-Stars: Silver Slugger and four-time Gold Glove–winner second baseman Brandon Phillips; Silver Slugger and four-time Gold Glove–winner shortstop Brandon Crawford, who won the World Series twice with the San Francisco Giants; and National League Cy Young–winning pitcher Brandon Webb, who led the National League in wins twice with the Arizona Diamondbacks.

Many of the toughest Brandons have been drawn to the football field. Guard Brandon Scherff played in five Pro Bowls (so far!), and six-time Pro Bowl wide receiver Brandon Marshall was the 2012 Pro Bowl MVP, co-led the NFL in touchdowns in 2015, and set NFL records for most receptions in a game (twenty-one) and most seasons (six) with over one hundred receptions.

On the field, the track, the ice, the court, or the mat, a Branden, Brandon, or Brendon in your family will excel, achieving princely success and reaching the top of the hill.

Brandon Crawford, Baseball (Shortstop), San Francisco Giants, USA, 2011–current

Brendon Hartley, Auto Racing (FIA World Endurance Championship), New Zealand, 2002–current

Brandon "The Beast" Marshall, Football (Wide Receiver), Denver Broncos, USA, 2006–2018

Brandon Phillips, Baseball (Second Baseman), Cincinnati Reds, USA, 2002–2018

Brandon "B-Roy" Roy, Basketball (Shooting Guard), Portland Trail Blazers, USA, 2006–2013

Brandon Scherff, Football (Guard), Washington Redskins, USA, 2015–current

Brendan Shanahan, Ice Hockey (Left Wing), Detroit Red Wings, Canada, 1987–2009

Brandon Wagner, Wheelchair Basketball, Canada, 2007–2012

Brandon Webb, Baseball (Pitcher), Arizona Diamondbacks, USA, 2003–2009

BRETT

You don't need to have ancestors from Great Britain or Brittany in France to name a future champion in your family Brett, though it doesn't hurt, seeing as the origin of the name is the Middle English word for someone from those locations. A handful of Bretts have made a big impact in a variety of fields: NHL Hall of Fame right wing Brett Hull has a Stanley Cup win along with nine All-Star appearances, Australian cricketer Brett Lee was ranked among the fastest bowlers in the world, barefoot water skier Brett Wing racked up multiple world championships and records, and Brett Moffitt has thus far won a dozen races and a championship in the NASCAR Truck Series. Probably the most popular Brett in recent years is NFL quarterback Favre, whose twenty-year career saw him score eleven Pro Bowl appearances, a Super Bowl championship, and tons of other awards, records, and recognitions.

Brett Favre, Football (Quarterback), Green Bay Packers, USA, 1991–2010

Brett Hull, Ice Hockey (Right Wing), St. Louis Blues, Canada, 1986–2005

Brett Lee, Cricket (Bowler), New South Wales Men's Cricket Team, Australia, 1997–2012

Brett Moffitt, Auto Racing (NASCAR), USA, 2012–current

Brett Wing, Water Skiing, Australia, 1975–1982

BRIAN/BRYAN

Brian and Bryan come from an unknown Irish/Breton origin, possibly from an Old Celtic root for "high" or "noble." With its enduring popularity across different countries and eras, it's unsurprising to see professional athletes and sports stars with this name succeeding in a wide range of "fields," with some singular standouts in cricket (top-ranked batsman and record-holder Brian Lara of Trinidad and Tobago), skiing (US six-time Paralympic Games gold-medalist Brian Santos), and strength athletics (four-time World's Strongest Man-winner Brian Shaw). Brian is also a popular name among figure skaters, with gold medalist champions Canadian Brian Orser, French Brian Joubert, and American Brian Boitano.

Over on the ice, the Stanley Cup has gone to teams with defenseman Brian Campbell (four-time All-Star), right wing Bryan Hextall (three-time All-Star), and one of the top one hundred players in NHL history center Bryan Trottier, who has nine All-Star appearances and six Stanley Cup wins. Finally, the gridiron has seen epic plays by Pro-Bowlers Super Bowl-winner linebacker Bryan Cox (three times) and defensive legend Chicago Bears linebacker Brian Urlacher (eight times).

A kid you name Brian or Bryan can definitely find success playing sports alongside others or figure skating!

Brian Boitano, Figure Skating, USA, 1979–1994

Brian Campbell, Ice Hockey (Defense), Chicago Blackhawks, Canada, 1999–2017

Bryan Cox, Football (Linebacker), New England Patriots, USA, 1991–2002

Bryan Hextall, Ice Hockey (Right Wing), New York Rangers, Canada, 1933–1948

Brian Joubert, Figure Skating, France, 1988–2010

Brian Lara, Cricket (Batsman), Trinidad and Tobago National Cricket Team, Trinidad and Tobago, 1987-2007

Brian Orser, Figure Skating, Canada, 1980–1988

Brian Santos, Para-Alpine Skiing, USA, 1984–1995

Brian Shaw, Strength Athletics (Strongman), USA, 2005–current

Bryan Trottier, Ice Hockey (Center), New York Islanders, Canada, 1975–1994

Brian Urlacher, Football (Linebacker), Chicago Bears, USA, 2000–2012

BRUCE

Often considered a Scottish name, Bruce came over with the Normans having previously been a place name for people from Brix in Normandy (and possibly meaning "willow land"). Bruces have reached the pinnacle of athleticism in surfing (champion big wave specialist Bruce Irons), baseball (World Series-winner and six-time All-Star pitcher Bruce Sutter), wrestling (Bruce Baumgartner, who has a huge gold medal record count at Olympic Games, World Championships, World Cups, and more), esports (Taiwanese *Street Fighter* champion Bruce "GamerBee" Hsiang), football (career sack record-setting defensive end Bruce Smith, who scored eleven Pro-Bowl appearances), and water skiing (Hall of Famer Australians trick champion Bruce Cockburn and jump specialist Bruce Neville). Finally, two Bruces have really left a huge mark on the world since their too short but brilliant careers. Bruce McLaren was a championship Formula 1 racer and car designer, whose team and company bearing his name have gone on to be synonymous with the pinnacle of automobile racing and production. And arguably the most iconic person with this name of all time is Bruce Lee, martial arts legend, instructor, actor, director, and more.

Give your child the name Bruce and the drive to excel, and maybe introduce him to karate or racing to see if he has an affinity.

Bruce Baumgartner, Freestyle Wrestling, USA, 1983–1996

Bruce Cockburn, Water Skiing, Australia, 1951–1975

Bruce "GamerBee" Hsiang, Esports (*Street Fighter*), Taiwan, 2014–current

Bruce Irons, Surfing, USA, 1999–2008

Bruce Lee (Lee Jun-fan), Martial Arts, USA, 1941–1973

Bruce McLaren, Auto Racing (Formula 1), New Zealand, 1958–1970

Bruce Neville, Water Skiing, Australia, 1985–2001

Bruce Smith, Football (Defensive End), Buffalo Bills, USA, 1985–2003

Howard Bruce Sutter, Baseball (Pitcher), Chicago Cubs, USA, 1976–1988

BUCK/BUCKY

Buck can refer to a bunch of different things, including various male animals, adventurous youths, money, furniture, gymnastic or automotive equipment, and more. Correspondingly, there are numerous origins for the term all the way back to the Proto-Indo-European language. In modern times, Buck, and the more familiar Bucky, can be a name on its own or a nickname for just about anyone, which makes it perfect if you're looking for something cool to call your kid regardless of their birth name.

Bucks have reached fame and glory on land and on sea with two-time NASCAR Cup Series champion and Hall of Famer Elzie "Buck" Baker, and Robert "Buck" Halperin, whose incredible life included champion-level sailing along with a stint as an NFL quarterback. Bucks on the baseball diamond made a splash in the early days, particularly at first base with nine-time All-Star and World

Series champ Frank "Buck" McCormick and thirteen-time All-Star and three-time Negro World Series champ Walter "Buck" Leonard.

Give your kid the nickname Buck to inspire steady hands and quick moves at first base or beyond, or go for Bucky to inspire a love of speed and tricks like ten-time X Games gold-medalist skateboarder Charles "Bucky" Lasek!

Elzie "Buck" Baker Sr., Auto Racing (NASCAR), USA, 1949–1976

Robert "Buck" Halperin, Sailing, USA, 1959–1963

Charles "Bucky" Lasek, Skateboarding, USA, 1987–2013

Walter "Buck" Leonard, Baseball (First Baseman), Homestead Grays, USA, 1934–1950

Frank "Buck" McCormick, Baseball (First Baseman), Cincinnati Reds, USA, 1934–1948

BUDDY

Like *Buck/Bucky*, Buddy is a fun nickname that can go with any name, regardless of gender. Give it to a child you think will be particularly friendly, or who may have the passion for sports and athletics like heavyweight boxer and actor Jacob "Buddy" Baer, nineteen-time NASCAR Cup Series-winner Elzie "Buddy" Baker (son of Buck Baker), MLB's two-time All-Star second baseman Charles "Buddy" Myer and five-time All-Star third baseman David "Buddy" Bell, and legendary nine-ball player Cecil "Buddy" Hall.

Jacob "Buddy" Baer, Boxing (Heavyweight), USA, 1934–1942

Elzie "Buddy" Baker Jr., Auto Racing (NASCAR), USA, 1959–1992

David "Buddy" Bell, Baseball (Third Baseman), Cleveland Indians, USA, 1972–1989

Cecil "Buddy" Hall, Pool (Nine-Ball), USA, 1962–2011

Charles "Buddy" Myer, Baseball (Second Baseman), Washington Senators, USA, 1925–1941

BUTCH

Originally a nickname for butchers, Butch has become a classic English moniker for all sorts of different names, as well as people in general, with no real rhyme or reason governing its usage. In sports, Butches are most often found in team sports, which makes sense as comraderie can lead to giving each other nicknames. South African fly-half/inside center Andrew "Butch" James won the 2007 Rugby World Cup, and MLB catcher Harold "Butch" Wynegar received two All-Star selections during his early career with the Minnesota Twins.

Some Butches really like to go fast, like sprinter Harry "Butch" Reynolds, whose Olympic gold medal and three world championships came from 4x400 meter relay events, while among the most accurate can be counted Olympic team gold- and bronze-medalist archer Richard "Butch" Johnson.

The ice rink is where two Canadian champions with this nickname have dominated with four Stanley Cups apiece: All-Star center Robert "Butch" Goring and legendary four-time All-Star Montreal Canadiens defenseman and Hall of Famer Émile "Butch" Bouchard.

Whether your last name is similar to *Butcher*, *Bouchard*, or the like, or your son just has a tough demeanor, then Butch may be a suitable nickname for him. He may end up being a sturdy ice hockey player, enjoy precision sports or going fast, or something else entirely, but he's likely to be a staunch and supportive member of his team.

Joseph Émile "Butch" Bouchard, Ice Hockey (Defense), Montreal Canadiens, Canada, 1941–1956

Robert "Butch" Goring, Ice Hockey (Center), New York Islanders, Canada, 1969–1987

Andrew "Butch" James, Rugby (Fly-Half/Inside Center), Sharks, South Africa, 2000–2013

Richard "Butch" Johnson, Archery, USA, 1995–2012

Harry "Butch" Reynolds Jr., Track & Field (Sprinting), USA, 1987–1999

Harold "Butch" Wynegar Jr., Baseball (Catcher), Minnesota Twins, USA, 1976–1988

BYRON

From a humble origin in an English place name and Old English roots meaning "place of the cow sheds" comes the powerful name Byron. On tennis courts, Zimbabwean Byron Black ranked number one in the world in doubles with twenty-two titles and a Grand Slam win.

While chances are good that a little Byron in your family will enjoy playing tennis with his friends, he could also go solo and excel all on his own just like golfer Byron Nelson, who ranks among the best players ever having won sixty-four professional events and five majors and setting numerous records during his relatively short career in the 1930s and '40s!

Byron Black, Tennis, Zimbabwe, 1991–2002

John Byron Nelson Jr., Golf, USA, 1932–1946

GIRLS

BABE

See *Mildred* for Mildred "Babe" Didrikson Zaharias.

BEATRIX

Looking for a name that has a great pedigree and a long history of usage in Europe but isn't heard every day in the US? Beatrix has uncertain origins, though many think it comes from a Latin word for "voyager" or "traveler." No matter the source, Beatrix has lots of related names including *Bea*, *Beatrice*, and *Beatriz*. Going back in time a bit, we can find some American sports pioneers with turn-of-the-twentieth-century golfer Beatrix Hoyt, who won the US Women's Amateur tournament three years running, and six-time national champion figure skater Beatrix Loughran, who is the only American to win three Olympic medals in the sport.

Beatrix Hoyt, Golf, USA, 1896–1900

Beatrix Loughran, Figure Skating, USA, 1922–1932

BECCA

Rebecca is a classic, beautiful name that dates all the way back to biblical Hebrew, but some *Rebeccas* deep down are really Beccas. A common short form, or even a name all on its own, Becca can be a little bit more relaxed while also a little tougher, as you can see in some really cool competitors like US Women's Championship curler Becca Hamilton, World Marathon Challenge runner Becca Pizzi (who also manages an ice cream parlor!), record-holding powerlifter and strongwoman Becca Swanson, and American sabre fencer Becca Ward, who has a World Championship gold medal and two Olympic bronzes.

Rebecca "Becca" Hamilton, Curling (Second), USA, 2010–current

Rebecca "Becca" Pizzi, Marathon, USA, 1997–current

Rebecca "Becca" Swanson, Strength Athletics, USA, 2002–current

Rebecca "Becca" Ward, Fencing (Sabre), USA, 2006–2008

BECKIE/BECKY

The more common diminutive of *Rebecca*—more popular than *Becca*—has traditionally been Becky, and it even has its own variant in Beckie. Athletes with these names are far-ranging, coming in first place and winning big in everything from cycling (like Welsh seven-time World Champion medalist track cyclist Becky James) to ice hockey (like Canadian three-time Olympic gold-medalist and four-time world champion defense player Becky Kellar-Duke).

A Becky or Beckie in your family can succeed at anything she puts her mind, skills, and determination to, but don't be surprised if she prefers succeeding alongside her teammates. Give her a wide range of sports to try, especially soccer; she may turn out to be a valuable defender like American four-time NWSL Defender of the Year and seven-time NWSL Best XI center back Becky Sauerbrunn, whose trophy, medal, and award collection includes three NWSL Championships, an NWSL Challenge Cup, International Champions Cup, four CONCACAF Women's Championships, five SheBelieves Cups, three Algarve Cups, two Four Nations Tournament championships, Olympic gold and bronze medals, and two FIFA Women's World Cups!

Rebecca "Becky" James, Track Cycling, Wales, 2009–2016

Rebecca "Becky" Kellar-Duke, Ice Hockey (Defense), Burlington Barracudas, Canada, 1997–2010

Rebecca "Becky" Sauerbrunn, Soccer (Center Back), FC Kansas City, USA, 2005–current

BERYL

The unisex Beryl is a "jewel" name related to the crystal that appears naturally in clear, blue, green, yellow, red, and black varieties. In the sporting world, women with this name are purely focused on going fast and winning races, with examples like Deaflympics gold-medalist sprinter Beryl Wamira of Kenya; Beryl Swain, who was the first woman to compete in the Isle of Man TT motorcycle race solo in 1962; and seven-time world title-winning British cyclist Beryl Burton! Pick the name Beryl for a child destined for speed, whether that's on the track, in the water, or on wheels.

Beryl Burton, Road/Track Cycling, England, 1956–1986

Beryl Swain, Motorcycle Racing (Tourist Trophy), England, 1960–1962

Beryl Wamira, Track & Field (Sprinting), Kenya, 2013–current

BETH

Beth can stand on its own, be a shortened form of names like *Elizabeth*, or show up combined with a secondary name like *Anne*. All of these appear in American athletics starting with two ladies whose careers began in the 1970s; golfer Beth Daniel won thirty-three LPGA Tour events, while Beth Heiden was a multi-talented competitor who won World Championships in both speed skating *and* cycling. In the pool, Beth Botsford scored gold twice in 1996 in backstroke.

Coincidentally, the US women's field hockey team that won bronze at the 1984 Los Angeles Olympics included two Beths: Beth Anders and Beth Beglin.

Calling a daughter Beth should help her succeed, especially in swimming or team sports played on fields.

Elizabeth "Beth" Anders, Field Hockey (Sweeper), USA, 1984

Elizabeth "Beth" Beglin, Field Hockey (Midfielder), USA, 1980–1988

Beth Anne Botsford, Swimming (Backstroke), USA, 1996–2006

Beth Daniel, Golf, USA, 1978–2009

Elizabeth "Beth" Heiden, Speed Skating/ Road Cycling, USA, 1976–1983

BETSY

Most often a short form of *Elizabeth* (Hebrew for "God is my abundance" or "God is my oath"), Betsy can feel like an old-fashioned name, but it's ready for a big comeback. Consider it especially if your family is a fan of rowing or golf, seeing as your daughter will find excellent role models like Olympic gold-medalist coxswain Betsy Beard and golfers Betsy King and Betsy Rawls, who both won multiple major championships on the LPGA Tour.

Elizabeth "Betsy" Beard, Rowing, USA, 1984–1988

Betsy King, Golf, USA, 1977–2005

Elizabeth "Betsy" Rawls, Golf, USA, 1951–1970

BETTY

The name Betty, like *Betsy*, can be given to a child on its own or serve as a shortened form of other names, in this case a long list including *Beatriz*, *Beatrice*, *Bethany*, *Elizabeth*, and more. Because of the range of names involved, you can find Bettys from lots of different places. From the Commonwealth of Australia came ICC Cricket Hall of Famer Betty Wilson (the first woman to take a hat-trick in a women's Test and the only one until 2004) and world record-setting sprinter Betty Cuthbert, who collected four Olympic gold medals. Hammer thrower Betty Heidler has won multiple medals across Olympics, World Championships, and more for Germany, and American professional golfer Betty Jameson was one of the founders of the LPGA.

Elizabeth "Betty" Cuthbert, Track & Field (Sprinting), Australia, 1956–1964

Betty Heidler, Track & Field (Hammer Throw), Germany, 2003–2016

Elizabeth "Betty" Jameson, Golf, USA, 1945–1970

Elizabeth "Betty" Wilson, Cricket (Bowler/ Fielder), Victoria Women's Cricket Team, Australia, 1948–1958

BILLIE

While it was once mainly given to boys, Billie has become a name typically given to girls. It can appear on its own, attached to another name like *Jean*, or serve as a nickname for *Wilhelmina* (from Germanic for "resolute protector") or other names. There have been two iconic Billies in sports, both truly inspirational. Billie Fleming began her cycling career in 1932 and specialized in long-distance riding, eventually setting a record for cycling over 29,600 miles in one year! That record was only overtaken in 2015, one year after Fleming passed away at the age of one hundred. Of course, the most famous Billie is tennis superstar Billie Jean King. Her list of accomplishments is long, including winning thirty-nine Grand Slam titles and reaching the number one ranking in the world. King is also known for participating in the highly publicized "Battle of the Sexes" match against Bobby Riggs in 1973.

A girl named Billie in your family is sure to take her interests and passions to the limit, both in athletics and causes she believes in.

Lilian "Billie Fleming" Bartram, Long Distance Cycling, England, 1932–1940

Billie Jean King, Tennis, USA, 1959–1990

BIRGIT/BRIDGETTE/BRIGID/BRIGIT

From the Emerald Isle comes the family of similar-sounding names that include Birgit, Bridgette, Brigid and Brigit. Whichever variation you prefer, the name originates in Gaelic from a root meaning "power," "strength," "vigor" and "virtue." That's a powerful starting place for a little girl, one who can walk in the footsteps of previous champions like Kenyan marathon runner Brigid Kosgei (Olympic silver and four-time World Marathon Majors gold-winner), German soccer striker Birgit Prinz (three-time FIFA World Player of the Year, three-time Olympic bronze-medalist, and two-time FIFA World Cup-winner), and basketball forward Bridgette Gordon, who won Olympic gold with the American team. Interestingly, women with these names have had lots of success with water, either in it like Australian water polo Olympic gold-medalist Bridgette Gusterson, or on it like canoe sprinter Brigit Fischer, who won eight Olympic gold medals and twenty-eight World Championship gold medals for Germany.

Brigit Fischer, Sprint Canoeing, Germany, 1978–2005

Bridgette Gordon, Basketball (Forward), Sacramento Monarchs, USA, 1988–1998

Bridgette Gusterson, Water Polo (Center Forward), Australia, 1995–2000

Brigid Kosgei, Marathon, Kenya, 2016–current

Birgit Prinz, Soccer (Striker), Eintracht Frankfurt, Germany, 1993–2011

BOBBI/BOBBIE

Bobbi/Bobbie (along with other variants) is another name that has been traditionally used as a short form or nickname, particularly for *Barbara* or *Roberta*, or used on its own. There are a handful of ladies with this name in the sporting universe, and among them are some really impressive trailblazers. Track and field athlete Fanny "Bobbie" Rosenfeld made a name for herself in the 1920s, excelling at multiple sports and winning silver and gold medals in sprinting at the 1929 Olympic Games. Roberta "Bobbi" Gibb was the first woman to complete the Boston Marathon and is recognized as the women's winner for the first three years (1966–1968).

Giving your child the name (or nickname) Bobbi/Bobbie can instill in her a drive to win—and maybe change the world while she's at it.

Roberta "Bobbi" Gibb, Marathon, USA, 1966–1968

Fanny "Bobbie" Rosenfeld, Track & Field (Sprinting), Canada, 1923–1933

BONNIE

While those familiar with traditional Scottish music and slang may know of the word "bonnie" as an adjective for someone or something pretty or attractive, it actually comes from a Latin word meaning simply "good." Bonnies aren't just nice to look at; they can also be fierce competitors. An inspirational success story, Bonnie Blair was a dominant speed skater in her heyday, winning eight gold medals in Olympic Games and World Championships.

Bonnie Blair, Speed Skating, USA, 1984–1995

BRANDI/BRANDIE

Its origin in Dutch for "burnt wine" may not sound super inspirational on its own, but any child you name or nickname Brandi or Brandie will have some pretty cool role models to look up to. Golfer Brandie Burton collected five LPGA Tour wins and became the youngest female golfer to win over $1 million, and Brandi Chastain's stellar soccer career included two Olympic gold medals and two FIFA Women's World cup wins!

Brandie Burton, Golf, USA, 1990–2000

Brandi Chastain, Soccer (Defender/Midfielder/Forward), San Jose CyberRays, USA, 1988–2010

BREANNA/BRIANA/BRIANNA

A lot of interesting names come about as different versions of previously existing names, which is the case for Brianna. Originally a feminine version of the name *Brian*, Brianna entered common usage in the sixteenth century and has many different regional and spelling variants, including Breanna and Briana. Athletes with these names are especially successful in team sports, with world-class American competitors like soccer goalkeeper Briana Scurry (winner of the 1999 FIFA Women's World Cup and two Olympic gold medals); ice hockey forward Brianna Decker (Olympic Gold-medalist, six-time World Championship-winner), who scored the first hat trick in the NWHL; and basketball power forward Breanna Stewart, who has three All-Star appearances, two WNBA championships, and two gold medals each at Olympic Games and World Championships!

Pick your favorite version of the name Brianna for your child and get her into team sports early!

Brianna Decker, Ice Hockey (Forward), Boston Pride, USA, 2009–current

Briana Scurry, Soccer (Goalkeeper), Atlanta Beat, USA, 1994–2010

Breanna Stewart, Basketball (Power Forward), Seattle Storm, USA, 2016–current

BRENDA

Brenda may not stand out as a name of mystery, but there are some really interesting questions as to where it comes from. Options include a feminine form based on Old Nordic *Brandr* (meaning "torch" or "sword"), or less likely from the Gaelic name *Brendan*. Whatever the true source, Brenda has become a name of champions, from Dutch tennis legend Brenda Schultz-McCarthy, who reached the number nine rank in the world and was recorded with the eighth-fastest serve by a woman ever, to water polo legend Brenda Villa, who won gold medals at the Olympics, World Championships, Pan American Games, FINA World Cup, and FINA World League!

Will a Brenda in your family feel at home in the water, or will she find success on the tennis court? Who knows!

Brenda Schultz-McCarthy, Tennis, Netherlands, 1986–2008

Brenda Villa, Water Polo (Attacker), USA, 1999–2012

BRIT/BRITT

Arising as short forms of names like *Birgit*, *Birgitta*, *Brittany/Brittney*, and others are Brit and Britt, though of course they're fully functional as names all on their own. The biggest concentration of winning Brits and Britts have occurred in winter sports, with Swedish Olympic gold- and two-time silver-medalist cross-country skier Britt Strandberg; Norwegian Paralympian Britt Mjaasund Øyen, who won two gold medals in cross-country skiing and eight golds, two silvers, and a bronze in ice sledge speed racing; and cross-country skier Brit Pettersen of Norway, who won a gold medal and two bronzes at the Olympics; a gold, a silver, and two bronzes from World Championships; and fifteen World Cup events!

While a Brit or Britt in your family has a strong chance of enjoying skiing and other cold weather activities, she could also branch out into other sports, such as orienteering like Norwegian relay world champion Brit

Volden; soccer like Norwegian defender Brit Sandaune, who won six league championships and Olympic gold and bronze medals; or water-skiing like American trick skier Britt Larsen-Kovak, who set multiple records and won three Masters' championships and two medals of each color at World Championships, sustaining a long dynasty alongside her identical twin sister, Tawn.

Brit Larsen-Kovak, Water Skiing, USA, 1984–1997

Britt Mjaasund-Øyen, Cross-Country Skiing/Ice Sledge Speed Racing, Norway, 1980–1994

Brit Pettersen Tofte, Cross-Country Skiing, Norway, 1980–1988

Brit Sandaune, Soccer (Defender), SK Trondheims-Ørn, Norway, 1985–2004

Britt Strandberg, Cross-Country Skiing, Sweden, 1960–1968

Brit Volden, Orienteering, Norway, 1979–1987

BRITTANY/BRITTNEY

Hearing the name Brittany/Brittney may conjure up images of a pop singer, but its origin stretches back to the Brittany region of France. If you're a fan of athletic endeavors and sports you may think of other people, because there are some pretty amazing Brittanys and Brittneys out there. Brittany Force is a NHRA drag racer who won the NHRA Drag Racing Series Top Fuel championship in 2017. On the court, basketball phenom Brittney Griner has collected seven WNBA All-Star appearances and a championship, plus two Olympic Games and two World Cup gold medals. Brittany Bowe is a multitalented athlete with six World Championships gold medals in speed skating, and also eight more World Championships golds in inline speed skating. Brittney Reese is famous for her incredible long jump career with an Olympic gold, three World Indoor Championships, four World Championships, and the American indoor record.

Pick a favorite spelling of Brittany or Brittney (or other variants like *Britney*) for your kid and she's sure to find success in her chosen field.

Brittany Bowe, Basketball (Point Guard)/Inline Skating/Speed Skating, USA, 2002–current

Brittany Force, Auto Racing (NHRA), USA, 2013–current

Brittney Griner, Basketball (Center), Phoenix Mercury, USA, 2013–current

Brittney Reese, Track & Field (Long Jump), USA, 2008–current

C

BOYS

CAL

The origin of the name *Calvin* may be surprising to some people, coming from Latin by way of French and meaning "bald." That's just one name that contributes to the legendary moniker Cal, sometimes a name on its own and sometimes a short form for *Caleb*, *Callum*, *Calvin*, etc. Cals have dominated various sports, like two-time NHL All-Star center/two-time Stanley Cup champion Cal Gardner, and football's Cal Hubbard, who was a four-time All-Pro tackle and four-time NFL champion. The name is probably most associated with baseball's Cal Ripken Jr., who racked up an incredible nineteen All-Star appearances in his twenty-one seasons with the Baltimore Orioles. His list of accomplishments includes two MVPs, the record for consecutive games played, a World Series championship, and more.

Will your Cal be the next powerhouse baseball player or a champion in another field? There's only one way to find out!

Calvin "Cal" Gardner, Ice Hockey (Center), Toronto Maple Leafs, Canada, 1945–1961

Robert Calvin "Cal" Hubbard, Football (Tackle), Green Bay Packers, USA, 1927–1936

Calvin "Cal" Ripken Jr., Baseball (Shortstop/Third Baseman), Baltimore Orioles, USA, 1981–2001

CALE

If you're a fan of names that begin with "C" and want your kid to be a speed demon, then consider calling him Cale! Most often a short form of or nickname for *Caleb*, *Charles*, or others, Cale has made a big mark around the NASCAR track starting in the late 1950s with one of the most famous drivers in the sport's history, William Caleb "Cale" Yarborough. Cale made his NASCAR Cup Series debut in 1957, and in his thirty-one-year career, scored eighty-three wins and three consecutive championships! He is tied for sixth place on the all-time winner's list, and he holds a host of other achievements and awards in NASCAR and beyond.

William Caleb "Cale" Yarborough, Auto Racing (NASCAR), USA, 1957–1988

CARL

Coming from the same Germanic root meaning "free man" as the name *Charles* is Carl. When it comes to sports and athleticism, Carls gravitate toward two things: speed and accuracy. On the baseball diamond, screwball pro Carl Hubbell was a nine-time All-Star and World Series-winning pitcher for the New York Giants, while Boston Red Sox slugger Carl Yastrzemski holds a host of records and awards along with his massive eighteen All-Star appearances. Back in the early twentieth century, Carl Osburn became the Olympic Games's most winning sport shooter, capturing eleven medals (five of them gold) in shooting events between 1912 and 1924. Last, but certainly not least, is the track and field phenom Carl Lewis, who collected ten World Championship medals and ten Olympic Games medals (nearly all of them gold) in a variety of events and set multiple world records, including the indoor long jump that he continues to hold to this day!

A Carl in your family is destined to feel the need for speed, whether that's on foot or in shooting or throwing a ball.

- **Carl Hubbell**, Baseball (Pitcher), New York Giants, USA, 1928–1943
- **Frederick Carlton "Carl" Lewis**, Track & Field (Sprinting/Long Jump), USA, 1979–1997
- **Carl Osburn**, Sport Shooting (Rifle), USA, 1912–1924
- **Carl Yastrzemski**, Baseball (Left Fielder/First Baseman), Boston Red Sox, USA, 1961–1983

CARLOS

Just as *Carl* comes from the same root as *Charles*, Carlos is a Portuguese and Spanish variant from the same family. Athletes with this name have excelled in many different fields, with singular examples reaching their summit, including Filipino gymnast Carlos Yulo, who won four medals in recent World Championships; Venezuelan world champion trick water skier Carlos Suarez; two-time NBA All-Star power forward Carlos Boozer, who also won Olympic gold in basketball; and 2008 Tour de France-winner Carlos Sastre of Spain. Two men named Carlos have made big impacts in soccer: Tevez (FIFA Club World Cup- and Olympic gold-winner) and Valderrama (top-ranked South American footballer) of Argentina and Colombia, respectively.

American baseball has seen quite a few champs named Carlos, with three-time All-Stars second baseman Baerga of Puerto Rico, Panamanian grand slam slugger Lee, and three from Venezuela: batting champion González of the Colorado Rockies, shortstop Guillén, and Chicago Cubs pitcher Zambrano. Puerto Rican switch hitter and record-holding base stealer Carlos Beltrán leads the pack with nine All-Star appearances and a World Series win.

You don't need to be Spanish, Venezuelan, Caribbean, or South American to choose the winning name Carlos for a child in your family; if you do, just don't be surprised if the little one really likes T-ball.

- **Carlos Baerga**, Baseball (Second Baseman), Cleveland Indians, Puerto Rico, 1990–2001
- **Carlos Beltrán**, Baseball (Outfielder), New York Mets, Puerto Rico, 1998–2017
- **Carlos Boozer Jr.**, Basketball (Power Forward), Utah Jazz, USA, 2002–2017
- **Carlos González**, Baseball (Outfielder), Colorado Rockies, Venezuela, 2008–2019
- **Carlos Guillén**, Baseball (Shortstop), Detroit Tigers, Venezuela, 1998–2011
- **Carlos Lee**, Baseball (Left Fielder/First Baseman), Milwaukee Brewers, Panama, 1999–2012
- **Carlos Sastre**, Road Cycling, Spain, 1998–2011
- **Carlos Suarez**, Water Skiing, Venezuela, 1971–1979
- **Carlos Tevez**, Soccer (Forward), Manchester City Football Club, Argentina, 2001–current
- **Carlos Valderrama**, Soccer (Midfielder), Asociación Deportivo Cali, Colombia, 1981–2002

Carlos Yulo, Artistic Gymnastics, Philippines, 2018–current

Carlos Zambrano, Baseball (Pitcher), Chicago Cubs, Venezuela, 2001–2012

CARLTON

Combining the "free man" root of *Carl/ Charles* with an Old English word for "settlement" gives us the name Carlton, also used as a place name in Europe. There are two notable Carltons in athletics: Carlton "Lucky" Lowe had a long career and won gold in the Water Ski World Championships, and MLB Hall of Famer Carlton Fisk was an eleven-time All-Star catcher playing for both Boston Red and Chicago White Sox.

A little boy named Carlton may naturally gravitate toward high-speed water sports or team sports like baseball!

Carlton Fisk, Baseball (Catcher), Boston Red Sox, USA, 1969–1993

Carlton Wayne "Lucky" Lowe, Water Skiing, USA, 1970–1993

CARMELO

Do you hope for a kid who specializes in playing basketball? Consider the name Carmelo, a Spanish and Italian version of *Carmel* (Hebrew for "garden"). The most famous Carmelo is the ten-time NBA All-Star and four-time Olympic medalist small forward/power forward Carmelo Anthony.

Carmelo Anthony, Basketball (Small Forward/Power Forward), Denver Nuggets, USA, 2003–current

CHARLES/CHARLIE

Charles, coming from the same Proto-Germanic for "free man" as *Carl* and other names, has long been a popular name throughout Europe and North America. It's fitting, then, that plenty of men with this name have found success in a multitude of athletic endeavors, and the same goes for those named or called the more familiar (and unisex) Charlie. Just a few of these include early 1900s seven-time Olympic medalist (four of them gold) swimmer Charlie Daniels; ice dancer Charlie White, who's won one of each Olympic medal and multiple golds at Worlds Championships, Four Continents Championships, and Grand Prix Finals; four-time Olympic gold-winning Dutch equestrian Charles de Mortanges; Canadian former record holder speed skater Charles Hamelin, who collected nineteen gold medals across Olympics, World Championships, and World Team Championships (fifty-two medals in total); and Charles Smith, whose third consecutive water polo Olympic gold medal made him the oldest winner in his sport.

Meanwhile, multiple men with these names have held places of pride in track and field (American high jump phenom Charles Austin, who won gold at the Olympics, World Championships, World Indoor Championships, and World Cup Championship, and the father/son sprinting Olympic gold-winning duo of Charles Jenkins Jr. and Sr.), and baseball (four-time All-Star Colorado Rockies batting champion Charlie Blackmon and six-time All-Star, World Series–winning Detroit Tigers second baseman Charlie Gehringer).

Even among all of these greats, some stand above for their achievements as well as their dedication and larger-than-life personalities. Charles "Karch" Kiraly is synonymous with volleyball, having won Olympic gold in both indoor and outdoor events. Charles Barkley is one of basketball's most famous greats, achieving eleven All-Star appearances and two Olympic gold medals with the "Dream Team" before becoming a TV personality.

Let all of these inspire a Charles or Charlie in your family to achieve great things in life, whether that's in sports or some other worthy passion!

Charles Austin, Track & Field (High Jump), USA, 1991-1999

Charles Barkley, Basketball (Power Forward/ Small Forward), Philadelphia 76ers, USA, 1984-2000

Charles "Charlie" Blackmon, Baseball (Outfielder), Colorado Rockies, USA, 2011-current

Charles "Charlie" Daniels, Swimming (Freestyle), USA, 1903-1908

Charles "Charlie" Gehringer, Baseball (Second Baseman), Detroit Tigers, USA, 1924-1942

Charles Hamelin, Speed Skating, Canada, 2004-current

Charles "Chip" Jenkins Jr., Track & Field (Sprinting), USA, 1992

Charles "Charlie" Jenkins Sr., Track & Field (Sprinting), USA, 1955-1958

Charles "Karch" Kiraly, Volleyball (Outside Hitter), USA, 1981-2007

Charles de Mortanges, Equestrian (Eventing), Netherlands, 1924-1936

Charles Smith, Water Polo (Goalkeeper), England, 1908-1920

Charles "Charlie" White Jr., Ice Dancing, USA, 1992-2017

CHASE

You don't have to come from a family of hunters to name a child Chase, a name that comes from a Latin origin meaning "to pursue" or "to catch" and first saw common usage as a descriptor for hunters. Your Chase might be interested in auto racing, baseball, or swimming based on the champions who have used it! Chase Elliott (son of Bill Elliott) is a NASCAR Cup Series racer who, in his seven seasons thus far, has racked up thirteen wins and a championship; Chase Utley was a six-time All-Star and World Series-winning second baseman; and Chase Kalisz's ongoing swimming career has already yielded records and gold medals at Olympic Games, World Championships, and Pan Pacific Championships!

William "Chase" Elliott II, Auto Racing (NASCAR), USA, 2013-current

Chase Kalisz, Swimming (Breaststroke/ Butterfly/Medley), USA, 2013-current

Chase Utley, Baseball (Second Baseman), Philadelphia Phillies, USA, 2003-2018

CHRIS

Christians, *Christophers*, and the like are cool, but dudes who go by the unisex short form Chris are a breed unto themselves. A little bit wild, they show up to break the mold and leave an indelible mark on their respective fields, just as a Chris in your family will. He'll be able to look up to impactful athletes like Jamaican cricketer Chris Gayle, who's considered one of the all-time greatest batsmen; five-time X Games gold-medalist skateboarder Chris Cole; esports fighting game champion Chris "NYChrisG" Gonzalez; twenty-two-time winner of the highly dangerous cheese rolling competition at Cooper's Hill Chris Anderson; and Hall of Fame horse racing jockey Chris Antley, who won a staggering 3,480 races in his seventeen year career.

Chrises have made it big in cycling (four-time Tour de France General Classification-winner Chris Froome and Chris Hoy, who has six Olympic and eleven World Championship gold medals), and running sports (Bahamian sprinter Chris Brown, who won gold at the Olympics, World Championships, and World Indoor Championships, and pioneer duathlon/triathlon athlete Chris Mosier). And on the ice, six-time All-Star, Stanley Cup-winner, and gold medalist defenseman Chris Pronger was considered one of the greatest (and one of the dirtiest) in ice hockey, while Chris Chelios set records for his lengthy and momentous career during which the defenseman won a World Cup of Hockey gold medal, played in eleven NHL All-Star Games, won three Stanley Cup championships, and earned a place in the Hockey Hall of Fame.

Here in the US, multiple Chrises have excelled in the traditionally most popular professional sports. The hardwood courts of the NBA have witnessed the achievements of eleven-time All-Star point guard Chris Paul and center/power forward Chris Bosh, who has a stellar eleven All-Star appearances and two NBA championships. The most successful athletes going by this name in baseball are pitchers and include three-time All-Star and two-time World Series champ Chris Carpenter, and seven-time All-Star and World Series champion Chris Sale! Last, but certainly not least, are the gridiron Chrises: three-time Pro Bowl running back Chris Johnson; cornerback Chris McAlister, who scored his three Pro Bowl appearances and Super Bowl championship with the Baltimore Ravens; and Denver Broncos cornerback Chris Harris Jr., who has four Pro Bowl appearances and a Super Bowl win.

Chris Anderson, Cheese Rolling, England, 2004–current

Christopher "Chris" Antley, Horse Racing (Jockey), USA, 1982–1999

Christopher "Chris" Bosh, Basketball (Center/Power Forward), Miami Heat, USA, 2003–2017

Christopher "Chris" Brown, Track & Field (Sprinting), Bahamas, 2005–2016

Christopher "Chris" Carpenter, Baseball (Pitcher), Toronto Blue Jays, USA, 1997–2012

Christos "Chris" Chelios, Ice Hockey (Defense), Detroit Red Wings, USA, 1984–2010

Chris Cole, Skateboarding, USA, 2000–current

Christopher "Chris" Froome, Road Cycling, England, 2007–current

Christopher "Chris" Gayle, Cricket (Batting All-Rounder), Jamaica National Cricket Team, Jamaica, 1998–current

Christopher "Chris" (NYChrisG) Gonzalez, Esports (Fighting Games), USA, 2011–current

Christopher "Chris" Harris Jr., Football (Cornerback), Denver Broncos, USA, 2011–current

Chris Hoy, Track Cycling, Scotland, 2000–2012

Christopher "Chris" Johnson, Football (Running Back), Tennessee Titans, USA, 2008–2017

Christopher "Chris" McAlister, Football (Cornerback), Baltimore Ravens, USA, 1999–2009

Chris Mosier, Running (Duathlon/Triathlon), USA, 2010–current

Christopher "Chris" Paul, Basketball (Point Guard), Los Angeles Clippers, USA, 2005–current

Christopher "Chris" Pronger, Ice Hockey (Defense), St. Louis Blues, Canada, 1993–2011

Christopher "Chris" Sale, Baseball (Pitcher), Chicago White Sox, USA, 2010–current

CHRISTIAN

A traditional baptismal name meaning "follower of Jesus Christ," Christian appears in many different countries and societies. Just some of those who have pursued high-level athletics and sports include French fencer Christian d'Oriola, who won four Olympic gold medals and eight World Championships with the foil; current world record-holder in twenty-five meter rapid fire pistol shooting and Olympic gold-medalist Christian Reitz of Germany; and triple jump phenom Christian Taylor, who has the second longest jump record and multiple gold medals from the Olympics and World Championships.

Whatever a little Christian in your family is into, encourage him to try out fencing, sport shooting, and jumping.

Christian d'Oriola, Fencing (Foil/Épée), France, 1947–1958

Christian Reitz, Sport Shooting (Pistol), Germany, 2008-current

Christian Taylor, Track & Field (Triple Jump), USA, 2011-current

CHRISTOPHER

Even moreso than *Chris*, the name Christopher is primarily used by Christians because it's Greek for "Christ-bearer." There definitely aren't as many top-ranked athletes who go by the full name, but those who do have spread across quite a few countries and disciplines to snatch glory and accolades. Australian cyclist Christopher Scott sped to an impressive ten Paralympic Games medals (six of which were gold) with another dozen at World Championships, Christopher Dean was a champion ice dancer who won Olympic gold and four gold medals at World Championships, X Games and World Championships ski cross-winner Christopher Del Bosco competed for Canada, Christopher "GeT_RiGhT" Alesund is an esports champion in *Call of Duty: Global Offensive*, and horse racing jockey Christopher Emigh has won more than four thousand races in his ongoing career!

But that's not all. Among the soccer greats, striker Christopher Katongo had over one hundred caps for Zambia and scored over 120 goals between clubs and international play.

Naming your son Christopher will give him strong shoulders to bear the weights of the world, and quite possibly a sporting spirit that could steer him toward team sports, cycling, skiing, or even competitive video games!

Christopher "GeT_RiGhT" Alesund, Esports (*Call of Duty: Global Offensive*), Sweden, 2007-current

Christopher Dean, Ice Dancing, England, 1980-1994

Christopher Del Bosco, Skiing, USA, 2006-2016

Christopher Emigh, Horse Racing (Jockey), USA, 1989-current

Christopher Katongo, Soccer (Striker), Jomo Cosmos, Zambia, 2001-2017

Christopher Scott, Para-Cycling, Australia, 1988-2008

CHRISTY

A unisex nickname that can work for any "Chris-" name, Christy has phenomenal sports credentials that can inspire a boy in your family, whether he plays golf, baseball, or something else entirely. Coming out of Ireland were not one but two champion golfers named Christy O'Connor, and when their careers overlapped, they were given the nicknames "Junior" and "Senior" to tell them apart. The younger won sixteen professional events while the elder took home a staggering sixty-four wins. Meanwhile, on the baseball diamond in the early twentieth century, fans cheered on New York Giants pitcher Christy Mathewson, whose two World Series championships; two Triple Crowns; rankings as National League wins leader four times, ERA leader five times, and strikeout leader five times; two no-hitters; and more led to his place on the all-time greats list and his induction into the first class of the Baseball Hall of Fame!

Christopher "Christy" Mathewson, Baseball (Pitcher), New York Giants, USA, 1900-1916

Christopher "Christy Junior" O'Connor, Golf, Ireland, 1967-1992

Patrick Christopher "Christy Senior" O'Connor, Golf, Ireland, 1951-1977

CHUCK

Chuck, often a nickname for *Charles/Charlie*, is a cool name that's often associated with things like nunchaku and Chuck Taylor All-Stars shoes. If there's one thing that links athletes with this name, it's being tough, a quality that will surely extend to a little Chuck in your family as well. Chuck Stearns was nicknamed "Mr. Consistency" for his absolute domination in water skiing for years, and then there's four foot, eleven-and-a-half inch weightlifter Chuck "Mighty Mite" Vinci, who set records and won two Olympic gold medals; just before the weigh-in for the first one, he was a pound-and-a-half over so he spent the next hour running and exercising, and when that wasn't quite enough, a last-minute haircut let him squeak by! In the NFL, the ferocious Chuck "Concrete Charlie" Bednarik played both offense and defense in his thirteen-season career with the Philadelphia Eagles, earning eight Pro Bowl appearances and two NFL championships. Martial arts have produced arguably the most famous Chucks, with UFC legend and MMA Light Heavyweight Champion Chuck Liddell and US Air Force air policeman-turned-karate champion and martial arts innovator-turned-action movie star Chuck Norris.

Charles "Chuck" Bednarik, Football (Linebacker/Center), Philadelphia Eagles, USA, 1949–1962

Charles "Chuck" (The Iceman) Liddell, MMA (Heavyweight), USA, 1998–2018

Carlos "Chuck" Norris, Karate, USA, 1965–1969

Chuck Stearns, Water Skiing, USA, 1957–1985

Charles "Chuck" Vinci Jr., Weightlifting, USA, 1955–1960

CLYDE

Having tall people in your family and coming from Scotland isn't required for naming a child Clyde, which comes from a Celtic place name for people living near the river Clyde that passes through Glasgow, but it couldn't hurt. Either way, your little Clyde is likely to enjoy basketball if the incredibly talented former stars of the sport with that name are any indication. Clyde Lovellette was a star center in the 1950s and early '60s, earning four All-Star appearances, three NBA championships, and an Olympic gold medal; seven-time All-Star and two-time NBA champion point guard Walt "Clyde" Frazier spent most of his twelve seasons with the New York Knicks; and Hall of Fame inductee Clyde Drexler is considered one of the greatest players of all time with his ten All-Star appearances, NBA championship, and Olympic gold medal with the 1992 "Dream Team." Outside of the basketball court, Clyde Walcott was ranked the top batsman in the world during his cricket career, and he was the first person to score five centuries in a single Test during a series playing against Australia in 1955.

Clyde Drexler, Basketball (Shooting Guard/Small Forward), Portland Trail Blazers, USA, 1983–1998

Walt "Clyde" Frazier, Basketball (Point Guard), New York Knicks, USA, 1967–1979

Clyde Lovellette, Basketball (Center), Boston Celtics, USA, 1951–1964

Clyde Walcott, Cricket (Wicketkeeper), Barbados National Cricket Team, Barbados, 1941–1964

COLIN

A name with stronger popularity in England and Wales than the US, Colin comes to us from two different European sources; it's a derivative of both an Old French shortened form of *Nicholas* (from roots meaning "victory of the people") and a Gaelic name meaning "whelp" or "cub." As you might expect, there are famous Colins in traditionally European sports like cricket and soccer. Hall of Famer Colin Cowdrey was an early record setter on the cricket field as the first person to play one hundred Test matches, taking 120 catches as a fielder, and the first batsman to make centuries against all the other current teams. Midfielder Colin Bell earned a Hall of Fame spot with his forty-eight appearances with the England national football team and 177 total career goals, and forward Colin Clarke became one of Northern Ireland's all-time top scorers with 147 career goals.

New Zealand's "All Blacks" rugby has seen its champion Colins as well, with the famously tough Meads, who played in fifty-five Test matches, and Slade, whose 2011 and 2015 Rugby World Cup wins puts him in the rarified air of only twenty players who have won multiple.

All of these suggest that naming a son Colin will give him toughness and speed, while taking inspiration from NFL quarterback and activist Colin Kaepernick will give him the conviction to help others and the inner strength to stand up for his beliefs, no matter the opposition.

- **Colin Bell**, Soccer (Midfielder), Manchester City Football Club, England, 1963–1980
- **Colin Clarke**, Soccer (Forward), Southampton Football Club, Northern Ireland, 1980–1993
- **Michael "Colin" Cowdrey (Baron Cowdrey of Tonbridge)**, Cricket (Batsman), Kent County Cricket Club, England, 1950–1975
- **Colin Kaepernick**, Football (Quarterback), San Francisco 49ers, USA, 2011–2016
- **Colin Meads**, Rugby (Lock), King Country Rugby Football Union, New Zealand, 1955–1973
- **Colin Slade**, Rugby (First Five-Eighth), Section Paloise, New Zealand, 2006–current

CONNOR/CONOR

If you're Irish or of Irish descent and a dog person, there really isn't a better fit for you than the name Connor/Conor because it comes from Old Irish roots for "lover of hounds" or "lover of wolves"! In ice hockey you'll find Edmonton Oilers center Connor McDavid, who has four All-Star appearances and a World Championship gold medal. Meanwhile Conor Dwyer of the US brought home multiple gold medals in freestyle swimming from the Olympics and various World Championships, and Conor McGregor is a modern-day MMA legend, having held the UFC featherweight and lightweight championships at the same time and becoming the world's highest paid athlete in 2021 with various high-profile bouts and exhibitions.

- **Conor Dwyer**, Swimming (Freestyle), USA, 2010–2019
- **Connor McDavid**, Ice Hockey (Center), Edmonton Oilers, Canada, 2015–current
- **Conor McGregor**, MMA (Featherweight/Lightweight/Welterweight), Ireland, 2008–current

CRIS/CRISTIANO

A shared Italian and Portuguese variant of the name *Christian*, Cristiano is famous around the world for representing one man, and that, of course, is Cristiano Ronaldo. Solidly ranked as one of the greatest players of all time, Ronaldo has a huge list of achievements and awards, not least of which are his over eight hundred senior career goals, thirty-two trophies, five Ballon d'Or awards, and over eleven hundred career appearances. Fast, strong, and accurate, there's nothing Cristiano can't do, and he's still going strong at both Al-Nassr and the Portugal national football team, so there's no telling the heights he'll reach!

Before you buy cleats and a soccer ball for a little Cristiano or Cris in your family, keep in mind that there are also great role models in other sports, like football (eight-time Pro Bowl wide receiver Cris Carter) and auto racing (Champ Car champion Cristiano da Matta).

- **Graduel Christopher "Cris" Carter**, Football (Wide Receiver), Minnesota Vikings, USA, 1987–2002
- **Cristiano da Matta**, Auto Racing (Champ Car), Brazil, 1999–2006

Cristiano Ronaldo dos Santos Aveiro, Soccer (Forward), Real Madrid Club de Fútbol, Portugal, 2001–current

CURT/CURTIS

Curt (different from *Kurt*) most often appears as a short form of Curtis, which comes to modern times via a long path from the Spanish *Cortés*, with a root meaning "polite" or "courteous." Curts and Curtises in sports are always a little bit extra, as you can see with kickboxer Curtis Bush, who added an acting career to his five world title wins, and three-time All-Star and Olympic gold medal-winning ice hockey goaltender Curtis "Cujo" Joseph, who used Stephen King's iconic ferocious dog character on his face masks. They're joined on the leaderboards by five-time NFL Pro Bowl running back Curtis Martin and Hall of Fame golfer Curtis Strange who won seventeen times on the PGA Tour.

A Curt or Curtis in your family will be athletic, unique, and if he plays baseball, hopefully more like the philanthropic three-time All-Star slugger Curtis Granderson than the controversial and outspoken six-time All-Star and three-time World Series champion pitcher Curt Schilling.

Curtis Bush, Kickboxing (Welterweight/Middleweight), USA, 1979–1999

Curtis Granderson Jr., Baseball (Outfielder), New York Yankees, USA, 2004–2019

Curtis Joseph, Ice Hockey (Goaltender), Toronto Maple Leafs, Canada, 1989–2009

Curtis Martin Jr., Football (Running Back), New York Jets, USA, 1995–2006

Curt Schilling, Baseball (Pitcher), Boston Red Sox, USA, 1988–2007

Curtis Strange, Golf, USA, 1976–2005

CY

Cy is not a name that's very popular these days, but it's definitely deserving of a comeback! It's often, but definitely not always, a short form or nickname for other names like *Cyril*, *Cyrus*, and *Seymour*. Looking back at the Cys in sports shows us that the nickname was used for people with all sorts of different names. Of course there was four-time Stanley Cup-winning NHL left wing Cyril "Cy" Denneny, but the name is most common among baseball players and, most famously, World Series-winner Denton "Cy" Young, whose incredible pitching achievements and records inspired the MLB's Cy Young Award for best pitchers.

No matter what you name your child, you can use the fun nickname Cy and make sure to encourage throwing practice.

Cyril "Cy" Denneny, Ice Hockey (Left Wing), Ottawa Senators, Canada, 1914–1929

Denton "Cy" Young, Baseball (Pitcher), Boston Americans, USA, 1890–1911

GIRLS

CAITLIN/CAITLYN/KAITLIN/KAITLYN

Caitlin has a family of associated names with different spellings, in this case all coming through a convoluted pathway of Old French and Irish variants of *Katherine*. Champion women with these names have won big on land, in the water, and on ice and snow. The first group includes Olympic gold-medalist decathlete and record setter Caitlyn Jenner; and two-time Netball World Champion goal shooter Caitlin Bassett of Australia. On the water, sprint canoeist Caitlin Regal of New Zealand has paddled to an Olympic win and a world championship, while American swimmer Kaitlin Sandeno set records on her way to winning Olympic gold and five world championships.

For those who like it a bit colder, there are the winter sports enthusiasts like Olympic gold-medalist snowboarder Kaitlyn Farrington; ice hockey defense player Caitlin Cahow, who was part of three World Women's Championship teams and won a 4 Nations Cup; and Canadian curler Kaitlyn Lawes, who has two Olympic golds and a world championship in her medal collection.

There are as many sports to excel in as different versions of the Caitlin family of names, so whichever one you may pick for a daughter will give her a drive to succeed in whatever field she chooses.

Caitlin Bassett, Netball (Goal Shooter), Australia, 2005–current

Caitlin Cahow, Ice Hockey (Defense), USA, 2006–2013

Kaitlyn Farrington, Snowboarding, USA, 2009–2015

Caitlyn Jenner, Track & Field (Decathlon), USA, 1970–1976

Lesley Kaitlyn Lawes, Curling (Third), Canada, 2009–current

Caitlin Regal, Sprint Canoeing, New Zealand, 2015–current

Kaitlin Sandeno, Swimming (Butterfly/Freestyle/Medley), USA, 1999–2007

CAMILLA/CAMILLE

A name with ancient origins, Camilla is a feminine form of the Roman cognomen (a hereditary part of a triple word name) *Camillus*. As it passed down to modern times, it split into a French version, Camille, and other assorted variants like Camilla. Ladies with this name are versatile athletes, making waves on the water and on land with stand outs including World Championship gold medal-winner badminton player Camilla Martin of Denmark; French swimmer Camille Muffat, who won Olympic gold in 400 meter freestyle and a World Championship in 200 meter; five-time World Champion and Hall of Fame water skier Camille Duvall, nicknamed "the Golden Goddess"; and ultramarathon runner Camille Herron, who has won five World Championship gold medals.

Whether you're descended from Romans, French, or just regular Americans, choose the name Camilla or Camille for your daughter and sign her up for swimming lessons!

Camille Duvall, Waterskiing, USA, 1975–1987

Camille Herron, Ultramarathon, USA, 2011–current

Camilla Martin, Badminton, Denmark, 1989–2004

Camille Muffat, Swimming (Freestyle/Medley), France, 2005–2014

CANDACE/CANDICE

If you're hoping for a tall, athletic daughter with royal bearing, consider giving her the name Candace or Candice! Appearing in the New Testament, the name comes from an ancient title for queens in what is now modern-day Ethiopia as it was translated into Greek. Women with these names today gravitate toward basketball. Among the best of the best are Candace Parker, who has thus far racked up six WNBA All-Star appearances and two championships (mostly while playing for the Los Angeles Sparks) along with two Olympic gold medals, and seven-time All-Star and WNBA champion power forward Candice Dupree.

Candice Dupree, Basketball (Power Forward), Phoenix Mercury, USA, 2006–current

Candace Parker, Basketball (Center/Power Forward/Guard), Los Angeles Sparks, USA, 2016–current

CANDIE/CANDY

Originating as a diminutive of *Candace*, the name Candy is super sweet whether you go with the more traditional spelling or with Candie. While *Candaces* are known for being tall and playing basketball, girls who go by Candie and Candy have more varied athletic interests, such as golf, like Candie Kung who won five professional events, or swimming, like Olympic gold-medalist synchronized swimmer Candy Costie!

Candace "Candy" Costie, Synchronized Swimming, USA, 1982–1984

Candie Kung (Kung I-Ping), Golf, USA, 2001–2019

CARINA

The name Carina comes from an ancient Latin word meaning "beloved." That language also had the word *carina* meaning "keel of a ship" (where we get the name of the constellation that includes the star Canopus), which is interesting because one of the superlative athletes with this name is Germany's Olympic gold-medalist and two-time World Champion rower Carina Bär! Other luminaries so-named include Dutch Carina Benninga, who has an Olympic gold medal and two World Cup championships in field hockey, and German ski jumper Carina Vogt, who also won Olympic gold along with five World Championship titles.

Carina Bär, Rowing, Germany, 2010–current

Carina Benninga, Field Hockey (Midfielder), Netherlands, 1983–1991

Carina Vogt, Ski Jumping, Germany, 2012–current

CARLI/CARLY

The name Carli/Carly has followed the same convoluted route as the name *Carl*, coming from *Charles* and its origin in a root for "free man" or "warrior." On the other hand, they can also serve as shortened or pet names for *Carla* or *Caroline*.

There have been three iconic American athletes with these names who made big impacts in different events. Freestyle swimmer Carly Piper scored gold at the 2004 Athens Olympic Games, setting a world record with her 4x200 meter freestyle relay teammates. At those same games, Carly Patterson dominated the gymnastics events, winning the all-around gold; she also won multiple gold medals at other championships from 2003 to 2004! Last but certainly not least, Carli Lloyd was a standout star of the United States National Soccer Team, earning two Olympic gold medals, two FIFA Women's World Cups, and two FIFA Player of the Year awards.

Pick a version of Carli or Carly for a child in your family and she's sure to be fast, agile, and a great team player.

Carli Lloyd, Soccer (Midfielder/Forward), Western New York Flash, USA, 1999–2021

Carly Patterson, Artistic Gymnastics, USA, 2000–2004

Carly Piper, Swimming (Freestyle), USA, 2004–2008

CARMELITA

Carmelita is a Spanish feminine diminutive of the name *Carmel*, which means "garden" in Hebrew and appears as the name of a mountain in the Old Testament. Will naming a daughter Carmelita give her the ability to run fast and beat the competition? It might if she takes after Carmelita Jeter, a top-tier American sprinter whose accomplishments include winning one of each medal at the 2012 London Olympic Games, as well as nine World Championship medals (three of them golds)!

Carmelita Jeter, Track & Field (Sprinting), USA, 2007–2017

CAROL/CAROLE

A unisex name traditionally descending from the same *Carl/Charles/Carolus* "free man" lineage as *Carly*, Carol—and its lesser-seen variant Carole—can also be short for names like *Caroline*. Where have we seen athletes with these names winning big? All-rounder Carole Hodges won the 1993 Women's World Cup with the England Women's Cricket Team; Carol Huynh was the first Canadian woman to win Olympic gold in wrestling; figure skater Carol Heiss won Olympic gold in Squaw Valley in 1960, as well as five World Championships; and Hall of Fame golfer Carol Mann racked up thirty-eight LPGA Tour wins and two championships!

Carol (or Carole) could be a good choice for you if you're hoping for a daughter to excel on the links, the ice, the field, or the mat.

Carol Heiss, Figure Skating, USA, 1953–1960

Carole Hodges, Cricket (All-Rounder), Lancashire and Cheshire Women's Cricket Team, England, 1976–1993

Carol Huynh, Freestyle Wrestling, Canada, 2000–2012

Carol Mann, Golf, USA, 1960–1981

CAROLINA/CAROLINE/KAROLINA

As you can see with names like *Carly* and *Carol*, there is an entire pantheon of variations and derivations that come from the Latin name *Carolus* by way of *Charles*, *Carl*, etc. Another feminine diminutive is Carolina, part of a family that includes Karolina and Caroline (pronunciations may vary depending on the specific country and language of origin).

Athletes with these names have risen to the top of a wide range of fields all over Europe and North America. Spanish badminton champion Carolina Marín was the top-ranked player in the world (and considered one of the best ever) and had a huge gold medal count at the Olympics and World Championships. Cypriot visually impaired swimmer Karolina Pelendritou won the moniker "Princess of the Pool" over her long career with her three Paralympic Games and three World Championship gold medals, while Russian gymnast Karolina Sevastyanova reportedly ate only buckwheat for six months before the 2012 Olympic Games . . . and she won the gold. Canadian ice hockey forward Caroline Ouellette won Olympic gold at four different Games, as well as six World Championships, and Karolina Arewång-Höjsgaard of Sweden is an orienteering world champion!

Track and field competitions have seen winners in the pentathlon and heptathlon with Swedish Carolina Klüft (nine gold medals across various events), and in the long jump with Polish two-time Paralympic Games gold-medalist and three-time World Champions gold-medalist Karolina Kucharczyk. Last but not least is tennis, whose luminaries have included Dane Caroline Wozniacki, who won thirty career titles and spent seventy-one weeks at the world top spot.

Pick your favorite version and pronunciation of Carolina/Caroline for your daughter and watch her thrive!

- **Karolina Arewång-Höjsgaard**, Orienteering, Sweden, 2003–2010
- **Carolina Klüft**, Track & Field (Heptathlon/Long Jump), Sweden, 2003–2011
- **Karolina Kucharczyk**, Track & Field (Long Jump), Poland, 2011–current
- **Carolina Marín**, Badminton, Spain, 2009–current
- **Caroline Ouellette**, Ice Hockey (Forward), Montreal Stars, Canada, 1999–2018
- **Karolina Pelendritou**, Swimming (Breaststroke), Cyprus, 1999–current
- **Karolina Sevastyanova**, Rhythmic Gymnastics, Russia, 2012
- **Caroline Wozniacki**, Tennis, Denmark, 2005–2020

CAROLYN

A unique English variant of *Caroline*, the name Carolyn can give your daughter a particular fondness for competing alongside partners and teammates, especially on the hardwood court, on the baseball diamond, or in the pool! She can walk, or swim, in the footsteps of women like world champion basketball guard Carolyn Jones-Young; All-American Girls Professional Baseball League All-Star pitcher and champion Carolyn Morris, who threw a perfect game and three no-hitters with the Rockford Peaches; and Canadian two-time Olympic gold-medalist and three-time world champion synchronized swimmer Carolyn Waldo.

- **Carolyn Jones-Young**, Basketball (Guard), Portland Fire, USA, 1999–2002
- **Carolyn Morris**, Baseball (Pitcher), Rockford Peaches, USA, 1944–1946
- **Carolyn Waldo**, Synchronized Swimming, Canada, 1984–1988

CASTER

While *Castor* is known for its origin in Greek mythology (he and his twin brother, Pollux, had several adventures), Caster is a household name among sports enthusiasts for the incredible South African runner Caster Semenya. She has blazed her way through events ranging from 400 meter to 1500 meter, collecting gold medals in the Continental Cup, African Games and Championships, Commonwealth Games, World Championships, and Olympic Games, and her career is far from over! She's a model of athletic prowess and grace under pressure.

A Caster in your family will be fast as lightning and a beacon for equality.

- **Mogkadi Caster Semenya**, Track & Field (Middle-Distance Running), South Africa, 2009–current

CATE/CATERINE/CATHARINE/CATHERINE/CATHY

Catherine is an interesting name because of its obscure origins. It came about as a French variant of *Katherine*, which comes from Ancient Greek . . . but we don't know the original meaning. The sources get even more murky with later connections to an entirely different Greek word for "pure." Regardless of its true origins that we may never discover, girls and women named Catherine have proven powerful competitors and winners in many fields.

Singular Catherines and Catharines at the top of their games include soccer Olympic gold-winner defender Catherine "Cat" Whitehill; Canadian cross-country cyclist Catharine Pendrel, who has two World Championships and an Olympic Games bronze medal; early American speed skating legend Catherine "Kit" Klein, who won Olympic gold in 1932 and the World Finals in 1936; French six-time

World Champion archer Cathérine Pellen; and Olympic gold-medalist and four-time National Pro Fastpitch champion softball pitcher Catherine "Cat" Osterman.

Meanwhile, we can find winners and champions in ice hockey with American right wing/center Catherine "Cammi" Granato, who won Olympics and World Women's Championships gold and silver medals. In track and field history, Catherine Lavender was part of the American 4x100 meter relay team that won gold at the 1952 Helsinki Olympic Games, sprinter and Australian indigenous person Catherine "Cathy" Freeman won Olympic gold and silver and multiple gold medals at World Championships, and Colombian Caterine Ibargüen has excelled at multiple events with triple jump gold medals at the Olympic Games and World Championships.

When it comes to combative sports, you better bring your A-game when going up against people like French judoka Catherine Fleury-Vachon, who won gold medals at the 1992 Barcelona Olympic Games and 1989 World Judo Championships. The largest concentration of top-ranked Catherines can be found in the pool, from Paralympic Games gold-medalist Catherine Huggett of Australia to a trio of American two-time Olympic gold-medalists Cathy Ferguson, Catherine "Cathy" Carr, and Catherine Fox.

Name a daughter Catherine (or some other form like Caterine and she may find a love of swimming, sparring, running, or more!

Catherine "Cathy" Carr, Swimming (Breaststroke), USA, 1960–1973

Cathy Ferguson, Swimming (Backstroke), USA, 1963–1967

Catherine Fleury-Vachon, Judo, France, 1989–1995

Catherine Fox, Swimming (Freestyle), USA, 1995–1998

Catherine "Cathy" Freeman, Track & Field (Sprinting), Australia, 1990-2003

Catherine "Cammi" Granato, Ice Hockey (Right Wing/Center), USA, 1990-2005

Catherine Huggett, Swimming (Backstroke/Freestyle), Australia, 1988–1992

Caterine Ibargüen, Track & Field (Triple Jump/Long Jump), Colombia, 2002-current

Catherine "Kit" Klein, Speed Skating, USA, 1932–1936

Catherine Lavender, Track & Field (Sprinting), USA, 1951–1952

Catherine "Cat" Osterman, Softball (Pitcher), USA, 2007–2015

Cathérine Pellen, Archery, France, 1988–2002

Catharine Pendrel, Cross-Country Cycling, Canada, 2008–current

Catherine "Cat" Whitehill, Soccer (Defender), Boston Breakers, USA, 2005-2015

CHANTAL/CHANTELLE

I don't think people today connect the name Chantal with stone, per its origin in an Old Occitan root for a "stony" place, but competitors with this name (and the variant Chantelle) are stone-cold winners. Australian Chantelle Newbery is an Olympic gold-medalist in 10-meter platform diving, Italian-American kickboxer and actor Chantal Ughi has won seven Muay Thai world championships, Canadian Chantal Petitclerc won a massive twenty-one Paralympic Games medals in wheelchair racing (fourteen of them gold), and multi-talented Canadian model, actor, and jockey Chantal Sutherland has won over 1,060 races thus far in her ongoing career.

Whether you live in a place with lots of stones or not, you can give the name Chantal or Chantelle to a girl in your family who may find her place riding horses, diving, or taking apart opponents in the octagon.

Chantelle Newbery, Diving, Australia, 1998-2006

Chantal Petitclerc, Wheelchair Racing, Canada, 1992–2008

Chantal Sutherland, Horse Racing (Jockey), Canada, 2000–current

Chantal Ughi, Kickboxing (Super Lightweight), Italy, 2005–current

CHARLEY/CHARLIE

Charlie in all its forms is more known as a "boy" name, but it's famously unisex. It can be short for a wide variety of names, including *Charlotte* and *Charlene*, and it can stand on its own. Current athletes making this name famous include LPGA tour-winning golfer Charley Hull and auto racing star Charlie Martin, who competes in the BritCar Endurance Championship. Both are known for their activism as well, Hull for gender equality in golf clubs and Martin for transgender and LGBT acceptance in sports.

Charley Hull, Golf, England, 2013–current

Charlie Martin, Auto Racing (BritCar), England, 2006–current

CHARLOTTE

Another feminine form of *Charles* is Charlotte, which, while a tad old-fashioned, is ready for its comeback with a young athlete in your family. She'll have some truly inspirational role models to look up to, like Australian rugby player Charlotte Caslick, who won Olympic gold in rugby sevens; three-time Olympic gold and two-time World Championship equestrian dressage-winner Charlotte Dujardin of Great Britain; and Swedish skier Charlotte Kalla, whose three Olympic golds and three World Championships are just part of her stellar twenty-two medal count. Last but not least is the phenom Charlotte "Lottie" Dod, who won the first of her five Wimbledon Ladies' Singles Championships at age fifteen and later in life switched to different sports, even winning an Olympic silver medal in archery!

Charlotte Caslick, Rugby (Five-Eighth/Fullback), Australia Women's National Rugby Sevens Team, Australia, 2013–current

Charlotte "Lottie" Dod, Tennis/Archery, England, 1883–1911

Charlotte Dujardin, Equestrian (Dressage), England, 2011–current

Marina "Charlotte" Kalla, Skiing, Sweden, 2003–current

CHERYL/SHERYL

The modern name Cheryl (sometimes spelled Sheryl) has a couple possible derivations: most consider it an evolution of *Cherie* from the French word meaning "beloved" or "darling," or it may come from *Charles* like quite a few of the other "C" names above. While there are a couple winning Cheryls and Sheryls in curling and netball, there's an excellent chance that if you give one of these names to a daughter in your family, she'll end up loving basketball like small forward and Olympic Games gold medal-winner Cheryl Miller, four-time All-Star forward and three-time WNBA champion Cheryl Ford, and shooting guard/small forward Sheryl Swoopes, who has six All-Star appearances and four championships!

Cheryl Ford, Basketball (Forward), Detroit Shock, USA, 2003–2013

Cheryl Miller, Basketball (Small Forward), USC, USA, 1982–1986

Sheryl Swoopes, Basketball (Shooting Guard/Small Forward), Houston Comets, USA, 1997–2011

CHLOE

The fertility origins of Chloe (with or without accents on the "e") and its basis in an Ancient Greek word for a "new green shoot" may give a girl with this name a green thumb, but she'll also enjoy rugged play and sports if she's anything like Australian Olympic gold-medalists rugby forward Chloe Dalton and pentathlete

Chloe Esposito. Not to mention American snowboarder Chloe Kim, whose incredible career has already included an Olympic gold medal, two World Championship golds, and five gold medals at X Games.

Chloe Dalton, Rugby (Forward), Australia Women's National Rugby Sevens Team, Australia, 2014–current

Chloe Esposito, Track & Field (Pentathlon), Australia, 2008–2016

Chloe Kim, Snowboarding, USA, 2013–current

CHRIS

The unisex Chris, as you might expect, is a name that comes from "Christ," usually by way of longer forms like *Christina/Christine*. However, sometimes champions just need a short and quick name, especially if they're particularly adept at dealing with fast-traveling balls in sports. A Chris in your family may gravitate toward baseball, like 1954 All-American Girls Professional Baseball League champion catcher Chris Ballingall, or excel at tennis, like Christine "Chris" Evert, who won 157 singles titles and eighteen Grand Slam singles and was ranked number one in the world multiple times.

Chris Ballingall, Baseball (Catcher), Kalamazoo Lassies, USA, 1953–1954

Christine "Chris" Evert, Tennis, USA, 1972–1989

CHRISSIE/CHRISSY/CHRISTIE/CHRISTY

Along with *Chris*, there's a series of short forms and nicknames for "Christ"-based names that include Chrissie, Christie, and Christy. At one time these may have been considered informal and relaxed, but the athletes who have gone by them are anything but. These include super welterweight title-holding boxing champ Christy Martin; World Championship cyclist Chrissy Redden of Canada; American Olympic Games gold-medalist softball shortstop/outfielder Christie Ambrosi; American soccer defender Christie Pearce, who won three Olympic gold medals and two FIFA Women's World Cups; and four-time Ironman Triathlon World Champion and multiple record-holder Chrissie Wellington of England.

Christie Ambrosi, Softball (Shortstop/Outfielder), USA, 1996–2000

Christy Martin, Boxing (Middleweight/Welterweight), USA, 1989–2012

Christie Pearce, Soccer (Center Back), SkyBlue Football Club, USA, 1997–2010

Chrissy Redden, Cross-Country Cycling, Canada, 2000–2003

Christine "Chrissie" Wellington, Triathlon, England, 2006–2011

CHRISTINE/KRISTINA

A variety of names have descended from the Middle Ages moniker *Christian*, itself referring to people of the Christian faith. Some of the most popular feminine variants around the world include Kristina and Christine, so it should come as no surprise that athletes with those names have made a big impression too.

Scattered across a huge range of disciplines are Olympic gold-medalist weightlifter Christine Girard of Canada; Canadian Olympic gold medal-winning soccer forward and holder of the record for international goals (men or women—188 in total!) Christine Sinclair; Kristina Šmigun-Vähi of Estonia, who won two Olympic Games gold medals, a World Championship, and more in cross-country skiing; and Canadian speed skating legend Christine Nesbitt, whose Olympic gold and eight World Championships are just part of her huge eighteen-medal count in international events.

In rowing, there are two-time World Champion Kristina Larsen of Australia and

Germany's Kristina Mundt, who has two Olympic gold medals and two World Rowing Championships. On the tennis courts, Kristina "Kiki" Mladenovic claimed the world's top spot in doubles in 2019 with twenty-four titles, and Christine Ohuruogu of Great Britain ran to four Olympic medals, including a gold, ten World Championships podiums (three of them gold), and many more accolades at international events!

Whether you prefer Christine or Kristina, giving your daughter one of these classic names will add a bit of speed and tenacity to a noble spirit.

Christine Girard, Weightlifting, Canada, 2001–2012

Kristina Larsen, Rowing, Australia, 1995–2003

Kristina "Kiki" Mladenovic, Tennis, France, 2009–current

Kristina Mundt, Rowing, Germany, 1985–1994

Christine Nesbitt, Speed Skating, Canada, 2003–2015

Christine Ohuruogu, Track & Field (Sprinting), England, 2004–2018

Christine Sinclair, Soccer (Forward), Portland Thorns Football Club, Canada, 2001–current

Kristina Šmigun-Vähi, Cross-Country Skiing, Estonia, 1993–2010

CLAIRE/CLARESSA

"Clear," "bright," and even "famous" are the meanings of the ancient Latin word *clarus* that has led to a family of modern names including Claire. Athletic exemplars with these names include American swimming butterfly stroke competitor Claire Donahue, who won an Olympic gold medal and World Championship with her medley team. Meanwhile, cricketer Claire Taylor established herself as one of the top batters of her generation by being the first woman named *Wisden* Cricketer of the Year and 2009 ICC Women's Cricketer of the Year, winning the 2009 Women's Cricket World Cup and the very first Women's World Twenty20 in the same year, and being inducted into the ICC Hall of Fame.

If you like these names but are looking for something even more unique, consider a variant like Claressa, made famous by the indomitable Claressa Shields. A boxer and mixed martial artist, Shields has a solid gold medal count of five (two at the Olympics, two World Championships, and one at Pan American Games) and has held multiple titles in both sports and in multiple weight classes!

Claire Donahue, Swimming (Butterfly/Medley), USA, 2008–2014

Claressa Shields, Boxing/MMA (Middleweight/Lightweight), USA, 2012–2016

Samantha Claire Taylor, Cricket (Batter), Berkshire Women's Cricket Team, England, 1993–2011

CLAUDIA

Claudia is an ancient name, one of the noble houses (*gens*) of ancient Rome. It's also the feminine form of the name *Claudius*, which was Latin for "lame"—a far cry from the incredible and amazing abilities of Claudias from around the world, like Olympic gold-medalist and three-time World Champion gymnast Claudia Presăcan of Romania; Costa Rican freestyle swimmer Claudia Poll, who captured Olympic gold and five World Championships; and Austrian paraplegic alpine monoskier Claudia Lösch, who collected seven Paralympic Games medals (two of them gold) and six World Championship golds along with a silver!

Claudia is clearly an awesome name with ancient history and some solid athletic muscle behind it, but it's especially fitting for anyone with German lineage. That country has produced Tour de l'Aude– and Giro d'Italia Femminile-winning cyclist Claudia Lichtenberg; Olympic and World Championship gold-medalist shot putter Claudia Losch; cross country skier Claudia Nystad, who won six medals at Olympic Games (two of them gold) and five World Championship medals; and the massively successful speed skater Claudia Pechstein, whose lengthy medal count includes five gold out of a total nine Olympic medals and six golds out of an incredible forty-one World Championship medals.

Claudia Lichtenberg, Road Cycling, Germany, 2006–2017

Claudia Lösch, Alpine Skiing, Austria, 2006–2015

Claudia Losch, Track & Field (Shot Put), Germany, 1983–1990

Claudia Nystad, Cross-Country Skiing, Germany, 1998–2015

Claudia Pechstein, Speed Skating, Germany, 1988–2017

Claudia Poll, Swimming (Freestyle), Costa Rica, 1993–2001

Claudia Presăcan, Artistic Gymnastics, Romania, 1994–2000

CONNIE

Connie is another unisex name that originated as a short form of numerous names (including *Conrad*, *Constance*, *Cornelia*, and *Cornelius*), but has come to stand on its own. Constance "Connie" Wisniewkski was an early baseball pioneer, earning four All-Star appearances, two championships, and a number of records in the All-American Girls Professional Baseball League in the 1940s and '50s. More recent champion Connies include Canadian curler Connie Laliberte, who won one of each medal in World Championships; the multi-talented cyclist and speed skater Connie Carpenter-Phinney, who rode to an Olympic gold medal and World Championship; and nine-time Paralympics Games gold-medalist in wheelchair racing Connie Hansen of Denmark.

Connie Carpenter-Phinney, Road Cycling, USA, 1972–1984

Connie Hansen, Wheelchair Racing, Denmark, 1984–1992

Connie Laliberte, Curling (Skip), Canada, 1984–2000

Constance "Connie" Wisniewkski, Baseball (Pitcher/Outfielder), Grand Rapids Chicks, USA, 1944–1952

CORTNEY/COURTNEY

The unisex Courtney (rarely Cortney) has a couple of possible, and very different, derivations, coming from either an Old French place name for people living in the Courtenay region, a Norman nickname meaning "short nose," or even an Irish word meaning "descendent of Curnan." Most Courtneys who have excelled in athletics and sports have been Americans, though they appear in many different disciplines. You can find exemplars like X Games gold-medalist surfing star Courtney Conlogue; three-time WNBA All-Star point guard Courtney Vandersloot, who won a championship with the Chicago Sky; two-time world champion gymnast Courtney Kupets; and water polo attacker Courtney Mathewson, who has gold medals from five different major international competitions.

Many Courtneys are focused entirely on speed. Track and field competitions have witnessed the accomplishments of Olympic gold-medalist and five-time World Champion sprinter Courtney Okolo. In the pool, freestyle swimmer Courtney Shealy has won two Olympic gold medals, while Paralympian Cortney Jordan has won a huge number of medals and World Championships in a variety of different strokes and race lengths. The fastest Courtney of all may be drag racer Courtney Force, the winningest female Funny Car driver in NHRA history, who has twelve victories achieved at over three hundred miles per hour.

Naming your daughter Courtney will surely instill in her a drive to succeed, and just maybe a love of going fast too!

Courtney Conlogue, Surfing, USA, 2004–current

Courtney Force, Auto Racing (NHRA), USA, 2011–2019

Cortney Jordan, Swimming (Backstroke/Freestyle/Medley), USA, 2006–2016

Courtney Kupets, Artistic Gymnastics, USA, 1999–2004

Courtney Mathewson, Water Polo (Attacker), USA, 2010–2016

Courtney Okolo, Track & Field (Sprinting), USA, 2015–current

Courtney Shealy, Swimming (Freestyle), USA, 2000–2003

Courtney Vandersloot, Basketball (Point Guard), Chicago Sky, USA, 2011–current

CRISTIANE

You don't have to be Brazilian to give the name Cristiane (a feminine form of the name *Christian* that originated in Brazil) to someone in your family, but if you do, she'll be absolutely unstoppable if she takes after the champion who has come before her. In the octagon, Cristiane "Cris Cyborg" Venâncio is an MMA legend with a 25–2–1 record, two World Jiu-Jitsu Championships, and a career that's seen her hold featherweight championships in all four major mixed martial arts organizations to become the only Grand Slam Champion in history!

Cristiane "Cris Cyborg" Venâncio, MMA (Featherweight), Brazil, 2005–current

CYNTHIA

Another name that reaches all the way back to ancient Greece and Greek mythology is Cynthia, which comes from an epithet honoring the goddess Artemis's birthplace on Mount Kynthos on the island of Delos. A patron deity of athletes (in particular racers and archers), Artemis can inspire a Cynthia in your family to athletic feats worthy of recognition alongside freestyle swimmer Cynthia Woodhead, who won three gold and two silver medals at World Championships when she was only fourteen years old; three-time All-Star and four-time WNBA champion Cynthia Cooper-Dyke of the Houston Comets (who also won Olympic gold); and five-time world champion in forms and weapons and five-time tournament Grand Master martial arts legend Cynthia Rothrock!

Cynthia Cooper-Dyke, Basketball (Point Guard/Shooting Guard), Houston Comets, USA, 1986–2003

Cynthia Rothrock (Foo Lok Law), Martial Arts, USA, 1981–1985

Cynthia Woodhead, Swimming (Freestyle), USA, 1978–1984

D

BOYS

DAIGO

Daigo is a Japanese masculine name that can be written with characters meaning "big" or "great" along with "me" or "enlightenment" and more. Naming your son Daigo may give him great enlightenment, but it's more likely to inspire in him a love of competition, possibly on the soccer field, behind the wheel, or even with a controller in his hand! We've seen such successes with athletes like two-time J.League Best XI right back Daigo Nishi, who has collected a J1 League championship, the J.League Cup three times, Emperor's Cup twice, Japanese Super Cup, and an AFC Champions League championship.

Daigo Saito is an international drifting driver who has won seventeen events and two championships in the D1 Grand Prix series and was the first driver ever to win both major drift events (D1GP and Formula D), while Daigo Umehara stands as one of the greatest (and longest-running) fighting game esports competitors who has won the Evolution Championship Series six times and Super Battle Opera championship twice, set a Guinness World Record for becoming the "most successful player in major tournaments of *Street Fighter*," and more!

- **Daigo Nishi**, Soccer (Right Back), Kashima Antlers, Japan, 2006–current
- **Daigo Saito**, Auto Racing (D1 Grand Prix), Japan, 2004–current
- **Daigo "The Beast" Umehara**, Esports (Fighting Games), Japan, 1997–current

DALE

You might not expect much of people named for a type of pleasant valley, but Dales come in all varieties and several categories of champion. Just look at Olympic and World Championship gold medal–winning skier Dale Begg-Smith, baseball slugger Dale Murphy (seven-time All-Star), and South African cricketer Dale Steyn, who's widely considered one of the best fast bowlers of all time.

Meanwhile, arguably the most famous Dales are concentrated in NASCAR! There you can find Dale Jarrett, with thirty-two Cup Series wins and a championship, and the father-son duo of Dale Earnhardt. The "Intimidator" was a feared driver throughout his twenty-six-year career, racing to a massive seventy-six wins and a record-tying seven championships before his untimely death on the track in 2001; his super popular son Dale Jr. had his own Cup career with twenty-six wins, as well as twenty-four wins and a championship in the Xfinity series.

A Dale in your family is likely to feel perfectly at home behind the wheel, but he may collect more than his share of speeding tickets.

Dale Begg-Smith, Skiing, Australia, 2006–2014

Ralph Dale Earnhardt Jr., Auto Racing (NASCAR), USA, 1996–current

Ralph Dale "Intimidator" Earnhardt Sr., Auto Racing (NASCAR), USA, 1975–2001

Dale Jarrett, Auto Racing (NASCAR), USA, 1982–2008

Dale Murphy, Baseball (Outfielder), Atlanta Braves, USA, 1976–1993

Dale Steyn, Cricket (Bowler), Titans, South Africa, 2003–2021

DAMIAN

With its origin in an Ancient Greek word for "conquering" and "overcoming," a Damian in your family is sure to make waves wherever he ends up, just as point guard Damian Lillard has in the NBA. Thus far, he's collected six All-Star appearances in his nine-year career with the Trail Blazers, as well as a gold medal at the 2020 Olympic Games and numerous awards and accolades.

Damian Lillard Sr., Basketball (Point Guard), Portland Trail Blazers, USA, 2012–current

DAN/DANNY

Some people go by the full name *Daniel* (biblical Hebrew meaning "God is my judge"), but some prefer more casual forms like Dan and Danny. Dan also has some derivations of its own, including an Old Norse source meaning "Danish person." So where do we see champion Dans and Dannys?

Dan Majerle collected three All-Star appearances during his stint with the Phoenix Suns, along with a World Championship with the US National Team; American speed skater Dan Jansen won Olympic gold and an assortment of medals at World Championships; five-time X Games skateboarding gold medalist Danny Way is the only person ever to ollie over the Great Wall of China; and decathlete Dan O'Brien won Olympic and World Championship gold while setting world records.

Some feel the need for speed, like Dan Gurney whose long list of auto racing accomplishments include co-winning the first-ever Cannonball Run and becoming one of only three drivers ever to win races in four major series. The more pugilistic competitors with these names include iconic wrestlers/mixed martial artists Dan Severn and Dan Henderson, who both held multiple different championship titles during their storied careers. Lastly, the gridiron has seen the exploits of Hall of Famer Dan Marino who earned nine Pro Bowl appearances and numerous awards with the Miami Dolphins on his way to becoming one of the most famous and highest-ranked quarterbacks of all time.

Whether you're going for a short form of *Daniel* or just using Dan or Danny on its own, a child so named in your family may gravitate toward racing, combat sports, or football, but has the chance to succeed in anything he sets his mind to!

Daniel "Dan" Gurney, Auto Racing (Formula 1), USA, 1959–1970

Daniel "Dan" Henderson, MMA (Welterweight/Middleweight/Heavyweight), USA, 1997–2016

Daniel "Dan" Jansen, Speed Skating, USA, 1982–1994

Daniel "Dan" Majerle, Basketball (Shooting Guard/Small Forward), Phoenix Suns, USA, 1988–2002

Daniel "Dan" Marino Jr., Football (Quarterback), Miami Dolphins, USA, 1983–1999

Daniel "Dan" O'Brien, Track & Field (Decathlon), USA, 1991-1996

Daniel "Dan" Severn, MMA (Heavyweight/Openweight)/Freestyle Wrestling, USA, 1994-2013

Danny Way, Skateboarding, USA, 1989-2009

DANIEL

Daniel, often a source for *Dan/Danny*, can make a big impact when used in its full form because it comes from biblical Hebrew, meaning "God is my judge," as well as the New Testament *Book of Daniel*.

With its international popularity, we can find Daniels excelling in a wide variety of disciplines, like Olympic and World Championship gold medal-winning discus thrower Daniel Ståhl of Sweden; all-time great handball player Daniel Narcisse, who won two Olympic gold medals and four World Championships; two-time World Poker Tour champion and six-time World Series of Poker-winner Daniel Negreanu; and the Brazilian swimming phenom Daniel Dias, who won fourteen gold Paralympics medals (out of twenty-seven total) and thirty-one World Championships!

Swedish Daniel Sedin and his twin brother, Henrik, were star players for the NHL's Vancouver Canucks, with Daniel earning three All-Star shots (along with gold medals for Sweden at Olympics and World Championships), while Daniel Alfredsson has gold and silver Olympic medals, silver and bronze medals from World Championships, and six All-Star appearances. The highest concentrations of Daniels have been on the soccer field, and two of them were defenders on Argentina's 1978 FIFA World Cup champion team! Daniel Killer had nearly thirty goals in his almost five hundred senior and national appearances, while captain Daniel Passarella won two World Cups, ranked as the top scoring defender during his career, and is widely considered the greatest South American defender in history.

Daniel Alfredsson, Ice Hockey (Right Wing), Ottawa Senators, Sweden, 1992-2014

Daniel Dias, Swimming (Backstroke/Breaststroke/Butterfly/Freestyle/Medley), Brazil, 2006-current

Daniel Killer, Soccer (Defender), Club Atlético Rosario Central, Argentina, 1970-1987

Daniel Narcisse, Handball (Center Back), France, 2000-2017

Daniel Negreanu, Card Gaming (Poker), USA, 1997-current

Daniel Passarella, Soccer (Center Back/Sweeper), Club Atlético River Plate, Argentina, 1971-1989

Daniel Sedin, Ice Hockey (Left Wing), Vancouver Canucks, Sweden, 1997-2018

Daniel Ståhl, Track & Field (Discus), Sweden, 2013-current

DARREL/DARRELL/DARRYL

A lot of names have variant versions, but few have quite as many as the Darrell family. The name comes from a Norman-French place name for a person from the Airelle region of France, and there are seemingly endless evolutions and variations. With rare exceptions, champion athletes with these names are Americans, though they've spread out to dominate numerous fields, including esports (fighting game expert and *Street Fighter* Zangief pro Darryl "Snake Eyez" Lewis, who has eleven tournament wins), horse racing (jockey Darrel McHargue, who won over 2,550 races in his sixteen-year career), and archery (two-time Olympic gold-medalist Darrell Pace).

Currently racing in NASCAR's elite Cup series is Darrell "Bubba" Wallace, the first African-American to win in multiple NASCAR series, while Darrell Waltrip made history there with his fourth-place record-tying eighty-four wins and three championships. Both football and baseball have athletes with these names as well, the former including four-time Pro Bowl cornerback for the Washington Redskins and two-time Super Bowl-winner Darrell Green. The latter has seen the likes of three very talented men whose lives were also marked with personal challenges: pitcher Darryl Kile (three-time All-Star), catcher Darrell Porter (four-time All-Star and World Series-winner), and the incomparable hitter Darryl Strawberry (eight-time All-Star and three-time World Series champion).

If you like the sound of Darrell you have lots of options as far as spellings and variant forms, and choosing one for your son will give him plenty of athletic opportunities. You may want to steer him more towards auto racing and football rather than baseball, though.

- **Darrell Green**, Football (Cornerback), Washington Redskins, USA, 1983–2002
- **Darryl Kile**, Baseball (Pitcher), Houston Astros, USA, 1991–2002
- **Darryl "Snake Eyez" Lewis**, Esports (Fighting Games), USA, 2010–current
- **Darrel McHargue**, Horse Racing (Jockey), USA, 1972–1988
- **Darrell Pace**, Archery, USA, 1972–1991
- **Darrell Porter**, Baseball (Catcher), Kansas City Royals, USA, 1971–1987
- **Darryl Strawberry**, Baseball (Right Fielder), New York Mets, USA, 1983–1999
- **William Darrell "Bubba" Wallace Jr.**, Auto Racing (NASCAR), USA, 2012–current
- **Darrell Waltrip**, Auto Racing (NASCAR), USA, 1972–2000

DAVE

There are lots of impressive athletes named *David* out there, but some of them prefer to go by the popular diminutive Dave. Singular Daves with notable careers include two-time American Olympic gold-medalist volleyball player Dave Saunders; Olympic gold-medalist freestyle wrestler and world champion Dave Schultz; freestyle swimmer Dave Walters, who won Olympic gold and four World Championships; American sailing legend Dave Curtis, whose medal count included thirteen World Championships (nine of them gold); ten-time World Champion archer (and considered one of the best ever) Dave Cousins; fiery and controversial golfer Dave Hill, who had thirteen PGA wins and six tour championships; and the legendary Scottish soccer player Dave Mackay, who had over six hundred appearances and nearly ninety goals in his senior and national career.

What happens when multiple Daves succeed in the same sport? Well, you get luminaries like basketball greats Dave Bing (seven-time All-Star point guard) and eight-time All-Star and two-time NBA champion center Dave Cowans, who spent a decade with the Boston Celtics. Canadian defenseman Dave Ritchie scored the very first goal in the NHL in 1917, paving the way for players like All-Star and "Miracle on Ice" Olympic gold-medalist right wing Dave Christian and four-time All-Star right wing Dave Taylor. The gridiron has seen plays by linebacker Dave Robinson, who had three Pro Bowl appearances, three NFL championships, and two Super Bowl wins; New York favorite punter Dave Jennings, who went to the Pro Bowl four times during his stint with the Giants; and seven-time Pro Bowl linebacker Dave Wilcox, who spent his entire career with the San Francisco 49ers. Last but not least, baseball has seen seven-time All-Star pitcher Dave Stieb; slugger Dave Parker, who got the nickname "the Cobra" along with his seven All-Star appearances and two World Series wins; and twelve-time All-Star hitter Dave Winfield.

If you name a son *David* but call him Dave, know that he'll have a bright future and probably gravitate toward team sports, and instill in him an indomitable spirit, like amputee legend Dave Stevens, the only college football and minor league baseball player without legs!

- **David "Dave" Bing**, Basketball (Point Guard), Detroit Pistons, USA, 1966–1978
- **David "Dave" Christian**, Ice Hockey (Right Wing), Washington Capitals, USA, 1980–1996
- **David "Dave" Cousins**, Archery, USA, 1998–2013
- **David "Dave" Cowens**, Basketball (Center), Boston Celtics, USA, 1970–1983
- **David "Dave" Curtis**, Sailing, USA, 1970–2002
- **James David "Dave" Hill**, Golf, USA, 1958–1987
- **David "Dave" Jennings**, Football (Punter), New York Giants, USA, 1974–1987
- **David "Dave" Mackay**, Soccer (Left Half/Sweeper), Tottenham Hotspur Football Club, Scotland, 1953–1972
- **David "Dave" Parker**, Baseball (Right Fielder/Designated Hitter), Pittsburgh Pirates, USA, 1973–1991
- **David "Dave" Ritchie**, Ice Hockey (Defense), Montreal Wanderers, Canada, 1914–1926
- **Richard David "Dave" Robinson**, Football (Linebacker), Green Bay Packers, USA, 1963–1974
- **David "Dave" Saunders**, Volleyball (Outside Hitter), USA, 1984–1988
- **David "Dave" Schultz**, Freestyle Wrestling, USA, 1980–1996
- **David "Dave" Stevens**, Baseball (Pinch Hitter), St. Paul Saints, USA, 1983–1996
- **David "Dave" Stieb**, Baseball (Pitcher), Toronto Blue Jays, USA, 1979–1998
- **David "Dave" Taylor**, Ice Hockey (Right Wing), Los Angeles Kings, Canada, 1977–1994
- **David "Dave" Walters**, Swimming (Freestyle), USA, 2008–2012
- **David "Dave" Wilcox**, Football (Linebacker), San Francisco 49ers, USA, 1964–1974
- **David "Dave" Winfield**, Baseball (Right Fielder), New York Yankees, USA, 1973–1995

DAVEY

Davids are ubiquitous and *Daves* show up in a lot of sports, but some athletes are just Daveys through and through. These unique characters include two MLB second basemen: four-time All-Star Davey Lopes, who has a World Series win, and four-time All-Star Davey Johnson, who has two World Series championships. Even they are not as fast as NASCAR Hall of Fame driver Davey Allison, who won nineteen races in his nine-year career.

- **David "Davey" Allison**, Auto Racing (NASCAR), USA, 1983–1993
- **David "Davey" Johnson**, Baseball (Second Baseman), Baltimore Orioles, USA, 1965–1978
- **David "Davey" Lopes**, Baseball (Second Baseman), Los Angeles Dodgers, USA, 1972–1987

DAVID

The biblical Hebrew name David (meaning "beloved") is perennially popular in many areas of the world, so it should come as no surprise that there are *a lot* of athletic champions with it. These range through disciplines and sports, including surfing (international champion David Nuuhiwa), freestyle skiing (two-time Olympic gold-medalist, World Champion, and four-time X Games-winner David Wise), synchronized diving (David Boudia, who won Olympic gold, silver, and bronzes), bowling (eleven-time PBA title-winner David Ozio), volleyball (Olympic gold-medalist, and World Cup and World League champion David Lee), squash (number one ranked, four-time World Champion David Palmer of Australia), rowing (Scottish

Paralympic Games gold-medalist and two-time World Champion David Smith), and boccia (David Smith, the most successful British player ever with three Paralympic gold medals, four World Championship wins, and more)!

Davids have many "beloved" sports and activities, like esports American *Halo* champion David "Walshy" Walsh), woodchopping (Australia's David Foster, who is the country's most successful athlete with over one thousand titles), lifting (Soviet weightlifter David Rigert, who won an Olympic gold medal and six World Championships while setting sixty-five world records), horse racing (Canadian jockey David Gall, who holds the fifth rank in lifetime wins with nearly 7,400), and figure skating (American Olympic-winner and three-time World Champion David Jenkins).

Golf has seen pros like ten-time South African PGA tour-winner David Frost, David Toms with thirteen wins, and former top-ranked David Duval with twenty wins, while rugby giants include record-breaking 1984 "grand slam"-winner David Campese of Australia. Some Davids have enjoyed driving really fast, like Scottish thirteen-time Formula 1 Grand Prix-winner David Coulthard; American motorcycle racer David Bailey, who won thirty Motocross races and four championships; and NASCAR legend David Pearson, who won 105 Cup Series races and three championships along with dozens of other accomplishments.

One of the most-winning Davids on the tennis court has been American paralyzed player David Wagner, who racked up an incredible 157 career titles in his race to the top spot in the world. Over on the basketball court were high-flying shooting guard David "Skywalker" Thompson, who had four All-Star appearances; and David Robinson, who played center for the San Antonio Spurs with ten All-Star selections and two championships. Gridiron football greats named David have included placekicker David Akers and guard David DeCastro, who have six Pro Bowl appearances each. In the pool, David Wilkie has been called the greatest Scottish swimmer with his one gold and two silver Olympic medals, three World Championships, and more; American David McCagg has a solid gold medal collection of four World Championships; and David Roberts of Wales has a massive sixteen Paralympics medals (eleven of them gold) and fifteen podium finishes at World Championships (eight of them gold)!

Track and field events have had their share of Davids with David Verburg, who has won gold medals at Olympics and various World Championships in 400 meter events; two-time Olympic gold-medalist and two-time World Champion in 800 meter David Rudisha of Kenya; Australian arm-amputee David Evans, who won two Paralympic Games gold medals and three World Championships in various running events; and English wheelchair racer David Weir, who has racked up ten Paralympics medals (six of them gold), eight World Championships medals (six of them gold), two World Cup wins, and more. America's pastime, on the other hand, has seen five-time All-Star pitcher David Price; five-time All-Star and five-time World Series champion pitcher David Cone; New York Mets third baseman David Wright, who set multiple franchise records and racked up seven All-Star appearances and other accolades; and the iconic ten-time All-Star and three-time World Series-winning hitter David "Big Papi" Ortiz.

There is a huge concentration of elite Davids in soccer (or football, depending on your locale). Just a few of the stand-outs in this group are FIFA World Cup-winning French striker David Trezeguet, who has scored over 260 goals; FIFA World Cup-winning and high-ranked Spanish striker David Villa, who has made nearly four hundred goals; and FIFA World Cup and two-time UEFA

European Championship-winning midfielder David Silva, who has over 716 appearances. Arguably the most famous and popular David in sports is midfielder David Beckham, whose epic twenty-year career has garnered nineteen major trophies, spots in multiple Halls of Fame, high rankings in best-of lists, records like being the first English player to win league titles in four different countries, and dozens of awards and accolades.

And then there are the many Davids in combat sports! They can be found in karate (Scottish two-time World Champion David Coulter) and judo (French judoka David Douillet, who won two Olympic gold medals, four World Championships, and more), while on the wrestling mat, Russian/Slovakian David Musulbes won Olympic gold and silver medals and two World Championships; and American David Taylor collected gold from Olympic Games, World Championships, World Cup, and more. And some of the best competitors in boxing have felt the ferocious fists of American two-time super middleweight champ (and currently ranked best in the world) David Benavidez, who has an astounding 25-0 record; British cruiserweight and heavyweight David Haye, who held multiple world titles; and six-time heavyweight title-holder David Tua of Samoa, who's famous for his incredible punching, ended his career with a 52-5-2 record.

As you can see, there is no limit to what a David can achieve and it'll be a wonder to watch a boy with that name in your family make his place in the world.

David Akers, Football (Placekicker), Philadelphia Eagles, USA, 1997–2013

David Bailey, Motorcycle Racing (AMA), USA, 1980–1986

David Beckham, Soccer (Midfielder), Manchester United Football Club, England, 1992–2013

Anthony David Benavidez, Boxing (Middleweight/Heavyweight), USA, 2015–current

David Boudia, Diving, USA, 2000–current

David Campese, Rugby (Wing/Fullback), Randwick District Rugby Union Football Club, Australia, 1982–1996

David Cone, Baseball (Pitcher), New York Mets, USA, 1986–2003

David Coulter, Karate, Scotland, 1975–1984

David Coulthard, Auto Racing (Formula 1), Scotland, 1993–2008

David DeCastro, Football (Guard), Pittsburgh Steelers, USA, 2012–2020

David Douillet, Judo, France, 1991–2000

David Duval, Golf, USA, 1993–2011

David Evans, Para-Athletics, Australia, 1991–1996

David Foster, Woodchopping, Australia, 1978–current

David Frost, Golf, South Africa, 1981–2012

David Gall, Horse Racing (Jockey), Canada, 1956–1999

David Haye, Boxing (Cruiserweight/Heavyweight), England, 2002–2018

David Jenkins, Figure Skating, USA, 1954–1960

David Lee, Volleyball (Middle Blocker), USA, 2001–2016

David McCagg, Swimming (Freestyle), USA, 1978–1982

David Musulbes, Freestyle Wrestling, Russia, 1994–2008

David Nuuhiwa, Surfing, USA, 1952–current

David "Big Papi" Ortiz, Baseball (Designated Hitter/First Baseman), Boston Red Sox, Dominican Republic, 1997–2016

David Ozio, Bowling, USA, 1985–1995

David Palmer, Squash, Australia, 1994–2011

David Pearson, Auto Racing (NASCAR), USA, 1960–1986

David Price, Baseball (Pitcher), Tampa Bay Rays, USA, 2008–current

David Rigert, Weightlifting, USSR, 1968–1980

David Roberts, Para Swimming, Wales, 1993–2010

David Robinson, Basketball (Center), San Antonio Spurs, USA, 1989–2003

David Rudisha, Track & Field (Sprinting), Kenya, 2009–2017

David Silva, Soccer (Midfielder), Manchester City Football Club, Spain, 2001–current

David Smith, Boccia, England, 2004–current

David Smith, Para Rowing, Scotland, 2006–2012

David Taylor, Freestyle Wrestling, USA, 2010–current

David "Skywalker" Thompson, Basketball (Shooting Guard), Denver Nuggets, USA, 1975–1984

David Toms, Golf, USA, 1989–2017

David Trezeguet, Soccer (Striker), Juventus Football Club, France, 1994–2014

Faumuina To'aletai Mafaufau David Tua, Boxing (Heavyweight), Samoa, 1992–2013

David Verburg, Track & Field (Sprinting), USA, 2013–current

David Villa Sánchez, Soccer (Striker), Valencia Club de Fútbol, Spain, 2000–2020

David Wagner, Tennis, USA, 1999–current

David "Walshy" Walsh, Esports (*Halo*), USA, 2004–2012

David Weir, Para-Athletics, England, 2002–current

David Wilkie, Swimming (Breaststroke/Medley), Scotland, 1969–1976

David Wise, Skiing, USA, 2012–current

David Wright, Baseball (Third Baseman), New York Mets, USA, 2004–2018

DEACON

Occasionally used as a proper first name, Deacon (from an Ancient Greek word for "messenger" or "servant") is more often a nickname. It was used by several early, record-setting American baseball players, including pitcher Charles "Deacon" Phillippe, who pitched a no-hitter in 1899. The most famous Deacon in sports is eight-time Pro Bowl defensive end David "Deacon" Jones, who played most of his career for the Los Angeles Rams, is widely ranked among the top defensive players of all time, and who coined the term "sack" as it pertains to football.

David "Deacon" Jones, Football (Defensive End), Los Angeles Rams, USA, 1961–1974

Charles "Deacon" Phillippe, Baseball (Pitcher), Pittsburgh Pirates, USA, 1899–1911

DEION/DION

Names like Deion and Dion share a common origin, having evolved from the Ancient Greek deity Dionysos. Now, you don't have to love wine and hard partying to bequeath one of these names to your child, and if you do, he may take after these multiple successful professional athletes. Three-time NHL All-Star and World Champion defenseman Dion Phaneuf dazzled on the ice, while traditional football has witnessed the expertise of Dion Dublin, who's scored 183 goals in 613 appearances! Deion Sanders, possibly the biggest star with a name from this group, was a multi-talented athlete in high school, going on to play multiple sports in college, including running track. He would go on to careers in not one but two professional sports, playing major league baseball for nine years and then dominating football with eight Pro Bowl appearances, two Super Bowl championships, and tons of accolades and accomplishments.

Dion Dublin, Soccer (Center-Forward/Center-Back), Aston Villa Football Club, England, 1988–2008

Dion Phaneuf, Ice Hockey (Defense), Calgary Flames, Canada, 2005–2019

Deion Sanders Sr., Football (Cornerback/Wide Receiver)/Baseball (Outfielder), Atlanta Falcons/Atlanta Braves, USA, 1989–2005/1989–2001

DENIS/DENNIS/DENYS

Like the *Deion/Dion* family of names, Dennis and its variants are also descendants of the Greek god Dionysos via the Latin name *Dionysius*. Among the athletes here we can see a bit more of the Dionysian influence with some bad boys among the champions, like undisputed world heavyweight kickboxing champion Dennis Alexio, who has held six titles in his MMA career and New Zealand's Denis "Denny" Hulme, whose gruffness behind the wheel earned him the nickname "the Bear" as he was winning eight races and a championship in Formula 1. Then there are six-time World Champion ski mountaineer Dennis Brunod of Italy; six-time All-Star and World Series champion pitcher Dennis Eckersley; six-time Pro Bowl safety Dennis Smith, who played his whole career with the Denver Broncos; basketball's five-time All-Star and three-time NBA champ Dennis Johnson; and swimmer Denys Dubrov of Ukraine, who has won eleven Paralympic Games medals (four of them gold) and two World Championships to date.

On European football fields, Scottish Denis Law is the third-ranked goal scorer in Manchester United history and a Ballon d'Or winner, while defender Denis Smith of Stoke City was renowned for being tougher than anyone else and suffering a staggering amount of injuries that earned him the *Guinness Book of Records* recognition as the most injured man in football.

Arguably the most famous, or maybe infamous, of this group is basketball bad boy Dennis Rodman. The "Worm" made his mark on the NBA as an aggressive defender and rebounder, racking up two All-Star appearances, five NBA championships, multiple awards . . . and plenty of controversies both on and off the court.

A Dennis (or Denis/Denys) in your family may not achieve the notoriety of a Rodman, but he'll be tough and daring, a challenge to keep up with but a formidable competitor.

- **Dennis Alexio**, MMA/Boxing (Heavyweight), USA, 1980–1999
- **Dennis Brunod**, Ski Mountaineering, Italy, 2001–2010
- **Denys Dubrov**, Swimming (Breaststroke/Butterfly/Freestyle/Medley), Ukraine, 2007–current
- **Dennis Eckersley**, Baseball (Pitcher), Oakland Athletics, USA, 1975–1998
- **Denis "Denny" Hulme**, Auto Racing (Formula 1), New Zealand, 1965–1974
- **Dennis Johnson**, Basketball (Point Guard/Shooting Guard), Boston Celtics, USA, 1976–1990
- **Denis Law**, Soccer (Center Forward), Manchester United Football Club, Scotland, 1956–1974
- **Dennis "Worm" Rodman**, Basketball (Power Forward/Small Forward), Chicago Bulls, USA, 1986–2006
- **Dennis Smith**, Football (Safety), Denver Broncos, USA, 1981–1994
- **Denis Smith**, Soccer (Defender), Stoke City Football Club, England, 1968–1983

DEREK/DERRICK

From the Germanic *Theodoric* (from roots meaning "ruler of people") came the name *Diederik*, which is the direct ancestor of Derek and Derrick. You don't have to be a ruler to succeed with one of these names, as we see with such varied professionals as British racing legend Derek Bell, whose victories included five 24 Hours of Le Mans, three Daytona 24, and two World Sportscar Championships; Hall of Fame cricket bowler Derek Underwood, who has nearly three hundred Test wickets; MMA heavyweight champ Derrick Lewis, who has the most knockouts in UFC history; and Canadian Olympic gold-medalist and World Champion rower Derek Porter.

American football is chock full of successful athletes with these names, including four-time Pro Bowl linebacker Derrick Johnson;

four-time Pro Bowl running back Derrick Henry, who has led the league in rushing and rushing touchdowns twice; nine-time Pro Bowler and record holder for most sacks in a game Derrick Thomas; and eleven-time Tampa Bay Buccaneers Pro Bowl linebacker and Super Bowl champion Derrick Brooks.

America's favorite pastime has probably the most famous Derek in modern sports. Derek Jeter began his twenty-year career with the New York Yankees in 1995; since then, the shortstop racked up fourteen All-Star appearances, five World Series wins, and a huge number of awards, records, and, of course, endorsements.

Derek Bell, Auto Racing (24 Hours of Le Mans), England, 1968–1974

Derrick Brooks, Football (Linebacker), Tampa Bay Buccaneers, USA, 1995–2008

Derrick Henry Jr., Football (Running Back), Tennessee Titans, USA, 2016–current

Derek Jeter, Baseball (Shortstop), New York Yankees, USA, 1995–2014

Derrick Johnson, Football (Linebacker), Kansas City Chiefs, USA, 2005–2018

Derrick Lewis, MMA (Heavyweight), USA, 2010–current

Derek Porter, Rowing, Canada, 1958–2000

Derrick Thomas, Football (Linebacker/ Defensive End), Kansas City Chiefs, USA, 1989–1999

Derek Underwood, Cricket (Bowler), Kent County Cricket Club, England, 1963–1987

DHANRAJ

Dhanraj (from roots meaning "ruler over money") may not be a commonly known name in the United States, but it has a famous athletic pedigree in India thanks to field hockey forward Dhanraj Pillay. Consistently ranked among the country's top players of all time, Pillay had a stellar senior career and scored 170 goals in his fifteen years with his national team, while also winning gold at Champions Challenge, Asia Cup, and Asian Games.

Dhanraj Pillay, Field Hockey (Forward), India Men's National Field Hockey Team, India, 1992–2005

DHYAN

As with *Dhanraj*, Dhyan (which can mean a form of meditation) is a super cool Indian name that has history with a massive sports star in field hockey, this time "magician" of the game Dhyan Chand. Feted as possibly the best player in his sport of all time, Dhyan was born with the surname Singh and was given his more well-known last name Chand (meaning "moon" in Hindi) from his teammates who watched him hone his skills by practicing hockey at night. He scored 570 goals with his national team and won gold medals at three consecutive Olympic Games; his list of accolades and honors is lengthy, and his birthday even became a national sports celebration in India!

Whether you're into meditation or appreciate field hockey, Dhyan can be a unique and cool name for your consideration.

Dhyan Chand, Field Hockey (Center Forward), India Men's National Field Hockey Team, India, 1926–1949

DICK

There are plenty of athletes named *Richard*, but some guys are just straight up Dicks. A diminutive for *Richard* that may have come about because it rhymes with "*Rick*" (though it can also be a Dutch short form of *Diederik*), Dick is a name for competitors with a style and personality all their own, including baseball Dicks like seven-time All-Star home run leader Allen and eight-time All-Star and two-time World Series–winning shortstop Groat.

Then there are some highly iconic auto racing and football-playing Dicks. Dick Trickle was a short track legend with over 1,200 wins under his belt and a wild personality that included a penchant for smoking in his cars. On the football field, offensive guard Dick Stanfel had five Pro Bowl appearances and two NFL championships, and Hall of Fame cornerback Dick "Night Train" Lane played in seven Pro Bowls while leading the league in interceptions twice and setting the record for most interceptions in a season (fourteen), while Dick Butkus may be the toughest Dick of all. During his nine years with the Chicago Bears, the linebacker earned eight Pro Bowl appearances and is credited with over one thousand tackles, earning him a fearsome and well-earned reputation.

Dick may not be the most fashionable name/nickname choice these days, but if you do give it to your son, he's sure to have tons of personality!

- **Richard "Dick" Allen**, Baseball (First Baseman/Third Baseman), Philadelphia Phillies, USA, 1963–1977
- **Richard "Dick" Butkus**, Football (Linebacker), Chicago Bears, USA, 1965–1973
- **Richard "Dick" Groat**, Baseball (Shortstop), Pittsburgh Pirates, USA, 1952–1967
- **Richard "Dick" (Night Train) Lane**, Football (Cornerback), Chicago Cardinals, USA, 1952–1965
- **Richard "Dick" Stanfel**, Football (Offensive Guard), Detroit Lions, USA, 1952–1958
- **Richard "Dick" Trickle**, Auto Racing (Short Track), USA, 1958–2002

DIEGO

Diego is a name with uncertain origins, possibly deriving from the Spanish *Santiago* (meaning "Saint Jacob") or a Greek root meaning "teaching." The name is especially popular in Spanish-speaking regions, and you can see successful athletes with it in a few different fields, like MMA (with Diego Sanchez, who's won Middleweight and Welterweight titles) and gymnastics (with Brazilian Olympic silver-medalist, two-time World Champion, and three-time World Cup-winner Diego Hypólito). A Diego in your family may find himself drawn to one of those sports, but it's more likely you'll find him kicking around a soccer ball . . .

Of course, international sports fans will know that Diegos are particularly concentrated in football/soccer. There are many stars with this name, including three-time UEFA Super Cup-winning striker Diego Costa of Brazil, whose goal count is 188 in 495 appearances; and Uruguayan Diego Forlán, whose many awards and more than 260 goals across senior and international appearances have earned him a place on many top forwards lists of his time. The most famous Diego was best known for his last name, Argentinian football legend Maradona. In his combined 694 appearances, Maradona scored 354 goals, and won everything from a FIFA World Cup to two Ballon d'Or awards, top scorer accolades, placement on all kinds of "best of" lists, and so much more. He was and continues to be beloved by fans all over the world for his playing and his vivacious character.

- **Diego da Silva Costa**, Soccer (Striker), Club Atlético de Madrid, S.A.D., Brazil, 2006–current
- **Diego Forlán**, Soccer (Forward), Club Atlético de Madrid, S.A.D., Uruguay, 1997–2018
- **Diego Hypólito**, Artistic Gymnastics, Brazil, 2002–2019
- **Diego Maradona**, Soccer (Attacking Midfielder/Second Striker), Società Sportiva Calcio Napoli, Argentina, 1976–1997
- **Diego Sanchez**, MMA (Welterweight), USA, 2002–current

DIRK

Like the *Derek* family of names, Dirk comes to us from the Dutch name *Diederik*, itself from the Germanic *Theodoric*, meaning "ruler of people." Dirks most often come from German or Dutch families, but not always, and if you add one to yours, he may very well excel in soccer or basketball if he takes inspiration from the following.

A Dutch athlete with international success was football striker/winger Dirk Kuyt, who scored 308 goals in 740 domestic and national appearances and collected various trophies and awards, including the League Cup, Turkish Cup, and Dutch Footballer of the Year in 2006. Meanwhile, the seven-foot-tall Dirk Nowitzki of Germany set and shattered records during his incredible twenty-one-year NBA career with the Dallas Mavericks; during that time, he had fourteen All-Star appearances, fifteen trips to the playoffs, an NBA championship, and tons of awards and accolades leading to his placement on top-ranked power forwards and European players lists.

Dirk Kuyt, Soccer (Striker/Winger), Liverpool Football Club, Netherlands, 1998–2018

Dirk Nowitzki, Basketball (Power Forward), Dallas Mavericks, Germany, 1994–2019

DOMINIC/DOMINIK/DOMINIQUE

While *Dominicus* was a name once given to Catholic children born on a Sunday, there are much cooler, modern, unisex versions like Dominic, Dominik, and the French variant Dominique. On the ice, Dominik Hašek of Czechoslovakia became known as one of the best goaltenders of all time, racking up six All-Star appearances and two Stanley Cup championships, as well as an Olympic gold medal with his native country's team. Dominic "Dom" DiMaggio was the youngest of three Major League Baseball brothers (including his older sibling Joe), batting eleven years for the Boston Red Sox and being selected as an All-Star seven times. Nine-time All-Star small forward Dominique Wilkins was known for his incredible slam dunks (winning two out of five contests).

Dominic "Dom" DiMaggio, Baseball (Center Fielder), Boston Red Sox, USA, 1940–1953

Dominik Hašek, Ice Hockey (Goaltender), Buffalo Sabres, Czechoslovakia, 1980–2011

Jacques Dominique Wilkins, Basketball (Small Forward), Atlanta Hawks, USA, 1982–1999

DON/DONALD

Don can be short for a variety of names, though it's most often used for Donald, which comes from Gaelic roots for "world ruler." They may not be world leaders, but some Dons and Donalds have been incredibly successful athletes, sometimes the best in the world!

Over on the football field, Don Hutson had a ten-year career with the Green Bay Packers, during which he earned four All-Star appearances and won three NFL championships, and five-time Pro Bowl wide receiver and Super Bowl champion Green Bay Packer Donald Driver is a star beyond the game with a series of kids' books. Baseball, too, has had a number of great Dons and Donalds, like four-time All-Star pitcher Don Sutton; iconic New York Yankees first baseman and batter Don Mattingly, who has six All-Star appearances; and nine-time All-Star Dodger pitcher and three-time World Series champ Don Drysdale.

Don Garlits and Don Prudhomme were both drag racing legends, while British driver and engineer Donald Campbell set multiple land and water world speed records with his custom-built "Bluebird" vehicles. Inside the ring, Don "the Dragon" Wilson is widely considered the best American kickboxer of all time, with eleven world championships and forty-seven knockout wins. Lastly, if you're a fan of cricket, you're certain to know a couple Dons from Australia: right-handed wicketkeeper Don Tallon's fifty-eight Test dismissals earned him a spot on many top

Test wicketkeeper lists, while batsman Don Bradman is always ranked among the top cricketers of all time and his Test batting average is considered a feat unparalleled by any professional athlete in any sport.

Whether a Don or Donald in your family learns to play cricket, enjoys martial arts, likes to drive fast, or participates in a team sport, he'll have a champion's spirit and do you proud.

Donald "Don" Bradman, Cricket (Batsman), South Australian Men's Cricket Team, Australia, 1927–1949

Donald Campbell, Speed Record Breaking, England, 1949–1967

Donald Driver, Football (Wide Receiver), Green Bay Packers, USA, 1999–2012

Donald "Don" Drysdale, Baseball (Pitcher), Brooklyn Dodgers, USA, 1956–1969

Donald "Don" Garlits, Auto Racing (Drag Racing), USA, 1954–1992

Donald "Don" Hutson, Football (End), Green Bay Packers, USA, 1935–1945

Donald "Don" Mattingly, Baseball (First Baseman), New York Yankees, USA, 1982–1995

Don Prudhomme, Auto Racing (Drag Racing), USA, 1962–1994

Donald "Don" Sutton, Baseball (Pitcher), Los Angeles Dodgers, USA, 1966–1988

Donald "Don" Tallon, Cricket (Wicketkeeper), Queensland Men's Cricket Team, Australia, 1933–1954

Donald "Don" (The Dragon) Wilson, Kickboxing, USA, 1974–2002

DORIAN

If you're a history buff or a fan of late nineteenth-century literature, then the name Dorian might really appeal to you, though it's also great for families who love sports and competition. The name can alternatively be traced back to the Dorians, a tribe in ancient Greece, or to Oscar Wilde's 1891 novel *The Picture of Dorian Gray*. In more recent times, the name has played a big part in winning medals and trophies. Sometimes this happens by way of team sports, such as rugby (English hooker Dorian "Nobby" West, who helped his teams to the Heineken Cup twice and the 2003 Rugby World Cup).

Dorians competing on their own have really shown the full range of skills and temperaments you might see in a son with this name, anything from racing across the waves—like Dutch two-time Olympic gold-medalist and two-time world champion windsurfer Dorian van Rijsselberghe—to maximizing the potential of his brain—like Romanian chess Grandmaster Dorian Rogozenco—to sculpting his body to perfection—like English bodybuilder Dorian Yates, whose six Mr. Olympia wins puts him among the greatest in his sport!

Dorian Rogozenco, Chess, Romania, 1994–current

Dorian van Rijsselberghe, Windsurfing, Netherlands, 2009–current

Dorian "Nobby" West, Rugby (Hooker), Leicester Tigers, England, 1997–2004

Dorian Yates, Bodybuilding, England, 1984–1997

DREW

Drew is usually, but not always, a short form of *Andrew* (from Greek for "manly", though there are potential sources for it in French and Irish as well). If you like the name for your son, he may enjoy being on the water or the ice, or staying dry and throwing a football. That's if he follows in the footsteps of iconic Drews before him like Australian rower Drew Ginn, who won three gold Olympic medals and five World Championships; five-time NHL All-Star defenseman Drew Doughty, who won two Stanley Cups and two Olympic gold medals for Canada; and NFL quarterbacks

Drew Bledsoe, who has four Pro-Bowl appearances and a Super Bowl win; and the record-breaking thirteen-time Pro Bowler, Super Bowl champion, and philanthropist Drew Brees.

- **Drew Bledsoe**, Football (Quarterback), New England Patriots, USA, 1993–2006
- **Drew Brees**, Football (Quarterback), New Orleans Saints, USA, 2001–2020
- **Drew Doughty**, Ice Hockey (Defense), Los Angeles Kings, Canada, 2008–current
- **Drew Ginn**, Rowing, Australia, 1995–2012

DEWAYNE/DWAYNE/DWYANE

Originally of Gaelic origin, Duane comes from the Irish "Saint Dubhán" and an original meaning of "dark." It has come to be popular in the United States and other parts of the world, and has evolved into many different spellings and variants. Athletes with these names are interesting and varied too, from soccer's Canadian goal scorer Dwayne De Rosario, whose successes made him Canada's top all-time scorer and the ninth highest scorer in Major League Soccer history, to racing legend DeWayne "Tiny" Lund, who won forty-one races and three championships in the NASCAR Grand American Series. In the US, the name is probably most synonymous with basketball giant Dwyane Wade (the unique spelling is a family name). The shooting guard earned a huge thirteen All-Star shots and won three NBA championships along with an Olympic gold medal.

- **Dwayne De Rosario**, Soccer (Attacking Midfielder/Forward), San Jose Earthquakes, Canada, 1997–2019
- **DeWayne "Tiny" Lund**, Auto Racing (NASCAR), USA, 1955–1975
- **Dwyane Wade Jr.**, Basketball (Shooting Guard), Miami Heat, USA, 2003–2019

DUKE

You don't have to have royalty in your lineage to name (or nickname) a kid Duke, which comes from the Latin word "dux" meaning "leader." A Duke in your family will be noble and brave, and may even revolutionize a sport. British boxer Duke McKenzie held titles in three different weight classes during his 39–7 career, and Hall of Fame center fielder and slugger Edwin "Duke" Snider earned eight All-Star appearances and won two World Series. Duke Paoa Kahinu Mokoe Hulikohola Kahanamoku, an actual Hawaiian noble born before the island nation became a state, excelled at swimming with three Olympic gold and two silver medals (and some incredible records) and helped popularize surfing as a sport around the world!

- **Duke Kahanamoku**, Swimming (Freestyle)/Surfing, USA, 1912–1932
- **Duke McKenzie**, Boxing (Flyweight/Bantamweight/Junior-Featherweight), England, 1982–1998
- **Edwin "Duke" Snider**, Baseball (Center Fielder), Brooklyn Dodgers, USA, 1947–1964

DWIGHT

Like the *Deion* family of names, Dwight comes ultimately from the name of the Greek god Dionysos, this time by way of the feminine form *Dionysia* and the medieval name *Diot*. What athletes might inspire a sporty young Dwight in your family? Depending on what type of athleticism he's into, maybe be boxer Dwight Qawi, who held both light heavyweight and cruiserweight world titles; Trinidadian soccer forward/midfielder Dwight Yorke, who scored nearly two hundred goals and won numerous awards; or Olympic gold-medalist and five-time World Champion long jumper Dwight Phillips.

Or, if he's a fan of popular American team sports, he may try to emulate the on-field accomplishments of four-time MLB All-Star pitcher and two-time World Series champion Dwight Gooden, seven-time NFL Pro Bowler and Super Bowl champion Dwight Freeney, or eight-time All-Star and NBA champion Dwight Howard!

Dwight Freeney, Football (Defensive End/ Outside Linebacker), Indianapolis Colts, USA, 2002-2017

Dwight Gooden, Baseball (Pitcher), New York Mets, USA, 1984-2000

Dwight Howard II, Basketball (Center/Power Forward), Orlando Magic, USA, 2004-current

Dwight Phillips, Track & Field (Long Jump), USA, 2003-2013

Dwight Qawi, Boxing (Light Heavyweight/ Cruiserweight), USA, 1978-1998

Dwight Yorke, Soccer (Forward/Midfielder), Aston Villa Football Club, Trinidad and Tobago, 1989-2009

GIRLS

DANICA

Danica has a very interesting origin, coming from a character in Slavic folklore. She was the "morning star" and sister to the sun—already a cool bit of inspiration for naming a child Danica . . . but then there's also the chance she'll grow up to be a speed demon like professional racecar driver and IndyCar race-winner Danica Patrick! Patrick raced in a number of different series from kart to stock, setting records and firsts for women in racing as she went, paving the way for more women in the sport.

Danica Patrick, Auto Racing (IndyCar), USA, 2000-2018

DANIELA

The biblical Hebrew name *Daniel* ("God is my judge") has spawned many alternate forms and versions over the years, including a number of feminine ones. Daniela is a neat one that's most popular in Europe, but it's just waiting for cool people to bring it to new places. Highly successful Danielas have included German two-time Olympic gold-medalist and World Champion speed skater Daniela Anschütz-Thoms; ski jumping two-time World Champion Daniela Iraschko-Stolz of Austria; and Swiss four-time Ironman World Champion Daniela Ryf. Gymnastics is a particular interest to Danielas, like Romanian Daniela Mărănducă, who won gold at World Artistic, and Aerobic Gymnastics World Championships, and Hall of Fame Romanian three-time Olympic gold-medalist and seven-time World Champion Daniela Silivaş!

Daniela Anschütz-Thoms, Speed Skating, Germany, 2003–2010

Daniela Iraschko-Stolz, Ski Jumping, Austria, 2011–current

Daniela Mărănducă, Aerobic/Artistic Gymnastics, Romania, 1991–2005

Daniela Ryf, Triathlon, Switzerland, 2010–2018

Daniela Silivaş, Artistic Gymnastics, Romania, 1985–1991

DANIELLE

Like *Daniela*, Danielle is a variant on the biblical Hebrew *Daniel*, and while it, too, is popular in Europe, it has seen much more usage in the United States. Also like *Danielas*, Danielles are good at a wide variety of sports and athletics, from basketball (three-time WNBA All-Star point guard Danielle Robinson) to golf (seven-time LPGA Tour-winner Danielle Ammaccapane). Bowler Danielle McEwan has won seven titles (including two majors) on the Professional Women's Bowling Association Tour; Danielle Scott-Arruda has a host of volleyball medals, including two Olympic golds and a World Championship; Dutch water polo player Daniëlle de Bruijn earned an Olympic gold medal; and Dutch soccer star Daniëlle van de Donk has scored over 130 goals in her combined 413 club and international career appearances while earning a UEFA Women's Championship and more.

Danielle Ammaccapane, Golf, USA, 1988–1998

Daniëlle de Bruijn, Water Polo (Field Player), Netherlands, 1997–2008

Danielle McEwan, Bowling, USA, 2012–current

Danielle Robinson, Basketball (Point Guard), San Antonio Stars, USA, 2011–current

Danielle Scott-Arruda, Volleyball (Middle Blocker), USA, 1994–current

Daniëlle van de Donk, Soccer (Midfielder/Winger), Arsenal Women Football Club, Netherlands, 2008–current

DANUTA

Danuta is a fun Polish name that has uncertain origins, possibly coming from a Lithuanian derivation of *Daniel*. Name your daughter Danuta (you can nickname her *Dan* or *Danny*) and introduce her to swordsmanship and paddling sports; she may turn out like Polish world champion épée fencer Danuta Dmowska or Hungarian sprint canoeist Danuta Kozák, who has won six Olympic gold medals and fifteen world championships!

Danuta Dmowska, Fencing (Épée), Poland, 2000–2005

Danuta Kozák, Sprint Canoeing, Hungary, 1996–current

DARA

An iconic short name that has risen independently in different parts of the world, Dara can be Irish from a root meaning "fruitful" or "fertile," Cambodian from Sanskrit meaning "star," Persian meaning "wealthy," and more. Daras from North America have reached Olympic podiums in two very distinct sports, with Canadian gold medalist freestyle skier Dana Howell, who won the very first ski slopestyle event in 2014, and American freestyle swimmer Dara Torres, who collected a set of four golds, four silvers, and four bronzes between 1984 and 2008!

A little girl named Dara will be the star of your family, competitive and successful, and probably enjoy water or winter sports.

Dara Howell, Freestyle Skiing, Canada, 2012–current

Dara Torres, Swimming (Freestyle), USA, 1983–2012

DARIA/DARJA/DARYA

Like *Dara*, the family of names including Daria, Darja, and Darya has unique origins and meanings in different parts of the world and in different languages. In this case, Daria is a feminine variant of *Darius*, which comes through Greek from a Persian name meaning "possessing goodness." Darja is an alternate Czech, Estonian, and Slovene version, while Darya can be a Belarusian, Russian, or Ukrainian version of Daria or come from a different Persian root for "sea" or "ocean."

What can you expect if you name your daughter one of these names? Regardless of which version you choose, she's likely to be agile, strong, and quick, with talents and a demeanor suited to gymnastics. At least that's what the overwhelming evidence points to! The cavalcade of elite rhythmic gymnasts (mainly from Russia) includes Daria Kondakova, who won four gold medals and eleven silvers at World Championships; Olympic gold-medalist and three-time world champion Daria Shkurikhina; four-time world champion and five-time Grand Prix Final-winner Darya Dmitriyeva; and Darja Varfolomeev of Germany, who in just a few years has already won six gold medals, four silvers, and a bronze at World Championships and thirteen golds, seven silvers, and seven bronzes at World Cup events.

If a Daria, Darja, or Darya in your family is not interested in gymnastics but rather winter sports, she can be inspired by Belarusian four-time Olympic gold-medalist and two-time world champion biathlete Darya Domracheva, who won thirty-four World Cup events with one overall title and five discipline titles.

Darya Dmitriyeva, Rhythmic Gymnastics, Russia, 2009–2013

Darya Domracheva, Biathlon, Belarus, 2006–2018

Daria Kondakova, Rhythmic Gymnastics, Russia, 2009–2012

Daria Shkurikhina, Rhythmic Gymnastics, Russia, 2006–2008

Darja Varfolomeev, Rhythmic Gymnastics, Germany, 2019–current

DARINA/DARYNA

Sometimes serving as diminutives of *Dariya* and sometimes coming from Irish roots for "fruitful" or "fertile" or Slavic for "gift," Darina and Daryna are two more cool "D" names that can really make a little girl in your family stand out from the crowd. She may be a gift to her teammates in sports like volleyball, swimming, or soccer, like Italian world champion outside hitter Darina Mifkova; Ukrainian backstroke swimmer Daryna Zevina, who won a set of each color medal from World Championships; and six-time Ukrainian Woman Footballer of the Year and Ukrainian Women's League Footballer of the Year forward Daryna Apanashchenko, who has won multiple championships and top scorer awards.

Daryna Apanashchenko, Soccer (Forward), Zvezda-2005 Perm, Ukraine, 2001–current

Darina Mifkova, Volleyball (Outside Hitter), Italy, 1990–2009

Daryna Zevina, Swimming (Backstroke), Ukraine, 2012–2022

DAWN

If you want a daughter who likes getting up early and sports that involve water, you may want to name her Dawn, which comes from an Old English root for "daybreak." There have been a couple of famous land-based athletes with this name—including runner Dawn Moncrieffe, who won a gold, bronze, and two silver medals at Deaflympics, and six-time WNBA All-Star point guard Dawn Staley—though the majority have found success in or on the water. Australian swimmer Dawn Fraser has a huge medal count, while Dawn Dawson has won two Expert Women's

Ski world championships on stand-up personal watercraft and women's sailing pioneer Dawn Riley took home world championships in the One Ton Cup and Women's World Cup.

- **Dawn Dawson**, Stand-Up Personal Watercraft Racing, USA, 1992–1992
- **Dawn Fraser**, Swimming (Freestyle), Australia, 1956–1964
- **Dawn Moncrieffe**, Track & Field (Middle-Distance Running), Canada, 1985–2001
- **Dawn Riley**, Sailing, USA, 1989–2003
- **Dawn Staley**, Basketball (Point Guard), Charlotte Sting, USA, 1994–2006

DEANNA

There are *Diana*s and then there are Deannas and DeAnnas, whose names are probably descended from *Diana* or possibly *Dean*. Two sports champions with these names have been Americans, though they have gone in very different directions. Track and field star DeAnna Price has won a World Championship and Continental Cup in the hammer throw and holds the American record (and second place in the world), and shooting guard/point guard Deanna Nolan scored five All-Star appearances and three WNBA championships in her eight-year career with Detroit Shock.

Whether you prefer the capital "A" in the middle or not, consider Deanna/DeAnna for your daughter and be ready to take her to the track or basketball court.

- **Deanna Nolan**, Basketball (Shooting Guard/Point Guard), Detroit Shock, USA, 2001–2013
- **DeAnna Price**, Track & Field (Hammer Throw), USA, 2015–current

DEBBIE/DEBI

*Deborah/Debra*s have their athletic claims to fame, but women with the shorter/more familiar forms—Debbies and Debis—have their own accomplishments. These come in various fields, starting with some water sports, like water skiing's two-time Ski Racing World Champion Debbie Nordblad (ranked among the most decorated US women water skiers) and three-time Olympic gold-medalist freestyle swimmer Debbie Meyer. On land, Debbies have won fame in cricket (New Zealand's Hall of Fame all-rounder Debbie Hockley), high jump (innovative Pan American gold-medalist Canadian Debbie Brill, who developed the "Brill Bend" technique), and track (Bahamian sprinter Debbie Ferguson-McKenzie, who won an Olympic medal of each color, two World Championships, and many more). Lastly, there are those who have excelled on ice and snow, like Olympic gold-medalist alpine skier Debbie Armstrong; World Champion figure skater Debi Thomas; and Canadian curling World Champion and Olympic Games demonstration gold medalist Debbie Jones-Walker.

- **Debra Rae "Debbie" Armstrong**, Alpine Skiing, USA, 1982–1988
- **Debbie Brill**, Track & Field (High Jump), Canada, 1968–1985
- **Debbie Ferguson-McKenzie**, Track & Field (Sprinting), Bahamas, 1995–2013
- **Deborah "Debbie" Hockley**, Cricket (All-Rounder), Canterbury Magicians, New Zealand, 1977–2000
- **Deborah "Debbie" Jones-Walker**, Curling (Second/Third), Canada, 1976–2012
- **Deborah "Debbie" Meyer**, Swimming (Freestyle), USA, 1967–1972
- **Debbie Nordblad**, Water Skiing, USA, 1981–2006
- **Dr. Debra "Debi" Thomas**, Figure Skating, USA, 1985–1991

DEBORAH/DEBRA

A nature name, Deborah stretches back to biblical Hebrew and means "bee." You can find Deborahs (and Debras) stinging the competition and buzzing their way to victory on land and sea, and even on horseback! Cricketer Debra Stock won the World Cup with England in 1993, British para-equestrian Deborah Criddle has collected four golds and two silver medals at the Paralympics, and Italian sport shooter Deborah Gelisio has a huge medal collection, including Olympic silver and multiple World Championships and World Cups. On and beneath the water, Cuban free diver Deborah Andollo has set multiple depth and breath records; Deborah Jiménez of Spain won Paralympic gold, silvers, and bronzes in breaststroke and freestyle swimming; and American sailor Deborah Capozzi has captured five Olympic medals (two of them gold), while Deborah Compagnoni has been ranked the best Italian female skier of all time with her three Olympic gold medals and three World Championships in Super-G, Slalom, and Giant Slalom.

A Deborah (or Debra) in your family will be a productive member of the hive and will stand out for her accomplishments in whatever field she chooses.

Deborah Andollo, Free Diving, Cuba, 1993–2000

Deborah Capozzi, Sailing, USA, 2005–2011

Deborah Compagnoni, Alpine Skiing, Italy, 1986–1999

Deborah Criddle, Para-Equestrian (Para-Dressage), England, 2000–2012

Deborah Gelisio, Sport Shooting (Trap), Italy, 2000–2017

Deborah Jiménez, Swimming (Breaststroke/Freestyle), Spain, 2000–2014

Debra Stock, Cricket (All-Rounder), Berkshire Women's Cricket Team, England, 1989–2004

DEMI

While Demi is a flexible name that can be used on its own or as a diminutive for names like *Demetria*, in most cases it is still descended from Ancient Greek roots and the name of the goddess of agriculture, Demeter. Demis haven't made a huge impact in the sporting world until recently, when Dutch road cyclist Demi Vollering won The Women's Tour 2021 and the 2023 Tour de France Femmes and English soccer left-back Demi Stokes won the FA Women's Super League (WSL) Cup three times, an FA WSL championship, and the FA Cup three times with Manchester City, as well as a UEFA Women's Championship with her national team!

Name or call your daughter Demi and be sure to teach her to ride a bike and play soccer; she may enjoy long rides up and down hills or playing defense on the field with her friends.

Demi Stokes, Soccer (Left-Back), Manchester City Women's Football Club, England, 2007–current

Adriana Geertruida "Demi" Vollering, Road Cycling, Netherlands, 2018–current

DENISE

From the French *Denis*, and ultimately from the Greek god Dionysos, comes the name Denise. Denises in the sports world aren't necessarily revelers in the tradition of Bacchus, but they do include an auto racing pioneer (American Denise McCluggage, who had wins at Sebring and the Monte Carlo Rally), and an Olympic gold-medalist and two-time World Champion heptathlete (British Denise Lewis, who set multiple records during her career).

Name your daughter Denise and she may follow in their footsteps!

Denise Lewis, Track & Field (Heptathlon), England, 1994–2004

Denise McCluggage, Auto Racing (Endurance/Grand Touring/Rally), USA, 1954–1969

DIANA

Dianas are all goddesses, naturally, with their name coming from the ancient Roman deity of the hunt and moon (from the Greek goddess Artemis). It's really interesting to see the notable athletic Dianas around the world, from India's record-setting cricket bowler Diana Edulji to Canadian soccer star and Olympic bronze-medalist midfielder Diana Matheson. Here in the US have been two great swimmers with this name; Diana Munz has one of each medal from the Olympics and six medals from World Championships (including a gold) in freestyle events, while long-distance swimmer Diana Nyad has set records and swam around the island of Manhattan, from Cuba to Florida, and more. Last but not least, Diana Taurasi is ranked among the greatest female basketball players of all time, and during her career with Phoenix Mercury, she's racked up ten All-Star appearances and three WNBA championships, not to mention a host of records, as well as five Olympic gold medals and three World Championships!

Even if she doesn't dive into swimming, basketball, soccer, or these other sports, a Diana in your family will be a powerful goddess in her own right.

- **Diana Edulji**, Cricket (All-Rounder), India Women's National Cricket Team, India, 1976–1991
- **Diana Matheson**, Soccer (Midfielder), Washington Spirit, Canada, 2003–2021
- **Diana Munz**, Swimming (Freestyle), USA, 1997–2004
- **Diana Nyad**, Long-Distance Swimming, USA, 1970–2013
- **Diana Taurasi**, Basketball (Point Guard/ Shooting Guard), Phoenix Mercury, USA, 2004–current

DOMINIQUE

The unisex Dominique comes from a name once given to Catholic children born on a Sunday, and it shares that origin with a variety of alternate spelling and pronunciation versions. Dominiques can succeed at anything, like snowboarding (Canadian X Games-winner and Olympic silver- and bronze-winning Dominique Maltais), but they appear mostly in gymnastics. The world stage has seen the amazing talents of two Americans who won Olympic gold as part of the "Magnificent Seven" in Atlanta in 1996 (Dominique Moceanu, who also had silver and bronze medals at World Championships, and Dominique Dawes, who collected three more bronze Olympic medals and three silver and one bronze at World Championships).

- **Dominique Dawes**, Artistic Gymnastics, USA, 1989–2000
- **Dominique Maltais**, Snowboarding, Canada, 2002–2014
- **Dominique Moceanu**, Artistic Gymnastics, USA, 1992–2006

DONNA

Donna can feel like an old-fashioned name (Italian for "woman"), though it's ready for a return to glory. If you give it to your daughter, she's likely to feel right at home in the water. That's if she takes after the premiere athlete with the name, American swimmer Donna de Varona, who won two gold medals each at the 1963 Pan American Games and the 1964 Olympic Games.

- **Donna de Varona**, Swimming (Freestyle/ Medley), USA, 1960–1964

DORIS

Doris comes from Ancient Greek roots (Doris was one of the sea god Okeanos's fifty nymph daughters), and its popularity in the US isn't quite what it once was. The 1940s saw athletes with this name surge to the forefront in two different sports: tennis and baseball. Doris Hart was the number one-ranked female tennis player in the world, and her many accomplishments include being the first player ever to achieve the mythical "Boxed Set" of Grand Slams, winning a title in singles, women's doubles, and mixed doubles at each of the four Grand Slam events. In the All-American Girls Professional Baseball League, Doris Sams was a powerful all-around player, pitching, batting, and more. She was selected for the All-Star team five times, pitched a perfect game, won batting titles during her career playing with the Muskegon Lassies and Kalamazoo Lassies, and, of course, was introduced to the National Women's Baseball Hall of Fame.

If Doris isn't too old-fashioned for you, then put it on your list of potential names for your daughter; she may turn out to love hitting balls with either bats or racquets!

Doris Hart, Tennis, USA, 1942–1955

Doris Sams, Baseball (Outfielder/Pitcher), Muskegon Lassies, USA, 1946–1953

DOROTHY

Another classical name that comes from Ancient Greek, Dorothy (meaning "god's gift") has had a very interesting history in athleticism with some incredible women. Dorothy "Dottie" Pepper was a champion golfer, winning seventeen LPGA Tour events (two of them major championships), while figure skater Dorothy Hamill was the darling of the United States in the mid-1970s with her win in the 1976 Winter Olympics, as well as her iconic style.

Notably, however, Dorothys have had a huge representation in softball and baseball! The All-American Girls Professional Baseball League featured three-time All-Star shortstop and two-time champ Dorothy Schroeder, who played in all twelve AAGPBL seasons; and seven-time All-Star (every year the league held it) Dorothy "Dottie" Kamenshek, who played first base for the Rockland Peaches. On the softball side, Dorothy "Dot" Wilkinson was a nineteen-time All-American catcher with the Phoenix Ramblers, as well as a two-time bowling champion (being inducted into the Halls of Fame for both sports), while more recently Dorothy "Dot" Richardson won two softball Olympic gold medals with the US team!

Whether you nickname her *Dot* or *Dottie* or just stick with Dorothy, it's a good bet your daughter will love to play catch in the backyard.

Dorothy Hamill, Figure Skating, USA, 1971–1976

Dorothy "Dottie" Kamenshek, Baseball (First Base), Rockford Peaches, USA, 1943–1953

Dorothy "Dottie" Pepper, Golf, USA, 1988–2004

Dorothy "Dot" Richardson, Softball (Shortstop), USA, 1980–2000

Dorothy "Dottie" Schroeder, Baseball (Shortstop), Fort Wayne Daisies, USA, 1943–1954

Dorothy "Dot" Wilkinson, Softball (Catcher)/Bowling, Phoenix Ramblers, USA, 1933–1965

E

BOYS

EARL

Germanic and Old English words like "jarl" have brought us the name Earl, meaning "nobleman" or "warrior." Whether your family includes royalty or not, Earl is a great name for a kid who will be athletic and competitive, like Earl Anthony, who is ranked among the top bowlers of all time with forty-three titles; four-time All-Star shooting guard/point guard and NBA champion Earl Monroe; and the original "Man of 1,000 Holds" World Heavyweight Champion wrestler Earl Caddock. Baseball's Earls have included five-time All-Star catcher Earl Battey Jr. and six-time All-Star slugger Earl Averill, while on the football field, defensive end Earl Faison was a five-time All-Star and champion in the American Football League with the San Diego Chargers, and back Earl "Dutch" Clark was an early NFL superstar with six first-team All-Pro selections and a championship in the 1930s.

- **Earl Anthony**, Bowling, USA, 1963–1997
- **Earl Averill**, Baseball (Center Fielder), Cleveland Indians, USA, 1929–1941
- **Earl Battey Jr.**, Baseball (Catcher), Washington Senators, USA, 1955–1967
- **Earl Caddock**, Wrestling (Heavyweight), USA, 1915–1922
- **Earl "Dutch" Clark**, Football (Back), Portsmouth Spartans, USA, 1931–1938
- **Earl Faison**, Football (Defensive End), San Diego Chargers, USA, 1961–1966
- **Vernon Earl Monroe**, Basketball (Shooting Guard/Point Guard), Baltimore Bullets, USA, 1967–1980

EARVIN

See *Magic* for Earvin "Magic" Johnson Jr.

ED

Ed is almost always a shortened form of a longer name, usually *Edward* or *Edmund* but potentially others. Eds are typically a bit more relaxed than *Edwards*, though not quite as free-wheeling as *Eddies*! In what athletic competitions can you find an Ed at the top of his game? You might look to ice hockey with goaltender Ed Belfour, who earned six All-Star selections and won a Stanley Cup and an Olympic gold medal. Eds are concentrated in gridiron football, with Dallas Cowboys three-time Pro Bowl defensive end and NFL champion Ed "Too Tall" Jones; Miami Dolphins guard Ed Newman, who had four Pro Bowl appearances and a Super Bowl championship; and nine-time Pro Bowl free safety and Super Bowl-winner Ed Reed, who set multiple records for interceptions and more.

If you name your kid an "Ed-" name and give him this nickname make sure to take him out to toss the pigskin around early!

Edward "Ed" Belfour, Ice Hockey (Goaltender), Dallas Stars, Canada, 1989–2008

Edward "Ed" (Too Tall) Jones, Football (Defensive End), Dallas Cowboys, USA, 1974–1989

Edward "Ed" Newman, Football (Offensive Guard), Miami Dolphins, USA, 1973–1984

Edward "Ed" Reed Jr., Football (Free Safety), Baltimore Ravens, USA, 2002–2013

EDDIE/EDDY

Just like *Ed*, Eddie and Eddy can be a short form of or nickname for any number of longer names like *Edward* and *Edmund*. Eddies are characters through and through, at once some of the most successful athletes and some of the most unique. Champion surfer Eddie Aikau saved over five hundred people as a lifeguard and gave his life trying to save sailors stranded at sea; shooting guard/small forward Eddie Jones earned three All-Star appearances in his fourteen years with the NBA; and seven-time NHL All-Star and two-time Stanley Cup-winning defenseman Eddie Shore was known for his hard hitting (and record-setting number of penalty minutes).

American football has witnessed the exploits of fullback Eddie Price (who earned three Pro Bowl appearances during his five years playing for the New York Giants) and four-time Pro Bowl running back Eddie George, while MLB fans have watched the plays of eight-time All-Star and World Series champ "Steady" Eddie Murray (who's ranked among the best-ever first basemen), and power hitter Eddie Mathews (who racked up twelve All-Star appearances, two World Series wins, multiple records and awards, and a reputation for threatening reporters who bothered him).

Two athletes really capture the spirit and possibility of the name Eddie and show what a boy with this name could accomplish. Michael "Eddie the Eagle" Edwards may not have been the most talented ski jumper in the world, but that didn't stop his enthusiasm for the event to make his way to the 1988 Winter Olympics; despite coming in last place, his successful jump placed him at number six on the all-time British ski jumpers list! On the flipside, Belgian cyclist Édouard "Eddy the Cannibal" Merckx is almost universally considered the pinnacle of his sport and the greatest of all time, having won 525 races, including eleven Grand Tours, four World Championships, and set many records that may never be topped.

Edward "Eddie" Aikau, Surfing, USA, 1959–1978

Edward "Eddie" Collins Sr., Baseball (Second Baseman), Philadelphia Athletics, USA, 1906–1930

Michael "Eddie the Eagle" Edwards, Ski Jumping, England, 1987–1989

Edward "Eddie" George Jr., Football (Running Back), Houston Oilers, USA, 1996–2004

Eddie Jones, Basketball (Shooting Guard/Small Forward), Los Angeles Lakers, USA, 1994–2008

Edwin "Eddie" Mathews, Baseball (Third Baseman), Boston Braves, USA, 1952–1968

Édouard "Eddy the Cannibal" Merckx, Road/Track Cycling, Belgium, 1965–1978

Edward "Eddie" Murray, Baseball (First Baseman/Designated Hitter), Baltimore Orioles, USA, 1977–1997

Edward "Eddie" Price, Football (Fullback), New York Giants, USA, 1950–1955

Edward "Eddie" Shore, Ice Hockey (Defense), Boston Bruins, Canada, 1924–1943

EDGAR

You may not be wealthy or wield spears, but you may decide that Edgar (from Old English roots for those two things) is a pretty cool name for your child who will have varied interests and passions. Successful athletic Edgars have come from various parts of the world and are spread across several unique fields, from freestyle skiing (French Olympic gold and bronze-medalist and three-time World Champion Edgar Grospiron) to soccer (Dutch midfielder Edgar Davids, whose fifty-six goals in 664 club and international appearances have put him on many top-ranked lists). On the baseball diamond, Colombian shortstop Édgar Rentería was selected as an All-Star five times and won two World Series, while seven-time All-Star third baseman Edgar Martínez earned numerous batting awards and accolades during his seventeen years with the Seattle Mariners. Last but least is horse racing jockey Edgar Prado of Peru, who has currently won over 7,400 races in his ongoing career!

Edgar Davids, Soccer (Defensive Midfielder), Amsterdamsche Football Club Ajax, Netherlands, 1991–2014

Edgar Grospiron, Freestyle Skiing, France, 1989–1995

Edgar Martínez, Baseball (Designated Hitter/Third Baseman), Seattle Mariners, USA, 1987–2004

Edgar Prado, Horse Racing (Jockey), Peru, 1986–current

Édgar Rentería, Baseball (Shortstop), St. Louis Cardinals, Colombia, 1996–2011

EDOARDO/EDUARDO/EDWARD

The classic Edward comes from the same Old English roots for "fortune" and "guard," similar to *Edgar*. And while lots of American and British Edwards go by short forms like *Ed* or *Eddie*, athletes in other countries use their full names more frequently; these include Edoardo and Eduardo. British weightlifter Edward Levy nabbed a World Weightlifting Championship way back in 1891, a few years before American pole vaulter Edward Cook won Olympic gold in 1908. Italian Edoardo Mangiarotti is a fencing legend, whose thirty-nine Olympic and World Championships gold medals make him the most decorated fencer of all time. Meanwhile, there have been tons of Edoardos and Eduardos in international football! Among the best of them have been top scorer Jonas Eduardo "Edu" Américo of Brazil, with 205 goals in his senior career and a FIFA World Cup; the second-highest goal scorer of America Football Club Eduardo "Edu" Coimbra (218 total goals); and Brazilian Eduardo da Silva, who played for Croatia and posted a huge 223 goals in 531 total appearances.

Depending on your native language and culture, you may prefer Edward, Eduardo, or Edoardo, but whichever one you choose for your son will give him fast feet and good coordination . . . or a blazing pitching arm like that of ten-time MLB All-Star New York Yankees pitcher Edward "Whitey" Ford, who won six World Series championships and a Cy Young award, was named World Series MVP, led the American League in wins three times and the MLB in ERA twice, and was inducted into the Baseball Hall of Fame.

Jonas Eduardo "Edu" Américo, Soccer (Forward), Santos Futebol Clube, Brazil, 1966–1985

Eduardo "Edu" Coimbra, Soccer (Attacking Midfielder), America Football Club, Brazil, 1966–1981

Edward Cook Sr., Track & Field (Pole Vault), USA, 1907–1911

Eduardo da Silva, Soccer (Forward), Građanski nogometni klub Dinamo Zagreb, Brazil, 2001–2018

Edward "Whitey" Ford, Baseball (Pitcher), New York Yankees, USA, 1950–1967

Edward Levy, Weightlifting, England, 1891–1896

Edoardo Mangiarotti, Fencing (Épée/Foil), Italy, 1935–1960

EDSON

See *Pelé* for Edson "Pelé" Arantes do Nascimento.

ELDRICK

See *Tiger* for Eldrick "Tiger" Woods.

ELGIN

One of the greatest basketball players ever got his name from a very interesting set of circumstances. Elgin Baylor was born in Washington, DC, and right from the start was set apart by his name, which his father chose from the name of his favorite watch! The Elgin National Watch Company was named for its location in Elgin, Illinois, and the city of Elgin, in turn, was named after a famous Protestant hymn named for the Scottish town of Elgin (with uncertain origins–possibly from roots meaning "beautiful valley"). That long and complicated trail gave us the NBA legend Elgin Baylor, who earned eleven All-Star appearances in his fourteen seasons playing small forward with the Minneapolis Lakers. Known for his hanging jump shot and running bank shot, Baylor set numerous scoring and rebounding records, some of which have lasted decades, and his most points scored in an NBA Finals game still stands!

No matter the original source, if you like the name Elgin and give it to your son, he'll be fast, accurate, and a great team player.

Elgin Baylor, Basketball (Small Forward), Minneapolis Lakers, USA, 1958–1971

EMERSON

Built from a classic English "son of" name construction, Emerson might be an obvious choice for your son if one of his parents is named *Emery* or *Emmerich*. But even without those names in the family, Emerson is a cool name that's been up in lights for a few different sports that can motivate and inspire your child. International football has had several players with this name, including notables from Brazil, like forward Emerson Sheik, who scored a massive 273 goals in his 554 club appearances. Two-time American Football League All-Star running back Emerson Boozer won both an AFL championship and a Super Bowl with the New York Jets, while Brazilian Emerson Fittipaldi was a two-time Formula 1 champion who won fourteen races in that series, along with two Indianapolis 500s, a CART championship, and many more.

Emerson Boozer, Football (Running Back), New York Jets, USA, 1966–1975

Emerson Fittipaldi, Auto Racing (Formula 1), Brazil, 1970–1996

Emerson Sheik, Soccer (Forward), Urawa Red Diamonds, Brazil, 1998–2018

EMIL/EMILE

While they're not pronounced exactly the same way, Emil and Emile share an ancient and noble source in a Roman family name that has as its root the word "rival." That's a perfect origin for the name of a fierce competitor, as your Emil or Emile will be once he chooses his preferred athletic endeavor. He may take after three-time AFL All-Star and champion linebacker of the Los Angeles Chargers Emil Karas; Czech four-time Olympic gold-medalist distance runner Emil Zátopek; and the incredibly successful Norwegian biathlete Emil Svendsen, whose massive medal collection includes four golds, three silvers, and a bronze from the Olympics and twelve golds, six silvers, and three bronzes from World Championships!

Interestingly, Emils are quite good at shooting at things. In the world of esports are champions Emil "Nyhrox" Pedersen of Norway and Emil "Magisk" Reif of Denmark, who have won at *Fortnite* and *Counter-Strike: Global Offensive*, respectively, while sport shooters winning big at Olympic Games and World Championships have included two-time gold medalist Emil Kellenberger of Switzerland and Sweden's Emil Martinsson, who set world records and collected nearly twenty medals at World Championship events (including ten golds).

- **Emil Karas**, Football (Linebacker), Los Angeles Chargers, USA, 1959–1966
- **Emil Kellenberger**, Sport Shooting (Rifle), Switzerland, 1899–1922
- **Emil Martinsson**, Sport Shooting (Running Target), Sweden, 2002–current
- **Emil "Nyhrox" Pedersen**, Esports (*Fortnite*), Norway, 2018–current
- **Emil "Magisk" Reif**, Esports (*Counter-Strike: Global Offensive*), Denmark, 2015–current
- **Emil Svendsen**, Biathlon, Norway, 2005–2018
- **Emil Zátopek**, Long-Distance Running, Czechoslovakia, 1946–1957

EMMANUEL

See *Manny* for Emmanuel "Manny" Pacquiao Sr.

EMMITT

Emmett is a typically masculine offshoot of the name *Emma* (from Germanic roots for "whole" or "universal"), though we're going to look at a couple really tough guys with the alternate form Emmitt. Cornerback Emmitt Thomas played thirteen seasons with the Kansas City Chiefs, along the way earning five Pro Bowl appearances, two AFL championships, and a Super Bowl win, not to mention team records and a spot in the Hall of Fame. A bit more recently, Emmitt Smith solidified his place as one of the best-ever running backs, with eight Pro Bowl selections, three Super Bowl championships, and a long list of accolades and records; he is still the NFL's all-time rushing leader!

The name Emmitt clearly gives you a drive to succeed, as well as the speed and strength to back it up.

- **Emmitt Smith III**, Football (Running Back), Dallas Cowboys, USA, 1990–2004
- **Emmitt Thomas**, Football (Cornerback), Kansas City Chiefs, USA, 1966–1978

ENZO

Enzo is a name shrouded in mystery—or at least competing origin stories. Some believe it's an Italian form of the German *Heinz*, while others think something similar with the Old German *Anzo*. Separately from all that, it can be a short form of a variety of longer names, including *Lorenzo* and *Vincenzo*.

When it comes to athleticism and competition, some Enzos excel beyond all expectation, leading the pack and setting the pace for everyone to come. Attacking midfielder Enzo Francescoli became one of the top-ranked South American soccer players and solidified his place on all-time great lists with his 237 goals in 647 club and international appearances, and Italian Enzo Maiorca overcame a fear of the ocean to become a world record-setting free diver! Arguably the best-known Enzo is Mr. Ferrari himself, an eleven-time winner in 1920s Grand Prix racing, who started his own race team and car company that's still synonymous with excellence and speed.

- **Enzo Ferrari**, Auto Racing (Grand Prix), Italy, 1919–1924
- **Enzo Francescoli**, Soccer (Attacking Midfielder), Club Atlético River Plate, Uruguay, 1980–1997

Vincenzo "Enzo" Maiorca, Free Diving, Italy, 1960–1988

ERIC/ERIK

Eric in all its variant forms (including Erik) is a mighty name, coming from an Old Norse name with roots meaning "always" and "ruler." Erics and Eriks in sports may not be rulers per se, but they've laid claim to plenty of records, championships, and the like. Running back Eric Dickerson was an All-Star in more than half of his eleven NFL seasons and set a record for single-season rushing; Eric Frenzel is one of the most successful Nordic combined skiers of all time, with six Olympic medals (three of them gold) and seventeen podiums at World Championships (seven of them wins); and Scottish runner Eric Liddell's road to an Olympic win was popularized in the film *Chariots of Fire*.

Both two-time All-Star slugger Eric Davis and three-time All-Star pitcher Éric Gagné won a World Series, and on two wheels, Belgium's Erik De Vlaeminck won seven cyclo-cross world championships and Erik Zabel appears on Germany's all-time best cyclist and cycling sprinter rankings for his 152 professional wins.

Meanwhile, history has shown us that Erics and Eriks really excel with ice skates! Canadian pairs figure skater Eric Radford has a full set of Olympic medals and two World Championships, while in speed skating fellow countryman Éric Bédard has two Olympic golds and seven World Championships on the short track and American long track skater Eric Heiden has an incredible five Olympic gold medals and seven World Championships. Those who have found glory in ice hockey include Swedish six-time All-Star defenseman Erik Karlsson; Canadian six-time All-Star center and Stanly Cup champion Eric Staal, who also has gold medals from the Olympics and a World Championship; and Canadian center Eric Lindros, who had seven All-Star appearances to go along with his silver and gold Olympic medals.

Pick your favorite version of Eric/Erik for your son who is sure to be the boss of your household and enjoy ice skating.

Éric Bédard, Speed Skating, Canada, 1998–2006

Eric Davis, Baseball (Outfielder), Cincinnati Reds, USA, 1984–2001

Erik De Vlaeminck, Cyclo-Cross, Belgium, 1966–1977

Eric Dickerson, Football (Running Back), Los Angeles Rams, USA, 1983–1993

Eric Frenzel, Nordic Combined Skiing, Germany, 2007–current

Éric Gagné, Baseball (Pitcher), Los Angeles Dodgers, Canada, 1999–2008

Eric Heiden, Speed Skating, USA, 1977–1980

Erik Karlsson, Ice Hockey (Defense), Ottawa Senators, Sweden, 2008–current

Eric Liddell, Track & Field (Sprinting), Scotland, 1924–1925

Eric Lindros, Ice Hockey (Center), Philadelphia Flyers, Canada, 1992–2007

Eric Radford, Figure Skating, Canada, 2005–2018

Eric Staal, Ice Hockey (Center), Carolina Hurricanes, Canada, 2003–current

Erik Zabel, Road Cycling, Germany, 1993–2008

ERNIE

Ernie is most often a nickname for *Ernest* (or more rarely other names like *Ernesto*), which comes from a Germanic root meaning "serious." Naming or calling your kid Ernie won't necessarily make him a serious person, but it will make him a serious competitor if he takes after champions like Canadian four-time World Champion curler Ernie Richardson and South African golf legend Ernie Els, who was ranked number one in the world with four major championships among his seventy wins.

Ernies have excelled in baseball, with gentle giant Ernie Lombardi scoring eight All-Star appearances and a World Series win as a catcher and Ernie Banks, who started in the Negro Leagues and ended up with fourteen MLB All-Star selections during his eighteen years with the Cubs (not to mention being ranked among the best baseball players ever). On the gridiron, lots of Ernies have taken the field, with some of the most impactful including five-time Pro Bowl fullback and multi-sport phenom Ernie Nevers (who also set multiple NFL records, including scoring forty points in a game) and nine-time Pro Bowl defensive tackle Ernie Stautner, who played his whole career with the Steelers.

Ernest "Ernie" Banks, Baseball (Shortstop/First Baseman), Chicago Cubs, USA, 1951–1971

Theodore Ernest "Ernie" Els, Golf, South Africa, 1989–2016

Ernesto "Ernie" Lombardi, Baseball (Catcher), Cincinnati Reds, USA, 1931–1947

Ernest "Ernie" Nevers, Football (Fullback), Chicago Cardinals, USA, 1926–1931

Ernest "Ernie" Richardson, Curling (Skip), Canada, 1959–1963

Ernest "Ernie" Stautner, Football (Defensive Tackle), Pittsburgh Steelers, USA, 1950–1963

EVAN

There are many variations and alternate forms of the name *John* around the world, including the Welsh Evan. Evans with athletic success run a pretty big gamut, from the graceful and artistic Olympic gold-medalist and World Champion figure skater Evan Lysacek to the tough-as-nails MMA fighter and UFC Middleweight Champion Evan Tanner and three-time All-Star third baseman Evan Longoria, who set multiple team records with the Tampa Bay Rays.

Evan Longoria, Baseball (Third Baseman), Tampa Bay Rays, USA, 2008–current

Evan Lysacek, Figure Skating, USA, 2004–2014

Evan Tanner, MMA (Middleweight/Heavyweight), USA, 1997–2008

EVANDER

The name Evander has some very cool origins. The most common background for it is a Latin descendent of Ancient Greek roots meaning "good man," though it can occasionally come about via a Scottish tradition from Norse roots for "bow" and "warrior."

Of course, the most famous Evander in the modern world is four-time world heavyweight boxing champion Evander Holyfield! The "Real Deal" began his boxing career in international bouts at Pan American Games and the Olympics before achieving undisputed champion status at cruiserweight and then moving up to the big time at heavyweight. He fought (and beat) some of the biggest names in boxing history, including Buster Douglas, George Foreman, Larry Holmes, Riddick Bowe, and Mike Tyson.

Naming your son Evander will give him the toughness and power of one of the greatest heavyweights in modern times.

Evander "The Real Deal" Holyfield, Boxing (Cruiserweight/Heavyweight), USA, 1984–2011

EVEL

Evel isn't really a name, but rather the nickname of the most famous and popular motorcycle stunt performer of all time. Robert "Evel" Knievel had quite a career bouncing from job to job before becoming a motorcycle racer and discovering the possibilities of doing stunts (and self-promotion). After some promising initial success, he aimed higher and bigger, and when a sponsor partner urged him to present a more daring name, "Evel" was born (the partner actually suggested "Evil," but Knievel didn't want that hard an edge). Evel would go on to jump over all manner of cars, buses, and both man-made and natural landmarks, becoming a household name for excitement and daring.

Evel could be a cool name or nickname for a child who will most definitely be a little daredevil.

Robert "Evel" Knievel, Motorcycle Stunt Performing, USA, 1965–1977

GIRLS

ECATERINA/EKATERINA/YEKATERINA

There are many variants and variations of the name *Catherine/Katherine* around the world, with Eastern Europe providing us with Ecaterina, Ekaterina, and Yekaterina. However, you don't need to have Romanian, Bulgarian, Macedonian, or Russian lineage to give one of these names to a girl in your family; they're cool, they have interesting nicknames like *Katya* and *Katyusha*, and they've all been used by inspirational athletes! Russian tennis player Ekaterina Makarova reached the top doubles spot in the world, with four Grand Slam championships and an Olympic gold medal; Bulgarian biathlete Ekaterina Dafovska scored Olympic gold; Yekaterina Gamova is a Russian two-time World Champion volleyball player; and Belarusian rower Ekaterina Karsten has accumulated a huge medal collection, with five from Olympic Games (including two golds), fifteen from World Championships (six of them gold), and more.

Among the most graceful of these competitors were two highly decorated Russians and a Romanian: record-setting, two-time Olympic-winner and four-time World Champion figure skater Ekaterina Gordeeva; rhythmic gymnast Ekaterina Selezneva, who won two World Championships and a Grand Prix Final; and Romanian gymnastics Hall of Famer Ecaterina Szabo, who took home a massive four Olympic golds and ten World Championship medals (including two golds).

Ekaterina Dafovska, Biathlon, Bulgaria, 1992–2006

Yekaterina Gamova, Volleyball (Opposite), Russia, 1999–2014

Ekaterina Gordeeva, Figure Skating, USSR, 1986–1994

Ekaterina Karsten, Rowing, Belarus, 1991–2017

Ekaterina Makarova, Tennis, Russia, 2004–2020

Ekaterina Selezneva, Rhythmic Gymnastics, Russia, 2013–current

Ecaterina Szabo, Artistic Gymnastics, Romania, 1983–1987

EDITA/EDITH/EDYTA

While they may not look or sound totally similar at first glance, Edita and Edyta are European variations on the name Edith, which comes from Old English roots for "wealth/fortune" and "battle." These names have won big with three world champions: Polish sprint canoeist Edyta Dzieniszewska, Lithuanian road cyclist Edita Pučinskaitė, and Dutch judoka Edith Bosch, who won a gold medal, four silvers, and three bronzes at International Judo Federation (IJF) Grand Slam events.

Teach a girl in your family named Edita, Edith, or Edyta to train hard and maximize her athletic abilities, but also to play fair and be vigilant.

Edith Bosch, Judo, Netherlands, 2000–2013

Edyta Dzieniszewska, Sprint Canoeing, Poland, 2005–current

Edita Pučinskaitė, Road Cycling, Lithuania, 1994–2010

EILEEN

See *Aileen*.

ELANA

Most often considered a descendent of the names *Elaine* or *Helen* (but can also be a variation of other names like *Elan*, *Alana*, or *Yelena*), Elana is an uncommon but pretty name that can give its owner stamina and a bit of a need for speed. These are especially true if she takes after record-breaking South African Olympic gold-medalist and World Half Marathon champion long-distance runner Elana Meyer or American bobsledder Elana Meyers Taylor, who's won eight podiums at World Championships (including four golds).

Elana Meyer, Long-Distance Running, South Africa, 1991–1999

Elana Meyers Taylor, Bobsleigh, USA, 2009–current

ELEANOR/ELINOR

Eleanor, coming from an Occitan name by way of Old French and appearing with the alternate spelling Elinor, can be viewed as an old-fashioned name, and it's true that many women who have had it instead go by a nickname or short form like *Ellie*. However, Eleanor and Elinor are absolutely the names of champions and pioneers with a diverse set of accomplishments. British ultramarathon runner Eleanor Robinson won two IAU 100 kilometer World Championships, along with a host of other races and record-setting events; and American two-time Olympic gold medal-winning freestyle swimmer Eleanor Garatti was inducted into the International Swimming Hall of Fame. Called the "Babe Ruth of the All-American Girls Professional Baseball League," Eleanor Callow was a four-time All-Star and three-time league champion as well as the all-time home run and triples leader.

Name your daughter Eleanor or Elinor and she'll be courageous, empowered, competitive, and someone who will reach for the sky.

Eleanor Callow, Baseball (Left Fielder), Rockford Peaches, Canada, 1947–1954

Eleanor Garatti, Swimming (Freestyle), USA, 1928–1932

Eleanor Robinson, Ultramarathon, England, 1983–2001

ELENA

In most parts of the world, Elena ultimately comes from the Ancient Greek name *Helen*, sometimes by way of the Eastern European *Yelena*. Just as the name appears all around the world, so, too, does it rank among the champions of various different sports and disciplines! Six-time All-Star and WNBA champion Elena Delle Donne had success on the international stage with a gold medal at an Olympic Games and a World Cup; Russian pairs figure skater Elena Berezhnaya reached the pinnacle with an Olympic gold, two world championships, and a Grand Prix Final win; and figure skater Elena Valova was an Olympic gold and silver-medalist and three-time world champion.

Among the most winning Elenas have been Russian gymnasts like three-time Olympic gold-medalist and two-time World Cup Final-winner Elena Mukhina, and Elena Zamolodchikova, who took home four Olympic medals (including two golds in 2000), seven World Championship medals (two golds), and five World Cup Finals (two more golds); rowers, like three-time Olympic gold-medalist and World Rowing Champion Elena Georgescu of Romania and Soviet seven-time world champion Elena Tereshina; and foil fencers, like Soviet Elena Belova, who took a stunning four Olympic gold medals and eight World Championships.

Will an Elena in your family find success in one of the sports we see here?

Elena Belova, Fencing (Foil), USSR, 1968–1980

Elena Berezhnaya, Figure Skating, Russia, 1983–2002

Elena Delle Donne, Basketball (Small Forward/Shooting Guard), Washington Mystics, USA, 2013–current

Elena Georgescu, Rowing, Romania, 1990–2008

Elena Mukhina, Artistic Gymnastics, USSR, 1975–1979

Elena Tereshina, Rowing, USSR, 1978–1987

Elena Valova, Figure Skating, Russia, 1979–1988

Elena Zamolodchikova, Artistic Gymnastics, Russia, 1999–2009

ELISA

Just one of many possible diminutives or evolutions of the name *Elisabeth/Elizabeth*, Elisa is most popular around Europe—particularly Italy when it comes to sports. That's the home country of volleyball world champion and World Championship MVP wing/spiker Elisa Togut and foil fencer Elisa Di Francisca, who fought her way to two gold medals and a silver at Olympic Games and a whopping nine golds, ten silvers, and ten bronzes at World Cup events!

Call your daughter Elisa and introduce her to swords and spiking; she too may become a champion in fencing or volleyball.

Elisa Di Francisca, Fencing (Foil), Italy, 2003–2019

Elisa Togut, Volleyball (Wing/Spiker), Italy, 1998–2005

ELISABETA

There aren't a ton of *Elizabeths* in the hallowed halls of major athletics (they typically prefer nicknames like *Betsy*), unlike the Romanian version Elisabeta. You don't need to be Romanian to give this name to a girl in your family, but if you do, she'll be fast and determined, especially while wielding an implement in her hand like two-time World Fencing Champion with the foil Elisabeta Guzganu-Tufan and Elisabeta Lipă, the winningest rower in Olympic history with five gold medals and a tremendous thirteen podium appearances at World Championships!

Elisabeta Guzganu-Tufan, Fencing (Foil), Romania, 1984–1995

Elisabeta Lipă, Rowing, Romania, 1982–2004

ELLE

If you want your daughter to be faster than fast, consider the name Elle (sometimes its own name from French "she," but more often a shortened form of *Eleanor/Elinor*, *Elizabeth*, or *Eloise*). A daughter with this name may take after multiple record-setting runner Elinor "Elle" St. Pierre or three-time Olympic gold-medalist and three-time World Champion rower Eleanor "Elle" Logan.

Eleanor "Elle" Logan, Rowing, USA, 2008–2016

Elinor "Elle" St. Pierre, Track & Field (Middle-Distance Running), USA, 2018–current

ELLEN

Ellen is a very versatile and worldly name, with a huge variety of potential origins. Its usage has come about as a descendant of *Helen* and *Eleanora*, and as a variation of other names like *Eleanor*, *Elena*, and *Elizabeth*. And while it once enjoyed a degree of popularity in the United States, it has become much more common in European countries, which is reflected in the multiple champion Ellens we can find in several different sports! Dutch cyclist Ellen van Dijk has a combined six World Championships on road and track along with dozens of other accolades; soccer forward Ellen White holds the record for most goals scored by an English player and has a record of 136 goals in 265 senior and national appearances; American Ellen Estes has a water polo World Championship, along with silver and bronze Olympic medals; Austrian foil fencer Ellen Preis won Olympic gold in 1932; and Dutch field hockey midfielder Ellen Hoog secured her place on the all-time greats lists of her sport by earning two gold medals each at the Olympics, World Cup, and Champions Trophy, scoring sixty goals on the Netherlands' National Women's Field Hockey Team.

Ellen Estes, Water Polo (Center), USA, 2000–2004

Ellen Hoog, Field Hockey (Midfielder), Netherlands, 2002–2017

Ellen Preis, Fencing (Foil), Austria, 1932–1948

Eleanora "Ellen" van Dijk, Road Cycling, Netherlands, 2006–current

Ellen White, Soccer (Forward), Manchester City Women's Football Club, England, 2005–current

ELLIE/ELLY

The sky is the limit when it comes to shortening "El-" names to the unisex Ellie (or more rarely Elly). No matter if you have an *Eloise*, *Elisa*, *Elena*, *Eleanor*, *Elizabeth*, or even *Michelle* or *Petronella*, you can call a daughter Ellie. If you do, she just might enjoy running or spending lots of time in the pool. That is, if she takes after track and field pros Ellie Greenwood of Scotland, who has two ultramarathon World Championship wins and records for long-distance running; two-time World Champion (1500-meter and 3000-meter) Elly van Hulst; or a large number of swimmers with these names, including English Paralympic gold-medalist and butterfly world record-holder Ellie Robinson; American swimmer Ellie Daniel, who took home Olympic gold, silver, and bronze; and incredibly successful Paralympian athletes like Australian Ellie Cole and British Ellie Simmonds who have dozens of medals at multiple events, including Paralympic gold and World Championships, along with world records.

Ellie Cole, Swimming (Backstroke/Butterfly/Freestyle), Australia, 2003–current

Eleanor "Ellie" Daniel, Swimming (Butterfly), USA, 1967–1972

Ellie Greenwood, Ultramarathon, Scotland, 2008–current

Eleanor "Ellie" Robinson, Swimming (Butterfly/Freestyle), England, 2015–current

Eleanor "Ellie" Simmonds, Swimming (Freestyle/Medley), England, 2008–2020

Elisa "Elly" van Hulst, Track & Field (Middle-Distance Running), Netherlands, 1984–1990

ELSIE

A diminutive of *Elizabeth*, the name Elsie has been around for a long time. It may feel a bit old-fashioned these days, but it's still fun and perky and can inspire a daughter to break out on her own, unleash her power in the water alongside her team, or hop in a car and race to victory! Some truly outstanding Elsies out there include turn-of-the-twentieth-century American sportswoman and top-ranked amateur golfer Elsie Cassatt, Olympic gold-medalist and two-time world champion water polo center back Elsie Windes, and race driver Elsie "Bill" Wisdom, who jumpstarted her career by winning the first women's race she entered at the famous Brooklands track, set speed records for women there, and won numerous times in women-only and mixed-gender races.

Elizabeth "Elsie" Foster Cassatt, Cricket/Golf, USA, 1893–1907

Elsie Windes, Water Polo (Center Back), USA, 2006–2012

Elsie "Bill" Wisdom, Auto Racing (Grand Prix), England, 1925–1955

EMILY

Just like *Emil/Emile*, Emily comes from the traditional Roman family name *Aemilius*, which in turn comes from a root meaning "rival." Emilys have found athletic rivals on the soccer field, with FIFA Women's World Cup-winner and two-time National Women's Soccer League champion defender/midfielder Emily Sonnett, and in the pool, with Olympic gold-medalist synchronized swimmer Emily LeSueur and Australian swimmer Emily Seebohm, who holds multiple records for her country and has won seven Olympic medals (three of them gold), twenty-four World Championship medals (five gold), and more. Rugby has seen dominant athletes with this name, including Emily Valentine, the earliest documented female rugby player, starting on her school's team at ten years old . . . in 1887!

An Emily in your family may express her athletic prowess in the water or on a field in a team sport, and just might be a pioneer at the same time.

Emily LeSueur, Synchronized Swimming, USA, 1996

Emily Seebohm, Swimming (Backstroke/Freestyle/Medley), Australia, 2007–current

Emily Scarratt, Rugby (Center/Fullback), Lichfield Ladies Rugby Union Football Club, England, 2015–current

Emily Sonnett, Soccer (Defender/Midfielder), Portland Thorns Football Club, USA, 2011–current

Emily Valentine, Rugby (Wing), Portora Royal School Wasps, Northern Ireland, 1887

EMMA

Emma's origins are Germanic from a root word meaning "universal." If there's anything that's "universal" connecting a girl named Emma with those who have succeeded in sports before her, it's her inner strength and ability to push beyond what others expect. You can see that spirit in Australian Olympic gold-medalist and three-time World Triathlon Series champion Emma Snowsill, and Australian swimmer Emma McKeon, who has won eleven Olympic medals (five of them gold), seventeen World Championship podiums (four gold), and multiple world records.

Emma McKeon, Swimming (Freestyle), Australia, 2012–current

Emma Snowsill, Triathlon, Australia, 2000–2012

ERICA/ERIKA

As you might be able to guess, Erica and Ericka are feminine variants of *Eric/Erik*, all of which draw their origin from Old Norse roots meaning "always" and "ruler." When it comes to the "rulers" of their sports and athletic fields, Russian épée fencer Erika Kirpu has one of each medal from World Championships and scored Olympic gold in 2020; Brazilian basketball center Érika de Souza has three All-Star appearances and a WNBA championship; Japanese swimmer Erika Nara took home two gold medals and three bronzes from the Paralympic Games; and American Erica Rose has two long-distance World Championship wins in swimming. On the racetrack, Erica Enders has crushed the competition in NHRA's Pro Stock with four championships and a string of records behind her, both for speed and for being the first woman to hit major milestones.

If you think you can handle an athletic and competitive girl "ruling" your household, then consider naming her Erica or Erika.

- **Érika de Souza**, Basketball (Center), Atlanta Dream, Brazil, 2002–current
- **Erica Enders**, Auto Racing (NHRA), USA, 2005–current
- **Erika Kirpu**, Fencing (Épée), Russia, 2012–current
- **Erika Nara**, Swimming (Freestyle), Japan, 2000–current
- **Erica Rose**, Swimming (Freestyle), USA, 1997–1998

ERIN

While the name Erin literally means "Irish" (from a Gaelic word meaning "of Ireland"), you don't have to be from the Emerald Isle to pass this iconic name to a girl in your family. Top Erins in sports are spread out across a huge landscape of athletic endeavors, from netball (two-time Netball World Champion Erin Bell of Australia) to luge (Olympic bronze-medalist and two-time World Champion Erin Hamlin). Australian Erin Phillips achieved success in basketball, where she's won two WNBA championships, Olympic gold, and a World Championship, while Canadian soccer goalkeeper Erin McLeod has won Olympic gold. New Zealander triathlon legend Erin Baker won 104 of the 121 races she entered, including a World Triathlon Championship, World Triathlon Duathlon Championship, and two Ironman World Championships, while American rower Erin Cafaro took home two Olympic gold medals and three World Rowing Championships. Erin Jauch is a three-time World Champion trampoline gymnast and Erin Popovich set multiple swimming records on her way to winning a staggering fourteen gold and five silver medals at the Paralympics.

- **Erin Baker**, Triathlon, New Zealand, 1984–1994
- **Erin Bell**, Netball, Australia, 2005–2018
- **Erin Cafaro**, Rowing, USA, 2006–2012
- **Erin Hamlin**, Luge, USA, 2006–2017
- **Erin Jauch**, Trampoline Gymnastics, USA, 2010–2016
- **Erin McLeod**, Soccer (Goalkeeper), Washington Freedom, Canada, 2004–current
- **Erin Phillips**, Basketball/Australian Rules Football, Indiana Fever, Australia, 2002–2016
- **Erin Popovich**, Swimming (Breaststroke/Butterfly/Freestyle), USA, 2000–2008

ESTHER

Esther is an ancient name, appearing in biblical Hebrew and possibly linked to an Old Persian root word for "star" (or related to the goddess Ishtar). Esthers are all goddesses in their own ways, and those who have become famous for their athletic accomplishments include Olympic gold-medalists like high jumper Esther Brand of South Africa and

American 4x100 meter relay racer Esther Jones. Esther Lofgren broke world records while rowing to an Olympic Games win and multiple World Rowing Championships, while on the tennis court Esther Vergeer of the Netherlands reached the top spot in the world with 136 career titles and seven gold medals at the Paralympic Games!

Esther Brand, Track & Field (High Jump), South Africa, 1940–1952

Esther Jones, Track & Field (Sprinting), USA, 1989–1992

Esther Lofgren, Rowing, USA, 2006–2012

Esther Vergeer, Wheelchair Tennis, Netherlands, 1995–2013

EVA

The name Eva is a variation on *Eve*, famous throughout the world for her biblical Hebrew origin (from a root meaning "to breathe" or "to live"). Eva has a bit more of a modern feel and has reached Olympic Games and World Championship podiums, world record lists, and more. The Swedish Curling Hall of Fame includes two-time Olympic gold-medalist and two-time World Champion Eva Lund; Czech snowboarder Eva Samková has Olympic and World Championship gold; gymnast Eva Bosáková, born in Czechoslovakia, collected fourteen medals across the two biggest international events; and Dutch field hockey midfielder Eva de Goede racked up three Olympic golds, two World Cup wins, three Champions Trophies, and more.

Any girl named Eva with an adventurous personality and competitive nature can look up to an absolute legend like multi-talented New Zealander Eva "Eve" Rimmer, who won thirty-two medals in major international events (twenty-two of them gold) in everything from javelin, shot put, and discus to pentathlon, swimming, and archery!

Eva Bosáková, Artistic Gymnastics, Czechoslovakia, 1957–1962

Eva de Goede, Field Hockey (Midfielder), Netherlands' National Women's Field Hockey Team, Netherlands, 2006–current

Eva Lund, Curling (Third), Sweden, 1993–2010

Eva "Eve" Rimmer, Para-Athletics/Swimming/Archery, New Zealand, 1968–1980

Eva Samková, Snowboarding, Czech Republic, 2013–current

EVELIN/EVELYN

There are a couple of different possible origins for the name Evelyn (and its related variants like Evelin and Evelyne), including an old Germanic form via Norman French or an Irish source. Wherever it came from, this family of names has driven athletes and great women to incredible feats, like American four-time World Champion cyclist Evelyn Stevens. Two hugely successful track and field athletes with world records under their belts bore versions of this name; German discus thrower Evelin Jahl won gold twice at the Olympics, and twice at the IAAF World Cup, while American Evelyn Ashford sprinted to four Olympic gold medals, three Goodwill Games wins, and more.

Evelyn Ashford, Track & Field (Sprinting), USA, 1976–1992

Evelin Jahl, Track & Field (Discus), Germany, 1976–1981

Evelyn Stevens, Road Cycling, USA, 2010–2016

EVGENIA/EVGENIIA/EVGENIYA

A family of names with small spelling differences—Evegnia, Evgeniia, and Evgeniya—comes from Eastern European evolutions of an ancient Roman name meaning "well born." These are mighty names, bringing their bearers to glory regardless of the circumstances of their birth, like Russian Paralympic gold-medalist and world champion sprinter Evgenia Trushnikova; Bulgarian short track speed skater Evgenia Radanova, who took home sixteen medals from World Championships, including two golds; and Ukrainian chess Woman Grandmaster Evgeniya Doluhanova.

There are two sports that athletes with these names have a particular fondness for, and they reflect the incredible grace and dexterity these athletes are capable of. Figure skating is the first, with Evgenia Shishkova, who won a gold medal each at World Championships and Grand Prix Final, and Evgenia Medvedeva, who won two golds at both of those. Rhythmic gymnastics is the other, with two of the all-time greats in five-time world champion Evgeniia Levanova and the incomparable Evgeniya Kanaeva, who shattered numerous world records on her way to winning two Olympic gold medals, seventeen world championships, three World Cup Finals, fifteen Grand Prix Finals, four World Games, and more!

Evgeniya Doluhanova, Chess, Ukraine, 2004–current

Evgeniya Kanaeva, Rhythmic Gymnastics, Russia, 2005–2012

Evgeniia Levanova, Rhythmic Gymnastics, Russia, 2016–2021

Evgenia Medvedeva, Figure Skating, Russia, 2004–2021

Evgenia Radanova, Short Track Speed Skating, Bulgaria, 1995–2010

Evgenia Shishkova, Figure Skating, Russia, 1991–1998

Evgenia Trushnikova, Para-Athletics, Russia, 2004–2016

F

BOYS

FABIAN

The name Fabian has a noble heritage, coming from a famous ancient Roman household, while also having a very down-to-earth origin in a word for "bean." Fabians are certainly not all bean farmers, though, with German athletes like Nordic combined skier Fabian Riesle, who has won four Olympic medals and six at World Championships (including three golds), and gymnast Fabian Hambüchen, who's collected a set of Olympic medals and nine podiums at World Championships. Meanwhile, quite a few Fabians are focused entirely on speed, with all thoughts put toward crossing that finish line. German slalom canoeist Fabian Dörfler has raced to three World Championships and six World Cup wins, wheelchair athlete Fabian Blattman of Australia has multiple world records to go along with his seven Paralympics medals and six from IPC Athletics World Championships (two golds at each), and Swiss quadruple time trial world champion cyclist Fabian Cancellara has captured two Olympic wins and four World Championships.

Clearly the name Fabian brings with it a love of going fast and trying to win!

- **Fabian Blattman**, Wheelchair Athletics, Australia, 1988–2000
- **Fabian Cancellara**, Road Cycling, Switzerland, 2001–2016
- **Fabian Dörfler**, Slalom Canoeing, Germany, 2001–2014
- **Fabian Hambüchen**, Artistic Gymnastics, Germany, 2003–2016
- **Fabian Riesle**, Nordic Combined Skiing, Germany, 2009–current

FEDOR/FYODOR

From a localized variation of the classic name *Theodore* (from Ancient Greek roots meaning "gift of god") comes the Russian royal name Fyodor and its popular alternate form Fedor. Once the name of tsars and Dostoyevsky, more recently it's been featured on Olympic Games podiums with winners like Dutch cyclist Fedor den Hertog, figure skater Fedor Klimov, and cross-country skiers Fyodor Simashev and Fyodor Terentyev (who are both World Champions). If you're a fan of mixed martial arts, there's only one Fedor of note and that's "the Last Emperor" Emelianenko! A heavyweight MMA fighter, sambo practitioner, and judoka, Fedor is widely considered one of the greatest mixed martial artists of all time, and on his way to a 40–6–1 record (as of this writing), he's accumulated multiple titles, championships, and medals at the highest levels of competition.

If you have Russian heritage in your family, then Fedor or Fyodor might be perfect for you, but even if you don't, naming a kid one of these can give him the dedication and power of an emperor and the fast hands and feet to along with it.

Fedor den Hertog, Road Cycling, Netherlands, 1968–1977

Fedor "the Last Emperor" Emelianenko, MMA (Heavyweight), USSR, 2000–current

Fedor Klimov, Figure Skating, USSR, 1994–2018

Fyodor Simashev, Cross-County Skiing, USSR, 1968–1974

Fyodor Terentyev, Cross-County Skiing, USSR, 1954–1958

FELIPE

The name *Philip* stretches back to Ancient Greek meaning "friend of horses," and in Spanish and Portuguese has found an alternate form in Felipe. There may not be horses involved in many of Felipes' careers, the most impressive of which include three-time All-Star slugger Felipe Alou's seventeen years in the MLB. On the other hand, there has been plenty of horsepower under the hoods of the various cars driven by Brazilian racers Felipe Nasr (two-time SportsCar champ) and Felipe Massa (eleven wins in Formula 1 and championships in Formula Chevrolet Brazil, Formula Renault 2000 Eurocup, Formula Renault 2000 Italy, and Euro Formula 3000).

If you like the name *Philip* but are looking for something a bit more unique, or your family is into horses (or race cars), Felipe might be perfect for you!

Felipe Alou, Baseball (Outfielder/First Baseman), Milwaukee Braves, Dominican Republic, 1958–1974

Felipe Massa, Auto Racing (Formula 1), Brazil, 1998–current

Felipe Nasr, Auto Racing (Formula 1), Brazil, 2008–current

FELIX

A truly happy-go-lucky name, Felix has been around since ancient Rome and means "lucky" or "prosperous" in Latin. It's not luck but skill and drive that elevates an athletic Felix to the top of the heap, and the list of the most successful of them include Austrian two-time World Champion figure skater Felix Kaspar; six-time All-Star MLB pitcher for the Seattle Mariners Félix Hernández, who pitched a perfect game and an immaculate inning; German soccer midfielder Felix Magath, who scored ninety-two goals in 463 club appearances and won a UEFA European Championship and European Cup Final; and Puerto Rican boxer Félix Trinidad, who won half a dozen titles in multiple weight classes on his way to a 42–3 record. Athletes named Felix range all the way to Austrian modern daredevil Felix Baumgartner, who is famous for jumping off of buildings, out of planes, and off of helium balloons in the stratosphere to set and break all manners of world records!

Felix Baumgartner, Daredevil, Austria, 1999–2014

Félix Hernández, Baseball (Pitcher), Seattle Mariners, Venezuela, 2005–2019

Felix Kaspar, Figure Skating, Austria, 1935–1938

Wolfgang Felix Magath, Soccer (Midfielder), Hamburger Sport-Verein e.V., Germany, 1972–1986

Félix Trinidad, Boxing (Welterweight/Middleweight), Puerto Rico, 1990–2008

FERNANDO

The name *Ferdinand* (from Germanic roots for "daring journey") isn't super popular these days, but the Spanish and Portuguese alternate form Fernando shows up quite a bit in countries where those languages are spoken. Some of the greatest Fernandos have even embraced the ancient source of their name and journeyed to victory, like Spanish two-time Formula 1 champion Fernando Alonso, who won thirty-two races. Where have other athletes with this name excelled?

Speed on the water has been the domain of two-time World Rowing Champion and Olympic silver-medalist Fernando Climent of Spain and Brazilian three-time paracanoe ICF Canoe Sprint World Champion Fernando Fernandes; and on the tennis court, Chilean Fernando González won eleven titles and an Olympic medal of each color!

It is perhaps not surprising that with the popularity of the name in Spanish- and Portuguese-speaking countries, Fernandos have left a major mark on the world of football/soccer. Some of the top Spanish strikers who have terrorized opposing teams include FIFA World Cup–winner Fernando Llorente, who has scored 208 goals in club and international appearances; 238 goal-scoring Fernando Morientes, who collected two Intercontinental Cups, an FA Cup, and a UEFA Super Cup; and Fernando Torres, who ended his illustrious career with over three hundred goals, an FA Cup, FIFA World Cup, two UEFA European Championships, and tons of personal awards and records!

You don't have to have a Spanish or Portuguese lineage to name a son Fernando, though if you do, you should probably prepare to watch a lot of soccer.

Fernando Alonso, Auto Racing (Formula 1), Spain, 1999–current

Fernando Climent, Rowing, Spain, 1977–1993

Fernando Fernandes, Paracanoeing, Brazil, 2010–current

Fernando González, Tennis, Chile, 1999–2012

Fernando Llorente, Soccer (Striker), Athletic Club, Spain, 2003–current

Fernando Morientes, Soccer (Striker), Real Madrid Club de Fútbol, Spain, 1993–2015

Fernando Torres, Soccer (Striker), Club Atlético de Madrid, S.A.D., Spain, 2000–2019

FLOYD

Fans of sports and athletics know that naming a kid Floyd (from a Welsh root for "gray") will give him indomitable strength and toughness with the ability to take a hit and keep on going. We see this in football, with Denver Broncos five-time Pro Bowl halfback Floyd Little, but even more so in boxing. Heavyweight Floyd Patterson had a tremendous boxing career in the 1950s and '60s after winning an Olympic gold medal, becoming the youngest-ever world heavyweight champion, holding that title twice, and finishing his career with a 55–8–1 record. Standing above them all is one of the highest-ranked boxers of all time, Floyd Mayweather Jr. The son of a boxer, Mayweather held no fewer than fifteen major world championships in five different weight classes, all with an undefeated record after boxing for nearly twenty years!

Floyd Little, Football (Halfback), Denver Broncos, USA, 1967–1975

Floyd Mayweather Jr., Boxing (Featherweight/Lightweight/Welterweight/Middleweight), USA, 1996–2015

Floyd Patterson, Boxing (Heavyweight), USA, 1952–1972

FRANCK/FRANK/FRANKIE

There are many variations of the name Frank, all of which trace their origins back to the Franks, a Germanic tribe of people who lived in Western Europe in the third and fourth centuries and who gave their name to the country of France. We're going to talk about sportsmen known as Franck, Frank, and Frankie, though all of these can be short or alternate forms of additional names like *Francis* and *Franklin*. So, where have these people made impacts in the world of athletic competition? A lot of places, as it turns out, from pistol shooting, with French Franck Dumoulin (who's won Olympic gold, two World Championships, and a World Cup), to horse racing, with world-renowned Italian jockey Frankie Dettori, who has over 3,290 wins thus far!

On the gridiron, Frank Gore is a five-time Pro Bowl running back and 49ers rushing yards leader and Frank Gifford is an eight-time Pro Bowler who won both a championship and the NFL Most Valuable Player Award in 1956, while on skis, German winter games legends Frank Luck and Frank Höfle have huge medal counts (in biathlon for the former, and in cross-country and biathlon Paralympics for the latter).

Franks in the world of combat sports are powerful heavyweights; Frank Mir was an MMA heavyweight champion and set lots of UFC firsts and records (including the fastest submission and only-ever toe hold finish); and Frank Gotch was the first American world heavyweight free-style wrestling champion. And when it comes to muscle, none did it better than legendary three-time Mr. Olympia bodybuilder Frank Zane, who won numerous competitions and was inducted into the International Federation of Bodybuilding and Fitness Hall of Fame.

Last but not least is America's favorite pastime and all-time great baseball Franks! Award-winning slugger Frank "the Big Hurt" Thomas was a five-time All-Star and won the Silver Slugger award four times, five-time All-Star second baseman Frank White won a World Series, fiery Venezuelan Frankie Rodríguez has earned six All-Star appearances and a World Series win, and iconic hitter Frank Robinson was an MVP in both leagues, a fourteen-time All-Star, a two-time World Series champion, and a member of multiple Halls of Fame.

A Franck, Frank, or Frankie in your family may gravitate toward skiing, combat sports, baseball, or some other sport or discipline, but no matter what he chooses, he'll be focused and hard-working, earning his accolades.

- **Lanfranco "Frankie" Dettori**, Horse Racing (Jockey), Italy, 1985–2023
- **Franck Dumoulin**, Sport Shooting (Pistol), France, 1992–2012
- **Francis "Frank" Gifford**, Football (Halfback/Wide Receiver), New York Giants, USA, 1952–1964
- **Franklin "Frank" Gore Sr.**, Football (Running Back), San Francisco 49ers, USA, 2005–2020
- **Frank Gotch**, Wrestling (Heavyweight), USA, 1899–1913
- **Frank Höfle**, Skiing/Biathlon/Road Cycling, Germany, 1984–2010
- **Frank Luck**, Biathlon, Germany, 1987–2004
- **Francisco "Frank" Mir III**, MMA/Boxing (Heavyweight), USA, 2001–current
- **Frank Robinson**, Baseball (Outfielder), Cincinnati Redlegs, USA, 1956–1976
- **Francisco "Frankie" Rodríguez**, Baseball (Pitcher), Anaheim Angels, Venezuela, 2002–2017
- **Frank Thomas Jr.**, Baseball (First Baseman/Designated Hitter), Chicago White Sox, USA, 1990–2008
- **Frank White Jr.**, Baseball (Second Baseman), Kansas City Royals, USA, 1973–1990
- **Frank Zane**, Bodybuilding, USA, 1961–1983

FRED

Freds are just . . . unique. The name can come from a wide variety of sources (including serving as a short form for *Frederick* or standing tall on its own) and has risen to the top of a huge number of different sports and athletic competitions. Freds have made the big time in team sports like Brazilian soccer striker Fred Guedes, who kicked over four hundred goals in his club and international career while racking up trophies like a Copa América and FIFA Confederations Cup, while some athletes with this name are all about speed, like English thirteen-time Champion Jockey Fred Archer, who won over 2,700 races.

Striving on their own to succeed against their opponents (or the environment) have been American golfer Fred Couples and British tennis star Fred Perry, who each reached the number one rank in the world with sixty-two career titles (how's that for a coincidence!); and English two-time World Billiards Champion and eight-time World Snooker Champion Fred Davis.

There are some sports in which multiple Freds have thrived, starting with cricket and the immensely popular batsman Fred Bakewell and his two-eyed stance, and Fred Trueman, who was the first person to take three hundred wickets in Test cricket and is ranked among the best bowlers of all time. And then there's football! Three-time AFL All-Star defensive back Fred Williamson won an AFL championship before becoming a successful Hollywood actor, Baltimore Colts defensive tackle Fred Miller had three Pro Bowl appearances and won Super Bowl V, four-time Pro Bowl defensive tackle Fred Williams had an NFL championship with the Chicago Bears, and five-time AFL All-Star tight end Fred Arbanas won three AFL championships before winning Super Bowl IV.

Frederick "Fred" Arbanas, Football (Tight End), Dallas Texans, USA, 1962–1970

Frederick "Fred" Archer, Horse Racing (Jockey), England, 1869–1886

Alfred "Fred" Bakewell, Cricket (Batsman), Northamptonshire County Cricket Club, England, 1928–1936

Frederick "Fred" Couples, Golf, USA, 1980–2010

Fred Davis, Snooker, England, 1948–1956

Frederico "Fred" Guedes, Soccer (Striker), Fluminense Football Club, Brazil, 2003–current

Fred Miller, Football (Defensive Tackle), Baltimore Colts, USA, 1963–1972

Frederick "Fred" Perry, Tennis, England, 1936–1959

Frederick "Fred" Trueman, Cricket (Bowler), Yorkshire County Cricket Club, England, 1949–1972

Fred Williams, Football (Defensive Tackle), Chicago Bears, USA, 1952–1965

Frederick "Fred" Williamson, Football (Defensive Back), Oakland Raiders, USA, 1960–1966

GIRLS

FABIANA

As with many traditionally feminine names, Fabiana is an alternate form of an originally masculine name, in this case stretching back to ancient Rome with the family name *Fabianus* (same as *Fabian*). In modern times, this name has achieved popularity in parts of Europe and especially in Brazil, where many of the athletic champions with it have competed and won. Volleyball has recently seen two rising stars named Fabiana, the recently retired Alvim (two Olympic gold medals and two World Championships) and the currently competing Claudino (two Olympic golds and seven World Grand Prix wins). At the absolute pinnacle of their respective fields are Czech boxer Fabiana Bytyqi, a powerhouse and current world atomweight champion with an unbeaten 15–0–1 record, and cyclist Fabiana Luperini, whose ten major wins include a record-setting five at the Giro d'Italia Femminile!

Fabiana is a super cool name that's not just restricted to people from Brazil, and with it a girl in your family will be strong and fast.

Fabiana Alvim, Volleyball (Libero), Brazil, 2002–2018

Fabiana Bytyqi, Boxing (Atomweight/Minimumweight), Czech Republic, 2015–current

Fabiana Claudino, Volleyball (Middle Blocker), Brazil, 2003–current

Fabiana Luperini, Road Cycling, Italy, 1993–2014

FALLON

A relatively modern name, Fallon has roots in Irish Gaelic and a word meaning "leader." If you name a daughter Fallon, I can't *guarantee* she'll lead, but if she's anything like these amazing ladies, she'll be tough and a pioneer going wherever she pleases. Former US Navy operations specialist Fallon Fox was the first openly transgender mixed martial artist (and a successful one with a 5–1 record), and professional rodeo cowgirl Fallon Taylor has numerous awards and accolades and was the 2014 Women's Professional Rodeo Association Barrel Racing World Champion!

Fallon Fox, MMA (Featherweight), USA, 2012–2014

Fallon Taylor, Rodeo, USA, 1995–current

FATIMA/FATMA

Fatima and its regional variant Fatma come from an Arabic root meaning "to abstain," and are popular names in Muslim populations and beyond. Interestingly, top athletes so named come from all different countries and excel in different sports and disciplines! They range from Spanish sport shooter Fátima Gálvez, who's won Olympic gold and a World Championship with the shotgun, to Portuguese long-distance runner Fátima Silva, who has five major marathon wins under her belt. British javelin thrower Fatima Whitbread currently has the third farthest women's throw and a World Championship; Turkish free diver Fatma Uruk recently set multiple world depth records with and without fins; Fatima de Melo has won a set of Olympic medals, a World Cup, and four Champions Trophies with the Netherlands field hockey team; and Egyptian Fatma Omar became a hugely successful powerlifter, winning four IPC World Championships and four Paralympic Games gold medals in successive events from 2000 to 2012.

Truly a global name, Fatima or Fatma is a

solid choice no matter where you live and will instill in a girl the courage to find her own unique place in the world.

Fatima de Melo, Field Hockey (Midfield/Backward), Netherlands, 1997–2011

Fátima Gálvez, Sport Shooting (Trap), Spain, 2010–current

Fatma Omar, Powerlifting, Egypt, 1998–current

Fátima Silva, Marathon, Portugal, 1999–2008

Fatma Uruk, Free Diving, Turkey, 2008–current

Fatima Whitbread, Track & Field (Javelin), England, 1978–1988

FELICE

If you're feeling lucky, and that your child might gravitate toward mixed martial arts or boating, you might want to take a look at the Italian/Spanish name Felice! It's a variant of *Felix*, which comes from a Latin root for "lucky" or "prosperous." The name is best known here in the United States for two-time World Champion and three-time bronze medalist rower Felice Mueller and Felice Herrig, who held the US kickboxing bantamweight title before switching to MMA and participating in some of the most exciting fights in recent UFC history.

Felice Herrig, MMA (Strawweight), USA, 2009–current

Felice Mueller, Rowing, USA, 2013–current

FIONA

A name traditionally associated with the Emerald Isle, Fiona is a feminine variant of the Old Irish *Fionn* meaning "fair" or "white." It has spread around the world and to this day sees a degree of popularity in a number of countries. When it comes to those whose focus lies in sports and athletics, any girls named Fiona can look up to Australian water polo FINA World Cup-winner Fiona Hammond; Scottish Olympic gold-medalist curler Fiona MacDonald; long jump legend Fiona May, who won two Olympic silver medals and three World Championships; and Ireland Women's National Rugby Union Team captain Fiona Coghlan, who scored the Women's Six Nations Championship, Grand Slam, and Triple Crown in 2013.

Fiona Coghlan, Rugby (Front Row/Prop), Leinster Rugby, Ireland, 2001–current

Fiona Hammond, Water Polo (Field Player), Australia, 2006

Fiona MacDonald, Curling (Second), Scotland, 2002

Fiona May, Track & Field (Long Jump), Italy, 1988–2005

FLORENCE

The spirit to compete at the absolute highest level and to be faster than anyone else in the world has driven two American women named Florence (from a Latin word for "flourishing"), who in turn inspired generations of girls and athletes. In the 1950s, Florence Chadwick took her love of swimming to the ocean and embarked on long distance treks, winning races and setting world records crossing the Bristol Channel, English Channel, Straits of Gibraltar, and more. A few decades later, Florence Griffith Joyner came on the scene and women's track and field would never be the same; "Flo-Jo" won three Olympic gold medals and two silvers, along with a gold and silver at World Championships, and on the way set multiple world records, including two that stand to this very day!

A Florence in your family will flourish and be an inspiration to everyone who knows her.

Florence Chadwick, Long-Distance Swimming, USA, 1950–1960

Florence "Flo-Jo" Griffith Joyner, Track & Field (Sprinting), USA, 1983–1988

FRANCENA/FRANCINA/FRANCINE

The Germanic tribe known as Franks have inspired many different modern names as they've evolved by way of the Latin *Franciscus*. One branch of that tree splits into the French *François/Françoise*, and then European forms like Francena, Francina, and Francine. These names are primed for a launch to glory, and a little athlete in your family can be part of that! She may grow up with a love of horses, like Canada's most-winning woman jockey of all time Francine Villeneuve, who won 1,001 races in her career; or she may want to run and jump herself, like track and field stars Francina "Fanny" Blankers-Koen, who famously won four Olympic gold medals for the Netherlands in 1948 as the "flying housewife"; and American sprinter Francena McCorory, who has ran to two Olympic gold medals, four World Championships, a World Relay Championship, and more.

Francina "Fanny" Blankers-Koen, Track & Field (Sprinting/Hurdling), Netherlands, 1946–1955

Francena McCorory, Track & Field (Sprinting), USA, 2011–2016

Francine Villeneuve, Horse Racing (Jockey), Canada, 1987–2012

FRANÇOISE

Like the trio of names above, the French Françoise can be traced back to the Germanic Franks and a whole host of related monikers. And also like *Francena/Francina/Francine*, Françoise is a bit of an old-fashioned name, but one that is ready for a comeback. The most recent athletic exemplar taking it to the world's stage was Cameroonian triple jumper Françoise Mbango Etone, who set records while winning two Olympic gold medals and two silvers at World Championships. Back in the 1960s and '70s, French Françoise Dürr was a big name in tennis, ranked number one in doubles with sixty titles!

Will a girl named Françoise in your family end up playing tennis or enjoying track and field events? Or will she find her own discipline to dominate and make her own?

Françoise Dürr, Tennis, France, 1965–1979

Françoise Mbango Etone, Track & Field (Triple Jump), Cameroon, 1996–2012

FRIDA/FRIEDA

Yet another set of names that have Germanic origins, Frida and Frieda have roots in a word meaning "peace," which is pretty neat. Alpine skiing is a draw to some women with these names, like Swiss World Champion Frieda Dänzer and Swedish Olympic gold-medalist Frida Hansdotter. Far from the snowy slopes, Freida Zamba created waves on the surfing scene, winning four World Surfing Championships on her way to becoming one of the highest ranked female surfers ever.

Name your daughter Frida or Frieda and she may spend all her free time in the water or up on mountains!

Frieda Dänzer, Alpine Skiing, Switzerland, 1956–1958

Frida Hansdotter, Alpine Skiing, Sweden, 2004–2019

Frieda Zamba, Surfing, USA, 1981–1988

G

BOYS

GABRIEL

Gabriel is a biblical Hebrew name of an archangel and messenger of the divine, with meanings interpreted as "messenger of God" or "God is my strength." As with many biblical names, Gabriel shows up around the world and has maintained a level of popularity throughout the years, so it's no surprise that we'd see champion athletes with it from a variety of countries. Canadian kickboxer Gabriel Varga embodies the "strength" aspect of the name with his multiple belts, while Swedish NHL All-Star left wing Gabriel Landeskog has had international glory winning a silver Olympic medal and two World Championships, and Brazilian three-time World Champion surfer and winner of the Quicksilver Pro Gold Coast Gabriel Medina is known for his iconic "backflip" move.

South America has also produced several top soccer pros, notably Brazilian rising star, Olympic gold-medalist, and Copa América-winning forward Gabriel de Jesus, and Argentinian all-time great striker Gabriel Batistuta (their top goal-scorer until Lionel Messi), who scored 350 goals across his club and international career and whose trophy case includes two Supercoppa Italianas, two Copa Américas, a FIFA Confederations Cup, and tons of personal awards.

Strength—and likely fast feet on the soccer field—is sure to be a quality in a little Gabriel in your family.

- **Gabriel Batistuta**, Soccer (Striker), Associazione Calcio Firenze Fiorentina, Argentina, 1988–2005
- **Gabriel de Jesus**, Soccer (Forward), Manchester City Football Club, Brazil, 2015–current
- **Gabriel Landeskog**, Ice Hockey (Left Wing), Colorado Avalanche, Sweden, 2009–current
- **Gabriel Medina**, Surfing, Brazil, 2011–current
- **Gabriel Varga**, Kickboxing, Canada, 2006–current

GALE

Any name can be used by anyone, and that's definitely true of the unisex Gale that's usually descended from a Middle English root for "jovial" (or sometimes as a short form of Galen from Greek for "tranquil"). There's little tranquility or joviality on the gridiron, however, where two Gales, both of whom played for only one team their whole career, have shone. Chicago Bears halfback and return specialist Gale Sayers set records right from his very first season and earned four Pro Bowl appearances in five years. Overlapping Sayers's career was that of guard Gale Gillingham, whose huge list of accolades during his ten years with the Green Bay Packers includes five Pro Bowl appearances, two NFL championships, and two Super Bowl wins.

Naming a son Gale may just be one of the best ways to prepare him for a love of football!

Gale Gillingham, Football (Guard), Green Bay Packers, USA, 1966–1976

Gale Sayers, Football (Halfback), Chicago Bears, USA, 1965–1971

GARETH

If your family has Welsh roots and likes soccer or rugby, there may be no better name choice for your son than Gareth. From uncertain roots (possibly from Old Welsh roots for "valor" or "hay lord"), the name has come to be most popular in England and especially Wales, and so it's no surprise that those are the home countries of champion Gareths. On the fields of international football has trod Welsh record-setting winger Gareth Bale, who is known for his speed and precision, which he's used to score nearly 220 goals as of this writing and earn two UEFA Super Cups, three FIFA Club World Cups, and many personal awards. Meanwhile, Welsh rugby stars include scrum half Gareth Edwards who is considered one of the greatest players of all time, with 426 points scored in 195 senior appearances, three Grand Slams, and more; Edwards even holds a record for British angling after landing a forty-five-pound pike!

Gareth Bale, Soccer (Winger), Real Madrid Club de Fútbol, Wales, 2006–current

Gareth Edwards, Rugby (Scrum Half), Cardiff Rugby Football Club, Wales, 1966–1978

GARRET/GARRETT

While it may sound like it's related to *Gareth*, the English name Garrett has the shared root for "spear" with the Germanic *Gerald* and *Gerard* and standouts like three-time All-Star and World Series champion slugger Garret Anderson and jockey Garrett Gomez who racked up an astounding 3,769 wins in his career.

Meanwhile, Garretts seem particularly suited to success on the water! Rowers Klugh and Miller have one of each Olympic medal and three World Rowing Championships, respectively; freestyle swimmer Weber-Gale has captured Olympic gold twice, as well as seven World Championships; and McNamara holds numerous surfing accolades, including the world record for the largest wave ever surfed and being the first to surf a tsunami created by calving glaciers!

Pick the name Garret or Garrett for a boy who will definitely love activities in and on water.

Garret Anderson, Baseball (Left Fielder), California Angels, USA, 1994–2010

Garrett Gomez, Horse Racing (Jockey), USA, 1988–2015

Garrett Klugh, Rowing, USA, 1999–2004

Garrett McNamara, Surfing, USA, 1978–current

Garrett Miller, Rowing, USA, 1997–2000

Garrett Weber-Gale, Swimming (Freestyle), USA, 2005–2013

GARRY/GARY

Gary may feel like an old-fashioned uncle's name, but it has a pretty cool origin in Norman French from Old Frankish roots meaning "spear" and "royal." Royal spearmen or not, Garys have made some pretty big marks in a lot of fields, and some may surprise you. There have been a whole lot of highly successful American football players with this name especially, with the greatest including cornerback Gary Green, who had five Pro Bowl appearances; four-time Pro Bowl defensive tackle and Super Bowl champ Gary "Big Hands" Johnson; wide receiver Gary Clark, who has four Pro Bowl appearances and two Super Bowl wins; and Super Bowl champion offensive tackle Gary Zimmerman, who went to the Pro Bowl a massive seven times!

American baseball has seen two supreme sluggers named Gary who both won a World Series, the nine-time All-Star (and only player ever to rack up one hundred RBIs in a season for five different teams) Gary Sheffield and the eleven-time All-Star catcher Gary "the Kid" Carter. Meanwhile, over on soccer fields of the world, Gary Lineker's combined 647 appearances and 329 goals and dozens of team and individual awards rank him among the top English strikers of all time.

Two marksmen named Gary Anderson have hit the bullseye in darts (Scottish two-time World Champion) and sport shooting (American two-time Olympic gold-medalist and six-time world record-setter). The flamboyant Gary Hall swam to ten Olympic medals (including five golds) and three World Championships, while point guard Gary "the Glove" Payton was a nine-time All-Star and NBA champion. Gary Sobers of Barbados routinely ranks at the top of all-time best cricket all-rounders lists with a number of records and achievements, and Russian chess Grandmaster Garry Kasparov held the number one spot in the world rankings for over twenty-one years!

If you're American and name your son Gary, he may very well enjoy football, but no matter what, he'll be a keen student of strategy in whatever sport or athletic domain he enjoys.

Gary Anderson, Darts, Scotland, 1996–current

Gary Anderson, Sport Shooting (Rifle), USA, 1962–1966

Gary "the Kid" Carter, Baseball (Catcher), Montreal Expos, USA, 1974–1992

Gary Clark, Football (Wide Receiver), Washington Redskins, USA, 1984–1995

Gary Green, Football (Cornerback), Kansas City Chiefs, USA, 1977–1985

Gary Hall Jr., Swimming (Freestyle), USA, 1996–2008

Gary "Big Hands" Johnson, Football (Defensive Tackle), San Diego Chargers, USA, 1975–1985

Garry Kasparov, Chess, USSR, 1976–current

Gary Lineker, Soccer (Striker), Leicester City Football Club, England, 1978–1994

Gary "the Glove" Payton Sr., Basketball (Point Guard), Seattle SuperSonics, USA, 1990–2007

Gary Sheffield, Baseball (Outfielder/Third Baseman), Los Angeles Dodgers, USA, 1988–2009

Garfield "Gary" Sobers, Cricket (All-Rounder), Barbados National Cricket Team, Barbados, 1952–1974

Gary Zimmerman, Football (Offensive Tackle), Minnesota Vikings, USA, 1984–1997

GENE

Formed as a diminutive of various names coming from Ancient Greek roots meaning "well born," including *Eugene* and *Eugenio*, Gene is uniquely American . . . and immensely successful! On the links, Gene Sarazen won forty-eight professional events and seven majors and remains one of only five golfers ever to complete a Career Grand Slam; in the ring, world heavyweight boxing champion Gene Tunney won eighty bouts and lost only one by decision; and on the gridiron, Oakland Raiders guard Gene Upshaw earned an AFL All-Star and six Pro Bowl selections, won an AFL championship and two Super Bowls, set the record for consecutive starts from the beginning of a career, and earned induction into the Pro Football Hall of Fame!

- **Eugenio "Gene" Sarazen**, Golf, USA, 1920–1956
- **James "Gene" Tunney**, Boxing (Heavyweight), USA, 1915–1928
- **Eugene "Gene" Upshaw Jr.**, Football (Guard), Oakland Raiders, USA, 1967–1981

GEORG/GEORGE/GEORGES

From the humblest of origins in Greek roots for "farmer" comes the name George (and its many variants, including Georg and Georges). A number of famous athletes and sports figures have taken that name from the fields of ancient Greece to modern competition. Among the solitary champions in their fields have been Jamaican sprinter George Rhoden, who won two Olympic gold medals; two-time World Champion Canadian water skier George Athans; Swiss gymnast Georges Miez, whose medal collection included eight from the Olympics (four gold) and three from World Championships; and German luge legend Georg Hackl, who has brought home three Olympic gold medals, ten World Championships, two World Cup championships, and more.

On four wheels, Belgian motocross racer Georges Jobé won five world championships. On bicycles, Belgian road and cyclo-cross racer Georges Ronsse won two World Championships and English George Mills won races on penny-farthings and set distance records in the 1800s, some of which were only broken in the twenty-first century. Swimming Georges have included a pair of two-time Olympic gold medalists in Canadian Hodgson and American Kojac.

Many Georges have been drawn to combat sports, including world-class mixed martial artist Georges St-Pierre, a UFC multiple world-champion-turned-actor (notably playing the "leaping" villain Georges Batroc in the Marvel Cinematic Universe). Of course, the most famous boxer with this name is American heavyweight George Foreman, Olympic gold-medalist, two-time world heavyweight champion, and promoter of the George Foreman Lean Mean Fat-Reducing Grilling Machine (George Foreman Grill)!

Georges also excel at major team sports like basketball, with early big man and pioneer center George "Mr. Basketball" Mikan, who had four NBA All-Star appearances and seven championships across the professional leagues of the time; six-time NBA All-Star George Yardley, who was the first player to score two thousand points in a single season; and George "the Iceman" Gervin, whose incredible consistency earned him twelve All-Star appearances during his NBA and ABA career. On the gridiron, four-time AFL All-Star quarterback and placekicker George Blanda collected three AFL championships and set multiple extra points records, and offensive tackle George Kunz was called to a huge seven Pro Bowls.

Liberian striker George Weah was considered one of the greatest African soccer players of all time, with over two hundred goals in 553 combined club and international appearances, an FA Cup, Ballon d'Or, ranking on the FIFA 100, and more—and that's all before he became the president of his country! Meanwhile, Northern Irish winger George Best, who famously played for Manchester United, regularly shows up on lists of the best-ever soccer players; during his career he scored 260 goals in over 740 appearances and earned a European Cup, two Charity Shields, a Ballon d'Or, and many, many more accolades and accomplishments.

On the baseball diamond, five-time All-Star third baseman George "Whitey" Kurowski won three World Series championships with the St. Louis Cardinals, and World Series champ George Brett—who is one of only five players ever with three thousand hits, three hundred home runs, and a career .300 batting average—had a stunning thirteen All-Star appearances. Standing above all these greats, though, is one of the most famous athletes of all times, and the absolute icon of his sport, George "Babe" Ruth. The larger-than-life "Bambino" played twenty-two seasons and set a staggering number of batting records along the way (many of which he still holds); he may have had only two All-Star appearances, but he was part of seven World Series championship teams.

Will a Georg, George, or Georges in your family reach the vaunted heights of athletes like George Best, George Foreman, or Babe Ruth? It's possible!

George Athans, Water Skiing, Canada, 1965–1979

George "Georgie" Best, Soccer (Winger), Manchester United, Ireland, 1963–1984

George Blanda, Football (Quarterback/Placekicker), Chicago Bears, USA, 1949–1975

George Brett, Baseball (Third Baseman/First Baseman), Kansas City Royals, USA, 1973–1993

George "Big George" Foreman, Boxing (Heavyweight), USA, 1967–1997

George "the Iceman" Gervin, Basketball (Shooting Guard/Small Forward), San Antonio Spurs, USA, 1972–1990

Georg Hackl, Luge, Germany, 1988–2006

George Hodgson, Swimming (Freestyle), Canada, 1912

Georges Jobé, Motorcycle Racing (Motocross), Belgium, 1979–1992

George Kojac, Swimming (Backstroke/Freestyle), USA, 1928–1932

George Kunz, Football (Offensive Tackle), Atlanta Falcons, USA, 1969–1980

George "Whitey" Kurowski, Baseball (Third Baseman), St. Louis Cardinals, USA, 1941–1949

Georges Miez, Artistic Gymnastics, Switzerland, 1924–1936

George "Mr. Basketball" Mikan, Basketball (Center), Minneapolis Lakers, USA, 1946–1956

George Mills, Endurance/Road Cycling, England, 1886–1895

George Rhoden, Track & Field (Sprinting), Jamaica, 1948–1952

Georges Ronsse, Road/Track Cycling, Belgium, 1926–1938

George "Babe" Ruth Jr., Baseball (Outfielder/Pitcher), New York Yankees, USA, 1914–1935

Georges "Rush" St-Pierre, MMA (Welterweight/Middleweight), Canada, 2002–2017

George Weah, Soccer (Striker), Associazione Calcio Milan, Liberia, 1985–2018

George Yardley III, Basketball (Forward/Guard), Detroit Pistons, USA, 1953–1962

GERD

You don't have to have a German heritage to name a son Gerd, but if you do, there's a good chance he'll like going fast, whether that's careening downhill on the slopes, blasting around a racetrack, or running around a soccer field. Gerd is often short for longer names like *Gerhard* or *Gerardus* (all built on an old Germanic root for "spear"), though it can stand on its own as well. In the wide world of sports, most successful athletes named or called Gerd hail from Germany, with few exceptions like Estonian Olympic gold-medalist and world champion discus thrower Gerd Kanter. Then there are two-time Olympic gold-winning rower Gerd Cintl; motorcycle racer Gerd Riss, whose list of over twenty championships includes eight different events; and para-alpine skier Gerd Schönfelder, who won an astounding sixteen gold medals, four silvers, and two bronzes at six different Paralympic Games. If you're a German soccer fan, you're sure to be familiar with striker Gerhard "Gerd" Müller, a legendary scorer whose career average of nearly one goal per game (over seven hundred scored!), FIFA World Cup win, UEFA European Championship, Intercontinental Cup win, Ballon d'Or, and multiple records have solidified his place among the best of all time.

Gerd Cintl, Rowing, Germany, 1958–1960

Gerd Kanter, Track & Field (Discus), Estonia, 2004–2018

Gerhard "Gerd" Müller, Soccer (Striker), Fußball-Club Bayern München e. V., Germany, 1963–1981

Gerd Riss, Motorcycle Racing (Speedway Grand Prix), Germany, 1984–2010

Gerd Schönfelder, Para-Alpine Skiing, Germany, 1992–2010

GLENN

Glenn is a pleasant-sounding place name, with origins in Gaelic for "valley." Glenns can lead pretty interesting lives, like Australian water ski jump champion Glenn Thurlow, who was the first man to jump over two hundred feet; and Northern Irish powerlifter Glenn Ross, who took home three World Strongman Cup championships. Australian fast bowler Glenn McGrath is among the top career wicket-taking cricket bowlers of all time, and Australian prop Glenn Lazarus was ranked among the best rugby league players and is the only player ever to win grand finals with three different clubs.

A Glenn in your family may gravitate toward a number of different sports (including some not typically popular in the US). And if you're open to nicknames, there are some great, inspiring options from three-time Olympic gold-medalist hurdler and sprinter Glenn "Jeep" Davis and iconic NASCAR racer Glenn "Fireball" Roberts.

Glenn "Jeep" Davis, Track & Field (Sprinting), USA, 1956–1960

Glenn Lazarus, Rugby (Prop), Brisbane Broncos, Australia, 1987–1999

Glenn McGrath, Cricket (Bowler), New South Wales Men's Cricket Team, Australia, 1992–2010

Edward Glenn "Fireball" Roberts Jr., Auto Racing (NASCAR), USA, 1950–1964

Glenn Ross, Powerlifting, Northern Ireland, 1995–2011

Glenn Thurlow, Water Skiing, Australia, 1976–2000

GORDON

Chances are you're probably not raising your kids in a European castle, but you can get that feeling by naming one of them Gordon! A name that comes from Scottish origins possibly meaning "spacious fort," Gordon inspires quickness, strength, and fast reaction times, especially on the ice. There's one Gordon who was so dominant in a sport he was nicknamed after it, Gordie "Mr. Hockey" Howe! An intimidating figure on the ice, Canadian Howe was selected as an NHL All-Star twenty-three times and was a four-time Stanley Cup–winner. He set (and still holds) numerous hockey records and is perpetually in the top rankings of best players ever.

Gordon "Gordie" (Mr. Hockey) Howe, Ice Hockey (Right Wing), Detroit Red Wings, Canada, 1946–1998

GRAEME/GRAHAM

Another place name based on a terrain type, Graham, and its variant Graeme, come from Scottish usage and Old English roots for "gravelly homestead." The most successful competitors with these two names seem to tend toward racing and going fast! The former includes cyclists like Australian two-time Olympic gold-medalist Graeme Brown and the unique Graeme Obree, who designed his own bike and riding style to break records and win two World Championships. On the Formula 1 circuit, British driver Graham Hill had fourteen wins and two championships (as well as being the only person ever to win the Triple Crown of Motorsport), all despite the fact that he didn't get his driver's license until he was twenty-four years old!

Last but not least are the cricketers, and again we see some of the best of the best. Graeme Hick holds numerous distinctions, including the record for playing in the most matches (in all cricket forms combined), scoring more than forty thousand first-class runs, exceeding twenty thousand runs in List A, scoring triple 100s in first-class cricket in three different decades, and ranking as the second run scorer of all time. Matching–and in some ways even exceeding–Hick's accomplishments is English captain and batsman Graham Gooch. A legend in his sport, Gooch holds the record for the most runs scored of all time–an astounding 67,057–while also scoring the most runs in List A specifically; his appearances were legendary and serve as examples of some of the finest playing of all time.

A cricket bat or a bicycle would be an appropriate gift for a young boy named Graham or Graeme, and if he does pursue a hobby or career in either field, he'll have some truly inspiring role models to look up to.

- **Graeme Brown**, Road/Track Cycling, Australia, 2002–2016
- **Graham Gooch**, Cricket (Batsman), Essex County Cricket Club, England, 1973–1995
- **Graeme Hick**, Cricket (Batsman), Worcestershire County Cricket Club, Rhodesia, 1983–2001
- **Norman Graham Hill**, Auto Racing (Formula 1), England, 1958–1975
- **Graeme "the Flying Scotsman" Obree**, Road/Track Cycling, Scotland, 1993–current

GREG

While some *Gregorys* prefer to use their full name–which stems from an Ancient Greek root meaning "to watch" by way of the Latin *Gregorius*–many athletes use the shortened form Greg instead. They're joined by men simply named Greg, a perfectly valid name on its own. Gregs can do most anything, with some specific preferences showing up among the herd, including the long jump (Olympic gold-medalists Bell and Rutherford from the US and UK, respectively) and track and field (American triple-World Champion hurdler Foster and Australian Paralympic gold-medalist wheelchair racer Smith). Bicycles have been the preferred vehicle for Belgian Olympic gold-medalist Van Avermaet and LeMond, whose two World Road Race Championships, three Tour de France general classifications, three World Championships, and more rank him among the best American cyclists of all time.

Then there are the more team sport-inclined athletes with this name, starting with football's famed Pittsburgh Steelers linebacker Greg Lloyd, who earned five Pro Bowl appearances. Over on the baseball diamond, Greg Luzinski batted his way to four All-Star games and a World Series championship, and eight-time All-Star and World Series-winner Greg Maddux set and continues to hold multiple pitching records. Meanwhile, Australian cricketer Greg Chappell was one of his country's all-time best batsmen and set a record for most catches in Test cricket.

Some Gregs have made a name for themselves at the pinnacle of their fields, like American surfer Greg Long, whose multiple major championship wins set him among the most skilled big wave surfers of all time, and Greg Bennett, who has a lengthy list of international triathlon wins. Hall of Fame golfer Greg Norman of Australia was the number one ranked player in the world for over six years, with a PGA career of twenty tournament wins and two majors. Last but not least is American Greg Louganis, whose four Olympic gold medals, five World Championships, and more put him firmly among the best divers of all time.

Whether you name your son *Gregory* and call him Greg, or just give him the shorter name outright, he'll have the drive of a champion and the potential to achieve worldwide fame!

Gregory "Greg" Bell, Football (Running Back), Buffalo Bills, USA, 1984–1990

Greg Bennett, Triathlon, Australia, 1990–2014

Gregory "Greg" Chappell, Cricket (Batsman), Somerset County Cricket Club, Australia, 1966–1984

Gregory "Greg" Foster, Track & Field (Hurdling), USA, 1977–1992

Gregory "Greg" LeMond, Road Cycling, USA, 1981–1994

Gregory "Greg" Lloyd Sr., Football (Outside Linebacker), Pittsburgh Steelers, USA, 1987–1998

Greg Long, Surfing, USA, 1996–current

Gregory "Greg" Louganis, Diving, USA, 1976–1988

Gregory "Greg" Luzinski, Baseball (Left Fielder/Designated Hitter), Philadelphia Phillies, USA, 1970–1984

Gregory "Greg" Maddux, Baseball (Pitcher), Atlanta Braves, USA, 1986–2008

Gregory "Greg" Norman, Golf, Australia, 1976–2009

Gregory "Greg" Rutherford, Track & Field (Long Jump), England, 2005–2018

Gregory "Greg" Smith, Wheelchair Racing/ Wheelchair Rugby, Australia, 1988–2012

Greg Van Avermaet, Road Cycling, Belgium, 2006–current

GUY

Are you hoping for a son who's way into ice hockey (especially if you're Canadian)? Then name your little guy Guy! This Norman French name that came from the Germanic *Wido* (same family as the Italian *Guido*) has been a mainstay among the highly successful Montreal Canadiens of the NHL. Four-time All-Star defenseman Guy Lapointe took home the Stanley Cup an incredible six times during his career from 1968 to 1984. Then there's one of the most highly ranked players in the NHL's history, six-time All-Star, five-time Stanley Cup champion, and multiple record-setting right wing Guy Lafleur! Now, if you live in a place where ice hockey isn't quite as popular, your Guy might take after a winner from a very different venue—rodeo star and eighteen-time Steer Roping World Champion Guy Allen.

Guy Allen, Rodeo (Steer Roping), USA, 1976–2016

Guy Lafleur, Ice Hockey (Right Wing), Montreal Canadiens, Canada, 1971–1991

Guy Lapointe, Ice Hockey (Defense), Montreal Canadiens, Canada, 1968–1984

GIRLS

GABBY/GABY

Thanks to its origin as the name of an archangel and messenger of God in the Hebrew Bible (meaning "God is my strength"), *Gabriel* is hugely popular around the world and has been adapted into many variations. Several of those—including *Gabriela/Gabriella* and *Gabriele/Gabrielle*—can be shortened to the fun and casual-sounding Gabby, or more rarely Gaby. If you give this name or nickname to your daughter, she'll embody both strength and grace, much like figure skaters German World Champion Gaby Seyfert and Canadian Olympic gold-medalist Gabby Daleman, as well as gymnast Gabby Douglas, who won three Olympic gold medals and two World Championships for the United States.

Gabrielle "Gabby" Daleman, Figure Skating, Canada, 2002–current

Gabrielle "Gabby" Douglas, Artistic Gymnastics, USA, 2008–2016

Gabriele "Gaby" Seyfert, Figure Skating, Germany, 1960–1970

GABRIELA/GABRIELLA

The feminine versions of the name *Gabriel* show up in a wider variety of sports and athletic disciplines, with Gabrielas and Gabriellas mainly across Europe excelling in unique solo competitions. These include equestrian dressage (West German Olympic gold-medalist and two-time World Champion Gabriela Grillo), ice dancing (French Olympic-winner and five-time World Champion Gabriella Papadakis), cross-country skiing (Italian Gabriella Paruzzi, whose Olympic medal count includes one gold and four bronzes), biathlon (Czech two-time World Champion Gabriela Soukalová), and sprint canoeing (Hungarian champion Gabriella Szabó, who won three Olympic events and nine World Championships). A little Gabriela or Gabriella in your family may find her calling in one of these or she may follow in the swift footsteps of track and field running stars like Italian Olympic gold-medalist and two-time World Champion Gabriella Dorio and Romanian Gabriela Szabo, whose medal count includes one of each Olympic award and a combined seven World Championships!

Gabriella Dorio, Track & Field (Medium-Distance Running), Italy, 1976–1984

Gabriela Grillo, Equestrian (Dressage), Germany, 1976–1982

Gabriella Papadakis, Ice Dancing, France, 1998–current

Gabriella Paruzzi, Cross-Country Skiing, Italy, 1991–2006

Gabriela Soukalová, Biathlon, Czechoslovakia, 2009–2017

Gabriella Szabó, Sprint Canoeing, Hungary, 2007–current

Gabriela Szabo, Long-Distance Running, Romania, 1994–2003

GABRIELE/GABRIELLE

Gabbys, *Gabys*, *Gabriela*s, and *Gabriella*s generally tend toward traditional athletic endeavors, while Gabrieles and Gabrielles stray a little further from the norm, so pick one of these names for a more adventurous and daring child. For every gymnast (East German Olympic gold-medalist Gabriele Fähnrich), rower (East German Gabriele Kühn, who won two Olympic events and a World Championship), and swimmer (two-time World Champion Gabrielle Rose of Brazil), there's a luge and bobsleigh champion (East German Gabriele Kohlisch, who has a long list of wins and championships), ski mountaineer (Swiss two-time World Champion Gabrielle Gachet), or dominant sport shooter (like Gabriele Kraushofer, who won a World Shooting Championship and six European championships).

- **Gabriele Fähnrich**, Artistic Gymnastics, Germany, 1984–1988
- **Gabrielle Gachet**, Ski Mountaineering, Switzerland, 1998–2012
- **Gabriele Kohlisch**, Luge/Bobsleigh, Germany, 1987–2000
- **Gabriele Kraushofer**, Sport Shooting (Handgun), Austria, 1992–2012
- **Gabriele Kühn**, Rowing, Germany, 1976–1980
- **Gabrielle Rose**, Swimming (Freestyle/Medley), Brazil, 1995–2003

GAIL/GAYLE

When it comes to variants and short forms of *Abigail* (from the biblical Hebrew for "my father's joy"), if *Abby*s and *Abbye*s are all about strength and toughness, then Gails and Gayles embody speed and flexibility. This can be seen in New Zealand's Gayle Broughton—a rugby sevens utility back covering multiple positions and winning Olympic gold and silver medals, as well as a Rugby World Cup Sevens championship—though it's perhaps best exemplified by Gail Devers. The American track and field legend captured the hearts of her countrymen as they watched her compete in the 1990s, winning sprint and hurdle events around the world. Among her long list of accomplishments are three Olympic gold medals and nine World Championships in her favorite events!

- **Gayle Broughton**, Rugby (Utility Back), Taranaki Rugby, New Zealand, 2014–2022
- **Yolanda Gail Devers**, Track & Field (Sprinting/Hurdling), USA, 1988–2004

GALINA

From far off Bulgaria and Russia comes the name Galina, which descends from an Ancient Greek name and root meaning "calm." Serenity and quiet are great, but you won't find those with a daughter to whom you give this name; instead, she'll be energetic and athletic, a sports star who will fight for success in her chosen field! That may be in a sport or event where other Galinas have trod before her, such as rhythmic gymnastics (like three-time world champion Galina Beloglazova and Olympic gold-medalist and two-time world champion Galina Shamrai), paddle and oar sports (like Olympic gold-medalist sprint canoeist Galina Kreft and two-time world champion rower Galina Yermolayeva), skiing (like Soviet cross-country skier Galina Kulakova, who won four golds, two silvers, and two bronzes from the Olympics and five golds, two silvers, and two bronzes from World Championships), or track and field (like Russian world champion sprinter Galina Malchugina, world champion long jumper Galina Chistyakova, and Olympic gold-medalist shot putter Galina Zybina).

Beyond those specific specialties, Galinas have shown their range in everything from speed skating to swimming, like Olympic gold-medalists skater Galina Stepanskaya and breaststroke expert Galina Prozumenschchikova, respectively; and cycling to fencing, like six-time sprint world champion Galina Yermolayeva and three-time Olympic gold-medalist and eight-time world champion foil phenom Galina Gorokhova, respectively.

- **Galina Beloglazova**, Rhythmic Gymnastics, USSR, 1982–1986
- **Galina Chistyakova**, Track & Field (Long Jump), USSR, 1984–1996
- **Galina Gorokhova**, Fencing (Foil), USSR, 1959–1972

Galina Kreft, Sprint Canoeing, USSR, 1974–1983

Galina Korchuganova, Aerobatics, USSR, 1959–1984

Galina Kulakova, Cross-Country Skiing, USSR, 1968–1982

Galina Malchugina, Track & Field (Sprinting), Russia, 1988–1998

Galina Prozumenschchikova, Swimming (Breaststroke), USSR, 1964–1973

Galina Shamrai, Artistic Gymnastics, USSR, 1950–1956

Galina Stepanskaya, Speed Skating, USSR, 1976–1978

Galina Yermolayeva, Sprint Cyclist, USSR, 1956–1973

Galina Yermolayeva, Rowing, USSR, 1970–1976

Galina Zybina, Track & Field (Shot Put), USSR, 1952–1964

GERTRUDE

It probably won't surprise you to learn that Gertrudes made their biggest mark a while ago, specifically around the turn of the twentieth century. The old-fashioned name comes from Germanic roots for "spear" and "strength," which is pretty cool, and trailblazers who bore it could be inspirations for a new generation of proud and daring young women. They can look up to athletes like Czech three-time World Champion table tennis player Gertrude Kleinová, or American Olympic gold-medalist freestyle swimmer Gertrude Ederle, who was the first woman to swim across the English Channel.

Gertrude Ederle, Swimming (Freestyle), USA, 1924–1926

Gertrude Kleinová, Table Tennis, Czechoslovakia, 1935–1937

GINA

If smaller women who are very competitive run in your family, you may want to consider naming a daughter Gina (or using that as a nickname while giving her one of the many names that end in "ina" or "nia"). The name hit international fame in the 1990s with Romanian gymnast Gina Gogean, whose massive thirty medals at major events included nine World Championship wins. Briefly overlapping her career was that of American super-bantamweight boxer Gina "Boom Boom" Guidi, who held a nearly undefeated 10-1-1 record, along with three World Championships.

Gina Gogean, Artistic Gymnastics, Romania, 1989–1998

Gina "Boom Boom" Guidi, Boxing (Super-Bantamweight), USA, 1995–2001

GINNY

Ginny is most often a nickname for *Virginia*, which comes from a traditional Roman family name and is related, but not actually from, Latin for "maid/virgin." The 1960s saw American swimmer Ginny Duenkel earning Olympic gold and setting records, and the '80s British equestrian eventing powerhouse Ginny Elliott winning three World Championships. More recently, American sport shooter Ginny Thrasher has won Olympic gold at the start of what's sure to be a huge career.

Will a Ginny in your family be the next world champion or Olympic winner? Only one way to find out!

Virginia "Ginny" Duenkel, Swimming (Backstroke/Freestyle), USA, 1963–1965

Virginia "Ginny" Elliott, Equestrian (Eventing), England, 1981–1990

Virginia "Ginny" Thrasher, Sport Shooting (Rifle), USA, 2016–current

GIOVANNA

Arising as a feminine version of the name *Giovanni* and ultimately from the same origin as *John*, meaning "God is gracious" in biblical Hebrew, Giovanna has reached a degree of popularity in Brazil, as well as Italy. Give this beautiful name to your daughter and she might excel at traditional sports, such as fencing, like Italian foil master Giovanna Trillini, who collected four gold medals, a silver, and three bronzes at Olympics; nine golds, five silvers, and five bronzes at World Championships; and four golds at Fencing World Cup events. On the other hand, your little Giovanna may strike out into something a bit more shiny, new, and revolutionary, like slacklining (balancing and performing tricks on a suspended webbing), following in the footsteps of Brazilian two-time world champion Giovanna Petrucci!

Giovanna Petrucci, Slacklining, Brazil, 2015–current

Giovanna Trillini, Fencing (Foil), Italy, 1987–2008

GISELA

A European variant of *Giselle*, Gisela gained popularity in the Netherlands, Germany, Portugal, and Spain before spreading beyond into the world. On podiums, medal counts, and trophies the name has appeared in a few very different sports and events; Argentinian doubles tennis player Gisela Dulko reached the number one spot in the world and won seventeen titles, and from Germany, track and field competitor Gisela Mauermayer won Olympic gold in the discus while Gisela Grothaus took home three gold medals and three silvers from Wildwater Canoeing World Championships!

Whether a Gisela in your family enjoys playing on the court, in track and field events, on the water, or somewhere else entirely, she'll be known for her success and fair play.

Gisela Dulko, Tennis, Argentina, 2001–2012

Gisela Grothaus, Wildwater Canoeing, Germany, 1970–1974

Gisela Mauermayer, Track & Field (Discus/Shot Put/Pentathlon), Germany, 1934–1938

GISELLE

From a humble origin in an Old German word for "hostage" or "pledge" comes the sporty name Giselle. Athletes with this name come in a couple different flavors, starting with excellent defenders who protect their team and give others the freedom to score. This is exemplified by field hockey defender English Olympic gold- and bronze-medalist Giselle Ansley. On the other hand, some Giselles charge ahead and give everything they have to reach victory, like Giselle Cole of Canada, who won three Paralympic gold medals in the long jump and sprinting, and Trinidadian boxer Giselle Salandy, who was the undefeated unified light middleweight world champion for three years and had a 16–0 record.

Don't be surprised if a daughter you name Giselle becomes a staunch protector and defender in her friend group . . . or an aggressive runner and fighter!

Giselle Ansley, Field Hockey (Defender), England, 2006–current

Giselle Cole, Para-Athletics, Canada, 1980

Giselle Salandy, Boxing (Welterweight/Middleweight), Trinidad and Tobago, 2000–2008

GLADYS

Another name that may be considered old-fashioned in the United States (like *Gertrude*), Gladys came about from an Old Welsh root for "country," though it also acquired a connection to the Roman *Claudia*. Athletes named Gladys have risen to the top in two countries, with world champion

Belgian archer Gladys Willems, as well as Canadian Gladys "Terrie" Davis, who held the first batting championship, played in the first All-Star game and won a league championship in the All-American Girls Professional Baseball League.

Bring back this classic name for a new generation by giving it to a daughter who may gravitate to bows and arrows or baseball.

Gladys "Terrie" Davis, Baseball (Shortstop/Outfield/Second Base), Rockford Peaches, Canada, 1943–1946

Gladys Willems, Archery, Belgium, 2003–2011

GRACE

A trio of elite competitors have shown that there is much grace under pressure to be found in the classic "virtue"-name of Grace, whether that's on the fairway with South Korean six-time PGA Tour-winner Grace Park, the netball court with World Netball Series champion Grace Kara of New Zealand, or on the mat with American two-time World Champion gymnast Grace McCallum.

A girl named Grace in your family will embody their same strength and drive to excel.

Grace Kara, Netball, New Zealand, 2005–current

Grace McCallum, Artistic Gymnastics, USA, 2018–current

Grace Park, Golf, South Korea, 1999–2012

GRETA/GRETE

With the origins of their names in forms of *Margaret* and *Margareta* that come from Greek for "pearl," it's interesting to see that athletes named Greta and Grete have found great success in competitions related to water and snow. Finnish sprint canoeist Greta Grönholm, Swedish diver Greta Johansson, and Danish freestyle swimmer Greta Andersen each have an Olympic gold medal in their respective disciplines. On the Norwegian slopes, freestyle skier Grete Eliassen has a pair of each medal color from the X Games, Grete Nykkelmo won a World Championship in both cross-country skiing and biathlon, and Grete Skjelbreid took home a tremendous eight World Championship biathlon titles.

Meanwhile on dry land, American Greta Neimanas has nine para-cycling medals from Track World Championships (including two golds), and Norwegian long-distance runner Grete Waitz has set numerous world records on her way to winning nine New York City Marathons, six World Championships, and more.

Whether you like Greta or Grete on its own or as a nickname for *Margaret*, you can encourage your little pearl to participate in water, snow, or track activities.

Greta Andersen, Swimming (Freestyle), Denmark, 1947–1964

Grete Eliassen, Freestyle Skiing, Norway, 2004–2013

Greta Grönholm, Sprint Canoeing, Finland, 1950

Anna Teresa Margareta "Greta" Johansson, Diving/Swimming (Breaststroke/Freestyle), Sweden, 1910–1913

Greta Neimanas, Para-Cycling, USA, 2006–2012

Grete Nykkelmo, Biathlon/Cross-Country Skiing, Norway, 1982–1992

Liv Grete Skjelbreid, Biathlon, Norway, 1995–2006

Grete Waitz, Long-Distance Running, Norway, 1972–1990

GUDRUN

Are you looking for a truly legendary name for your daughter, one that can inspire her with tales of old as well as more recent athletic successes? Then Gudrun may be perfect for you! With a name coming from Old Norse roots meaning "god's secret lore," Gudrun is a character in Norse mythology who was the wife of the great hero Sigurd.

Your daughter may be a team player, like Gudrun Scholz of Germany who won gold at the Women's Hockey World Cup and Indoor Nations Championship. On the other hand, a Gudrun in your family may be tough and strong like the mythical character, able to take down foes on her own like Norwegian four-time world champion freestyle wrestler Gudrun Høie!

Gudrun Høie, Freestyle Wrestling, Norway, 1989–1999

Gudrun Scholz, Field Hockey (Forward), Germany, 1963–1976

GUNDA

From an Old German word meaning "war" comes Gunda, which often appears as part of longer names, like *Hildegund*. A Gunda in your family will fight to victory in whatever field or sport inspires her, and she'll dominate it just like German speed skater Gunda Niemann-Stirnemann did hers by winning three gold medals, four silvers, and a bronze at Olympic Games; winning eight golds and two silvers at World Championships; winning a record ninety-eight golds in single World Cup events nineteen World Cup titles; setting eighteen world records; and holding the number one spot in the world for a staggering 2,958 days!

Gunda Niemann-Stirnemann, Speed Skating, Germany, 1987–2005

GWEN

The name Gwen by itself comes from an Old Welsh root meaning "white" or "blessed," but it can also be a short form of various names, including *Gwendolyn* and *Guinevere*. Gwens tend to enjoy the outdoors and a range of activities under the sun, which you can see in competitors like Olympic gold-medalist and two-time World Champion triathlete and marathon runner Gwen Jorgensen; track star Gwen Berry, who is ranked number six on the all-time hammer throw list and currently holds the world record for weight throw; and British para-athlete Gwen Buck whose extensive list of accolades includes Paralympic gold medals in table tennis, lawn bowls, and swimming!

Gwendolyn "Gwen" Berry, Track & Field (Hammer Throw), USA, 2011–current

Gwen Buck, Para-Athletics, England, 1964–1976

Gwen Jorgensen, Triathlon/Marathon, USA, 2010–current

H

BOYS

HAKEEM

Naming a son Hakeem will hopefully instill in him great wisdom because it comes from Arabic for "wise" (and was one of the ninety-nine names of Allah). There are some great athletes with this name, but one stands (literally) above the rest. At seven feet tall, Hakeem "the Dream" Olajuwon is a Houston, Texas phenomenon, having played basketball there for twenty seasons after emigrating from Nigeria. His NBA career cemented him as one of the best centers and overall players of all time, racking up twelve All-Star appearances and two back-to-back NBA championships. Hakeem revolutionized the position of center and broke down his play to a science, setting records and joining the US national basketball team to take home Olympic gold in 1996.

Hakeem Olajuwon, Basketball (Center), Houston Rockets, Nigeria, 1984–2002

HANK

Typically a nickname for people named *Henry* (going back to Germanic roots for "home" and "ruler"), Hank can also stand on its own or come from influences like the Dutch *Henk*. If you name your son Hank, there's a good chance he'll enjoy America's favorite pastime, as Hanks have proven some of the best baseball players of all time!

Hank Bauer, in his fourteen years in the MLB, had three All-Star appearances and was part of seven World Series–winning teams. Detroit Tigers Hall of Fame home run hitter Hank Greenberg would play in five All-Star games, win two World Series, top four home run and RBI leaderboards, and more. And then there's Hank Aaron, multiple batting-record setter and holder, twenty-five-time All-Star, World Series champion, one of the highest-ranked baseball players of all time, and so much more.

Henry "Hank" Aaron, Baseball (Right Fielder), Milwaukee Braves, USA, 1954–1976

Henry "Hank" Bauer, Baseball (Right Fielder), New York Yankees, USA, 1948–1961

Henry "Hank" Greenberg, Baseball (First Baseman), Detroit Tigers, USA, 1930–1947

HANS

Most popular in Western Europe but appearing throughout the world, the name Hans originated as a short form of the Germanic *Johannes* (which comes from the same biblical Hebrew "God is gracious" root as *John*). Top cyclists with this name include Swiss two-time World Champion Knecht and German

Olympic gold-medalist and three-time world champ Lutz, while American Dersch swam to Olympic gold at the 1992 Barcelona games. Hans Krankl is well known in Austria as one of that country's greatest-ever soccer players; the striker scored more than five hundred goals in over six hundred appearances!

Hans Dersch, Swimming (Breaststroke), USA, 1990–1992

Hans Knecht, Road Cycling, Switzerland, 1939–1949

Johann "Hans" Krankl, Soccer (Striker), Sportklub Rapid Wien, Austria, 1970–1989

Hans Lutz, Road/Track Cycling, Germany, 1973–1976

HAO

The sky's the limit when it comes to opportunities for a son you name Hao, who will try many things before finding his niche and becoming singular in his focus when it comes to competition; those are just some of the qualities that come with the Chinese name that can be written with characters meaning "vastness (of the sky)," "open-minded," or "straightforward." Haos have become masters of very different sports and events, from racewalking (like world champion Wang Hao) to chess (like Grandmaster Wang Hao, who won the 2019 FIDE Grand Swiss Tournament) and artistic gymnastics (like the five-time World Cup champion "King of Pommel Horse" Weng Hao).

If history is any indication, your little Hao may take a particular liking to water or racquet sports, in which case he'll follow in the footsteps of world champion sprint canoeists Liu Hao and Wang Hao, who won the 2019 Men's C-2 1000-meter event together, or not one but two table tennis champs named Wang Hao, the first of whom won a medal of each color at the World Table Tennis Championships between 1987 and 1993 and the second of whom is the legendary two-time Olympic gold-medalist, nine-time world champion, and seven-time World Cup-winner.

Liu Hao, Sprint Canoeing, China, 2018–current

Wang Hao, Chess, China, 2005–current

Wang Hao, Sprint Canoeing, China, 2017–current

Wang Hao, Table Tennis, China, 1987–1993

Wang Hao, Table Tennis, China, 1998–2014

Wang Hao, Track & Field (Racewalking), China, 2008–2010

Weng Hao, Artistic Gymnastics, China, 2016–current

HARMON

While it may sound similar to the word "harmony," the English name Harmon comes from the Germanic name *Hermann* with roots meaning "army man." Rather than joining the military, Harmon Killebrew joined a baseball team and became a dominant hitter in his era, with an astounding thirteen MLB All-Star appearances, multiple home run and RBI leaderboard rankings, hitting records, and more!

Harmon is a cool name that deserves another shot at the big leagues.

Harmon Killebrew Jr., Baseball (First Baseman/Third Baseman/Left Fielder), Washington Senators, USA, 1954–1975

HARRISON

Whether or not your name or your partner's name is *Harry*, Harrison (meaning "son of Harry") is a strong name for a kid who may run fast. They can find inspiration in competitors like six-time NFL Pro Bowl strong safety Harrison Smith of the Minnesota Vikings and track and field star Harrison Dillard, who won four Olympic gold medals in sprinting and hurdles.

William Harrison "Bones" Dillard, Track & Field (Sprint/Hurdling), USA, 1948-1953

Harrison Smith, Football (Strong Safety), Minnesota Vikings, USA, 2012-current

HARRY

From a Medieval English offshoot of the name *Henry* came Harry, a name that's garnered significant popularity in England and the United States. It follows, then, that those are the places where we've seen some Harrys who are titans of physical speed, strength, and power. These include four-time New York Giants All-Star catcher Harry "the Horse" Danning, Hall of Famer and welterweight world champion boxer Harry Lewis, and English soccer striker Harry Kane, who is the winner of a FIFA World Cup Golden Boot and considered one of the best in his position currently.

Name your son Harry and he may find enjoyment in combat sports or team sports like baseball or soccer.

Harry Danning, Baseball (Catcher), New York Giants, USA, 1933-1942

Harry Kane, Soccer (Striker), Tottenham Hotspur Football Club, England, 2009-current

Harry Lewis, Boxing (Welterweight), USA, 1903-1913

HENRIK

The name Henrik, related to *Henry* and popular in parts of Europe especially, has noble origins in Germanic roots for "home" and "ruler." The majority of athletic champions named Henrik hail from Sweden and can be found across a swathe of fields. Danes include handball champ Henrik Hansen, who won an Olympic gold medal as well as a World Championship, and *League of Legends* esports pro Henrik "Froggen" Hansen. Meanwhile, Sweden has produced Olympic gold-medalist and two-time World Champion sprint canoeist Henrik Nilsson, and soccer striker Henrik Larsson, who's considered one of the best Swedish players of all time, with over 470 goals scored in 874 club and international appearances.

In particular, Henriks seem predisposed to ice hockey! Center Henrik Zetterberg scored two All-Star appearances and a Stanley Cup win during his NHL career, along with winning Olympic gold and a World Championship for Sweden; three-time All-Star center Henrik Sedin also took home Olympic and World Championship gold; and New York Rangers goaltender Henrik Lundqvist had five All-Star appearances, an Olympic gold medal, and two World Championships (the second for inline hockey), and numerous records.

Henrik "Froggen" Hansen, Esports (*League of Legends*), Denmark, 2011-current

Henrik Hansen, Handball (Pivot), Denmark, 2004-current

Henrik Larsson, Soccer (Striker), The Celtic Football Club, Sweden, 1989-2013

Henrik Lundqvist, Ice Hockey (Goaltender), New York Rangers, Sweden, 2001-2020

Henrik Nilsson, Canoeing (Sprint), Sweden, 1997-2011

Henrik Sedin, Ice Hockey (Center), Vancouver Canucks, Sweden, 1997-2018

Carl Henrik Zetterberg, Ice Hockey (Center), Detroit Red Wings, Sweden, 1997-2018

HENRY

Henrys are "home rulers" like *Henrik*, with a wider distribution across Europe and the United States. Henrys love American football, with three-time Pro Bowl wide receiver Henry Ellard and four-time Pro Bowl defensive tackle Henry Jordan, who won no fewer than five NFL championships and the first two Super Bowls with the Green Bay Packers!

Then there are Henrys who just like to fight. Practitioners of the sweet science have included German light heavyweight champion of the world and Olympic gold-medalist Henry Maske, who ended his career with a phenomenal 31-1 record, and American Henry Jackson, who went by the name Henry Armstrong and held world championship titles in three different weight classes, while the octagon has witnessed the exploits of Olympic gold-medalist and UFC flyweight and bantamweight champion Henry Cejudo.

A Henry in your family who grows up big and strong may enjoy combat sports or football!

See *Lou* for Henry Louis "Lou" Gehrig.

- **Henry Cejudo**, MMA (Flyweight/Bantamweight), USA, 2005-2020
- **Henry Ellard**, Football (Wide Receiver), Los Angeles Rams, USA, 1983-1998
- **Henry "Armstrong" Jackson Jr.**, Boxing (Featherweight/Lightweight/Welterweight/Middleweight), USA, 1931-1945
- **Henry Jordan**, Football (Defensive Tackle), Green Bay Packers, USA, 1957-1969
- **Henry Maske**, Boxing (Light Heavyweight), Germany, 1990-2007

HERB/HERBIE

Definitely not a name we hear very often these days, at least in the United States, *Herbert* (from Germanic roots for "bright" and "army") and its short form Herb feel old-fashioned but still have a lot of life in them. This is especially true for a boy who may follow in the swift footsteps of athletic greats of the past! Jamaican Herb McKenley sprinted to a gold and three silver medals at the Olympics, British boxer Herbie Hide was a world heavyweight champion in the 1990s, Herb Thomas raced to forty-eight wins and two championships in NASCAR's top series, and five-time Pro Bowl cornerback Herb Adderley won a remarkable five NFL championships and three Super Bowls. Australian Herbs excel at rugby, with front row forward Herb Steinohrt, who is solidly ranked among the top forwards of all time, and cricket fans have enjoyed the exploits of batsmen like South African Herbie Taylor, who posted record scores against England and was the first player from his country to pass 2,500 Test runs.

- **Herbert "Herb" Adderley**, Football (Cornerback), Green Bay Packers, USA, 1961-1972
- **Herbert "Herbie Hide" Maduagwu**, Boxing (Cruiserweight/Heavyweight), Nigeria, 1989-2010
- **Herbert "Herb" McKenley**, Track & Field (Sprinting), Jamaica, 1948-1952
- **Herbert "Herb" Steinohrt**, Rugby (Forward), Toowoomba, Australia, 1922-1933
- **Herbert "Herbie" Taylor**, Cricket (Batsman), Natal, South Africa, 1909-1936
- **Herbert "Herb" Thomas**, Auto Racing (NASCAR), USA, 1949-1962

HIFUMI

For some, victory is as easy as "one, two, three," which just happens to be a translation of the characters you can use to write the Japanese unisex name Hifumi! A boy with this name in your family may push himself to conquer his opponents in mental or physical confrontations, just like 9-dan-ranked shogi player Hifumi Katō, who won eight major titles and twenty-three other championships and held the record for youngest player to go professional (at fourteen!) for over sixty years, or Olympic gold- and silver-medalist, four-time world champion, ten-time International Judo Federation (IJF) Grand Slam-winner, and IJF Grand Prix-winner Hifumi Abe!

- **Hifumi Abe**, Judo, Japan, 2015-current
- **Hifumi Katō**, Shogi, Japan, 1954-2017

HONUS

An uncommon nickname for *Hans* (from *Johannes* and ultimately biblical Hebrew meaning "God is gracious"), Honus has not seen much usage over the years, but it once was the talk of the town in America's pastime. Making his MLB debut in 1897, shortstop Honus Wagner was an early mega-star, racking up a World Series championship, a record eight National League batting championships, and five National League RBI and stolen base leader rankings during his career spent mostly with the Pittsburgh Pirates before later becoming one of the first class of players inducted into the Baseball Hall of Fame.

Name or call your son Honus and teach him the fundamentals of baseball; he'll be a star player on any team and become known for his position, and he'll be endlessly valuable to his teammates and friends (just like Wagner, whose 1909–1911 T206 baseball card sells for millions).

Johannes "Hans/Honus" Wagner, Baseball (Shortstop), Pittsburgh Pirates, USA, 1897–1917

GIRLS

HAILEY/HALEY/HALI/HAYLEY

An Old English town name meaning "hay clearing" has given us a whole family of unisex names like Hailie, Hailey, Haley, and Hayley. One famous athlete with this name deals with a lot of hay; rodeo star Hailey Kinsel has won three World Barrel Racing championships, multiple US titles, and more. Outside of the rodeo, most winners and champions with these names have found success in the water and on ice and snow, like Scottish Olympic gold-medalist curler Hailey Duff and American snowboarder Hailey Langland, who has already taken home one of each medal at the X Games since her career began in 2018.

Among the top ice hockey players in the last couple decades have been National Women's Hockey League All-Star forward Haley Skarupa, who's won an Olympic gold medal and three World Championships, as well as Canadian four-time Olympic gold-medalist and seven-time world champion center Hayley Wickenheiser, who was the first (non-goaltender) woman to play in professional men's hockey full-time. In the pool, multi-talented Hali Flickinger has three world championship wins, along with a national record in the 200-meter butterfly, and Haley Cope took her backstroke skills to four world championship wins.

Chances are good that a girl with a "Haley" style name in your family will find athletic success in water, ice, or snow, though her name's "hay" origin may draw her more to horses and rodeo activities.

Haley Cope, Swimming (Backstroke), USA, 2001–2004

Hailey Duff, Curling (Second/Third), Scotland, 2019–current

Hali Flickinger, Swimming (Butterfly/Freestyle), USA, 2016–current

Hailey Kinsel, Rodeo (Barrel Racing), USA, 2016–current

Hailey Langland, Snowboarding, USA, 2018–current

Haley Skarupa, Ice Hockey (Forward), Connecticut Whale, USA, 2012–current

Hayley Wickenheiser, Ice Hockey (Center), Canada, 1994–2017

HANA/HANNAH

With grace comes skill and success, and that's exactly what an athlete named Hannah (or the rarer form Hana) in your family will achieve! She'll follow in the footsteps of numerous competitors around the world with these names, mostly derived from biblical Hebrew for "grace," though there are other sources as well. The stellar Hanas and Hannahs who have excelled in physical endeavors include American Olympic and X Games gold-medalist and six-time World Cup-winning snowboarder Hannah Teter, and two two-time World Champions with Czech slalom canoeist Hana Koudelová and Slovak mountain bike orienteer Hana Bajtošová.

Czech Hana Mičechová won three World Championships in rhythmic gymnastics, American skier Hannah Kearney raced around moguls to nab an Olympic gold medal and three World Championships, and Irish rugby star Hannah Tyrrell's trophy shelf includes a Women's Six Nations Championship, Triple Crown, and FAI Women's Cup. Hannahs may have a slight proclivity toward swimming, as we can see with Scottish world champion medley swimmer Hannah Miley and five-time freestyle world champion Hannah Stockbauer of Germany!

Hana Bajtošová, Bike Orienteering, Slovakia, 2006–2009

Hannah Kearney, Skiing (Moguls), USA, 2005–2015

Hana Koudelová, Slalom Canoeing, Czechoslovakia, 1969–1971

Hana Mičechová, Rhythmic Gymnastics, Czechoslovakia, 1965–1967

Hannah Miley, Swimming (Freestyle/Medley), Scotland, 2008–2018

Hannah Stockbauer, Swimming (Freestyle), Germany, 1999–2005

Hannah Teter, Snowboarding, USA, 2002–current

Hannah Tyrrell, Rugby (Out-Half/Full-Back), Leinster Rugby, Ireland, 2009–current

HARRIET

If you have French lineage or want your daughter to be inspired to great feats, consider giving her the vintage name Harriet, which comes from a French family of names shared with *Henry* and Germanic roots for "home" and "ruler." There aren't a ton of Harriets with sports and athletic achievements, but the few are pretty rad. The most recent was Harriet Metcalf, who rowed to an Olympic gold medal at the 1984 Los Angeles games, and before her, sprinter Harriet Bland raised money with a hometown newspaper to get her to the 1936 Berlin Olympics where she won gold with the US women's relay team!

Harriet Bland, Track & Field (Sprinting), USA, 1932–1936

Harriet "Holly" Metcalf, Rowing, USA, 1981–1987

HAZEL

If brown hair and a love of tennis or rock climbing runs in your family, then Hazel might be an ideal choice to name your daughter! At one point considered an old-fashioned name (which comes from Old English and refers to the color brown and the tree by the same name), Hazel is poised for a comeback and can propel a girl to greatness on the court, up a mountainside, or anywhere else she feels drawn to practice her skills. She could take inspiration from fellow Hazels, including early-1900s tennis legend Hazel Hotchkiss Wightman, who won two Olympic gold medals, forty-five national titles, seventeen Grand Slam titles, and more; or British rock climber Hazel Findlay, who has conquered extreme routes all over the world and was the first woman to achieve numerous difficult climbs.

Hazel Findlay, Rock Climbing, England, 2010–current

Hazel Hotchkiss Wightman, Tennis, USA, 1909–1943

HEATHER

A nature and plant name, Heather comes from Middle English as a term for small shrubs that often have pink or white flowers and grow in rocky areas. Primarily from the Unites States, Canada, and the United Kingdom, Heathers have reached the pinnacle in a few different sports and athletic events. Heather Petri won four Olympic medals (including a gold) and three World Championships for the USA in water polo, and Canadian Heather Moyse conquered the bobsleigh with two Olympic gold medals and six World Cups. Meanwhile, the United States Women's National Soccer Team won three Olympic gold medals in a row with both Heather Mitts and Heather O'Reilly, the latter who also took home a FIFA Women's World Cup and more.

There is nothing that can get in the way of a girl named Heather, especially if she sets her eye on athleticism or group sports!

Heather Mitts, Soccer (Defender), Philadelphia Charge, USA, 2004–2012

Heather Moyse, Bobsleigh/Rugby (Fullback), Canada, 2005–2014

Heather O'Reilly, Soccer (Midfielder), SkyBlue Football Club, USA, 2002-2019

Heather Petri, Water Polo (Attacker), USA, 2000–2012

HEIDI

From German roots comes the name Heidi, originally a diminutive of the name *Adelheid* and introduced to the world via Johanna Spyri's 1880 novel *Heidi* and its Shirley Temple film adaptation in 1937. In Europe, Heidis have made a big impact in skiing with German Olympic gold-medalist alpine skier Biebl and five-time world champion cross-country skier Weng of Norway. But that's not all! There have also been German Olympic gold-medalist and world champion fencer Heidi Schmid and Swedish Heidi Andersson, who won an astounding eleven arm wrestling world championships!

You don't need to be from Europe or a fan of skiing to name a daughter Heidi; she may even smash her foes in arm wrestling.

Heidi Andersson, Arm Wrestling, Sweden, 1999–2015

Heidi Biebl, Alpine Skiing, Germany, 1960–1964

Adelheid "Heidi" Schmid, Fencing (Foil), Germany, 1957–1968

Heidi Weng, Cross-Country Skiing, Norway, 2010–current

HELEN

Helen of Troy may be most known for her beauty and bringing down an ancient empire, but modern athletes with the name (possibly related to light and brightness, less likely the moon) are famous for their skills and successes in all manner of sports and athletics. The majority of champion Helens have been Americans, except in the case of field hockey, where we've seen Olympic gold-medalists Helen Volk of Zimbabwe and midfielder Helen Richardson-Walsh of England. Helen Stephens, famous for her nickname the "Fulton Flash," won two sprinting gold medals at the 1936 Berlin Olympics; Helen Nicol (sometimes known as Nickie Fox) was an All-American Girls Professional Baseball League all-star pitcher and three-time AAGPBL champion; and Helen Maroulis has wrestled her way to an Olympic gold medal, three world championships, and more. Meanwhile, tennis courts have witnessed the glory of Helen Wills, whose thirty-one Grand Slams and multiple records and firsts came alongside her dual number one ranks in singles *and* doubles.

Helen "Nickie Fox" Nicol, Baseball (Pitcher), Kenosha Comets, USA, 1943–1952

Helen Maroulis, Freestyle Wrestling, USA, 2011-current

Helen Richardson-Walsh, Field Hockey (Midfielder), England, 1999–2016

Helen "Fulton Flash" Stephens, Track & Field (Sprinting), USA, 1936

Helen Volk, Field Hockey (Various), Zimbabwe, 1980

Helen Wills, Tennis, USA, 1919–1938

HELENA

Helens have their various sports, while Helenas have theirs, like Czech Helena Fibingerová who set no fewer than three world records and won a World Championship in the shot put. Most Helenas have found success on water and ice! Finnish cross-country skier Helena Takalo took home four Olympic and five world championships medals (one and two golds, respectively), Swedish water skier Helena Kjellander was a four-time world champion specializing in the slalom, and Australian Helena Brunner set records on her way to winning five Paralympic gold medals.

Choose the name Helena for a daughter who will love the water in any form, and who may also like throwing heavy objects.

Helena Brunner, Swimming (Backstroke/Freestyle), Australia, 1984

Helena Fibingerová, Track & Field (Shot Put), Czechoslovakia, 1974–1983

Helena Kjellander, Water Skiing, Sweden, 1991–1997

Anni Helena Takalo, Cross-Country Skiing, Finland, 1970–1982

HELENE

An old-fashioned variation of the name *Helen*, Helene doesn't have as much representation in the world of athletics, though its bearers have made some unique marks on the world. Controversial German Olympic gold-medalist fencer Helene Mayer is considered one of the greatest foilists of all time, American freestyle swimmer Helene Madison swept three gold medals at the 1932 Olympic Games, and Austrian figure skater Helene Engelmann spun and jumped to an Olympic gold medal and three World Championships.

Helene, then, is a perfect name for an aspiring swordswoman, swimmer, or skater!

Helene Engelmann, Figure Skating, Austria, 1913–1924

Helene Madison, Swimming (Freestyle), USA, 1930–1936

Helene Mayer, Fencing (Foil), Germany, 1928–1936

HENRIETA/HENRIETTA

Another name with the same Germanic roots for "home" and "ruler" as *Harriet*, Henrietta also feels old-fashioned but, at the same time, could be hip and ready for a comeback. In the last few decades, we've seen Hungarian Gymnastics Hall of Famer Henrietta "Heni"

Ónodi win gold in vault events at Olympic Games, World Championships, and World Cup Finals, while Slovak skier Henrieta Farkašová (with a rarer version of the first name) has proven her motto "impossible is nothing" with an incredible eleven Paralympic Games gold medals and seventeen world championships in various events.

Bring back Henrietta, pick a fun nickname for it, and introduce your daughter to skiing and gymnastics!

Henrieta Farkašová, Alpine Skiing, Slovakia, 2009–current

Henrietta "Heni" Ónodi, Artistic Gymnastics, Hungary, 1986–1997

HILARY

Interested in raising a genial child who likes ice skating and scoring goals? Consider the name Hilary, a unisex (originally masculine) moniker that comes from a root meaning "cheerful." She can look up to Hilary Knight, a powerful ice hockey forward whose trophy shelf includes an NCAA National Championship, an Olympic gold medal, eight World Championships, scoring champion awards, and more.

Hilary Knight, Ice Hockey (Forward), Boston Pride, USA, 2006–current

HITOMI

A traditional Japanese name, Hitomi can be written with symbols meaning "pupil of the eye," "wisdom," "beautiful," and more. Whichever inspiration you like, the name can provide an indomitable spirit, as seen in Japanese wrestling phenom Hitomi Obara, who took home gold from the 2012 London Olympic Games and had an unbroken streak of World Championship wins in her eight competitions from 2000 to 2011.

Hitomi Obara, Freestyle Wrestling, Japan, 2000–2012

HOLLY

A pretty nature name coming from Old English for the tree, Holly has a pretty tough reputation thanks to one Holly Holm. The "Preacher's Daughter" is way more than a triple threat, with long lists of achievements in boxing, kickboxing, and mixed martial arts; one of the greatest of all time, Holm has held multiple boxing world title belts and an MMA bantamweight championship!

Holly, then, is a perfect name for a little girl who will appreciate nature and be able to take care of herself in any situation.

Holly "the Preacher's Daughter" Holm, MMA/Boxing (Bantamweight/Featherweight/Welterweight/Middleweight), USA, 2001–current

HOPE

A "virtue" name meaning exactly what it sounds like, Hope has enjoyed moderate and steady popularity in the United States over the years. English midfielder Hope Powell won two FA Women's Cups, and American goalkeeper Hope Solo is world-renowned for her two Olympic gold medals, a World Cup championship, FIFA Women's World Cup, Golden Glove award, and more.

Definitely get a young Hope in your family a soccer ball to kick around!

Hope Powell, Soccer (Midfielder), Charlton Athletic Women's Football Club, England, 1978–1998

Hope Solo, Soccer (Goalkeeper), Seattle Reign Football Club, USA, 1996–2016

I

BOYS

IAN

Like *John*, Ian descends from the biblical Hebrew *Yohanan*, meaning "God is gracious," this time via Scottish Gaelic and then English. There have been quite a lot of Ians in professional sports over the years, taking wins, medals, and championships around the world, and they're all great inspirations for a competitive Ian in your family. Some of these include rugby union wing Ian Smith, who captained the Scotland national team to a Triple Crown and set a record for twenty-four international tries; English seventeen-time professional golf-winner Ian Poulter; American three-time esports *Call of Duty* world champion Ian "Crimsix" Porter, who holds the record for most tournament wins in that game; Australian three-time world champion kickboxer Ian "Powerhouse" Jacobs, who is best-known for achieving the fastest KO in kickboxing history; and four-time Olympic gold-medalist and three-time world champion sprint canoeist Ian Ferguson of New Zealand.

Fans of swimming are sure to know American three-time Olympic-winner and eight-time World Champion Ian Crocker, and Australian phenom Ian Thorpe, whose medal shelf includes five Olympic golds, thirteen world championship wins, and numerous world records. In international soccer (or "football," if you prefer), Welsh forward Ian Rush set goal records for Liverpool and the Wales national team, and midfielder Ian Callaghan had an astounding 983 total appearances (including a record for Liverpool). Lastly, cricket, too, has seen its share of impressive Ians, like English Botham, whose ranking among the best all-rounders of all time stems from holding the most Test wickets between 1986 and 1988, being only the second person to score one hundred runs and take ten wickets in one Test match (a "match double").

- **Ian Botham**, Cricket (All-Rounder), Somerset County Cricket Club, England, 1974–1993
- **Ian Callaghan**, Soccer (Midfielder), Liverpool Football Club, England, 1959–1981
- **Ian Crocker**, Swimming (Butterfly/Freestyle), USA, 2000–2008
- **Ian Ferguson**, Sprint Canoeing, New Zealand, 1983–1990
- **Ian "Powerhouse" Jacobs**, Kickboxing (Middleweight/Heavyweight), Australia, 1988–2009
- **Ian "Crimsix" Porter**, Esports (*Call of Duty*), USA, 2008–current
- **Ian Poulter**, Golf, England, 1995–current

Ian Rush, Soccer (Forward), Liverpool Football Club, Wales, 1978-2000

Ian Smith, Rugby (Wing), Scotland National Rugby Union Team, Scotland, 1923–1933

Ian Thorpe, Swimming (Freestyle), Australia, 1998-2012

ICHIRO

As with most Japanese names, Ichiro can be translated into various things depending on which characters are used to write it. The most common is a combination of "one" and "son," and in this vein, the name has traditionally been given to firstborn sons. Ichiro Ogimura was a legendary table tennis player, taking home twenty medals from world championship competitions, with twelve of them being wins; he was also a major player in the "Ping Pong Diplomacy" actions of athletes getting rival countries together via sporting events and leading to better relations between the United States and China. Meanwhile, baseball legend Ichiro Suzuki played in both Major League Baseball in North America and Nippon Professional Baseball in Japan, earning a combined seventeen All-Star appearances, seventeen Gold Glove awards, and nine batting championships, along with a Japan Series championship, three Silver Sluggers, and more.

Choose Ichiro for a child in your family who will make an impact at home and around the world, whether that's in table tennis, baseball, or any other field he decides to pursue.

Ichiro Ogimura, Table Tennis, Japan, 1953–1965

Ichiro Suzuki, Baseball (Right Fielder), Seattle Mariners, Japan, 1992–2019

IMRAN

The name Imran, Arabic for "prosperity" or "exalted nation," has some international fame for its bearers. The most well-known athlete with this name is Pakistan's Imran Khan, a Hall of Fame cricket all-rounder who was on the Cricket World Cup-winning team in 1992, was the second fastest to achieve an "all-rounder's triple" (three thousand runs and three hundred wickets) in seventy-five Tests, and is considered one of the greatest players of all time.

Whether your family has a love for cricket or not, a child you name Imran will have big accomplishments ahead of him on and off the field.

Imran Khan, Cricket (All-Rounder), Worcestershire County Cricket Club, Pakistan, 1971–1992

ISAAC

See *Vivian* for Isaac Vivian "Viv" Richards.

ISAIAH/ISIAH

From biblical Hebrew and a prophet's name meaning "God is salvation," Isaiah (and its alternate form Isiah) has appeared in various places around the world, though when it comes to champion athletes, they're all American, like powerful and fast NFL linebacker Isiah "Butch" Robertson who had six Pro Bowl appearances. Most famous of athletes with this name is NBA point guard Isiah Thomas, whose illustrious career included twelve All-Star appearances and two NBA championships with the Detroit Pistons.

Pick Isaiah or Isiah for a boy in your family who will be focused and determined, and introduce him to basketball!

Isiah "Butch" Robertson, Football (Linebacker), Los Angeles Rams, USA, 1971–1982

Isiah Thomas III, Basketball (Point Guard), Detroit Pistons, USA, 1981–1994

IVAN/IVÁN

The name Ivan may summon images of beefy Russians (and boxers who don't care whether their opponents live or not), but the Slavic moniker appears in quite a few cultures and languages thanks to its descent from the same biblical Hebrew roots for "God is gracious" that *John* shares. Ivans (with or without the accent) have risen to the top of an astonishing array of sports and athletic disciplines, including Italian two-time Giro d'Italia-winning cyclist Basso; American four-time NHL All-Star defenseman and two-time Stanley Cup–winner Johnson; American driver "Ironman" Stewart, who won eighty-two races and ten points championships in off-road racing; and Bulgarian esports legend "MinD_ContRoL" Ivanov, who has won over $4.5 million in *Dota 2* tournaments.

Among the best of the best, Puerto Rican Iván Rodríguez was a fourteen-time MLB All-Star catcher and World Series–winner, Czech tennis champion Ivan Lendl spent 270 weeks ranked number one in the world, Soviet freestyle wrestler Ivan Yarygin won every major competition (including two Olympic golds, a World Championship, and five World Cups) for a decade except for two second place finishes, long jumper Iván Pedroso of Cuba leapt to an Olympic gold medal and nine world championship wins, and Russian sprint canoeist Ivan Shtyl won a staggering seventeen World Championships.

There is one sport in which multiple Ivans have found a lot of success, and that's international soccer. Winger Ivan Perišić is considered one of the best Croatian players of all time, with a combined club and international 662 appearances with 171 goals; and Chilean striker Iván Zamorano scored 383 goals in 690 total appearances and was named to the FIFA 100 list.

Ivans are strong and capable of anything from cycling to video games, maybe slightly leaning toward success in soccer.

Ivan Basso, Road Cycling, Italy, 1999–2015

Ivan "MinD_ContRoL" Ivanov, Esports (*Dota 2*), Bulgaria, 2013–current

Ivan Johnson, Ice Hockey (Defense), New York Rangers, USA, 1925–1944

Ivan Lendl, Tennis, Czechoslovakia, 1978–1994

Iván Pedroso, Track & Field (Long Jump), Cuba, 1991–2007

Ivan Perišić, Soccer (Winger), Football Club Internazionale Milano, Croatia, 2007–current

Iván Rodríguez, Baseball (Catcher), Texas Rangers, Puerto Rico, 1991–2011

Ivan Shtyl, Sprint Canoeing, Russia, 2004–current

Ivan "Ironman" Stewart, Auto Racing (Off-Road), USA, 1973–1999

Ivan Yarygin, Freestyle Wrestling, USSR, 1970–1980

Iván Zamorano, Soccer (Striker), Real Madrid Club de Fútbol, Chile, 1985–2003

GIRLS

INES/INEZ

Ines and Inez, with options for accents depending on your language, are international versions of the classic virtue name *Agnes* that comes from an Ancient Greek root meaning "chaste." Athletes with these names have turned their attention to a number of fields, with some traditional ones like field hockey (Argentinian World Cup- and Champions Trophy-winner Inés Arrondo), racewalking (Portuguese World Champion Inês Henriques), and swimming (German two-time Olympic gold-medalist Ines Diers and Ines Geissler, who won Olympic gold and two world championships). Then there are those who travel down more unique paths, like five-time world champion nine-pin bowler Ines Maričić and ice climber Ines Papert, who won three Ice Climbing World Cup trophies.

An Ines or Inez in your family may pick a path less traveled, or she may join up to play a popular team sport, like two-time All-American Girls Professional Baseball League championship first basewoman Inez "Lefty" Voyce, whose teams made it to the playoffs in all of her eight seasons!

Inés Arrondo, Field Hockey (Field Player), Argentina, 1999-2004

Ines Diers, Swimming (Freestyle), Germany, 1980-1981

Ines Geissler, Swimming (Butterfly), Germany, 1980-1983

Inês Henriques, Track & Field (Racewalking), Portugal, 2001-current

Ines Maričić, Nine-Pin Bowling, Germany, 2010-current

Ines Papert, Ice Climbing, Germany, 1996-current

Inez "Lefty" Voyce, Baseball (First Base), Grand Rapids Chicks, USA, 1946-1953

INGRID

The name Ingrid brings to mind Northern European climes—and for good reason; popular in Germany and Scandinavia, it comes from Old Norse roots meaning "Ing [a Germanic fertility god] is beautiful." Athletes have elevated this name to podiums in a wide range of sports and events, primarily in team and relay events, including mountain bike orienteering (Finnish two-time relay world champion Ingrid Stengård), sprinting (German Olympic 4x100-meter relay gold medalist and world champion Ingrid Auerswald), water polo (Dutch three-time World Cup champion Ingrid Leijendekker), field hockey (German two-time World Cup champion and two-time Indoor Nations champion defender Ingrid Bruckert), equestrian events (German two-time Olympic team eventing gold-medalist and two-time World Equestrian Games champion Ingrid Klimke), and biathlon (Norwegian four-time relay world champion and eleven-time World Cup champion Ingrid Landmark Tandrevold).

You don't have to have European heritage (or be a pagan) to name a daughter Ingrid, but if you do, she's likely to enjoy playing with friends and on teams. However, she may break out of the pack to achieve greatness on her own. If so, she can be inspired by highly successful long-distance runner Ingrid Kristiansen of Norway, who won World Championships, World Cross Country Championships, World Road Race Championships, the Boston Marathon twice, the Chicago Marathon, the Houston Marathon twice, the London Marathon four times, the New York City Marathon, and the Stockholm Marathon three times!

Ingrid Auerswald, Track & Field (Sprinting), Germany, 1980–1988

Ingrid Bruckert, Field Hockey (Defender), Germany, 1976–1984

Ingrid Klimke, Equestrian (Eventing), Germany, 1999–current

Ingrid Kristiansen, Long-Distance Running, Norway, 1980–1993

Ingrid Leijendekker, Water Polo (Field Player), Netherlands, 1992–2000

Ingrid Stengård, Mountain Bike Orienteering, Finland, 2006–2010

Ingrid Landmark Tandrevold, Biathlon, Norway, 2018–current

IREEN/IRENE

Ireen and Irene are popular names in parts of Europe, though they can appear in lots of other places as well. They come to us from Ancient Greek roots and the divine representation of peace. Peace is great, though Ireens and Irenes still have a highly competitive nature and will leave it all on the track, field, or court to win the day. Dutch field hockey defender Ireen van den Assem won gold with her team at the 2018 World Cup, and Irene de Kok took home two world championships in judo. Meanwhile, World Netball Champion and two-time World Netball Series–winner Irene van Dyk of New Zealand is considered one of the top goal-shooters of all time, holding the record for most international appearances of any player ever, and Dutch speed skater Ireen Wüst solidified her place as one of the top speed skaters of all time with a collection of thirteen Olympic medals (six of them gold) and forty-five podiums at world championships with twenty-two wins!

Irene de Kok, Judo, Netherlands, 1984–1992

Ireen van den Assem, Field Hockey (Defender), Netherlands, 2018–current

Irene van Dyk, Netball, New Zealand, 1994–2016

Ireen Wüst, Speed Skating, Netherlands, 2005–2022

IRENA/IRINA/IRYNA

If *Ireen/Irene* isn't exotic enough for you, then consider one of the variant forms Irena, Irina, or Iryna! Many successful athletes with these names have been from various places in Eastern Europe, including three-time World Champions like diver Irina Lashko, Czech slalom canoeist Irena Pavelková, and Ukrainian freestyle wrestler Iryna Merleni, who also took home a gold and a bronze medal from the Olympics, while Soviet rhythmic gymnast Irina Deriugina had four world championship wins, three second place finishes, and a third.

On the track and the field, Soviet Irina Press won Olympic gold in hurdles and the pentathlon, German long-distance runner Irina Mikitenko won multiple major marathons, and Irena Szewińska of Poland sprinted to three gold medals, a silver, and two bronzes. Figure skating, too, has seen two champion Irinas with Russian two-time World Champion and four-time Grand Prix–winner Slutskaya and the legendary Soviet Rodnina, who won three successive Olympic gold medals and ten successive World Championships!

If an Irina in your family tends more toward mental pursuits, she can take inspiration from chess Grandmaster Irina Krush, the first American woman to achieve that rank.

Irina Deriugina, Rhythmic Gymnastics, USSR, 1972–1982

Irina Krush, Chess, USA, 1998–current

Irina Lashko, Diving, Russia/Australia, 1991–2004

Iryna Merleni, Freestyle Wrestling, Ukraine, 2000–2008

Irina Mikitenko, Long-Distance Running, Germany, 1996–2014

Irena Pavelková, Slalom Canoeing, Czechoslovakia, 1990–2012

Irina Press, Track & Field (Hurdling/ Pentathlon), USSR, 1960–1967

Irina Rodnina, Figure Skating, USSR, 1967–1980

Irina Slutskaya, Figure Skating, Russia, 1984–2006

Irena Szewińska, Track & Field (Sprinting/ Long Jump), Poland, 1964–1980

ISABELL/ISABELLE

While some "I" names are geographically concentrated in Eastern Europe, Isabell and Isabelle head west. Descending through a medieval variation of *Elizabeth* (from biblical Hebrew for "my God is an oath"), these names are seen most often in sports figures from France and Canada, particularly Québec.

France produced world champions like slalom canoeist Isabelle Despres and handball star Isabelle Wendling, while snowboarder Isabelle Blanc won Olympic gold and two World Championships on parallel slalom. From Canada, Isabelle Chartrand blocked opponents and prevented goals on her way to an ice hockey Olympic gold medal and a World Championship, and Isabelle Charest raced to three speed skating world champion titles, while Isabell Werth of Germany holds the record for most equestrian Olympic medals won with twelve (seven of them gold), not to mention her nine World Championships and five World Cup wins.

An Isabell or Isabelle in your family will have her pick of what she wants to do, from canoeing to speed skating and beyond!

Isabelle Blanc, Snowboarding, France, 1999–2003

Isabelle Charest, Speed Skating, Canada, 1994–2002

Isabelle Chartrand, Ice Hockey (Defense), Laval Le Mistral, Canada, 1995–2010

Isabelle Despres, Slalom Canoeing, France, 1995–2005

Isabelle Wendling, Handball (Pivot), France, 1999–2008

Isabell Werth, Equestrian (Dressage), Germany, 1989–current

J

BOYS

JACK

A perennial favorite in the US and the UK, Jack is traditionally a diminutive of *John* (from biblical Hebrew roots for "God is gracious") but can also stand on its own. There are tons of Jacks who have excelled in competitive events around the world in a variety of fields, including Chinese contract bridge World Bridge Federation grand master Jie "Jack" Zhao, American track and field star Jack Yerman (who won Olympic gold in the 4x400-meter relay and set numerous world records), record-setting three-time Olympic gold-medalist rower Jack Beresford, and six-time NBA All-Star small forward Jack Twyman.

There are numerous sports in which Jacks have found success, like baseball (with pitcher Morris, who earned five All-Star appearances and won four World Series). On the cricket pitch, two batsmen named Jack have scored big: Australian Fingleton collected five Test centuries (including an unbeaten century against the English bodyline attacks during the Ashes) and was the first player to score centuries in four consecutive Test innings) and English Hobbs became ranked among the top batsmen of all time, with numerous scoring and century-making records that stand to this day.

On the gridiron, defensive end Jack Youngblood played in seven Pro Bowls, quarterback Jack Kemp had seven AFL All-Star appearances and two championships, and both linebackers Jack Ham and Jack Lambert won four Super Bowl championships with eight and nine Pro Bowl appearances, respectively.

The fastest Jacks have included Australian Formula 1 legend Jack Brabham, who went from a career as a mechanic and engineer to winning fourteen top-level races and three F1 championships. Heavyweight champion Jack Dempsey is ranked among the top boxers and punchers of all time, alongside fellow champ Jack Johnson, who was the first African-American world heavyweight title-holder. Last but certainly not least is Jack Nicklaus, arguably the greatest golfer of all time, with 117 professional wins leading to an incredible eighteen major championships!

Jacks, whether given that name or just called that by way of *John*, are filled with potential. The world is theirs to conquer as they choose!

Jack Beresford, Rowing, England, 1920–1940

John "Jack" Brabham, Auto Racing (Formula 1), Australia, 1955–1970

William "Jack" Dempsey, Boxing (Heavyweight), USA, 1914-1927

John "Jack" Fingleton, Cricket (Opening Batsman), New South Wales Men's Cricket Team, Australia, 1928–1940

Jack Ham Jr., Football (Linebacker), Pittsburgh Steelers, USA, 1971–1982

John "Jack" Hobbs, Cricket (Opening Batsman), Surrey County Cricket Club, England, 1905–1934

John "Jack" Johnson, Boxing (Heavyweight), USA, 1897–1931

Jack Kemp, Football (Quarterback), Buffalo Bills, USA, 1957–1969

John "Jack" Lambert, Football (Linebacker), Pittsburgh Steelers, USA, 1974–1984

John "Jack" Morris, Baseball (Pitcher), Detroit Tigers, USA, 1977–1994

Jack Nicklaus, Golf, USA, 1961–2005

John "Jack" Twyman, Basketball (Small Forward), Rochester Royals, USA, 1955–1966

Jack Yerman, Track & Field (Sprinting), USA, 1959–1960

Herbert Jackson "Jack" Youngblood, Football (Defensive End), Los Angeles Rams, USA, 1971–1984

Jie "Jack" Zhao, Contract Bridge, China, 1998–current

JACKIE/JACKY

The unisex Jackie and Jacky may sound alike, but they have different sources, with the former originating as a nickname for *Jack* and the latter being a diminutive for *Jacques* (from biblical Hebrew *Jacob*). While *Jack*s are all over the board with respect to their sporting careers, Jackies and Jackys are more focused on a handful of disciplines.

On international racetracks, Belgian Jacky Ickx finished first in eight Formula 1 races and won the distinguished 24 Hours of Le Mans race six times (still the second highest record), while British Jackie Stewart's twenty-seven Formula 1 wins earned him three championships. Meanwhile, all fans of America's pastime know the name Jackie Robinson. After playing one season in the Negro leagues, Robinson joined the Brooklyn Dodgers in 1947 and became the first African American in Major League Baseball since 1884. Aside from that historic note, Jackie had a stellar career, earning a Rookie of the Year Award, six All-Star appearances, a batting championship, a World Series championship, and more.

Choose the name Jackie or Jacky for a boy in your family who may want to play ball or drive fast and who has the potential to change the game.

Jacques "Jacky" Ickx, Auto Racing (Formula 1), Belgium, 1966–1979

Jack "Jackie" Robinson, Baseball (Second Baseman), Brooklyn Dodgers, USA, 1945–1956

John "Jackie" (the Flying Scott) Stewart, Auto Racing (Formula 1), Scotland, 1965–1973

JAKE

Most often a short form of *Jacob*, sometimes short for other names like *Jakobus* or *Giacobbe*, and also frequently used on its own, Jake is a very popular moniker in English-speaking countries. In America, lots of Jakes have earned All-Star selections and championships in baseball and football, though the success of athletes with the name has also spread far and wide into a number of other sports and events. These include Jakes who have won big alongside teammates, like Canadian rower Jake Wetzel, whose Olympic gold and silver medals and three World Championship gold medals came in team events; and three-time team world champion recurve archer and four-time World Cup team gold-medalist Jake Kaminski.

On the flipside, some Jakes have made a name for themselves all on their own! This has happened in everything from wake-surfing (like Pro Skim world champion Jake Caster) to freestyle wrestling (like Olympic gold-medalist Jake Varner), skateboarding (like Australian big air pioneer Jake Brown who was the first person to complete a 720-degree rotation without grabbing his board and won two medals of each color at X Games) to boxing (with the iconic "Raging Bull" himself Jake LaMotta who won the world middleweight championship title in 1949, accumulated an 83–19–4 record, and was inducted into the inaugural class of the International Boxing Hall of Fame).

America's pastime is chock full of Jakes. San Diego Padres infielder Jake Cronenworth has already had two All-Star selections in his career, while legendary pitcher Jake Peavy had three while winning two World Series championships (with the Red Sox and Giants), a National League Cy Young award, and a Gold Glove and leading the National League in wins and strikeouts twice and the MLB in ERA twice!

Finally, we come to gridiron greats and a cavalcade of Pro Bowlers. Long snapper Jake McQuaide has had two Pro Bowl appearances, offensive tackle Jake Long had four, and 1970s free safety and punt returner Jake Scott earned five during his career while also winning two Super Bowl championships with the Miami Dolphins and being named Super Bowl MVP.

Football and baseball may be natural interests for a boy you name Jake, but he'll have the skills and competitive nature to find success in any event!

Jake Brown, Skateboarding, Australia, 1996–2013

Jake Caster, Wake Surfing, USA, 2016–current

Jacob "Jake" Cronenworth, Baseball (Infielder), San Diego Padres, USA, 2020–current

Jake Kaminski, Archery, USA, 2010–2017

Giacobbe "Jake" LaMotta, Boxing (Middleweight/Light Heavyweight), USA, 1941–1954

Jake Long, Football (Offensive Tackle), Miami Dolphins, USA, 2008–2016

Jacob "Jake" McQuaide, Football (Long Snapper), St. Louis Rams, USA, 2011–current

Jacob "Jake" Peavy, Baseball (Pitcher), San Diego Padres, USA, 2002–2016

Jacob "Jake" Scott III, Football (Free Safety/ Punt Returner), Miami Dolphins, USA, 1969–1978

Jacob "Jake" Varner, Freestyle Wrestling, USA, 2011–2016

Jacob "Jake" Wetzel, Rowing, Canada, 1999–2008

JAMES

The name of presidents, kings, actors, musicians, and more, James is another descendant of the biblical Hebrew *Jacob*. Just as many men named James have appeared in politics and media, so, too, have they become famous for their athletic achievements in a wide variety of places and events. American James "Clayster" Eubanks is a three-time *Call of Duty* esports World Champion, visually impaired British cyclist James Ball took home four Para-Cycling Track World Championships, British Formula 1 superstar James Hunt won ten races and a championship racing against his friend and rival Niki Lauda, and cricket has seen few talents like English bowler James Anderson, whose list of accomplishments includes being the all-time number one Test wicket-taker, the only fast bowler to take more than six hundred Test wickets, the third highest all-time wicket-taker, and more.

Football, soccer, and basketball have seen top athletes with this name, with eight-time Pro Bowl wide receiver James Lofton; UEFA Super Cup– and FIFA Club World

Cup-winning midfielders James Milner of England and James Rodríguez of Columbia; seven-time All-Star and three-time NBA champion Los Angeles Lakers small forward James Worthy; and ten-time All-Star shooting guard James Harden.

Apparently, athletes named James also really like to row, as we can see with world champions James Renforth, James Clarke, and James McRae, along with British two-time Olympic gold-medalist and six-time World Champion James Cracknell and Australian James Tomkins, whose medal count includes three Olympic wins and an unbroken streak of seven World Championships.

You definitely want to teach a James in your family to swim early on, though he may decide to pursue other athletic endeavors, like basketball, soccer, football, or even auto racing. If he's especially tough, he may even learn the sweet science like undisputed world heavyweight champion boxer James "Buster" Douglas, who exploded into popularity with his upset over Mike Tyson in 1990!

James Anderson, Cricket (Bowler), Lancashire County Cricket Club, England, 2000–current

James Ball, Para-Cycling, Wales, 2012–current

James Clarke, Rowing, England, 2007–2010

James Cracknell, Rowing, England, 1996–2004

James "Buster" Douglas, Boxing (Heavyweight), USA, 1981–1999

James "Clayster" Eubanks, Esports (*Call of Duty*), USA, 2010–current

James Harden Jr., Basketball (Shooting Guard), Houston Rockets, USA, 2009–current

James Hunt, Auto Racing (Formula 1), England, 1973–1979

James Lofton, Football (Wide Receiver), Green Bay Packers, USA, 1978–1993

James McRae, Rowing, Australia, 2005–2014

James Milner, Soccer (Midfielder/Winger/Full-Back), Liverpool Football Club, England, 2001–current

James Renforth, Rowing, England, 1868–1871

James Rodríguez Rubio, Soccer (Midfielder/Winger), Real Madrid Club de Fútbol, Columbia, 2006–current

James Tomkins, Rowing, Australia, 1985–2004

James Worthy, Basketball (Small Forward), Los Angeles Lakers, USA, 1982–1994

JAMIE

Jamie originated in Scotland as a diminutive for *James* and later became a unisex name used all on its own. Just as with *James*, Jamies are famous all over and for quite a few different things. In his ongoing auto-racing career, Australian Jamie Whincup has accumulated 124 wins and a record seven championships in the Supercars Championship series; British tennis star Jamie Murray (brother of fellow champ Andy Murray) won seven Grand Slams, the Davis Cup, and more on his way to a world number one ranking in doubles; and Australian centers have reached the pinnacle in rugby and field hockey with top-ranked record setter Jamie "Killer" Lyon (Super League and Challenge Cup Champion) and Jamie Dwyer (Olympic gold-medalist, two-time World Cup-winner, and six-time Champions Trophy-winner), respectively. On international tracks, Welsh sprinter Jamie Baulch won two World Championships in the late 1990s, while American Jamie Connolly left Harvard to participate in the 1896 Athens Olympic Games and won the first gold medal in modern history!

Encourage a young Jamie in your family, who may become a pioneer and world champion!

Jamie Baulch, Track & Field (Sprinting), Wales, 1996–2003

James "Jamie" Connolly, Track & Field (Triple Jump), USA, 1896–1900

Jamie Dwyer, Field Hockey (Center), Australia, 1998–current

Jamie Lyon, Rugby (Center/Five-Eighth), Manly Sea Eagles, Australia, 2000–2016

Jamie Murray, Tennis, Scotland, 2004–current

Jamie Whincup, Auto Racing (Supercars), Australia, 2002–current

JAN

Whether you pronounce it with a starting "J" or "Y" sound, the unisex name Jan ultimately comes from the same root as *John*, biblical Hebrew for "God is gracious." Name a child Jan and introduce him to an array of traditional team sports early; he may find he likes soccer, like the Czech national team's top-scoring striker Koller or Slovenian Oblak, who's ranked among the top modern goalkeepers, or football, like four-time Pro Bowl placekicker and Super Bowl champion Stenerud. Alternatively, he may gravitate toward other athletic events with inspirations like Jan Železný, who won three Olympic gold medals and three World Championships in javelin; or Olympic gold-medalist triathlete and three-time Ironman World Champion Jan Frodeno; Tour de France, Olympic, and World Championship-winner Jan Ullrich; and two-time Olympic gold-medalist, three-time World Cup-winner, and seven-time World Champion luger Jan Behrendt from Germany.

Jan Behrendt, Luge, Germany, 1988–1998

Jan Frodeno, Triathlon, Germany, 2002–current

Jan Koller, Soccer (Striker), Ballspielverein Borussia 09 e. V. Dortmund, Czechoslovakia, 1994–2011

Jan Oblak, Soccer (Goalkeeper), Club Atlético de Madrid, S.A.D., Slovenia, 2009–current

Jan Stenerud, Football (Placekicker), Kansas City Chiefs, Norway, 1967–1985

Jan Ullrich, Road Cycling, Germany, 1995–2006

Jan Železný, Track & Field (Javelin), Czech Republic, 1987–2006

JARED/JARROD/JARRYD

From a biblical Hebrew name meaning "descent" or "going down" comes the modern Jared, which has morphed into variants like Jarrod and Jarryd.

Gridiron football is a team sport featuring dynamic Jareds, including three-time Pro Bowl quarterback Jared Goff, who shares NFL records for most completions in a regular season game (forty-five) and most pass attempts with a perfect passer rating (thirty-three); and five-time Pro Bowl defensive end Jared Allen, who led the NFL in sacks twice, shares records for most career safeties (four) and most safeties in a season (two).

Then there's a trio of the fastest competitors with three different versions of the name. Jarrod Shoemaker ran and biked to a win at the Duathlon World Championship; Australian racewalker Jared Tallent collected a gold medal, two silvers, and a bronze from the Olympics and two golds, a silver, and three bronzes at World Race Walking Cup events; and Paralympic sprinter Jarryd Wallace, whose incredible success story went from losing a leg to winning multiple gold medals at World Para Athletics Championships and Parapan American Games, breaking multiple world records, giving a TED Talk on mastering transitions, and more.

Whether you choose the classic Jared for your son or one of the more unique variants like Jarrod, Jarryd, or Jered, he'll have plenty of champions to inspire him!

Jared Allen, Football (Defensive End), Minnesota Vikings, USA, 2004–2015

Jared Goff, Football (Quarterback), Los Angeles Rams, USA, 2016–current

- **Jarrod Shoemaker**, Duathlon, USA, 2002–2014
- **Jared Tallent**, Track & Field (Racewalking), Australia, 2006–2021
- **Jarryd Wallace**, Track & Field (Sprinting), USA, 2011–current

JASON

While the Jason of Ancient Greek mythology was a problematic hero, more recent athletes with the classical name have proven brave, wise, and highly skilled in their respective fields. Nowhere is this more obvious than on the Major League Baseball diamond, where fans have witnessed the accomplishments of Boston Red Sox catching-legend Jason Varitek, who had two World Series wins in addition to three All-Star appearances, and five-time All-Star first baseman and powerful hitter Jason Giambi.

Beyond baseball, you can find inspirational Jasons in many other places. Jason Kelce is a seven-time NFL Philadelphia Eagles Pro Bowl center and Super Bowl champion, English rugby star Jason Leonard won four Grand Slams and the 2003 Rugby World Cup, South African batsman Jason Roy was on the 2019 Cricket World Cup champion team and holds the ODI scoring record for England, point guard Jason Kidd scored ten All-Star appearances and an NBA championship with the Dallas Mavericks, and English cyclist Jason Kenny holds the British Olympic medal record with seven golds and two silvers, as well as three World Championships and more.

An athletic Jason in your family may excel in any of these traditional sports and events, though he also may focus his talents and abilities into more unique and modern fields, perhaps taking inspiration from American top-ranked esports competitor Jason "Mew2King" Zimmerman, who has won more than seventy *Super Smash Bros.* tournaments!

- **Jason Giambi**, Baseball (First Baseman/Designated Hitter), New York Yankees, USA, 1995–2014
- **Jason Kelce**, Football (Center), Philadelphia Eagles, USA, 2011–current
- **Jason Kenny**, Track Cycling, England, 2006–2020
- **Jason Kidd**, Basketball (Point Guard), Phoenix Suns, USA, 1994–2013
- **Jason Leonard**, Rugby (Prop), Harlequins, England, 1982–2004
- **Jason Roy**, Cricket (Batsman), Surrey County Cricket Club, South Africa, 2008–current
- **Jason Varitek**, Baseball (Catcher), Boston Red Sox, USA, 1997–2011
- **Jason "Mew2King" Zimmerman**, Esports (*Super Smash Bros.*), USA, 2005–current

JAYSON

A modern and cool variant of *Jason*, Jayson is a name that brings with it brains and brawn, sheer power and speed, and pinpoint dexterity. We can see this in winners and champions like Filipino chess Grandmaster Jayson Gonzales; Scottish World Blackball Champion pool player Jayson Shaw, who has won the Mosconi Cup five times and many other tournaments and set the world record for the highest run in 14.1 straight pool at 714; and Boston Celtics four-time All-Star small forward/power forward Jayson Tatum, who was named All-Star MVP and won an Olympic gold medal with Team USA!

- **Jayson Gonzales**, Chess, Philippines, 1996–2018
- **Jayson Shaw**, Pool (Nine-Ball/Ten-Ball), Scotland, 2010–current
- **Jayson Tatum**, Basketball (Small Forward/Power Forward), Boston Celtics, USA, 2017–current

JEFF

The medieval name *Geoffrey* and uncertain Germanic roots including "peace" have given us the moniker *Jeffrey*, but those who go by the short form Jeff (a perfectly good name on its own) have really made their marks in the world of sports and athletics. These champions can be spotted across the wide world of sports from wrestling (American heavyweight Olympic gold-medalist Blatnick) to volleyball (World Champion and Olympic Games-winner Stork), skeleton (Canadian two-time World Champion Pain), para-athletics (Canadian Adams, whose thirteen Paralympic Games medals include three wins), and soccer (five-time MLS champion Agoos).

On the football field, Jeff Garcia tied for longest touchdown pass at ninety-nine yards and had four Pro Bowl appearances, and six-time Pro Bowl center Jeff Saturday played nearly his entire career with the Indianapolis Colts (and won a Super Bowl with them).

Jeffs have found a calling in America's pastime, with two-time All-Star third baseman Cirillo; first baseman and outfielder "Mr. Marlin" Conine, who earned two All-Star appearances and won two World Series; four-time Houston Astros All-Star first baseman and three-time Silver Slugger Bagwell; and second baseman Kent, who had five All-Star appearances, earned four Silver Slugger awards, and was named the 2000 National League MVP.

A little Jeff in your family may take inspiration from any of those athletes or set out on his own path. Or he may want to take things fast and follow in the tire tracks of NASCAR legend Jeff Gordon, whose ninety-three Cup series wins on his way to four championships puts him third on the all-time winner's list.

Jeffrey "Jeff" Adams, Para-Athletics, Canada, 1988–2008

Jeffrey "Jeff" Agoos, Soccer (Defender), DC United, USA, 1988–2005

Jeffrey "Jeff" Bagwell, Baseball (First Baseman), Houston Astros, USA, 1991–2005

Jeffrey "Jeff" Blatnick, Greco-Roman Wrestling, USA, 1980–1987

Jeffrey "Jeff" Cirillo, Baseball (Third Baseman), Milwaukee Brewers, USA, 1994–2007

Jeffrey "Jeff" Conine, Baseball (First Baseman/Left Fielder), Florida Marlins, USA, 1990–2007

Jeffrey "Jeff" Garcia, Football (Quarterback), San Francisco 49ers, USA, 1994–2011

Jeffrey "Jeff" Gordon, Auto Racing (NASCAR), USA, 1993–2015

Jeffrey "Jeff" Kent, Baseball (Second Baseman), San Francisco Giants, USA, 1992–2008

Jeffrey "Jeff" Pain, Skeleton, Canada, 1995–2010

Jeffrey "Jeff" Saturday, Football (Center), Indianapolis Colts, USA, 1998–2012

Jeffrey "Jeff" Stork, Volleyball (Setter), USA, 1986–1992

JEREMY

Jeremy has its origins in biblical Hebrew for "God will exalt" by way of the name *Jeremiah*, and there's a number of athletes with this name who have made incredible accomplishments all on their own or with the support of their teams, like NBA champion and Asian-American basketball pioneer Jeremy Lin, four-time NFL Pro Bowl tight end and two-time Super Bowl champ Jeremy Shockey, and controversial but highly successful nine-time NHL All-Star center Jeremy Roenick.

On world championship stages have stood Jeremys like American skier Jeremy Bloom, French Olympic gold-medalist and four-time World Champion swimmer Jérémy Stravius, and American sprinter Jeremy Wariner, whose medal take included three

Olympic golds and six world championships. Meanwhile, motocross and supercross legend Jeremy McGrath racked up eighty-nine wins, seven Supercross championships, an X Games gold medal, and more.

Especially if you're an American sports fan, Jeremy might be a great pick for a son who will grow up to be a memorable champion.

Jeremy Bloom, Skiing, USA, 1997–2010

Jeremy Lin, Basketball (Point Guard), Toronto Raptors, USA, 2010–2022

Jeremy McGrath, Motocross/Supercross, USA, 1989–2006

Jeremy Roenick, Ice Hockey (Center), Chicago Blackhawks, USA, 1988–2009

Jeremy Shockey, Football (Tight End), New York Giants, USA, 2002–2011

Jérémy Stravius, Swimming (Backstroke/Butterfly/Freestyle), France, 2009–2019

Jeremy Wariner, Track & Field (Sprinting), USA, 2005–2015

JERRY

A perfectly fine name on its own, Jerry also serves as a nickname for a range of other names, from *George* and *Gerald* to *Jeremy* and *Jerome*. This classic American name brings with it a legacy of toughness and tenacity, especially when it comes to basketball and football. The number one Jerry on the hardwood was Jerry West. One of the all-time greatest all around players and scorers, "Mr. Clutch" was a fourteen-time All-Star and NBA champion (and highly successful executive later) with the Los Angeles Lakers, as well as an Olympic gold medalist. Meanwhile, over on the football field, wide receiver Jerry Rice earned thirteen Pro Bowl appearances and three Super Bowl wins in his twenty seasons, setting multiple records and solidifying his place among the top players of all time!

Jerry Rice, Football (Wide Receiver), San Francisco 49ers, USA, 1985–2005

Jerome "Jerry" (Mr. Clutch) West, Basketball (Point Guard), Los Angeles Lakers, USA, 1960–1974

JESSE

Possibly coming from a root for "gift" or "God's gift," the biblical Hebrew name Jesse has come to embody not only general athleticism but also striving against the odds and having great success in unexpected places. Baseball has seen its share of Jesses with early champs Barnes and "Crab" Burkett, and two-time All-Star, two-time World Series champion pitcher Orosco, whose lengthy career included playing a record 1,252 games across four decades. Another long string of victories came to an athlete born Jesse Kuhaulua in Hawaii, but who became the champion sumo wrestler known as Takamiyama Daigorō in Japan; he set multiple records during his twenty-year career and was the first wrestler born outside Japan to claim the top division championship. Finally there's legendary track and field athlete Jesse Owens. Best known for winning four gold medals to become the most successful athlete at the 1936 Olympic Games in Berlin, Owens was a huge upset to Hitler's plans for the event. One year earlier, Jesse also made history by breaking three world records and tying another, all in under an hour!

A Jesse in your family will be a champion and a trailblazer, finding success wherever he seeks it.

Jesse Barnes, Baseball (Pitcher), New York Giants, USA, 1915–1927

Jesse "Crab" Burkett, Baseball (Left Fielder), Cleveland Spiders, USA, 1890–1905

Jesse Kuhaulua (Takamiyama Daigorō), Sumo, USA, 1964–1984

Jesse Orosco, Baseball (Pitcher), New York Mets, USA, 1979–2003

James "Jesse" Owens, Track & Field (Sprinting/Long Jump), USA, 1935–1936

JIM

Jim is a classic diminutive form of *James*, but there is nothing small about the accomplishments achieved by athletes who have gone by this name. Primarily Americans, these Jims have excelled in many sports starting with golf and Jim Furyk, who won twenty-nine professional events and tied for the lowest PGA Tour score. Some Jims excel in America's pastime–like five-time All-Star power hitter Jim Thorne and Jim Palmer, whose no-hitter, awards, six All-Star appearances, three World Series championships, and more place him high on the all-time pitchers list–while some others are fighters-turned-actors, like karate champion and action star Jim Kelly and late-nineteenth century World Heavyweight Champion boxer Jim Corbett.

Jims have made big impacts in American football, like quarterback Jim Kelly (five-time Pro Bowler) and, of course, Cleveland Browns fullback Jim Brown, who consistently appears at the top of greatest NFL players lists thanks to his nine Pro Bowl invitations, NFL championship, and numerous records.

In the 1960s, Scottish Formula 1 racing legend Jim Clark won twenty-five races and two championships in only seventy-two starts, earning a spot on many all-time greatest driver lists. Finally, there's Jim Thorpe, whose athleticism could not be contained to just one, two, or even three disciplines. In the early 1900s, Thorpe played professional football, baseball, and basketball, and won Olympic gold medals in decathlon and pentathlon!

Be sure to introduce a Jim in your family to a wide range of sports and athletics; he may find one to pursue that surprises you, or he may excel at a number of them.

- **James "Jim" Brown**, Football (Fullback), Cleveland Browns, USA, 1957–1965
- **James "Jim" Clark Jr.**, Auto Racing (Formula 1), Scotland, 1960–1968
- **James "Gentleman Jim" Corbett**, Boxing (Heavyweight), USA, 1884–1903
- **James "Jim" Furyk**, Golf, USA, 1992–2020
- **James "Jim" Kelly**, Football (Quarterback), Buffalo Bills, USA, 1984–1996
- **James "Jim" Kelly**, Karate, USA, 1972–2013
- **James "Jim" Palmer**, Baseball (Pitcher), Baltimore Orioles, USA, 1965–1984
- **James "Jim" Thorne**, Baseball (First Baseman/ Third Baseman), Cleveland Indians, USA, 1991–2012
- **James "Jim" Thorpe (Wa-Tho-Huk)**, Track & Field/Football/Baseball/Basketball, USA, 1912–1928

JIMMIE

If you call or name your son Jimmie, don't be surprised if he gravitates toward baseball or racing. He'll have Major League Baseball role models to look up to, like two-time All-Stars outfielder Jimmie Hall and catcher Jimmie Wilson (who also won two World Series), as well as famed power hitter Jimmie Foxx, who had nine All-Star appearances, two World Series championships, a Triple Crown, batting champion and home run leader awards, and more. On the racetrack, Jimmie Johnson drove the 48 car to eighty-three wins and seven championships in NASCAR's top series, ranking him sixth in overall wins and tied for first in championships (on top of that, he was the only driver to win five championships consecutively!).

- **James "Jimmie" Foxx**, Baseball (First Baseman), Boston Red Sox, USA, 1925–1945
- **Jimmie Hall**, Baseball (Outfielder), Minnesota Twins, USA, 1963–1970
- **Jimmie Johnson**, Auto Racing (NASCAR), USA, 1998–2020
- **James "Jimmie" Wilson**, Baseball (Catcher), Philadelphia Phillies, USA, 1923–1940

JIMMY

The last of the *James* diminutives and nicknames, Jimmy may seem super casual, but athletes with this name have found serious success on fields, tracks, courses and courts. Cornerback Jimmy Johnson (not to be confused with Jimmie Johnson above) was a five-time Pro Bowler during his career with the San Francisco 49ers; six-time NBA All-Star small forward Jimmy Butler won an Olympic gold medal with Team USA; English striker Jimmy Greaves stands among England's top goal scorers, having scored 513 times in 765 club and international appearances; Jimmy Shea took home an Olympic win and a set of each medal at World Championships in skeleton; and tennis giant Jimmy Connors set records holding the number one spot in the world for 160 consecutive weeks (268 total), eight major titles, and more.

Jimmy Butler Jr., Basketball (Small Forward), Chicago Bulls, USA, 2011–current

James "Jimmy" Connors, Tennis, USA, 1972–1996

Jimmy Greaves, Soccer (Striker), Tottenham Hotspur Football Club, England, 1957–1980

James "Jimmy" Johnson, Football (Cornerback/Safety/Wide Receiver), San Francisco 49ers, USA, 1961–1976

James "Jimmy" Shea Jr., Skeleton, USA, 1997–2002

JOE

A classic American name, Joe is most often a short form for *Joseph* and sometimes other names like *Joel*. To say there have been *many* successful athletes known as Joe is an understatement, and while there are concentrations in boxing, baseball, and football, there are some outliers and unique Joes as well. These include seven-time NBA All-Star Joe Johnson; world renowned early-twentieth century three-time World Heavyweight Wrestling Champion Joe Stecher; American karate and kickboxing legend Joe Lewis, who was twice voted the greatest fighter in karate history; and record-setting English cricket top-order batsman and captain Joe Root, who was the top run-scorer on the way to winning the 2019 Cricket World Cup.

Joe Weatherly entertained NASCAR audiences in the 1950s and '60s, not only by winning twenty-five races and two championships in the top series, but also by his silly antics that led to his nickname the "Clown Prince of Racing," while dragster driver Joe Amato racked up fifty-two wins, five championships, and numerous records during his stellar eighteen-year career. Over on the ice of the NHL have been big Joes, with Canadian six-time All-Star center and Olympic champion Thornton, and Canadian three-time All-Star Colorado Avalanche center Sakic, who took home gold medals from the Olympics, World Championships, and World Cup, as well as two Stanley Cup trophies.

There are two legendary heavyweight boxing world champions who stand first and foremost in peoples' minds. Smokin' Joe Frazier won an Olympic gold medal in 1964 before his professional boxing career, during which he'd achieve a 32-4-1 record, become the first opponent to beat Muhammad Ali, hold the world championship from 1970–1973, and secure his place on lists of top heavyweights of all time. Even higher on those lists is Joe Louis Barrow, whose 66-3 record career included the longest-ever stretch holding the world heavyweight champion title (1937–1949, nearly twelve years) and successfully defending a title from the most consecutive challenges (twenty-five).

Up next are Joes in America's pastime, and while there have been a great many, these stand at the top. Minnesota Twins catcher and first baseman Joe Mauer had six All-Star appearances and won three Golden Gloves, five Silver Sluggers, and an MVP; and shortstop Joe Cronin was a seven-time All-Star during his twenty-year career. Ten-time All-Star second baseman (and ranked among the best-ever players at that position) and slugger Joe Morgan played for twenty-two seasons, accumulating two World Series championships, two MVPs, and more. Last but not least, the "greatest living ballplayer" of his era, New York Yankees' Joltin' Joe DiMaggio set numerous records on his way to becoming one of the greatest players of all time and had thirteen All-Star appearances (every year he played), nine World Series championships, tons of awards, and famously set and still holds the record for the longest hitting streak at a staggering fifty-six games!

The final set of Joes found their fame on the gridiron of American football and while there have been many NFL champions with this name, these are the greatest. "Mean" Joe Greene anchored the Pittsburgh Steelers' defensive line for thirteen years, garnering ten Pro Bowl appearances and winning four Super Bowls on the way to being considered one of the greatest defensive linemen of all time. Arguably the two most famous football Joes were both quarterbacks; Joe Namath played for the New York Jets before and after the AFL-NFL merger, and while his achievements "only" include two AFL MVPs, a single Pro Bowl appearance, one AFL championship, and one Super Bowl win, Namath was massively popular. Two years after Namath's retirement, Joe Montana came onto the scene, and during his sixteen seasons with the San Francisco 49ers and Kansas City Chiefs, he went to the Pro Bowl eight times and won the Super Bowl four times, claiming numerous passing titles along the way.

A small name, Joe carries with it a tremendous potential, and a boy with that name in your family may be a ball player, a fighter, racecar driver, or anything else he wants to be!

Joe Amato, Auto Racing (NHRA), USA, 1983–2001

Joseph "Joe" Louis Barrow, Boxing (Heavyweight), USA, 1934–1951

Joseph "Joe" Cronin, Baseball (Shortstop), Boston Red Sox, USA, 1926–1945

Joseph "Joltin' Joe" DiMaggio, Baseball (Center Fielder), New York Yankees, USA, 1936–1951

Joseph "Smokin' Joe" Frazier, Boxing (Heavyweight), USA, 1965–1981

Charles "Mean Joe" Greene, Football (Defensive Tackle), Pittsburgh Steelers, USA, 1969–1981

Joe Johnson, Basketball (Shooting Guard/Small Forward), Atlanta Hawks, USA, 2001–2022

Joseph "Joe" Lewis, Karate/Kickboxing, USA, 1965–1983

Joseph "Joe" Mauer, Baseball (Catcher/First Baseman), Minnesota Twins, USA, 2004–2018

Joseph "Joe" Montana Jr., Football (Quarterback), San Francisco 49ers, USA, 1979–1994

Joe Morgan, Baseball (Second Baseman), Cincinnati Reds, USA, 1963–1984

Joseph "Broadway Joe" Namath, Football (Quarterback), New York Jets, USA, 1965–1977

Joseph "Joe" Root, Cricket (Top-Order Batsman), Yorkshire County Cricket Club, England, 2009–current

Joseph "Joe" Sakic, Ice Hockey (Center), Colorado Avalanche, Canada, 1988–2009

Joseph "Joe" Stecher, Catch Wrestling, USA, 1912–1934

Joseph "Joe" Thornton, Ice Hockey (Center), San Jose Sharks, Canada, 1997–current

Joseph "Joe" Weatherly, Auto Racing (NASCAR), USA, 1952–1964

JOEY

An even more familiar nickname for *Joseph* than *Joe*, Joey may sound a bit juvenile, but when it comes to competition, Joeys don't mess around! First off, they like to go fast, and you can see examples of this with NASCAR driver Joey Logano, who has won thirty races in the Xfinity series and thirty-two races and two championships in the elite Cup series; and on skates with Olympic gold-, silver-, and bronze-medalist speed skater and World Sprint Championship-winner Joey Cheek and Joey Mantia, whose medal count includes three gold medals and a bronze on the ice in World Championships and nine World Championship golds, three silvers, and three bronzes in inline skating.

Joeys are celebrated on the baseball field, like Cincinnati Reds mainstay first baseman Joey Votto, who has earned six All-Star selections, a Gold Glove, a National League Hank Aaron award, and a National League MVP, and Joeys who also work well on teams include Canadian three-time Paralympic gold-medalist wheelchair basketball player Joey Johnson and four-time NFL Pro Bowl linebacker Joey Porter, who won Super Bowl XL with the Pittsburgh Steelers.

A Joey in your family, then, is likely to have a love of speed in various forms or enjoy playing and working with friends. On the other hand, he could find great success competing on his own in something unique and exciting, like competitive eating, where Joey Chestnut–one of the all-time greatest–has set world records eating dozens of foods including, of course, hot dogs (seventy-six in ten minutes)!

William Joseph "Joey" Cheek, Speed Skating, USA, 2002–2008

Joseph "Joey" Chestnut, Competitive Eating, USA, 2005–current

William Joseph "Joey" Dunlop, Motorcycle Racing (Tourist Trophy), Northern Ireland, 1976–2000

Joey Johnson, Wheelchair Basketball, Canada, 1996–2012

Joseph "Joey" Logano, Auto Racing (NASCAR), USA, 2005–current

Joey Mantia, Speed Skating/Inline Speed Skating, USA, 2010–current

Joseph "Joey" Porter Jr., Football (Linebacker), Pittsburgh Steelers, USA, 1999–2011

Joseph "Joey" Votto, Baseball (First Baseman), Cincinnati Reds, Canada, 2007–current

JOHN

Can a kid you name John grow up to be a football star or a wildly popular (and just plain wild) tennis pro? It's possible! With roots in biblical Hebrew for "God is gracious," the name John has been popular for generations and shows up across the sporting and athletic world, sometimes even in surprising places. "John John" Florence has dominated pipe surfing with five Triple Crowns of Surfing championships, two World Championships, and more; and wrestler John Smith brought home Olympic gold twice along with four World Championships. Pitcher John Smoltz was an eight-time All-Star and World Series champion in his twenty-two MLB seasons, while fellow ball-thrower John Elway is ranked among the all-time best football quarterbacks and won nine Pro Bowl appearances and two Super Bowls with the Denver Broncos!

On the snooker circuit, Englishman John Spencer won three World Championships and Scottish John Higgins holds the number three all-time rank with thirty-one tournament titles, while in the National Hockey League are two Canadian star centers with three-time Stanley Cup-winner John Madden and six-time All-Star and Olympic gold-medalist John Tavares.

A couple of basketball-playing Johns are ranked among the all-time best in their positions, including ten-time All-Star Utah

Jazz point guard John Stockton and Boston Celtics small forward John Havlicek, who had thirteen All-Star appearances and won a massive eight NBA championships, while the fastest Johns in the world include American seventeen-time champion and 155-time NHRA- and AHRA-winning drag racer John Force and British John Surtees, who won seven Grand Prix motorcycle world championships on two wheels before switching to four in Formula 1, where he achieved six wins and the 1964 championship! Finally, there's tennis and two more men who achieved the pinnacle by being ranked number one in the world in both singles *and* doubles. John Newcombe achieved this during his career in the 1960s and '70s, overlapping with the undisputed bad boy of the sport, John McEnroe. "Johnny Mac" won a staggering 155 singles and doubles titles, the most of any man in the Open Era, and held both number one ranks at the same time!

John Elway Jr., Football (Quarterback), Denver Broncos, USA, 1983–1998

John "John John" Florence, Surfing, USA, 2005–current

John Force, Auto Racing (NHRA), USA, 1978–current

John Havlicek, Basketball (Small Forward), Boston Celtics, USA, 1962–1978

John Higgins, Snooker, Scotland, 1992–current

John Madden, Ice Hockey (Center), New Jersey Devils, Canada, 1997–2012

John McEnroe, Tennis, USA, 1978–2006

John Newcombe, Tennis, Australia, 1967–1981

John Smith, Freestyle Wrestling, USA, 1987–1992

John Smoltz, Baseball (Pitcher), Atlanta Braves, USA, 1988–2009

John Spencer, Snooker, England, 1968–1992

John Stockton, Basketball (Point Guard), Utah Jazz, USA, 1984–2003

John Surtees, Auto/Motorcycle Racing (Formula 1), England, 1952–1972

John Tavares, Ice Hockey (Center), New York Islanders, Canada, 2009–current

JOHNNY

A popular diminutive of *John*, Johnny is a name utilized by some unique characters who could definitely inspire a young athlete. NHL's "most gentlemanly player" Johnny "Hockey" Gaudreau has six All-Star appearances in his career with the Calgary Flames, and quarterback Johnny Unitas solidified his place among the best NFL football players of all time with ten Pro Bowl appearances, three NFL championships, a Super Bowl win, and multiple records, while on the baseball diamond you've got ten-time All-Star first baseman and five-time World Series champion Johnny Mize and catcher Johnny Bench, who had fourteen All-Star appearances and two World Series wins during his career with the Cincinnati Reds, leading many to consider him among the top players in his position.

A Johnny in your family could even "star" in multiple disciplines, like five-time Olympic gold-medalist swimmer Johnny Weissmuller, who also played Tarzan and Jungle Jim in the movies!

Johnny Bench, Baseball (Catcher), Cincinnati Reds, USA, 1967–1983

John "Johnny" Gaudreau, Ice Hockey (Left Wing), Calgary Flames, USA, 2014–current

John "Johnny" Mize, Baseball (First Baseman), St. Louis Cardinals, USA, 1936–1953

John "Johnny" Unitas, Football (Quarterback), Baltimore Colts, USA, 1955–1973

Johnny Weissmuller, Swimming (Freestyle), USA, 1921–1928

JONATHAN

While it may sound similar to *John*, the name Jonathan comes from a different biblical Hebrew root meaning "God has given." Whether God-given or not, exceptional athletic ability has graced a number of Jonathans. Canadian center Jonathan Toews was called up to six NHL All-Star games and won three Stanley Cups, two Olympic gold medals, and a World Championship; offensive tackle Jonathan Ogden was an eleven-time Pro Bowler and Super Bowl champ during his career with the Baltimore Ravens; and cold weather athlete Jonathan Wyatt of New Zealand ran his way to seven Mountain Running World Cup wins!

Jonathans seem to have a particular penchant for track and field events, with Brazilian World Champion discus thrower Jonathan de Souza Santos; British high jumper Jonathan Broom-Edwards, who took home gold from the 2019 World Championships and 2020 Paralympic Games; and fellow British triple jumper Jonathan Edwards, who has an Olympic gold medal, two World Championships, and set the world record in 1995 that he still holds today.

A Jonathan in your family will enjoy competing (and winning) in the outdoors, whether he's throwing, jumping, playing a team sport, or even running through the ice and snow.

- **Jonathan Broom-Edwards**, Track & Field (High Jump), England, 2013–current
- **Jonathan Edwards**, Track & Field (Triple Jump), England, 1995–2003
- **Jonathan Ogden**, Football (Offensive Tackle), Baltimore Ravens, USA, 1996–2008
- **Jonathan de Souza Santos**, Track & Field (Discus/Shot Put), Brazil, 2008–2015
- **Jonathan Toews**, Ice Hockey (Center), Chicago Blackhawks, Canada, 2007–current
- **Jonathan Wyatt**, Mountain Running, New Zealand, 1994–2009

JORDAN

Jordan comes from a Hebrew root for "flow down" or "descend," which makes sense because it's the name of a river in Israel and a nearby country. Thanks to ancient people making pilgrimages to the river and then naming their sons and daughters after it, there are Jordans all over the world . . . and some of them have made it big in athletics!

American golfer Jordan Spieth has won thirteen times on the PGA Tour; esports veteran Jordan "n0thing" Gilbert has multiple major tournament wins playing *Counter-Strike: Global Offensive*; English soccer midfielder Jordan Henderson has won a FIFA Club World Cup, UEFA Super Cup, and League Cup while scoring forty-one goals in over six hundred senior and international appearances; and freestyle wrestler Jordan Burroughs has brought home an Olympic gold medal, five World Championships, and two World Cup wins for the USA.

You don't have to visit a famous river to name your child Jordan, but if you do, he might take to video games, soccer, wrestling, or more!

- **Jordan Burroughs**, Freestyle Wrestling, USA, 2007–current
- **Jordan "n0thing" Gilbert**, Esports (*Counter-Strike: Global Offensive*), USA, 2008–2019
- **Jordan Henderson**, Soccer (Midfielder), Liverpool Football Club, England, 2008–current
- **Jordan Spieth**, Golf, USA, 2012–current

JOSE/JOSÉ

Depending on your family's background or preference, you may accent your José or not, but either way, it originates as a Spanish and Portuguese variant of *Joseph*. It's no surprise, then, that many champion athletes with this name come from predominantly Spanish-speaking countries, though you can find Joses just about everywhere and in an interesting range of sports. Panamanian-American horse racing jockey Jose Lezcano has racked up over three thousand wins so far in his nearly twenty-year career, and Filipino pool pro Jose Parica has won over one hundred tournaments in multiple countries, making him one of the most renowned nine-ball players of all time.

Some especially tough Josés find their calling in combat sports and are considered among the best ever, like Mexican World Welterweight Champion boxer José Nápoles, who retired with an 81-7 record, while others achieve glory on the soccer field, like Brazilian striker José "Mazzola" Altafini, who scored over three hundred goals in more than six hundred senior and international appearances, had a FIFA World Cup win in 1958, and scored records in multiple series.

Professional baseball brings in stellar talent from all over, and that can be seen in the starting lineup of players with this name. The best of the best include highly decorated Dominican six-time All-Star right fielder, third baseman, and power hitter José Bautista, whose list of awards and career highlights is lengthy; controversial slugger and record setter (and famous steroid user) José Canseco, who also had six All-Star appearances as well as two World Series wins; and Venezuelan eight-time Houston Astros All-Star second baseman José Altuve, whose short stature belies an incredible career with multiple Silver Sluggers, a Gold Glove, Hank Aaron Award, batting championships, stolen base leader rankings, a World Series championship, and much more!

José "Mazzola" Altafini, Soccer (Striker), Associazione Calcio Milan, Brazil, 1956–1980

José Altuve, Baseball (Second Baseman), Houston Astros, Venezuela, 2011–current

José Bautista, Baseball (Right Fielder/Third Baseman), Toronto Blue Jays, Dominican Republic, 2004–2018

José Canseco, Baseball (Outfielder/ Designated Hitter), Oakland Athletics, USA, 1985–2001

Jose Lezcano, Horse Racing (Jockey), USA, 2004–current

José Nápoles, Boxing (Welterweight), Mexico, 1958–1975

Jose Parica, Pool (Nine-Ball), Philippines, 1973–2011

JOSEF

If you like the name *Joseph* but it isn't quite right for you and your family, then consider the international variant Josef. A son you name Josef may excel at things like gymnastics, volleyball, auto racing, canoeing, or soccer, if he is inspired by some of the following champions. Swiss gymnast Josef Stalder revolutionized his sport (creating the stalder circle skill) and has taken home Olympic gold, American IndyCar driver Josef Newgarden has won twenty-five races and two championships, and Czech sprint canoeist Josef Dostál has a huge medal collection that includes four Olympic medals and eleven from World Championships with five wins! Soccer fans are sure to be familiar with Venezuelan striker Josef Martínez, who has had massive success in the United States winning the MLS Cup, US Open Cup, the MLS Golden Boot, MVP, and more, as well as Czechoslovakian Ballon d'Or-winner Josef Masopust, who stands among the greatest midfielders of all time (and was included in the FIFA 100).

Josef Dostál, Sprint Canoeing, Czech Republic, 2012–current

Josef Martínez, Soccer (Striker), Atlanta United Football Club, Venezuela, 2010–current

Josef Masopust, Soccer (Midfielder), Dukla Prague, Czechoslovakia, 1950–1970

Josef Newgarden, Auto Racing (IndyCar), USA, 2005–current

Josef Stalder, Artistic Gymnastics, Switzerland, 1948–1952

JOSEPH

While most successful athletes named Joseph prefer to go by the short form *Joe*, there are a few who kept to the original, which comes from biblical Hebrew meaning "God will increase/add." Not a *Joe* but rather a "Doc," Joseph Alexander was a three-time NFL All-Pro guard in the early 1920s and part of the 1925 NFL champion New York Giants team. Much more recently, esports star Joseph "Mang0" Marquez has established himself as one of the all-time *Super Smash Bros. Melee* greats, with numerous major tournament wins since 2008.

If it seems like a young Joseph in your family prefers to be called by his full name, consider introducing him to football, swimming, or video games!

Joseph "Doc" Alexander, Football (Guard), New York Giants, USA, 1921–1927

Joseph "Mang0" Marquez, Esports (*Super Smash Bros. Melee*), USA, 2007–current

JOSH

The name Josh has traditionally been used as a short form of *Joshua* (or sometimes *Joseph*), though it's increasingly given to children all on its own. Joshes in sports are predominantly Americans in baseball, though there are interesting outliers, like UFC Heavyweight Champion and MMA legend Josh Barnett.

America's pastime is another favorite of Joshes. Pitcher Josh Hader had four All-Star appearances, and three-time Silver Slugger Award-winning outfielder and batting champion Josh Hamilton had five. Back in the 1930s and '40s, Negro leagues catcher Josh Gibson had twelve All-Star selections, two Negro World Series wins, two batting Triple Crowns, nearly eight hundred home runs, and more, leading him to be considered one of the greatest players of his era and still ranking among the best players ever.

If he follows after any of these men, an athletic Josh in your family is likely to enjoy baseball, so make sure to teach him to throw, catch, bat, and run.

Joshua "Josh" Barnett, MMA (Heavyweight), USA, 1997–current

Joshua "Josh" Gibson, Baseball (Catcher), Homestead Grays, USA, 1930–1946

Joshua "Josh" Hader, Baseball (Pitcher), Milwaukee Brewers, USA, 2017–current

Joshua "Josh" Hamilton, Baseball (Outfielder), Texas Rangers, USA, 2007–2015

JOSHUA

*Josh*es may tend toward baseball, but athletes going by the full name Joshua (from biblical Hebrew meaning "God is salvation") are a bit more wide-ranging. Inspire a boy to reach for the brass ring in sport shooting, sprinting, or soccer with the name Joshua and he may take after Irish Olympic gold-medalist shooter Joshua Millner, American World Champion sprinter Joshua Johnson, or German UEFA Super Cup and FIFA Club World Cup–winning defensive midfielder and right-back Joshua Kimmich!

Joshua Johnson, Track & Field (Sprinting), USA, 2001–2004

Joshua Kimmich, Soccer (Defensive Midfielder/Right-Back), Fußball-Club Bayern München e. V., Germany, 2013–current

Joshua Millner, Sport Shooting (Rifle), Ireland, 1908

JUAN

John isn't the only massively popular name descended from the Hebrew *Yochanan* by way of the Latin *Iohannes*, and you don't necessarily need to speak Spanish to pass on the related name Juan. If you do give this name to a son, you're probably going to want to introduce him to soccer, baseball, R/C cars, and video games (with a particular slant toward fighting games). That's especially true if he takes after or finds inspiration in people like Mexican nine-time world champion boxer Juan Manuel Márquez, who held four different weight class championships at once, and American esports champion and Jigglypuff master Juan "Hungrybox" DeBiedma, who has ranked among the top five *Super Smash Bros.* players since 2013.

When it comes to speed, the fastest Juans include Argentinian Formula 1 legend Juan Manuel Fangio, who raced to five championships with twenty-four wins in the 1950s. Then there are Juans who have reached the summit on the baseball diamond and soccer field. Dominican pitcher Juan Marichal threw a no-hitter in 1963 and had ten All-Star appearances, and second baseman Juan Padilla won two Olympic gold medals for Cuba. Last but not least are three flavors of midfielder, with Spanish UEFA European Champion and FIFA World Cup 2010-winner Juan Mata, Olympic gold-medalist and Intercontinental Cup-winner Juan Román Riquelme, and Juan Sebastián Verón, who won a UEFA Cup and UEFA Super Cup on his way to being included in the prestigious FIFA 100 list.

- **Juan "Hungrybox" DeBiedma**, Esports (*Super Smash Bros.*), USA, 2007–current
- **Juan Manuel Fangio**, Auto Racing (Formula 1), Argentina, 1950–1958
- **Juan Marichal**, Baseball (Pitcher), San Francisco Giants, Dominican Republic, 1960–1975
- **Juan Manuel Márquez**, Boxing (Featherweight/Lightweight/Welterweight), Mexico, 1993–2014
- **Juan Mata**, Soccer (Midfielder), Manchester United Football Club, Spain, 2006–current
- **Juan Padilla**, Baseball (Second Baseman), Cuba, 1987–1999
- **Juan Román Riquelme**, Soccer (Midfielder), Club Atlético Boca Juniors, Argentina, 1996–2015
- **Juan Sebastián Verón**, Soccer (Midfielder), Club Estudiantes de La Plata, Argentina, 1994–2017

JULIO

A Spanish evolution of the Roman name *Julius*, Julio is naturally popular around the world among Spanish-speaking communities. On national and international stages, three Julios have charged ahead of their respective packs in three different sports. American seven-time Pro Bowl wide receiver Quintorris "Julio" Jones has set many receiving records, and Brazilian top-ranked soccer goalkeeper Júlio César helped his teams to numerous championships, including a FIFA Club World Cup, Copa América, and two FIFA Confederations Cups, while also winning multiple goalkeeper awards during his 673 appearances. Perhaps best known among sports fans is Julio César Chávez, the Mexican boxer who held world championships in three different weight classes during his career and, with a number of records and a 107-6-2 career, is considered one of the best boxers of all time.

The inspirations are there for a little Julio in your family, so see if he likes football or soccer (and save boxing for later).

- **Júlio César**, Soccer (Goalkeeper), Football Club Internazionale Milano, Brazil, 1997–2018
- **Julio César Chávez**, Boxing (Featherweight/Lightweight/Welterweight), Mexico, 1980–2005
- **Quintorris "Julio" Jones Jr.**, Football (Wide Receiver), Atlanta Falcons, USA, 2011–current

JULIUS

The name Julius stretches way back to ancient Rome, though its origins are unclear and possibly come from a root for "downy-bearded" or relating to the god Jupiter. The latter is an interesting connection to one of the world-class athletes with this name, because like the deity hurled thunderbolts, Kenyan track and field competitor Julius Yego is a world-champion javelin thrower! If you name your kid Julius, he might gravitate toward sports like volleyball, football, or basketball, like Olympic and world champion volleyball player Julius Brink of Germany, nine-time Pro Bowl defensive end Julius Peppers, and, of course, Dr. J himself, eleven-time All-Star and three-time champion Julius Erving, who still holds multiple records and is considered among the greatest players (and especially dunkers) of all time.

Julius Brink, Volleyball (Defender), Germany, 2005–2012

Julius "Dr. J" Erving II, Basketball (Small Forward), Philadelphia 76ers, USA, 1971–1987

Julius Peppers, Football (Defensive End), Carolina Panthers, USA, 2002–2018

Julius Yego, Track & Field (Javelin), Kenya, 2008–current

JUNIOR

Junior has long been a suffix for sons named after their fathers, but it's also a nickname and, in some cases, a name all on its own! A Junior in your family will take after those in sports who were tough and fast, like NASCAR's Junior Johnson, who won fifty races and proved the technique of drafting in the 1950s and '60s; second and third baseman Junior Gilliam, who had three All-Star appearances in the Negro leagues before two in the MLB and four World Series championships playing for the Dodgers; and twelve-time Pro Bowl linebacker and NFL Hall of Famer Junior Seau.

James "Junior" Gilliam, Baseball (Second Baseman/Third Baseman), Brooklyn Dodgers, USA, 1946–1966

Robert "Junior" Johnson Jr., Auto Racing (NASCAR), USA, 1953–1966

Tiaina "Junior" Seau Jr., Football (Linebacker), San Diego Chargers, USA, 1990–2009

JUSTIN

Fairness is key in sports, and Justins are the perfect embodiment of that with their name coming from a Latin root for "just." Justins have concentrated in a trio of sports, while individual exemplars include Canadian NHL All-Star right wing Justin Williams, who won three Stanley Cups and two World Championships; English ten-time PGA Tour event-winner and Olympic gold-medalist golfer Justin Rose; nine-time EVO tournament-winning esports fighting games pro Justin "Jwong" Wong; and American sprinting phenom Justin Gatlin, who raced to five Olympic medals (including one gold), six World Championships, and two World Athletics Relay wins.

Rugby is huge in Australia and New Zealand, so it's no surprise that Justins would succeed in that version of football. Australian center/fullback Justin Hodges won two NRL Premierships with the Sydney Roosters and Brisbane Broncos, while rugby union halfback Justin Marshall of New Zealand was a five-time Super 12 champion and five-time Tri-Nations champion. On the baseball diamond, nine-time All-Star pitcher Justin Verlander has won a World Series, pitched three no-hitters, and more. Lastly, top Justins on the football field have included linebacker Justin Houston, who tied for most career safeties and most safeties in a season while earning four Pro Bowl appearances, and five-time Pro Bowl Baltimore Ravens placekicker and Super Bowl champion Justin Tucker, who holds records for most accurate NFL kicker, longest field goal, and more.

Justin Gatlin, Track & Field (Sprinting), USA, 2003–2020

- **Justin Hodges**, Rugby (Center/Fallback), Brisbane Broncos, Australia, 2000–2015
- **Justin Houston**, Football (Linebacker), Kansas City Chiefs, USA, 2011–current
- **Justin Marshall**, Rugby (Halfback), Crusaders, New Zealand, 1995–2010
- **Justin Rose**, Golf, England, 1998–current
- **Justin Tucker**, Football (Placekicker), Baltimore Ravens, USA, 2012–current
- **Justin Verlander**, Baseball (Pitcher), Detroit Tigers, USA, 2005–current
- **Justin Williams**, Ice Hockey (Right Wing), Los Angeles Kings, Canada, 2000–2020
- **Justin "Jwong" Wong**, Esports (Fighting Games), USA, 2003–current

GIRLS

JACKIE/JACQUELINE/JACQUIE

Like *James*, Jacqueline (and its most common nicknames Jackie and Jacquie) is descended from the Latin *Iacobus* and, ultimately, the biblical Hebrew name *Jacob*. When it comes to competitive women with these names, speed is the name of the game. American cyclist Jacquie Phelan dominated cyclo-cross in the 1980s and helped popularize women's mountain biking, Jacqueline "Jacka" Lölling has taken home three skeleton world championships to her home country Germany, and Australian swimmer Jacqueline "Jacqui" Freney has raced to a record eight Paralympic gold medals in one Games.

Probably the most famous Jackie in the world of athletics is American track and field competitor Jackie Joyner-Kersee, who captivated audiences everywhere with her heptathlon and long jump appearances at the Olympics. Her medal count includes three Olympic golds, a silver, and two bronzes, as well as four world championships, and more. In fact, Joyner-Kersee still holds the world record for the heptathlon!

Name a daughter Jacqueline or call her the unisex Jackie and she's sure to be a fast kid; introduce her to a wide range of sports and she's sure to go far.

- **Jacqueline "Jacqui" Freney**, Swimming (Backstroke/Freestyle/Medley), Australia, 2008–2016
- **Jacqueline "Jackie" Joyner-Kersee**, Track & Field (Heptathlon/Long Jump), USA, 1984–2000

Jacqueline "Jacka" Lölling, Skeleton, Germany, 2009–current

Jacquie Phelan, Cyclo-Cross, USA, 1982–2009

JAIME/JAMIE/JAYME

Whether you spell it Jaime, Jamie, or Jayme, a name in this family that you give to a little girl will inspire her to heights of achievement, and she'll have some pretty amazing inspirations to follow. American water polo goalkeeper Jaime Komer won two team world championships, Jayme Richardson has ridden to three world championships, and Canadian Jamie Salé won gold in figure skating at the Olympics, World Championships, Grand Prix Finals, and more. When the international women's auto racing W Series began in 2019, British Jamie Chadwick was the inaugural champion, and she's since raised her stats to eleven wins and two championships, while over on the slopes American slopestyle snowboarder Jamie Anderson has two Olympic gold medals and a massive haul from the Winter X Games, including eight wins.

Jamie Anderson, Snowboarding, USA, 2004–current

Jamie Chadwick, Auto Racing (W Series), England, 2013–current

Jaime Komer, Water Polo (Goalkeeper), USA, 2005–2009

Jayme Richardson, Para-Cycling, Australia, 2008–2014

Jamie Salé, Figure Skating, Canada, 1994–2002

JAN

Unlike the masculine form of *Jan* that comes from the same root as *John*, the feminine version is most often a short form for names like *Janet* and *Janice*. In the world of powerlifting, this name means incredible strength and determination. Janice "Jan" Todd began lifting in 1973 and, in her competitive career, which started in 1975, broke or set sixty national and world records! The *Guinness Book of World Records*–named "strongest woman in the world" also became the first woman to lift the Dinnie Stones in Scotland, and she'd remain the only one to do so until 2018. A Jan in your family will naturally be strong and competitive, but also smart and academic, just like Todd, who got her PhD and became a professor of kinesiology and health education.

Janice "Jan" Todd, Powerlifting, USA, 1975–1996

JANE/JAYNE

The family of names derived from the biblical Hebrew *Yochanan* is expansive, and one branch produced both *John* and Jane (via the Old French *Jehanne*). Some Janes are all about endurance and pacing themselves, like Estonian long-distance runner Jane Salumäe, whose marathon wins include Rome, Monaco, Los Angeles, and Vienna, while others focus on speed and teamwork, like American freestyle swimmer Jane Barkman, who twice won Olympic gold in the 4x100-meter relay, setting records both times. There are also some interesting variations on the name, like Jayne, which can inspire grace and perfection as it did with British ice dancer Jayne Torvill, who won four world championships, as well as an Olympic gold medal with perfect scores.

Jane Barkman, Swimming (Freestyle), USA, 1968–1972

Jane Salumäe, Long-Distance Running, Estonia, 1994–2004

Jayne Torvill, Ice Dancing, England, 1971–1994

JANET

Medieval English gave us the name Janet as a nickname for *Jane*, though both are considered a bit old-fashioned these days. Three Janets made sports headlines in the second half of the twentieth century, with Janet Watt of New Zealand winning gold in badminton at the Deaflympics, auto racing pioneer Janet Guthrie becoming the first woman to compete in the Indianapolis 500 and Daytona 500 and to lead a lap in NASCAR's premier series, and freestyle swimmer Janet Evans taking home four gold medals at the Olympic Games, five world championships, and multiple world records.

Whether in the pool, on the track, or over a net, a child you name Janet will have the will and skill to succeed.

Janet Evans, Swimming (Freestyle), USA, 1987–1994

Janet Guthrie, Auto Racing (NASCAR), USA, 1976–1980

Janet Watt, Badminton, New Zealand, 1985

JANICA

Does your family like winter sports, going fast, and unique names that start with "J"? Then Janica might be perfect for your daughter! Ultimately from the same origin as *John* in biblical Hebrew for "God is gracious," Janica has appeared as a Croatian and Slovene diminutive of *Jana*, a Finnish variant of *Janika*, and more. The world was introduced to the name in the late 1990s by Croatian alpine ski racer Janica Kostelić, a mighty force on the slopes who set numerous records on the way to winning four gold medals and two silvers at the Olympics, five world championships, and no fewer than thirty golds, sixteen silvers, and nine bronzes at World Cup events, including three overall titles and seven discipline titles.

Janica Kostelić, Alpine Ski Racing, Croatia, 1998–2007

JAYNA

An uncommon variation of *Jane*, the name Jayna carries a fierce determination, endurance, and a love of competing in the cold. That's especially true if a girl takes after Canadian ice hockey right wing Jayna Hefford! Hefford had a tremendous career in the National Women's Hockey League and Canadian Women's Hockey League, but she's best known for her international play; as part of the Canadian team, she won a 4 Nations Cup, seven world championships, and four Olympic gold medals . . . in four successive Olympic Games from 2002 to 2014!

Jayna Hefford, Ice Hockey (Right Wing), Brampton Thunder, Canada, 1996–2014

JEAN

The next Medieval English name in the *Jane* family is Jean, which can take a girl to any heights she should choose. British ice dancer Jean Westwood made a clean sweep of gold medals at four successive world championships (1952–1955), and American wheelchair racer Jean Driscoll has a collection of twelve medals from Paralympic Games (including five golds) in different events and eight wins at the Boston Marathon. If you're a fan of America's pastime you may be familiar with Jean Faut, a four-time All-Star pitcher in the All-American Professional Baseball League who won two championships, threw two perfect games and two no-hitters, and set numerous records on her way to being ranked among the best players in the league.

Jean Driscoll, Wheelchair Racing, USA, 1988–2000

Jean Faut, Baseball (Pitcher), South Bend Blue Sox, USA, 1946–1953

Jean Westwood, Ice Dancing, England, 1951–1955

JEANETTE

Jeannettes are calculating and precise, able to hit exact marks and wow their audiences. Jeannette Stewart-Wood of the UK was the 1967 water skiing World Champion, culminating a career of top marks in slalom and jumping, and Jeanette "Black Widow" Lee has won dozens of pool championships and a gold medal at the World Games to become the top-ranked female player in the 1990s.

Jeanette "Black Widow" Lee, Pool (Nine-Ball), USA, 1989–current

Jeannette Stewart-Wood, Water Skiing, England, 1963–1968

JELENA

A variant of the name *Yelena* across Eastern Europe, Jelena has strong roots in Lithuania, Croatia, Serbia, and Slovenia, where it has become popularly linked to similar-sounding Slavic words meaning "deer" and "fir tree." Top-tier athletes named Jelena have competed in places where you're not likely to see either fir trees or deer, from tennis courts (where Serbian Jelena Janković reached the world number one singles spot and won fifteen titles) to the streets of New York City (where Latvian long-distance runner Jeļena Prokopčuka won the New York Marathon twice) and even the boxing ring (where Canadian pugilist Jelena Mrdjenovich has won more than forty bouts and held multiple world championship titles in three different weight classes!).

If a young Jelena in your family loves to be out in nature, that's great; on the other hand, she may prefer city running, tennis, or even martial arts.

Jelena Janković, Tennis, Serbia, 2000–2022

Jelena Mrdjenovich, Boxing (Featherweight/Lightweight), Canada, 2003–current

Jeļena Prokopčuka, Long-Distance Running, Latvia, 2000–2016

JENNIE/JENNY

While most people think of Jenny as a diminutive of *Jennifer*, the name actually came about as a nickname for *Jane*, and originally the more popular spelling was Jennie. Nowadays, Jenny has taken the lead and can stand on its own, but we see athletes with both of these versions reaching the pinnacles of their respective disciplines. Cyclist Jennie Reed has numerous World Cup wins and a keirin world championship; German speed skater Jenny Wolf set speed records on her way to winning a World Sprint Championship and four World Single Distance Championships; Australian four-time Women's National Basketball League All-Star center and two-time champion Jenny Whittle brought home a World Cup with her national team; and softball pitcher and Olympic gold-medalist Jennie Finch crushed the competition in National Pro Fastpitch with a perfect season, two perfect games, multiple records, and more.

There have been two American swimming champions with the name Jenny: Kemp, who won Olympic gold in 1972, and Thompson, who broke almost half-a-dozen world records and took home twelve Olympic medals (eight of them gold) and thirty-two from World Championships (including eighteen wins).

A girl you name Jenny (or Jennie) can do it all, but definitely teach her how to swim.

Jennie Finch, Softball (Pitcher), Chicago Bandits, USA, 2004–2010

Jennifer "Jenny" Kemp, Swimming (Backstroke/Freestyle), USA, 1972–1975

Jennie Reed, Track Cycling, USA, 1998–2011

Jennifer "Jenny" Thompson, Swimming (Butterfly/Freestyle), USA, 1987–2004

Jennifer "Jenny" Whittle, Basketball (Center), Brisbane Blazers, Australia, 1994–2006

Jenny Wolf, Speed Skating, Germany, 2002–2011

JENNIFER

With a name that comes from the same Welsh roots for "white phantom" as *Guinevere* of King Arthur fame, a plucky young Jennifer in your family is likely to enjoy running around outdoors and playing physical team sports. This is especially true if she's inspired to compete by champion athletes with that name who have come before, and there have been many! Softball shortstop Jennifer McFalls was an Olympic gold-medalist, Scottish curler Jennifer Dodds has taken home Olympic gold and a World Mixed Doubles Championship, and Jennifer Hermoso is the all-time highest-scoring soccer player for Barcelona and Spain, with over 240 goals in her over 350 senior and international appearances.

Jennifer Suhr reached the rank of number one pole vaulter in the world with a win each at Olympic Games and World Championships, water skier Jennifer Calleri-Schwenk won four consecutive overall Barefoot Water Ski World Championships, Canadian Jennifer Heil preferred the cold with Olympic gold and four world championships in moguls skiing, and Canadian Women's Hockey League All-Star forward Jennifer Botterill won gold at three Olympic Games and five World Championships with her national team. But for many, the name Jennifer in athletics will bring to mind tennis singles superstar Capriati, who ranked number one in the world with three Grand Slam wins, fourteen career titles, and an Olympic gold medal.

Jennifer Botterill, Ice Hockey (Forward), Mississauga Chiefs, Canada, 1997–2011

Jennifer Calleri-Schwenk, Water Skiing, USA, 1978–1996

Jennifer Capriati, Tennis, USA, 1990–2004

Jennifer "Jenn" Dodds, Curling (Third), Scotland, 2011–current

Jennifer Heil, Skiing (Moguls), Canada, 2002–2011

Jennifer Hermoso, Soccer (False 9/Attacking Midfielder), Fútbol Club Barcelona Femení, Spain, 2004–current

Jennifer McFalls, Softball (Shortstop), USA, 1996–2000

Jennifer "Jenn" Suhr, Track & Field (Pole Vaulting), USA, 2004–2022

JESSI/JESSIE

Jessi and Jessie originated as diminutives of *Jean*, *Jessica*, and other "J" names, though they can certainly be used on their own as well. If you're looking to name a child Jessi or Jessie, consider getting her ice skates or R/C cars if she takes inspiration from people like Jessi Combs and Jessie Vetter. Combs was an off-road auto racing champion and women's land speed record-breaker, while ice hockey goaltender Vetter won six world championships with the US women's team.

Jessi Combs, Auto Racing (Off-Road), USA, 2011–2019

Jessica "Jessie" Vetter, Ice Hockey (Goaltender), Minnesota Whitecaps, USA, 2006–current

JESSICA

The exact origins of the name Jessica are unknown, though theories include Hebrew roots meaning either "gift," "wealthy," or "to behold." Regardless of where it comes from, Jessica is a marvelous moniker that's seen usage by some very cool athletes in the United States and elsewhere. ESPN sportscaster Jessica Mendoza was a National Pro Fastpitch softball league champion outfielder and Olympic gold-medalist; Brazilian mixed martial artist and Jiu-Jitsu black belt Jéssica Andrade held the UFC Women's Strawweight championship; Britain's Jessica Ennis-Hill took home Olympic gold in the heptathlon, as well as World Championships in that event and the pentathlon; and American soccer forward Jessica McDonald was part of teams winning two National Women's Soccer League Championships and the 2019 FIFA Women's World Cup.

Italian trap shooting markswoman Jessica Rossi hit the bullseye on an Olympic gold medal, four World Championships, two World Cups, and more; Australian canoeist Jessica Fox became the most decorated world champion in her sport with twelve wins (as well as an Olympic gold medal); and American swimmer Jessica Long has a staggering medal count of fifty-one golds, twenty-three silvers, and seven bronzes across Paralympic Games and World Championships thus far!

There are a lot of events that Jessicas have dominated, and a girl with this name in your family may find success in the pool, on the field or track, or even in the ring.

Jéssica Andrade, MMA (Strawweight/Flyweight/Bantamweight), Brazil, 2011-current

Jessica Ennis-Hill, Track & Field (Heptathlon/Pentathlon), England, 2004-2016

Jessica "Jess" Fox, Slalom Canoeing, Australia, 2009-current

Jessica Long, Swimming (Backstroke/Breaststroke/Butterfly/Freestyle), USA, 2004-current

Jessica McDonald, Soccer (Forward), North Carolina Courage, USA, 2010-current

Jessica Mendoza, Softball (Outfielder), USSSA Pride, USA, 2004-2012

Jessica Rossi, Sport Shooting (Trap), Italy, 2008-current

JILL

Jill is a direct descendent of *Gillian*, a medieval English name based on *Julian*, which in turn reaches back to the Roman *Julius*. There is uncertainty as to the roots of that name, with one possibility being a reference to the god Jupiter. If that is the case, Jill Mills is a great modern paragon of divine strength; she was the 2003 World Powerlifting champion and twice-crowned World's Strongest Woman! Trading some strength for speed is American Olympic gold-medalist bobsledder Jill Bakken.

No matter what sport or athletic endeavors she pursues, a Jill in your family will carry on this legacy with strength, speed, and grace.

Jill Bakken, Bobsled, USA, 1994-current

Jill Mills, Powerlifting, USA, 1995-2005

JOAN

Another descendent of the *John* family of names through the feminine form *Joanna*, Joan is now seen as old-fashioned, but it's ready for a comeback with your daughter. This is especially true if she enjoys running or hitting balls, like distance runner Joan Benoit, who has won numerous marathons (including the first Boston Marathon) and set records in her incredibly long career, or legendary softball pitcher Joan Joyce, who was an eighteen-time ASA National Women's Major Fastpitch All-Star and twelve-time champion, set numerous pitching and hitting records that still stand today, and even struck out both Ted Williams and Hank Aaron!

Joan Benoit, Long-Distance Running, USA, 1979-2019

Joan Joyce, Softball (Pitcher), Raybestos Brakettes, USA, 1954-1975

JOANE/JOANNE

Another *Yochanan*-based name is Joane/JoAnne, ideally suited for a girl who likes riding her bicycle or hitting balls on the links. Spanish cyclist Joane Somarriba took home one of each color medal from the Road World Championships, while American golf icon JoAnne Carner won forty-three LPGA Tour events and was inducted into the World Golf Hall of Fame.

JoAnne Carner, Golf, USA, 1970–1992

Joane Somarriba, Road Cycling, Spain, 1988–2005

JOANNA/JOHANNA

Through Latin and Greek, and ultimately from the biblical Hebrew *Yochanan*, meaning "god is gracious," come the two forms of Joanna and Johanna, which are mainly popular in Western Europe. This versatile and pretty name may be best for a runner, like Olympic gold-medalist hurdlers Joanna Hayes and Johanna Klier of Germany; a cyclist who follows in the pedals of English five-time World Champion and record-setting two-time Olympic gold-medalist Joanna Rowsell; or a tough fighter, like top-ranked kickboxer and MMA star Joanna Jędrzejczyk of Poland, who won five World Muay Thai Championships and was the UFC Women's Strawweight title holder.

If you're a fan of nicknames, then Johanna may be perfect for you because Olympic gold medalists with that name in the Netherlands go by lots of them! There's World Cup champion field hockey defender Johanna "Janneke" Schopman, speed skater Johanna "Ans" Schut, and freestyle swimmer Johanna "Jopie" Selbach. But even without a nickname, Johanna Sjöberg of Sweden won five World Championships in the pool.

Joanna Hayes, Track & Field (Hurdling), USA, 1999–2014

Joanna Jędrzejczyk, MMA/Kickboxing (Bantamweight/Featherweight/Strawweight/Flyweight), Poland, 2012–2022

Johanna Klier, Track & Field (Hurdling), Germany, 1976–1980

Joanna Rowsell, Road/Track Cycling, England, 2006–2017

Johanna "Janneke" Schopman, Field Hockey (Defender), Netherlands, 2001–2010

Johanna "Ans" Schut, Speed Skating, Netherlands, 1968–1971

Johanna "Jopie" Selbach, Swimming (Freestyle), Netherlands, 1934–1936

Johanna Sjöberg, Swimming (Butterfly/Freestyle), Sweden, 1995–2005

JODIE

Jodie is a unisex name that came about as a diminutive of "J" names like *Judy*, *Judit/Judith*, and *Joseph*. Jodies have found particular success in some European team sports and in the water, with champion athletes like Australians Jodie Cooper, who won thirteen international surfing events; iconic cricket captain Jodie Fields, who took her national team to both the ICC Women's World Twenty20 and the ICC Women's World Cup within a matter of months; and freestyle swimmer Jodie Henry, whose medal haul included three golds from the Olympics and five world championships.

Jodie Cooper, Surfing, Australia, 1983–2002

Jodie Fields, Cricket (Wicketkeeper/Batter), Queensland Women Cricket Team, Australia, 2001–2017

Jodie Henry, Swimming (Freestyle), Australia, 2002–2009

JORDAN/JORDIN/JORDYN

Jordan is a unisex name popular around the world thanks to pilgrims naming their children after the river with that name in Israel, while the feminine version has some interesting variants in spellings with Jordin and Jordyn. Most of the highly successful athletes with these names come from the United States, with the notable exception of Canada Women's National Soccer Team forward and Olympic gold-medalist Jordyn Huitema. Point guard Jordin Canada won two WNBA Championships with the Seattle Storm; volleyball setter Jordyn Poulter captured Olympic gold; outside hitter Jordan Larson has volleyball wins at the Olympics, World Championships, and World Grand

Prix; and two-time world champion and three-time World Cup-winner "Fierce Five" gymnast Jordyn Wieber won gold with her team at the 2012 Summer Olympics.

Whichever version of the name Jordan you prefer, a young athlete in your family with it has a good chance to excel as a team player in indoor events like basketball, gymnastics, or volleyball.

Jordin Canada, Basketball (Point Guard), Seattle Storm, USA, 2018–current

Jordyn Huitema, Soccer (Forward), Paris Saint-Germain Féminine, Canada, 2018–current

Jordan Larson, Volleyball (Outside Hitter), USA, 2009–2020

Jordyn Poulter, Volleyball (Setter), USA, 2013–current

Jordyn Wieber, Artistic Gymnastics, USA, 2011–2015

JOSEFINA/JOSEPHINE

There are many variants in various languages of the name *Joseph*, and the feminine ones include Josefina and Josephine. Any of these beautiful names would be a good pick for an active daughter who likes to run around outside, ride a bicycle, or swim, especially if she takes inspiration from such competitors as Australian two-time world champion track cyclist Josephine "Josie" Tomic; Mexican multi-discipline athlete Josefina Cornejo, who won eight Paralympics gold medals in various fields, including pentathlon and throwing events; and four-time Champions Trophy-winning field hockey forward Josefina Sruoga of Argentina.

Josefina Cornejo, Para-Athletics/Swimming (Backstroke/Freestyle), Mexico, 1976–1980

Josefina Sruoga, Field Hockey (Forward), Argentina, 2009–2015

Josephine "Josie" Tomic, Track Cycling, Australia, 2004–2012

JOY

All children are a joy, and some are even named that! A Joy in your family can strive to be like American soccer star Joy Fawcett, the United States Women's National Soccer Team's highest-scoring defender and winner of two Olympic gold medals and two FIFA Women's World Cups.

Joy Fawcett, Soccer (Defender), San Diego Spirit, USA, 1987–2004

JOYCE

While Joyce may include "joy," it does not come from the same source as that name but rather a convoluted path through Old French and Latin to an ancient Breton name meaning "lord." Some Joyces love going long distances, like Australian cyclist Joyce Barry, who set numerous records in the 1930s, and multiple marathon-winning Joyce Chepchumba of Kenya; and others are all about the surf and sun, like surfing pioneer Joyce Hoffman, who had numerous firsts for women in her field and was a US and World Champion!

Joyce Barry, Road/Track Cycling, Australia, 1936–1938

Joyce Chepchumba, Long-Distance Running, Kenya, 1995–2004

Joyce Hoffman, Surfing, USA, 1964–1971

JUDIT/JUDITH

The Tribe of Judah in biblical Hebrew is the source of the name Judith, as well as its alternate form Judit. Women with these names have been true inspirations, competing at the top levels of their chosen events, such as swimmers like Hungarian Olympic freestyle gold-medalist Judit Temes and Australian Judith Young, who won twelve medals from Paralympic Games and six from World Championships and Games for the Disabled (two golds at each).

Other Judits and Judiths have excelled at everything from rowing (like eight-time Olympic gold-medalist and world champion Judith Zeidler) to cycling (like Judith Arndt of Germany, who won three gold medals, three silvers, and three bronzes from Road World Championships and a gold, four silvers, and a bronze from Track World Championships), orienteering (like Swiss four-time world champion and World Games gold-medalist Judith Wyder), and long-distance running (like Judit Földing-Nagy of Hungary, who won marathons in Paris, Lisbon, Monaco, and Reims).

If a Judit or Judith in your family is less physical and more into mental exercises, she can find the ultimate inspiration in Hungarian chess legend Judit Polgár! Polgár broke the record for the youngest person to achieve the rank of Grandmaster and went on to become the youngest player in the FIDE top 100, the only woman to reach the top ten players in the world, the world's top-ranked woman from 1989 to 2014, the winner of numerous tournaments and matches against other top players, and an inductee into the World Chess Hall of Fame.

- **Judith Arndt**, Road/Track Cycling, Germany, 1995–2012
- **Judit Földing-Nagy**, Marathon, Hungary, 1990–2012
- **Judit Polgár**, Chess, Hungary, 1986–2014
- **Judit Temes**, Swimming (Freestyle), Hungary, 1952–1954
- **Judith Wyder**, Orienteering, Switzerland, 2011–current
- **Judith Young**, Swimming (Backstroke/Breaststroke/Freestyle), Australia, 1988–1996
- **Judith Zeidler**, Rowing, Germany, 1988–1992

JUDY

A very common English diminutive of *Judith*, Judy has a competitive power all its own and has reached international podiums for a variety of events. Canadian Judy Diduck's defense on the ice helped her national teams to four ice hockey world championships and a ringette world championship, and British pilot Jude Leden won two hang gliding world championships, a paragliding world championship, and multiple records, including becoming the first woman to hang glide over the English Channel.

Judys have excelled at a couple of very different types of events. The strongest women with this name include English three-time world champion powerlifter Judy Oakes. Meanwhile, golf has seen not one but two five-time professional event winners with Judy Dickinson and Judy Kimball (who won the 1962 LPGA Championship), as well as the iconic World Golf Hall of Famer Judy Rankin, who won twenty-eight events!

Watch out for any interest a young Judy in your family may show in lifting weights or playing golf, but let her explore all kinds of athletic and competitive avenues to find her favorite; she may like swimming, ice hockey, or even hang gliding!

- **Judy Dickinson**, Golf, USA, 1977–2000
- **Judy Diduck**, Ringette/Ice Hockey (Defense), Edmonton Chimos, Canada, 1990–1998
- **Judy Kimball**, Golf, USA, 1961–1988
- **Judy Leden**, Hang Gliding/Paragliding, England, 1982–current
- **Judy Oakes**, Powerlifting/Weightlifting/Shot Put, England, 1978–2000
- **Judy Rankin**, Golf, USA, 1962–1983

JULIA

Fast moving and faster reflexes seem to be the birthright of women named Julia, a feminine variant of the Roman *Julius*, which may come from a root for "downy bearded" or from the god Jupiter. Swedish esports champ Julia "juliano" Kiran switched from a successful *Counter-Strike* run to embark on a career playing *Valorant*, American Julia Mancuso skied to Olympic gold, and Julia Wilson of Australia is a two-time rowing world champion.

Julia "juliano" Kiran, Esports (*Counter-Strike/ Valorant*), Sweden, 2010–current

Julia Mancuso, Alpine Skiing, USA, 1999–2016

Julia Wilson, Rowing, Australia, 1999–2004

JULIANA/JULIANNA

Another set of variations on the *Julius* theme are the names Juliana and Julianna. There are definitely trends in the sports that women with these names have succeeded in, which may map to what a Juliana or Julianna in your family will enjoy doing. Other than Brazil's volleyball world champion Juliana Silva, it's fight or ride. In the MMA octagon, Brazilian Juliana Velasquez was the Bellator Women's Flyweight World Champion and has a 12–1 record, while Ultimate Fighter Julianna Peña was the UFC Women's Bantamweight Champion. On two wheels, American Juliana "Juli" Furtado is a three-time mountain biking world champion, and British-German Juliana Buhring is an ultra-endurance cyclist who has set multiple records, including the fastest global circumnavigation by a woman!

Juliana Buhring, Ultra-Endurance Cycling, Germany/England, 2012–current

Juliana "Juli" Furtado, Road/Mountain Cycling, USA, 1989–1996

Juliana Silva, Beach Volleyball, Brazil, 2005–2015

Julianna Peña, MMA (Bantamweight), USA, 2009–current

Juliana Velasquez, MMA (Flyweight), Brazil, 2014–current

JULIE

Like *Juliana/Julianna*, Julie is another variant of the Roman name *Julius* and has uncertain origins. Julies in athletics have made big strides in several disparate areas. Sharpshooter Julie Golob is an IPSC Handgun World Shoot winner, visually impaired Canadian para-cyclist Julie Cournoyer won two medals of each color at the Paralympic Games, and American ice hockey forward Julie Chu has a huge medal collection, including five wins and four second place rankings in World Championships, and three golds and seven silvers in the 4 Nations Cup.

Finally, the United States Women's National Soccer Team has a strong tradition of excellence, and not one but two Julies have been prominent members of that illustrious group. Midfielder Julie Foudy's soccer career from 1988 to 2004 included two Olympic Games wins and two FIFA Women's World Cup championships, while Julie Ertz, who plays in both midfielder and defender positions, also has two FIFA Women's World Cup wins!

I can't guarantee that a girl you name Julie will set records playing in professional sports, or win major international events as a soccer star, but she will have the tenacity and drive to succeed in whatever field she chooses.

Julie Chu, Ice Hockey (Forward), Montreal Stars, USA, 1999–2017

Julie Cournoyer, Para-Cycling, Canada, 1996–2002

Julie Ertz, Soccer (Midfielder/Defender), Chicago Red Stars, USA, 2013–current

Julie Foudy, Soccer (Midfielder), San Diego Spirit, USA, 1988–2004

Julie Golob, Sport Shooting (Handgun), USA, 1999–current

JUSTINE

From a Latin root meaning "just" (as in "fair") comes the name Justine, and two athletes have become inspirations for anyone else given this classic moniker. Canadian moguls skier Justine Dufour-Lapointe has made history multiple times with achievements at young ages, including a World Cup win, Olympic gold, and a world championship. And on the tennis court, Justine Henin of Belgium is known for her signature one-handed backhand and has reached the world number one ranking with forty-three singles titles, winning seven Grand Slams and an Olympic gold medal.

Justine Dufour-Lapointe, Freestyle Skiing, Canada, 2010–current

Justine Henin, Tennis, Belgium, 1999–2011

K

BOYS

KAI

Kai is a very interesting name, used for both boys and girls in a variety of cultures: in Hawaiian, it comes from a root for "sea"; in Chinese, it can mean such inspirational concepts as "triumph" and "victory"; and in Western Europe, uncertain sources have led to its popularity. Just as the sources and meanings for Kai are so varied, so, too, are the sports in which Kais have excelled over the years. These range from bouldering to para-athletics, as evidenced by Kai Harada of Japan and gold-medalist Zong Kai of China, respectively.

Kai Verbij of the Netherlands has skated to a World Sprint Championships win and four gold medals at the World Single Distance Championships, Chinese synchro and springboard diver Qin Kai won two gold medals at the Olympics and seven at World Championships, and artistic gymnast Zou Kai (also from China) set records with his massive medal haul, including five golds and a bronze at the Olympics and five golds and two silvers at World Championships.

A young Kai in your family may find success in a field that surprises you!

- **Kai Harada**, Rock Climbing, Japan, 2017–current
- **Qin Kai**, Diving, China, 2006–2016
- **Kai Verbij**, Speed Skating, Netherlands, 2011–current
- **Zong Kai**, Para-Athletics, China, 2008
- **Zou Kai**, Artistic Gymnastics, China, 2006–2014

KAREEM

Whether you prefer the spelling Kareem or Karim, the classic Arabic name comes from a root meaning "generous" and "noble." Athletes with this name have made a mark on soccer, football, and equestrian events, but one rises above them all—of course we're talking about basketball legend Kareem Abdul-Jabbar! One of the greatest players of all time, Abdul-Jabbar played center for twenty seasons with the Milwaukee Bucks and Los Angeles Lakers, and during that time racked up nineteen All-Star appearances, six NBA Championships, and numerous awards, accolades, and records. In fact, he still holds NBA records for all-time points scored, successful field goals, and career wins! Outside of the game, the skyhook virtuoso has also been a martial artist, actor, author, activist, and more.

Name your child Kareem (or Karim) and he, too, will be a "noble" champion on and off the court.

Kareem Abdul, Basketball (Center), Los Angeles Lakers, USA, 1969–1989

KARL

The name *Carl* comes from a Germanic root for "free man" by way of *Charles*, and Karl with a "K" is a popular German and Scandinavian variant. Successful Karls in sports tend to be hard-hitting and exceedingly accurate, attributes that may be shared by a young Karl in your family. Soccer stars from Germany include FIFA World Cup–winning striker Karl-Heinz Riedle, and forward Karl-Heinz Rummenigge, who in 688 club and international appearances won an Intercontinental Cup, UEFA European Championship, a spot on the FIFA 100, and two Ballon d'Or awards. Austrian figure skater Karl Schäfer took home two Olympic gold medals and seven World Championship wins, while Swiss sharpshooter Karl Zimmermann amassed an incredible thirty World Championships (along with seventeen second place finishes and twenty thirds). Probably the most famous Karl in the United States is "the Mailman," NBA power forward Karl Malone. Playing most of his career with the Utah Jazz, Malone was a fourteen-time All-Star and two-time Olympic gold-medalist, and his numerous career stats and records (including the most free throws shot and made, and third in all-time scoring) have him firmly on lists of all-time best players.

Karl "The Mailman" Malone, Basketball (Power Forward), Utah Jazz, USA, 1985–2004

Karl-Heinz Riedle, Soccer (Striker), Werder Bremen, Germany, 1983–2001

Karl-Heinz "Kalle" Rummenigge, Soccer (Forward), Bayern Munich, Germany, 1974–1989

Karl Schäfer, Figure Skating, Austria, 1927–1936

Karl Zimmermann, Sport Shooting, Switzerland, 1921–1947

KELLY

Based on an old Irish name, the unisex Kelly may come from roots from "bright-headed," "war/strife," or "church." Kelly Slater is often hailed as the king of surfing, having won major events all around the world. A winner of three Triple Crowns of Surfing and two X Games gold medals, Slater's fifty-six wins on the World Surf League Championship Tour earned him eleven championships.

Name a child Kelly and bring him (or her!) to the beach early!

Robert Kelly Slater, Surfing, USA, 1989–current

KEN

Ken most often shows up as a short form of the Irish-based *Kenneth*, but it can also be a diminutive of other names with "Ken" in them, and in Japan, it's a popular name that can be written with characters meaning "healthy" or "strong." Just as its origins are varied, so, too, are the places where Kens have made a name for themselves, like snooker (twenty-four-time tournament-winner and 1997 World Champion Doherty of Ireland) and esports ("LiquidKen" Hoang, who has dominated the *Super Smash Bros. Melee* scene and is considered one of its best ever players).

In more mainstream events, MMA legend Ken Shamrock helped popularize the discipline and was the first UFC Superfight Champion; Canadian ice hockey goaltender Ken Dryden was a five-time All-Star and six-time Stanley Cup-winner with the Montreal Canadiens; Australian Ken Rosewall reached the world tennis singles number one spot with twenty-three wins at Majors, eight Grand Slams, fifteen Pro Slams, and more; and Ken Norton, one of the few competitors to defeat

Muhammad Ali, is remembered as one of the greatest heavyweight boxers of all time!

Meanwhile, there's a particular concentration of Kens in baseball! Those with three All-Star appearances include Silver Slugger third baseman Ken Caminiti, World Series champion right fielder and designated hitter Ken Singleton, and outfielder Ken Griffey Sr., who won two World Series. Of course, they're all overshadowed by the latter's son; Hall of Fame center fielder Ken Griffey Jr. was selected to the All-Star game thirteen times in his twenty-two seasons, took home seven Silver Sluggers and ten Gold Gloves, and still stands high in the rankings of home run hitters.

Ken is a fun name on its own and a perfect short form for a bunch of names, and it's perfect for a kid who will have athletic tendencies and who may just follow in the footsteps of his father (and exceed them!).

- **Kenneth "Ken" Caminiti**, Baseball (Third Baseman), San Diego Padres, USA, 1987–2001
- **Ken Doherty**, Snooker, Ireland, 1990–current
- **Kenneth "Ken" Dryden**, Ice Hockey (Goaltender), Montreal Canadiens, Canada, 1970–1979
- **George Kenneth "Ken" Griffey Jr.**, Baseball (Center Fielder), Seattle Mariner, USA, 1989–2010
- **George Kenneth "Ken" Griffey Sr.**, Baseball (Outfielder), Cincinnati Reds, USA, 1973–1991
- **Ken "LiquidKen" Hoang**, Esports (*Super Smash Bros. Melee*), USA, 2003–current
- **Kenneth "Ken" Norton Sr.**, Boxing (Heavyweight), USA, 1967–1981
- **Kenneth "Ken" Rosewall**, Tennis, Australia, 1956–1980
- **Kenneth "Ken" Shamrock**, MMA (Heavyweight), USA, 1993–2016
- **Kenneth "Ken" Singleton**, Baseball (Right Fielder), Baltimore Orioles, USA, 1970–1984

KENNY

Kennys are almost universally diminutives of *Kenneths*, and they bring the competitive among them to some of the same areas we saw with *Kens*. Drag racer Kenny "Bud King" Bernstein had a colorful career with six NHRA championships and the distinction of being the first driver in that series to break the three hundred miles per hour mark. A Kenny in your family may have a similar need for speed, especially if he inherits it from his dad like Kenny Roberts Jr., whose eight wins and a championship in Grand Prix motorcycle racing came after watching his dad win twenty-four times and capture three championships!

Champion Kennys without wheels include five-time Pro Bowl Seattle Seahawks strong safety Kenny Easley; six-time MLB All-Star center fielder Kenny Lofton, who won four Gold Gloves and five American League stolen base leader rankings; and Kenny Harrison, who long jumped to an Olympic gold medal and world championship.

- **Kenneth "Kenny" Bernstein**, Auto Racing (Drag Racing), USA, 1978–2011
- **Kenneth "Kenny" Easley Jr.**, Football (Strong Safety), Seattle Seahawks, USA, 1981–1987
- **Kenny Harrison**, Track & Field (Triple Jump), USA, 1991–1996
- **Kenneth "Kenny" Lofton**, Baseball (Center Fielder), Cleveland Indians, USA, 1991–2007
- **Kenneth "Kenny" Roberts**, Motorcycle Racing (Grand Prix), USA, 1974–1983
- **Kenneth "Kenny" Roberts Jr.**, Motorcycle Racing (Grand Prix), USA, 1993–2007

KEVIN

All children should be beloved, and that's especially true of little Kevins, whose name comes from Irish roots for "beloved birth." Athletes with this name have found tremendous success in quite a few fields, and with some noteworthy concentrations. The range is wide and international, from esports champ Kevin "PPMD" Nanney, whose tournament wins and world rankings in *Super Smash Bros. Melee* placed him in the elite "Five Gods of Melee," to English rugby star and captain Kevin Sinfield, whose epic kicking helped him to two Challenge Cups, seven Super League championships, and more.

Kevins seem to have a love of sports that take place on water and ice. Ice hockey left wing Kevin Stevens had three All-Star appearances and won the Stanley Cup twice; German Kevin Kuske became the winningest Olympic bobsledder, with four gold medals to go with his seven world championships; and totally blind Australian water skier Kevin Murfitt was inducted into the sport's Hall of Fame for his nine world championships and numerous records. But if your little Kevin isn't a fan of watersports, he may want to check out some racing, perhaps getting inspiration from NASCAR fan-favorite Kevin Harvick, who has won at all levels of competition, including sixty wins and a championship in the Cup Series and two championships in the Xfinity series.

If your son Kevin is more a fan of team sports, he may take after English forward Kevin Keegan whose 275 combined goals earned him a spot on the FIFA 100 list and two Ballon d'Or awards. Closer to home, NBA basketball has featured a quartet of top players with this name. Five-time All-Star and NBA champion power forward/center Kevin Love won Olympic gold, while the Boston Celtics won three NBA championships in the 1980s with seven-time All-Star power forward Kevin McHale on the team. More recently, Kevin Durant has played small forward and power forward to two NBA championships while appearing in twelve All-Star games and winning three Olympic gold medals and a World Championship. Last but not least is the great Kevin Garnett, a fifteen-time All-Star power forward who won an NBA championship and an Olympic gold medal, was a four-time rebounding champion, and even played himself in the critically acclaimed film *Uncut Gems*!

Kevin Durant, Basketball (Small Forward/Power Forward), Golden State Warriors, USA, 2007–current

Kevin Garnett, Basketball (Power Forward), Boston Celtics, USA, 1995–2016

Kevin "Happy" Harvick, Auto Racing (NASCAR), USA, 1992–current

Joseph Kevin Keegan, Soccer (Forward), Liverpool Football Club, England, 1968–1985

Kevin Kuske, Bobsled, Germany, 2002–2018

Kevin Love, Basketball (Power Forward/Center), Minnesota Timberwolves, USA, 2008–current

Kevin McHale, Basketball (Power Forward), Boston Celtics, USA, 1980–1993

Kevin Murfitt, Water Skiing, Australia, 1993–2005

Kevin "PPMD" Nanney, Esports (*Super Smash Bros. Melee*), USA, 2009–2016

Kevin Sinfield, Rugby (Loose Forward/Fly-Half), Leeds Rhinos, England, 1997–2016

Kevin Stevens, Ice Hockey (Left Wing), Pittsburgh Penguins, USA, 1987–2002

KHALED/KHALID

With a name coming from an Arabic root for "lasting forever" or "eternal," your kid could race to everlasting fame! That's what has happened with athletes named Khaled and Khalid, particularly record-setting runners Khalid Khannouchi, who won the London and Chicago marathons (the latter multiple times), and Moroccan 10,000-meter Olympic gold-medalist Khalid Skah. On the other hand, your Khaled or Khalid may anchor a team like Bangladeshi cricket wicketkeeper Khaled Mashud, who won the 1997 ICC trophy.

Khalid Khannouchi, Long-Distance Running, USA, 1994–2012

Khaled Mashud, Cricket (Wicketkeeper), Rajshahi Division Cricket Team, Bangladesh, 1995–2011

Khalid Skah, Track & Field (Middle-Distance Running), Morocco, 1990–1996

KIRBY

A unisex name with strong feminine and masculine traditions, Kirby reaches back to an Old Norse place name for a "church settlement." Your proximity to a church notwithstanding, Kirby is a name with close ties to baseball, so you should definitely get a little boy (or girl) with that name in your family into little league as soon as possible. In Major League Baseball, pitcher Kirby Higbe had two All-Star appearances and was a National League strikeout leader in the 1940s; on the other side of the plate, the ten-time All-Star center fielder and Minnesota Twins legend Kirby Puckett won two World Series, six Golden Gloves, and six Silver Slugger awards with a batting championship, RBI leader rank, and records posted along the way.

Walter Kirby Higbe, Baseball (Pitcher), Brooklyn Dodgers, USA, 1937–1950

Kirby Puckett, Baseball (Center Fielder), Minnesota Twins, USA, 1984–1995

KJETIL

The name Kjetil comes from an Old Norse word for "kettle," originally used in religious ceremonies, and later became a word for "helmet." Helmets have been used by some of the top-tier athletes with this name (all of whom come from Norway), notably alpine skiers Kjetil Jansrud, who took home Olympic gold and a World Championship, and four-time Olympic gold-medalist, five-time world champ, and twenty-one-time World Cup-winner Kjetil Aamodt. Sometimes Kjetils stray off the beaten path, like ski orienteering world champion Ulven, or find their place on the water, like two-time world champion rower Borch.

Kjetil Aamodt, Alpine Skiing, Norway, 1988–2007

Kjetil Borch, Rowing, Norway, 2001–current

Kjetil Jansrud, Alpine Skiing, Norway, 2003–2022

Kjetil Ulven, Ski Orienteering, Norway, 1988–2002

KLAUS

Popular in Germany and some surrounding countries, the name Klaus originated as a short form for *Nicholas* (from Greek roots for "victory of the people"). Victory is exactly what we're interested in here, and we see it achieved by competitors with this name from Germany, Italy, and Austria. They're split between soccer (with seven-time Bundesliga and FIFA World Cup 1990-winning defender Klaus "Auge" Augenthaler), swimming (with Italian freestyle world champion Klaus Lanzarini), and winter sports (with world champion and two-time World Cup-winning Nordic combined skier Klaus Sulzenbacher and Olympic gold-medalist and world champion luger Klaus Bonsack).

If you're a fan of those events, then Klaus might be a good choice for a child in your family!

Klaus "Auge" Augenthaler, Soccer (Defender), Fußball-Club Bayern Munich e. V., Germany, 1976–1991

Klaus Bonsack, Luge, Germany, 1963–1972

Klaus Lanzarini, Swimming (Freestyle), Italy, 2000–2006

Klaus Sulzenbacher, Nordic Combined Skiing, Austria, 1983–1991

KOBE

Kobe is a unisex name that has appeared in various languages and cultures around the world, coming from a diminutive of the biblical Hebrew *Jacob*, meaning "tortoise" or "turtle" in Swahili, and probably best known as the name of a large city in Japan (and the beef that comes from its area). When it comes to sports, there's one man known internationally by the first name alone: Los Angeles Lakers shooting guard Kobe Bryant. Ranked as one of the greatest players of all time and the best of his generation, Kobe had an incredibly successful twenty-year career in the NBA, with eighteen All-Star appearances, five championships, and a long list of awards, records, and accomplishments, including two Olympic gold medals.

Whether you like the name because of how it sounds, its many origins, or how it honors the late basketball star, a child you give it to will reach the absolute pinnacle of his or her chosen field and become synonymous with it.

Kobe Bryant, Basketball (Shooting Guard), Los Angeles Lakers, USA, 1996–2016

KOJI

As with all Japanese names, Koji can mean different things depending on the kanji characters used to write it, but Koji is a particularly pleasant one because it can include characters like "prosperity," "good luck," "happiness," and "peace." All of our examples of champion Kojis come from Japan and they feature in some traditional and unexpected events. Koji Murofushi was an Olympic gold-medalist and world champion hammer thrower, table tennis legend Koji Kimura won four world championships in the 1960s, and Takanohana Kōji (Kōji Hanada) was a sumo wrestling yokozuna with a massive twenty-two tournament championships.

Koji is a great name even if you're not Japanese, and one that will inspire a child to compete and learn about his nation's unique events.

Koji Kimura, Table Tennis, Japan, 1961–1967

Koji Murofushi, Track & Field (Hammer Throw), Japan, 1993–2013

Takanohana Kōji (Kōji Hanada), Sumo Wrestling, Japan, 1988–2003

KURT

Another name that brings with it endless opportunity in any field, Kurt comes from either Germanic roots for "brave" and "counsel" or Turkish roots for "wolf" and has been seen across a number of sports. On the team sports side of things, famously undrafted quarterback Kurt Warner had four Pro Bowl appearances, was MVP in the Super Bowl that his team won, and was a member of two major Halls of Fame; and soccer winger Kurt Hamrin ranks among the top players from Sweden, with over 260 goals in his club and international career and winning two Coppa Italias, a UEFA Cup Winners' Cup, and more. If your Kurt is more independent, then he may take after Olympic gold-medalist and World Champion freestyle wrestler Kurt Angle (who went onto a long career in professional wrestling); NASCAR Cup Series champion Kurt Busch, who won thirty-four races in the sport's top series; and four-time Canadian world champion figure skater Kurt Browning.

Kurt Angle, Freestyle Wrestling, USA, 1995–1996

Kurt Browning, Figure Skating, Canada, 1985–1994

Kurt Busch, Auto Racing (NASCAR), USA, 1997–current

Kurt Hamrin, Soccer (Winger), ACF Fiorentina, Sweden, 1952–1972

Kurtis "Kurt" Warner, Football (Quarterback), St. Louis Rams, USA, 1994–2009

KYLE

Some associate the name Kyle with energy drinks and juvenile behavior, but it's clear from the facts that it's actually a noble name that can inspire all manner of athleticism, competition, and success! From Scottish usage and Gaelic roots in place names for "channel" or "narrows," Kyle has appeared on leaderboards in a staggering number of events. Australian Kyle Chalmers swam to Olympic gold and two world championships in freestyle (with more medals in medley and butterfly too); Kyle Clemons sprinted to a 4x400-meter relay win at the 2016 Rio de Janeiro Olympic Games and three different World Championships; top-ranked freestyle wrestler Kyle "Snyderman" Snyder is an Olympic gold-medalist and three-time world champion; point guard Kyle Lowry has made six All-Star appearances and has an NBA championship and an Olympic gold medal; and Canadian rower Kyle Hamilton's medal collection includes a gold from the 2008 Beijing Olympics, three World Rowing Championships, and eight podiums from the World Rowing Cup (including four golds).

Kyle "Ksharp" Miller and Kyle "Bugha" Giersdorf may never have gone up against each other, but they're both champion esports players; the former won three major *Counter-Strike* events while the latter is a *Fortnite* player with three FNCS championships and a win at the inaugural Fortnite World Cup. And then there are the fastest Kyles! On two wheels, Australian Kyle Baldock has won multiple BMX events, while NASCAR's elite Cup Series features champions Kyle Larson (currently one championship and eighteen wins) and Kyle Busch (currently two championships and sixty wins, with similar honors in other series as well).

On the ice, left wing Kyle Calder was a member of the Canadian 2003 World Champion team and fellow Canadian left wing Kyle Clifford won two Stanley Cups with the Los Angeles Kings. Finally, Kyle is a name that has appeared consistently in the NFL. Kyle Rote Sr. played for the New York Giants in the 1950s, earning four Pro Bowl appearances and an NFL championship; defensive tackle Kyle Williams went to six Pro Bowls while playing thirteen seasons with the Buffalo Bills; and Kyle Juszczyk is a nine-time Pro Bowl fullback currently playing for the San Fransisco 49ers.

- **Kyle Baldock**, BMX, Australia, 2009–current
- **Kyle Busch**, Auto Racing (NASCAR), USA, 1998–current
- **Kyle Calder**, Ice Hockey (Left Wing), Chicago Blackhawks, Canada, 1999–2012
- **Kyle Chalmers**, Swimming (Butterfly/Freestyle), Australia, 2014–current
- **Kyle Clemons**, Track & Field (Sprinting), USA, 2012–2016
- **Kyle Clifford**, Ice Hockey (Left Wing), Los Angeles Kings, Canada, 2009–current
- **Kyle "Bugha" Giersdorf**, Esports (*Fortnite*), USA, 2018–current
- **Kyle Hamilton**, Rowing, Canada, 2002–2008
- **Kyle Juszczyk**, Football (Fullback), San Francisco 49ers, USA, 2016–current
- **Kyle Larson**, Auto Racing (NASCAR), USA, 2011–current
- **Kyle Lowry**, Basketball (Point Guard), Toronto Raptors, USA, 2006–current
- **Kyle "Ksharp" Miller**, Esports (*Counter-Strike*), USA, 2001–2008
- **William Kyle Rote Sr.**, Football (Halfback/Wide Receiver), New York Giants, USA, 1951–1961
- **Kyle (Snyderman) Snyder**, Freestyle Wrestling, USA, 2015–current
- **Kyle Williams**, Football (Defensive Tackle), Buffalo Bills, USA, 2006–2018

KYRIE

The unisex Kyrie can be a derivative of a Christian prayer title from Greek meaning "Lord, have mercy" or an invented name, but either way it brings to mind just one person in the wild world of sports. Kyrie Irving has been a staple of the NBA since his introduction in 2011. Playing for the Cleveland

Cavaliers, Boston Celtics, and, most recently, the Brooklyn Nets, Irving has played in nine All-Star games, won an NBA championship, and joined the 50-40-90 club. On the international stage playing for the United States, he's also won an Olympic gold medal and a World Cup!

Working hard and flying high are traits that a kid you name Kyrie will share with the basketball star.

Kyrie Irving, Basketball (Point Guard), Cleveland Cavaliers, USA, 2011-current

KYUNG

As with many South Korean names, Kyung can mean a variety of things depending on which characters are used to write it; in this case, the characters include "scenery," "view," "honor," or "respect." These meanings are further compounded with different second syllables that make unique forms. Athletes with these names seem to gravitate toward archery in particular, with a trio of two-time world champions in Lee Kyung-chul, Kim Kyung-ho, and Park Kyung-mo, whose medal collection includes two Olympic golds, four world championships, and a World Cup win. Outside of the archery range, speed skater Song Kyung-taek has raced to four wins at World Championships.

Kyung with its different forms is a highly flexible name, and with it, a young athlete will have the keen eye and steady hand of an archer.

Kim Kyung-ho, Archery, South Korea, 1993-1997

Lee Kyung-chul, Archery, South Korea, 1995

Park Kyung-mo, Archery, South Korea, 1993-2008

Song Kyung-taek, Speed Skating, South Korea, 2003-2008

GIRLS

KAITLIN/KAITLYN

See *Caitlin/Caitlyn/Kaitlin/Kaitlyn.*

KAORI

The characters used to write the Japanese name Kaori can mean a variety of things—including the popular translations "fragrance" and "weaving"—and grace, agility, and quick moves are signatures of the athletes with this name. Singles figure skater Kaori Sakamoto has won two world championships and a gold medal at the Four Continents Championships, while the rest are fearsome fighters on the mat. Judo is a particular favorite, as shown by Kaori Yamaguchi, who won a gold medal and four silvers at World Championships, and Kaori Matsumoto, whose medal count includes a gold and a bronze from Olympic Games; two golds and a bronze from World Championships; two golds and a silver from World Masters; and more. Last but certainly not least is record-breaking freestyle wrestler Kaori Icho, who won four Olympic gold medals and ten world championships!

Naming a daughter Kaori will give her confidence, strength, and individuality, and she'll excel at one-on-one confrontations and overcoming her opponents.

Kaori Icho, Freestyle Wrestling, Japan, 2002-2019

Kaori Matsumoto, Judo, Japan, 2008-2019

Kaori Sakamoto, Figure Skating, Japan, 2004-current

Kaori Yamaguchi, Judo, Japan, 1978-1988

KAREN

From Danish origins, Karen is one of many names derived from *Katherine*. Hardly ones to ask for the manager, women with this name have made incredible strides and attained top honors in water skiing (Australian two-time World Overall Women's Champion Karen Neville), trampoline gymnastics (Canadian two-time world champion Karen Cockburn), and cricket (Australian two-time Women's Cricket World Cup-winner Karen Rolton, who holds her country's record for most runs in women's Test cricket).

Two Karens who have made a big impact on field hockey are Karen Haude, who won the Women's Hockey World Cup and Indoor Nations Championship with the West Germany team, and Australian midfielder Karen Smith, who's won a World Cup and three Champions Trophy tournaments. American cyclist Karen Kurreck is a world champion in both road bicycle and cyclo-cross racing, while in the pool, Karen Moe set records and won an Olympic gold medal in butterfly, and English freestyle swimmer Karen Pickering claimed three short course world championship wins; combine their skills and you've got one of the toughest Karens around, Ironman World Champion and two-time ITU Triathlon World Champion Karen Smyers.

Take back the glory and pride of the name Karen by giving it to your daughter and instilling in her a drive to compete and win.

Karen Cockburn, Trampoline Gymnastics, Canada, 2000–2017

Karen Haude, Field Hockey (Defender), Germany, 1967–1984

Karen Kurreck, Road/Track Cycling, USA, 1993–2018

Karen Moe, Swimming (Butterfly), USA, 1970–1972

Karen Neville, Water Skiing, Australia, 1979–1991

Karen Pickering, Swimming (Freestyle), England, 1986–2002

Karen Rolton, Cricket (Batter), South Australia Women Cricket Team, Australia, 1994–2011

Karen Smith, Field Hockey (Midfielder), Australia, 1997–2006

Karen Smyers, Triathlon, USA, 1990–1999

KARIN

Another variation of the name *Katherine*, Karin has Swedish origins but can be found anywhere from Germany to Brazil. It's a pretty name without all of the baggage that comes with the more well-known *Karen*, and might bring with it a talent for skating, volleyball, or gymnastics. That's especially true if a girl with this name takes after German three-time Olympic gold-medalist speed skater Karin Enke; Brazilian volleyball middle blocker Karin Rodrigues, who won two World Grand Prix tournaments; and world and Olympic champion artistic gymnasts Karin Lindberg of Sweden and Karin Büttner-Janz of Germany!

Karin Büttner-Janz, Artistic Gymnastics, Germany, 1967–1972

Karin Enke, Speed Skating, Germany, 1977–1988

Karin Lindberg, Artistic Gymnastics, Sweden, 1948–1956

Karin Rodrigues, Volleyball (Middle Blocker), Brazil, 1996–2000

KAROL

The uncommon feminine name Karol can be a diminutive of names like *Karoline*, be a variant of *Carol*, or be combined with secondary names like *Ann*. Choosing the name Karol for a girl in your family can give her a love of ice skating, riding bicycles, or playing in the ocean . . . and if she takes any of those hobbies seriously, she could achieve great things like American world champion pairs figure skater Karol Kennedy, Canadian three-time road bicycle racing world champion Karol-Ann Canuel, or Brazilian free-diver Karol Meyer, who has set eight world records, including the deepest apnea free dive (328 feet) and static apnea with pure oxygen (eighteen minutes, thirty-two seconds)!

Karol-Ann Canuel, Road Cycling, Canada, 2010–2021

Karol Kennedy, Figure Skating, USA, 1946–1952

Karoline "Karol" Meyer, Diving, Brazil, 1998–2010

KAROLINA

See *Carolina/Caroline/Karolina*.

KATARINA/KATERINA/KATHARINA/KATRINA

With a name as historically popular as *Katherine*, it's no surprise to see lots of variants popping up in different places and in different languages. What is surprising, though, is the huge assortment of sports and athletic events in which singular Katarinas, Katerinas, Katharinas, and Katrinas have made powerful impacts. Under the umbrella of track and field alone have been Greek pole vaulter Katerina Stefanidi, who has won Olympic and World Championship gold; English heptathlon and pentathlon world champion Katarina Johnson-Thompson; and Australian multi-talented para-athlete Katrina Webb, who took home seven medals from Paralympic Games (including three golds) and five from the World Para Athletics Championships.

Estonian left-handed épée fencer Katrina Lehis won Olympic gold in 2020, Czech rifle sport shooter Kateřina Emmons has collected one of each medal from the Olympics and a World Championship, Katrina Rore's defense helped her New Zealand team win the World Netball Series and Netball World Cup, and Katrina Powell and the Australian Hockeyroos won two Olympic gold medals, a World Cup, and three Champions Trophies. Last but not least are some of the winningest athletes with these names: American basketball forward Katrina McClain, who was named USA Basketball's Female Athlete of the Year twice as her teams won two Olympic gold medals and two FIBA World Championships, German four-time world champion ski jumper Katharina Althaus, and internationally beloved figure skater Katarina Witt, who won two Olympic gold medals and four world championships.

If you like the name *Katherine* but are looking for something a bit more unique, you may find a winner in the Katarina/Katerina/Katharina/Katrina family—and a winner is exactly what a little girl with that name will turn out to be.

Katharina Althaus, Ski Jumping, Germany, 2012–current

Kateřina Emmons, Sport Shooting (Rifle), Czech Republic, 2002–current

Katarina Johnson-Thompson, Track & Field (Heptathlon/Pentathlon/Long Jump), England, 2012–current

Katrina Lehis, Fencing (Épée), Estonia, 2015–current

Katrina McClain, Basketball (Forward), USA, 1983–1987

Katrina "Triny" Powell, Field Hockey (Striker), Australia, 1996–2003

Katrina Rore, Netball, New Zealand, 2005–current

Katerina Stefanidi, Track & Field (Pole Vaulting), Greece, 2011–current

Katrina Webb, Para-Athletics, Australia, 1996–2004

Katarina Witt, Figure Skating, Germany, 1978–1994

KATE/KATI/KATIE

As we see throughout this section, there are many names in the *Katherine* family, and just as many diminutives and nicknames for them, including Kate and Katie. Whether they're standing on their own as names or short forms for others, Kates and Katies have reached summits, stood on podiums, and taken home medals from lots of different events. In track and field, Katie Nageotte has pole vaulted to an Olympic gold medal and a recent win at World Championships, while British pentathlete Kate Allenby took home four world championships and two World Cup Final wins. Other solo competitors include German biathlete Kati Wilhelm, who raced and shot her way to seven Olympic medals (including three golds) and thirteen medals from World Championships (five of them being wins), and rock-climbing pioneer and author Katie Brown, who won two X Games events, the Rock Master, and a World Cup.

Kates and Katies excel in team sports too, like ice hockey (Olympic gold-medalist left wing and IIHF Ice Hockey Women's World Champion Katie King-Crowley), skeleton (two-time world champion racer Katie Uhlaender, who has won medals in both single and team events), rowing (world champion and three-time World Rowing Cup-winner Kate Johnson), and field hockey (Australian midfielder Kate Starre, who helped lead her team to two Olympic gold medals, two World Cups, and four Champions Trophy wins).

Women with these names have embarked on certain sports careers and won big, including basketball's five-time WNBA All-Star shooting guard/small forward Katie Douglas, who won the 2012 WNBA championship with the Indiana Fever, and seven-time All-Star and two-time champ Katie Smith, who played with team USA and won three Olympic gold medals and two World Cup championships. American soccer defender Kate Markgraf had a record 201 international caps and won two Olympic gold medals, the FIFA Women's World Cup, and more, while facing off in combat sports are some of the toughest Kates and Katies, like world champion British judoka Kate Howey and Irish boxer Katie Taylor, who currently has a perfect 21-0 record, an Olympic gold medal, five World Championship wins, and all four major world boxing titles!

A particular concentration of champions with these names is in the swimming pool. Freestyle swimmer Kate Ziegler has world championship gold medals in 400-, 800-, and 1500-meter events (five in total); and Katie Hoff raced to eight wins at World Championships in freestyle and medley events. But the undisputed queen of the pool is freestyle swimmer Katie Ledecky, who holds numerous records, won numerous awards, and has a massive forty-two medals from major international events, including seven wins at Olympics and nineteen at World Championships.

There are tons of great athletic inspirations for a daughter named Kate or Katie, no matter what sport or event she ends up favoring. But it's still a good idea to teach her how to swim right away.

Katherine "Kate" Allenby, Track & Field (Pentathlon), England, 1997–2004

Katie Brown, Rock Climbing, USA, 1995–2009

Kathryn "Katie" Douglas, Basketball (Shooting Guard/Small Forward), Orlando Miracle, USA, 2001–2014

Kathryn "Katie" Hoff, Swimming (Freestyle/Medley), USA, 2004–2015

Kate Howey, Judo, England, 1989–2004

Katherine "Kate" Johnson, Rowing, USA, 1993–2004

Kathryn "Katie" King-Crowley, Ice Hockey (Left Wing), USA, 1997–2006

Kathleen "Katie" Ledecky, Swimming (Freestyle), USA, 2012–current

Kathryn "Kate" Markgraf, Soccer (Defender), Chicago Red Stars, USA, 1998–2010

Kathryn "Katie" Nageotte, Pole Vaulting, USA, 2013-current

Katie Smith, Basketball (Shooting Guard/ Small Forward), Minnesota Lynx, USA, 1996–2013

Kate Starre, Field Hockey (Midfielder), Australia, 1991–2000

Katie Taylor, Boxing (Lightweight/ Welterweight), Ireland, 2005–current

Katie Uhlaender, Skeleton, USA, 2003–current

Kati Wilhelm, Biathlon, Germany, 1995–2010

Kate Ziegler, Swimming (Freestyle), USA, 2004–2015

KATERINE/KATHERINE/KATHRIN/KATRIN

Countless "C" and "K" names are related to the central Katherine family, all of which are rooted in Ancient Greek but have uncertain origins; it may come from words meaning "each," "torture," or "my consecration of your name" or from a connection to the goddess Hecate. The meaning "pure" sounds nice, but it was added to the name later when it was mistakenly connected to a similar-sounding word. Katherine has worldwide popularity and has been adapted into dozens of variant forms, including Katerine, Kathrin, and Katrin. And of course with all that variation, we see women with these names excelling in a large number of sports and events, though some intriguing patterns and concentrations emerge.

If you've got a little girl with one of these names in your family, you can expect big things from her, even if you don't know exactly where she's headed. It could be anything from speed skating (like German Olympic gold-medalist Katrin Mattscherodt) to cycling (like Dutch Paralympic Games gold-medalist Kathrin Goeken), biathlon (like German Katrin Apel, who collected a tremendous four world championships and four Olympic medals, including two golds, in her career), cricket (like fast bowler Katherine Brunt, who won two World Cups and a T20 World Cup), and esports (like Kat "Mystik" Gunn, whose tournament achievements led her to win season two of WCG Ultimate Gamer and be named the Guinness World Records 2016 highest-earning female gamer).

On the other hand, there are certain events that seem to draw in Katherines and the rest more than others. These include alpine ski racing, with world champions Kathrin Hölzl of Germany and Kathrin Zettel of Austria, and track and field, with Paralympic Games 200-meter gold-medalist Katrin Green; two-time world champion sprinter Katrin Krabbe; and distance runner Katrin Dörre-Heinig, who won both the Tokyo and London Marathons three times! Others gravitate toward swimming, like German backstroke world champion Kathrin Zimmermann; Australian two-time Paralympic gold-medalist Katherine Downie, who set three world records; two-time Olympic gold-winner and world champion freestyle swimmer Katrin Meissner of Germany; and Canadian four-time freestyle world champion Katerine Savard.

Very interestingly, it is on the water with paddles and oars that we see the biggest concentrations of champion athletes with names in the Katherine family! On the rowing side, we see German two-time Olympic gold-medalist and two-time world champion Katrin Rutschow-Stomporowski; British Katherine Grainger, whose one Olympic gold medal sits in her collection next to six wins at World Championships; and German four-time Olympic gold-medalist and eight-time world champion Kathrin Boron. Meanwhile, canoeing has witnessed the exploits of German four-time world champion Kathrin Giese; nine-time world champion Katrin Borchert, who competed for both Germany and Australia; and German Katrin

Wagner-Augustin, whose medal collection includes a staggering six from the Olympic Games (four of them gold) and twenty-eight from World Championships (ten of them gold and sixteen silver)!

Katrin Apel, Biathlon, Germany, 1994–2005

Katrin Borchert, Sprint Canoeing, Germany/Australia, 1988–2004

Kathrin Boron, Rowing, Germany, 1990–2008

Katherine Brunt, Cricket (All-Rounder), Yorkshire Women's Cricket Team, England, 2004–current

Katrin Dörre-Heinig, Marathon, Germany, 1984–2000

Katherine Downie, Swimming (Backstroke/Freestyle), Australia, 2011–current

Kathrin Giese, Sprint Canoeing, Germany, 1981–1986

Kathrin Goeken, Road Cycling, Netherlands, 2012

Katherine Grainger, Rowing, Scotland, 1997–2016

Katrin Green, Track & Field (Sprinting), Germany, 2008–2012

Katherine "Mystik" Gunn, Esports (*Dead or Alive/Halo*), USA, 2006–current

Kathrin Hölzl, Alpine Ski Racing, Germany, 2006–2012

Katrin Krabbe, Track & Field (Sprinting), Germany, 1988–1991

Katrin Mattscherodt, Speed Skating, Germany, 2003–2010

Katrin Meissner, Swimming (Freestyle), Germany, 1987–2003

Katrin Rutschow-Stomporowski, Rowing, Germany, 1994–2004

Katerine Savard, Swimming (Butterfly/Freestyle), Canada, 2010–current

Katrin Wagner-Augustin, Sprint Canoeing, Germany, 1997–2013

Kathrin Zettel, Alpine Ski Racing, Austria, 2005–2015

Kathrin Zimmermann, Swimming (Backstroke), Germany, 1983–1988

KATHY

Another classical diminutive of *Katherine*, Kathy may sound traditional to modern ears, but it's still a powerhouse and can instill in a girl a love for competing, whether it's in cycling, kickboxing, or golf. She can see the glory of her name in Australian Olympic gold-medalist racing cyclist Kathy Watt; five-time world champion martial artist Kathy Long, who had an 18–1 kickboxing record; and all-time top-ranked golfer Kathy Whitworth, who won eighty-eight times on the LPGA Tour (including six majors) and was inducted into the World Golf Hall of Fame.

Kathy Long, Kickboxing, USA, 1989–1992

Kathryn "Kathy" Watt, Road/Track Cycling, Australia, 1990–2008

Kathrynne "Kathy" Whitworth, Golf, USA, 1958–2005

KAY

A short and sporty name on its own, or a diminutive of everything from *Katherine* to *Kathleen*, Kay can propel a girl to push herself to be the best at her chosen field, conquering the opposition or overcoming people telling her that she can't do it. In the 1980s Irish wheelchair racer Kay McShane set a record for three consecutive wins at the London Marathon half a century after Kay Petre of Canada helped prove that women have what it takes to be race drivers, battling for speed records and winning races at Brooklands in the 1930s.

Kay McShane, Wheelchair Racing, Ireland, 1984–1988

Kathleen "Kay" Petre, Auto Racing (Grand Prix), Canada, 1933–1937

KELLY

Whether it comes from Irish roots meaning "bright headed," "war/strife," or "church," the unisex name Kelly has done it all. It's helped teams win trophies, with athletes like world champion ice hockey forward Kelly Stephens-Tysland; indoor volleyball opposite spiker and setter Kelly Murphy, who took home a world championship and a World Grand Prix title with the American team; and New Zealand versatile rugby union and sevens star Kelly Brazier, whose championship collection includes an Olympic gold medal, two Women's Rugby World Cups, two Rugby World Cup Sevens, and more.

Kellys can also do it all on their own, with individual winners like British two-time Olympic gold-medalist runner Kelly Holmes; Estonian freestyle skier Kelly Sildaru, who's taken home a halfpipe world championship, nine medals from the Winter X Games (including six golds), and more; seven-time Winter X Games-winner and Olympic gold-medalist snowboarder Kelly Clark; and bowler Kelly Kulick, who has won ten professional titles, a PBA Tour event, three World Tenpin Bowling Championships, two World Games, and more!

- **Kelly Brazier**, Rugby (Second Five-Eighth/First Five-Eighth), Otago Rugby Football Union, New Zealand, 2004–current
- **Kelly Clark**, Snowboarding, USA, 1999–2019
- **Kelly Holmes**, Track & Field (Middle-Distance Running), England, 1993–2004
- **Kelly Kulick**, Bowling, USA, 2001–current
- **Kelly Murphy**, Volleyball (Opposite Spiker/Setter), USA, 2012–current
- **Kelly Sildaru**, Freestyle Skiing, Estonia, 2017–current
- **Kelly Stephens-Tysland**, Ice Hockey (Forward), USA, 2004–2006

KERRI/KERRY

From an old Gaelic place name and a root for "black" comes the unisex name Kerry (and its alternate spelling Kerri). There's a good chance a daughter with one of these names will be graceful and powerful, enjoying her time in the sun and the spotlight. On the beach, Australian volleyball player Kerry Pottharst scored Olympic gold in 2000, just as the absolutely dominating career of American Kerry Walsh Jennings began. Walsh Jennings would go on to win three consecutive Olympic Games beach volleyball gold medals, along with three World Championships, forty-four Beach Volleyball World Tours, a record-setting 112 match/nineteen tournament streak, and much more. Meanwhile, if you were an American in 1996 you likely watched Kerri Strug clinch the Olympic gold medal for her gymnastics team known as the "Magnificent Seven." In one of the most famous Olympic moments in modern history, Strug performed a final vault with an injured ankle in order to beat the Russian team, and had to be carried by her coach to the medal podium.

- **Kerri Pottharst**, Beach Volleyball, Australia, 1982–2003
- **Kerri Strug**, Artistic Gymnastics, USA, 1990–1997
- **Kerry Walsh Jennings**, Beach Volleyball, USA, 2000–current

KIM

Used on its own and as a short form for other names before being associated primarily with *Kimberly*, the unisex Kim has various origins and derivations in different places, including the Sino-Vietnamese meaning "gold" or "metal." Some Kims are fast, like Belgian Kim Gevaert, who sprinted to Olympic gold in 2008; and tennis phenom Kim Clijsters, who battled Justine Henin and Serena Williams to reach the number one spot in the world in both singles and doubles. Other Kims focus on accuracy, like double trap and skeet shooter Kim Rhode, who has set records with her six Olympic Games medals (three of them gold) and five from World Championships (including two wins).

Whether you're using Kim as a short form, nickname, or given name, it can give a girl in your family the flexibility to succeed wherever she goes!

Kim Clijsters, Tennis, Belgium, 1997–2022

Kim Gevaert, Track & Field (Sprinting), Belgium, 2002–2008

Kimberly "Kim" Rhode, Sport Shooting (Double Trap/Skeet), USA, 1992–current

KRISTI/KRISTIE

Just like *Kate* and *Katie*, Kristi and Kristie can be diminutive forms of various other names like *Christina*, *Christine*, or *Kristina*, or they can be used as names on their own. Whichever you may prefer, a Kristi or Kristie in your family might find success on the soccer field, the wrestling mat, the skating rink, the basketball court, or even water skis.

This is especially true if she takes after winners like Houston Dash midfielder Kristie Mewis, who's scored nearly fifty goals on her way to a CONCACAF Women's Championship and NWSL Challenge Cup Championship; world champion and eight-time Masters Water Ski Tournament-winner Kristi Overton Johnson; wrestler Kristie Marano, who collected nine medals at World Championships (including two golds); Olympic gold-medalist and two-time world champion figure skater Kristi Yamaguchi; and basketball stars Kristi Harrower, a point guard who won a world championship for Australia, and three-time WNBA All-Star and two-time champion point guard/shooting guard Kristi Toliver.

Kristi Harrower, Basketball (Point Guard), Bendigo Spirit, Australia, 1991–2009

Kristie Marano, Freestyle Wrestling, USA, 1996–2006

Kristen "Kristie" Mewis, Soccer (Midfielder), Houston Dash, USA, 2013–current

Kristi Overton Johnson, Water Skiing, USA, 1983–2005

Kristi Toliver, Basketball (Point Guard/Shooting Guard), Washington Mystics, USA, 2009–current

Kristine "Kristi" Yamaguchi, Figure Skating, USA, 1989–1992

KRISTIN

If you're hoping for a daughter who loves to swim and go fast, consider naming her Kristin (a variant form of *Christina*). She may take after German swimming Hall of Famer Kristin Otto, who became the first woman to win six gold medals at an Olympic Games (in 1988)! She also took home seven gold medals (and two silvers) from World Championships and set multiple world records along the way.

Kristin Otto, Swimming (Backstroke/Butterfly/Freestyle), Germany, 1982–1989

KRISTINA

See *Christine/Kristina*.

KRISTINE

Depending on what part of the world you're in, Kristine can be derivative of names like *Christina* and *Christine*. In some cases, that can also have an influence on which sports may be preferred by girls with that name. For example, there are the Kristines of Denmark and Norway who excel at handball! These include two-time Olympic gold-medalists Kristine Andersen of Denmark and Kristine Lunde-Borgersen (also a world champion) of Norway.

What about Americans with these names? They've excelled in rowing, with Kristine

Norelius, who won gold at the 1984 Olympic Games, and Kristine O'Brien, who took home world championships in eight and coxless four; swimming, with Kristine Quance, who scored an Olympic gold medal with her medley team in 1996; and soccer, with two-time Olympic gold-medalist and two-time FIFA Women's World Cup-winning forward and midfielder Kristine Lilly.

Kristine Andersen, Handball (Playmaker), Denmark, 1996–2004

Kristine Lilly, Soccer (Forward/Midfielder), USA, 1994–2011

Kristine Lunde-Borgersen, Handball (Center Back), Norway, 2001–2018

Kristine Norelius, Rowing, USA, 1980–1984

Kristine O'Brien, Rowing, USA, 2015–current

Kristine Quance, Swimming (Breaststroke/Medley), USA, 1991–1998

KRISZTINA

Maybe your family is Hungarian, or maybe you're just a fan of alternate forms of *Christina*; either way, Krisztina is a cool formation that may give a daughter an excitement for sports in the water or on the ice. That's especially true if she follows in the footsteps of Hungarian superstars like world champion ice dancer Krisztina Regőczy, record-setting five-time Olympic gold-medalist and two-time world champion backstroke swimmer Krisztina Egerszegi, or famed sprint canoeist Krisztina Fazekas-Zur, who has two Olympic wins along with eight world championships!

Krisztina Egerszegi, Swimming (Backstroke/Butterfly/Medley), Hungary, 1981–1996

Krisztina Fazekas-Zur, Sprint Canoeing, Hungary, 1990–current

Krisztina Regőczy, Ice Dancing, Hungary, 1969–1980

KSENIA/KSENIYA

Unless your heritage includes Eastern European, you may not be familiar with the name Ksenia/Kseniya, but in Russia and surrounding countries, it has enjoyed a good deal of popularity. A variant form of a Greek name that means "hospitality," the name Ksenia has appeared on podiums and leader boards for several different athletic competitions, from sprint canoeing (world champion Ksenia Kurach) to handball (Kseniya Makeyeva, who won a world championship), archery (two-time world champion Ksenia Perova), figure skating (Olympic gold-medalist and Grand Prix Final-winner Ksenia Stolbova), fencing (three-time world champion wheelchair competitor Ksenia Ovsyannikova), and mountain bike orienteering (four-time world champion Ksenia Chernykh)!

Ksenias in particular are known for their grace, agility, and power, like two-time world champion artistic gymnasts Ksenia Semyonova and Ksenia Afanasyeva; and rhythmic gymnasts Ksenia Dzhalaganiya, who won a World Championship, three-time world champion Ksenia Poliakova, and Ksenia Dudkina, whose two World Championship wins bracketed her 2012 Olympic gold medal in group all-around.

If you're looking for a name that's exotic to most Americans' ears but with a strong history of athletic accomplishments (and gymnastic glory in particular), Ksenia may be just the one for you!

Ksenia Afanasyeva, Artistic Gymnastics, Russia, 2007–2016

Ksenia Chernykh, Mountain Bike Orienteering, Russia, 2004–2010

Ksenia Dudkina, Rhythmic Gymnastics, Russia, 2011–2013

Ksenia Dzhalaganiya, Rhythmic Gymnastics, Russia, 1993–2003

Ksenia Kurach, Sprint Canoeing, Russia, 2018–current

Kseniya Makeyeva, Handball (Pivot), Russia, 2006–current

Ksenia Ovsyannikova, Wheelchair Fencing (Foil/Épée), Russia, 2015–current

Ksenia Perova, Archery, Russia, 2010–current

Ksenia Poliakova, Rhythmic Gymnastics, Russia, 2016–2019

Ksenia Semyonova, Artistic Gymnastics, Russia, 2006–2011

Ksenia Stolbova, Figure Skating, Russia, 2011–2020

KYOKO

Like other Japanese names, Kyoko can be written with characters with various meanings, in this case including "capital city," "respectful," "apricot," "mirror," or "child." Two Kyokos have made athletic history on the international scene, and utilizing their name may grace a little girl with an affinity for the water or strength and power: swimmer Kyoko Iwasaki won the 200-meter breaststroke event at the 1992 Barcelona Olympic Games when she was only fourteen years old, while freestyle wrestler Kyoko Hamaguchi took home five World Championship wins (out of ten podium appearances).

Kyoko Hamaguchi, Freestyle Wrestling, Japan, 1996–2010

Kyoko Iwasaki, Swimming (Breaststroke), Japan, 1992–1995

L

BOYS

LADAINIAN

Some names have a long and complicated history stretching back centuries and multiple languages, while others have come to be much more recently and offer lots of promise for the future. LaDainian falls into that second group, and any boy given that name would be lucky to follow in the fast footsteps of NFL Hall of Fame running back LaDainian Tomlinson! A five-time Pro Bowler, Tomlinson played most of his career with the San Diego Chargers and racked up accolades like NFL MVP, Offensive Player of the Year, rushing yards leader, scoring leader, and more.

- **LaDainian Tomlinson**, Football (Running Back), San Diego Chargers, USA, 2001–2011

LANCE

Originally coming from a Germanic root meaning "land" and later associated with the weapon of the same name, Lance is a powerful and swift name. Here in the United States, this name has appeared at the pinnacle of two popular sports, as well as one that's a little more exotic. Chicago Bears linebacker Lance Briggs was a nine-time Pro Bowler in the 2000s and early 2010s, while in the '60s and early '70s, wide receiver Lance "Bambi" Alworth was a seven-time AFL All-Star who led in receiving yards, receptions, and receiving touchdowns three times each, and won both an AFL Championship and a Super Bowl. On the baseball diamond, outfielder and first baseman Lance Berkman had six All-Star appearances and was on the 2011 World Series Championship team, while about twenty years earlier, Lance Parrish was an eight-time All-Star catcher who won the 1984 World Series and was awarded three Gold Gloves and six Silver Sluggers. Up in the frozen north, dog musher Lance Mackey won both the Yukon Quest and the famous Iditarod Trail Sled Dog Race four times!

Teach your Lance good sportsmanship so he grows up to be a fair-minded competitor, and not a cheater like another, infamous Lance.

- **Lance "Bambi" Alworth**, Football (Wide Receiver), San Diego Chargers, USA, 1962–1972
- **William Lance Berkman**, Baseball (Outfielder/First Baseman), Houston Astros, USA, 1999–2013
- **Lance Briggs**, Football (Linebacker), Chicago Bears, USA, 2003–2014
- **Lance Mackey**, Dog Sled Racing, USA, 2001–2020

Lance Parrish, Baseball (Catcher), Detroit Tigers, USA, 1977–1995

LARRY

Traditionally a diminutive of *Laurence/Lawrence* (from a Roman place name and possibly the "laurel"), Larry can arise as a nickname from names like *Lazarus* or even just stand on its own. Larrys are especially prominent in sports here in the United States, with a number of champions spread out across baseball, football, basketball, and more. Bodybuilder Larry Scott was the very first Mr. Olympia winner in 1965 (and became the first two-time winner the following year), and Larry Myricks was a two-time World Cup–winner and two-time world champion long jumper. Ice hockey has seen Larry Robinson, whose ten All-Star appearances and six Stanley Cup wins put him in the ranks of the all-time best players.

On the baseball diamond, Larrys have prospered in multiple positions. Atlanta Braves third baseman and left fielder Larry "Chipper" Jones had a huge eight All-Star appearances, a World Series championship, MVP, batting championship, and more, while center fielder Larry Doby made history as the second black player in Major League Baseball (and the first in the American League) while going on to score a total of eight All-Star selections, championships in both the Negro World Series and World Series, home run leader and RBI leader titles, and more.

Hall of Fame Miami Dolphins fullback Larry Csonka played in five Pro Bowls and won two Super Bowls; guard Larry Allen had eleven Pro Bowl selections in his long career, which was played mostly with the Dallas Cowboys, who he won a Super Bowl with; and Arizona Cardinals wide receiver Larry Fitzgerald's eleven Pro Bowl games came with receptions and receptions touchdown leader spots, and a number of awards and NFL records.

While one basketball player certainly stands at the top of the Larry rankings, he's not the only one who made it big in the NBA. There's also point guard Larry Brown, whose career in the 1960s included three American Baseball Association All-Star selections, an ABA championship, and a gold medal at the 1964 Olympic Games in Tokyo. Of course, there's no discussion of NBA legends without Boston Celtics small forward/power forward Larry Bird. Ranked among the top basketball players of all time, Bird has an extensive list of accomplishments and accolades, including twelve All-Star appearances, three NBA championships, multiple MVPs, Hall of Fame inductions, an Olympic gold medal he received as part of the 1992 "Dream Team," and many more.

Whether you name him *Laurence*, *Lawrence*, *Lazarus*, or just Larry, a boy with this name in your family can achieve great things, especially if he's backed up by a solid team. Or he may just be a natural-born fighter with incredible stamina and longevity, like world heavyweight champion boxer Larry Holmes, one of the top-ranked fighters of all time; he held the elite championship from 1978 to 1985 at the end of his incredible forty-eight straight wins, finishing out his career with a 69–6 record.

Larry Allen Sr., Football (Guard), Dallas Cowboys, USA, 1994–2007

Larry Bird, Basketball (Small Forward/Power Forward), Boston Celtics, USA, 1979–1992

Lawrence "Larry" Brown, Basketball (Point Guard), Oakland Oaks, USA, 1967–1972

Larry Csonka, Football (Fullback), Miami Dolphins, USA, 1968–1979

Lawrence "Larry" Doby, Baseball (Center Fielder), Cleveland Indians, USA, 1942–1962

Larry Fitzgerald Jr., Football (Wide Receiver), Arizona Cardinals, USA, 2004–2020

Larry Holmes, Boxing (Heavyweight), USA, 1973-2002

Larry "Chipper" Jones Jr., Baseball (Third Baseman/Left Fielder), Atlanta Braves, USA, 1993–2012

Larry Myricks, Track & Field (Long Jump), USA, 1976–1991

Larry Robinson, Ice Hockey (Defense), Montreal Canadiens, Canada, 1973–1992

Larry Scott, Bodybuilding, USA, 1959–1980

LARS

Lars originated as a Scandinavian offshoot of the name *Laurence/Lawrence*, and today it enjoys popularity throughout Western Europe. Three Olympic gold-medalists and world champions have gone by this moniker and may inspire a young Lars in your family to excel in throwing, swimming, or a combination of seemingly unrelated events. These are five-time world champion German discus thrower Lars Riedel; Swedish swimmer Lars Frölander, who stood on the podium three times at the Olympics (one gold and two silvers) and twenty-one times at World Championships (including nine wins); and Swedish pentathlete Lars Hall, who won two Olympic gold medals and six world championships!

Lars Frölander, Swimming (Butterfly/Freestyle), Sweden, 1992–2012

Lars Hall, Track & Field (Pentathlon), Sweden, 1949–1953

Lars Riedel, Track & Field (Discus), Germany, 1990–2006

LAURENCE/LAWRENCE

Laurences and Lawrences may not all come from ancient Laurentum in Italy, but the "laurels" origin of the name helps explain their athletic achievements and will inspire the same in a boy you give one of these names to. New York Giants outside linebacker Lawrence "L.T." Taylor scored big with ten Pro Bowl appearances, two Super Bowl wins, three NFL Defensive Player of the Year titles, and more. A notable character was American track and field star Laurence "Lon" Myers in the 1880s, whose long list of world and national records was matched only by the uniqueness of some of his accomplishments, including setting the world quarter-mile record missing a shoe and winning a race by running sideways.

The most famous Lawrence in sports is rarely remembered for his real name, but rather for his distinctive nickname. Baseball Hall of Famer Lawrence "Yogi" Berra is counted among the best catchers and overall players of all-time, and in his nineteen seasons, he racked up eighteen All-Star appearances, a record ten World Series wins, three American League MVP selections, and more! Also famous for his off-the-field antics and sayings, Berra, despite his relatively short stature, was a giant figure in baseball whose personality and play will stay strong in the hearts and minds of fans forever.

Lawrence "Yogi" Berra, Baseball (Catcher), New York Yankees, USA, 1946–1965

Laurence "Lon" Myers, Track & Field (Sprinting/Middle-Distance Running), USA, 1880–1887

Lawrence "L.T." Taylor, Football (Outside Linebacker), New York Giants, USA, 1981–1993

LEBRON

LeBron can be traced back to Spanish roots for "hare" and French for "brown," but the path forward for a LeBron in your family is clear if he follows in the enormous footsteps of LeBron James. Ranked among the greatest basketball players of all time, LeBron's achievements are legendary; these include eighteen All-Star selections, four NBA Championships (with three different teams), four MVP awards and four NBA Finals MVPs, Scoring Champion and Assists Leader titles, three medals from the Olympic Games (including two golds), and many more.

LeBron James Sr., Basketball (Small Forward), Los Angeles Lakers, USA, 2003–current

LEE

The unisex name Lee stretches back to an Old English word for "clearing," which makes sense when you look at the champions with that name and their successes on fields, pitches, and tracks. Some gravitate toward team sports, like seven-time MLB All-Star relief pitcher and four-time saves leader Lee Smith; and English rugby champion Lee Smith, who collected wins in three Grand Finals, a Federation Shield, and the 2008 World Cup Challenge.

Meanwhile, Lees who have competed on their own have absolutely dominated their respective sports, like bodybuilder Lee Haney, who holds the co-record for most Mr. Olympia wins (eight), and NASCAR legend Lee Petty, whose career began with the start of the stock car racing company and included fifty-four wins and three championships in the elite series. Finally, golf has seen the highest highs of English Lee Westwood (world number one in 2010, with forty-four professional wins) and American Lee Trevino, who's ranked among the all-time greats with his ninety-two professional wins (including twenty-nine on the PGA Tour), six major championships, and induction into the Hall of Fame.

Name a little one Lee and let him loose; he may find his stride lifting weights, hitting holes in one, or playing with friends on a team!

Lee Haney, Bodybuilding, USA, 1982–1991

Lee Petty, Auto Racing (NASCAR), USA, 1949–1961

Lee Smith, Baseball (Relief Pitcher), Chicago Cubs, USA, 1980–1997

Lee Smith, Rugby (Wing/Fullback/Center), Leeds Rhinos, England, 2005–current

Lee Trevino, Golf, USA, 1960–1976

Lee Westwood, Golf, England, 1993–current

LEIGHTON/LLEYTON

A name with very humble origins, *Layton* was a place name for English "towns with leek gardens" and a name for the people who lived there; in modern times, it has been adapted into variants like Leighton and Lleyton, and, more importantly, it has climbed to the highest of heights. Australian tennis pro Lleyton Hewitt reached the number one singles rank in the world with thirty titles and two Grand Slams, and Welsh darts player Leighton Rees held the world top spot and won the very first British Darts Organization World Professional Darts Championship.

Lleyton Hewitt, Tennis, Australia, 1998–2020

Leighton Rees, Darts, Wales, 1970–1991

LENNOX

When sports fans hear the name Lennox, they probably don't think of elm trees in Scotland, but Gaelic is the primary source for its origin. Instead, the one man who comes to mind is Lennox "the Lion" Lewis, the last undisputed heavyweight world champion boxer! Lewis, with dual Canadian and British citizenship, retired from the sweet science with an incredible 41-2-1 record, having won an Olympic gold medal, the heavyweight world championship three times, and more.

Gift your son the name Lennox to instill in him the patience, endurance, and power to rise to the top of his chosen field.

Lennox "the Lion" Lewis, Boxing (Heavyweight), Canada/England, 1989–2003

LEONARD

Leonard has a pretty cool origin, with Germanic roots meaning "brave lion," but the name does not appear frequently among top athletes. A notable example, however, was Maple Leafs and Red Wings icon Leonard Kelly, better known as "Red." Playing in defense and center positions, Kelly was selected six times to the NHL All-Star game and won the Stanley Cup eight times, four times each with his two teams! Being a part of those dynasties and his long career of consistent playing led to his induction in the Hall of Fame.

Whether your Leonard sports a hair color-themed nickname or not, he'll have focus and determination—and probably enjoy ice skating.

Leonard "Red" Kelly, Ice Hockey (Defense/Center), Toronto Maple Leafs, Canada, 1947–1967

LEO/LIONEL

Some animals are so regal and so majestic that they inspire us to name children after them, and that's definitely the case with lions. There are many "lion" derived names around the world, and it just so happens that one of them was given to arguably the greatest footballer (or soccer player, depending on where you're from) of all time. Argentinian-born Lionel Messi, then only sixteen years old, took the world by storm when he joined Barcelona C and started racking up impressive stats. His transition from youth to adult player came quickly with a fierce training regimen, and he signed on with the senior team on his eighteenth birthday in 2005. If the rest is history, it's a glorious one, with a long list of achievements including goal records, championships, special awards, and more, just some of which include winning La Liga ten times, Copa del Rey seven times, Supercopa de España seven times, UEFA Champions League four times, UEFA Super Cup three times, FIFA Club World Cup three times, 2022 FIFA World Cup, Ballon d'Or seven times, and many more player awards and accolades.

Give your child a leonine spirit and drive to excel with the name Lionel (and nickname Leo)!

Lionel "Leo" Messi, Soccer (Forward), Fútbol Club Barcelona, Argentina, 2003–current

LEROY

See *Satchel* for Leroy "Satchel" Paige.

LEW

Lew is most often seen as a classic short form of *Lewis*, but it can also be given as a name on its own or as a variant of other names, like *Lev*. Aside from Australian tennis pro Lew Hoad, who reached the singles world number one spot in 1953, the rest of the champion Lews have been Americans, and their fields vary from basketball (1948 Olympic gold-medalist guard Lew Beck) to golf (Lew Worsham, who had thirteen wins in professional series, including six on the PGA Tour and the US Open in 1947) and boxing (Hall of Fame lightweight puncher Lew Jenkins, who held the World Lightweight Championship in 1940 and knocked out fifty-two of his seventy-four wins).

As you can see by those dates, the name Lew is due for a comeback!

Lewis "Lew" Beck Jr., Basketball (Guard), USA, 1948

Lewis "Lew" Hoad, Tennis, Australia, 1950–1973

Lew Jenkins, Boxing (Lightweight), USA, 1935–1950

Lewis "Lew" Worsham Jr., Golf, USA, 1935–1956

LEWIS

While *Lews* have been more prevalent in the United States, competitors and pioneers going by the full name Lewis have mostly come from the United Kingdom. Rugby seems to be a sport popular with men named Lewis, including Lewis Jones, who was Leeds Rhinos's first player to score over one thousand points and who won the championship with them in 1961, and flanker Lewis "Mad Dog" Moody, who led his teams to multiple Premierships and the 2003 World Cup.

When it comes to pure speed, though, no Lewis can compare with British Formula 1 giant Lewis Hamilton. Starting at an early age with remote-control cars and go-karts, Hamilton rose through the ranks and entered the premier racing series in 2007. Since then, he's racked up a record 103 wins and a record-tying seven championships—and he's still racing!

You don't have to be British to name a kid Lewis, but if you do, there's a good chance he'll be independent and daring and, of course, he'll like to go fast.

- **Lewis Hamilton**, Auto Racing (Formula 1), England, 2007–current
- **Benjamin Lewis Jones**, Rugby (Full-Back/Center/Wing), Leeds Rhinos, Wales, 1950–1969
- **Lewis "Mad Dog" Moody**, Rugby (Flanker), Leicester Tigers, England, 1996–2012

LIAM

Liam is a great name for a team player who loves to be out on the field with his friends. Originating as a short form for *William* in Ireland, Liam has spread to popularity across the United Kingdom and has appeared on leaderboards in cricket (bowler Liam Plunkett, who won the 2019 Cricket World Cup with the England cricket team) and sprint canoeing (British Olympic gold-medalist and two-time world champion Liam Heath).

International football has seen the exploits of many Liams, with a standout like English defender Ridgewell, who had success in Major League Soccer with an All-Star selection and an MLS Cup win with the Portland Timbers. Then there are the champions with this name who have starred in rugby, with some of the top contenders including English prop Liam Watts, who earned a spot on the Super League Dream Team and won the Challenge Cup with Hull Football Club; and fullback Liam Williams of Wales, whose list of trophies features a Pro12 Grand Final, 2019 premiership and European Rugby Champions Cup, a Grand Slam, and the 2019 Six Nations Championship!

- **Liam Heath**, Sprint Canoeing, England, 2009–2022
- **Liam Plunkett**, Cricket (Bowler), Durham County Cricket Club, England, 2003–current
- **Liam Ridgewell**, Soccer (Defender), Portland Timbers, England, 2002–2020
- **Liam Watts**, Rugby (Prop), Hull Football Club, England, 2007–current
- **Liam Williams**, Rugby (Fullback), Scarlets, Wales, 2010–current

LORENZO

The origins of *Laurence* stretch back to ancient Rome, while later, the variant form Lorenzo appeared in Italian and Spanish. If a Lorenzo in your family takes athletic inspiration from others with his name, he'll definitely be a dedicated team player and work well with others. American football has seen the exploits of four-time Pro Bowl fullback Lorenzo Neal, and Italian volleyball sensation Lorenzo Bernardi sits on many best-ever lists with his accomplishments, including two World Championship wins, a World Cup, and five World League wins.

- **Lorenzo Bernardi**, Volleyball (Outside Hitter), Italy, 1984–2007
- **Lorenzo Neal**, Football (Fullback), San Diego Chargers, USA, 1993–2009

LOU

A classic unisex name that can be a short form for *Louis*, *Luigi*, and others, Lou is primarily known in baseball, but that's not all. Let's not forget bodybuilder Lou Ferrigno, who won the Mr. Universe competition twice before kicking off a career as the Hulk. Multiple Lous have made their mark on the baseball diamond and were inducted into the Hall of Fame, like Cleveland Indians shortstop Lou Boudreau who had eight All-Star appearances, grabbed the American League batting champion title, and was named AL MVP the year he won the World Series (1948). Of course, topping the charts is New York Yankees first baseman Lou Gehrig. In his seventeen seasons with the team, he racked up seven All-Star selections, six World Series championships, a batting champion title, three home run leader rankings, a Triple Crown, MVPs, and numerous records. The teammate of Babe Ruth has also attained legendary status for how he dealt with the onset of amyotrophic lateral sclerosis (Lou Gehrig's disease) and the world-famous speech he gave upon his retirement.

While a young man you name Lou may not achieve such lofty heights, hopefully he will embody the sportsmanship and striving for success we see here.

Louis "Lou" Boudreau, Baseball (Shortstop), Cleveland Indians, USA, 1938–1952

Louis "Lou" Ferrigno Sr., Bodybuilding, USA, 1972–1995

Henry Louis "Lou" Gehrig, Baseball (First Baseman), New York Yankees, USA, 1923–1939

LOUIS

The name Louis has an interesting origin story coming from a French version of a Latinized version of *Ludwig*, which in turn comes from Germanic roots for "famous battle." A Louis in your family may be inspired by the "battle" part, or he may prefer to go fast. That aspect of athletes named Louis shows itself in Olympic gold-medalist sprinter Louis "Pinky" Clarke; race car driver Louis Meyer, who was the first person to win the Indianapolis 500 three times; and French three-time Tour de France–winner and world champion cyclist Louis "Louison" Bobet.

Louis "Louison" Bobet, Road Cycling, France, 1946–1961

Louis "Pinky" Clarke, Track & Field (Sprinting), USA, 1924

Louis Meyer, Auto Racing (Indianapolis 500), USA, 1928–1939

LUCAS/LUKAS/ŁUKASZ

Lucas comes to us from an ancient place name for people from Lucania in Italy, and European variants include the popular Lukas (commonly found in Germany, Scandinavia, and Lithuania) and Łukasz (from Poland). It's not too surprising, then, that the majority of highly successful athletes with these names have made their fame on the football (soccer) field, though that's not all. Polish kickboxer Łukasz Jarosz held the World Super Heavyweight championship, Danish esports champ Lukas "gla1ve" Rossander was on the team that first won four *Counter-Strike: Global Offensive* Major Championships, and Brazilian volleyball middle blocker Lucas Saatkamp has won an Olympic gold medal, a World Championship, a World Cup, three World Grand Champions Cups, and more.

Heading to the soccer field, there's a big list of champions with these names, with the hightest ranks including UEFA Super Cup and FIFA World Cup–winning defender Lucas Hernandez of France; Spanish right winger and back Lucas Vázquez, who grabbed trophies for four UEFA Champions Leagues, three La Liga, three UEFA Super Cups, and three FIFA Club World Cups; and Polish forward Lukas Podolski, who has scored over 260 goals on his way to winning an FA Cup, FIFA World Cup, and more.

Whichever spelling you prefer (and don't sleep on the cool Łukasz version), a Lucas name can give your son the speed and coordination to play and enjoy soccer or any other sport!

- **Lucas Hernandez**, Soccer (Defender), Fußball-Club Bayern München e. V., France, 2014–current
- **Łukasz Jarosz**, Kickboxing (Heavyweight), Poland, 2006–current
- **Lukas Podolski**, Soccer (Forward), Arsenal Football Club, Poland, 2003–current
- **Lukas "gla1ve" Rossander**, Esports (*Counter-Strike: Global Offensive*), Denmark, 2012–current
- **Lucas Saatkamp**, Volleyball (Middle Blocker), Brazil, 2004–current
- **Lucas Vázquez**, Soccer (Right Winger/Right-Back), Real Madrid Club de Fútbol, Spain, 2010–current

LUIGI

While here in the United States, the name might be most famous for the video game brother of Mario, Luigi is a classic Italian variant of the name *Louis*. Luigis are known for their athletic accomplishments. The Italian 1936 Berlin Olympics 8-meter class sailing team included two Luigis (De Manincor and Poggi) who went home with gold medals, while, similarly, gymnasts Luigi Cambiaso and Luigi Maiocco won Olympic team gold together in 1920 and 1924 (with Maiocco having picked up a third in 1912). Separated by a few more years were 1948 Olympic gold-medalist épée fencer Luigi Cantone and two-time sabre world champion Luigi Tarantino, who won in the '90s.

As you might expect, an Italian name like Luigi has featured prominently in soccer over the years, and in fact, the 1934 FIFA World Cup champion team had two of them, defender Luigi Allemandi and midfielder Luigi Bertolini! Two years later, midfielder Luigi Scarabello would take home an Olympic gold medal in 1936, while in the 1990s, defender Luigi Apolloni had a tremendous career with Parma, winning two Coppa Italias, a Supercoppa Italiana, two UEFA Cups, a UEFA Cup Winner's Cup, and a UEFA Super Cup.

You don't have to be of Italian heritage to give the name Luigi to your son, but if you do, you should definitely teach him the fundamentals of soccer; he's likely to enjoy that sport.

- **Luigi Allemandi**, Soccer (Defender), Football Club Internazionale Milano, Italy, 1919–1939
- **Luigi Apolloni**, Soccer (Defender), Parma Calcio 1913, Italy, 1984–2001
- **Luigi Bertolini**, Soccer (Midfielder), Juventus Football Club, Italy, 1924–1940
- **Luigi Cambiaso**, Artistic Gymnastics, Italy, 1920–1924
- **Luigi Cantone**, Fencing (Épée), Italy, 1948
- **Luigi De Manincor**, Sailing, Italy, 1936–1948
- **Luigi Maiocco**, Artistic Gymnastics, Italy, 1912–1924
- **Luigi Poggi**, Sailing, Italy, 1936–1948
- **Luigi Scarabello**, Soccer (Midfielder), Genoa Cricket and Football Club, Italy, 1933–1947
- **Luigi Tarantino**, Fencing (Sabre), Italy, 1995–2012

LUIS/LUÍS

Another variant of *Louis*, Luis is Spanish and sometimes features an accent. As we'll see with the internationally famous athletes with this name, a boy named Luis is likely to enjoy playing with friends outdoors, either on the baseball diamond or soccer field.

Heading out to America's pastime, we start off with three-time All-Stars like Cuban two-time American League ERA leader Luis Tiant, and Dominican second baseman Luis Castillo, who won a World Series with the Florida Marlins and earned two stolen base leader titles and three Gold Glove Awards, while left fielder Luis Gonzalez earned five All-Star selections along with a World Series win and a Silver Slugger. Standing above the rest is Venezuelan Luis Aparicio, the Hall of Fame shortstop who played in no fewer than thirteen All-Star games, won the 1966 World Series with the Baltimore Orioles, and whose other accolades include nine Gold Glove Awards and nine AL stolen base leader titles.

The list of international football players named Luis (and Luís) who have won big is *extensive*. Just a few from the very top include Argentinian midfielder Luis Monti (Coppa Italia, Central European International Cup, two FIFA World Cup All-Star Team appearances, and FIFA World Cup), Spanish midfielder Luis Suárez (two La Liga, two European Cups, two Intercontinental Cups, and Ballon d'Or), and Portuguese winger Luís Figo (four La Liga, two Copas del Rey, UEFA Cup Winner's Cup, two UEFA Super Cups, Intercontinental Cup, and Ballon d'Or)!

- **Luis Aparicio**, Baseball (Shortstop), Chicago White Sox, Venezuela, 1956–1973
- **Luis Castillo**, Baseball (Second Baseman), Florida Marlins, Dominican Republic, 1996–2010
- **Luís Figo**, Soccer (Winger), Fútbol Club Barcelona, Portugal, 1989–2009
- **Luis Gonzalez**, Baseball (Left Fielder), Arizona Diamondbacks, USA, 1990–2008
- **Luis Monti**, Soccer (Midfielder), Juventus Football Club, Argentina, 1921–1939
- **Luis Suárez**, Soccer (Midfielder), Football Club Internazionale Milano, Spain, 1953–1973
- **Luis Tiant**, Baseball (Pitcher), Boston Red Sox, Cuba, 1964–1982

LUKE

An English variant of *Lucas*, the name Luke is popular in the United States and various places around the world. Interestingly, there are lots of Lukes who have made powerful impacts in rugby! If a Luke in your family is tough and enjoys getting into the scrum, he may take after champions like English hooker Luke Cowan-Dickie, whose senior career accolades include two Six Nations Championships, Autumn Nations Cup, and two Premierships; lock Luke Romano, who won the 2015 Rugby World Cup with the New Zealand team; and English Luke Thompson, who's played prop and lock and won two Super League Grand Finals.

We also see Lukes on the field, rink, and track. On the gridiron, Carolina Panthers linebacker Luke Kuechly had seven Pro-Bowl appearances along with a slew of awards, while ice hockey greats include American Paralympic Games gold-medalist and two-time world champion ice sledge hockey player Luke McDermott. Lastly, no Lukes are faster on two wheels than a trio of Australians riding team pursuit: Olympic gold-medalist Luke Roberts, world champion Luke Durbridge, and two-time world champion Luke Davison.

Other team players include seven-time MLB All-Star Chicago White Sox shortstop Luke Appling, who twice held the American League batting champion title, and Luke Doerner (field hockey winner of the 2010 World Cup and five Champions Trophies).

- **Lucius "Luke" Appling**, Baseball (Shortstop), Chicago White Sox, USA, 1930–1950
- **Luke Cowan-Dickie**, Rugby (Hooker), Exeter Chiefs, England, 2010–current
- **Luke Davison**, Road/Track Cycling, Australia, 2011–current
- **Luke Doerner**, Field Hockey (Defender), Tassie Tigers, Australia, 2006–2012
- **Luke Durbridge**, Road/Track Cycling, Australia, 2010–current
- **Luke Kuechly**, Football (Linebacker), Carolina Panthers, USA, 2012–2019
- **Luke McDermott**, Ice Sledge Hockey, USA, 2015–current

- **Luke Roberts**, Road/Track Cycling, Australia, 1998–2013
- **Luke Romano**, Rugby (Lock), Crusaders, New Zealand, 2009–current
- **Luke Thompson**, Rugby (Prop/Lock), St Helens R.F.C., England, 2013–current

GIRLS

LAILA/LAYLA

Some names bring with them ideals of grace, speed, or endurance, but Laila and Layla are pure toughness. You wouldn't necessarily expect that from their origins—Layla meaning "night" in Arabic and a form of Laila coming from Old Norse for "blessed"—but we definitely see that in two American champion boxers! Laila Ali went undefeated in her twenty-four-bout career, holding the light heavyweight title and multiple super middleweight titles, while Layla McCarter fought her way to world titles in five different weight classes with forty-four wins; both are ranked among the top female boxers of all time!

- **Laila Ali**, Boxing (Middleweight/ Heavyweight), USA, 1999–2007
- **Layla McCarter**, Boxing (Featherweight/ Lightweight/Welterweight/Middleweight), USA, 1998–current

LARISA/LARISSA

You probably don't hear the name Larisa/ Larissa very often unless you're a fan of Greek history (it was a city in Thessaly), Greek mythology (she was a nymph), or astronomy (it's one of the moons of Neptune). Coming from a root for "citadel," the name has a powerful athletic history in Russia, though it can turn up anywhere, like with Brazilian world champion and World Tour Finals-winning volleyball player Larissa França. Then there are five-time Olympic gold-medalist and eleven-time world champion cross-country skier Larisa Lazutina; and artistic gymnasts two-time Olympic Games-winner Larisa

Petrik and world champion Larisa Latynina, whose medal collection includes nine winning titles each from both the Olympics and World Championships (and fourteen more podium appearances)!

Larisa/Larissa is a cool name with an interesting ancient pedigree, and can give a girl poise, assertiveness, and, quite possibly, a love of gymnastics.

- **Larissa França**, Beach Volleyball, Brazil, 2004–current
- **Larisa Latynina**, Artistic Gymnastics, USSR, 1953–1966
- **Larisa Lazutina**, Cross-Country Skiing, Russia, 1984–2002
- **Larisa Petrik**, Artistic Gymnastics, USSR, 1965–1970

LAURA

Like *Laurel*, Laura comes from Latin for the "laurel" tree, which has been a source of trophies for athletic competitors both literally and figuratively for thousands of years. Where might a Laura in your family earn her laurels? If she follows in the footsteps of others with her name, she may be a team player, like German volleyball world champion and Olympic gold-medalist Laura Ludwig, and softball outfielder Laura Berg, who won three gold medals at Olympic Games and four world championships. On the other hand, she could compete all on her own, like foil fencer Laura Badea-Cârlescu, who won a full set of Olympic medals and nine World Championship medals (including two wins) for Romania, and English golf legend Laura Davies, who has won eighty-seven pro events, including twenty on the LPGA Tour and four majors! German biathlete Laura Dahlmeier and British cyclist Laura Kenny have won both on their own and with teams, the former earning two Olympic gold medals and seven world championships and the latter matching the world championship number with five wins at Olympic Games. Meanwhile, Lauras from different countries have made big impacts on international soccer. German goalkeeper Laura Benkarth defended her teams on the way to an Olympic gold medal and a UEFA Women's Championship; and French center back Laura Georges was named to the FIFA Women's World Cup All-Star Team and won two UEFA Women's Champions Leagues and two Cyprus Cups!

- **Laura Badea-Cârlescu**, Fencing (Foil), Romania, 1994–2004
- **Laura Benkarth**, Soccer (Goalkeeper), SC Freiburg, Germany, 2009–current
- **Laura Berg**, Softball (Outfielder), WPSL Gold, USA, 1994–2001
- **Laura Dahlmeier**, Biathlon, Germany, 2013–2019
- **Laura Davies**, Golf, England, 1985–2010
- **Laura Georges**, Soccer (Center Back), Olympique Lyonnais Féminin, France, 2003–2018
- **Laura Kenny**, Road/Track Cycling, England, 2010–current
- **Laura Ludwig**, Beach Volleyball, Germany, 2004–current

LAUREN

A name with ancient roots (coming from a variant of *Laurence*, and thus the root "from Laurentum" in Italian), Lauren has had unisex uses in modern times. There are quite a few Laurens who have achieved athletic superiority in a bunch of different disciplines, and so offer many potential inspirations for a sporting girl in your family. These range from English cricket batter and wicketkeeper Lauren Winfield-Hill, who won the 2017 World Cup, to Australian world champion and World Cup Final gold-medalist artistic gymnast Lauren Mitchell; and Australian basketball phenom Lauren Jackson, whose lengthy list of accomplishments and accolades includes a World Cup, six WNBL and seven WNBA All-Star appearances, five WNBL championships, two WNBA championships, MVPs, and scoring titles.

Some Laurens prefer competing in the cold–like world champions Lauren Gibbs (bobsleigh) and Lauren Gray (curling) of America and Scotland, respectively, and Canadian eight-time Paralympic Games gold-medalist para-alpine skier Lauren Woolstencroft–while others prefer to face-off against their opponents in the ring, like taekwondo practitioner Lauren Burns (who won an Olympic gold medal for Australia), as well as Olympic gold-medalist and world champion middleweight boxer Lauren Price of Wales. International soccer has seen some highly successful competitors with this name as well, including the highly decorated forward/midfielder Lauren Holiday, who is the winner of two Olympic gold medals, two NWSL Championships, three Four Nations Tournaments, the FIFA World Cup 2015, a spot on the FIFA Women's World Cup All-Star Team, and so much more.

Lastly, Laurens seem to enjoy competing (and winning!) in the water. These include Olympic gold–medalist and two-time world champion water polo player Lauren Wenger, and American rower Lauren Schmetterling, who won a gold medal at the 2016 Olympic Games and three world championships. And then there are the swimmers themselves, with world champions like British Lauren Steadman (who also scored a Paralympic Games win in the triathlon), freestyle swimmer Lauren Boyle of New Zealand, and American freestyle Olympic gold-medalist Lauren Perdue.

As you can see, a Lauren can find great success in whichever field she chooses!

Lauren Boyle, Swimming (Freestyle), New Zealand, 2006-2017

Lauren Burns, Taekwondo, Australia, 1996-2000

Lauren Gibbs, Bobsled, USA, 2016-current

Lauren Gray, Curling (Third/Lead), Scotland, 2011-current

Lauren Holiday, Soccer (Forward/Midfielder), FC Kansas City, USA, 2009-2015

Lauren Jackson, Basketball (Power Forward/Center), Seattle Storm, Australia, 1997-current

Lauren Mitchell, Artistic Gymnastics, Australia, 2007-2016

Lauren Perdue, Swimming (Freestyle), USA, 2010-2012

Lauren Price, Boxing (Middleweight), Wales, 2011-current

Lauren Schmetterling, Rowing, USA, 2013-current

Lauren Steadman, Swimming/Triathlon, England, 2008-current

Lauren Wenger, Water Polo (Defender), USA, 2002-2012

Lauren Winfield-Hill, Cricket (Batter/ Wicketkeeper), Oval Invincibles, England, 2007-current

Lauren Woolstencroft, Para-Alpine Skiing, Canada, 2002-2010

LAURENCE

If you're looking for a unique "L" name that can bring with it a competitive nature, love of speed, and a familiarity in the water, then Laurence might be perfect for you! Descended from an ancient name for people from Laurentum in Italy, Laurence is unisex and has been featured on international sprint canoe podiums with Canadian Laurence Lapointe, who won an astounding eleven gold medals at Canoe Sprint World Championships.

Laurence Lapointe, Sprint Canoe, Canada, 2010-current

LAURIE

Originating as a short form of names like *Laura* and *Laurence*, Laurie has long since established itself as a name all on its own. We can see a pair of champion athletes with this name from North America, with American Olympic gold-medalists ice hockey forward Laurie Baker and artistic gymnast Laurie Hernandez.

Name your daughter Laurie, or another "L" name with Laurie as a nickname, and she may very well prefer cold sports or competitive gymnastics.

Laurie Baker, Ice Hockey (Forward), USA, 1994–2002

Lauren "Laurie" Hernandez, Artistic Gymnastics, USA, 2012–2016

LAVONE

A variant of *Lavonne*, which comes from the same linguistic family as *Yvonne*, and ultimately from a Germanic root for the "yew" tree, Lavone may sound like an outdated name, but it certainly could be an inspirational moniker for a family of baseball lovers. In the 1940s, Lavone "Pepper" Paire was a catcher and infielder in the All-American Girls Professional Baseball League, winning the championship with the Racine Belles in 1946 and earning a spot on the 1948 All-Star team. The National Women's Baseball Hall of Famer also topped leaderboards in RBIs and fielding percentage!

Lavone "Pepper" Paire, Baseball (Catcher/Infielder), Racine Belles, USA, 1944–1953

LEANNE

Originating as a combination of two separate names (*Lee* and *Anne*), Leanne has made appearances at the top levels of two very different sports. Leanne Wong is a recent world champion artistic gymnast, while Leanne Barrette has won twenty-six titles on the Professional Women's Bowling Association Tour, including three Player of the Year awards and induction into the PWBA Hall of Fame.

A little Leanne in your family may find fame and fortune in gymnastics or bowling, or another field as unique as she is!

Leanne Barrette, Bowling, USA, 1987–current

Leanne Wong, Artistic Gymnastics, USA, 2019–current

LEAH

The biblical Hebrew name Leah has somewhat uncertain origins, most often attributed to a Hebrew root meaning "weary" but possibly coming from an Akkadian word for "cow." No matter its origins, Leahs are going places and taking accolades, propelling women to success in their preferred fields (or tracks or courses). Leah Neuberger won gold at the World Table Tennis Championships, race car driver Leah Pruett has won thirteen races across two elite series and a championship in Top Fuel, and English midfielder/center back Leah Williamson has a trophy case full of soccer accomplishments, including two FA Women's Cups, two FA WSL Cups, a SheBelieves Cup, and a UEFA Women's Championship!

Give your little Leah open roads and see how far she'll travel.

Leah Neuberger, Table Tennis, USA, 1947–1956

Leah Pruett, Auto Racing (Top Fuel), USA, 2013–current

Leah Williamson, Soccer (Midfielder/Center Back), Arsenal Women Football Club, England, 2014–current

LEE/LEE-

The Western unisex name Lee may come from Old English for "clearing," but champion athletes who go by this name have won their events on sea, ice, and in the gym. These include American Olympic gold-medalist and world champion foil fencer Lee Kiefer, Israeli four-time Windsurfing World Championship-winning Lee Korzits, and speed skater Chun Lee-kyung of South Korea, who took home four Olympic gold medals (and a silver), along with twenty-three medals from individual world championships (including nine wins) and six from World Team Championships!

Whether you like the Old English or the Korean version, Lee is a great name for an adventurous and ambitious child.

Chun Lee-kyung, Speed Skating, South Korea, 1990–1998

Lee Kiefer, Fencing (Foil), USA, 2010–current

Lee Korzits, Windsurfing, Israel, 2003–2013

LEI

If you're hoping for a daughter who's strong and daring, the unisex name Lei might be perfect for you. A popular Chinese name, Lei can have various meanings, including "bud" and "pile of stones." Chinese athletes in the 2000s proved the power of the name with two-time world champion weightlifter Wang Lei and mountain climber Cao Lei, the first Chinese woman (and first Asian-American) to conquer the Seven Summits of the world, ski to both North and South Poles, and accomplish the fabled "Explorer's Grand Slam."

Cao Lei, Weightlifting, China, 2001–2010

Wang Lei, Mountaineering, China, 2003–2010

LEILANI

Originating in Hawaii, the name Leilani can mean "royal offspring" or "heavenly flowers." Other than its pretty sound and meaning, the name brings with it a depth of possibility and hope for the future. This is exemplified in such stellar icons as squash World Doubles Championship-winner Leilani Rorani of New Zealand, and three-time American-Australian Women's National Basketball League All-Star point guard and three-time WNBL champion Leilani Mitchell.

Leilani Mitchell, Basketball (Point Guard), Canberra Capitals, Australia/USA, 2008–current

Leilani Rorani, Squash, New Zealand, 1996–2002

LENA

Arising as a short form for a number of very different names, including *Helena*, *Magdalena*, and *Yelena*, Lena has also grown into its own as a full-fledged name. Lenas from all around the world have achieved fantastic successes and accomplishments and are great role models for little girls who share their name. They could inspire her to try out gymnastics, like Belarusian artistic gymnast Lena Piskun, who won world championships on the vault and uneven bars; mixed martial arts, like Ukrainian WBC Muaythai World Featherweight Champion Lena Ovchýnnikova; or windsurfing, like Turkish Professional Windsurfers Association World Cup gold-medalist and two-time International Funboard Class Association slalom world champion Lena Erdil.

Interestingly, the name seems to bring with it a degree of accuracy and can make your daughter into a markswoman, like American sport shooter Lena Miculek, who has won gold at the International Practical Shooting Confederation (IPSC) Rifle World Shoot and three gold medals at the IPSC Shotgun World Shoot, and Lena Neuner of Germany, who put herself at the top of all-time greatest biathletes with two Olympic gold medals (and a silver), a record twelve golds, four silvers, and a bronze from World Championships, and, at World Cup events, thirty-four wins, three overall titles, and seven discipline titles.

- **Lena Erdil**, Windsurfing, Turkey, 2006–current
- **Lena Miculek**, Sport Shooting (Rifle/Shotgun), USA, 2011–current
- **Magdalena "Lena" Neuner**, Biathlon, Germany, 2006–2012
- **Oléna "Lena" Ovchýnnikova**, Kickboxing/MMA (Featherweight), Ukraine, 2006–current
- **Elena "Lena" Piskun**, Artistic Gymnastics, Belarus, 1993–1997

LETICIA

The Spanish Leticia evolved from the Latin root of *Letitia*, meaning "happiness." Brazil has given us some very inspirational Leticias, like six-time X Games gold-medalist and World Skateboarding Championship-winning street skateboarder Letícia Bufoni and Leticia Ribeiro, who became one of the top-ranked female jiu-jitsu black belts of all time with more than a dozen wins at World Championships and World Cups.

It may not be in martial arts or skateboarding, but a Leticia in your family is sure to discover her happiness through competition and athleticism.

- **Letícia Bufoni**, Skateboarding (Street), Brazil, 2007–current
- **Leticia Ribeiro**, Jiu-Jitsu, Brazil, 1996–2014

LIDIA/LIDIYA/LYDIA

The name Lydia stretches back to ancient times and the town of that name in Asia Minor, while different languages and regions in Europe would go on to create variant forms Lidia and Lidiya. Athletic Lidias, Lidiyas, and Lydias from all over the world have been scoring goals, winning races, and setting records in a huge variety of fields, including marathon running (like Romanian world champion Lidia Şimon), weightlifting (like Spanish Olympic gold-medalist and two-time world champion Lydia Valentín), and soccer (like Australian goalkeeper Lydia Williams, who defended her teams on their way to winning two W-League Premierships).

Meanwhile, a number of competitors with these names have gravitated toward events in the water or on ice and snow. These include Olympic gold-medalists Lydia Jacoby (swimming) from the United States and Lydia Lassila (freestyle skiing) of Australia, Israeli two-time world champion yacht sailor Lydia Lazarov, and the massively successful Soviet speed skater Lidiya Skoblikova, who won all six Olympic events she entered, as well as dozens of world championships.

If you fancy the name Lydia, you have some very interesting options for its spelling, and any girl you give that name to should be introduced to swimming, boating, and skiing as early as possible.

- **Lydia Jacoby**, Swimming (Breaststroke), USA, 2020–current
- **Lydia Lassila**, Freestyle Skiing, Australia, 2002–current
- **Lydia Lazarov**, Yachting, Israel, 1966–1970
- **Lidia Şimon**, Marathon, Romania, 1994–2012
- **Lidiya Skoblikova**, Speed Skating, USSR, 1959–1969
- **Lydia Valentín**, Weightlifting, Spain, 2002–current
- **Lydia Williams**, Soccer (Goalkeeper), Canberra United Football Club, Australia, 2005–current

LILIA

Floral names are popular all over the world, and a uniquely European form of *Lily* gives us the name Lilia. Sure to stand out in your daughter's class and team roster, this name can instill in her grace, flexibility, speed, and strength, especially if she follows in the footsteps of Cuban three-time Olympic gold-medalist volleyball player Lilia Izquierdo; artistic gymnast Lilia Podkopayeva of Ukraine, who won two Olympic golds and a silver, as well as five medals at World Championships; and Bulgarian six-time world champion rhythmic gymnast Lilia Ignatova, one of the so-called "Golden Girls of Bulgaria."

Lilia Ignatova, Rhythmic Gymnastics, Bulgaria, 1980–1986

Lilia Izquierdo, Volleyball (Setter), Cuba, 1992–2000

Lilia Podkopayeva, Artistic Gymnastics, Ukraine, 1993–1997

LILIANA

If you like the name *Lillian* but want something a little more unique for your daughter, consider the variant Liliana. Introduce a girl with that name to boats and she may find them exactly her speed, like three-time Olympic champion rower Liliana Gafencu of Romania!

Liliana Gafencu, Rowing, Romania, 1996–2004

LILLIAN

Can a name inspire someone to win Olympic gold? It just might in the case of Lillian, which may have come from a diminutive of *Elizabeth* or a variation of *Lily*. It has appeared at the top of podiums at Olympic Games multiple times, starting with early women's athletics pioneer Lillian Copeland (discus throw gold in 1932) and swimmer Lillian "Pokey" Watson (4x100-meter freestyle in 1964 and 200-meter backstroke in 1968), who won her first gold at only fourteen years old and set multiple world records in her career.

Lillian Copeland, Track & Field (Discus/Javelin/Shot Put), USA, 1928–1935

Lillian "Pokey" Watson, Swimming (Backstroke/Freestyle), USA, 1964–1968

LILY

A floral name like *Rose* and *Poppy*, Lily has spawned many variants (see several throughout this section), but the original still maintains popularity around the world. In recent years, Lilys have won in all sorts of athletic competitions, including rugby (Australian forward Lily Dick, who took home the 2022 Rugby Sevens World Cup), field hockey (English Olympic gold-medalist midfielder/forward Lily Owsley), and rowing (British Lily van den Broecke, who won gold at both Paralympic Games and World Championships).

Going back a ways, the name was also used by some incredibly brave and inspirational pioneers in women's sports. In 1906, Hungarian Lily Kronberger became the first women's world champion figure skater, going on to take home three more golds and two bronzes in total. And in 2002, the English Football Hall of Fame inducted one woman in its inaugural class, Lily Parr, who played soccer in the first half of the twentieth century against women and men, playing in over four hundred games and scoring over nine hundred goals!

With that pedigree, Lily is a great name for a future athlete and leader in her field.

Lily Dick, Rugby (Forward), Queensland Reds, Australia, 2015–current

Lily Kronberger, Figure Skating, Hungary, 1906–1911

Lily Owsley, Field Hockey (Midfield/Forward), England, 2013–current

Lilian "Lily" Parr, Soccer (Winger), Dick, Kerr Ladies F.C., England, 1919–1951

Lily van den Broecke, Rowing, England, 2011–2012

LINDSAY/LINDSEY/LYNDSEY

Coming from an Old English place name referring to the area around Lincoln Island, Lindsay has spread around the world and to multiple variants, including Lindsey and Lyndsey. American athletes with these names have gone on to great success in a number of fields, with some truly stand-out champions who are household names among fans. Some of the winners in different fields include five-time WNBA All-Star and four-time champion point guard Lindsay Whalen (who also won a pair each of Olympic gold medals and world championships), three-time X Games vertical skateboarding gold-medalist Lyndsey "Lyn-Z" Hawkins, two-time Olympic gold-medalist and seven-time world champion swimmer Lindsay Benko, and tennis great Lindsay Davenport, who reached the world number one spot in both singles and doubles (with fifty-five and thirty-eight titles, respectively), won an Olympic gold medal, and earned many more accolades.

Two Americans of this family of names have crushed it in soccer: two-time Olympic gold-medalist forward/winger Lindsay Tarpley and multi-position player Lindsey Horan, whose lengthy list of major wins and championships includes NWSL Champions, NWSL Challenge Cup, UEFA Women's Champions, two CONCACAF Women's Championships, and the 2019 FIFA Women's World Cup! And then there are the cold-weather athletes, like Olympic gold-medalist and two-time world champion Lindsey Vonn (alpine skiing), and Lindsey Jacobellis, who became the female snowboard cross competitor with the most medals and awards, with two Olympic golds and a silver, six world championship wins (and a bronze), and twelve medals at the X Games, ten of them being gold!

Any Lindsay-type name is a great contender for a kid who loves to play outside, whether that's on the tennis court, soccer field, or snow. And with the many different spelling variations, there's a perfect Lindsay, Lindsey, or Lyndsey for your family!

Lindsay Benko, Swimming (Freestyle/Backstroke), USA, 1997–2004

Lindsay Davenport, Tennis, USA, 1993–2011

Lyndsey "Lyn-Z" Hawkins, Skateboarding, USA, 1995–current

Lindsey Horan, Soccer (Forward/Midfielder), Portland Thorns FC, USA, 2012–current

Lindsey Jacobellis, Snowboarding, USA, 2003–current

Lindsay Tarpley, Soccer (Forward/Winger), USA, 1998–2011

Lindsey Vonn, Alpine Skiing, USA, 2000–2019

Lindsay Whalen, Basketball (Point Guard), Minnesota Lynx, USA, 2004–2016

LISA

The name *Elizabeth* (from biblical Hebrew meaning "my God is an oath") has spawned multiple diminutives and nicknames that have gone on to become popular monikers themselves, including Lisa. This short name is quite popular among successful athletes, with multiple examples from North America, Western Europe, Australia, and New Zealand. They're also spread out in many different sports, showing just how much potential a Lisa has in finding her perfect game and excelling in it. Surfer Lisa Andersen has won four world championships, Danish Lisa Gjessing is a Paralympic Games gold-medalist and four-time world champion para-taekwondo competitor, and sprint canoeist Lisa Carrington took the title of New Zealand's winningest Olympian, with five golds and a silver, to go along with her massive nineteen podium appearances (twelve of them wins) at World Championships.

Lisas also shine when it comes to team efforts! Lisa Raymond reached the number one tennis doubles rank in the world with seventy-nine titles and multiple records, German Lisa Buckwitz won Olympic gold in the two-woman bobsleigh, pitcher Lisa Fernandez threw her way to three Olympic softball gold medals, and Australian field hockey forward Lisa Powell won two Olympic golds and two World Cups. At the absolute top of their games have been Australian cricket all-rounder Lisa Sthalekar, who was on the teams winning the 2005 World Cup, 2010 World Twenty20, and 2013 Women's Cricket World Cup; and eight-time WNBA All-Star and two-time champion Los Angeles Sparks center Lisa Leslie, who racked up four Olympic gold medals, two world championships, and many more.

There are a couple places where multiple Lisas have excelled, the first being archery, with Canadian Lisa Buscombe, who won gold at World Field Archery Championships and World Games, and German Lisa Unruh, who won at a World Cup Final, The World Games, and a World Championship. Track and field events have also been popular with athletes of this name, with Canadian six-time Paralympic gold-medalist wheelchair sprinter Lisa Franks; Australian Lisa "the Cheetah" Llorens, who took home four Paralympic Games and four world championship golds in sprinting and jumping events; and Australian five-time Paralympic gold-medalist and five-time world champion sprinter Lisa McIntosh.

Lisa Andersen, Surfing, USA, 1987–2001

Lisa Buckwitz, Bobsleigh, Germany, 2015–current

Lisa Buscombe, Archery, Canada, 1984–1987

Lisa Carrington, Sprint Canoeing, New Zealand, 2009–current

Lisa Fernandez, Softball (Pitcher/Third Base), USA, 1990–2008

Lisa Franks, Wheelchair Racing, Canada, 2000–2004

Lisa Gjessing, Para-Taekwondo, Denmark, 2013–current

Lisa Leslie, Basketball (Center), Los Angeles Sparks, USA, 1997–2009

Lisa "The Cheetah" Llorens, Track & Field (High Jump/Long Jump), Australia, 1994–2004

Lisa McIntosh, Para-Athletics, Australia, 1998–2006

Lisa Powell, Field Hockey (Forward), Australia, 1990–2000

Lisa Raymond, Tennis, USA, 1989–2015

Lisa Sthalekar, Cricket (All-Rounder), New South Wales Women Cricket Team, Australia, 1997–2013

Lisa Unruh, Archery, Germany, 2008–current

LIZ/LIZZIE/LIZZY

Not only athletic prowess and success, but records and firsts are the purview of girls nicknamed (or sometimes just named) Liz, Lizzie, or Lizzy. Racing driver Liz Halliday-Sharp set the bar for women in the American Le Mans Series with six wins (the most at the time), Australian four-time WNBA All-Star center Liz Cambage set the league's single-game scoring record, and, way back in 1898, pitcher and infielder Lizzie Arlington became the first woman to play in men's professional baseball when she took the field with the Reading Coal Heavers!

English cyclist Lizzie Deignan has wins on road and track, including three world championships; British breaststroke and freestyle swimmer Liz Johnson collected one of each color medal at the Paralympic Games, along with four golds and three bronzes at World Championships; and British skeleton racer Lizzy Yarnold ended her career with a huge collection of two Olympic gold medals, a gold and two bronzes from World Championships, and a gold and silver from World Cup!

Elizabeth "Lizzie" Arlington, Baseball (Pitcher/Infielder), Reading Coal Heavers, USA, 1891–1898

Elizabeth "Liz" Cambage, Basketball (Center), Las Vegas Aces, Australia, 2007–current

Elizabeth "Lizzie" Deignan, Road/Track Cycling, England, 2008–current

Elisabeth "Liz" Halliday-Sharp, Auto Racing (American Le Mans Series), USA, 2001–2010

Elizabeth "Liz" Johnson, Swimming (Breaststroke/Freestyle), Wales, 2001–2012

Elizabeth "Lizzy" Yarnold, Skeleton, England, 2010–2018

LOGAN

While it's more known as a masculine name (especially with comic book characters like X-Men's Wolverine), the unisex Logan comes from Gaelic roots for "little hollow." In addition to having a cool-sounding name, a little Logan will exhibit precision, speed, and tenacity, all qualities exemplified by American volleyball outside hitter Logan Tom. Among her many accomplishments are three Volleyball World Grand Prix championships and numerous MVP awards.

Logan Tom, Volleyball (Outside Hitter), USA, 2002–2019

LOLO/LORI

Lori arose as a diminutive of names like *Laura*, *Lauren*, and *Lorraine* and has appeared on the athletic world stage with very impressive women, including Olympic gold-medalists Lori Dupuis of Canada and Lori Chalupny of the United States; the former an ice hockey forward who won three world championships and the latter a soccer midfielder who was on the roster for America's 2015 FIFA Women's World Cup win. But in some circles, the most famous Lori goes by a nickname; Lolo Jones has won world championships in both hurdling and bobsledding!

Name your daughter Lori to give her a champion's spirit (and potentially an affinity for ice hockey or soccer), and there's a built-in nickname with Lolo that can also give her a desire to go really fast.

Lori Chalupny, Soccer (Midfielder), Chicago Red Stars, USA, 2006–2015

Lori Dupuis, Ice Hockey (Forward), Brampton Thunder, Canada, 1995–2002

Lori "Lolo" Jones, Track & Field (Hurdling)/ Bobsleigh, USA, 2002–current

LOUISE

As you might expect, Louise is a variant of the French name *Louis*, which in turns comes from Germanic roots for "famous in battle." A Louise in your family may become just that, especially if she takes after three women who achieved renown on the battlefields of tennis courts, racetracks, and golf courses. When Louise "the first lady of racing" Smith entered the 1949 Daytona Beach Road Course NASCAR race, she helped set the record for three women participating in one race, tied for the second woman in NASCAR's top series, and would go on to win thirty-eight races across her seven-year driving career. More recently, Australian wheelchair racer and activist Louise Sauvage has amassed a huge collection of trophies and titles, with thirteen medals at the Paralympic Games (nine of them gold), eleven wins at the World Para Athletics Championships, two gold medals and a bronze at the Olympics (demonstration sports), four World Athletics Championships, and wins at four Boston Marathons, the Los Angeles Marathon, and the Berlin Marathon, and more. Lastly, Louise Suggs pioneered the sport of golf for women when she co-founded the LGPA Tour in 1950 and ultimately won sixty-one times at professional events and was inducted into the World Golf Hall of Fame.

Alix Louise Sauvage, Wheelchair Racing, Australia, 1990–2004

Louise Smith, Auto Racing (NASCAR), USA, 1949–1956

Mae Louise Suggs, Golf, USA, 1948–1960

LUCIA

The Roman name *Lucius* (from a root meaning "light") has evolved into the feminine form Lucia, which pops up in a number of Romance languages around the world, and Lucias from two different countries have become champions in three different sports. Romanian Lucia Toader has rowed with her teams to two World Rowing Championship wins, while among fight fans, Lucia is synonymous with the "Most Dangerous Woman in the World," Dutch kickboxer and boxer Lucia Rijker. She went 36–0 with four kickboxing world championships before switching over to standard boxing, where she'd win all seventeen bouts and hold multiple world titles.

Lucia is a beautiful name in any language, and a girl with that name in your family will bring light and happiness . . . and possibly an unbeaten record smashing her opponents in the ring!

Lucia Rijker, Boxing (Lightweight/Welterweight)/Kickboxing, Netherlands, 1982–2004

Lucia Toader, Rowing, Romania, 1984–1987

LUCY

An English variant of *Lucia*, Lucy is often seen as an old-fashioned name and, not surprisingly, hasn't made a very big impact in popular sports. The major exception to that is English soccer defender Lucy Bronze. She's an excellent inspiration for an athletic (and potentially soccer-loving) Lucy in your family due to her successes on the field, including two FA WSL Cups, two Women's FA Cups, three UEFA Women's Champions Leagues, a SheBelieves Cup, UEFA Women's Championship, two selections to the FIFA Women's World Cup All-Star Squad, the Best FIFA Women's Player award, and many more!

Lucia "Lucy" Bronze, Soccer (Right-Back), Olympique Lyonnais Féminin, England, 2007–current

LUDMILA/LUDMILLA/LYUDMILA

A family of names that has never reached a high degree of popularity in the United States, Ludmila/Ludmilla/Lyudmila come from Slavic roots for "favor of the people" and have appeared almost exclusively in Eastern Europe. There, women with these names have made powerful impacts on several sports, especially artistic gymnastics and track and field. Outliers include Soviet Olympic gold-medalist and World Cup-winning volleyball player Lyudmila Chernyshyova; Czech four-time world champion slalom canoeist Ludmila Polesná; and figure skating legend Ludmila Belousova, who won two Olympic gold medals and four world championships competing for the USSR and later Switzerland.

The fastest of the track and field athletes with these names have sprinted with Olympic gold-medalist Lyudmila Kondratyeva of the USSR, and hurdled with Ludmila Engquist, who won an Olympic Games event and three world championships. Finally, there's artistic gymnastics, a field that Russians have long excelled in. Lyudmila Gromova was part of the team that won the all-around Olympic gold in 1964, and a few years later, the reign of Ludmilla Tourischeva began. She would amass a staggering nine medals from Olympic Games (including four golds), eleven from World Championships (seven of them wins), five World Cup Finals, and multiple records for her incredible successes.

You don't need a Russian or Czech background to name a daughter Ludmila, Ludmilla, or Lyudmila, but it will definitely stand out as something unique. There's no guarantee it'll give her a leaning toward running track or gymnastics, but it will give her a fierce determination and serious work ethic.

Ludmila Belousova, Figure Skating, USSR/Switzerland, 1954–1969

Lyudmila Chernyshyova, Volleyball (Outside Hitter), USSR, 1973–1981

Ludmila Engquist, Track & Field (Hurdling), USSR/Sweden, 1988–2002

Lyudmila Gromova, Artistic Gymnastics, USSR, 1964

Lyudmila Kondratyeva, Track & Field (Sprinting), USSR, 1974–1988

Ludmila Polesná, Slalom Canoeing, Czechoslovakia, 1961–1975

Ludmilla Tourischeva, Artistic Gymnastics, USSR, 1967–1976

LYN/LYNN/LYNNE

With names derived from a Welsh root for "lake," it's interesting to see top athletes with successes in water-based sports! These include world champion slalom canoeist Lyn Ashton and two-time world champion surfer (and the first women to win twice) Lynne Boyer.

Of course, people with names in the Lynn family can't be contained just to watersports, and so we also see winners like Lyn Gunson of New Zealand, who won one of each color medal from the World Netball Championships, as well as a gold at the World Games; and three-time World Cross Country Championships-winner Lynn Jennings.

You have multiple options when it comes to spelling a "Lynn" sounding name, and if you give one to your daughter, I recommend teaching her to swim as early as possible—she may take to the water and find her favorite sport there!

Caroline Louise "Lyn" Ashton, Slalom Canoeing, USA, 1972–1973

Lynne Boyer, Surfing, USA, 1978–1979

Lyn Gunson, Netball, New Zealand, 1974–1985

Lynn Jennings, Long-Distance Running, USA, 1978–1999

LYNETTE/LYNNETTE

In most cases, Lynette/Lynnette is a diminutive of *Lynn*, though it can also be traced back to a Welsh root meaning "likeness." Giving a girl one of these names apparently imbues her with precision, pinpoint accuracy, and a skill for scoring with balls. At least that's the lesson we can take from two-time world champion and Olympic demonstration gold-medalist taekwondo practitioner Lynnette Love; Scottish world champion pool player Lynette Horsburgh; and Olympic gold-medalist and World Cup-winning basketball guard Lynette Woodard, who became the first woman on the Harlem Globetrotters!

Lynette Horsburgh, Snooker/Pool (Eight-Ball), Scotland, 1991–2015

Lynnette Love, Taekwondo, USA, 1987–1992

Lynette Woodard, Basketball (Guard), Cleveland Rockers, USA, 1983–1999

M

BOYS

MAGIC

The name, the title, the myth, and the legend, Magic applies to only one man. A basketball phenom early in his life, Earvin Johnson Jr. gained the nickname "Magic" while playing in high school, and it would become the primary way the world would know him. Magic's NBA career is legendary, with twelve All-Star appearances, three MVPs, two steals leader and four assists leader rankings, five championships, and more, all with the Los Angeles Lakers. Oh, and he also scored an Olympic gold medal and was inducted into the basketball Hall of Fame.

Magic is not a name a lot of people can pull off, but if you think your son is going to reach the pinnacle of his sport or profession, then give it a go! Also recommended as a nickname for kids named *Earvin*.

Earvin "Magic" Johnson Jr., Basketball (Point Guard), Los Angeles Lakers, USA, 1979–2000

MAGNUS

Especially popular in Scandinavian countries, the name Magnus comes directly from ancient Latin meaning "great." The greatness of competitive athletes named Magnus can't be overstated, with examples like Nordic combined skier Magnus Moan, who won Olympic gold and a world championship for Norway; and Swedish two-time World Men's Handball Championship-winning center back/line player Magnus Wislander, who has scored over one thousand goals in over 380 matches.

A Magnus in your family will balance brains and brawn, taking inspiration from Norwegian five-time World Chess Champion Grandmaster Magnus Carlsen, 1998 World's Strongest Man and arm-wrestling champion Magnus Samuelsson of Sweden, and Icelandic four-time World's Strongest Man Magnús Ver Magnússon, who's ranked among the top strongmen and powerlifters of all time.

Sven Magnus Carlsen, Chess, Norway, 2004–current

Magnus Moan, Nordic Combined Skiing, Norway, 2002–2019

Magnus Samuelsson, Strongman, Sweden, 1995–2008

Magnús Ver Magnússon, Strongman, Iceland, 1985–2005

Hans Einar Magnus Wislander, Handball (Center Back/Line Player), Sweden, 1983–2005

MAHENDRA

If you're searching for a standout "M" name that can inspire in your child a competitive edge and a well-rounded set of athletic skills, consider looking to South Asia and the highly celebrated Mahendra. From a Sanskrit root for "great" combined with the sky father deity Indra, Mahendra is famous around the world for one man, Mahendra Singh Dhoni. Better known as MS, Dhoni is considered one of the greatest cricketers of all time with a lengthy list of awards, achievements, and records, not least of which include scoring over ten thousand runs in ODI, winning a combined six Indian Premier League and Champions League T20 championships with the Channai Super Kings, and, while playing with and captaining the Indian national cricket team, winning two Asia Cups, the 2007 ICC World Twenty20, 2011 Cricket World Cup, 2013 ICC Champions Trophy, and more!

Mahendra Singh "MS" Dhoni, Cricket (Wicketkeeper Batsman), Chennai Super Kings, India, 1999–current

MAL

Typically a short form for a variety of names starting with "Mal-" (especially *Malcolm*), Mal is a versatile name that is due for a new surge in popularity; the two champion Mals had careers in the mid- and late-twentieth century and are absolutely worthy of inspiring a new generation. Mal Whitfield had an incredible life, serving with the Tuskegee Airmen and flying as a tail gunner in the Korean War and gaining track and field fame with three Olympic gold medals (and a silver and bronze) in 800-meter and 4x400-meter relay and an 880-yard world record. Over in Australia, rugby center Mal Meninga became ranked among the best players of all time with numerous wins and records, including becoming the only player to participate in four Kangaroo Tours (while captaining two of them), being inducted into the Australian Rugby Hall of Fame, and being added to the list of Immortals, Australian's top rugby players.

Malcolm "Mal" Meninga, Rugby (Center), Souths Logan Magpies, Australia, 1979–1994

Malvin "Mal" Whitfield, Track & Field (Sprinting), USA, 1948–1952

MALCOLM/MALCOM

You don't need to have Scottish, Irish, or Catholic roots to enjoy the name Malcolm (from Gaelic for "disciple of Saint Columba") or its lesser-seen variant Malcom, and it's come to have some storied successes in a few different athletic fields. Gridiron football has recently seen the actions of New England Patriots Super Bowl champion wide receiver Malcolm Mitchell, who became a celebrated children's book author, as well as two-time Pro Bowl safety and two-time Super Bowl champion Malcolm Jenkins. Brazilian soccer forward/winger Malcom Filipe Silva de Oliveira's successes (including winning a Russian Cup, three Russian Super Cups, and an Olympic gold medal) have made him known among fans the world over as simply "Malcom," while Barbadian cricketer Malcolm Marshall reached the heights of bowler rankings with the highest Test bowling average (among bowlers who have taken at least two hundred wickets) and induction in the ICC Cricket Hall of Fame.

A Malcolm (or Malcom) in your family may take after one of those athletes and compete and triumph in a more traditional sport.

Malcolm Butler, Football (Cornerback), New England Patriots, USA, 2014–current

Malcolm Jenkins, Football (Safety), Philadelphia Eagles, USA, 2009–2021

Malcolm Marshall, Cricket (Bowler), Hampshire County Cricket Club, Barbados, 1977–1995

Malcolm Mitchell, Football (Wide Receiver), New England Patriots, USA, 2016–2017

Malcom Filipe Silva de Oliveira, Soccer (Forward/Winger), Football Club Zenit, Brazil, 2014–current

MANFRED

Manfred is definitely not a name you hear very often in the United States, but it has a cool origin in Old Germanic roots for "man of peace" and has exemplified the ambitions of some very successful German athletes. If you were to choose this name for your son (and potentially give him the nickname *Manny*), he may look to events like boxing, bobsleigh, biathlon, or volleyball like Olympic welterweight gold-medalist pugilist Manfred Wolke; world champion bobsledder Manfred Schumann; biathlete Manfred Beer, who won two world championships; and four-time Paralympic standing volleyball gold-medalist Manfred Kohl.

Manfred Beer, Biathlon, Germany, 1974–1979

Manfred Kohl, Standing Volleyball, Germany, 1988–2000

Manfred Schumann, Bobsleigh, Germany, 1974–1979

Manfred Wolke, Boxing (Welterweight), Germany, 1968–1972

MANNY

Manny is traditionally a diminutive of *Emmanuel* or *Manuel*, though it has been used for other names and has appeared on its own as well. A little boy named or nicknamed Manny should definitely be taught the fundamentals of baseball because that is the sport where the most athletes with his name have found great successes. These include three-time Gold Glove and two-time Silver Slugger award-winning second baseman Manny Trillo of Venezuela, who had four All-Star appearances and two World Series wins; six-time All-Star third baseman/shortstop and Platinum Glove Manny Machado; and Dominican-American outfielder Manny Ramirez, whose power hitting scored him nine Silver Slugger awards, two AL Hank Aaron awards, a batting championship, two World Series championships, twelve All-Star appearances, and more!

On the other hand, your Manny might be super tough, more like the most famous athlete with this name, boxer Manny Pacquiao. Ranked among the top boxers of all time, the Filipino southpaw known as "PacMan" reached unparalleled heights in his long career, amassing a 62-8-2 record and becoming the first person to win world championships in eight different weight classes!

Manuel "Manny" Machado, Baseball (Third Baseman/Shortstop), Baltimore Orioles, USA, 2012–current

Emmanuel "Manny" (PacMan) Pacquiao Sr., Boxing (Flyweight/Super Bantamweight/Featherweight/Lightweight/Welterweight/Middleweight), Philippines, 1995–2021

Manuel "Manny" Ramirez, Baseball (Outfielder), Boston Red Sox, Dominican Republic, 1993–2011

Jesús Manuel "Manny" Trillo, Baseball (Second Baseman), Philadelphia Phillies, Venezuela, 1973–1989

MANUEL

While most *Manny*s gravitate toward America's pastime, Manuels (whose name is a Portuguese and Spanish descendent of *Emmanuel*, from Hebrew meaning "God is with us") can most often be found on the soccer field. International football has witnessed such greats as Brazilian two-time FIFA World Cup champion right winger Manuel "Garrincha" dos Santos, who was named to the FIFA World Cup All-Star Team twice and had numerous awards and accolades; and German top-ranked goalkeeper Manuel Neuer, who, in over eight hundred appearances to date, has filled his trophy case with two FIFA Club World Cups, a FIFA World Cup, the Best FIFA Men's Goalkeeper award, a FIFA World Cup Golden Glove, selections on two FIFA World Cup All-Star Teams and a FIFA World Cup Dream Team, and more!

If your Manuel is a rare one who doesn't like to kick a ball around, perhaps water or winter sports will be more to his liking. This is especially true if he takes inspiration from such greats as Spanish water polo legend Manuel Estiarte (who played in 580 games) and Austrian ski jumper Manuel Fettner, both of whom won Olympic gold and a world championship, or German world champion and two-time World Cup champion bobsledder Manuel Machata.

- **Manuel "Garrincha" dos Santos**, Soccer (Right Winger), Botafogo de Futebol e Regatas, Brazil, 1951–1972
- **Manuel Estiarte**, Water Polo (Center Forward), Spain, 1975–2000
- **Manuel Fettner**, Ski Jumping, Austria, 2013–current
- **Manuel Machata**, Bobsleigh, Germany, 2005–2015
- **Manuel Neuer**, Soccer (Goalkeeper), Fußball-Club Bayern München e. V., Germany, 2004–current

MANZOOR

Another name not often encountered in the United States, Manzoor (Arabic for "seen" or "visible") will certainly stand out in your kid's class roll call. It should also give him an enjoyment of running and playing outside with friends because it's known in international field hockey for two very prominent Pakistani players. Manzoor Atif scored Olympic gold in 1960 between two silver medals; a generation later, Manzoor "Junior" Hussain set records and achieved amazing plays on his way to Olympic gold and bronze, in addition to two Hockey World Cup wins, two Champions Trophies, and more.

- **Manzoor Atif**, Field Hockey (Fullback), Pakistan, 1956–1964
- **Manzoor "Junior" Hussain**, Field Hockey (Forward/Striker), Pakistan, 1975–1984

MARC

Part of a family of names that descend from the Roman god Mars, Marc can be traced to Catalan, French, Welsh, and other languages and societies. As varied as the places and peoples where Marc is popular, so, too, are the sports in which competitors with it have stood on podiums and taken home honors. These range from volleyball, with Olympic gold-medalist Marc Waldie; to judo, as exemplified by French Olympic champion Marc Alexandre; and ice hockey, with Canadian two-time All-Star and Stanley Cup–winning center Marc Savard.

Spanish champions include three-time NBA All-Star center Marc Gasol, who won an NBA championship and two World Cups; and motorcycle racer Marc Márquez, who has set numerous records for his accomplishments, including numerous wins and championships in multiple series. Last but not least, Canadian speed skater Marc Gagnon was an international star in the 1990s, winning three gold and two silver Olympic medals, twenty-nine medals at World Championships (fourteen of them golds), and five more golds and a silver at World Team Championships.

There are no boundaries on the width and breadth of where a Marc might travel and succeed, making his mark on the world wherever he so chooses.

- **Marc Alexandre**, Judo, France, 1984–1988
- **Marc Gagnon**, Speed Skating, Canada, 1993–2002
- **Marc Gasol**, Basketball (Center), Memphis Grizzlies, Spain, 2003–current
- **Marc Márquez**, Motorcycle Racing (MotoGP), Spain, 2008–current

Marc Savard, Ice Hockey (Center), Boston Bruins, Canada, 1997–2011

Marc Waldie, Volleyball (Middle Blocker), USA, 1984

MARCEL

Marcel comes from *Marcellus*, which in turn originated with a Roman diminutive of the name *Marcus*. And just as with *Marcs*, Marcels have hit it off across a wide world of sports over the years! They range from Belgian world champion road cyclist Marcel Kint to swimmer Marcel Wouda, who won two world championships for the Netherlands; and Canadian eight-time NHL All-Star center Marcel "Little Beaver" Dionne, whose incredible scoring ability earned him induction into the Hockey Hall of Fame and a spot on the "100 Greatest NHL Players" of all-time list.

When it comes to Marcels considered to be among the absolute best at what they did, Austrian alpine ski racer Marcel Hirscher amassed a huge collection of medals, including two golds and one silver from the Olympics, seven golds and four silvers from World Championships, and sixty-seven total medals from World Cup events, while French soccer center-back/defensive midfielder Marcel Desailly scored thirty goals in nearly eight hundred senior and international appearances while racking up a Supercoppa Italiana, FA Cup, UEFA Super Cup, FIFA World Cup, UEFA European Championship, two FIFA Confederations Cups, and placements on the FIFA World Cup All-Star Team and FIFA 100.

Name your kid Marcel and watch out for any particular athletic interest he may express; he's likely to pick his favorite early and have lots of fun!

Marcel Desailly (Odenke Abbey), Soccer (Center-Back/Defensive Midfielder), Chelsea Football Club, France, 1986–2006

Marcel "Little Beaver" Dionne, Ice Hockey (Center), Los Angeles Kings, Canada, 1971–1989

Marcel Hirscher, Ski Racing, Austria, 2007–2019

Marcel Kint, Road Cycling, Belgium, 1935–1951

Marcel Wouda, Swimming (Medley), Netherlands, 1992–2000

MARCO/MARKO

Another name that comes from the Roman war god Mars (like so many in this section) is Marco/Marko, the spelling differing depending on which country you come from or which language your ancestors spoke. In recent times, athletic Marcos and Markos have made impacts on multiple sports, with a couple of interesting concentrations. Ice hockey right wing Marko Anttila won an Olympic gold medal and two world championships for Finland; Italian archer Marco Galiazzo shot his way to two Olympic golds and a silver, two wins and two second places at World Championships, and a World Cup; and German endurance auto racer Marco Werner sped to three American Le Mans Series championships and wins at 24 Hours of Daytona and 24 Hours of Le Mans three times!

On the water, two Yugoslavians have taken home a sprint canoeing world championship (Marko Novaković and Marko Tomićević), while the cycling world has witnessed the stunning 2011 scratch race World Championship win by Kwok Ho-Ting Marco of Hong Kong and the exploits of Italian superstar Marco Pantani (winner of the Tour de France and Giro d'Italia). And then there's soccer, or what these competitors would call "football!" Italian midfielder Marco Tardelli scored seventy-two goals while winning the European Cup, UEFA Cup, UEFA Winner's Cup, UEFA Super Cup, and FIFA World Cup, while Marco van Basten of the Netherlands stands among the top-ranked strikers of all time with his three hundred goals and huge list of wins and awards, including three European Cups, three European Supercups, a UEFA European Championship, and three Ballon d'Or trophies while being named 1992 FIFA World Player of the Year, UEFA Best Player of the Year three times, European Top Scorer, and many more.

Definitely get your little Marco (or Marko) out on the soccer field early to see if he likes it, though you may find his preferences lean more toward things like canoeing or cycling!

Marko Anttila, Ice Hockey (Right Wing), Helsingin Jokerit, Finland, 2003–current

Marco Galiazzo, Archery, Italy, 1999–current

Kwok Ho-Ting Marco, Road/Track Cycling, Hong Kong, 2007–2014

Marko Novaković, Sprint Canoeing, Yugoslavia, 2012–current

Marco Pantani, Road Cycling, Italy, 1992–2003

Marco Tardelli, Soccer (Midfielder/Defender), Juventus Football Club, Italy, 1972–1988

Marko Tomićević, Sprint Canoeing, Yugoslavia, 2009–current

Marcel "Marco" van Basten, Soccer (Striker), Amsterdamsche Football Club Ajax, Netherlands, 1981–1995

Marco Werner, Auto Racing (Endurance Racing), Germany, 1993–2010

MARCUS/MARKUS

Marcus was an ancient Roman name (and most likely came from the war god Mars), and it later got a variant form in Markus that's traditionally popular in Estonia, Finland, Germany, and Scandinavia. Regardless, both versions have spread around the world, as well as around the world of athletics. They can be found in ice hockey, with Swedish five-time NHL All-Star left wing Markus Näslund; skiing, with German world champion and two-time Olympic gold-medalist alpine racer Markus Wasmeier; sprint canoeing, with Swedish Olympic-winner and three-time world champion Markus Oscarsson; and even snowboarding, with Norwegian world champion and six-time X Games gold-medalist Marcus Kleveland!

In the NFL, cornerback Marcus Peters was selected to three Pro Bowls, and six-time Pro Bowl running back Marcus Allen was a Super Bowl XVIII champion and MVP; held numerous distinctions, including rushing touchdowns leader, rushing yards leader, and scoring leader; and was inducted into the Pro Football Hall of Fame.

Name your son Marcus (or Markus if you're looking for something a bit different) to give him lots of potential; he may gravitate toward classic American team sports or find himself in something else entirely.

Marcus Allen, Football (Running Back), Los Angeles Raiders, USA, 1982–1997

Marcus Kleveland, Snowboarding, Norway, 2013–current

Markus Näslund, Ice Hockey (Left Wing), Vancouver Canucks, Sweden, 1990–2010

Markus Oscarsson, Sprint Canoeing, Sweden, 1995–2011

Marcus Peters, Football (Cornerback), Kansas City Chiefs, USA, 2015–current

Markus Wasmeier, Alpine Ski Racing, Germany, 1983–1994

MARIO

Traditionally an Italian and Spanish evolution of the ancient Roman name *Marius* (probably related to the god Mars), Mario may be most famous for a certain video game character, but in certain circles, it's synonymous with incredible athletes. This is most notable in a couple of places; first off, auto racing! On tracks around the world, Mario Andretti raced to victories across multiple series and events, including Formula 1, NASCAR Cup Series, IndyCar, Indianapolis 500, and more; with nearly 110 total wins, Andretti collected championships in Formula 1, IndyCar, and IROC. As far as athletes who enjoy colder sports, the top Mario will always be Canadian Hall of Fame center Mario Lemieux, a ten-time All-Star, multiple record holder, and winner of two Stanley Cups, an Olympic gold medal, World Cup, and more.

Going around the wide world of sports, we find Marios in events like football (four-time Pro Bowl defensive end Mario Williams), mixed martial arts (Submission Fighting world champion and three-time World Jiu-Jitsu Champion Mário Sperry of Brazil), and skiing (Austrian Nordic combined two-time Olympic gold-medalist and two-time world champion Mario Stecher).

With a name that's popular in European countries, it's no surprise that Marios have made their impact on soccer in a big way. Just some of the top international football stars and champions include Argentinian striker/attacking midfielder Mario Kempes (scored 354 goals, named to the FIFA World Cup All-Star Team, and won the UEFA Winners' Cup, UEFA Super Cup, and FIFA World Cup 1978), Yugoslavian striker Mario Mandžukić (261 goals, UEFA Champions League, UEFA Super Cup, and FIFA Club World Cup), and Brazilian forward/left wing Mário Zagallo (FIFA World Cup All-Star Team and winner of two FIFA World Cups).

A Mario in your family has unlimited potential and could end up loving any number of sports, either traditional or more esoteric. He may follow in the footsteps of the giants in ice hockey, auto racing, or soccer.

- **Mario Andretti**, Auto Racing (Formula 1), USA, 1960–1994
- **Mario Kempes**, Soccer (Striker/Attacking Midfielder), Valencia Club de Fútbol, Argentina, 1970–1996
- **Mario Lemieux**, Ice Hockey (Center), Pittsburgh Penguins, Canada, 1984–2006
- **Mario Mandžukić**, Soccer (Striker), Juventus Football Club, Yugoslavia, 2004–2021
- **Mário Sperry**, MMA (Heavyweight), Brazil, 1994–2015
- **Mario Stecher**, Nordic Combined Skiing, Austria, 1994–2015
- **Mario Williams**, Football (Defensive End), Houston Texans, USA, 2006–2016
- **Mário Zagallo**, Soccer (Forward/Left Wing), Botafogo de Futebol e Regatas, Brazil, 1951–1965

MARK

If you thought the name *Marc* has succeeded in a huge range of places, wait till you see Mark! From the same family of names coming from the ancient Roman name *Marcus*, Mark has enjoyed popularity around the world for a very long time. And with that spread and usage, it should come as no surprise that the name appears on the lists of top athletes in international sports and events. We'll get to concentrations of Marks, but looking at the full list is stunning. It includes basketball (four-time NBA All-Star and world champion point guard Mark Price), speed skating (Dutch Olympic gold-medalist and world champion Mark Tuitert), surfing (Australian four-time world champion Mark Richards), golf and bowling (Mark O'Meara and Mark Roth, respectively, who both won thirty-four times at professional events), freestyle wrestling (Olympic gold-medalist and two-time world champion Mark Schultz), and snowboarding (Canadian phenom Mark McMorris, who has taken home a world championship and over twenty medals from the X Games, including eleven golds). Marks can excel in any situation with brains, like Russian chess Grandmaster Mark Taimanov, or brawn, like Arnold Strongman Classic–winner and World Powerlifting Champion Mark Henry.

Marks have raced on four wheels and in pools to great successes, like NASCAR legend Mark Martin, who won forty Cup races and forty-nine Xfinity races, as well as five IROC championships. Swimmers on leaderboards with this name include German three-time breaststroke world champion Mark Warnecke; English freestyle and butterfly swimmer Mark Foster, who collected sixteen medals from World Championships (including six golds); and nine-time Olympic gold-medalist Mark Spitz, who set numerous records in his stellar career.

Finally, we come to team sports in which champion Marks have been truly plentiful. Gridiron football has three-time Pro Bowlers Mark Andrews (Baltimore Ravens tight end), Mark Ingram II (running back), and quarterback Mark Brunell, who was selected for the Pro Bowl three times, won a Super Bowl, and lead the NFL in passing yards. Ice hockey has also seen Marks rise to the top, with three-time All-Star Mark Giordano; world champion left wing Mark Recchi, who played in seven All-Star games and won the Stanley Cup three times on his way to being inducted into the Hall of Fame; and—standing above these champions as one of the greatest players of all time—sixteen-time All-Star center Mark Messier, who won two Stanley Cups and set numerous records in his NHL career.

Last but not least is America's pastime and a whole slew of Marks. First baseman Mark Texeira had three All-Star appearances and a World Series championship, along with five Gold Glove and three Silver Slugger awards; five-time All-Star and World Series-winner Mark Buehrle pitched his way to four Gold Gloves, a no-hitter, and a perfect game; and first baseman Mark McGwire had massive success with twelve All-Star appearances, two World Series championships, multiple Silver Slugger awards and home run leader rankings (though with the eternal asterisk beside his name because of his admitted steroid use).

Name your kid Mark and his future is his to craft!

- **Mark Andrews**, Football (Tight End), Baltimore Ravens, USA, 2018–current
- **Mark Brunell**, Football (Quarterback), Jacksonville Jaguars, USA, 1993–2011
- **Mark Buehrle**, Baseball (Pitcher), Chicago White Sox, USA, 2000–2015
- **Mark Foster**, Swimming (Butterfly/Freestyle), England, 1985–2007
- **Mark Giordano**, Ice Hockey (Defense), Calgary Flames, Canada, 2004–current
- **Mark Henry**, Powerlifting/Weightlifting, USA, 1990–2002
- **Mark Ingram II**, Football (Running Back), New Orleans Saints, USA, 2011–current
- **Mark Martin**, Auto Racing (NASCAR), USA, 1977–2013
- **Mark McGwire**, Baseball (First Baseman), Oakland Athletics, USA, 1986–2001
- **Mark McMorris**, Snowboarding, Canada, 2010–current
- **Mark Messier**, Ice Hockey (Center), Edmonton Oilers, Canada, 1978–2004
- **Mark O'Meara**, Golf, USA, 1980–current
- **William Mark Price**, Basketball (Point Guard), Cleveland Cavaliers, USA, 1986–1998
- **Mark Recchi**, Ice Hockey (Right Wing), Philadelphia Flyers, Canada, 1988–2011
- **Mark Richards**, Surfing, Australia, 1974–1982
- **Mark Roth**, Bowling, USA, 1970–2009
- **Mark Schultz**, Freestyle Wrestling, USA, 1982–1988
- **Mark Spitz**, Swimming (Butterfly/Freestyle), USA, 1965–1972
- **Mark Taimanov**, Chess, USSR, 1948–1971
- **Mark Texeira**, Baseball (First Baseman), New York Yankees, USA, 2003–2016
- **Mark Tuitert**, Speed Skating, Netherlands, 2003–2014
- **Mark Warnecke**, Swimming (Breaststroke), Germany, 1988–2005

MARTIN

A name that comes from ancient Latin and the war god Mars is a good match for someone who plays the rough game of ice hockey, and we can see that in Martins from Canada: right wing St. Louis, who earned six All-Star appearances, a Stanley Cup win, an Olympic gold medal, and induction into the Hall of Fame; and nine-time All-Star New Jersey Devils goaltender and Hall of Famer Brodeur, who took home two Olympic golds and three Stanley Cups and literally changed the game with the introduction of the "Brodeur Rule," which limits where goaltenders can operate! No less rugged and tough are rugby players like the English pair of top-ranked Martin Johnson, who played lock and won the Rugby World Cup and Six Nations Championship in 2003, and wing Martin Offiah, whose incredible list of accomplishments includes scoring more than five hundred tries, seven Championships, two Premierships, four Challenge Cups, three Regal Trophies, a Lancashire Cup, two World Club Challenges, and more.

There's a conspicuous number of Martins who excel in the cold, including three-time ski jumping world champion Martin Höllwarth; cross country skier Martin Johnsrud Sundby, who took home five medals from Olympic Games (including two golds) and nine from World Championships (four of them golds) for his home country of Norway; German ten-time Paralympic gold-medalist and two-time world champion monoskier Martin Braxenthaler; and French biathlete Martin Fourcade, who collected five gold medals and two silvers from the Olympics and an astounding thirteen golds, ten silvers, and five bronzes from World Championship events!

Martins can also stray from the pack and find their own ways in the world, making a name for themselves in fields from canoe sprinting, like Czech two-time world champion Martin Fuksa to wrestling, with Hall of Fame heavyweight Martin "Farmer" Burns, who was the World Catch-as-Catch-Can Champion and World Light Heavyweight Champion in the late 1800s.

- **Martin Braxenthaler**, Para-Alpine Skiing, Germany, 1998–2010
- **Martin Brodeur**, Ice Hockey (Goaltender), New Jersey Devils, Canada, 1991–2015
- **Martin "Farmer" Burns**, Wrestling (Heavyweight), USA, 1879–1897
- **Martin Fourcade**, Biathlon, France, 2008–2020
- **Martin Fuksa**, Sprint Canoeing, Czech Republic, 2013–current
- **Martin Höllwarth**, Ski Jumping, Austria, 1992–2008
- **Martin Johnson**, Rugby (Lock), Leicester Tigers, England, 1989–1999
- **Martin Offiah**, Rugby (Wing), Wigan Warriors, England, 1987–2002
- **Martin St. Louis**, Ice Hockey (Right Wing), Tampa Bay Lightning, Canada, 1997–2015
- **Martin Johnsrud Sundby**, Cross-Country Skiing, Norway, 2005–2021

MARVIN

The name Marvin has murky roots, probably coming either from Old Welsh roots for "bone marrow," "sea," "noble," "wish," or "young goat," or instead from Old English for "famous friend." Whichever it is, the name is now considered pretty old-fashioned and not super "cool," but it's ready for a comeback and can inspire a young boy to run fast or study the sweet science. On the gridiron, five-time Pro Bowl offensive tackle Marvin Powell Jr. played nearly his entire career with the New York Jets, and Indianapolis Colts wide receiver Marvin Harrison Sr. led in receiving yards and receptions while scoring eight Pro Bowl appearances and a Super Bowl win in 2007.

In the boxing ring, Marvins have really shined, going back to Marvin Camel, who became the cruiserweight world champion in 1980 and the first boxer to hold that title from two different sanctioning bodies. Also in the 1980s, "Marvelous" Marvin Hagler solidified his ranking among the all-time best with a staggering 62-3-2 record and a seven-year stint as the undisputed middleweight world champion. Most recently, Filipino Marvin Sonsona became the world super flyweight champ with a (current) 22-1-1 record.

- **Marvin Camel**, Boxing (Light Heavyweight/Cruiserweight), USA, 1973–1990
- **"Marvelous" Marvin Hagler**, Boxing (Middleweight), USA, 1973–1987
- **Marvin Harrison Sr.**, Football (Wide Receiver), Indianapolis Colts, USA, 1996–2008
- **Marvin Powell Jr.**, Football (Offensive Tackle), New York Jets, USA, 1977–1986
- **Marvin Sonsona**, Boxing (Welterweight/Featherweight/Bantamweight/Flyweight), Philippines, 2007–current

MAT/MATT

Matthew is a perfectly good name, and one that's seen a lot of athletic successes; however, many people with that name prefer to go by the most common short form, Matt. This name has a huge number of winners and champions associated with it across a range of sports! We'll get to the events with multiple Matts involved, but first off are the individuals who have conquered their respective fields, like Mat (a variant of Matt) Hoffman, a two-time X Games gold-medalist BMX vert ramp rider; Australian Matt Ryan, who is a three-time Olympic gold-medalist in equestrian eventing; and two-time UFC Welterweight Champion Matt Hughes, whose dominating career (45-9 record) has earned him a Hall of Fame induction and a common placement on top MMA fighter lists.

Canadian ice hockey greats include two-time All-Star, Olympic gold-medalist, and two-time world champion center and right wing Matt Duchene, while American soccer stars include center-back Matt Hedges (three-time MLS All-Star, US Open Cup, and CONCACAF Gold Cup) and Sporting Kansas City defender Matt Besler (four-time MLS All-Star, MLS Cup, and two CONCACAF Gold Cups). In NASCAR, Matt Kenseth had a tremendous Cup career with thirty-nine wins and the Winston Cup championship in 2003. Jumping into the swimming pools of international competitions, freestyle and medley swimmer Matt Biondi stood on ten Olympic Games podiums (with eight golds) and eleven World Championships (six wins), while Australian Matt Cowdrey broke records with a tremendous twenty-three medals from Paralympic Games (thirteen of them gold) and thirty from World Championships (twenty-three gold)!

Matts really congregate in team sports: baseball and gridiron football. Baseball Matts have been making their marks since the early days, with late 1800s pitcher Matt Kilroy pitching a no-hitter in 1886 and setting the still-standing MLB record for most strikeouts in a single season (513, though under the original rules). In the years since, the best of the best have included five-time All-Star third baseman and World Series champion Matt Williams, who collected four Gold Gloves and four Silver Sluggers while leading the National League in RBIs in 1990 and home runs in 1994; and seven-time All-Star left fielder Matt Holliday, who won the World Series in 2011 and four Silver Slugger awards and was RBI leader and batting champ in 2007.

Last but not least are the roughest and toughest Matts on the American football field! Atlanta Falcons quarterback Matt Ryan has had four Pro Bowl appearances while winning multiple titles and awards for his throwing, and at the height of six Pro Bowl games apiece are Minnesota Vikings outside linebacker Matt Blair and Super Bowl champion center Matt Birk.

If you name (or nickname) a child Matt, his potential can go in any number of directions. It's likely he'll enjoy team sports like football or baseball, but the sky's the limit!

Matthew "Matt" Besler, Soccer (Defender), Sporting Kansas City, USA, 2009–2021

Matthew "Matt" Biondi, Swimming (Freestyle/Butterfly), USA, 1984–1992

Matthew "Matt" Birk, Football (Center), Minnesota Vikings, USA, 1998–2012

Albert Matthew "Matt" Blair, Football (Outside Linebacker), Minnesota Vikings, USA, 1974–1985

Matthew "Matt" Cowdrey, Swimming (Backstroke/Butterfly/Freestyle), Australia, 2004–2015

Matthew "Matt" Duchene, Ice Hockey (Center/Right Wing), Colorado Avalanche, Canada, 2009–current

Matthew "Matt" Hedges, Soccer (Center-Back), FC Dallas, USA, 2009–current

Mat Hoffman, BMX, USA, 1986–current

Matthew "Matt" Holliday, Baseball (Left Fielder), St. Louis Cardinals, USA, 2004–2018

Matthew "Matt" Hughes, MMA (Welterweight), USA, 1998–2013

Matthew "Matt" Kenseth, Auto Racing (NASCAR), USA, 1988–2020

Matthew "Matt" Kilroy, Baseball (Pitcher), Baltimore Orioles, USA, 1886–1898

Matthew "Matt" Ryan, Equestrian (Eventing), Australia, 1992–2004

Matthew "Matt" Ryan, Football (Quarterback), Atlanta Falcons, USA, 2008–current

Matthew "Matt" Williams, Baseball (Third Baseman), San Francisco Giants, USA, 1987–2003

MATTHEW

Many Matthews eschew the full version of their name for the shorter *Matt*, but there are standouts that keep the original, which comes to us via Greek from biblical Hebrew meaning "gift of God." Some Matthews have definitely used their gifts to excel in athletics and sporting endeavors, like Australian top-ranked opening batsman Matthew Hayden, who led his national team to winning the 2003 and 2007 Cricket World Cups; Matthew Emmons, who is a sport shooting Olympic rifle gold-medalist; esports *Overwatch* pro Matthew "super" DeLisi, who won three major events; and English four-time Olympic gold-medalist rower and ten-time world champion Matthew Pinsent.

If swimming is your Matthew's gift, he may follow in the wake of Australian winners like freestyle world champion Matthew Abood; or Matthew Dunn, who won eight world championships in freestyle and medley. Or your Matthew may be fast and tough and prefer playing on the field with his friends, like four-time Pro Bowl Baltimore Ravens linebacker Matthew Judon and New England Patriots wide receiver Matthew Slater, who has played in ten Pro Bowls and won three Super Bowls!

Matthew Abood, Swimming (Freestyle), Australia, 2009–current

Matthew "super" DeLisi, Esports (*Overwatch*), USA, 2016–2022

Matthew Dunn, Swimming (Freestyle/Medley), Australia, 1991–1999

Matthew Emmons, Sport Shooting (Rifle), USA, 2002–current

Matthew Hayden, Cricket (Opening Batsman), Queensland Cricket Team, Australia, 1991–2012

Matthew Judon, Football (Linebacker), Baltimore Ravens, USA, 2016–current

Matthew Pinsent, Rowing, England, 1990–2004

Matthew Slater, Football (Wide Receiver), New England Patriots, USA, 2008–current

MATTHIAS/MATTIAS

From a Greek variant of the same origin as *Matthew*, Matthias and Mattias are names more familiar among European athletes than North American ones, but either one would make a great pick for a kid who is interested in things like building up his strength, taking care of horses, ice skating, or playing soccer with his friends. Matthias Baumann of Germany and Austrian-German Matthias Steiner both won Olympic gold medals, the former in equestrian team eventing and the latter in weightlifting, while ice hockey defenseman Mattias Öhlund won the 1998 World Championship and a 2006 Olympic gold medal for his home country of Sweden. Meanwhile, Germany has produced soccer stars like center-back Matthias Ginter (who won a DFL-Supercup, FIFA Confederations Cup, and the FIFA World Cup in 2014) and defensive midfielder/sweeper Matthias Sammer (who is the winner of Bundesliga three times, DFL-Supercup twice, UEFA Champions League, UEFA European Championship, US Cup, and the coveted Ballon d'Or in 1996).

- **Matthias Baumann**, Equestrian (Eventing), Germany, 1988–1992
- **Matthias Ginter**, Soccer (Center-Back), Borussia Verein für Leibesübungen 1900 e. V. Mönchengladbach, Germany, 2012–current
- **Kenneth Mattias Öhlund**, Ice Hockey (Defense), Vancouver Canucks, Sweden, 1992–2011
- **Matthias Sammer**, Soccer (Defensive Midfielder/Sweeper), Sportgemeinschaft Dynamo Dresden e.V., Germany, 1985–1998
- **Matthias Steiner**, Weightlifting, Austria/Germany, 2001–2013

MAX

Max is a highly versatile unisex name, often serving as a short form of *Maximilian*, *Maxwell*, and others, while also appearing on its own. In Germany, there's an interesting grouping of winners with this name in sprint canoeing, with Max Lemke (Olympic gold and three world championships), Max Rendschmidt (three Olympic wins and five at World Championships), and Max Hoff (one of each medal at the Olympics and seven golds and five silvers at World Championships).

Here in the United States, America's pastime has seen the exploits of two-time All-Star and World Series champion infielder Max Muncy; and starting pitcher Max Scherzer, who has played in eight All-Star games and won a World Series and whose trophy case includes three Cy Young awards; he also pitched two no-hitters; was the wins leader four times, National League strikeout leader three times, and MLB strikeout leader once; and tied for pitching the most immaculate innings and striking out the most players in a nine-inning game!

The name pops up singly in a few different sports, with three-time NFL Pro Bowl center and Super Bowl champion Max Unger and Belgian-Dutch Formula 1 phenom Max Verstappen, who has won thirty-five races and two championships. Boxing witnessed the rise and stardom of two heavyweights from across the Atlantic, Max Baer of the United States and Max Schmeling of Germany. With 68–13–2 and 56–10–4 records (respectively), both attained the lofty title of World Heavyweight Champion, fighting each other as well as luminaries like James Braddock and Joe Louis. The 1933 fight between Baer and Schmeling was world-famous; to many, it represented the struggle of Jewish people against the Nazis, although it would be revealed later that the German boxer actually helped smuggle Jewish children out of Germany at great risk to himself.

Whatever longer name you give a child, the short form Max may inspire a boxer's aggression, racecar driver's need for speed, sprint canoeist's love of water, or baseball player's agility and skill!

Maximilian "Max" Baer, Boxing (Heavyweight), USA, 1929–1941

Max Hoff, Sprint Canoeing, Germany, 2009–current

Max Lemke, Sprint Canoeing, Germany, 2017–current

Maxwell "Max" Muncy, Baseball (Infielder), Los Angeles Dodgers, USA, 2015–current

Max Rendschmidt, Sprint Canoeing, Germany, 2013–current

Maxwell "Max" Scherzer, Baseball (Pitcher), Washington Nationals, USA, 2008–current

Maximilian "Max" Schmeling, Boxing (Heavyweight), Germany, 1924–1948

Maxwell "Max" Unger, Football (Center), Seattle Seahawks, USA, 2009–2018

Max Verstappen, Auto Racing (Formula 1), Belgium/Netherlands, 2014–current

MAXIMILIAN

While many people go by the shorter nickname *Max*, some amazing men are Maximilians through and through. The name has a very strong heritage, descending from the Roman name *Maximus* and meaning "greatest"—a quality that a trio of athletes have brought to the world's stage in three unique events. On the water, Singaporean kitesurfer Maximilian Maeder won gold and silver in Sailing World Championships to become the youngest world champion at sixteen, German rower Maximilian Reinelt collected gold and silver medals from Olympics and two golds and three silvers from World Championships, and German track cyclist Maximilian Levy won four world championships and earned three silver medals and three bronzes.

If you name your son Maximilian and continue to call him by the full version of the name, be sure to teach him how to ride a bike and introduce him to water sports!

Maximilian Levy, Track Cycling, Germany, 2004–2021

Maximilian Maeder, Kitesurfing, Singapore, 2018–current

Maximilian Reinelt, Rowing, Germany, 2010–2016

MEL/MELVIN

Melvin and its short form Mel (from Norman French and a place name meaning "bad town") aren't exactly topping the charts of popular baby names these days. If you choose this old-fashioned name for a boy in your family, there's a good chance he'll find his calling in the pool, on the baseball diamond, or on the football field. That is especially true if he's like world champion and two-time Olympic gold-medalist swimmer Melvin Stewart Jr. or power hitting legend Mel Ott, who played in eleven consecutive All-Star games, won a World Series in 1933, led the National League in home runs six times, and was inducted into the Hall of Fame.

On the gridiron, four-time Pro Bowl return specialist Mel Gray led the NFL in kickoff return yards in 1991, and Pittsburgh Steelers cornerback Mel Blount was inducted into the Hall of Fame after playing in five Pro Bowls, winning four Super Bowls, and leading the NFL in interceptions in 1975.

Melvin "Mel" Blount, Football (Cornerback), Pittsburgh Steelers, USA, 1970–1983

Melvin "Mel" Gray, Football (Wide Receiver), St. Louis Cardinals, USA, 1971–1985

Melvin "Mel" Ott, Baseball (Right Fielder), New York Giants, USA, 1926–1947

Melvin Stewart Jr., Swimming (Butterfly/Freestyle), USA, 1986–1994

MICHAEL

Perpetually among the top baby names around the world, Michael comes to us from biblical Hebrew meaning "who is like God." With its international popularity, you can expect the list of famous and successful athletes with this name to be pretty extraordinary. Michaels who are masters of their fields include top-ranked English world champion and Grand Slam of Darts-winner Michael Smith; Hawaiian-Chinese surfer Michael Ho, who won the Duke Classic, Hawaiian Triple Crown, Pipe Masters, and World Cup; Australian six-time world champion road and track cyclist Michael Hepburn; and German three-time Olympic gold-medalist and three-time world champion horseback rider Michael Jung.

Some Michaels thrive in the cold with events like alpine skiing (Australian two-time Paralympic gold-medalist Michael Norton) and biathlon (Michael Greis of Germany, who won three times at Olympic Games and World Championships). Cricket fans will be familiar with Australian middle-order batter Michael Clarke (winner of two Cricket World Cups), while international swimming has seen German three-time Olympic gold-medalist and five-time world champion Michael Gross and freestyle innovator Michael Klim of Australia, who took home six medals from the Olympics, including two golds, and twenty-five medals from World Championships. Top-tier track and field lists include Olympic gold-medalist and two-time world champion sprinter Michael Norman, and Michael Walker of the UK, who won five Paralympic gold medals in shot put, discus throw, club throw, and javelin. Then there are Michaels on baseball diamonds and rugby pitches: five-time All-Star and World Series champion left fielder Michael Brantley; seven-time All-Star infielder, Gold Glove-winner, and AL batting champ Michael Young; Australian flanker Michael Hooper (who won the 2014 Super Rugby Champions and 2015 Rugby Championship); and superstar Michael Jones of New Zealand (whose lengthy list of accomplishments includes winning two Super 12 championships, two Tri-Nations, and the 1987 Rugby World Cup).

Even more Michaels have appeared on the fields of soccer and gridiron football! Liverpool legend and FIFA 100 striker Michael Owen's trophy collection included an FA Cup, UEFA Cup, UEFA Super Cup, and the coveted Ballon d'Or; and Danish attacking midfielder/forward Michael Laudrup ranks among the best players ever with a senior and international career of 726 appearances capturing La Liga five times, Copa del Rey, UEFA Super Cup, Intercontinental Cup, and FIFA Confederations Cup while being named to the FIFA World Cup All-Star Team and FIFA 100. Switching from one football to another, we see return specialist Michael Bates, who played in five Pro Bowls, and seven-time Pro Bowl New York Giants defensive end Michael Strahan, who twice led the NFL in sacks, set records in sacks, won Super Bowl XLII, and was inducted into the Hall of Fame.

While all of those are impressive, some Michaels stand at the absolute pinnacle of their events and will go down in history among the greatest of the great. German-born Michael Schumacher started racing karts when he was only four years old, and he'd go on to win a record-tying seven Formula 1 championships between 1994 and 2004. Just as fast on a different kind of track, Michael Johnson was the king of sprinting in his era, winning four Olympic gold medals and fifty-six World Championship gold medals between 1991 and 2000 and setting multiple world records. Only one person could be known instantly by his first name alone in an entire professional sport, and that would be Michael Jordan. Regularly considered one of the greatest basketball players of all time, "Air Jordan" played from 1984 to 2003 (with a couple short breaks) and dominated the NBA with the Chicago Bulls, winning six championships. Finally, there's United States swimming phenomenon Michael Phelps, who won a record-shattering twenty-eight Olympic medals—twenty-three of which were gold—and dozens more at World Championships.

Naming your son Michael won't necessarily make him the absolute best, fastest, and most successful in his chosen field, but he'll put in the work and be a champion in whatever he decides to pursue. Introduce him to a wide range of sports early on so he can find his favorite!

Michael Bates, Football (Return Specialist), Carolina Panthers, USA, 1993–2003

Michael Brantley Jr., Baseball (Left Fielder), Cleveland Indians, USA, 2009–current

Michael Clarke, Cricket (Batsman), Australia, 2003–2015

Michael Greis, Biathlon, Germany, 2000–2012

Michael Gross, Swimming (Butterfly/Freestyle), Germany, 1981–1991

Michael Hepburn, Cycling (Road & Track), Australia, 2009–current

Michael Ho, Surfing, USA, 1976–current

Michael Hooper, Rugby (Flanker), Australia Wallabies, 2011–current

Michael Johnson, Track & Field (Sprinting), USA, 1991–2000

Michael Jones, Rugby (Flanker/Number 8), Auckland Rugby Union, New Zealand, 1985–1999

Michael Jordan, Basketball (Shooting Guard), Chicago Bulls, USA, 1984–2003

Michael Jung, Equestrian (Eventing), Germany, 2008–current

Michael Klim, Swimming (Freestyle), Australia, 1994–2007

Michael Laudrup, Soccer (Attacking Midfielder/Forward), Fútbol Club Barcelona, Denmark, 1981–1998

Michael Norman Jr., Track & Field (Sprinting), USA, 2018–current

Michael Norton, Alpine Skiing, Australia, 1986–1995

Michael Owen, Soccer (Striker), Liverpool Football Club, England, 1996–2013

Michael Phelps II, Swimming (Backstroke/Butterfly/Freestyle/Medley), USA, 2000–2016

Michael Schumacher, Auto Racing (Formula 1), Germany, 1991–2012

Michael Smith, Darts, England, 2008–current

Michael Strahan, Football (Defensive End), New York Giants, USA, 1993–2007

Michael Walker, Para-Athletics, England, 1988–1992

Michael Young, Baseball (Infielder), Texas Rangers, USA, 2000–2013

MICHEL

There are many variations of the name *Michael*, and Michel is a French one that has seen some popularity across the world as a flexible unisex name. In the world of sports, two men exemplify the winning spirit embodied in the name, with the most recent competitor being Dutch speed skater Michel Mulder, who has won Olympic gold and bronze as well as two gold medals at World Sprint Championships. Meanwhile, French soccer midfielder Michel Platini is counted among the sport's all-time greats, and during his senior and international career 653 appearances, he won numerous titles and awards, including the European Cup, European Cup Winners' Cup, European Super Cup, Intercontinental Cup, UEFA, and European Championship; he was also named to the FIFA World Cup All-Star Team twice, FIFA World Cup All-Time Team, FIFA 100, and FIFA World Cup Dream Team, and was awarded the coveted Ballon d'Or three times!

Could a Michel in your family rise to greatness on skates or the soccer field? Teach him the basics early on and see where his true talents can take him.

Michel Mulder, Speed Skating, Netherlands, 2007–current

Michel Platini, Soccer (Midfielder), Association Sportive Nancy Lorraine, France, 1972–1988

MICK

An old diminutive of *Michael*, Mick is a name that brings with it a love of the ocean and surfing, but with an important acknowledgement of the dangers that one can find there. That's the lesson Australian three-time world champion surfer Mick Fanning learned when he survived a shark attack unscathed during a competition in 2015! Fanning's career would include twenty-two wins on the World Surf League Championship Tour and induction into the Surfers' Hall of Fame.

Michael "Mick" Fanning, Surfing, Australia, 2002–2018

MICKEY

Most often a diminutive of the name *Michael*, the unisex Mickey can also be just fine on its own. About a century of American sports has told us one thing: a Mickey's place is almost always on the baseball diamond! That goes back at least to 1925 and the beginning of catcher Mickey Cochrane's career, which included two All-Star appearances, three World Series championships, and induction into the Baseball Hall of Fame. In the 1940s and '50s, Mickey Vernon played first baseman for a variety of teams beginning with the Washington Senators, and across his twenty-year career, he was the American League batting champion twice, played in seven All-Star games, and won the World Series in 1960 with the Pittsburgh Pirates.

Last but certainly not least is the most famous Mickey in all of sports: New York Yankees slugger Mickey Mantle. Considered one of the greatest players of all time, Mantle's record speaks for itself; the power hitter played in sixteen All-Star games; won seven World Series; held the top spot on batting champion, home run leader, and RBI leader boards; won a Triple Crown; took home a Gold Glove; set numerous MLB records; and was inducted into the Hall of Fame, among even more achievements.

Of course, Mickeys don't *have* to play baseball, and yours may find success in another field, like boxing if he takes after the world welterweight and middleweight champion Mickey Walker, who boxed in the early 1900s and cemented his name on all-time greats lists with an unofficial 131-25-6 record!

Gordon "Mickey" Cochrane, Baseball (Catcher), Philadelphia Athletics, USA, 1925–1937

Mickey Mantle, Baseball (Center Fielder), New York Yankees, USA, 1951–1968

James Barton "Mickey" Vernon, Baseball (First Baseman), Washington Senators, USA, 1939–1960

Edward "Mickey" Walker, Boxing (Welterweight/Middleweight/Heavyweight), USA, 1919–1935

MIGUEL

While *Mickey* is a popular American diminutive of *Michael*, Miguel is a Portuguese and Spanish variant of the classic name. Also like *Mickeys*, Miguels are prominent in America's pastime, with Dominican shortstop Miguel Tejada, who played in six All-Star games, won two Silver Slugger awards, and was the League RBI leader in 2004; and Venezuelan twelve-time All-Star first and third baseman Miguel Cabrera, whose lengthy MLB career has seen him win a World Series, seven Silver Sluggers, two AL Hank Aaron awards, four AL batting championships, two AL home run leaderboards, two AL RBI charts, and more.

A Miguel in your family may find baseball to be his calling or go into another team sport, like soccer, in which case, he can look up to Mexican right-back Miguel Layún, who in his senior and international career has won a Copa MX, two CONCACAF Champions Leagues, CONCACAF Gold Cup, and CONCACAF Cup. If he is more independent, he might find his place in solo competitions, like Spanish road racing cyclist Miguel Induráin, whose epic career included an Olympic gold medal and world championship, two Giro d'Italia wins, and five at the Tour de France with the record for most consecutively!

José Miguel Cabrera, Baseball (First Baseman/Third Baseman), Detroit Tigers, Venezuela, 2003–current

Miguel Induráin, Road Cycling, Spain, 1978–1996

Miguel Layún, Soccer (Right-Back), Club de Fútbol América S.A. de C.V., Mexico, 2006–current

Miguel Tejada, Baseball (Shortstop), Baltimore Orioles, Dominican Republic, 1997–2013

MIKA

Another variation of *Michael*, the Scandinavian name *Mikael* was translated into the Finnish Mika. Most successful athletes named Mika do come from Finland, but the name is certainly not restricted to usage there. As you might expect, some of the Finnish champions made their mark in cold weather sports, like NHL All-Star center and world champion Mika Zibanejad and dual Olympic gold-medalists and world champions Mika Hannula (ice hockey right wing) and Mika Laitinen (ski jumper).

If your Mika doesn't like the cold, he may prefer indoor events like pool (Mika Immonen, who won world championships in both nine- and ten-ball) or bowling (fourteen-time Professional Bowlers Association event-winner Mika Koivuniemi, who has bowled twenty-nine perfect games). Track and field is an option, too, as it was for world champion shot putter Mika Halvari, and there's always the chance he may just like to go fast and put pedal to the medal like racing driver Mika Häkkinen, who won twenty races and two championships in Formula 1!

Mika Häkkinen, Auto Racing (Formula 1), Finland, 1975–2007

Mika Halvari, Track & Field (Shot Put), Finland, 1993–2000

Mika Hannula, Ice Hockey (Right Wing), IF Malmö Redhawks, Sweden, 2000–2014

Mika Immonen, Pool (Nine-Ball/Ten-Ball), Finland, 1991–current

Mika Koivuniemi, Bowling, Finland, 2001–2018

Mika Laitinen, Ski Jumping, Finland, 1990–2000

Mika Zibanejad, Ice Hockey (Center), New York Rangers, Sweden, 2010–current

MIKAEL/MIKHAIL

Two more variants of the name *Michael* are similar in sound if not spelling; Mikael hails from Breton, Finnish, and Scandinavian, while Mikhail is Belarusian and Russian. You may be able to guess some of the sports and events competitors with these names have excelled in because they're pretty traditional for inhabitants of the colder climes of Europe. In ice hockey, we have Finnish two-time world champion center Mikael Granlund and right wing Mikael Samuelsson, who won an Olympic gold medal and world championship for Sweden, as well as the Stanley Cup with the Detroit Red Wings.

Mikaels and Mikhails can excel in any competition, from the physical to the mental, as you can see with French soccer defender Mikaël Silvestre, who won an FA Cup, UEFA Champions League, Intercontinental Cup, and the FIFA Confederations Cup twice; Russian two-time Olympic gold-medalist and two-time world champion gymnast Mikhail Voronin; and three-time world champion and chess Grandmaster Mikhail Botvinnik, who became the sixth World Chess Champion.

A child with one of these names in your family may take after one of these top-notch competitors, and he may reach the absolute pinnacle of his field, like Canadian freestyle skier Mikaël Kingsbury, who became the most medaled mogul skier of all time with three podiums from the Olympics (one gold) and thirteen from World Championships, including eight wins!

Mikhail Botvinnik, Chess, Russia, 1925–1970

Mikael Granlund, Ice Hockey (Center/Right Wing), Minnesota Wild, Finland, 2008–current

Mikaël Kingsbury, Skiing (Freestyle), Canada, 2010–current

Karl Mikael Samuelsson, Ice Hockey (Right Wing), Detroit Red Wings, Sweden, 1996–2015

Mikaël Silvestre, Soccer (Defender), Manchester United Football Club, France, 1996–2014

Mikhail Voronin, Artistic Gymnastics, Russia, 1966–1972

MIKE

Mike is mostly, but not *always*, a short form of *Michael*, though it can be a nickname for other names or even be a name all on its own. And just like *Michael*s, Mikes have no boundaries on where their talents and successes lie, achieving greatness in all sorts of places. Even the range of those who have competed on their own is broad, from two-time world champion long jumper Mike Powell, to top-ranked doubles tennis player Mike Bryan, who set records with eighteen major men's titles, 123 ATP titles, and 506 weeks in the world's top spot. Some of the toughest Mikes go into combat sports, like Greek eighteen-time world champion kickboxer Mike Zambidis; and boxing heavyweight world champion Mike Tyson.

Plenty of Mikes are all about going fast, whether that's via a horse, motorcycle, bike, or race car. BMX rider Mike King rode to a mountain bike world championship, horse racing jockey Mike Smith has won more than 5,600 races, and British motorcycle racer Mike Hailwood racked up seventy-six wins in the Grand Prix series on his way to nine championships. On four wheels, British racer Mike Conway has dominated recent World Endurance Championship seasons with seventeen wins and two championships since 2020.

How about Mikes who play best with others? Six-time Pro Bowl Tampa Bay Buccaneers fullback Mike "A-Train" Alstott won Super Bowl XXXVII, and Hall of Famer Mike Ditka was a feared tight end, with five Pro Bowl appearances, an NFL championship, and a Super Bowl championship, before an equally dazzling coaching career. Nearly all of the most successful Mikes in ice hockey have been Canadians, with All-Star center, Stanley Cup-winner, and Olympic gold-medalist Richards; two-time All-Star, world champion, and Olympic gold-medalist goaltender Smith; and New York Islanders right wing Bossy, who played in seven All-Star games, won four Stanley Cups, and was inducted into the Hall of Fame; they're joined on the leaderboard by American eight-time All-Star center and Hall of Famer Mike Modano, who won the Stanley Cup in 1999, and set multiple NHL records.

Last but not least are the Mikes in America's pastime. Among the best of the best have been ten-time All-Star Los Angeles Angels center fielder Mike Trout, who hit his way to nine Silver Sluggers and two Hank Aaron Awards, and two incredible twelve-time All-Stars and Hall of Famers: catcher Mike Piazza, who collected ten Silver Sluggers, and 1980 World Series champion Philadelphia Phillies third baseman Mike Schmidt, whose accolades include ten Gold Gloves, six Silver Sluggers, hitting four home runs in one game, and leading the National League four times in RBIs and eight times in home runs!

Michael "Mike" (A-Train) Alstott, Football (Fullback), Tampa Bay Buccaneers, USA, 1996–2007

Michael "Mike" Bossy, Ice Hockey (Right Wing), New York Islanders, Canada, 1977–1987

Michael "Mike" Bryan, Tennis, USA, 1998–2020

Michael "Mike" Conway, Auto Racing (FIA World Endurance Championship), England, 2001–current

Michael "Mike" Ditka, Football (Tight End), Chicago Bears, USA, 1961–1972

Stanley Michael "Mike" Hailwood, Motorcycle Racing (Grand Prix), England, 1958–1967

Michael "Mike" King, BMX, USA, 1984–2004

Michael "Mike" Modano Jr., Ice Hockey (Center), Dallas Stars, USA, 1989–2011

Michael "Mike" Piazza, Baseball (Catcher), New York Mets, USA, 1992–2007

Michael "Mike" Powell, Track & Field (Long Jump), USA, 1988–2001

Michael "Mike" Richards, Ice Hockey (Center), Los Angeles Kings, Canada, 2005–2016

Michael "Mike" Schmidt, Baseball (Third Baseman), Philadelphia Phillies, USA, 1972–1989

Mike Smith, Ice Hockey (Goaltender), Calgary Flames, Canada, 2002–current

Michael "Mike" Smith, Horse Racing (Jockey), USA, 1991–current

Michael "Mike" Trout, Baseball (Center Fielder), Los Angeles Angels, USA, 2011–current

Michael "Iron Mike" Tyson, Boxing (Heavyweight), USA, 1985–2005

Michalis "Mike" Zambidis, Kickboxing (Welterweight/Middleweight), Greece, 2000–2015

MING

An ideal name for a family who tends to have tall children and for a child who will be a dedicated and successful team player, Ming is Chinese and can be written in different characters that can be translated as "bright/clear" or "inscribe/engrave." Seven-foot six-inch Hall of Fame basketball center Yao Ming bridged eastern and western sports worlds with three FIBA Asia Cup gold medals, numerous awards and accomplishments in the Chinese Basketball Association, eight NBA All-Star selections during his career with the Houston Rockets, and much more!

Yao Ming, Basketball (Center), Houston Rockets, China, 1997–2011

MITSUO

Just like all Japanese names, Mitsuo can be written with various characters that have different meanings, in this case "light/ray," "three," or "fullness/satisfy" plus "male," "husband," "hero/leader," or "center/middle." We find a notable *three* Mitsuos as exemplars in their respective fields: welterweight freestyle wrestler Mitsuo Ikeda won Olympic gold in 1956, artistic gymnast Mitsuo Tsukahara innovated new skills on his way to five Olympic gold medals and four world championships, and Kashima Antlers soccer midfielder Mitsuo Ogasawara had nearly eight hundred senior and international appearances, during which he was named to the J.League Best Eleven six times and won four Emperor's Cups, five J.League Cups, four Japanese Super Cups, and AFC Asian Cup 2004!

The name Mitsuo is not confined to Japan, and if you choose it for your son, he, too, may become a *hero* as a gymnast, playing soccer, or wrestling.

Mitsuo Ikeda, Freestyle Wrestling (Welterweight), Japan, 1956–1964

Mitsuo Ogasawara, Soccer (Midfielder), Kashima Antlers, Japan, 1998–2010

Mitsuo Tsukahara, Artistic Gymnastics, Japan, 1968–1978

MO

Mo is most often a short form of longer names, ranging from *Mariano* to *Mohamed*. Whether used as a diminutive or given to a child directly, this short "M" name is built for speed, which we can see in the professional athletes and world champions who have used it. On the baseball diamond, Mo Rivera was a thirteen-time All-Star relief pitcher for the New York Yankees; won five World Series, multiple MVPs, and other awards; and was inducted into the Baseball Hall of Fame. International football fans are familiar with the exploits of Egyptian forward Mo Salah (scoring over three hundred goals, an FA Cup, UEFA Champions League, UEFA Super Cup, FIFA Club World Cup, and more), and Mo Farah is the winningest track distance runner (and British track athlete) of all time with four Olympic gold medals and six world championships!

Mohamed "Mo" Farah, Long-Distance Running, England, 2005–current

Mariano "Mo" Rivera, Baseball (Relief Pitcher), New York Yankees, Panama, 1995–2013

Mohamed "Mo" Salah, Soccer (Forward), Liverpool Football Club, Egypt, 2010–current

MOHAMMAD/MOHAMMED/MUHAMMAD

From Arabic for "commendable" or "praised" and the name of the prophet and founder of Islam, Muhammad has the unique distinction of being the most popular name in the world, especially when you factor in the many regional and spelling variations, like Mohamed, Mohammad, and Mohammed. Athletes with these names have had success in multiple sports, some of which are especially popular in specific parts of the world. These include Indonesian three-time world champion badminton player Mohammad Ahsan, Indian field hockey Olympic gold-medalists Mohammed Hussain and Mohammed Shahid, and, in cricket, world top-ranked ODI bowler Mohammed Siraj of India.

For most, though, hearing the name in the context of competition and winning brings to mind just one champion, and that's Muhammad Ali. Consistently ranked among the best boxers of all time, Ali won an Olympic gold medal, ended his professional career with a 56–5 record, fought in some of the biggest and most watched bouts of all time, and is the only three-time heavyweight world champion! He was able to accomplish all of that even while missing out on almost four years of boxing in his twenties because of his protest against the Vietnam War and refusing the draft. Ali wasn't an important figure just in the ring and for his anti-war messaging, though; he was heavily involved in philanthropy, activism, art, and even international diplomacy!

The Muhammad family of names has a beautiful history and can inspire a strong competitive nature, hopefully leading a boy in your family to become the greatest himself.

Mohammad Ahsan, Badminton, Indonesia, 2008–current

Muhammad Ali (Cassius Clay Jr.), Boxing (Heavyweight), USA, 1954–1981

Mohammed Hussain, Field Hockey (Full-Back), India, 1934–1936

Mohammed Shahid, Field Hockey (Forward), India, 1979–1989

Mohammed Siraj, Cricket (Bowler), Royal Challengers Bangalore, India, 2015–current

MOISÉS/MOSES

Are you looking for a classic name with ancient roots that can inspire a child to be a great team player? Then consider Moses (biblical Hebrew from uncertain origins—likely either an Egyptian root for "son" or a Hebrew one for "deliver"), or its Spanish/Portuguese variant Moisés. The latter made a big impact on baseball with Dominican-American slugger Moisés Alou, who played for multiple teams during his seventeen seasons while racking up six All-Star appearances, a World Series win, and two Silver Slugger awards. Inside on the hardwood court, basketball center Moses Malone had a stellar twenty-year career during which he was selected as an All-Star thirteen times, led the NBA in rebounds six times, won multiple MVPs and an NBA championship, and more, all propelling him to be inducted into the Basketball Hall of Fame and considered one of the greatest players of all time. Moseses can even be pioneers and firsts, like Moses Fleetwood Walker, who was the first African-American to play in Major League Baseball; he played catcher for the Toronto Blue Stockings all the way back in 1884.

Moisés Alou, Baseball (Outfielder), Montreal Expos, USA, 1990–2008

Moses Malone, Basketball (Center), Philadelphia 76ers, USA, 1974–1995

Moses Fleetwood Walker, Baseball (Catcher), Toledo Blue Stockings, USA, 1881–1889

MORRIS

Maurice is not a name you hear very often these days, nor is its variant Morris, a name that to some may evoke imagery of a bygone era. And indeed, the American Olympic champions with this name had their successes more than one hundred years ago, but they were really impressive; Morris Kirksey ranks among the rarest of the rare with Olympic gold medals in two totally different events (in this case the 4x100-meter relay and rugby), while Marine Corps sharpshooter Morris "Bud" Fisher took his elite, record-breaking rifle skills to the international stage with five gold medals across two different Olympic Games in the 1920s!

Morris "Bud" Fisher, Sport Shooting (Rifle), USA, 1916–1934

Morris Kirksey, Track & Field (Sprinting)/Rugby, USA, 1920–1921

MUGGSY

See *Tyrone* for Tyrone "Muggsy" Bogues.

MUSTAFA/MUSTAPHA

Every son is his family's "chosen one," and that's exactly the Arabic meaning of the name Mustafa/Mustapha. Athletes with this princely moniker have made strides in several different fields, from para-athletics, like Moroccan Paralympic gold- and silver-medalist distance runner Mustapha El Aouzari and French six-time Paralympic gold-medalist wheelchair racer Mustapha Badid, to chess, like three-time Turkish Chess Champion and Grandmaster Mustafa Yılmaz. Among the greatest of the great are Turkish freestyle wrestler Mustafa Dağıstanlı, who won two Olympic gold medals, three world championships, and gold and silver at World Cup events, and was named CAF Champions League best goalkeeper three times and Moroccan League best goalkeeper twice and set multiple Moroccan and African goalkeeper records!

Give your son a chosen destiny and a powerful, competitive spirit with the name Mustafa or Mustapha.

Mustapha Badid, Para-Athletics, France, 1984–1996

Mustapha Chadili, Soccer (Goalkeeper), Raja Club Athletic, Morocco, 1992–2011

Mustafa Dağıstanlı, Freestyle Wrestling, Turkey, 1954–1960

Mustapha El Aouzari, Para-Athletics, Morocco, 2004

Mustafa Yılmaz, Chess, Turkey, 2008–current

GIRLS

MADDIE/MADDY

Maddie and Maddy can be diminutives of any "Mad-" name, including but not limited to *Madeline*, *Madison*, and *Maddison*, or even a variation of *Magdalen*. Giving one of those nicknames to your daughter (or even naming a girl Maddie or Maddy straight out!) may give her a love of hockey and defending her teammates like a couple of Olympic gold-medalists: English EuroHockey champion field hockey goalkeeper Maddie Hinch and two-time world champion ice hockey goaltender Maddy Rooney. On the other hand, your Maddie or Maddy may find her calling in just about any sport, from baseball, like three-time All-American Girls Professional Baseball League All-Star third base player and two-time champion Maddy English, to freestyle skiing, like Olympic gold-medalist and five-time X Games champion Maddie Bowman!

Maddison "Maddie" Bowman, Freestyle Skiing, USA, 2012–2018

Madeline "Maddy" English, Baseball (Third Base), Racine Belles, USA, 1943–1951

Madeline "Maddie" Hinch, Field Hockey (Goalkeeper), Tilburg Hockey Club, England, 2008–current

Madeline "Maddy" Rooney, Ice Hockey (Goaltender), Team ADIDAS, USA, 2015–current

MAGGIE

Originally a diminutive of the name *Margaret*, Maggie can be seen as a traditional name in the US and UK, but it's certainly sporting! This is especially true in artistic gymnastics, with world champion Maggie Nichols; rugby, with English Hall of Fame flanker Maggie Alphonsi, who won seven Six Nations titles, six Grand Slams, and the 2014 Women's Rugby World Cup; and water polo, with Maggie Steffens, who won four world championships and three Olympic gold medals (setting a record for the most goals scored by a single player in women's Olympic water polo in the process).

Whether a Maggie in your family gravitates toward gymnastics, rugby, water polo, or some other sport, she's sure to make her mark and have a lasting legacy.

Margaret "Maggie" Alphonsi, Rugby (Flanker), Saracens W.R.F.C., England, 2003–2014

Margaret "Maggie" Nichols, Artistic Gymnastics, USA, 2013–2020

Margaret "Maggie" Steffens, Water Polo (Driver), USA, 2010–current

MALAIKA

Are you looking for a cool "M" name that'll stand out on the playground and will inspire in a girl a love of running, jumping, and playing in the sun? Malaika, derived from Arabic and meaning "angel" in Swahili, could be a great fit for you! In athletic circles, you can find examples with baseball infielder Malaika Underwood, who won the 2006 Women's Baseball World Cup with the American team, and German Olympic gold-medalist and two-time world champion long jumper Malaika Mihambo.

Malaika Mihambo, Track & Field (Long Jump), Germany, 2013–current

Malaika Underwood, Baseball (Infield), USA, 2006–2015

MANUELA

A feminine variant of the masculine name *Manuel*, Manuela has a strong Spanish and

Portuguese tradition but shows up across Europe. The champion ladies with this name show just how varied and multi-talented a Manuela can be, and one in your family can excel, compete, and win in anything! Just ask Portuguese world champion marathon runner Manuela Machado; Italian two-time Olympic gold-medalist cross-country skier Manuela Di Centa; and German sprint canoeist Manuela Mucke, whose medal count includes two Olympic golds and thirteen podiums at World Championships (two of them golds).

Manuela Di Centa, Cross-Country Skiing, Italy, 1980–1998

Manuela Machado, Marathon, Portugal, 1990–2000

Manuela Mucke, Sprint Canoeing, Germany, 1995–2003

MAREN

You don't have to come from German or Danish stock to name a kid Maren, which is an interesting descendent of *Maria* or *Marina*. Marens have a slight predisposition to rowing events, like world champion rower Maren Derlien and two-time world champion sprint canoeist Maren Knebel (both from Germany), or winter sports, like German world champion biathlete Maren Hammerschmidt, and Norwegian ski jumper Maren Lundby, who won Olympic gold, two world championships, and thirty World Cup events, including a record three consecutive overall titles!

Maren Derlien, Rowing, Germany, 1999–2008

Maren Hammerschmidt, Biathlon, Germany, 2011–current

Maren Knebel, Sprint Canoeing, Germany, 2005–2010

Maren Lundby, Ski Jumping, Norway, 2009–current

MARGARET

Margaret has very ancient roots in Indo-Iranian languages meaning "pearl," and while some go by the nickname *Maggie*, others have brought the full name into the spotlight and onto sporting podiums around the world. There have been pioneers and groundbreakers, like rifle markswoman and US Army shooting instructor Margaret Murdock, who became the first woman to win an Olympic shooting medal in 1976. Other sharpshooting Margarets include champion Paralympians Margaret Maughan of Great Britain, who is the winner of a gold medal in archery, swimming, dartchery, and lawn bowls, and Margaret Harriman of South Africa, who took home seven Paralympic archery gold medals; three golds, a silver, and a bronze in lawn bowls; and a gold and a bronze in dartchery.

Margarets aren't limited; they have the capability to excel in any field or sport, just like backstroke and freestyle swimmer Margaret Hoelzer, who scored eleven medals from World Championships (including six golds), and Australian tennis phenom Margaret Court, who reached the world number one spot in both singles and doubles and won a record sixty-four major titles!

Margaret Court, Tennis, Australia, 1960–1977

Margaret Harriman, Archery/Dartchery/Lawn Bowls, South Africa, 1960–1996

Margaret Hoelzer, Swimming (Backstroke/Freestyle), USA, 2002–2008

Margaret Maughan, Archery/Swimming/Dartchery/Lawn Bowls, England, 1960–1980

Margaret Murdock, Sport Shooting (Rifle), USA, 1966–1976

MARGIT

Margaret is popular around the world, so much so that it has several variants in different languages and cultures, including the Hungarian and Scandinavian Margit. This shorter form is flexible and fast, like the people who have brought it to the forefront of events like field hockey, with German Hockey World Cup–winner Margit Müller; artistic gymnastics, with Hungarian two-time Olympic gold-medalist Margit Korondi; and luge, with German four-time world champion and Olympic gold-medalist Margit Schumann!

Margit Korondi, Artistic Gymnastics, Hungary, 1952–1956

Margit Müller, Field Hockey (Defender), Germany, 1960–1980

Margit Schumann, Luge, Germany, 1972–1980

MARGO/MARGOT

From a French derivation of the name *Margaret*, Margot and Margo embody the spirit of athletic excellence, as well as a drive to be the first. Polish basketball center Margo Dydek dominated the WNBA as the league's tallest player (seven feet, two inches), earning two All-Star selections and setting a record for all-time blocks, while Dutch field hockey defender Margot van Geffen has won a Champions Trophy, two World Cups, and two Olympic gold medals. Then there are the American pioneers, rock climber Margo Hayes, who was the first woman to climb a 9a+ graded route, and Margo Oberg, who became the first professional woman surfer in the world and the first woman to be paid for surfing while being named Women's World Champion twice and winning six world championships and two World Contests!

Małgorzata "Margo" Dydek, Basketball (Center), Utah Starzz, Poland, 1998–2008

Margo Hayes, Rock Climbing, USA, 2015–current

Margo Oberg, Surfing, USA, 1965–1991

Margot van Geffen, Field Hockey (Defender), Hockeyclub's-Hertogenbosch, Netherlands, 2011–current

MARIA/MARIIA/MARIYA

The name Maria can be traced back through Latin and Greek and all the way to biblical Hebrew *Miryam*, which has uncertain origins, possibly coming from roots meaning "sea of bitterness," "rebelliousness," or "wished for child," though there's strong evidence it comes from an Egyptian root word for "beloved" or "love." Maria has propagated throughout much of the world, and it has plenty of variants of its own, including Mariia and Mariya. Most of the successful athletes with these names originate in Eastern Europe, but there are also plenty from other parts of the globe.

Women with these names who have become known for their sport include Azerbaijani wrestler Mariya Stadnik, who won two world championships and numerous gold medals at Grand Prix, Golden Grand Prix, and others; Olympic gold-medalist and four-time world champion sprint canoeist Mariya Shubina of the Soviet Union; and record-breaking Italian athlete Maria Scutti, who won fifteen medals at one Paralympic games (including ten golds) across four different areas! There are even competitors known for their minds, like Ukrainian Women's World Chess Champion and Grandmaster Mariya Muzychuk. Meanwhile, few Marias are as famous as Russian tennis superstar Sharapova, former world number one and one of only ten women to win a career Grand Slam on her way to thirty-six titles.

Then there are champions in sports like rowing, with Maria Dumitrache of Romania, who won Olympic gold and two world championships; and synchronized swimming, with Russian three-time Olympic gold-medalists Mariya Kiselyova and Mariya Gromova, who also took home three world championships. And trios have appeared in track and field events (with three Olympic gold-medalists: Soviet 400-meter runner Mariya Pinigina, Russian five-time world champion high jumper Mariya Lasitskene, and 800-meter runner

Maria Mutola of Mozambique, who set records as she took home ten world championships and four World Cup wins), and alpine skiing (with Spanish six-time World Cup-winner María José Rienda Contreras, Swiss three-time world champion and twenty-five-time World Cup-winner Maria Walliser, and Maria Höfl-Riesch of Germany, who took home three Olympic gold medals, two world championships, and a massive eighty-one World Cup medals).

The largest concentration of athletes with these names appears in Russian gymnastics, with rhythm competitors Mariya Netesova (Olympic gold medalist), Mariia Kravtsova (three-time world champion), and Maria Tolkacheva (Olympic gold medalist and eleven-time world champion), and Soviet artistic gymnast Maria Gorokhovskaya, who took home a world championship and set a record for most medals won by a woman at an Olympic Games (two golds and five silvers in 1952) that held until 2021.

Whichever version of the name Maria you may prefer, it can give a little girl the drive to succeed in any number of endeavors, especially sports!

- **Maria Magdalena Dumitrache**, Rowing, Romania, 1998–2001
- **Maria Gorokhovskaya**, Artistic Gymnastics, USSR, 1947–1954
- **Mariya Gromova**, Synchronized Swimming, Russia, 2004–2012
- **Maria Höfl-Riesch**, Alpine Ski Racing, Germany, 2001–2014
- **Mariya Kiselyova**, Synchronized Swimming, Russia, 2000–2004
- **Mariia Kravtsova**, Rhythmic Gymnastics, Russia, 2016–2018
- **Mariya Lasitskene**, Track & Field (High Jump), Russia, 2014–current
- **Maria Mutola**, Track & Field (Sprinting), Mozambique, 1988–2008
- **Mariya Muzychuk**, Chess, Ukraine, 2002–current
- **Mariya Netesova**, Rhythmic Gymnastics, Russia, 2000
- **Mariya Pinigina**, Track & Field (Sprinting), USSR, 1983–1988
- **María José Rienda Contreras**, Alpine Skiing, Spain, 1994–2011
- **Maria Scutti**, Athletics/Swimming/Fencing/Table Tennis, Italy, 1958–1962
- **Maria Sharapova**, Tennis, Russia, 2001–2020
- **Mariya Shubina**, Sprint Canoeing, USSR, 1958–1966
- **Mariya Stadnik**, Freestyle Wrestling, Azerbaijan, 2008–current
- **Maria Tolkacheva**, Rhythmic Gymnastics, Russia, 2013–current
- **Maria Walliser**, Alpine Skiing, Switzerland, 1983–1990

MARIANA

Typically a descendant of the Roman name *Marius* by way of *Marianus*, Mariana can also come from a combination of the popular names *Maria* and *Ana*. Either way you come upon it, Mariana is a beautiful name that can give your daughter a drive to go fast, especially when she's in the water or on two wheels! Mariana Ribeiro of Brazil has swum to three freestyle gold medals and two backstroke bronze medals at World Para Swimming Championships, while Colombian BMX racer Mariana Pajón has powered her way to two gold medals and a silver at the Olympics; six golds and four bronzes at World Championships; three golds, two silvers, and a bronze at World Cup events; and more.

- **Mariana Pajón Londoño**, BMX, Colombia, 2010–current
- **Mariana Ribeiro**, Swimming (Freestyle/Backstroke), Brazil, 2020–current

MARIANNE

The French name Marianne has two distinct

origins, in some cases coming as a diminutive of *Marie* and in others formed as a combination of the names *Marie* and *Anne*. Marianne may be more popular in certain parts of the world than it is in the United States, but it's a solid pick for a family of sports fans. Your Marianne may be an Olympic gold-medalist team player like Dutch soccer striker Marianne Pettersen, who won the 1995 FIFA Women's World Cup, and Brazilian four-time World Grand Prix-winning volleyball wing spiker Marianne Steinbrecher. Or she may excel on her own like speed skaters Marianne St-Gelais of Canada (world champion) and Marianne Timmer of the Netherlands (three Olympic gold medals and three world championships), or the world top-ranked cyclist Marianne Vos of the Netherlands, who has won eight cyclo-cross world championships, three world championships in road racing, Olympic gold and two world championships on the track, three general classifications at the Giro d'Italia Femminile, and more!

- **Marianne Pettersen**, Soccer (Striker), Asker Fotball, Norway, 1997–2007
- **Marianne St-Gelais**, Speed Skating, Canada, 2010–2018
- **Marianne Steinbrecher**, Volleyball (Wing Spiker), Brazil, 1996–2021
- **Maria Aaltje "Marianne" Timmer**, Speed Skating, Netherlands, 1997–2011
- **Marianne Vos**, Road/Track Cycling, Netherlands, 2002–current

MARIE/MARIE-

One of the most flexible names around, Marie comes from Czech and French variations of *Maria* and can be combined with a number of other French names to create forms like Marie-Claire, Marie-Claude, Marie-José, Marie-Laure, Marie-Louise, and Marie-Philip. Most, but not all, of the top athletes with Marie names are from France or Canada, and they range across several different disciplines. In and on the water, there have been Canadian two-time Paralympic gold-medalist swimmer Marie Claire Ross and German five-time world champion rower Marie-Louise Dräger, and in the cold, we have French X Games gold-medalist SuperPipe skier Marie Martinod and French biathlete Marie Habert, who won Olympic gold and five world championships. France has also given us a notable runner, with sprinter Marie-José Pérec, who won three Olympic gold medals and two world championships in the 1990s.

French judoka Marie-Claire Restroux won an Olympic gold medal and a world championship, and her fellow countrywoman Marie-Laure Norindr became an esports fighting game champion under the name "Kayane" and was named the most successful female competitor in fighting game tournaments by Guinness World Records! Lastly, Canadian ice hockey forward Marie-Philip Poulin is ranked among the best players of all time with three Olympic gold medals, ten medals from world championships (including three golds), and more.

Choose Marie or a Marie- combo name for a daughter for a talented and ambitious competitor who may gravitate toward water sports, cold weather events, judo, or esports!

- **Marie-Louise Dräger**, Rowing, Germany, 1999–2019
- **Marie Habert**, Biathlon, France, 2007–2018
- **Marie Martinod**, Freestyle Skiing, France, 2006–current
- **Marie-Laure "Kayane" Norindr**, Esports (Fighting Games), France, 2001–current
- **Marie-José Pérec**, Track & Field (Sprinting), France, 1991–2000
- **Marie-Philip Poulin**, Ice Hockey (Forward), Les Canadiennes de Montréal, Canada, 2008–current
- **Marie-Claire Restroux**, Judo, France, 1995–1999

Marie Claire Ross, Para-Swimming, Canada, 1992–1998

MARIEL

Originally created as a diminutive for *Mary* with a dash of *Muriel* thrown in, Mariel is an uncommon name for an extraordinary daughter. Her interests may tend toward the uncommon as well (like sword fighting!), but that's where she'll excel and maybe even break records. That's exactly the case with fencing legend Mariel Zagunis, whose sabre skills have led her to win a pair each of Olympic gold and bronze medals (becoming the first-ever American fencing gold medalist) and four golds, five silvers, and four bronzes from World Championships!

Mariel Zagunis, Fencing (Sabre), USA, 2000–current

MARINA

Does your family come from Roman stock, love the sea, or enjoy volleyball, ice dancing, or skiing of various kinds? Well then Marina might be a great name for your daughter! A feminine version of the Roman family name *Marinus* that comes from either *Marius* or a root meaning "of the sea," Marina shows up in three pairs of top athletes. There are Russian world champion volleyball setters Marina Akulova and Marina Sheshenina, skiers German Olympic gold-medalist alpine skier Marina Kiehl and Swiss two-time world champion water skier Marina Doria, and ice dancers Olympic gold-medalist, world champion, and Grand Prix Final–winner Marina Anissina and Marina Klimova, who won Olympic gold and three world championships.

Marina Akulova, Volleyball (Setter), Russia, 2001–2012

Marina Anissina, Ice Dancing, France/Russia, 1993–2002

Marina Doria, Water Skiing, Switzerland, 1953–1960

Marina Kiehl, Alpine Skiing, Germany, 1982–1988

Marina Klimova, Ice Dancing, USSR, 1983–1996

Marina Sheshenina, Volleyball (Setter), Russia, 2003–2018

MARIT

Another variant of the name *Margaret*, Marit comes from Norwegian and Swedish; unsurprisingly, it shows up most in Scandinavian countries. But it's ready for a boost in popularity anywhere around the world, especially for athletic and ambitious little girls following in the footsteps of stellar sports figures like Dutch Olympic gold-medalists Marit van Eupen (three-time world champion rower) and Marit Bouwmeester (four-time world champion Laser Radial class sailor), as well as Norwegian cross-country skier Marit Bjørgen, who won fifteen medals at Olympic Games (including eight golds) and twenty-six at World Championships (eighteen of them gold) while setting records for the most Olympic medals of any winter athlete, most all-time Cross-Country World Cup wins (114 with four overall titles), and the most successes of any Cross-Country World Cup sprinter.

Marit Bjørgen, Cross-Country Skiing, Norway, 2000–2022

Marit Bouwmeester, Sailing (Laser Radial), Netherlands, 2010–current

Marit van Eupen, Rowing, Netherlands, 2000–2008

MARJORIE

Like *Marit*, Marjorie is a variant of *Margaret*, in this case coming from medieval English. And while Marits tend toward skiing, sailing, and rowing, Marjories tend to find their successes in curling, diving, and sprinting! Canadian Marjorie "Marj" Mitchell won a curling world championship, American diver Marjorie Gestring nabbed Olympic gold in the 3-meter springboard in 1936, and Marjorie Jackson-Nelson set records in Australia during her sprinting career in the 1950s while winning two Olympic gold medals on the international stage.

Marjorie Gestring, Diving, USA, 1936–1948

Marjorie Jackson-Nelson, Track & Field (Sprinting), Australia, 1950–1954

Marjorie "Marj" Mitchell, Curling (Skip), Canada, 1975–1980

MARNIE

The origins of the name Marnie may be uncertain (it may come from a variant of *Marina*), but its track record is not. Marnie McGuire of New Zealand and Marnie Peters of Canada are famous for their accuracy, the former winning six professional golf tournaments and the latter taking home a wheelchair basketball gold medal each from the Paralympic Games and Wheelchair Basketball World Championships. Peters's speed and strength was matched by her fellow countrywoman Marnie McBean, who won three Olympic gold medals (and a bronze) in rowing.

Whether she follows these stellar athletes in rowing, golf, or basketball or forges her own path, a Marnie in your family will have the drive to succeed and the skills to back it up.

Marnie McBean, Rowing, Canada, 1989–1999

Marnie McGuire, Golf, New Zealand, 1986–2003

Marnie Peters, Wheelchair Basketball, Canada, 1995–2004

MARTA

Martha (from Aramaic for "lady" or "mistress") may not have a substantial athletic pedigree, but its variant Marta sure does. Ladies with this name have appeared on podiums across the world's stage, conquering a number of different sports and events, from handball (world champion Norwegian-Croatian center back Marta Tomac) to sprint canoeing (Polish world champion Marta Walczykiewicz). Italians with this name have made waves, like beach volleyball defender Marta Menegatti, who has collected sixteen medals on the World Tour (including two wins), and two-time world champion alpine skier Marta Bassino, who won six World Cup slalom events. However, only one athlete is known by the name Marta all on its own, and that's Brazil's record-setting soccer forward Marta Vieria da Silva. In her long senior and international career, she's already racked up almost three hundred goals, a UEFA Women's Cup, six Best FIFA Women's Player awards, a FIFA Women's World Cup Golden Boot, a FIFA Women's World Cup Golden Ball, and more!

You should definitely teach a Marta in your family how to play soccer; she, too, may end up becoming one of the best players of all time!

Marta Bassino, Alpine Skiing, Italy, 2014–current

Marta Vieria da Silva, Soccer (Forward), Umeå IK, Brazil, 2000–current

Marta Menegatti, Beach Volleyball, Italy, 2006–current

Marta Tomac, Handball (Center Back), Norway/Croatia, 2006–current

Marta Walczykiewicz, Sprint Canoeing, Poland, 2008–current

MARTINA/MARTINE

Like *Martin* and other related names, Martina and Martine descend from Roman sources and Mars, the god of war. Girls with these names aren't necessarily warlike, but they do have a fighting instinct when it comes to competition, confidence, and teamwork. Those who have come before have made it big in such varied fields as wrestling (Canadian three-time world champion Martine Dugrenier) and discus (German Olympic gold-medalist and two-time world champion Martina Hellmann).

German VfL Wolfsburg soccer striker Martina Müller scored 175 goals during her career, winning Bundesliga twice, the UEFA Women's Champions League twice, and the FIFA World Cup twice; Slovakian swimmer Martina Moravcová took home twenty-two medals from World Championships (including seven wins); and Czech speed skater Martina Sáblíková raced to seven medals at Olympic Games (three of them gold) and over thirty at world championships (twenty-one of them being wins)! Italian Martinas in particular seem to excel at rhythmic gymnastics, as proven by teammates Santandrea and Centofanti, winners of ten (four golds) and twelve (five golds) medals from World Championships, respectively.

Any parent of a Martina would be remiss if they didn't at least introduce her to tennis, in case she'll follow in the footsteps of a couple all-time greats who share her name. Martina Hingis of Switzerland held the world number one singles spot for 209 weeks with five major titles and the doubles number one standing with twenty overall titles, all while achieving the record of the youngest-ever Grand Slam champion. Meanwhile, Martina Navratilova secured her place among the top tennis players of all time with the second-longest stretch at the world singles number one ranking (332 weeks), winning eighteen major titles, and holding the record for longest doubles number one spot (237 weeks) with forty-one titles! The left-handed player set numerous records and she is also one of only three to achieve a career "Boxed Set" by winning Grand Slams in singles, same-sex doubles, and mixed doubles.

Martina Centofanti, Rhythmic Gymnastics, Italy, 2015–current

Martine Dugrenier, Freestyle Wrestling, Canada, 2005–2012

Martina Hellmann, Track & Field (Discus), Germany, 1983–1992

Martina Hingis, Tennis, Switzerland, 1994–2017

Martina Moravcová, Swimming (Butterfly/Freestyle/Medley), Slovakia, 1992–2008

Martina Müller, Soccer (Striker), Verein für Leibesübungen Wolfsburg e. V., Germany, 1998–2015

Martina Navratilova, Tennis, Czechoslovakia/USA, 1974–2006

Martina Sáblíková, Speed Skating, Czech Republic, 2005–current

Martina Santandrea, Rhythmic Gymnastics, Italy, 2016–current

MARY

One of the most consistently popular girl names in the Western world, Mary topped the charts of baby names in the United States from 1880 to 1961, and only fell out of the top ten in 2009. An English variant of the name *Maria*, its relatively few instances among top athletes is a bit surprising compared to its general usage, but it has been borne by some pretty iconic and inspirational women. These include world champion freestyle skier Mary Jo Tiampo; Northern Irish Olympic gold-medalist pentathlete Mary Peters; two-time world champion middle-distance runner and multiple world record-setter Mary Decker; two-time Olympic gold-medalist tennis star Mary Joe Fernández; Indian six-time world champion boxer Mary Kom, who is the only boxer of any gender to win eight World Championship medals; and swimmer Mary Meagher, who won five medals at the Olympics (three of them gold) and nine at World Championships.

Mary is now a traditional name in the United States and other Western countries, but it has plenty of sporting life left in it. A daughter with this name in your family may gravitate toward one of the events these Marys have excelled in or find her own niche and set her own world records.

- **Mary Decker**, Track & Field (Middle-Distance Running), USA, 1973–1999
- **Mary Joe Fernández**, Tennis, USA, 1986–2000
- **Mangte "Mary" Kom**, Boxing (Atomweight/Flyweight), India, 2000–current
- **Mary Meagher**, Swimming (Butterfly/Freestyle), USA, 1979–1988
- **Mary Peters**, Track & Field (Pentathlon), Northern Ireland, 1966–1974
- **Mary Jo Tiampo**, Freestyle Skiing, USA, 1986

MARY LOU

There are many versions of the name *Mary* with second parts, but one of them stands above the rest when it comes to famous athletes. Mary Lou may feel old-fashioned now, but it has been shouted by American sports fans on two notable occasions. First was in 1953, when Mary Lou Studnicka pitched during the All-American Girls Professional Baseball League championship, taking the Grand Rapids Chicks to victory over the Kalamazoo Lassies. A bit more recently, Mary Lou Retton became America's darling when she won Olympic gold at the 1984 Los Angeles Olympic Games, becoming the first American woman to win the gymnastics all-around; she'd also collect two silver and two bronze medals at those games.

Name your daughter Mary Lou and excited fans will one day call out her name too!

- **Mary Lou Retton**, Artistic Gymnastics, USA, 1983–1986
- **Mary Lou Studnicka**, Baseball (Pitcher), Grand Rapids Chicks, USA, 1951–1953

MAUREEN

Another traditional "M" name for girls, Maureen comes from an Anglicized form of an Irish diminutive for *Mary*. In the middle of the 1900s, Maureen Connolly was an American tennis star known as "Little Mo," who had an incredible start to a career that was sadly cut short by an accident. Rising to the world number one singles spot with nine major singles titles, Little Mo set records as the first woman to win a Grand Slam, as well as the first (and still only!) player of any gender to win a title without losing a single set at all four major championships. More recently, Indonesian Maureen "Alice" Stephany has been climbing the esports ranks as she dominates *PUBG Mobile* tournaments across Southeast Asia and beyond.

You, too, can bring the name Maureen into the twenty-first century by giving it to a girl who may excel at tennis, esports, or anything else she puts her mind to.

- **Maureen "Little Mo" Connolly**, Tennis, USA, 1949–1955
- **Maureen "Alice" Stephany**, Esports (*PUBG Mobile*), Indonesia, 2019–current

MAYA

Maya is a truly international name, appearing in numerous cultures around the world with origins including a Hebrew root for "water," Sanskrit root for "illusion" or "magic," and Greek root for "good mother." Varied, too, are the sports that champion Mayas have dominated, like skeleton (with Swiss racer Maya Pedersen-Bieri, who has won an Olympic gold medal and two world championships) and swimming (with the multi-talented Maya DiRado, who took home four medals from the Olympics (two of them gold) and a gold and a silver at World Championships). Meanwhile, Brazilian Maya Gabeira has reached the pinnacle of surfing by winning seven world championships and setting a Guinness World Record for surfing the biggest wave, and six-time WNBA All-Star Minnesota Lynx small forward Maya Moore won four championships along with two world championships and two Olympic gold medals!

Consider Maya for a girl in your family and introduce her to plenty of sports so she can find her favorite.

Madeline "Maya" DiRado, Swimming (Backstroke/Freestyle/Medley), USA, 2012–2016

Maya Gabeira, Surfing, Brazil, 2004–current

Maya Moore, Basketball (Small Forward), Minnesota Lynx, USA, 2011–2018

Maya Pedersen-Bieri, Skeleton, Switzerland, 1995–current

MCKAYLA/MICHAELA/MIKAELA/ MYKAYLA

With the long-time, international popularity of the name *Michael* (from biblical Hebrew meaning "who is like God"), it's no surprise that there would arise feminine versions of it, and there are multiple spellings to choose from! Whether you like McKayla, Michaela, Mikaela, MyKayla, or another variant for your child, there's a decent chance she'll end up enjoying one of three very specific sports (if she follows in the footsteps of those who have come before her).

Boxing fans have enjoyed watching the pugilistic power of highly ranked fighters Swedish WBC light middleweight champion Mikaela Laurén (32-6 record) and unified super featherweight world champion Mikaela Mayer (17-1). Then there are the American artistic gymnasts MyKayla Skinner, winner of a team world championship and All-Around World Cup, and iconic "not impressed" Olympic gold-medalist and three-time world champion McKayla Maroney. Last but decidedly not least are the alpine skiers: three-time world champion and three-time World Cup-winning Michaela Kirchgasser; Michaela Dorfmeister, who won two Olympic gold medals, two world championships, and twenty-five World Cup gold medals; and record-breaking Mikaela Shiffrin, whose two Olympic gold medals ties her for most alpine skiing wins for any American, seven world championship wins and fourteen medals overall leads American rankings, and eighty-eight World Cup golds (of 138 total medals) are the most of any skier of any gender in the world!

Michaela Dorfmeister, Alpine Skiing, Austria, 1991–2006

Michaela Kirchgasser, Alpine Skiing, Austria, 2001–2018

Mikaela Laurén, Boxing (Welterweight/ Middleweight), Sweden, 2009–current

McKayla Maroney, Artistic Gymnastics, USA, 2011–2016

Mikaela Mayer, Boxing (Featherweight/ Lightweight), USA, 2017–current

Mikaela Shiffrin, Alpine Skiing, USA, 2011–current

MyKayla Skinner, Artistic Gymnastics, USA, 2012–2021

MEAGAN/MEGAN/MEGHAN

If *Margaret* is a bit too old-fashioned for you, you may prefer one of the variants of Megan, a Welsh diminutive of the classic "pearl" moniker. There are just about as many differently spelled versions as you can imagine, with Meagan, Megan, and Meghan showing up on rolls of prominent athletes in the United States, Canada, and Australia. Some of these who have risen to the top of the ranks in their individual events include Canadian pairs figure skater Meagan Duhamel, who won one of each color medal at the Olympics and two world championships; Australian five-time World Cup champion (two Women's Cricket World Cups and three Women's T20 World Cups) cricket bowler Megan Schutt; and American rower Meghan Musnicki, who has collected two Olympic gold medals and five world championships.

Two sports have seen a pair of champions with these names, starting with ice hockey forwards Meghan Agosta of Canada, who has won three Olympic gold medals and two world championships, and American Meghan Duggan, whose stellar career saw her teams win Olympic gold and seven world championships. American soccer fans are very familiar with two members of the FIFA Women's World Cup 2015 championship team: Meghan Klingenberg and Megan Rapinoe. The former is a left back who has won the NWSL Championship twice, CONCACAF Women's Championship, and SheBelieves Cup, while the latter is an international superstar midfielder/winger whose long list of accomplishments includes an Olympic gold medal, the Women's Cup, two FIFA Women's World Cups, three CONCACAF Women's Championship, four SheBelieves Cups, The Best FIFA Women's Player 2019, FIFA Women's Cup Golden Ball and Boot in 2019, and the Ballon d'Or Féminin.

A Meagan, Megan, or Meghan in your family won't necessarily be a world champion ice hockey or soccer player, but she will be a fierce competitor who will fight for her team and family on and off the field.

- **Meghan Agosta**, Ice Hockey (Forward), Montréal Stars, Canada, 2006–current
- **Meghan Duggan**, Ice Hockey (Forward), Boston Blades, USA, 2006–2020
- **Meagan Duhamel**, Figure Skating, Canada, 1988–2018
- **Meghan Klingenberg**, Soccer (Left Back), Portland Thorns FC, USA, 2011–current
- **Meghan Musnicki**, Rowing, USA, 2010–current
- **Megan Rapinoe**, Soccer (Midfielder/Winger), OL Reign, USA, 2006–current
- **Megan Schutt**, Cricket (Bowler), South Australia Women Cricket Team, Australia, 2009–current

MEG

When it comes to the *Megan* family of names, there's one traditional nickname that sets some girls apart, and that, of course, is Meg. If your little one prefers the short form, or if you give her that name without a longer version, she may become an athletic legend like American golfer Meg Mallon, who won twenty professional events (four of them major championships) and was inducted into the World Golf Hall of Fame, or Australian cricket batter Meghann "Meg" Lanning, who has won two Women's Cricket World Cups and five Women's World Twenty20 championships while setting the record for most Women's ODI centuries!

- **Meghann "Meg" Lanning**, Cricket (Top-Order Batter), Victoria Cricket Women Team, Australia, 2008–current
- **Meg Mallon**, Golf, USA, 1987–2010

MELISSA

From Greek for "bee," the name Melissa has long enjoyed popularity in the United States and shows up in places like Canada and Australia as well. Where have Melissas buzzed their way to wins and championships? Everywhere from sprinting (with world champion Melissa Jefferson of the USA) to beach volleyball (with world champion Melissa Humana-Paredes of Canada), swimming (with Australian two-time Paralympics gold-medalist Melissa Carlton) to paratriathlons (with three-time world champion Melissa Stockwell), alpine skiing (with Australian four-time winner of the World Para Alpine Skiing Championships Melissa Perrine), and water polo (with American Melissa Seidemann, whose medal count includes three golds each from the Olympic Games and World Championships, as well as a World Cup!).

While a Melissa can clearly succeed in any traditional sport she enjoys, there are also those who gravitate toward more unique and extreme events, so your Melissa may take after women like aerobatic pilot and women's Wingsuit B.A.S.E. race world champion Melissa Andrzejewski.

Melissa Andrzejewski, Extreme Sports, USA, 2006–current

Melissa Carlton, Swimming (Butterfly/Freestyle), Australia, 1991–2000

Melissa Humana-Paredes, Beach Volleyball, Canada, 2015–current

Melissa Jefferson, Track & Field (Sprinting), USA, 2022–current

Melissa Perrine, Alpine Skiing, Australia, 2009–current

Melissa Seidemann, Water Polo (Center/Defender), USA, 2010–current

Melissa Stockwell, Triathlon, USA, 2008–current

MERLENE

A unique soundalike to *Marlene* that comes from *Merle* and Old Irish roots for "bright sea," Merlene is a name pretty much guaranteed to impart a love of running and going fast! Give her running shoes and teach her about the exploits of Jamaican sprinters Merlene Frazer, who won the 4x100-meter relay at the 1991 World Championships, and Merlene Ottey, whose incredible thirty-plus-year career included twenty-one medals from World Championships (six of them gold) and multiple world records.

Merlene Frazer, Track & Field (Sprinting), Jamaica, 1991–2001

Merlene Ottey, Track & Field (Sprinting), Jamaica/Slovenia, 1979–2012

MERYL

The name Meryl comes from Old Irish roots meaning "bright sea" by way of the name *Muriel*, and it's an ideal one for a family that enjoys dancing, ice skating, and healthy competition. It's the name of ice dancer Meryl Davis, who won a full set of medals from the Olympics, two golds and two silvers from World Championships, five golds and a bronze from Grand Prix Finals, and more! Davis was ranked at the top of the world standings for five seasons, and, with partner Charlie White, set multiple records for their achievements as well as the longevity of their career.

Meryl Davis, Ice Dancing, USA, 2006–2017

MIA

A fun and short modern descendent of the name *Maria*, Mia has had noteworthy popularity in Scandinavia and is homophonous with an Italian word for "mine." International Mias have conquered primarily European sports, with Swedish two-time Women's EHF Champions League–winner and 1994 World Handball Player of the Year Mia Hermansson-Högdahl and Mia Audina of Indonesia (and later the Netherlands), who was ranked the number one badminton player in the world and who won two Uber Cups.

Here in the United States, our Mias are tough and super competitive. Boxer Mia St. John fought her way to super welterweight and lightweight world championships with a 49-14-2 record, and soccer forward/midfielder Mia Hamm is ranked as one of the greatest soccer players of all time whose career included two Olympic gold medals, two FIFA Women's World Cup wins, two FIFA World Player of the Year awards, being named to the FIFA 100, and becoming the first woman inducted into the World Football Hall of Fame!

A scrappy and ambitious Mia in your family may find an international sport she enjoys, giving her all to win big.

Mia Audina, Badminton, Indonesia/Netherlands, 1994–2006

Mariel "Mia" Hamm, Soccer (Forward/Midfielder), Washington Freedom, USA, 1987–2004

Mia Hermansson-Högdahl, Handball (Right Wing), Sweden, 1984–2000

Mia St. John, Boxing (Welterweight/Lightweight/Featherweight), USA, 1997–2016

MICHELE/MICHELLE

As the Beatles knew, the name Michelle comes from French, and ultimately from a variant of the name *Michael*. Whether they spell it with one "l" or two, athletes with this name from around the world have conquered a number of different sports, with a couple of interesting concentrations. Singular competitors include eight-time Japan Pro Softball League champion and two-time Olympic gold-medalist pitcher Michele Smith; five-time world champion and Grand Prix Final-winning figure skater Michelle Kwan; and Australian horse racing jockey Michelle Payne, who has over 760 career wins.

Meanwhile, pairs of Michelles have been champion swimmers and soccer players. Canadian Michelle Toro is a world champion freestyle swimmer, and in the 1980s and '90s, Michelle Smith became Ireland's most successful Olympian, with three gold medals and a bronze. On international football fields, Australian striker Michelle Heyman is the W-League's all-time top scorer with two W-League Premierships, two W-League Championships, and two W-League Golden Boot awards, while American midfielder/forward Michelle Akers ranks among the best players ever, having earned an Olympic gold medal, won two FIFA Women's World Cups, been included in the FIFA 100, and named FIFA Female Player of the Century.

A daughter you name Michele or Michelle has her pick of athletic or other endeavors, but she may find soccer or swimming to her liking.

Michelle Akers, Soccer (Midfielder/Forward), Tyresö Fotbollsförening, USA, 1985–2000

Michelle Heyman, Soccer (Striker), Canberra United Football Club, Australia, 2008–current

Michelle Kwan, Figure Skating, USA, 1994–2006

Michelle Payne, Horse Racing (Jockey), Australia, 2004–current

Michele Smith, Softball (Pitcher), Toyota Shokki, USA, 1992–2002

Michelle Smith, Swimming (Butterfly/Freestyle/Medley), Ireland, 1983–1998

Michelle Toro, Swimming (Freestyle), Canada, 2014–current

MICKEY

Mickey is typically seen as a boy's name, but it can be a fun unisex diminutive for anyone! It even holds a special place in the heart of golf fans for the World Golf Hall of Famer Mary "Mickey" Wright. Despite having a relatively short competitive career, Wright dominated the links with ninety wins, eighty-two of them on the LPGA Tour, and thirteen of those being major championships. To this day she's considered one of the best golfers of all time, and she's a great role model for a young Mickey in your family.

Mary "Mickey" Wright, Golf, USA, 1954–1969

MILDRED

Chances are good that these days you don't know any young people named Mildred, an old-fashioned name if we've ever heard one. But the name is powerful (coming from Old English and roots meaning "gently strength") and has a very distinct athletic heritage, used with fun nicknames in baseball and track and field and by one of the most impressive sportswomen of the twentieth century. The All-American Girls Professional Baseball League (1943–1954) featured numerous star players named Mildred, including Canadian

All-Star third basewoman Millie Warwick, who set a single season hitting streak record; and All-Star Grand Rapids Chicks pitcher and league champion Mid Earp, who pitched a no-hitter in 1948.

Millie McDaniel set a world record when she won the gold medal in high jump at the 1956 Olympic Games, following in the footsteps of the incredibly multi-talented Babe Didrikson Zaharias, who won Olympic gold medals in 80-meter hurdles and javelin in 1932. Babe's skills went far beyond just track and field events; she also played basketball and baseball, but she is best known for her stellar golf career! She was a founding member of the Ladies Professional Golf Association (LPGA), winning the majority of her forty-eight professional events on that tour, including ten majors.

The name Mildred is definitely ready for a comeback, and it brings with it several fun nicknames (including *Millie*, *Mid*, and *Babe*) and a penchant for baseball, running, and playing in the sun.

Mildred "Mid" Earp, Baseball (Pitcher), Grand Rapids Chicks, USA, 1947–1950

Mildred "Millie" McDaniel, Track & Field (High Jump), USA, 1953–1956

Mildred "Millie" Warwick, Baseball (Third Base), Rockford Peaches, Canada, 1943–1944

Mildred "Babe" Didrikson Zaharias, Track & Field/Golf, USA, 1930–1955

MISSY

Typically a diminutive of the name *Melissa*, Missy is a fun, feminine moniker. If athletes are any indication, the name comes along with a love of speed, whether that's shooting through the water or blasting over mountainsides! Mountain Bike Hall of Famer Missy Giove rode to two World Cup wins and a world championship, while Missy Franklin set multiple world records on her way to collect five Olympic gold medals (in backstroke, freestyle, and medley) and eleven world championships.

Melissa "Missy" Franklin, Swimming (Backstroke/Freestyle/Medley), USA, 2010–2018

Melissa "Missy" Giove, Mountain Biking, USA, 1993–2002

MISTY

While *Missy* came about as a nickname for *Melissa*, Misty with a "t" is a name all on its own and arose from the meteorological adjective in Old English. There's plenty of moisture in the air where Mistys like to play and compete; Olympic gold-medalist and world champion Misty Hyman is a swimmer, and Misty May-Treanor, who won three Olympic gold medals and the Beach Volleyball World Championships three times with partner Kerri Jennings, is a legendary beach volleyball player.

Misty Hyman, Swimming (Backstroke/Butterfly), USA, 1995–2000

Misty May-Treanor, Beach Volleyball, USA, 1999–2012

MOLLY

Molly originally arose as a medieval diminutive of *Mary*, though in modern times it's used plenty on its own and can even be used as a nickname for other names. Three Mollys from three different countries have reached the heights of their careers in three different sports. Molly Taylor has driven through the ranks of Australian rally racing, becoming the first woman to win the Australian Rally Championship in 2016 and going on to become the 2021 Extreme E champion; three-time world champion biathlete Martina "Molly" Beck was the first German to win the Biathlon World Cup overall in 2003; and ice hockey player Molly Engstrom's stellar performance playing defense led to winning four world championships and the 4 Nations Cup.

Whether you name your daughter Molly or just use it as a nickname, she will undoubtedly find her own unique place in the world, excelling in whatever field she chooses!

Martina "Molly" Beck, Biathlon, Germany, 2000–2010

Molly Engstrom, Ice Hockey (Defense), Brampton Thunder, USA, 2001–2018

Molly Taylor, Auto Racing (Rally), Australia, 2010–current

MONICA/MONIKA

Monica/Monika is a name with uncertain origins, thought by many to come from Berber or Phoenician languages. It later became associated with words in other languages, like "one" in Greek and "advisor" in Latin and saw its popularity in English rise in the eighteenth century. In modern times, Monicas and Monikas have proven versatile and powerful, embodying strength and physicality, like Ms. Fitness Olympia and two-time World Pro Figure champion Monica Brant, as well as brains and strategy, like Polish chess Woman Grandmaster and Grandmaster Monika Soćko. On ice, German speed skater Monika Pflug and curler Monika Wagner are Olympic gold-medalists and world champions (two for Wagner).

A Monica or Monika can succeed at any endeavor she puts her mind to, whether physical or mental, though she may have a particular penchant for tennis. Sports fans will know Monica Seles of Yugoslavia, whose singles career took off with fifty-three titles (nine of them majors) and the world's number one spot! Ranked among the best players of all time, Seles was set to have a lifetime of achievements before being attacked and injured, but even then, she bravely returned to the court for more wins.

Monica Brant, Bodybuilding, USA, 1991–2016

Monika Pflug, Speed Skating, Germany, 1971–1988

Monica Seles, Tennis, Yugoslavia/USA, 1989–2003

Monika Soćko, Chess, Poland, 1995–current

Monika Wagner, Curling (Second/Third), Germany, 1980–2012

MYRTLE

Being named after a bush doesn't sound terribly exciting, but the name Myrtle (from Greek for "the shrub") has a long history and was once pretty popular. It appeared among top athletes in 1928, when Canadian multi-talented competitor Myrtle Cook sprinted to Olympic gold; 1934, when English cricketer Myrtle Maclagan played in the very first women's Test match before going on to captain the English team and score two Test centuries; and 1988, when English weightlifter Myrtle Augee won an International Powerlifting Federation world championship!

Pick this old-fashioned name for a daughter who will bring it into the twenty-first century and who may appreciate running fast, team sports, or lifting weights.

Myrtle Augee, Powerlifting, England, 1986–2002

Myrtle Cook, Track & Field (Sprinting), Canada, 1928–1937

Myrtle Maclagan, Cricket (All-Rounder), Surrey Women's Cricket Team, England, 1934–1951

N

BOYS

NAIM

We kick off the boys "N" names with a descendant of the traditional Arabic Na'im, which comes from a root meaning "at ease," "happy," or "tranquil." In the 1980s and '90s, Turkish Naim Süleymanoğlu became an icon for short kings everywhere when the four-foot ten-inch weightlifter known as "Pocket Hercules" set forty-six world records and cemented himself as the best pound-for-pound lifter of all time, with three Olympic gold medals and seven world championships.

You can't go wrong with this pleasant name that's perfectly ideal for a family of short, strong men.

Naim Süleymanoğlu, Weightlifting, Turkey, 1982–2000

NAP

Nap is an old-fashioned nickname for *Napoléon* and other names that are not heard much these days, but trust me when I say it used to be all the rage. Nap was a hallmark of baseball players in the first half of the twentieth century! National Baseball Hall of Fame second baseman Napoléon "Nap" Lajoie was a three-time RBI leader, AL home run leader, AL batting champion, and Triple Crown winner at the turn of the century; and Brooklyn starting pitcher George Napoléon "Nap" Rucker led the National League in shutouts, WAR, complete games, and innings pitched and pitched a no-hitter in 1908.

Whether you're giving it as a diminutive to a little Napoléon in your family or just a fun name in general, Nap can inspire dreams of making it big in America's pastime.

Napoléon "Nap" Lajoie, Baseball (Second Baseman), Cleveland Naps, USA, 1896–1916

George Napoléon "Nap" Rucker, Baseball (Pitcher), Brooklyn Superbas, USA, 1907–1916

NAT/NATE

Most often short forms of names like *Nathan* and *Nathaniel*, Nat and Nate are fully functional on their own and are ideal for a boy who will get into combat sports, play on water or ice, or be a sturdy team player. Among the toughest athletes with these names has been MMA fighter Nate Marquardt, who held the Strikeforce Welterweight championship and the Pancrase Middleweight championship three times. In and on the water,

Australian surfer Nat Young and American freestyle swimmer Nate Dusing each captured two world championships, three-time world waterskiing champion Nate Smith set the world slalom record, freestyle skier "Nate Dog" Roberts won world championship gold and bronze in moguls, and snowboarder Nate Holland collected seven golds and two bronzes in snowboard cross at the X Games.

Nats and Nates also excel when playing with others, as we can see by concentrations of them in basketball and football. The gridiron has seen the exploits of two-time Pro Bowlers Nate Kaeding (placekicker) and Nate Odomes (interceptions co-leader cornerback), while on the hardwood, six-time All-Star point guard Nate Archibald led the league in scoring and assists and won the 1981 championship with the Boston Celtics and seven-time All-Star center/power forward Nate Thurmond was the first player to achieve the lofty quadruple-double!

Your job as a parent of a Nat or Nate is clear: provide him with access to a pool and the slopes, be open to any interest he shows in martial arts, and teach him to be a good team player.

- **Nathaniel "Nate" Archibald**, Basketball (Point Guard), Cincinnati Royals, USA, 1970–1984
- **Nathaniel "Nate" Dusing**, Swimming (Freestyle/Medley), USA, 1997–2005
- **Nate Holland**, Snowboarding, USA, 2007–current
- **Nathaniel "Nate" Kaeding**, Football (Placekicker), San Diego Chargers, USA, 2004–2013
- **Nathan "Nate" Marquardt**, MMA (Lightweight/Middleweight/Welterweight), USA, 1999–current
- **Nathaniel "Nate" Odomes**, Football (Cornerback), Buffalo Bills, USA, 1987–1996
- **Nathan "Nate" Roberts**, Freestyle Skiing, USA, 1999–current
- **Nate Smith**, Water Skiing, USA, 2010–current
- **Nathaniel "Nate" Thurmond**, Basketball (Center/Power Forward), San Francisco Warriors, USA, 1963–1977
- **Robert Harold "Nat" Young**, Surfing, Australia, 1965–1979

NATHAN

A perennial popular choice for parents in the United States and Australia, Nathan comes to English from biblical Hebrew meaning "he gave." If there's anything Nathans are given, it's the ability to find their particular sport to excel in—and there are lots of choices out there. Nathan Cohen of New Zealand rowed to two world championships and a gold medal at the Olympics; Nathan Chen is carving up the figure skating world with three Grand Prix Finals and world championships each, plus an Olympic gold medal; Canadian six-time All-Star Colorado Avalanche ice hockey center Nathan MacKinnon has won the Stanley Cup and a world championship; and freestyle swimmer Nathan Adrian has (thus far) collected eight medals from the Olympics (five of them gold) and nineteen from World Championships, with fifteen of them being wins!

In Australia in particular, Nathans are unsurprisingly dominant in local favorite sports like cricket and rugby. Some of these include the 2019 Australian Men's Test Player of the Year, Nathan Lyon, who has been named to three ICC Test Teams of the Year; and Parramatta Eels second-row Nathan Hindmarsh, who won two Tri-Nations, a Rugby League Four Nations championship, and a World Cup and holds multiple records as the first player to make ten thousand, eleven thousand, and twelve thousand tackles.

Outside of Australia, naming a son Nathan can give your son an appreciation for figure skating, ice hockey, or swimming, while down under, he's more likely to appreciate more local pastimes.

Nathan Adrian, Swimming (Freestyle), USA, 2008–current

Nathan Chen, Figure Skating, USA, 2007–current

Nathan Cohen, Rowing, New Zealand, 2000–2013

Nathan Hindmarsh, Rugby (Second-Row), Parramatta Eels, Australia, 1998–2012

Nathan Lyon, Cricket (Bowler), South Australia Cricket Team, Australia, 2008–current

Nathan MacKinnon, Ice Hockey (Center), Colorado Avalanche, Canada, 2013–current

NED

Possibly arising from smooshing together the term "mine Ed," Ned started off as a diminutive of names like *Edmund* and *Edward*, though it's expanded to be used on its own as well. Ned may not be a very common name heard these days, but it does pop up in the sporting world from time to time! In the 1950s, pitcher Ned Garver was an MLB All-Star while Ned Jarrett was tearing up the tracks of NASCAR, winning fifty races and two championships in the elite Grand National series over a thirteen-year career and earning a place in the Motorsports Hall of Fame of America. Ned has even made the leaderboards of lacrosse recently, with seven-time All-Star and two-time World Lacrosse Champion Ned Crotty.

Whether it's a nickname for an *Edmund* or *Edward*, or just a Ned on its own, give this name to your son who will be a strong competitor in his favorite field.

Ned Crotty, Lacrosse (Attack), Chrome Lacrosse Club, USA, 2010–2022

Ned Garver, Baseball (Pitcher), St. Louis Browns, USA, 1948–1961

Ned Jarrett, Auto Racing (NASCAR), USA, 1952–1966

NELSON

You don't need to be named *Neil* to name a son Nelson, though that's where the English patronymic comes from. If you do, he may swim like a fish or enjoy driving fast, if he's anything like two-time Olympic gold-medalist swimmer Nelson Diebel, Colombian Paralympic gold-medalist and eleven-time world champion swimmer Nelson Crispín, or Brazilian father-and-son racing duo Nelson Piquet (twenty-three wins and three championships in Formula 1) and Nelson Piquet Jr. (three wins and a championship in Formula E).

If he doesn't feel the need for speed or the allure of the water, there are plenty of other fun things a Nelson in your family may enjoy. Athletes with this name have found success in many different fields, including wrestling (like Soviet two-time world champion Nelson Davidyan), bowling (like Nelson "Bo" Burton Jr., who won eighteen titles), track and field (like Portuguese Olympic gold-medalist, world champion, and World Indoor Tour-winning triple jumper Nelson Évora), baseball (like Dominican seven-time All-Star designated hitter/right fielder Nelson Cruz Jr., whose career included four Silver Slugger awards, becoming the AL home run leader and RBI leader, and winning the World Baseball Classic), and even memory games (like Grand Master of Memory and five-time USA Memory Champion Nelson Dellis)!

Nelson "Bo" Burton Jr., Bowling, USA, 1964–1997

Nelson Crispín, Swimming (Breaststroke/Butterfly/Freestyle/Medley), Colombia, 2011–current

Nelson Cruz Jr., Baseball (Designated Hitter/Right Fielder), Texas Rangers, Dominican Republic, 2005–current

Nelson Davidyan, Greco-Roman Wrestling, USSR, 1964–1981

Nelson Dellis, Memory Sports, USA, 2009–current

Nelson Diebel, Swimming (Breaststroke), USA, 1989–1992

Nelson Évora, Track & Field (Triple Jump), Portugal, 2004–2021

Nelson Piquet, Auto Racing (Formula 1), Brazil, 1971–1991

Nelson Piquet Jr., Auto Racing (Formula E), Brazil, 1993–current

NEYMAR

Some names date back to ancient times, while others are modern inventions that only reach a wide audience when they're championed by an athlete in a major international sport. The latter is exactly the case with Neymar, a Brazilian name that may come from a combination of the Roman gods Neptune and Mars. Forward Neymar da Silva Santos Júnior has been setting records for years, having started his professional career at the age of seventeen. Since then, he's scored over one hundred goals for three different clubs, more than seventy-five with Brazil, and won dozens of trophies, including La Liga twice, Copa del Rey three times, UEFA Champions League, FIFA Club World Cup, and FIFA Confederations Cup. Considered one of the greatest players in the history of the sport, Neymar has earned the FIFA Confederations Cup Golden Ball and Bronze Shoe, FIFA and World Cup Bronze Boot, and recognition on the FIFA Confederations Cup Dream Team and FIFA World Cup Dream Team.

If you like Roman mythology, astronomy, or soccer, then Neymar might be a good choice for naming an athletic and ambitious son in your family!

Neymar da Silva Santos Júnior, Soccer (Forward), Santos Futebol Clube, Brazil, 2009–current

NICHOLAS/NICOLAS

There are names that seem destined to stand upon podiums and receive medals and awards, and that could be said for Nicholas, which comes from Ancient Greek roots meaning "victory of the people" or "people of victory." With its long history, Nicholas has spawned multiple spelling variants, the most common of which is Nicolas. Kenyan hurdler Nicholas Bett became a world champion in 2015, and American rower Nicholas Anderson reached that mark three times in the late 1990s, while French soccer forward Nicolas Anelka scored over 220 goals in nearly 750 senior and international appearances while racking up three FA Cups, a UEFA Champions League, UEFA European Championship, and FIFA Confederations Cup. Tennis, meanwhile, is a particular favorite of athletes named Nicolas, with Chilean two-time Olympic gold-medalist Nicolás Massú and French doubles player Nicolas Mahut, who held the number one spot in the world for thirty-nine weeks, won thirty-seven titles and five Grand Slams, and played in the longest match in history (183 games, over eleven hours)!

If your son prefers the full version of Nicolas or Nicholas, there's a good chance he may be fast on his feet and quick on the ball, but also able to go the distance and play for days.

Nicholas Anderson, Rowing, USA, 1997–2000

Nicolas Anelka, Soccer (Forward), Chelsea Football Club, France, 1996–2015

Nicholas Bett, Track & Field (Hurdling), Kenya, 2011–2018

Nicolas Mahut, Tennis, France, 2000–current

Nicolás Massú, Tennis, Chile, 1997–2013

NICK

Nicholas may mean "victory of the people," but Nick is the obvious champion when it comes to which name is used by more sports champions. Such wins, championships, and awards have happened in numerous sports and events, ranging from strength sports (with world champion powerlifter Nick Best)

to soccer (with six-time MLS All-Star goalkeeper Nick Rimando, who has won the CONCACAF Gold Cup and the MLS Cup twice), skiing (with four-time X Games gold-medalist Nick Goepper), pool (with eight-time straight pool and nine-ball world champion Nick Varner), and tennis (with three-time Paralympic gold-medalist Nick Taylor, who reached the doubles number one rank with twelve Grand Slams).

British Nicks riding to victories include two-time Olympic gold-medalist equestrian show jumper Nick Skelton while in the water, Hungarian water polo player Miklós "Nick" Martin won two Olympic gold medals before defecting to the United States, Nick Thoman swam to two world championships and Olympic gold in the 4x100-meter medley, and Australian Nick Green rowed to two Olympic gold medals and four world championships!

Nicks do tend toward a few sports over all the others, with a pair of victors appearing in golf with the record-breaking duo of World Golf Hall of Famers Nick Faldo of England (forty-three wins, six majors) and Nick Price of Zimbabwe (forty-eight wins, three majors).

Meanwhile, the most Nicks in one sport accumulate on the gridiron of American football! Three-time Pro Bowlers include San Francisco 49ers defensive end Nick Bosa, 1990 NFL scoring leader placekicker Nick Lowery, and Super Bowl XLV champion Green Bay Packers free safety Nick Collins. Nick Chubb is a four-time Pro-Bowl Cleveland Browns running back and center Nick Mangold was selected seven times during his career with the New York Jets.

Whether it's his given name or a nickname, an athletic boy named Nick is likely to enjoy playing with his friends on a football team, but he certainly has the capability to branch out into any sport or discipline!

Nick Best, Powerlifting, USA, 1996–current

Nicholas "Nick" Bosa, Football (Defensive End), San Francisco 49ers, USA, 2019–current

Nicholas "Nick" Chubb, Football (Running Back), Cleveland Browns, USA, 2018–current

Nicholas "Nick" Collins, Football (Free Safety), Green Bay Packers, USA, 2005–2011

Nicholas "Nick" Faldo, Golf, England, 1977–2015

Nicholas "Nick" Goepper, Freestyle Skiing, USA, 2013–current

Nicholas "Nick" Green, Rowing, Australia, 1990–1998

Dominic "Nick" Lowery, Football (Placekicker), Kansas City Chiefs, USA, 1978–1996

Nicholas "Nick" Mangold, Football (Center), New York Jets, USA, 2006–2016

Miklós "Nick" Martin, Water Polo (Field Player), Hungary, 1952–1956

Nicholas "Nick" Price, Golf, Zimbabwe, 1977–2009

Nicholas "Nick" Rimando, Soccer (Goalkeeper), Real Salt Lake, USA, 2000–2019

Nicholas "Nick" Skelton, Equestrian (Show Jumping), England, 1978–2017

Nick Taylor, Wheelchair Basketball (Shooting Guard)/Golf, Australia, 2005–current

Nicholas "Nick" Thoman, Swimming (Backstroke), USA, 2007–2012

Nick Varner, Pool (Nine-Ball), USA, 1971–2011

NICKY

Nicky is another fun diminutive for "Nic-" names, and a boy you call Nicky could very well want to be a race car or motorcycle driver! On and off racetracks, motorcycle racer Nicky Hayden won the 2016 MotoGP World Championship, while Welsh rally co-driver Nicky Grist took the checkered flag in twenty-one races and won the 1993 World Rally Championship.

Nicholas "Nicky" Grist, Auto Racing (Rally), Wales, 1985–2006

Nicholas "Nicky" Hayden, Motorcycle Racing (MotoGP World Championship), USA, 1998–2017

NICO

With yet another short form of *Nicholas*, Nicos continue the need for speed. German slalom canoeist Nico Bettge has a gold and six silver medals from World Championships, Spanish motorcycle racer Nico Terol rode to thirteen wins and the 2011 125cc World Championship, and German-Finnish Formula 1 driver Nico Rosberg sped to twenty-three wins and the 2016 championship.

It is possible that a Nico in your family won't have a racing bug; instead, he might just create his own sport altogether, like Nico Broekhuysen of Netherlands did in 1902 when he adapted the Swedish game "ring-boll" into korfball!

Nico Bettge, Slalom Canoeing, Germany, 2000–current

Nicolaas "Nico" Broekhuysen, Korfball, Netherlands, 1902–1934

Nico Rosberg, Auto Racing (Formula 1), Germany, 2005–2016

Nicolás "Nico" Terol, Motorcycle Racing (125cc World Championship), Spain, 2004–current

NICOLAI/NICOLAJ/NIKOLAI/NIKOLAJ/NIKOLAY

The name *Nicholas* has many variants around the world, and in Eastern Europe, that's reflected in the family of names that includes Nicolai, Nicolaj, Nikolai, Nikolaj, and Nikolay. It should come as no surprise, then, what kinds of sports athletes with these names have conquered. Blind cross-country skier Nikolay Polukhin won Paralympic gold, and Olympic gold-medalists include Soviet water polo player Nikolay Melnikov and figure skater Nikolai Panin-Kolomenkin, who was Russia's first athlete to win that elite award in 1908 in the incredibly challenging special figures event.

Tough, fast, and strong describe many of these athletes, including Estonian two-time world champion épée fencer Nikolai Novosjolov; Russian two-time world heavyweight champion boxer Nikolai Valuev, who, at seven feet, is the tallest to hold that title; Olympic gold-medalist and three-time world champion weightlifter Nikolaj Pešalov; Soviet wrestler Nikolay Balboshin, who swept every event he entered at Olympic Games and World Championships (one gold and five golds, respectively); and record-setting Soviet artistic gymnast Nikolai Andrianov, whose massive medal haul includes fifteen from the Olympics (seven of them gold) and thirteen from World Championships.

Ice hockey is another sport you'd expect people in cold weather countries to enjoy, and Russians with the Nikolai family of names definitely show up in those rosters with a pair of two-time world champions in left wing Nikolay Kulemin and right wing Nikolay Zherdev, as well as four-time NHL All-Star goaltender Nikolai Khabibulin, who won both a Stanley Cup and an Olympic gold medal.

While a name like Nikolai might seem to impart strength and dogged determination on the ice or snow, it can also represent quick thinking and even faster reflexes, proven by Danish esports legends like three-time *League of Legends* League Championship Series champion Nicolaj "Jensen" and Nicolai "dev1ce" Reedtz, whose *Counter-Strike: Global Offensive* exploits include wins at four Major Championships, two Majors MVP awards, and consistent rankings among the best players in the world!

Nikolai Andrianov, Artistic Gymnastics, USSR, 1971–1980

Nikolay Balboshin, Greco-Roman Wrestling, USSR, 1972–1984

Nicolaj "Jensen" Jensen, Esports (*League of Legends*), Denmark, 2012–current

Nikolai Khabibulin, Ice Hockey (Goaltender), Tampa Bay Lightning, Russia, 1994–2014

Nikolay Kulemin, Ice Hockey (Left Wing), Toronto Maple Leafs, Russia, 2003–current

Nikolay Melnikov, Water Polo (Field Player), USSR, 1972

Nikolai Novosjolov, Fencing (Épée), Estonia, 2001–current

Nikolai Panin-Kolomenkin, Figure Skating, Russia, 1901–1912

Nikolaj Pešalov, Weightlifting, Croatia, 1989–2004

Nikolay Polukhin, Cross-Country Skiing, Russia, 2010

Nicolai "dev1ce" Reedtz, Esports (*Counter-Strike: Global Offensive*), Denmark, 2013–current

Nikolai Valuev, Boxing (Heavyweight), Russia, 1993–2009

Mykola "Nikolay" Zherdev, Ice Hockey (Right Wing), Columbus Blue Jackets, Russia, 2002–current

NIGEL

The history of the name Nigel goes back as far as medieval times and a Latinization of *Neil*, though the origins of that one are lost to time. Nigel's popularity among the British hasn't quite made it to this side of the Atlantic, though there are several truly inspiring athletes and competitors who could inspire anyone anywhere to give the name to their child. The variety of events that Nigels have dominated are extreme, ranging from the purely physical boxing (with Nigel Benn, who won world championships in two different weight classes) to the entirely mental chess (with child prodigy/Grandmaster Nigel Short). The most famous sporting Nigel is racing driver Mansell, one of the most decorated of all time, with thirty-one wins and a championship in Formula 1 and five wins.

Nigel Benn, Boxing (Middleweight), England, 1987–1996

Nigel Mansell, Auto Racing (Formula 1), England, 1976–1995

Nigel Short, Chess, England, 1975–current

NIKI

While most "Nic-" and "Nik-" names get diminutives like *Nick* and *Nicky*, there's one Niki that really stands out from the crowd. In 1971, Austrian racing driver Andreas Nikolaus "Niki" Lauda joined the Formula 1 series and quickly made a name for himself as a dedicated, and fast, competitor. His career reached stellar heights (twenty-five wins and three championships driving for both Ferrari and McLaren) as well as disastrous lows (a horrific crash with toxic fume inhalation and burns). Lauda helped raise the profile of the sport with his famous rivalry with James Hunt.

The name Niki definitely has a different feel from Nicky, and any kid lucky enough to be called that will be a force of nature, fast, smart, and determined to win.

Andreas Nikolaus "Niki" Lauda, Auto Racing (Formula 1), Austria, 1971–1985

NIKITA

The *Nikolai* family of names is Eastern Europe's evolution of *Nicholas/Nicolas*, but Russia has also given us the name Nikita, which comes from the same Greek root meaning "winner" or "victor." Athletes named Nikita are absolutely victors, from Olympic gold-medalist soccer forward Nikita Simonyan, who won two Soviet Cups, four Soviet Top Leagues, and multiple goal scorer awards, to two-time Olympic gold-medalist and World Team Trophy-winning ice dancer Nikita Katsalapov and artistic gymnast Nikita

Nagornyy, who has taken home Olympic gold and three world championships. There's even a pair of winners in ice hockey, with world champion defenseman Nikita Nikitin and four-time NHL All-Star Tampa Bay Lightning right wing and two-time Stanley Cup-champion Nikita Kucherov.

Nikita Katsalapov, Ice Dancing, Russia, 2010-current

Nikita Kucherov, Ice Hockey (Right Wing), Tampa Bay Lightning, Russia, 2011-current

Nikita Nagornyy, Artistic Gymnastics, Russia, 2015-current

Nikita Nikitin, Ice Hockey (Defense), Columbus Blue Jackets, Russia, 2002-current

Nikita Simonyan, Soccer (Forward), FC Spartak Moscow, USSR, 1946-1959

NIKLAS

We're nearly done with names based on *Nicholas*, and here we come to the Scandinavian favorite Niklas. The history of athletes with this name gives us an indication that a Niklas is most at home in a team setting, working together with his teammates to defeat their opponents. German soccer center-back Niklas Süle has defended his teams on their way to winning the Bundesliga five times, as well as the UEFA Champions League, UEFA Super Cup, FIFA Club World Cup, and FIFA Confederations Cup, while Olympic gold medals have been won by German field hockey midfielder Niklas Meinert, Danish three-time world champion handball goalkeeper Niklas Landin Jacobsen, and Swedish six-time world champion and record-setting curling skip Niklas Edin.

In particular, this *Nicholas* variant excels at ice hockey! Swedish ice stars include Olympic gold-medalist right wing Niklas Eriksson, three-time Stanley Cup-champion defenseman Niklas Hjalmarsson, and defenseman Niklas Kronwall, whose list of awards includes an Olympic gold medal, a world championship, and the Stanley Cup.

Johan Niklas Edin, Curling (Skip), Sweden, 2005-current

Niklas Eriksson, Ice Hockey (Right Wing), Leksands Idrottsförening, Sweden, 1987-2007

Niklas Hjalmarsson, Ice Hockey (Defense), Chicago Blackhawks, Sweden, 2004-2023

Niklas Kronwall, Ice Hockey (Defense), Detroit Red Wings, Sweden, 1999-2019

Niklas Landin Jacobsen, Handball (Goalkeeper), Denmark, 2006-current

Niklas Meinert, Field Hockey (Midfielder), Germany, 2003-2008

Niklas Süle, Soccer (Center-Back), Fußball-Club Bayern München e. V., Germany, 2012-current

NIKOLA

Our final entry based on *Nicholas* is the Danish and Slovene Nikola. The NBA has imported some of the tallest Nikolas around to play center, like Serbian five-time All-Star Denver Nuggets Nikola Jokić (six feet, eleven inches), while Serbian setters have made big strides on the international volleyball scene with Olympic gold-medalist Nikola Grbić. Some of the most successful athletes with this name include Serbian two-time Olympic gold-medalist, world champion, and two-time World League champion water polo center-back Nikola Jakšić, and French handball center-back Nikola Karabatić, who has solidified his position as one of the all-time greats, with three Olympic gold medals (and a bronze) and seven podiums at World Championships (four of them wins).

If your family comes from Eastern Europe or you want to add a little flair to your kid's *Nicholas*-based name, then Nikola might be just right for you. A boy with this name may find his niche in a European sport or something closer to home (like basketball if he's particularly tall).

Nikola Grbić, Volleyball (Setter), Serbia, 1987-2014

Nikola Jakšić, Water Polo (Center-Back), Serbia, 2013–current

Nikola Jokić, Basketball (Center), Denver Nuggets, Serbia, 2012–current

Nikola Karabatić, Handball (Center Back), France, 2000–current

NOLAN

The name Nolan, from an Irish root for "famous" or "loud," is definitely best for a boy who will either love to play sports on ice (especially if he's Canadian) or find his place on the baseball diamond! That's especially true if he's anything like world champion curler Nolan Thiessen. Meanwhile, two Nolans have made big impacts on America's pastime. Third baseman Nolan Arenado played most of his career with the Colorado Rockies, and during his decade-plus career, he has played in seven All-Star games, claimed the NL RBI leader twice and NL home run leader three times, and earned five Silver Sluggers, six Platinum Gloves, and ten Gold Gloves; he also hit for the cycle twice and was on the 2017 World Baseball Classic championship team. And then, of course, there's record-setting eight-time All-Star pitcher Nolan Ryan. Known as the "Ryan Express," the National Baseball Hall of Famer won the 1969 World Series, was the NL ERA leader twice and strikeout leader eleven times, and still holds records for seven career no-hitters, over 5,700 career strikeouts, and more. With consistent play (and fastballs over one hundred miles per hour) for a record-tying twenty-seven seasons, Nolan Ryan is considered one of the game's all-time greats.

Nolan Arenado, Baseball (Third Baseman), Colorado Rockies, USA, 2013–current

Lynn Nolan "Ryan Express" Ryan Jr., Baseball (Pitcher), California Angels, USA, 1966–1993

Nolan Thiessen, Curling (Lead), Canada, 2004–2016

NORBERT

Nobert, from Old German roots for "north" and "bright," is uncommon in the United States but has enjoyed popularity in a number of European countries. And if the records of champion athletes with this name are anything to go by, a boy you name Norbert could have a *very* bright future indeed. Athlete Norberts include German Olympic gold-medal pistol sport shooter Klaar; Manchester United soccer defensive midfielder "Nobby" Stiles, who won the FA Cup, European Cup, and FIFA World Cup in the 1960s and '70s; and German three-time world champion rower Keßlau.

Pairs of Norberts have stood on podiums in front of the world for their successes in water polo and luge. In the pool, driver Norbert Hosnyánszky won Olympic gold and a world championship, and wing/driver Norbert Madaras took home two of each, while on the luge track, Italian two-time world champion Norbert Huber racked up ten World Cup wins and German Norbert Hahn won two times at both Olympic Games and World Championships.

Norbert Hahn, Luge, Germany, 1973–1980

Norbert Hosnyánszky, Water Polo (Driver), Hungary, 2003–current

Norbert Huber, Luge, Italy, 1983–1999

Norbert Keßlau, Rowing, Germany, 1983–1989

Norbert Klaar, Sport Shooting (Pistol), Germany, 1976

Norbert Madaras, Water Polo (Wing/Driver), Hungary, 2001–2018

Norbert "Nobby" Stiles, Soccer (Defensive Midfielder), Manchester United Football Club, England, 1960–1975

NORMAN

You don't have to come from the frozen north lands to name your son Norman, though that is the Scandinavian origin of the name with a Germanic root meaning "northman." From sports history, we can see that Normans are particularly drawn to ice hockey and basketball, so you're strongly urged to introduce a Norman in your family to skating and the fundamentals of dribbling and shooting. The NHL has seen Canadian All-Star and two-time Detroit Red Wings Stanley Cup-champion goaltender Norman "Normie" Smith, who set the league record for most saves in a single game (ninety-two), while on the hardwood, three-time All-Star point guard Norman "Norm" Van Lier led the league in assists in 1971.

Norman "Normie" Smith, Ice Hockey (Goaltender), Detroit Red Wings, Canada, 1931–1945

Norman "Norm" Van Lier, Basketball (Point Guard), Chicago Bulls, USA, 1989–1990

NOVAK

In the United States, Novak (from a Serbian root meaning "new") is much more often a surname than a given name, but that's not the case in Eastern Europe. Soccer defender Novak Roganović helped bring the name to an international stage when he won Olympic gold with the Yugoslavian team in 1960, but no one has done more to popularize it than tennis singles world number one Novak Djokovic! The Serbian tennis star has held that world top-spot for a record number of weeks with ninety-three titles and counting, and he shows no sign of slowing down!

A Novak in your family may not become one of the greatest players of all time, but he's sure to make a mark wherever his athletic interests drive him; perhaps introduce him to soccer and tennis and see if he follows in Roganović or Djokovic's footsteps.

Novak Djokovic, Tennis, Serbia, 2003–current

Novak Roganović, Soccer (Defender), Fudbalski klub Vojvodina, Yugoslavia, 1954–1965

GIRLS

NADIA

The name Nadia has a couple of origins from different parts of the world. Arising in western Europe from a diminutive of *Nadezhda* (which means "hope" in Bulgarian and Russian), it also has Arabic roots meaning "tender" or "delicate." In the 1970s, one athlete's incredible achievements brought the name to international fame. At the 1976 Montréal Olympic Games, Romania's artistic gymnastics team included then fourteen-year-old Nadia Comăneci, a child prodigy. Not only did she win three gold medals, a silver, and a bronze at the Games, but she also scored the world's first Olympic gymnastics perfect score! Comăneci would go on to win a total of nine Olympic medals (including five golds), two golds and two silvers at World Championships, two golds and a silver at the World Cup, and a grand total of nine perfect scores at the Olympics!

A Nadia in your family will surely share in Comăneci's grace and strength, making her a powerful force in whatever sport she loves.

Nadia Comăneci, Artistic Gymnastics, Romania, 1970–1984

NADINE

A variant and French diminutive of *Nadia*, the name Nadine has made waves on multiple continents and in several different athletic competitions. It has run the gamut of both individual and team sports, the former including Dutch world champion pentathlete Nadine Broersen, two-time Olympic gold-medalist and four-time world champion dressage equestrian Nadine Capellmann of Germany, and South African water skier Nadine de Villiers, who stands as one of the best barefoot skiers of all time, with eight world barefoot records, ten World Barefoot Championships, and induction into the International Waterski and Wakeboard Federation Hall of Fame.

On the team side, German field hockey striker Nadine Ernsting-Krienke won the Champions Challenge, a Champions Trophy, and Olympic gold and silver; and German soccer goalkeeper Nadine Angerer became known as one of the best goalkeepers of all time, with an incredible trophy collection including the UEFA Women's Cup, five UEFA European Football Championships, two FIFA World Cups, and more while being named to the FIFA Women's World Cup All-Star Team twice, FIFA Women's World Cup Best Goalkeeper, and FIFA World Player of the Year!

Name your daughter Nadine and introduce her to the wide world of sports; she's sure to find at least one that she loves to participate in.

Nadine Angerer, Soccer (Goalkeeper), 1. Frauenfußballclub Turbine Potsdam 71 e. V., Germany, 1995–current

Nadine Broersen, Track & Field (Pentathlon), Netherlands, 2012–current

Nadine Capellmann, Equestrian (Dressage), Germany, 1997–current

Nadine Ernsting-Krienke, Field Hockey (Striker), Germany, 1990–2007

Nadine de Villiers, Water Skiing, South Africa, 1997–2002

NAN

While in the Western world Nan has served as a diminutive of both *Ann* and *Nancy*, in China it is also a type of wood and can be used to convey a wish for health and strength. Strength is definitely an attribute of two Chinese athletes who can be an inspiration to a Nan in your family; Zhang Nan was a world champion artistic gymnast, while Wang Nan's table tennis achievements of four Olympic gold medals, fifteen world championships, and five World Cup wins set her among the greatest top-ranked players of all time!

Name your daughter Nan and give her the vitality of wood and the athletic acumen of competitors who have come before her.

Wang Nan, Table Tennis, China, 1994–2008

Zhang Nan, Artistic Gymnastics, China, 2002–2009

NANA

The unisex Nana has numerous origins and usages around the world, from a Greek diminutive of *Ioanna* to examples in Georgia and Japan. Those last two are where we see Nanas compete and win at high levels with both brains and strength! Georgia is home to two recent chess Woman Grandmasters, Woman International Master Nana Alexandria and International Master Nana Ioseliani. Those are both great inspirations for a young girl excited about chess or other mentally challenging games, while Japanese volleyball middle blocker and winner of the Montreaux Volley Masters Nana Iwasaka is a paragon of physical proficiency and domination.

Nana Alexandria, Chess, Georgia, 1966–2006

Nana Ioseliani, Chess, Georgia, 1978–2003

Nana Iwasaka, Volleyball (Middle Blocker), Japan, 2009–2021

NANCY

An old-fashioned name that reached its pinnacle of popularity in the United States in the 1940s and '50s, Nancy has medieval origins as a diminutive of *Annis* (from *Agnes*) or *Ann* (from *Hannah*). Athletes here and in Canada have continued the awesomeness of Nancys into the modern era, with Canadian alpine skier Nancy Greene Raine winning Olympic gold and two World Championships in 1968, golf megastar Nancy Lopez starting her road to fifty-one professional wins (three of them majors) in 1977, Basketball Hall of Fame point guard Nancy "Lady Magic" Lieberman winning a world championship in 1979 and the Women's American Basketball Association championship in 1984, and volleyball opposite Nancy Metcalf winning the World Grand Prix in 2012.

A Nancy in your family can continue the name's prominence in the twenty-first century, whether she becomes a champion skier, golfer, basketball player, volleyball player, or something else entirely.

Nancy Greene Raine, Alpine Skiing, Canada, 1959–1968

Nancy Lieberman, Basketball (Point Guard), Dallas Diamonds, USA, 1980–2008

Nancy Lopez, Golf, USA, 1974–2008

Nancy Metcalf, Volleyball (Opposite), USA, 2000–2014

NAOMI/NOEMI

The name Naomi (and subsequently its variant Noemi) has two very different origins, arising both from biblical Hebrew with a root meaning "pleasantness" and from Japanese in a form that can be written with characters meaning "straight" or "direct" plus "beautiful." Will the name Naomi or Noemi make your daughter into an Olympic gold-medalist water polo defender? Maybe not, but it did work in the cases of both Australian World Cup–winner Naomi Castle and Italian world champion Noémi Tóth!

Or maybe your daughter will get into sports like archery, tennis, or field hockey, like British World Games gold-medalist archer Naomi Folkard; Dutch hockey midfield/forward Naomi van As, who won two Olympic gold medals, two World Cups, and three Champions Trophies; or number one singles tennis player in the world Naomi Osaka, whose on-the-court achievements include four Grand Slams.

Naomi Castle, Water Polo (Defender), Australia, 1995–2004

Naomi Folkard, Archery, England, 2000–current

Naomi Osaka, Tennis, Japan, 2013–current

Noémi Tóth, Water Polo (Defender), Italy, 1994–2004

Naomi van As, Field Hockey (Midfield/Forward), Netherlands, 1999–current

NATALIA/NATALIYA/NATALYA

Latin Christian tradition created the name Natalia from the word for "Christmas Day," and ever since, it has spread far and wide in the world with numerous variants in different places, including Nataliya and Natalya. Many of the sports that athletes with this family of names have succeeded in are classic Russian-beloved events, though there are some interesting outliers too. Ukrainian weightlifter Nataliya Skakun became a world champion in 2003 and won gold at the 2004 Olympic Games; Russian wrestler Natalia Vorobieva took home Olympic gold and silver, as well as two world championships; Russian water skier Natalia Roumiantseva set five world records on her way to four world championships; and Russian synchronized swimmer Natalia Ishchenko's medal collection includes five golds from Olympic Games and nineteen from World Championships.

Eastern European Natalias, Nataliyas, and Natalyas have had successes in some common areas, which may point to some fields a daughter you give one of these names may share! Maybe she'll enjoy throwing heavy objects and follow in the footsteps of Russian Olympic gold-medalist discus thrower

Natalya Sadova, or Soviet shot putter Natalya Lisovskaya, who added three world championships to her own Olympic gold medal. Or a Natalia in your family may find she likes to tackle numerous outdoor sports in one, like Russian Olympic gold-medalist biathlete Natalya Snytina and Ukrainian Nataliya Dobrynska, who became an Olympic gold-medalist heptathlete and world champion pentathlete.

If you're set on the name Natalia specifically, introduce your daughter to gymnastics; she may be inspired by the Soviet trio of Natalia Lashchenova (team Olympic gold medal and world championship), Natalia Kuchinskaya (Olympic gold in team and balance beam and world championships in uneven bars, balance beam, and floor exercise), and Natalia Yurchenko (all-around and two team world championships and all-around, vault, and balance beam World Cup Final gold medals)!

- **Nataliya Dobrynska**, Track & Field (Heptathlon/Pentathlon), Ukraine, 2004–2013
- **Natalia Ishchenko**, Synchronized Swimming, Russia, 2004–2016
- **Natalia Kuchinskaya**, Artistic Gymnastics, USSR, 1965–1968
- **Natalia Lashchenova**, Artistic Gymnastics, USSR, 1988–1991
- **Natalya Lisovskaya**, Track & Field (Shot Put), USSR, 1985–2002
- **Natalia Roumiantseva**, Water Skiing, USSR, 1979–1997
- **Natalya Sadova**, Track & Field (Discus), USSR/Russia, 1989–2010
- **Nataliya Skakun**, Weightlifting, Ukraine, 2003–2004
- **Natalya Snytina**, Biathlon, Russia, 1994
- **Natalia Vorobieva**, Freestyle Wrestling, Russia, 2012–current
- **Natalia Yurchenko**, Artistic Gymnastics, USSR, 1978–1986

NATALIE

Like the *Natalia* family of names, Natalie comes from an ancient Latin term for "Christmas Day." Of course, you don't have to celebrate that holiday to enjoy one of these names, and they have lots of history in athletics and sports around the world to inspire a girl to greatness in any field she chooses. She may be a team player like Australian beach volleyball Olympic gold-medalist Natalie Cook, two-time world champion water polo defender/center-forward Natalie Golda, and Australian world champion doubles squash player and two-time World Team Champion Natalie Grinham.

On the other hand, your Natalie may gravitate toward competing independently, like Czech world champion pentathlete Natalie Dianová, world champion figure roller-skater Natalie Dunn, German two-time World Road Champion and three-time World Track Champion para-cyclist Natalie Simanowski, and German luger Natalie Geisenberger, who has straddled both worlds with six Olympic gold medals and nine world championships in singles and team relay, which makes her one of the top athletes of all time in her field.

Natalies do tend slightly toward certain sports, and we can find pairs of them in the highest levels of cricket, with all-rounders Natalie Brown (run-scoring leader, 2017 County Championship, and Women's Twenty20 Cup) and Natalie "Nat" Sciver-Brunt (captain of 2017 Women's Twenty20 Cup championship team); ice hockey, with forwards Natalie Darwitz (three-time world champion) and Natalie Spooner (two-time world champion, two-time Olympic gold-medalist, and Clarkson Cup-winner); and basketball, with wheelchair player Natalie Schneider (Paralympic gold-medalist and Wheelchair Basketball World Champion) and forward Natalie Williams (four-time All-Star, Olympic gold-medalist, and two-time World Cup-winner).

But the overwhelming choice for Natalies appears to be swimming! Get a Natalie in your family into the pool early so she can grow up to be like two-time world champion Natalie Hinds; record-setting Natalie Coughlin, who won twelve medals at the Olympics (three of them gold) and twenty-eight from World Championships (ten of them wins!); and South African Natalie du Toit, whose medal haul includes a staggering thirteen golds and two silvers from Paralympic Games and a dozen golds, one silver, and one bronze from World Championships!

Natalie Brown, Cricket (All-Rounder), Lancashire Women's Cricket Team, England, 2006–current

Natalie Cook, Beach Volleyball, Australia, 1996–2012

Natalie Coughlin, Swimming (Backstroke/Butterfly/Freestyle/Medley), USA, 2001–2015

Natalie Darwitz, Ice Hockey (Forward), Minnesota Whitecaps, USA, 1998–2010

Natalie Dianová, Track & Field (Pentathlon), Czech Republic, 2009–2012

Natalie Dunn, Roller Skating, USA, 1963–1980

Natalie Geisenberger, Luge, Germany, 2007–current

Natalie Golda, Water Polo (Defender/Center-Forward), USA, 2003–2008

Natalie Grinham, Squash, Australia, 1995–2014

Natalie Hinds, Swimming (Freestyle/Butterfly), USA, 2020–current

Natalie Schneider, Wheelchair Basketball (Forward), USA, 2008–current

Natalie "Nat" Sciver-Brunt, Cricket (All-Rounder), Surrey Women's Cricket Team, England, 2010–current

Natalie Simanowski, Road/Track Cycling, Germany, 2006–2008

Natalie Spooner, Ice Hockey (Forward), Toronto Furies, Canada, 2007–current

Natalie du Toit, Swimming (Breaststroke/Butterfly/Freestyle), South Africa, 2002–2012

Natalie Williams, Basketball (Forward), Utah Starzz, USA, 1996–2005

NATASA/NATASCHA/NATASHA

There are numerous names across the world that look and sound similar to Natasha, though some have distinctly different origins. Natasha and Natascha are Russian, Dutch, and German descendants of *Natalia/Nataliya/Natalya* (Latin for "Christmas Day"), while Natasa is a Greek diminutive of *Anastasia* (which means "resurrection"). Champion athletes with these three names have arisen in numerous countries, tackling a number of different sports and dominating the competition. Natasha Kaiser-Brown sprinted to a track and field world championship, Belarusian tennis player Natasha Zvereva hit the world number one ranking with eighty titles (eighteen Grand Slams), and Russian boxer Natascha Ragosina held numerous super middleweight and heavyweight world championship belts by the end of her incomparable 22–0 career.

Bulgarian sprint canoeist Natascha Janakieva became a world champion in 1977, while Hungarian Natasa Dusev-Janics collected five Olympic medals, including three golds, and thirty-five medals from World Championships (twenty of them being wins), in the 2000s. Canoeing may be a fun hobby for a Natasha (of any spelling), or she may find a team sport in which to excel, like Olympic gold-medalist and three-time world champion softball infielder Natasha Watley, who won World Cup gold, two World Cup Championships, and three National Pro Fastpitch championships, and English soccer striker Natasha Dowie, whose achievements include a Women's FA Cup, FA Women's National League Cup, FA Women's Super League twice, W-League Premiership, and multiple FA Women's league and W-League individual awards!

Natasha Dowie, Soccer (Striker), Liverpool Football Club Women, England, 2004–current

Natasa Dusev-Janics, Sprint Canoeing, Hungary, 2001–2019

Natascha Janakieva, Sprint Canoeing, Bulgaria, 1972–1982

Natasha Kaiser-Brown, Track & Field (Sprinting), USA, 1991–1997

Natalia "Natascha" Ragosina, Boxing (Super Middleweight/Heavyweight), Russia, 2004–2009

Natasha Watley, Softball (Infield), USSSA Pride, USA, 2004–2017

Natalya "Natasha" Zvereva, Tennis, Belarus, 1988–2002

NELLIE/NELLY

Traditionally diminutives of *Nell* and other names, Nellie and Nelly are perfectly fine on their own and can inspire a girl to lofty athletic goals in any field, though particularly in sports that start with "G." At least that's what we've seen with women like golfer Nelly Korda, who has won twelve professional events, including one major and an Olympic gold medal, and Soviet artistic gymnast Nellie Kim, who took to the world's stage in the 1970s and '80s with five Olympic gold medals (and the second-ever perfect score) and five world championships for team, vault, and floor!

Nellie Kim, Artistic Gymnastics, USSR, 1973–1980

Nelly Korda, Golf, USA, 2016–current

NICOLA/NIKOLA

Nicola and Nikola are unisex names more prevalent in Europe than the US. They come from diminutives and alternatives to *Nicholas*, with Nicola from French and Nikola from Czech, German, Polish, and Slovak. If you're looking for a name that will make your daughter strong, tough, and able to stand up to any threat, one of these might just do the trick; they have proven powerful with British world champion judoka Nicola Fairbrother, British two-time Olympic gold-medalist and world champion boxer Nicola Adams, and Austrian five-time world champion wrestler Nikola Hartmann!

On the other hand, there's nothing stopping a Nicola from achieving her dreams no matter where they take her, which might be in swimming (like British two-time freestyle world champion Nicola Jackson) or even bridge (like English top-ranked Woman World Grand Master Nicola Smith).

Nicola Adams, Boxing (Flyweight), England, 2007–2019

Nicola Fairbrother, Judo, England, 1989–1999

Nikola Hartmann, Freestyle Wrestling, Austria, 1993–2000

Nicola Jackson, Swimming (Freestyle/Butterfly), England, 1999–2002

Nicola Smith, Bridge, England, 1965–current

NICOLE

Victory is assuredly in the future of any girl named Nicole, athletic or otherwise, because her name comes from a French feminine form of *Nicholas* (from roots for "victory" and "people"). American Nicoles have had great success in fencing and volleyball with foil world champion Nicole Ross, and world champion libero Nicole Davis, who won three World Grand Prix. Internationally, Australian rugby wing Nicole Beck won the 2009 Rugby Sevens World Cup and a gold medal at the 2016 Olympic Games, Welsh Nicole Cooke is an Olympic gold-medalist cyclist who won a UCI Road World Championship and two UCI Women's Road World Cup overalls, and German dressage equestrian Nicole Uphoff has collected four gold medals from Olympic Games and three from World Championships!

Nicole Beck, Rugby (Wing), Sydney University Football Club, Australia, 2008–current

Nicole Cooke, Road Cycling, Wales, 1999–2013

Nicole Davis, Volleyball (Libero), USA, 2005–2015

Nicole Ross, Fencing (Foil), USA, 2011–current

Nicole Uphoff, Equestrian (Dressage), Germany, 1987–2013

NINA

The name Nina began as a short form of longer appellations like *Antonina* and *Giannina*, but there's nothing small about the potential a Nina embodies! The majority of champion Ninas have come from Eastern Europe, specifically the Soviet Union, with world champion speed skater Nina Statkevich, Olympic gold-medalist and handball world champion Nina Lobova, and two-time Olympic gold-medalist and team volleyball world champion Nina Smoleyeva.

Some Ninas have focused on agility, like 1950s Soviet two-time Olympic gold-medalist artistic gymnast and world champion Nina Bocharova, and Belgian Nina Derwael, who recently won Olympic gold and two world championships on the uneven bars, as well as three World Cups. Others enjoy their time on the slopes, like Chinese three-time aerial skiing world champion Li Nina and Soviet cross-country skiers Nina Fyodorova (Olympic gold medalist and two-time world champion) and Nina Gavrylyuk (who's taken home four medals from Olympic Games, three of them gold, and eleven medals for World Championships, including six wins).

Track and field events also attract Ninas, including Soviets like Olympic gold-medalist sprinter Nina Zyuskova and discus thrower Nina Ponomaryova, whose first of two Olympic gold medals was the first won by a Soviet athlete.

Interestingly, the biggest concentration of Ninas have been rowers and paddlers! Soviet sprint canoeists on the international stage have included world champions Nina Gruzintseva and Nina Doroh, while three-time world champion Nina Gopova also took home gold and silver from the Olympics. And in rowing events, German world champion Nina Gäßler joins Soviets Nina Frolova (four world championships) and Nina Umanets (five wins at World Championships)!

Nina Bocharova, Artistic Gymnastics, USSR, 1948–1956

Nina Derwael, Artistic Gymnastics, Belgium, 2013–current

Nina Doroh, Sprint Canoeing, USSR, 1977–1979

Nina Frolova, Rowing, USSR, 1970–1982

Nina Fyodorova, Cross-Country Skiing, USSR, 1970–1980

Nina Gäßler, Rowing, Germany, 2004–2005

Nina Gavrylyuk, Cross-Country Skiing, USSR/Russia, 1987–2003

Nina Gopova, Sprint Canoeing, USSR, 1973–1980

Nina Gruzintseva, Sprint Canoeing, USSR, 1955–1968

Li Nina, Freestyle Skiing, China, 2002–2010

Nina Lobova, Handball (Goalkeeper), Ukraine/USSR, 1976–1982

Nina Ponomaryova, Track & Field (Discus), USSR, 1948–1966

Nina Smoleyeva, Volleyball, USSR, 1968–1978

Nina Statkevich, Speed Skating, USSR, 1970–1974

Nina Umanets, Rowing, USSR, 1977–1983

Nina Zyuskova, Track & Field (Sprinting), USSR, 1979–1980

NING

An uncommon Chinese first name that can mean "peaceful," Ning can impart on a girl fast hands and the skills to win across the table from her opponents in any setting! A girl you name Ning can find inspiration in two-time Olympic gold-medalist and world champion badminton player Zhang Ning and the massively successful (though somewhat contentious) table tennis maven Ding Ning, who took home four medals from Olympic Games (three of them gold), sixteen from World Championships (eight of them wins), and ten golds at World Cup events!

Ding Ning, Table Tennis, China, 2009-2021

Zhang Ning, Badminton, China, 1993-2008

NINO

You may not be familiar with the name Nino, which is Georgian and possibly comes from a place name for Nineveh in ancient Assyria. But be advised, this name does not miss. It's the name of Olympic gold-medalist and six-time World Shooting Champion pistol sport shooter Nino Salukvadze, the first woman to compete in *nine* different Olympic Games. And that's not all—it's the name of five different Georgian chess luminaries: Woman Grandmaster Nino Khomeriki, Woman Grandmaster and International Master Nino Gurieli, two-time French Women's Chess Champion and Woman Grandmaster Nino Maisuradze, four-time Georgian Women's Chess Champion and Grandmaster Nino Batsiashvili, and Nino Khurtsidze, who achieved the ranks of Woman Grandmaster and International Master while winning the Georgian Women's Chess Championship five times and the overall Georgian Chess Championship once!

If you name a daughter Nino, you're absolutely required to teach her how to play chess.

Nino Batsiashvili, Chess, Georgia, 2012-current

Nino Gurieli, Chess, Georgia, 1976-current

Nino Khomeriki, Chess, Georgia, 2018-current

Nino Khurtsidze, Chess, Georgia, 1989-2018

Nino Maisuradze, Chess, Georgia/France, 2009-current

Nino Salukvadze, Sport Shooting (Pistol), Georgia, 1988-current

NNEKA

A beautiful and exotic name, Nneka comes from the Igbo language and means "mother is supreme." Nigerian lineage is not a prerequisite for naming a daughter Nneka, but if you do, she may turn out to be the ultimate team player, pressing her advantage and protecting those around her. These traits are on full display in American seven-time WNBA All-Star Los Angeles Sparks power forward Nneka Ogwumike, who won two World Cups with the USA Basketball Women's National Team and was league MVP the year her team won the championship.

Nnemkadi "Nneka" Ogwumike, Basketball (Power Forward), Los Angeles Sparks, USA, 2012-current

NOELLE

Noelle is a festive name like *Natalie*, this time coming from French for "Christmas." Celebrating Christmas is not a requirement for using this name in your family, but it's ideal for people who like cold weather or who tend to be very tall. At least that's the impression we get from looking at athletes like WNBA champion point guard/shooting guard Noelle Quinn and two-time world champion skeleton racer Noelle Pikus-Pace!

Noelle Pikus-Pace, Skeleton, USA, 2005-2014

Noelle Quinn, Basketball (Point Guard/ Shooting Guard), Seattle Storm, USA, 2007-2018

NORMA

Later associated with the masculine name *Norman*, Norma was created by Felice Romani for his opera by the same name in 1831. Here in the United States, the name is often considered old-fashioned, but it does have some interesting athletic history around the world in track and field events, with Australian Olympic gold-medalist sprinter Norma Croker, and bowls, with Norma Shaw of England, who won a World Indoor Bowls Championship gold medal and three golds, five silvers, and four bronzes at World Bowls Championships!

Bring the name Norma to a new generation by giving it to your daughter; she'll be fast on her feet and enjoy rolling balls indoors and out.

Norma Croker, Track & Field (Sprinting), Australia, 1956-1960

Norma Shaw, Bowls, England, 1981-2000

O

BOYS

OLAF/OLOF

The mighty name Olaf, with interesting variants like Olof, stretches back to Old Norse from roots meaning "ancestor's descendant" (which is kind of redundant). These names may conjure up images of frozen locales, and that's where success has been found by athletes like German Olympic gold-medalist speed skater Olaf Zinke, and German bobsledder Olaf Hampel, who raced to a pair of Olympic gold medals and a pair of world championships! A boy named Olaf or one of its variants doesn't *have* to play in the cold; he may prefer indoor sports like *Counter Strike: Global Offensive*- legend Olof "olofmeister" Gustafsson, whose numerous international tournament wins and two majors landed him the title of best player in the world in 2015.

Olof "olofmeister" Gustafsson, Esports (*Counter Strike: Global Offensive*), Sweden, 2010-current

Olaf Hampel, Bobsleigh, Germany, 1994-1998

Olaf Zinke, Speed Skating, Germany, 1983-1994

OLE

From the same Old Norse roots as *Olaf* comes the Danish and Norwegian favorite Ole. How do athletes with this name compare to their compatriots? Oles are especially keen-eyed and love to go fast, traits that you'll surely see in a son named Ole. He may take after Danish motorcycle speedway racer Ole Olsen, whose lengthy list of achievements includes three Speedway World Championships, three Speedway World Team Cups, seven Golden Helmets, and more; soccer forward Ole Gunnar Solskjær, who won two FA Cups, a UEFA Champions League, and an Intercontinental Cup; five-time Olympic gold-medalist rifle sport shooter Ole Lilloe-Olsen; or biathlete Ole Einar Bjørndalen, who's considered one of the best ever in his sport, with thirteen Olympic medals (eight of them golds), forty-eight medals from World Championships (winning twenty-one times), and more!

Ole Einar Bjørndalen, Biathlon, Norway, 1993-2017

Ole Lilloe-Olsen, Sport Shooting (Rifle), Norway, 1920-1924

Ole Olsen, Motorcycle Racing (Speedway), Denmark, 1967-1983

Ole Gunnar Solskjær, Soccer (Forward), Manchester United Football Club, Norway, 1990-2007

OLEG

Like *Olaf* and *Ole*, Oleg comes from Old Norse, but in this case, from a root meaning "blessed" and evolving into Russian. In the world of sports, Olegs have displayed ferocity and focus in multiple areas, with exemplars like Russian NHL All-Star, two-time Stanley Cup-champion, and world champion ice hockey defenseman Oleg Tverdovsky; Ukrainian artistic gymnast Oleg Vernyayev, who has won both a world championship and Olympic gold medal; three-time World Allround Champion speed skater Oleg Goncharenko; and Soviet Ballon d'Or-winning soccer forward Oleg Blokhin, who had 764 appearances, scored 325 goals, and won Soviet Top League eight times, Soviet Cup five times, USSR Super Cup three times, UEFA Cup Winners Cup twice, and UEFA Super Cup.

Oleg Blokhin, Soccer (Forward), Football Club Dynamo Kyiv, USSR/Ukraine, 1969–1990

Oleg Goncharenko, Speed Skating, USSR, 1953–1962

Oleg Tverdovsky, Ice Hockey (Defense), Mighty Ducks of Anaheim, Russia, 1992–2013

Oleg Vernyayev, Artistic Gymnastics, Ukraine, 2011–current

OLEKSANDR

The independent people of Ukraine have given us the name Oleksandr, which comes from the Greek *Alexander* meaning "defending" or "defender of men." Interestingly, there have been a number of unique para-athletes with this name who have had major athletic successes, including four-time Paralympic gold-medalist and two-time world champion swimmer Oleksandr Mashchenko; two-time gold medalist runner Oleksandr Driha; multi-sport throwers Oleksandr Iasynovyi, who won Paralympic gold and a world championship in discus with a world record; and Oleksandr Doroshenko, who collected three medals from Paralympic Games (two of them gold) and five from World Championships (three gold)!

The name has also been championed by Olympic gold-medalist pistol sport shooter Oleksandr Petriv; "Ukraine's Strongest Man" Oleksandr Lashyn, who won twice at World Strongman Federation events; and Olympic gold-medalist and world champion boxer Oleksandr Usyk, who has held world titles in both cruiserweight and heavyweight divisions and (currently) has not lost a single professional match!

Whether you have Ukrainian ancestry, are looking for a different take on *Alexander*, or just happen to like Oleksandr, the name can inspire a young athlete to any height.

Oleksandr Doroshenko, Para-Athletics, Ukraine, 2002–2014

Oleksandr Driha, Track & Field (Middle-Distance Running), Ukraine, 2004

Oleksandr Iasynovyi, Para-Athletics, Ukraine, 2000–2011

Oleksandr Lashyn, Strength Athletics, Ukraine, 2008–current

Oleksandr Mashchenko, Swimming (Breaststroke/Butterfly/Freestyle), Ukraine, 2000–current

Oleksandr Petriv, Sport Shooting (Pistol), Ukraine, 2008–current

Oleksandr Usyk, Boxing (Cruiserweight/Heavyweight), Ukraine, 2006–current

OLIVER

The origins of the internationally popular name Oliver are lost to time, but theories include a Germanic lineage similar to *Olaf* or a Frankish source. No matter where it came from, the name is going places and already has a tremendous athletic history in a wide range of sports and events. Olivers have excelled on their own in things like weightlifting (with Nigerian snatch world champion Oliver Orok), sport shooting (with German world champion Oliver Geis), pool (with German nine-ball and two-time straight pool world champion Oliver Ortmann), and swimming (with Ollie Hynd of the United Kingdom, who set multiple world records on his way to collecting six Paralympic Games medals, including three golds, and six from World Championships, with four wins).

When it comes to team players, there have been American 1924 Olympic gold-medalist 4x400-meter relay-winner Oliver Macdonald; Hungarian two-time Olympic gold-medalist water polo champion Olivér Halassy; and two-time NHL All-Star defenseman Oliver Ekman-Larsson, who won two world championships with his native Swedish team.

Olivers have appeared in numerous sports including equestrian events, with American jockey Oliver Lewis, who won the first Kentucky Derby, and British eventing Olympic gold-medalist Oliver Townend. In the boxing ring, Oliver McCall held the WBC heavyweight title and beat Lennox Lewis, while way back in the 1904 Olympic Games, Oliver Kirk won the featherweight division and subsequently lost ten pounds in two weeks to win the bantamweight! International soccer fans will be familiar with legendary German goalkeeper Oliver Kahn, whose achievements include eight Bundesliga titles, six DFB-Pokal, a UEFA Cup, UEFA Champions League, the 2002 FIFA World Cup Golden Ball, a spot on the FIFA 100 list, and more.

Last but certainly not least are all of the Olivers who have rowed and paddled to victory! The best of the best include Olympic gold-medalist sprint canoeists Oliver Fix (two-time world champion) and Oliver Kegel (four-time world champion), and rowers Oliver Cook (a Paralympic gold-medalist world champion), Oliver James (three-time world champion), and Oliver "Ollie" Stanhope (Paralympic gold-medalist and five-time world champion).

Raise your Oliver with lessons of fair play and sportsmanship and he'll go far in his chosen field, whether it's rowing, boxing, equestrian events, soccer, or anything else he sets his mind to!

Oliver Cook, Rowing, England, 2007–current

Oliver Ekman-Larsson, Ice Hockey (Defense), Arizona Coyotes, Sweden, 2010–current

Oliver Fix, Slalom Canoeing, Germany, 1990–1996

Oliver Geis, Sport Shooting (Pistol), Germany, 2013–current

Olivér Halassy, Water Polo (Field Player), Hungary, 1928–1938

Oliver "Ollie" Hynd, Swimming (Backstroke/Freestyle/Medley), England, 2011–current

Oliver James, Rowing, England, 2013–current

Oliver Kahn, Soccer (Goalkeeper), FC Bayern Munich, Germany, 1987–2008

Oliver Kegel, Sprint Canoeing, Germany, 1985–1994

Oliver Kirk, Boxing (Bantamweight/Featherweight), USA, 1904–1919

Oliver Lewis, Horse Racing (Jockey), USA, 1875

J. Oliver Macdonald, Track & Field (Sprinting), USA, 1924

Oliver McCall, Boxing (Heavyweight), USA, 1985–2018

Oliver Orok, Weightlifting, Nigeria, 1984

Oliver Ortmann, Pool (Straight/Nine-Ball), Germany, 1985–current

Oliver "Ollie" Stanhope, Rowing, England, 2017–current

Oliver Townend, Equestrian (Eventing), England, 2005–current

OLIVIER

While most people in the United States will be more familiar with *Oliver*, Olivier is a popular French (meaning "olive tree") and Dutch version. Oliviers from France (and a couple other places) have had successes in multiple sports, with some notable concentrations. First, there are singular winners and champions like 2014 EVO Champion fighting games pro Olivier "Luffy" Hay, Canadian Olympic gold-medalist and four-time world champion speed skater Olivier Jean, and France's top soccer goal scorer Olivier Giroud, who played striker for Arsenal and AC Milan and has scored over three hundred goals in senior and international play, four FA Cups, UEFA Champions League, UEFA Europa League, FIFA World Cup 2018, and more.

In general, though, it seems that Oliviers like to go fast, riding to win on land and at sea! Exemplars of this trend include race drivers Olivier Pla, who won two Le Mans Series races and a championship, and Olivier Gendebien of Belgium, who raced to a then-record of four 24 Hours of Le Mans victories; and Olivier de Kersauson, who set speed records sailing around the world and winning two Jules Verne Trophies!

If you like the name Oliver but feel it's a bit too commonplace, or if you have French lineage, then Olivier might be a good option for your son. Introduce him to skating, soccer, big wheels, and the like and he may just race his way into the record books!

Olivier Gendebien, Auto Racing (24 Hours of Le Mans), Belgium, 1955–1961

Olivier Giroud, Soccer (Striker), Arsenal Football Club, France, 2005–current

Olivier "Luffy" Hay, Esports (Fighting Games), France, 2009–current

Olivier Jean, Speed Skating, Canada, 2007–current

Olivier de Kersauson, Sailing, France, 1973–2005

Olivier Pla, Auto Racing (Le Mans Series), France, 2000–current

OMAR

A Middle Eastern name that has traveled the world, Omar can be traced back to Arabic for "populous" or "flourishing" or to biblical Hebrew for "speak." An Omar in your family could very well flourish in team sports, as Omars before him have in baseball and soccer! He'd be in good company with MLB three-time All-Star shortstop Omar Vizquel, who won eleven Gold Gloves across his lengthy career, and Cuban two-time Olympic gold-medalist second baseman and three-time Baseball World Cup champion Omar Linares.

Meanwhile, international football fans have cheered on American CONCACAF Gold Cup Best XI and four-time MLS Best XI center-back Omar Gonzalez (three MLS Cups, CONCACAF Champions League, and two CONCACAF Gold Cups), and legendary Italian-Argentinian Ballon d'Or and Serie A Golden Boot-winning forward Omar Sívori (three Serie A, three Coppa Italia, South American Championship, and a place on the FIFA 100).

Your little Omar has endless possibilities in front of him as he runs toward his bright future, just like Jamaican Olympic gold-medalist and two-time world champion hurdler Omar McLeod.

Omar Gonzalez, Soccer (Center-Back), LA Galaxy, USA, 2009–current

Omar Linares, Baseball (Second Baseman), Vegueros de Pinar del Río, Cuba, 1982–2002

Omar McLeod, Track & Field (Hurdling), Jamaica, 2015–current

Enrique Omar Sívori, Soccer (Forward), Juventus Football Club, Italy/Argentina, 1954–1969

Omar Vizquel, Baseball (Shortstop), Cleveland Indians, Venezuela, 1989–2012

OSAMU

"Discipline," "study," "logic," and "reign" are great words to describe the life of a champion athlete, and they happen to be the meanings of characters used to write the Japanese name Osamu. A focused and diligent Osamu can achieve anything, whether it's physical perfection (like super bantamweight world champion boxer Osamu Sato or Olympic gold-medalist and two-time world champion wrestler Osamu Watanabe, who never lost a bout) or mental prowess (like 9-dan ranked shoji player Osamu Nakamura, who has won over eight hundred games and eleven tournaments).

Osamu Nakamura, Shogi, Japan, 1980–current

Osamu Sato, Boxing (Super Bantamweight), Japan, 1995–2004

Osamu Watanabe, Freestyle Wrestling, Japan, 1962–1964

OSCAR/ÓSCAR/OSKAR/OSZKAR

There's a possibility that the name Oscar comes from Old Irish roots for "deer friend" or Old English for "God" and "spear," but as it has spread around the world, it split into numerous variants, including Oskar, Oszkar, and Óscar. With the broad number of versions comes an equally wide array of sports these names have conquered, from fencing (with Hungarian two-time Olympic gold-medalist sabre fencer Oszkár Gerde) to Greco-Roman wrestling (with Finnish world champion and two-time Olympic gold-medalist Oskari Friman), curling (with Swedish Olympic-winner and six-time world champion skip/third Oskar Eriksson), and soccer (with Brazilian 2014 FIFA World Cup All-Star Team attacking midfielder Oscar dos Santos Emboaba Júnior, who has won a Premier League, Football League Cup, UEFA Europa League, and FIFA Confederations Cup).

There has been a pair of elite road cyclists from Spain: three-time world champion Óscar Freire, and Óscar Pereiro, who won the Tour de France in 2006. Basketball fans will be familiar with Olympic gold-medalist point guard Oscar Robertson, who was a twelve-time NBA All-Star, MVP, and champion with six assists leader rankings and the distinction of being the first (and still one of only two) player to average a triple-double for an entire season. Last but certainly not least on the list of world-famous Oscars is the Golden Boy himself, boxer Oscar De La Hoya. The Los Angeles-born fighter finished his 39-6 record career with an Olympic gold medal, having won eleven world titles in six different weight classes (three of them lineal), and a secure spot on lists of the best-ever boxers.

There's a range of spellings and variations to choose from if you like the name Oscar for your son, as well as a world of possibilities for him with regards to sports and athletics. He may be a tough boxer, a fast cyclist, an agile basketball player, or anything else he wants to be!

Oscar dos Santos Emboaba Júnior, Soccer (Attacking Midfielder), Chelsea Football Club, Brazil, 2008–current

Oskar Eriksson, Curling (Skip/Third), Sweden, 2008–current

Óscar Freire, Road Cycling, Spain, 1998–2012

Oskar "Oskari" Friman, Greco-Roman Wrestling, Finland, 1915–1928

Oszkár Gerde, Fencing (Sabre), Hungary, 1908–1912

Oscar De La Hoya, Boxing (Featherweight/Lightweight/Welterweight/Middleweight), USA, 1992–2008

Óscar Pereiro, Road Cycling, Spain, 2004–2010

Oscar Robertson, Basketball (Point Guard), Cincinnati Royals, USA, 1960–1974

OTTO

Originally a German diminutive of numerous names, Otto comes from an Old Frankish root meaning "wealth" or "fortune." Athletic competition may not bring an Otto in your family great wealth, but he's sure to have fun playing his favorite games or events, and he may find fame like Norwegian four-time Olympic gold-medalist rifle sport shooter Otto Olsen or American five-time Pro Bowl Cleveland Browns quarterback Otto Graham, who won three NFL championships; was a three-time NFL MVP, passing touchdowns leader, and two-time passing yards leader; and was inducted into the Pro Football Hall of Fame!

Otto Graham, Football (Quarterback), Cleveland Browns, USA, 1946–1955

Otto Olsen, Sport Shooting (Rifle), Norway, 1920–1924

OZZIE

Ozzie is typically a diminutive for names like *Osborn*, *Oswald/Oswaldo*, and others, but it can be a nickname for all sorts of "O" first names and last names, or even be used as a name all on its own. An Ozzie in your family (whether that's his legal name or a nickname) is likely to be a team player with fast hands and excellent reflexes. If he's on the bigger and tougher side, he may enjoy football like three-time Pro Bowl Cleveland Browns tight end Ozzie Newsome, but otherwise his talents may bring him success on the baseball diamond. There he can follow in the footsteps of shortstops like Venezuelan three-time All-Star, Gold Glove-winner, and two-time World Series champion Ozzie Guillén, or Hall of Famer Ozzie Smith, who racked up fifteen All-Star appearances, a World Series win, thirteen Gold Glove Awards, and more!

Oswaldo "Ozzie" Guillén, Baseball (Shortstop), Chicago White Sox, Venezuela, 1985–2000

Ozzie Newsome Jr., Football (Tight End), Cleveland Browns, USA, 1978–1990

Osborne "Ozzie" Smith, Baseball (Shortstop), St. Louis Cardinals, USA, 1978–1996

GIRLS

OKSANA

A most genial name, Oksana is a Ukrainian classic that originally comes from an Ancient Greek word meaning "hospitality," and a number of athletic Oksanas from Ukraine, Russia, and other European countries have achieved huge successes on the world's stage. Oksanas are nothing if not adaptable and multi-talented, ranging from Russian Olympic gold-medalist and three-time world champion weightlifter Oksana "Oxana" Slivenko to épée fencer Oksana Yermakova, who won two Olympic gold medals and five medals from World Championships (two wins) and Russian fitness competitor Oksana Grishina, whose trophy case includes the 2006 Overall Fitness World Championship, ten Arnold Classics, and four Ms. Fitness Olympias.

A young girl with this name has a long lineage of ice skating and gymnastics champions to be inspired by, if that's where her interests and talents lie. On the ice, Ukrainian figure skater Oksana Baiul captured gold at both Olympics and World Championships before becoming a popular media figure in America, while top-tier Russian ice dancers include Oksana Grishuk, who won two Olympic gold medals, four world championships, and two Grand Prix Finals. Meanwhile, Olympic gold-medalist, three-time world champion, and World Cup Final-winning artistic gymnast Oksana Chusovitina has competed for the USSR, Uzbekistan, and Germany; Oksana Omelianchik took home three world championships and a World Cup Final gold medal for the Soviet Union; and Ukrainian rhythmic gymnast Oksana Skaldina won six gold medals at World Championships and four at World Cup Finals!

- **Oksana Baiul**, Figure Skating, Ukraine, 1991–1994
- **Oksana Chusovitina**, Artistic Gymnastics, USSR/Uzbekistan/Germany, 1990–current
- **Oksana Grishina**, Fitness Competition, Russia, 1993–2017
- **Oksana Grishuk**, Ice Dancing, Russia, 1988–1998
- **Oksana Omelianchik**, Artistic Gymnastics, USSR, 1985–1989
- **Oksana Skaldina**, Rhythmic Gymnastics, Ukraine, 1988–2014
- **Oksana "Oxana" Slivenko**, Weightlifting, Russia, 2001–current
- **Oksana Yermakova**, Fencing (Épée), Russia/Estonia, 1991–2005

O-KYEONG

If you're looking for a unique "O" name that can give a girl a strong drive toward teamwork, ambition, success, and even politics, then O-Kyeong might be a cool match. Hopefully she'll have the wins and career to back it up, like South Korean handball player Lim O-Kyeong, who won a gold medal and two silvers at the Olympics before becoming a member of the National Assembly of the Republic of Korea!

- **Lim O-Kyeong**, Handball (Center Back), South Korea, 1992–2008

OLENA

Another Ukrainian name like *Oksana*, Olena is a variant on the Ancient Greek *Helen*. While in Greek mythology Helen launched a thousand ships that led to the Trojan War, modern day Olenas have been fighters, shooters, skiers, and even gymnasts. Kickboxer and MMA fighter Oléna "Lena"

Ovchynnikova has won multiple International Sport Karate Association gold medals, as well as the WBC Muaythai World Featherweight Championship belt; biathlete Olena Bilosiuk won Olympic gold and a world championship; Olena Iurkovska has three Paralympic gold medals in the biathlon, as well as two Paralympic golds in cross-country skiing; and rhythmic gymnast Olena Vitrychenko has a collection of twenty-three medals from World Championships (nine of them wins) and eleven from Grand Prix Finals (five golds).

Whether a fighter, gymnast, or skier, an Olena in your family will discover her talent and take it to the highest heights!

Olena Bilosiuk, Biathlon, Ukraine, 2007–current

Olena Iurkovska, Biathlon/Cross-Country Skiing, Ukraine, 2002–2010

Oléna "Lena" Ovchynnikova, Kickboxing/MMA (Featherweight/Flyweight), Ukraine, 2006–current

Olena Vitrychenko, Rhythmic Gymnastics, Ukraine, 1986–2000

OLGA

The Russian name Olga (from Old Norse for "holy" or "blessed") may seem quaint or old-fashioned in the United States, but it continues to be a force of nature in Europe and is ready for a revival here. A girl named Olga may follow in the footsteps of previous champions with her name, being blessed with excitement for track and field events, skiing, or gymnastics. From Russia, Olga Kaniskina racewalked to an Olympic gold medal and a world championship; she's in good company with Kazakh Olympic gold-medalist and world champion triple jumper Olga Rypakova.

Some Olgas prefer wintry conditions (like Austrian alpine skier Olga Pall, who won Olympic gold in 1968, and Russian two-time Olympic gold-medalist and three-time world champion biathlete Olga Zaitseva, whose top successes came in the twenty-first century), while for others it's all about the allure of athletic expression through artistic gymnastics (like Hungarian portable apparatus Olympic gold-medalist Olga Tass and Soviet Olga Korbut, whose four Olympic gold medals, two Olympic silver medals, and four medals from World Championships were earned on the vault, floor exercise, balance beam, and with her teams).

Olga Kaniskina, Track & Field (Racewalking), Russia, 2006–2012

Olga Korbut, Artistic Gymnastics, USSR, 1969–1977

Olga Pall, Alpine Skiing, Austria, 1968–1970

Olga Rypakova, Track & Field (Triple Jump), Kazakhstan, 2005–2023

Olga Tass, Artistic Gymnastics, Hungary, 1948–1960

Olga Zaitseva, Biathlon, Russia, 2000–2015

OLHA

The Russian language gave us *Olga*, but another interesting variant of *Helga* comes from Ukraine in the form of Olha. You can help bring this name to prominence by giving it to a little girl who may find inspiration in a trio of outstanding competitors: world champion triple jumper Olha Saladukha, Olympic gold-medalist handball player Olha Zubaryeva, and sabre fencer Olha Kharlan, whose current medal count includes a gold, a silver, and two bronzes from Olympic Games and six golds, seven silvers, and two bronzes from World Championships!

Olha Kharlan, Fencing (Sabre), Ukraine, 2006–current

Olha Saladukha, Track & Field (Triple Jump), Ukraine, 2006–2021

Olha Zubaryeva, Handball (Right Back), USSR/Ukraine, 1980

OLIVE

You don't have to love eating olives to name a daughter after the Mediterranean fruit, but if you do, she might be an early, and fast, walker. That's especially true if she takes after her predecessor, Irish world champion racewalker Olive Loughnane!

Olive Loughnane, Track & Field (Racewalking), Ireland, 1999-2012

OLIVIA

From an ancient Latin root for the olive tree and popularized in England at the start of the seventeenth century by Shakespeare himself, Olivia remains one of the most frequently used names for baby girls. Interestingly, and despite its overall popularity, Olivia is not a name that shows up very often on lists of top athletes. When it does, Olivias have a tendency toward pushing themselves hard (like British Para Powerlifting World Cup-winner and World Para Powerlifting Champion Olivia Broome and American three-time world champion rower Olivia Coffey), or toward sprinting (like Belgian 4x100-meter relay Olympic gold-medalist Olivia Borlée and Welsh track and field athlete Olivia "Livvy" Breen, who won World Para Athletics Championships in the same event and the long jump).

An Olivia in your family can continue the tradition of athletic excellence displayed by these women, finding success in track and field events, rowing, or powerlifting, or discovering her talents in another field altogether.

Olivia Borlée, Track & Field (Sprinting), Belgium, 2006-2016

Olivia "Livvy" Breen, Track & Field (Sprinting/Long Jump), England, 2012-current

Olivia Broome, Powerlifting, England, 2017-current

Olivia Coffey, Rowing, USA, 2013-current

OSLEIDYS

A Spanish-Caribbean name of uncertain origin (possibly from a combination of the prefix "Os-" and a variant of "lady"), Osleidys is cool and unique, something that will definitely stand out in class roll call. It can also give a girl a powerful throwing arm and the love of playing in the outdoors, as evidenced by Cuban Olympic gold-medalist and two-time world champion javelin thrower Osleidys Menéndez!

Osleidys Menéndez, Track & Field (Javelin), Cuba, 1997-2009

P

BOYS

PAAVO

Paul is a great name, but maybe you're looking for something a little different or you have Estonian or Finnish ancestry. Either way, you may want to check out the name Paavo! Coming from the cold north, the name might inspire your son to love winter sports like Finnish Paavos before him, including Olympic gold-medalist cross-country skier Paavo Lonkila or world champions Paavo Korhonen (Nordic combined skiing) and Paavo Puurunen (biathlon).

If he prefers indoor events, though, artistic gymnastics might be more his lane, like Paavo Aaltonen, who won a world championship on the horizontal bar and Olympic gold on the vault, pommel horse, and with his team.

And then there's track and field! Paavo Yrjölä set three official world records and won the decathlon at the 1928 Olympic Games in Amsterdam, and he's in good company with the legendary runner Paavo Nurmi. Between 1920 and 1934, the "Flying Finn" won nine gold and three silver medals from Olympic Games in middle- and long-distance events while setting twenty-two world records and running undefeated in 121 races. With a lifetime of competition and supporting athletics, Nurmi has gone down as one of the greatest athletes of all time, and he and the other Paavos here are great inspirations for a little boy who shares their name.

- **Paavo Aaltonen**, Artistic Gymnastics, Finland, 1948–1952
- **Paavo Korhonen**, Nordic Combined Skiing, Finland, 1952–1960
- **Paavo Lonkila**, Cross-Country Skiing, Finland, 1950–1952
- **Paavo "the Flying Finn" Nurmi**, Track & Field (Middle-/Long-Distance Running)/Cross-Country Running, Finland, 1920–1934
- **Paavo Puurunen**, Biathlon, Finland, 1995–2006
- **Paavo Yrjölä**, Track & Field (Decathlon), Finland, 1924–1932

PABLO

One of the many variants of the original Roman name that became the modern *Paul*, the Spanish Pablo is a perfect name for a kid who's going to be in the middle of the action, anchoring his team, whether it's in sports, academics, or anything else. He'll be in good company with Venezuelan-American two-time MLB All-Star Pablo Sandoval, who played at third base, first base, and catcher while earning three World Series rings and being named World Series MVP, and soccer midfielders Pablo Mastroeni (MLS Best XI and winner of the MLS Cup and three CONCACAF Gold Cups) and Pablo Aimar (Supercopa Sudamericana, La Liga twice, UEFA Cup, and UEFA Super Cup)!

Pablo Aimar, Soccer (Midfielder), Valencia Club de Fútbol, Argentina, 1996–2018

Pablo Mastroeni, Soccer (Midfielder), Colorado Rapids, USA, 1995–2013

Pablo Sandoval Reyes, Baseball (Third Baseman/First Baseman/Catcher), San Francisco Giants, Venezuela, 2008–2021

PÁDRAIG

From the Emerald Isle comes the name Pádraig, a traditional Irish variant of *Patrick*. Consider this name if you're hoping your son will be accurate and great at getting a ball exactly where it needs to go! He can take inspiration from athletes like FA Cup Golden Ball soccer striker Pádraig Amond, who has won a League of Ireland First Division championship, FAI Cup, and League of Ireland Cup, along with multiple regional player of the year awards, as well as golfer Pádraig Harrington, who has won thirty-seven professional events and three majors and who was inducted into the World Golf Hall of Fame in 2024.

Pádraig Amond, Soccer (Striker), Newport County Association Football Club, Ireland, 2006–current

Pádraig Harrington, Golf, Ireland, 1995–current

PAOLO

There are lots of evolutions of the name *Paul* around the world, from the Roman *Paulus* and a root meaning "small" or "humble." Like *Paavo* in Finland, Paolo is the Italian version, and it has a number of examples in sports with a clear concentration in soccer, or football if you're outside of the United States. There are individual examples as well, such as world champions triple jumper Paolo Camossi, rower Paolo Di Girolamo, and racewalker Paolo Grecucci, as well as two-time world champion épée fencer Paolo Pizzo.

Paolos have definitely made their mark on the fields of international football, with two top-ranked Italians with dozens of trophies, awards, and accolades between them. AC Milan defender Paolo Maldini is famous for his longevity, playing in over one thousand total appearances and winning numerous titles; he was also named to the FIFA World Cup All-Star Team twice, the FIFA World Cup Dream Team, FIFA XI, and FIFA 100 and was given the Bravo Award, FIFA Order of Merit, and more. Last but certainly not least is striker Paolo Rossi, one of the greatest players of all time. His long list of trophies includes the 1982 FIFA World Cup, while he was awarded the FIFA World Cup Golden Boot, FIFA World Cup Golden Ball, Ballon d'Or, and World Soccer Awards Player of the Year and was included in the FIFA XI twice and FIFA 100.

A little Paolo in your family should definitely be given a soccer ball as soon as possible, though you should also be on the lookout in case he develops an interest in something like track and field, rowing, running, or fencing.

Paolo Camossi, Track & Field (Triple Jump), Italy, 1995–2006

Paolo Di Girolamo, Rowing, Italy, 2013

Paolo Grecucci, Track & Field (Racewalking), Italy, 1975–1983

Paolo Maldini, Soccer (Defender), Associazione Calcio Milan, Italy, 1984–2009

Paolo Pizzo, Fencing (Épée), Italy, 2009–current

Paolo Rossi, Soccer (Striker), L.R. Vicenza, Italy, 1973–1987

PAT

Pat is the go-to unisex nickname for a variety of names, including *Patrice*, *Patricio*, and *Patrick*. And while we see a lot of range among athletes with those longer names, guys who go by Pat alone are almost all about toughness and giving and taking hits. They also can display courage and dedication that's above and beyond the norm, which is a great thing to inspire in a little Pat in your family!

Super featherweight Pat Manuel is the first openly trans professional boxer and currently holds a 3-0 record, and Australian Man of Steel award-winning rugby player Pat Richards has accumulated points scorer titles along with a Premiership, two Super League Grand Finals, and two Challenge Cups. On the gridiron, Indianapolis Colts punter Pat McAfee had two Pro Bowl appearances; Pat Williams was a three-time Pro Bowl defensive tackle with the Buffalo Bills and Minnesota Vikings; and Pat Tillman left his job playing safety for the Arizona Cardinals to defend his country while speaking truth to power.

- **Patricio "Pat" Manuel**, Boxing (Super Featherweight), USA, 2008–current
- **Patrick "Pat" McAfee**, Football (Punter), Indianapolis Colts, USA, 2009–2016
- **Patrick "Pat" Richards**, Rugby (Fullback/Center), Wigan Warriors, Australia, 2000–2016
- **Patrick "Pat" Tillman Jr.**, Football (Safety), Arizona Cardinals, USA, 1998–2001
- **Patrick "Pat" Williams Sr.**, Football (Defensive Tackle), Minnesota Vikings, USA, 1997–2010

PATRIC/PATRICK/PATRIK

Patricius was a stately Roman name (from a root meaning "nobleman"), and it has made its way to the twenty-first century in the form of the ubiquitous Patrick, as well as the lesser heard Patric and Patrik variants. These names have risen to great heights in sports around the world, with many of them appearing in team sports! This definitely suggests that if you name a son Patrick (or one of the other spellings), he'll be a dedicated team player, working well with his teammates on and off the field to have fun and achieve success.

Patrics, Patricks, and Patriks have won medals and awards in track and field (like American two-time Olympic gold-medalist shot putter Parry O'Brien), figure skating (like Canadian Patrick Chan, who took home a gold and two silvers from the Olympics, five medals from World Championships (three of them wins), and four medals from Grand Prix Finals), and even esports (like Swedish *Counter-Strike: Global Offensive* major champion Patrik "f0rest" Lindberg). On the hardwood courts, Canadian wheelchair basketball player Patrick Anderson won three Paralympic gold medals, while one of the most famous players of all time is eleven-time All-Star New York Knicks center Patrick Ewing, who won two Olympic gold medals with the USA team and was inducted into the Basketball Hall of Fame.

But that's not nearly all; numerous athletes with these names are concentrated in the trio of football, ice hockey, and soccer. Gridiron players include four-time Pro Bowl Baltimore Ravens fullback Patrick Ricard; seven-time Pro Bowl San Francisco 49ers middle linebacker and two-time NFL tackles leader Patrick Willis; and six-time Pro Bowl quarterback Patrick Mahomes, who has won three Super Bowls, been named MVP twice and Super Bowl MVP three times, led in passing yards and passing touchdowns (twice), and more.

Some dudes with these names excel on the ice, like Swedish two-time Stanley Cup-winner and world champion right wing Patric Hörnqvist; nine-time All-Star Chicago Blackhawks right wing and three-time Stanley Cup champion Patrick Kane; and Canadian Hall of Fame goaltender Patrick Roy, who played in eleven All-Star games, won four Stanley Cup championships, set several league records, and more.

On the other hand, some Patricks have become superstars on soccer fields, like Cameroonian Olympic gold-medalist striker Patrick M'Boma, Dutch FIFA 100 striker Patrick Kluivert (UEFA Champions League, UEFA Super Cup, Intercontinental Cup, and UEFA Euro 2000 Golden Boot), and legendary French midfielder Patrick Vieira, who has won five FA Cups, FIFA Confederations Cup, the FIFA World Cup 1998, and more while being named to the FIFA World Cup All-Star Team and FIFA 100!

- **Patrick Anderson**, Wheelchair Basketball, Canada, 1997–2012
- **Patrick Chan**, Figure Skating, Canada, 1996–2018
- **Patrick Ewing Sr.**, Basketball (Center), New York Knicks, Jamaica/USA, 1985–2002
- **Patric Hörnqvist**, Ice Hockey (Right Wing), Pittsburgh Penguins, Sweden, 2005–current
- **Patrick Kane II**, Ice Hockey (Right Wing), Chicago Blackhawks, USA, 2007–current
- **Patrick Kluivert**, Soccer (Striker), Fútbol Club Barcelona, Netherlands, 1994–2008
- **Patrik "f0rest" Lindberg**, Esports (*Counter-Strike/Counter-Strike: Global Offensive*), Sweden, 2005–current
- **Patrick Mahomes II**, Football (Quarterback), Kansas City Chiefs, USA, 2017–current
- **Patrick M'Boma**, Soccer (Striker), La Berrichonne de Châteauroux, Cameroon, 1992–2005
- **William Patrick "Parry" O'Brien**, Track & Field (Shot Put), USA, 1952–1964
- **Patrick Ricard**, Football (Fullback), Baltimore Ravens, USA, 2017–current
- **Patrick Roy**, Ice Hockey (Goaltender), Montreal Canadiens, Canada, 1984–2003
- **Patrick Vieira**, Soccer (Midfielder), Arsenal Football Club, France, 1993–2011
- **Patrick Willis**, Football (Linebacker), San Francisco 49ers, USA, 2007–2014

PATRICE/PATRÍCIO

The modern forms and derivations of the ancient Latin name *Patricius* (from a root word meaning "nobleman") are many, with a couple of the most common being Patrice and Patrício. Athletes with these names have conquered a few different fields with impressive successes; Brazilian MMA fighter Patrício "Pitbull" Freire has held two different Bellator belts and is considered the best in his weight class, French ten-time world champion Patrice Martin is a record-setting water skier, and Canadian three-time NHL All-Star Boston Bruins center Patrice Bergeron has won the Stanley Cup, a world championship, and two Olympic gold medals.

Olympic success for French Patrices continues onto the soccer field with striker Patrice Garande, who won a gold medal in 1984, while left-back Patrice Evra made the most of his 815 senior and international appearances, winning Premier League five times, Coppa Italia twice, Supercoppa Italiana, UEFA Champions League, and the FIFA Club World Cup.

A Patrice or Patricio in your family may stand out in a world of Patricks, and he's likely to enjoy playing soccer (though he might prefer something like ice hockey, water skiing, or MMA instead).

- **Patrice Bergeron**, Ice Hockey (Center), Boston Bruins, Canada, 2003–current
- **Patrice Evra**, Soccer (Left-Back), Manchester United Football Club, France, 1998–2018
- **Patrício "Pitbull" Freire**, MMA (Featherweight/Lightweight), Brazil, 2004–current
- **Patrice Garande**, Soccer (Striker), Association de la Jeunesse Auxerroise, France, 1978–1995
- **Patrice Martin**, Water Skiing, France, 1979–1996

PAU

The name *Paul* may come from a Latin root meaning "small" or "humble," but it turns out that the Catalan and Occitan version Pau is perfect for a boy who enjoys a sport that's primarily played by tall people: basketball! Shooting guard Pau Ribas has been a huge force in European basketball, winning the FIBA EuroCup, EuroCup twice, and gold medals in both EuroBasket and World Cup. The seven-foot-tall power forward/center Pau Gasol also had a lot of success in Spanish basketball (including three EuroBasket golds and a World Cup win), though he's better known for his NBA career, during which he racked up six All-Star appearances and two NBA championships!

- **Pau Gasol Sáez**, Basketball (Power Forward/ Center), Los Angeles Lakers, Spain, 1998–2021
- **Pau Ribas Tossas**, Basketball (Shooting Guard), FC Barcelona Bàsquet, Spain, 2005–current

PAUL

The name Paul, descended from a Roman family name and a Latin root meaning "small" or "humble," has enjoyed significant popularity in the United States and around the world; in fact, from 1880 to 2000, it was among the top one hundred names given to American babies! Naturally, with so many Pauls running around, a number of them are going to end up as athletes, and a fair few of those have been destined for true greatness. Some are team players supporting their mates and working together, like three-time Olympic gold-medalist double sculls rower Paul Costello; Australian Paralympic gold-medalist and four-time world champion tandem cyclist Paul Clohessy; Dutch tennis pro Paul Haarhuis, who reached the world number one doubles spot with fifty-four titles and six Grand Slams; and Irish rugby lock Paul O'Connell, whose massive trophy collection includes three United Rugby Championships, three Six Nations Championships, a Grand Slam, and four Triple Crowns.

Some Pauls straddle the line, competing on their own and with teams, like Belgian pistol and rifle sport shooter Paul Van Asbroeck, who won a full set of Olympic medals in individual and team events; épée fencer Paul Anspach, who won four Olympic medals with the Belgian team and a gold on his own; Italian singles and doubles luger Paul Hildgartner, who won two Olympic gold medals and two world championships; and Welsh swimming prodigy Paul Radmilovic, who won three Olympic gold medals with the Great Britain water polo team and another in the 4x200-meter freestyle.

On the links, American Paul Azinger has won sixteen professional events (one major) and English Paul Casey has won a huge twenty-one, while gridiron greats include two-time AFL All-Star and three-time AFL champion punter and linebacker Paul Maguire, and Hall of Fame Green Bay Packers running back, halfback, and kicker Paul Hornung, who played in two Pro Bowls, won four NFL championships and a Super Bowl, and led the league in rushing touchdowns and scoring (three times)!

International football fans have cheered for English midfielders like Paul Scholes (FA Cup three times, UEFA Champions League twice, and FIFA Club World Cup), Manchester United's Paul Pogba of France (Golden Boy, Coppa Italia twice, Supercoppa Italiana twice, UEFA Europa League, UEFA Nations League, and FIFA World Cup 2018), and, of course, top-ranked German Paul Breitner, who won the Bundesliga five times, La Liga twice, Copa del Rey, and FIFA World Cup 1974 while being honored as a FIFA World Cup All-Star and placed on the FIFA World Cup All-Time Team and FIFA 100.

Tough Pauls on skates include Paralympic gold-medalist and world champion ice sledge hockey goalie Paul Rosen; seven-time All-Star left wing Paul Kariya, who won Olympic gold and a world championship; and Hall of Fame defenseman Paul Coffey, who played in fourteen All-Star games, won the Stanley Cup four times, and set numerous NHL records.

*Pau*s are definitely basketball players, but what about Pauls? Five-time All-Star shooting guard/point guard Paul Westphal won the NBA championship in 1974 with the Boston Celtics and was inducted into the Basketball Hall of Fame, eight-time All-Star small forward Paul George won Olympic gold with the American team in 2016, and Hall of Fame small forward Paul Pierce played in ten All-Star games and, in 2008, became an NBA champion and the NBA Finals MVP.

Last but not least are the Pauls who have played in America's pastime! They include six-time All-Stars Paul Konerko (World Series champion first baseman) and Paul Derringer (two-time World Series–winning pitcher); and seven-time All-Stars first baseman Paul Goldschmidt (NL MVP, NL home run leader, NL RBI leader, four Gold Gloves, five Silver Sluggers, and two Hank Aaron awards) and record-setting Hall of Fame designated hitter and infielder Paul Molitor (World Series champion, World Series MVP, four Silver Slugger awards, and more).

There is nothing stopping a Paul from finding and succeeding at his favorite sport, so make sure to introduce a son with this name to lots of different events so he can find his!

- **Paul Anspach**, Fencing (Épée), Belgium, 1909–1928
- **Paul Azinger**, Golf, USA, 1981–2009
- **Paul Breitner**, Soccer (Left-Back/Midfielder), Fußball-Club Bayern München e. V., Germany, 1970–1983
- **Paul Casey**, Golf, England, 2000–current
- **Paul Clohessy**, Track Cycling, Australia, 1992–2000
- **Paul Coffey**, Ice Hockey (Defense), Edmonton Oilers, Canada, 1980–2001
- **Paul Costello**, Rowing, USA, 1920–1928
- **Samuel Paul Derringer**, Baseball (Pitcher), Cincinnati Reds, USA, 1931–1945
- **Paul George**, Basketball (Small Forward), Indiana Pacers, USA, 2010–current
- **Paul Goldschmidt**, Baseball (First Baseman), Arizona Diamondbacks, USA, 2011–current
- **Paul Haarhuis**, Tennis, Netherlands, 1989–2003
- **Paul Hildgartner**, Luge, Italy, 1971–1988
- **Paul Hornung**, Football (Running Back/Halfback/Kicker), Green Bay Packers, USA, 1957–1967
- **Paul Kariya**, Ice Hockey (Left Wing), Mighty Ducks of Anaheim, Canada, 1994–2010
- **Paul Konerko**, Baseball (First Baseman), Chicago White Sox, USA, 1997–2014
- **Paul Maguire**, Football (Punter/Linebacker), Buffalo Bills, USA, 1960–1970
- **Paul Molitor**, Baseball (Designated Hitter/Infielder), Milwaukee Brewers, USA, 1978–1998
- **Paul O'Connell**, Rugby (Lock), Munster Rugby, Ireland, 2001–2017
- **Paul Pierce**, Basketball (Small Forward), Boston Celtics, USA, 1998–2017
- **Paul Pogba**, Soccer (Midfielder), Manchester United Football Club, France, 2011–current
- **Paolo "Paul" Radmilovic**, Water Polo/Swimming, Wales, 1901–1929
- **Paul Rosen**, Ice Sledge Hockey (Goalie), Canada, 2001–2010
- **Paul Scholes**, Soccer (Midfielder), Manchester United Football Club, England, 1993–2013
- **Paul Van Asbroeck**, Sport Shooting (Pistol/Rifle), Belgium, 1900–1936
- **Paul Westphal**, Basketball (Shooting Guard/Point Guard), Phoenix Suns, USA, 1972–1984

PAULO

Galician and Portuguese have given us the *Paul* variant Paulo, which in the sporting world has proven a favorite of soccer players from Portugal and Argentina! These include Portuguese players Paulo Sousa (Guerin d'Oro midfielder) and Paulo Futre (two-time Portuguese Footballer of the Year winger; winner of Primeira Liga twice, European Cup, and Copa del Rey twice; and named to World Soccer 100 Greatest Footballers of All Time); and Argentinian Supercoppa Italiana all-time top scoring forward/midfielder Paulo Dybala, whose trophy collection features four Coppa Italia titles, three Supercoppa Italiana, and FIFA World Cup 2022.

Get a Paulo in your family out on the soccer field early and cheer him on to victory!

- **Paulo Dybala**, Soccer (Forward/Midfielder), Juventus Football Club, Argentina, 2011–current
- **Paulo Jorge dos Santos Futre**, Soccer (Winger), Club Atlético de Madrid, S.A.D., Portugal, 1983–1998
- **Paulo Carvalho de Sousa**, Soccer (Midfielder), Juventus Football Club, Portugal, 1989–2002

PAVEL/PAWEL

The last of the many variants and versions of the original Roman name that became *Paul* are the similar-sounding Pawel and Pavel. Some athletes with these names embark on careers on their own, earning individual glory like two five-time world champions: Polish hammer thrower Paweł Fajdek, and Russian épée fencer Pavel Kolobkov, who also took home a gold, two silvers, and three bronze medals from Olympic Games. Others succeed on their own and find victory alongside their teammates, like Soviet track and field star Pavel Lednyov, whose seven medals in the pentathlon from the Olympics (two gold) and nine from World Championships (six gold) came in individual and team victories.

Russian players are famous for their ice hockey exploits, and Pavels are no exception. Four-time NHL center Pavel Datsyuk skated to two Stanley Cup wins along with an Olympic gold medal and a world championship with his national team, while fellow world champion right wing Pavel Bure's seven All-Star selections and phenomenal play earned him an induction into the Hockey Hall of Fame. Quite possibly the most famous sports Pavel is Czech soccer midfielder Nedvěd, whose 760 senior and international appearances rocketed him to the upper echelons of footballers with a lengthy list of accolades, including winning the UEFA Cup Winners' Cup and UEFA Super Cup; earning awards like the Golden Ball six times, Guerin d'Oro, UEFA Club Best Midfielder of the Year, World Soccer Awards Player of the Year, Golden Foot, and Ballon d'Or; and being included in the FIFA 100!

Teach a young Pavel or Pawel to succeed on his own and with his friends and he'll be ready for anything that comes his way, whether that's on the ice, on a soccer field, or in any other field he chooses.

- **Pavel Bure**, Ice Hockey (Right Wing), Vancouver Canucks, Russia, 1987–2003
- **Pavel Datsyuk**, Ice Hockey (Center), Detroit Red Wings, Russia, 1996–2021
- **Paweł Fajdek**, Track & Field (Hammer Throw), Poland, 2011–current
- **Pavel Kolobkov**, Fencing (Épée), Russia, 1988–2008
- **Pavel Lednyov**, Track & Field (Pentathlon), USSR, 1968–1980
- **Pavel Nedvěd**, Soccer (Midfielder), Juventus Football Club, Czech Republic, 1990–2009

PEDRO

Stones are not typically thought of as being particularly fast, but athletes named Pedro (a Portuguese and Spanish version of *Peter*, which comes from "stone" in Greek) definitely are, whether on foot, throwing something through the air, or behind the wheel! These include Mexican 24 Hours of Le Mans–champion and two-time winner on the Formula 1 circuit Pedro Rodríguez de la Vega; Cuban-Portuguese Olympic gold-medalist and world champion triple jumper Pedro Pichardo; Dominican-American Baseball Hall of Famer and eight-time MLB All-Star pitcher Pedro Martínez, who led the MLB in wins and AL in strikeouts three times while winning a World Series, three Cy Young awards, and a Triple Crown; and Spanish soccer forward/winger Pedro Rodríguez Ledesma, whose lengthy career and 840 senior and international appearances brought him trophies like La Liga five times, Copa del Rey three times, Supercopa de España four times, UEFA Europa League, UEFA Champions League three times, UEFA Super Cup three times, FIFA Club World Cup twice, UEFA European Championship, and the 2010 FIFA World Cup.

Name your son Pedro and see how fast he can go!

Pedro Martínez, Baseball (Pitcher), Boston Red Sox, Dominican Republic/USA, 1992–2009

Pedro Pichardo, Track & Field (Triple Jump), Cuba/Portugal, 2013–current

Pedro Rodríguez Ledesma, Soccer (Forward/Winger), Fútbol Club Barcelona, Spain, 2005–current

Pedro Rodríguez de la Vega, Auto Racing (Formula 1), Mexico, 1950–1971

PELÉ

Few names in history are as closely connected to a specific sport as Pelé, the quintessential master of soccer and one of the greatest sportsmen of all time. Named after inventor Thomas Edison, Brazilian Edson Arantes do Nascimento learned to play football as a youth and was given the nickname Pelé (different stories offer different origins for the moniker, though the legend himself has stated it didn't mean anything and had no translation in Portuguese). He was so good at the game that he went pro with Santos at only fifteen years old, starting an incredible career that would see him earn countless accolades and be called the greatest player of all time. A versatile striker and playmaker with epic skills, Pelé set the Guinness World Record for most career goals scored in football (1,279 goals in 1,363 games), is the only player to have won three FIFA World Cups, and is considered by many to be a paragon of skill and sportsmanship. He was lauded by his teammates and opponents during his career and after, and the list of his awards and achievements is too long to include here but feature countless top-scorer and best-player awards, induction into multiple Halls of Fame, and so much more.

Pelé is a glorious nickname for a son whether or not he's named Edson. He should be introduced to soccer as early as possible, but no matter what sport he ends up loving, he'll develop fine skills as well as a good attitude about winning and losing. He'll hit leaderboards in goals or points and be a powerful, versatile presence on the field.

Edson "Pelé" Arantes do Nascimento, Soccer (Forward), Santos Futebol Clube, Brazil, 1956–1977

PETE

A great many Petes around the world are actually *Peters*, but the diminutive works for other names, too, including *Petros*. There are many fields in which a solitary Pete has climbed to the top ranks, from diving (with Canadian two-time Olympic gold-medalist Ulise "Pete" Desjardins) to rodeo events (with Canadian four-time World Champion Bronc Rider and ProRodeo Hall of Famer Pete Knight), basketball (with five-time NBA

All-Star and Hall of Fame shooting guard Pete Maravich), rowing (with British three-time Olympic gold-medalist and five-time world champion Pete Reed), and, of course, tennis (with Petros "Pete" Sampras, whose number one ranking, sixty-four titles (fourteen majors), and multiple records have placed him among the all-time greatest players).

Meanwhile, Petes seem particularly drawn to the sport of baseball! Three-time All-Star outfielder Harold Patrick "Pistol Pete" Reiser was an NL batting champion and two-time NL stolen base leader in the 1940s, five-time All-Star infielder James "Pete" Runnels was the AL batting champion in 1960 and 1962, and Hall of Fame pitcher Grover Cleveland "Old Pete" Alexander solidified his ranking among top players with the 1926 World Series championship, three Triple Crowns, and achieving NL wins leader six times, NL ERA leader four times, and NL strikeout leader six times.

Whether your son is a *Peter*, *Petros*, or another name entirely, the nickname Pete can give him a love of athletics and a spirit of competition—enrollment in T-ball is highly recommended! One word of warning: teach him fairness, sportsmanship, and following the rules so his athletic achievements are never overshadowed . . . like what happened to seventeen-time MLB All-Star Pete Rose, who had an incredible career but lost out on being inducted into the Baseball Hall of Fame because of his gambling.

Grover Cleveland "Old Pete" Alexander, Baseball (Pitcher), Chicago Cubs, USA, 1911–1930

Ulise "Pete" Desjardins, Diving, USA, 1924–1928

Peter "Pete" Knight, Rodeo (Bronc Riding), Canada, 1924–1937

Peter "Pete" Maravich, Basketball (Shooting Guard), New Orleans Jazz, USA, 1970–1980

Peter "Pete" Reed, Rowing, England, 2005–2018

Harold Patrick "Pete" Reiser, Baseball (Outfielder), Brooklyn Dodgers, USA, 1940–1952

Peter "Pete" Rose Sr., Baseball (Outfielder/ Infielder), Cincinnati Reds, USA, 1963–1986

James "Pete" Runnels, Baseball (Infielder), Boston Red Sox, USA, 1951–1964

Petros "Pete" Sampras, Tennis, USA, 1988–2003

PETER

A rock may not appear to be the most inspiring source for an active and winning name, but Peter's Ancient Greek origin of "stone" hasn't stopped the name from rolling to great heights! Some Peters are tough and strong—like Dutch heavyweight martial artist Peter Aerts, who tops kickboxing all-time greats charts with his multiple championships, while others focus on speed—like Slovakian three-time World Road Race Champion cyclist Peter Sagan and three-time Olympic gold-medalist middle-distance runner Peter Snell.

If you're Hungarian and like accents in your names, then your son might enjoy playing in the pool and join the ranks of water polo players like Olympic gold-medalist Péter Rusorán, and Péter Biros, whose trophy case holds a world championship, three Olympic gold medals and a World Cup.

Peters can also succeed in any field or event that fits their talents and interests; they can gain inspiration through predecessors like German five-time world champion foil fencer Peter Joppich and Danish esports pro Peter "dupreeh" Rasmussen, who has won four major *Counter-Strike: Global Offensive* championships while earning two HTLV MVPs and seven Top 20 Player of the Year awards.

Peter Aerts, Kickboxing (Heavyweight), Netherlands, 1985–current

Péter Biros, Water Polo (Driver), Hungary, 1995–2015

Peter Joppich, Fencing (Foil), Germany, 2002-current

Peter "dupreeh" Rasmussen, Esports (*Counter-Strike: Global Offensive*), Denmark, 2012-current

Péter Rusorán, Water Polo (Field Player), Hungary, 1952-1972

Peter Sagan, Road Cycling, Slovakia, 2009-current

Peter Snell, Track & Field (Middle-Distance Running), New Zealand, 1960-1965

PEYTON

The unisex name Peyton has an uncertain origin, coming from an Old English place name for "Pæga's Town." Despite its humble beginnings, no one can deny the popularity and influence of its most famous bearer, Hall of Fame NFL quarterback Peyton Manning. An absolute dynamo on the field, "the Sheriff" was selected for the Pro Bowl fourteen out of his eighteen seasons, won two Super Bowls, and racked up a massive list of accomplishments, including Super Bowl MVP, NFL Most Valuable Player five times, NFL passing yards leader three times, NFL passing touchdowns leader four times, NFL completion percentage leader twice, and more. Peyton set multiple NFL records too, including most passing yards in a season and most passing touchdowns in a season!

A boy you name Peyton has a lot to look up to in Manning, and can take to heart lessons of hard work.

Peyton "the Sheriff" Manning, Football (Quarterback), Indianapolis Colts, USA, 1998-2015

PHIL

There may be multiple ways to spell *Philip*, but they all share one thing: they're frequently shortened to Phil! Phils have particular sets of skills that have seen them rise through the ranks in a few different sports, with some truly top contenders. There are team players like English rugby prop Phil Vickery, who won a Premiership, the Heineken Cup, and the 2003 World Cup; Olympic gold-medalist and world champion beach volleyball player Phil Dalhausser; and five-time MLB All-Star pitcher and Hall of Famer Phil Niekro, who won five Gold Gloves and a Roberto Clemente award in a career that saw him lead the National League in strikeouts and wins twice, as well as pitch a no-hitter in 1973!

Meanwhile, other Phils charge ahead on their own, like Olympic gold-medalist and world champion alpine ski racer Phil Mahre, who took home sixty-nine medals from World Cups (twenty-seven of them wins), and American auto racing legend Phil Hill, who achieved three wins and a championship in both 24 Hours of Le Mans and Formula 1.

Some of the most famous and exemplary Phils in sporting and competitive history include Canadian ten-time NHL All-Star center, two-time Stanley Cup champion, and Hall of Famer Phil Esposito; Phil Mickelson, who has won fifty-seven professional golf tournaments, including six majors; English sixteen-time world champion darts player Phil Taylor, who won 214 professional events, including eighty-five majors; and "Zen Master" Phil Jackson, who won two NBA championships as a player with the New York Knicks and then a further eleven as a coach for the Chicago Bulls and Los Angeles Lakers.

Any one of those can be a great inspiration for a young Phil looking for a sport or activity he likes. And if he happens to enjoy gambling, then he may take after ten-time World Series of Poker bracelet-winner and World Poker Title champion Phil Ivey, and Phil Hellmuth, who has won a record sixteen World Series of Poker bracelets!

Philip "Phil" Dalhausser, Beach Volleyball, USA, 2005-2020

Philip "Phil" Esposito, Ice Hockey (Center), Boston Bruins, Canada, 1963-1981

Phillip "Phil" Hellmuth Jr., Card Gaming (Poker), USA, 1987–current

Philip "Phil" Hill Jr., Auto Racing (Formula 1), USA, 1956–1967

Phillip "Phil" Ivey Jr., Card Gaming (Poker), USA, 1998–current

Philip "Phil" Jackson, Basketball (Power Forward), New York Nicks, USA, 1967–1980

Phillip "Phil" Mahre, Alpine Ski Racing, USA, 1975–1984

Philip "Phil" Mickelson, Golf, USA, 1992–current

Philip "Phil" Niekro, Baseball (Pitcher), Milwaukee Braves, USA, 1964–1987

Philip "Phil" Taylor, Darts, England, 1986–2018

Philip "Phil" Vickery, Rugby (Prop), Gloucester Rugby, England, 1995–2010

PHILIP/PHILIPP/PHILLIP

Why is Australian-American two-time Olympic gold-medalist equestrian eventer Philip Dutton the most Philip of them all? Philip (alternatively spelled Phillip or Philipp) comes from Ancient Greek roots meaning "friend of horses!" Of course, Philips of all varieties aren't bound to playing and competing with horses, but they do have unlimited athletic and sporting potential. Just ask champions like Swiss two-time Olympic gold-medalist snowboarder Philipp Schoch; eight-time Pro Bowl San Diego/Los Angeles Chargers quarterback Philip Rivers, who led the NFL in passing yards, completion percentage, and more; and top-ranked German soccer full-back Philipp Lahm, who was named to the FIFA World Cup All-Star Team twice, FIFA World Cup Dream Team, and FIFA FIFPro World XI twice for his incredible career that included winning Bundesliga eight times, DFL-Supercup three times, UEFA Champions League, UEFA Super Cup, FIFA Club World Cup, and FIFA World Cup 2014.

Phillip Dutton, Equestrian (Eventing), Australia/USA, 1996–current

Philipp Lahm, Soccer (Full-Back), Fußball-Club Bayern München e. V., Germany, 2001–2017

Philip Rivers, Football (Quarterback), San Diego Chargers, USA, 2004–2020

Philipp Schoch, Snowboarding, Switzerland, 2002–2007

PIERRE

A French version of the name *Peter* (from a Greek root meaning "stone"), Pierre is definitely more popular in certain parts of Europe and Canada. Pierres go back a ways, with Pierre de Coubertin co-founding the modern Olympic Games in 1896 (and winning a gold in literature in 1912). More recently, equestrian show jumper Pierre Durand won Olympic gold and a world championship, Pierre Vaultier became a world champion and two-time Olympic gold-medalist in snowboard cross, and pairs figure skater Pierre Brunet won five world championships and three Olympic medals (two of them gold) with his partner/wife!

International football fans have cheered on German midfielder/winger Pierre Littbarski to the 1990 FIFA World Cup, as well as French-Gabonese striker Pierre-Emerick Aubameyang to the DFL-Supercup twice and FA Cup while he was named African Footballer of the Year and Bundesliga Player of the Year. Last but not least, hardy Canadians have found success on the ice, including five-time NHL All-Star center Pierre Turgeon and eight-time All-Star defenseman and Stanley Cup–champion Pierre Pilote.

Whether you think he might like ice hockey, soccer, figure skating, equestrian events, or something else entirely, your son can take the name Pierre to heart with a steadfast dedication to playing hard and fair.

- **Pierre-Emerick Aubameyang**, Soccer (Striker), Ballspielverein Borussia 09 e. V. Dortmund, France/Gabon, 2008–current
- **Pierre Brunet**, Figure Skating, France, 1924–1935
- **Charles Pierre de Coubertin**, Literature, France, 1896–1912
- **Pierre Durand**, Equestrian (Jumping), France, 1988–1990
- **Pierre Littbarski**, Soccer (Midfielder/Winger), 1. Fußball-Club Köln 01/07 e. V., Germany, 1978–1997
- **Joseph Albert Pierre Pilote**, Ice Hockey (Defense), Chicago Blackhawks, Canada, 1955–1969
- **Pierre Turgeon**, Ice Hockey (Center), New York Islanders, Canada, 1987–2007
- **Pierre Vaultier**, Snowboarding, France, 1997–current

PIOTR/PYOTR

Like *Pierre* in French, Piotr and Pyotr are Belarusian/Polish and Russian evolutions of the name *Peter*. Nearly all of the top-level athletes with these European names are from Poland, with a couple of exceptions, and they span numerous categories and events.

There are many Piotrs and Pyotrs who have won with partners or teammates, including World League–winner and two-time world champion volleyball middle blocker Piotr Nowakowski, four-time world championship and multiple World Cup–winner wheelchair dancer Piotr Iwanicki, and Russian ski jumper Piotr Żyła, who took home seven medals from World Championships (three of them gold), six World Cup wins, and more in individual and team events.

Meanwhile, there are some particular sports that seem to attract men with these names and might be interesting for a boy in your family! If he likes to be on the water, he may enjoy canoeing, like two-time world champion sprint canoeists Piotr Siemionowski and Piotr Markiewicz. If he's more of a fun- (and compete-) in-the-sun type, he may gravitate toward running, like Soviet Pyotr Bolotnikov, who won Olympic gold in the ten thousand meters, and 4x400-meter sprinters Piotr Rysiukiewicz (world champion) and Piotr Haczek (two-time world champion).

The spirit of competition and winning goes beyond the pure physical, and a boy can find inspiration for mental prowess and success in International Solving Grandmaster Piotr Murdzia, who is considered among the top chess problem solvers of all time and has eight world championships under his belt.

- **Pyotr Bolotnikov**, Long-Distance Running, USSR, 1956–1965
- **Piotr Haczek**, Track & Field (Sprinting), Poland, 1996–2001
- **Piotr Iwanicki**, Wheelchair Dancing, Poland, 1999–2006
- **Piotr Markiewicz**, Sprint Canoeing, Poland, 1993–2001
- **Piotr Murdzia**, Chess, Poland, 1994–current
- **Piotr Nowakowski**, Volleyball (Middle Blocker), Poland, 2006–current
- **Piotr Rysiukiewicz**, Track & Field (Sprinting), Poland, 1994–2006
- **Piotr Siemionowski**, Sprint Canoeing, Poland, 2009–current
- **Piotr Żyła**, Ski Jumping, Poland, 2004–current

PUD

Pud may not sound like the most exciting nickname, but in the late 1800s, it was all the rage in professional baseball thanks to one James "Pud" Galvin. A star pitcher for a number of teams, Pud (who was said to have "made hitters look like *pudding*") set numerous records, threw two no-hitters in 1880 and 1884, and was the first winner of three hundred games.

I can't guarantee the name will bring your son great athletic success and induction into the National Baseball Hall of Fame like Galvin, but if you do decide to call your kid Pud, then enroll him in Little League and teach him the basics of pitching!

James Francis "Pud" Galvin, Baseball (Pitcher), Buffalo Bisons, USA, 1875–1892

PYRROS

The Greek name Pyrros (with alternate spellings Pyrrhus and Pyrrhos) comes from a root for "fire" and can mean "red-headed" or "flame-colored." You don't have to have Greek ancestry or hotheads in your family to name a child Pyrros, but if you do, he might just be stronger than you and take after Greek weightlifter Pyrros Dimas! Dimas, the most successful Greek Olympic athlete and renowned in his sport, lifted to three Olympic gold medals and a bronze, as well as three world championships and more.

Pyrros Dimas, Weightlifting, Greece, 1989–2004

GIRLS

PAM/PAMELA

Pams and Pamelas don't need to be sweet, though when the sixteenth century poet Sir Philip Sidney created the full name, he may have done it with the Greek roots for "all" and "honey" in mind. In more modern times, athletes with these names have found much sweet success on water and tracks! A girl you name Pam or Pamela may find watersports to her liking, in which case she can follow in the footsteps of people like world champion sailor Pamela Healy; Australian ASP World Tour 1990 surfing world champion Pam Burridge; and British two-time Paralympic gold-medalist and four-time world champion rower Pam Relph.

If she likes to stretch her legs, then your little Pam may instead be a track and field athlete like world champion sprinter Pam Marshall or Kenyan middle-distance runner Pamela Jelimo, who won Olympic gold and a world championship in the 800 meters.

But if water events and running aren't quite her speed, she may find her talents lie in tennis; she'll be in good company there with doubles world number one ranked Pam Shriver, who dominated the scene in the 1980s and '90s with 112 doubles titles (twenty-two of them majors) and an Olympic gold medal!

Pam Burridge, Surfing, Australia, 1977–1999

Pamela Healy, Sailing, USA, 1983–1992

Pamela Jelimo, Track & Field (Middle-Distance Running), Kenya, 2007–2012

Pam Marshall, Track & Field (Sprinting), USA, 1984–1988

Pamela "Pam" Relph, Rowing, England, 2010–2016

Pamela "Pam" Shriver, Tennis, USA, 1979–1997

PAOLA

As we saw in the "P–Boys" section, there are several variants of the name *Paul* out there, and that extends to feminine forms, too, like Paola. Most popular in Italy and Central and South America, Paola has appeared on the leaderboards of several disparate sports, with a particular concentration of Italian volleyball players! These include world champion blocker Paola Paggi and libero Paola Cardullo, who has a collection of gold medals from a World Championship, World Grand Champions Cup, and World Cup.

Other Paolas have found their success in everything from field hockey (like Argentinian World Cup and two-time Champions Trophy-winning goalkeeper Paola Vukojicic) to cycling (like cross country two-time Olympic gold-medalist and two-time world champion Paola Pezzo), archery (like five-time Paralympic gold-medalist Paola Fantato), tennis (like Argentinian former world doubles number one player Paola Suárez, who won forty-four titles and eight Grand Slams), and racquetball (like Mexican twelve-time world champion Paola Longoria).

Whether you're Italian, Mexican, Argentinian, or from anywhere else, consider the name Paola for an active and competitive daughter; she may be slightly predisposed to enjoy volleyball but can succeed at anything.

Paola Cardullo, Volleyball (Libero), Italy, 1996–current

Paola Fantato, Archery, Italy, 1988–2004

Paola Longoria López, Racquetball, Mexico, 2004–current

Paola Paggi, Volleyball (Blocker), Italy, 1996–current

Paola Pezzo, Cross-Country Cycling, Italy, 1993–2000

Paola Suárez, Tennis, Argentina, 1991–2014

Paola Vukojicic, Field Hockey (Goalkeeper), Argentina, 1998–2009

PAT

The first in a trio of related names, Pat is a unisex moniker that's typically, but by no means always, a diminutive of *Patricia*. Athletes going by Pat have been incredibly successful, reaching heights that few others do and shattering expectations. English race driver Pat Moss cemented her place in history as one of the greatest rally competitors, racing to five European Ladies' Rally Championships and three international event wins; diver Pat McCormick collected four gold medals across two Olympic Games and was famous for attempting dives that others feared to perform; and famously steel-willed golfer Pat Bradley won thirty-six professional events (six majors) and was inducted into the World Golf Hall of Fame.

A Pat in your family will find her own unique talent and take it all the way to the top!

Pat Bradley, Golf, USA, 1974–1995

Patricia "Pat" McCormick, Diving, USA, 1951–1956

Patricia "Pat" Moss, Auto Racing (Rally), England, 1954–1974

PATRICIA

The somewhat old-fashioned name Patricia comes from the same origin as *Patrick*, ultimately from an ancient Latin root meaning "nobleman." Patricia Miranda took her experience competing against boys in high school to the international stage of women's freestyle wrestling, where she won two World Cup gold medals, an Olympic bronze medal, and two silvers and a bronze at World Championships!

Choose the name Patricia for your daughter and she'll be another unstoppable force.

Patricia Miranda, Freestyle Wrestling, USA, 2000–2007

PATTI/PATTY

Patty (and its somewhat lesser used variant Patti) is best known as a diminutive of *Patricia*, though it actually came about as an evolution of *Matty* from the name *Martha*! And wouldn't you know it, like *Pat*s and *Patricia*s, American Pattis and Pattys are pretty incredible competitors, racking up wins, trophies, championships, and records. Patti McGee set a world record for the fastest girl on a skateboard (forty-seven miles per hour!) and became the first female professional skateboarder; Patti Catalano set records on her way to winning the Boston Marathon, the Honolulu Marathon four times, and more; and Olympic gold-medalist swimmer Patty Kempner set the 200-meter individual medley world record in 1957!

Skateboarding, running, and swimming are great activities that a Patty in your family may enjoy, though she'll definitely succeed in anything she chooses. But consider taking her out on the links where she may take after two absolute icons with her name, World Golf Hall of Famers Patty Sheehan and Patty Berg! Sheehan won forty-one professional events (six majors) and Berg won a staggering sixty-three with a record fifteen major titles.

Patricia "Patty" Berg, Golf, USA, 1940–1979

Patti Catalano, Long-Distance Running, USA, 1976–1985

Patricia "Patty" Kempner, Swimming (Breaststroke/Medley), USA, 1957–1960

Patti McGee, Skateboarding, USA, 1964–1965

Patty Sheehan, Golf, USA, 1980–2006

PAULA

A feminine version of *Paul* (from Latin for "small" or "humble"), the name Paula brings with it speed and accuracy. That can manifest in sinking putts (like golfer Paula Creamer, who has twelve professional wins with one major title), being in the right place at the right time on the court (like Volleyball World Grand Prix-winning middle blocker Paula Weishoff), or grappling and throwing opponents (like Argentinian Olympic gold-medalist and world champion judoka Paula Pareto, whose medal collection also includes nine from International Judo Federation Grand Slams and nine from Grand Prix events!).

Speed and endurance are key for Paulas who run, bike, and swim like Zimbabwean eight-time Ironman World Champion Paula Newby-Fraser, and British long-distance runner Paula Radcliffe, who won a marathon world championship, three World Cross Country Championships, three World Half Marathon Championships, multiple marathons around the world, and more, all while breaking and setting numerous world records.

Paula Creamer, Golf, USA, 2004–current

Paula Newby-Fraser, Triathlon, Zimbabwe, 1986–2002

Paula Pareto, Judo, Argentina, 2005–2021

Paula Radcliffe, Long-Distance Running, England, 1986–2015

Paula Weishoff, Volleyball (Middle Blocker), USA, 1981–1996

PEGGY

In medieval times, *Margaret*s were called *Meggy*, and that nickname somehow morphed into the variant Peggy. In modern times, this name has appeared in a few sports, though not very recently, so it's definitely due for a comeback. If you give the name (or nickname) to your daughter, she may find an interest in skateboarding, like Z-Boys member Peggy Oki; swimming, like German 10-kilometer open water world champion Peggy Büchse; or figure skating, like Olympic gold-medalist and three-time world champion ladies' skater Peggy Fleming.

Peggy Büchse, Swimming (Open Water), Germany, 1992–2002

Peggy Fleming, Figure Skating, USA, 1962–1968

Peggy Oki, Skateboarding, USA, 1974–1975

PETRA

Especially popular in certain parts of Europe, Petra is a feminine name derived from *Peter* (from a Greek root for "stone"). A girl you name Petra will be the rock on her team, whether that's in athletic competition, academic projects, or business. She can look up to a series of champion Petras in a few different sports, women who have shown a love of speed on land, in water, on wheels, and over snow and ice. These include German world champion 400-meter hurdler Petra Pfaff; German Olympic gold-medalist and world record-setting javelin thrower Petra Felke; Dutch Olympic gold-medalist breaststroke swimmer Petra van Staveren; and German track cyclist Petra Rossner, who won Olympic gold, a world championship, and a World Cup.

Petras seem to excel in the cold, and particularly in alpine skiing. German para-alpine skier Petra Merkert took home three gold medals from the 1976 Paralympic Games; Austrian Petra Kronberger won Olympic gold in slalom and alpine combined, a downhill world championship, and thirty-five medals at World Cups (sixteen of them gold) in the 1980s and '90s; and Slovakian Petra Vlhová is having a tremendous career with Olympic gold in slalom, giant slalom world championship, and sixty-six World Cup medals, including twenty-eight golds so far!

Petra Felke, Track & Field (Javelin), Germany, 1981–1992

Petra Kronberger, Alpine Skiing, Austria, 1987–1992

Petra Merkert, Alpine Skiing, Germany, 1976

Petra Pfaff, Track & Field (Hurdling), Germany, 1980–1983

Petra Rossner, Road/Track Cycling, Germany, 1988–2004

Petronella "Petra" van Staveren, Swimming (Breaststroke), Netherlands, 1981–1986

Petra Vlhová, Alpine Skiing, Slovakia, 2012–current

PIA

A "virtue" name, Pia is a feminine version of *Pius*, meaning "pious" in Latin. So where do Pias concentrate their athletic endeavors? Norwegian curler Pia Trulsen won a world championship with her team in 2015, Swedish sport shooter Pia Hansen took home Olympic gold in the double trap in 2000, and Swiss rower Pia Vogel sped to two world championships. Other absolute champion Swedes include chess legend Pia Cramling, who is the fifth woman ever to attain the rank of Grandmaster and has been ranked the number one woman player in the world three times!

With these examples and more, a girl you name Pia is sure to excel, whether that's with her brawn or her brain.

Pia Cramling, Chess, Sweden, 1984–current

Pia Hansen, Sport Shooting (Double Trap), Sweden, 2000–2004

Pia Trulsen, Curling (Lead), Norway, 2011–current

Pia Vogel, Rowing, Switzerland, 1994–2002

PICABO

Some of the coolest names come from the unlikeliest of sources, and that's the case with Picabo. The future alpine ski racer was allowed to choose her own name at three years old and was inspired by the nearby small town of Picabo, Idaho (Native American for "silver water"). Picabo Street became a world champion in the downhill in 1996 and then won Super-G Olympic gold in 1998; she collected a total of two medals at Olympic Games, three at World Championships, and seventeen at World Cups (nine wins)!

If you're looking for a fun, off-beat name that is unique and may inspire a love of cold weather and skiing, Picabo might be the perfect match for you.

Picabo Street, Alpine Skiing, USA, 1989–2002

PIERA

If you're not Italian you may be unfamiliar with the name Piera, a feminine version of *Pierangelo*, which comes from *Peter* and *Angelus*. Its complex origin notwithstanding, Piera is a hip name and a solid choice for someone who loves to play and compete. Italian athletes with it have appeared in international basketball, with 1938 EuroBasket gold-medalist Piera Verri; and in water sports, with Water Ski and Wake Sport Hall of Famer Piera Castelvetri, who won numerous Italian and European titles, as well as the women's tricks event at the 1959 World Championships.

Piera Castelvetri, Water Skiing, Italy, 1956–1960

Piera Verri, Basketball (Center), Reyer Venezia, Italy, 1932–1939

PIPPA

Traditionally more popular in the UK than the USA, Pippa arose as a nickname for *Philippa* (a feminine version of *Philip*, meaning "lover of horses"). It's a fun, sprightly moniker and great for a girl who likes to go fast and ride, especially on horses and sail boats! This is proven by a couple of English athletes, equestrian eventing rider Pippa Funnell, who became the first person to win the Rolex Grand Slam of Eventing, and Olympic gold-medalist and two-time world champion Yngling-class sailor Pippa Wilson.

Philippa "Pippa" Funnell, Equestrian (Eventing), England, 1997–current

Philippa "Pippa" Wilson, Sailing (Yngling), England, 2007–2010

POLINA

Grace, agility, and strength are hallmarks of girls and women named Polina, a European variant of *Paulina* or a diminutive of *Apollinariya*. This is proven by talented athletes like Soviet artistic gymnast Polina Astakhova, who dominated in the late 1950s and '60s with ten medals won at Olympic Games (five of them golds) and four medals won at World Championships (half of them gold)!

Polina Astakhova, Artistic Gymnastics, USSR, 1956–1967

POLLY

Just as *Peggy* came about as an evolution of *Meggy*, the name Polly began as a medieval variant of *Molly*! Most popular in English-speaking countries, Polly has solid athletic chops on the water. New Zealand sailor Polly Powrie won Olympic gold and silver in the 470 class, with six medals (two gold) at World Championships in 470 and 420, while British doctor Polly Swann became a world champion rower in 2013 and has won three gold medals at World Rowing Cups events.

A Polly in your family clearly should be introduced to water sports as early as possible!

Olivia Elizabeth "Polly" Powrie, Sailing, New Zealand, 2007–2017

Polly Swann, Rowing, England, 2009–current

PORTIA

A name that comes from the Latin word for "pig" may not seem like it's particularly befitting of athletes and sportswomen, but you'd be surprised. Name your daughter Portia and she may be the toughest on her team, giving and taking hits while moving the ball down the pitch toward victory. Look no further for evidence than New Zealand rugby wing Portia Woodman-Wickliffe, whose appearances with her national union and sevens teams have seen her win Olympic gold and silver medals, the Women's Rugby World Cup twice, Rugby World Cup Sevens twice, and more while setting records and racing to milestones, like being the first woman in sevens to score two hundred tries!

Portia Woodman-Wickliffe, Rugby (Wing), New Zealand Women's National Rugby Sevens Team, New Zealand, 2013–current

PRAPAWADEE

Sometimes a name really is the key to victory, and that's the case with Thai weightlifter Prapawadee Jaroenrattanatarakoon. Born Junpim Kuntatean, she won silver and bronze medals at World Championships but was looking for an edge to get her even greater success at the upcoming 2008 Olympic Games. On the recommendation of her fortune teller, she changed her name to Prapawadee Jaroenrattanatarakoon (possibly translated as "sparkling river-flow of brilliant prosperity") . . . and subsequently won Olympic gold!

If you're looking for the luckiest name around that can give your daughter strength and the determination to win, consider Prapawadee.

Prapawadee Jaroenrattanatarakoon, Weightlifting, Thailand, 2002–2012

PREETI

To have a daughter who will get great *enjoyment* from playing sports with friends, consider giving her the name Preeti, which comes from Sanskrit for "pleasure" or "joy." She may take after Indian athletes like cricket bowlers Preeti Dimri (who began playing all three international cricket formats within ten days) and Preeti Bose (who was on the 2016 Women's Asia Cup T20-winning team), as well as field hockey forward Preeti Dubey, who won the Asian Champions Trophy with the India team!

Preeti Bose, Cricket (Bowler), Haryana Women's Cricket Team, India, 2011–current

Preeti Dimri, Cricket (Bowler), Railways Women's Cricket Team, India, 1999–2015

Preeti Dubey, Field Hockey (Forward), India, 2014–2017

PRIYA

From Sanskrit meaning "beloved" comes the name Priya, a moniker that represents strength, determination, and the will and skill to succeed despite any hardships. Oh, and possibly a love of swimming and being in the water if Priya Cooper is any indication! The Australian swimming star didn't let cerebral palsy stand in her way of a competitive athletic career, winning an astonishing sixteen medals from Paralympic Games (nine of them gold) and ten more from World Championships (eight gold) while setting multiple world records.

Priya Cooper, Swimming (Backstroke/Freestyle/Medley), Australia, 1986–2000

PUNAM

The Hindi name Punam (alternatively spelled Poonam) has roots in Sanskrit for the "full moon," though girls with this name love to play and compete under the sun. Punams are powerful and strong, like Commonwealth

Games gold-medalist and Commonwealth Champion weightlifter Punam Yadav, and cricket batter Punam Raut, who set a world record (for any gender) of 320 opening runs in partnership with Deepti Sharma!

Whether she prefers competing on her own or alongside a team, a Punam in your family will have lots of fun and success . . . and not just every full moon.

Punam Raut, Cricket (Batter), IPL Trailblazers, India, 2009–current

Punam Yadav, Weightlifting, India, 2014–current

PURNIMA

Coming from the same Sanskrit "full moon" root as *Punam* comes Purnima, a name that can inspire a girl to shoot for the highest heights. That's exactly what we see in Indian archer Purnima Mahato, who won national championships and a gold medal at the International Archery Championships.

Purnima Mahato, Archery, India, 1993–2012

BOYS

QINAN

The unisex name Qinan (similar to the county Qin'an in the Chinese province of Gansu) appears in men's athletics when it comes to the top marksmen in the world. Rifle sport shooter Zhu Qinan won Olympic gold and silver medals, set multiple records, and took home multiple World Cup wins.

A boy (or girl) you name Qinan will be eagle-eyed and patient, waiting for the perfect moment to hit the target–whether that's in shooting or anything else in life.

Zhu Qinan, Sport Shooting (Rifle), China, 2000–2011

QINGQUAN

Like many Chinese names, Qingquan can have a variety of meanings, though from weightlifter Long Qingquan's example, we can see it inspire strength and dedication to one's craft. Long is a world champion and two-time Olympic gold-medalist who set the world record in the 56-kilogram class with a 307 kilogram total!

Long Qingquan, Weightlifting, China, 2008–2016

QUENTIN/QUENTON/QUINTON

There are numerous spelling variants of the name Quentin/Quenton/Quinton, though they all originate with the Roman name *Quintus*, which was generally assigned to a fifth-born child. Athletes with these names around the world have excelled in a quartet of sports, with French track cyclist Quentin Lafargue winning a 1-kilometer time trial world championship and biathlete Quentin Maillet accumulating a huge medal haul, including two golds and three silvers from Olympic Games, twelve total from World Championships (three golds), and lots more from World Cup events. On the team sport front, NFL Indianapolis Colts guard Quenton Nelson was selected for five Pro Bowls while South African cricket captain and wicket-keeper/batter Quinton de Kock rocketed to numerous benchmarks in centuries while collecting an IPL championship, multiple Man of the Match awards, the 2017 South African Cricketer of the Year title, and more.

Choose Quentin, Quenton, or Quinton for your son and he may show a preference for cycling, skiing, shooting, football, or even cricket!

Quinton de Kock, Cricket (Wicketkeeper/Batter), Mumbai Indians, South Africa, 2009–current

Quentin Lafargue, Track Cycling, France, 2014–current

Quentin Maillet, Biathlon, France, 2013–current

Quenton Nelson, Football (Guard), Indianapolis Colts, USA, 2018–current

QUINN

Quinn, another unisex "Q" name, comes from Old Irish and a root for either "sense/reason" or "chief." In professional sports, Quinns support their teammates, either stopping opponents from scoring or moving the ball and setting up assists. These two traits are embodied in Canadian NHL All-Star Vancouver Canucks defenseman Quinn Hughes, and point guard Quinn Buckner, who won an NBA championship with the Boston Celtics and an Olympic gold medal with the USA team.

Raise your Quinn with these ideals and he'll be a valuable part of successful teams wherever his interests take him.

William Quinn Buckner, Basketball (Point Guard), Milwaukee Bucks, USA, 1976–1986

Quintin "Quinn" Hughes, Ice Hockey (Defense), Vancouver Canucks, USA, 2019–current

GIRLS

QINAN

While sport shooter Zhu Qinan (see the "Q–Boys" section) is all about hitting the target, professional ice hockey player and Challenge Cup of Asia-winner Zhao Qinan shows off the defensive edge of this unisex name. Tough and fast, the Vanke Rays player can inspire solid teamwork in a girl (or boy!) you name Qinan.

Zhao Qinan, Ice Hockey (Defense), Shenzhen Vanke Rays, China, 2013–current

QINGSHUANG

For a girl who is at home on the ice and will achieve her own success, then help others realize their dreams, consider the name Qingshuang, which can be written in Chinese characters meaning "blue/green," "clean/pure," "frost/crystallized," "cheerful/happy," and more. Yue Qingshuang had only been curling for two years before she was called to join her nation's team at the 2002 Pacific Curling Championships, which was the start of an international career that would see her win six gold medals and three silvers at Pacific-Asia Championships and one medal of each color at World Championships! And once her competing days were over, Yue became a coach for the Chinese wheelchair curling team and guided them to gold medals at two Winter Paralympics.

Yue Qingshuang, Curling (Second), China, 2002–2013

QUINCY

You don't have to have five children to name one of them Quincy, a cool unisex name that comes from a Roman name traditionally given to the fifth-born child. A Quincy in your family will be outgoing and competitive, enjoying the sun and the surf . . . at least if he or she is anything like surfer Quincy Davis! Starting off her career in competitions against boys, Davis rose through the ranks until she was winning multiple Corona Extra Pro Surf Circuit events and more. Quincy is multitalented, with successful musical and fashion endeavors.

Quincy Davis, Surfing, USA, 2009–current

R

BOYS

RAFAEL/RAPHAEL

From the biblical Hebrew name meaning "God heals" come several different versions of Rafael and Raphael (with or without an accent). Just as the name has spread to different parts of the globe with different spellings, so, too, have top-tier athletes with these names proliferated in a variety of sports and competitions! These range from baseball (with Cuban-American four-time All-Star first baseman Rafael Palmeiro, who collected three Gold Gloves and a pair of Silver Sluggers) to MMA (with Brazilian-American World Jiu-Jitsu Champion and former UFC Lightweight Champion Rafael dos Anjos) and biathlon (with French eight-time world champion Raphaël Poirée, who also won forty-four World Cup events, including four overalls).

Where this name shows up the most is definitely soccer, better known internationally as football. Truly at the top of the game are players like Mexican CONCACAF Best Player and CONCACAF Best XI defender Rafael Márquez (who won La Liga four times, Copa del Rey, Supercopa de España three times, FIFA Club World Cup, FIFA Confederations Cup, and lots more) and French Real Madrid center-back Raphaël Varane, who was named to the UEFA Team of the Year, FIFA World Cup Fantasy Team, and FIFA World Cup Dream Team while winning UEFA Champions League four times, UEFA Super Cup three times, FIFA Club World Cup four times, FIFA World Cup 2018, and many more!

That's not all, though, as we take a look at two more unique champions. There's Raphaël Lévy of France, who is one of the greatest *Magic: The Gathering* collectable card game players in the world, with six Grand Prix victories and induction into the Magic: The Gathering Pro Tour Hall of Fame. Of course, no discussion of Rafaels is complete without talking about one of greatest tennis players of all time, Rafael Nadal. The Spanish singles player has been ranked number one in the world across 209 weeks; set numerous records, including being one of only two men to achieve Career Golden Slams in singles; and has won two Olympic gold medals and ninety-two singles titles, including thirty-six Masters.

Truly a boy named a variant of Rafael has endless potential in sports, career, and life.

Rafael dos Anjos, MMA (Welterweight/Lightweight), Brazil/USA, 2004–current

Raphaël Lévy, Card Gaming (*Magic: The Gathering*), France, 1997–current

Rafael Márquez, Soccer (Defender), Fútbol Club Barcelona, Mexico, 1996–2018

Rafael Nadal Parera, Tennis, Spain, 2001–current

Rafael Palmeiro Corrales, Baseball (First Baseman), Baltimore Orioles, Cuba/USA, 1986–2005

Raphaël Poirée, Biathlon, France, 1995–2007

Raphaël Varane, Soccer (Center-Back), Real Madrid Club de Fútbol, France, 2010–current

RAHUL

Most popular in South Asia, the name Rahul is thought to come from a Sanskrit root meaning "able" or "efficient." That most definitely describes Rahul Dravid, one of cricket's all-time greatest batsmen who has been nicknamed "The Wall" and "Mr. Dependable"! The 2002 ICC Champions Trophy-winner and 2004 ICC Player of the Year and Test Player of the Year scored a monumental 24,177 runs in international cricket and appears on numerous leaderboards and top ten standings; he is the fourth-highest run scorer in Test cricket, has had the most catches by any non-wicketkeeper, was part of the highest-scoring Test partnership, and more. Dravid's legacy was solidified even further with the Don Bradman Award and induction into the ICC Hall of Fame.

Naming a son Rahul won't necessarily make him an international cricket star, but it will make him able and efficient, a dependable part of his team, and a hard worker.

Rahul "the Wall"/"Mr. Dependable" Dravid, Cricket (Batsman), Karnataka Cricket Team, India, 1990–2013

RALF/RALPH

Ralph, and its alternate spelling Ralf, may seem like an old-fashioned name, but it has a pretty cool origin in Old Norse roots meaning "counsel" and "wolf." Ralfs and Ralphs in sports and athletics have been hungry like the wolf for wins and championships, which we can see in competitors like Canadian six-time NHL All-Star center and six-time Stanley Cup champion Ralph Backstrom; World Welterweight Champion and International Boxing Hall of Famer Ralph "Young Corbett III" Giordano, whose incredible 132-12-20 record ranks him among the best southpaws of all time; and German rapid-fire pistol sport shooter Ralf Schumann, whose medal collection includes three golds and two silvers from Olympic Games; four golds, a silver, and two bronzes from World Championships; and many more!

Italian-American Raffaele "Ralph" DePalma was a prolific racer in the early 1900s—reportedly winning 2,557 of the 2,889 races he entered—and won the 1915 Indianapolis 500. If a young Ralph in your family likes America's pastime, he may prefer hitting, like All-Star and NL batting champion Ralph "Road Runner" Garr and left fielder Ralph Kiner, who played in six All-Star games, led the National League in RBIs and home runs seven times, and was inducted into the Baseball Hall of Fame.

Ralph Backstrom, Ice Hockey (Center), Montreal Canadiens, Canada, 1956–1977

Raffaele "Ralph" DePalma, Auto Racing (Indianapolis 500), Italy/USA, 1909–1936

Ralph "Road Runner" Garr, Baseball (Outfielder), Atlanta Braves, USA, 1968–1980

Ralph "Young Corbett III" Giordano, Boxing (Welterweight/Middleweight), USA, 1919–1940

Ralph Kiner, Baseball (Left Fielder), Pittsburgh Pirates, USA, 1946–1955

Ralf Schumann, Sport Shooting (Pistol), Germany, 1985–2008

RAMON/RAMÓN

Ramon, from the same Germanic "counsel" and "protection" roots as the name *Raymond*, comes in two flavors: with or without the accent. The former appears more in

Spanish-speaking countries, though both versions can and do show up all around the world. If you name a son Ramon or Ramón, what sports may he gravitate toward? If he's like those who have come before him, it could be such varied events as fencing, kickboxing, or horse racing! From these fields, he can find inspiration from Cuban four-time Olympic gold-medalist fencer Ramón Fonst; Dutch eight-time Muay Thai world champion kickboxer Ramon Dekkers, who helped popularize the sport around the world; and Venezuelan jockey Ramón Domínguez, who won nearly five thousand races in his career.

Ramon Dekkers, Kickboxing, Netherlands, 1986–2006

Ramón Domínguez, Horse Racing (Jockey), Venezuela, 1996–2013

Ramón Fonst Segundo, Fencing (Foil/Épée), Cuba, 1900–1938

RANDY

Randy is traditionally a diminutive of names like *Randall*, *Randolph*, and others, though it can certainly stand on its own as well. Randy is tremendously popular among athletes, especially American ones, appearing all over the place in professional sports and many different events. Randys have had an impact on everything from pairs figure skating (with world champion Randy Gardner) to freestyle wrestling (with Olympic gold-medalist Randy Lewis), beach volleyball (with five-time world champion Randy Stoklos), and bowling (with thirteen-time PBA Tour-winner Randy Pedersen)!

Next let's see where multiple Randys have landed, starting with combat sports, like International Sport Karate Association World Heavyweight Muay Thai Champion kickboxer Randy Blake, who held two Xtreme Fighting League championships; and six-time UFC champion (heavyweight and light heavyweight) Randy "the Natural" Couture, who has gone from freestyle wrestling to service in the army to MMA fighting, acting, and more!

Lots of Randys love to play and compete outdoors, like Olympic gold-medalist shot putters Randy Matson and Randy Barnes; Paralympic gold-medalist wheelchair sprinter Randy Dorman; and Olympic gold-medalist long jumper Randy Williams. Then there are those who love to go fast, like fifteen-time national and world champion BMX racer Randy Stumpfhauser, and horse racing jockey Randy Romero, who won nearly 4,300 races in his thoroughbred career.

On the gridiron, Randys have been major playmakers, and the greatest include six-time Pro Bowl wide receiver and Hall of Famer Randy Moss, who led the NFL in receiving touchdowns six times; seven-time Pro Bowl Denver Broncos middle linebacker Randy Gradishar; and defensive tackle Randy "the Manster" White, whose thirteen years playing for the Dallas Cowboys resulted in nine Pro Bowl appearances, a Super Bowl championship, Super Bowl co-MVP award, and induction into the Pro Football Hall of Fame.

That just leaves America's pastime and another list of great Randys at the top of it; four-time All-Star Randy Myers led in saves three times and won the 1990 World Series, and Randy "the Big Unit" Johnson played in ten All-Star games; won the 2001 World Series, five Cy Young Awards, World Series MVP, and a Triple Crown; led the MLB in wins and nine times in strikeouts; threw a perfect game and a no-hitter (and hit a bird!); and was inducted into the Hall of Fame.

Randy is a great name with a huge lineage in sports and offers a lot of options, whether you want to use it as a nickname or give it to a son on its own. Your Randy has the potential to succeed in any field, whether athletic or otherwise, and if he works hard enough, he could become the next Natural, Manster, or Big Unit!

Eric Randolph "Randy" Barnes, Track & Field (Shot Put), USA, 1988–1996

Randy "Boom Boom" Blake, Kickboxing (Cruiserweight/Heavyweight), USA, 2007–current

Randall "Randy" (the Natural) Couture, MMA (Heavyweight), USA, 1997–2011

Randy Dorman, Para-Athletics, USA, 1988

Randy Gardner, Figure Skating, USA, 1973–1980

Randy Gradishar, Football (Middle Linebacker), Denver Broncos, USA, 1974–1983

Randall "Randy" (the Big Unit) Johnson, Baseball (Pitcher), Seattle Mariners, USA, 1988–2009

Randall "Randy" Lewis, Freestyle Wrestling, USA, 1980–1992

James Randel "Randy" Matson, Track & Field (Shot Put), USA, 1964–1972

Randy Moss, Football (Wide Receiver), Minnesota Vikings, USA, 1998–2012

Randall "Randy" Myers, Baseball (Pitcher), New York Mets, USA, 1985–1998

Randy Pedersen, Bowling, USA, 1985–2013

Randy Romero, Horse Racing (Jockey), USA, 1975–1999

Randy Stoklos, Beach Volleyball, USA, 1981–2008

Randall "Randy" Stumpfhauser, BMX, USA, 1988–2008

Randall "Randy" (the Manster) White, Football (Defensive Tackle), Dallas Cowboys, USA, 1975–1988

Randy Williams, Track & Field (Long Jump), USA, 1969–1987

RAÚL

Like *Randy* and numerous other "R" names, Raul comes from Old Norse roots for "counsel" and "wolf." One thing is apparent: add the accent to make it Raúl and you're looking at a potential star soccer player! It's likely a Raúl will be aggressive and looking to score, like three iconic forwards. Peruvian two-time MLS All-Star and CONCACAF Champions League Best XI Raúl Ruidíaz has won the MLS Cup and CONCACAF Champions League; Mexican Olympic gold-medalist and CONCACAF Gold Cup Golden Ball-winner Raúl Alonso Jiménez has taken home a CONCACAF Cup and a CONCACAF Gold Cup; and the man internationally known as Raúl (Raúl González) has a mighty record; in his over one thousand appearances, he scored nearly 450 goals; was awarded the Zarra Trophy four times, La Liga's Best Spanish Player a record five times, UEFA Club Forward of the Year three times, and FIFA 100 status; and won numerous trophies!

Raúl González Blanco, Soccer (Forward), Real Madrid Club de Fútbol, Spain, 1994–2015

Raúl Alonso Jiménez Rodríguez, Soccer (Forward), Wolverhampton Wanderers Football Club, Mexico, 2011–current

Raúl Mario Ruidíaz Misitich, Soccer (Forward), Seattle Sounders Football Club, Peru, 2008–current

RAY

While Ray is typically a diminutive of *Raymond*, it can serve the same function for other names, as well as stand on its own. And just as varied as its usage is the range of events and sports that Rays have conquered! Rays competing and winning on their own go back to the early 1900s with racecar driver Ray Harroun, who won the inaugural 1911 Indianapolis 500, and standing long jump, high jump, and triple jump specialist Ray Ewry, who proved to be the absolute best in the world by winning eight Olympic gold medals (and two at the 1906 Intercalated Games) and by setting multiple records.

Capturing wins and titles with their teammates have been men like English soccer left-back Ray Wilson, who won the 1966 FIFA World Cup; Australian four-time NSWRL premiership-winning rugby star Ray Price, who was awarded the Daily M and Rothmans Medals; and ten-time NBA All-Star shooting guard Ray Allen, who won NBA championships with the Boston Celtics and Miami Heat, as well as an Olympic gold medal!

A Ray in your family, whether nicknamed for *Raymond* or otherwise, may find his interests align with one of those varied sports, or he may dive into one of the fields where multiple Rays have succeeded before him. He may take a liking to cue sports, like three-time world champion straight pool pro Ray Martin, who earned his "Cool Cat" nickname by winning a tournament in California during an earthquake, or Welsh six-time World Snooker Champion Ray Reardon, who became the first player ranked number one in the world. If your son prefers playing in colder surroundings, he may find ice hockey more his speed, skating in the footsteps of Canadians Ray Whitney (two-time All-Star left wing and Stanley Cup champion) and Ray Bourque (thirteen-time All-Star defenseman and Stanley Cup champion, who is considered among the greatest players ever and was inducted into the Hockey Hall of Fame).

Several Rays have taken charge on the gridiron and can inspire a love of football in a young boy who shares their name, with Pro Football Hall of Famers like Raiders seven-time Pro Bowl and three-time Super Bowl champion punter Ray Guy, and middle linebacker Ray Lewis, whose seventeen-year career with the Baltimore Ravens saw him win two Super Bowls; earn thirteen Pro Bowl appearances; and be named a Super Bowl MVP, NFL Defensive Player of the Year twice, and NFL tackles leader.

Beyond all of that, there is a unique tradition among athletes known as Ray to reach the top of the rankings in the ring! This can be seen in boxing, with two of the all-time greatest, both nicknamed "Sugar." Sugar Ray Leonard took home an Olympic light welterweight boxing gold medal in 1976 before turning pro, ultimately accumulating a 36–3–1 record that included winning world championships five times in five different weight classes! Leonard routinely ranks among the top boxers of all time. His nickname, coined by a US Olympic Boxing Team coach, linked Leonard to the one-and-only Sugar Ray Robinson (Walker Smith Jr.). Robinson, often considered the best of the best, had a powerful amateur career before turning pro, with some estimations of an 85–0 record. As a professional boxer, he won welterweight and middleweight world championships seven times; achieved a record of 174 wins, nineteen losses, six draws, and two no contests; and was named everything from "fighter of the year" multiple times to "fighter of the century."

Walter Ray Allen Jr., Basketball (Shooting Guard), Milwaukee Bucks, USA, 1996–2014

Raymond "Ray" Bourque, Ice Hockey (Defense), Boston Bruins, Canada, 1979–2001

Raymond "Ray" Ewry, Track & Field (Standing Jumping), USA, 1900–1908

William Ray Guy, Football (Punter), Oakland Raiders, USA, 1973–1986

Ray Harroun, Auto Racing (Indianapolis 500), USA, 1903–1911

"Sugar" Ray Leonard, Boxing (Welterweight/Middleweight/Heavyweight), USA, 1972–1997

Raymond "Ray" Lewis Jr., Football (Middle Linebacker), Baltimore Ravens, USA, 1996–2012

Ray "Cool Cat" Martin, Pool (Straight), USA, 1968–1994

Raymond "Ray" Price, Rugby (Flanker/Breakaway/Lock), Parramatta Eels, Australia, 1971–1990

Raymond "Ray" Reardon, Snooker, Wales, 1967–1991

Walker "Sugar Ray Robinson" Smith Jr., Boxing (Lightweight/Welterweight/Middleweight/Heavyweight), USA, 1940–1965

Raymond "Ray" Whitney, Ice Hockey (Left Wing), San Jose Sharks, Canada, 1991–2014

Ramon "Ray" Wilson, Soccer (Left-Back), Huddersfield Town Association Football Club, England, 1952–1971

RAYMOND

The name Raymond may have evolved from Germanic roots for "counsel" and "protection," but in the modern-day, athletes with this name are precision attackers! When playing on a team, they can drive the ball forward or catch it to make touchdowns, like French FIFA World Cup All-Star Team and FIFA XI attacking midfielder Raymond Kopa, who won an Etoile d'Or, and six-time NFL Pro Bowl split end Raymond Berry, who won two NFL championships with the Baltimore Colts; led the NFL in receiving yards three times, receptions three times, and receiving touchdowns twice; and was inducted into the Pro Football Hall of Fame.

On the other hand, Raymonds who compete on their own can be fearsome opponents in the ring or octagon–skillfully finding their opponents' weaknesses–or marksmen with a keen eye and throwing hand, like World Association of Kickboxing Organizations world champion and Bellator Kickboxing Welterweight Champion Raymond Daniels and Dutch darts legend Raymond "Barney" van Barneveld, whose trophy case holds four world championships, two World Masters, two World Trophies, three International Darts League championships, four Finder Masters championships, and more!

Raymond Berry Jr., Football (Split End), Baltimore Colts, USA, 1955–1967

Raymond Daniels, Kickboxing/MMA (Welterweight), USA, 2006–current

Raymond Kopa, Soccer (Attacking Midfielder), Stade de Reims, France, 1949–1967

Raymond "Barney" van Barneveld, Darts, Netherlands, 1984–current

RED

Some nicknames are complicated, with convoluted origins in different languages and translations across history. And then some are just based on hair color! That's most often the case with "Red," though of course anyone is free to name their kids any way they like, and Red is a cool name on its own regardless. Hair color doesn't particularly matter more in one sport than another, though it's interesting to see just how many Reds there have been in baseball. Two of the greatest Hall of Fame MLB Reds are six-time All-Star and six-time World Series champion pitcher Red Ruffing, who led the American League in wins and strikeouts (all despite losing four toes as a child), and ten-time All-Star second baseman and NL stolen base leader Red Schoendienst, who won two World Series (and three more as a manager later).

Reds appearing at the top of other sports and events include stock car race driver Red Byron, who won NASCAR's first ever championship (Modified) and the first Strictly Stock championship (which would become the elite Cup Series) in 1948 and 1949, respectively; Dew Tour gold-medalist slopestyle snowboarder Red Gerard, who famously won an Olympic gold medal after waking up late and wearing a roommate's jacket; and, from Canada, six-time NHL All-Star, Stanley Cup champion, and Hall of Fame center Red Berenson and horse racing jockey Red Pollard, who is most famous for winning eighteen races with the legendary Seabiscuit.

See *Leonard* for Leonard "Red" Kelly.

Gordon "Red" Berenson, Ice Hockey (Center), St. Louis Blues, Canada, 1961–1978

Robert "Red" Byron, Auto Racing (NASCAR), USA, 1932–1951

Redmond "Red" Gerard, Snowboarding (Slopestyle), USA, 2017–current

John "Red" Pollard, Horse Racing (Jockey), Canada, 1925–1955

Charles Herbert "Red" Ruffing, Baseball (Pitcher), New York Yankees, USA, 1924–1947

Albert Fred "Red" Schoendienst, Baseball (Second Baseman), St. Louis Cardinals, USA, 1945–1963

REGGIE

Reggie is most often used as a diminutive of *Reginald* (from Germanic roots for "counsel," "power," or "authority"), though of course it can also be given to a child all on its own. Around the world, Reggies have varied sports interests, though here in the United States they're much more focused in a few popular team sports.

In the NBA, five-time All-Star shooting guard and three-point threat Reggie Miller became a member of the lofty 50–40–90 club, won an Olympic gold medal and FIBA world championship, continues to hold high rankings in three-point field goals and free throws, and was inducted into the Naismith Memorial Basketball Hall of Fame.

Moving outside, we'll take a look at gridiron football fields and top athletes there, like Indiana Colts six-time Pro Bowl wide receiver and Super Bowl champion Reggie Wayne, who led the league in receiving yards; and Hall of Fame defensive end Reggie White, who played in thirteen Pro Bowls, was named NFL Defensive Player of the Year twice, twice led the NFL in sacks, and won the Super Bowl with the Green Bay Packers in 1996.

Last but certainly not least are the baseball players named Reggies, notably seven-time All-Star outfielder Reggie Smith, who won a Gold Glove and the 1981 World Series with the Los Angeles Dodgers; and legendary Hall of Fame right fielder Reggie "Mr. October" Jackson, who played in fourteen All-Star games, won five World Series, was named World Series MVP twice, took home two Silver Sluggers, and led the American League in home runs four times and RBIs once!

Call a son Reggie and he's likely to enjoy playing on a team, finding his perfect position, and pulling his weight to help his teammates succeed.

Reginald "Reggie" (Mr. October) Jackson, Baseball (Right Fielder), Kansas City Athletics, USA, 1967–1987

Reginald "Reggie" Miller, Basketball (Shooting Guard), Indiana Pacers, USA, 1987–2005

Carl Reginald "Reggie" Smith, Baseball (Outfielder), Los Angeles Dodgers, USA, 1966–1984

Reginald "Reggie" Wayne, Football (Wide Receiver), Indianapolis Colts, USA, 2001–2014

Reginald "Reggie" White, Football (Defensive End), Philadelphia Eagles, USA, 1984–2000

REINER

If your family has German heritage and you love horses, then Reiner just might be the perfect name for your son! From Germanic roots for "counsel" and "army," this name hit the international stage in the 1960s with German equestrian dressage competitor Reiner Klimke. Over the course of his lengthy career, he would collect no fewer than six Olympic gold medals and six world championships, with additional bronze medals from both events too.

If you name a boy Reiner, you should definitely introduce him to horses and horseback riding!

Reiner Klimke, Equestrian (Dressage), Germany, 1960–1999

REX

A very old-fashioned name that was most popular from the 1920s to the '50s, Rex has extremely noble origins because it means "king" in Latin. Where have athletes with this name achieved royal glory? Early twentieth-century field hockey player Rex Norris won a gold medal with the India team at the 1928 Amsterdam Olympic Games, and Welsh rugby scrum half Rex Willis won four Five Nations Championships (and a Triple Crown and two Grand Slams along the way) in the 1940s and '50s.

Those are strong indicators that a boy named Rex will be a solid team player, though sometimes a Rex just needs to feel the wind in his face while going as fast as he can. That's borne out by NASCAR Grand National race driver Rex White, who, despite his small stature (135 pounds at five feet, four inches), had a towering career with twenty-eight wins and the 1960 championship.

Reginald "Rex" Norris, Field Hockey (Back/Half-Back), India, 1918–1928

Rex White, Auto Racing (NASCAR), USA, 1954–1964

William Rex Willis, Rugby (Scrum Half), Barbarian Football Club, Wales, 1949–1955

RICARDO

Portuguese and Spanish have given us Ricardo, a popular variation on *Richard* (from Old German meaning "brave" or "firm ruler"). Ricardos can mainly be found competing and winning outside in the sun, like Argentinian golfer Ricardo González, who has won twenty-eight professional events, and two Brazilian world champions named Ricardo Santos, one in windsurfing and the other in beach volleyball (the latter also won an Olympic gold medal)!

Meanwhile, the most famous Ricardo is better known as "Kaká," the Brazilian football attacking midfielder also known as Ricardo Leite, whose list of awards and trophies is extensive to say the least. Considered one of the greatest of his time (as well as all time), Kaká posted wins including a FIFA Club World Cup, FIFA Confederations Cup twice, and the 2002 FIFA World Cup, while his awards and accolades include a Ballon d'Or, FIFA World Player of the Year, FIFPro World Player of the Year, FIFPro World XI three times, UEFA Team of the Year three times, Bola de Ouro, Bola de Prata, FIFA Club World Cup Golden Ball, Time 100 twice, MLS All-Star three times, and many more.

The name Ricardo is definitely recommended for families who love soccer, but it's also great for anyone looking to have a competitive kid who will enjoy all sorts of interesting activities.

Ricardo González, Golf, Argentina, 1986–current

Ricardo "Kaká" Izecson dos Santos Leite, Soccer (Attacking Midfielder), Associazione Calcio Milan, Brazil, 2000–2017

Ricardo Santos, Beach Volleyball, Brazil, 2000–current

Ricardo Santos, Windsurfing, Brazil, 1999–current

RICHARD

Many Richards end up going by a diminutive or nickname (see *Dick*, *Rick*, *Richi/Richie*, and *Rickey/Ricky*), but there is a lot of strength and speed in the full name that comes from Old German roots for "brave ruler." These include pioneers and record setters, runners, drivers, riders, and more. Hungarian Greco-Roman wrestler Richárd Weisz took home Olympic gold in 1908, and, more recently, cornerback Richard Sherman secured his fame on the football field with five Pro Bowl appearances, an interceptions leader ranking, and a Super Bowl championship.

Many Richards love to go fast, sometimes on foot, like Kenyan world champion long-distance runner Richard Limo, British world champion sprinter Richard Kilty, and Olympic gold-medalist sprinter Richard "Torpedo" Thompson of Trinidad and Tobago. However, with horsepower, Richards really blow away the competition! English horse racing jockey Richard Johnson has over 3,800 wins, which rank him second overall in the National Hunt Racing series, while on the tracks of NASCAR, Richard Petty is and always will be the King. Petty set (and still holds) numerous records in stock car racing, his two hundred wins and seven championships in NASCAR's top series are still among the top rankings, and his name appears in numerous Halls of Fame and on top drivers of all time lists.

Name a son Richard and he's likely to love going fast; be prepared to zoom him around in his stroller before he graduates to bikes, horses, and, eventually, cars!

- **Richard Johnson**, Horse Racing (Jockey), England, 1994–2021
- **Richard Kilty**, Track & Field (Sprinting), England, 2012–current
- **Richard Limo**, Long-Distance Running, Kenya, 1999–2011
- **Richard Petty**, Auto Racing (NASCAR), USA, 1958–1992
- **Richard Sherman**, Football (Cornerback), Seattle Seahawks, USA, 2011–current
- **Richard "Torpedo" Thompson**, Track & Field (Sprinting), Trinidad & Tobago, 2007–current
- **Richárd Weisz**, Greco-Roman Wrestling, Hungary, 1899–1912

RICHI/RICHIE

You have many choices of nicknames when it comes to naming a kid *Richard* (as you can see throughout this chapter and beyond), each with their own specific style and athletic traditions. The lesser heard Richi is ideal for someone who loves to get out on the slopes, like German two-time world champion ski jumper Richard "Richi" Freitag, who took home sixteen World Cup wins, while the more standard Richie is perfect for a team player who wants to compete alongside his best friends and share in their victories!

Here in the United States, soccer midfielder Richie Williams won the MLS Cup three times, CONCACAF Champions' Cup, and CONCACAF Gold Cup, and baseball Hall of Famer Richie Ashburn led the National League in batting and stolen bases while earning six All-Star appearances.

Fans down under have rugby, with legendary New Zealand flanker/number 8 Richie McCaw, who is a three-time World Rugby Player of the Year and World Rugby Player of the Decade and has set multiple records and won an astounding number of championships and trophies, including two Rugby World Cups, National Provincial Championship five times, Super Rugby Championship four times, Tri-Nations seven times, three Grand Slams, the Bledisloe Cup eight times, and more!

- **Don Richard "Richie" Ashburn**, Baseball (Center Fielder), Philadelphia Phillies, USA, 1948–1962
- **Richard "Richi" Freitag**, Ski Jumping, Germany, 2010–2022
- **Richard "Richie" McCaw**, Rugby (Flanker/Number 8), Crusaders, New Zealand, 2000–2015
- **Richard "Richie" Williams**, Soccer (Midfielder), D.C. United, USA, 1992–2005

RICK

Rick is often a nickname for *Richard*, but not always. And like the champion athletes with that longer name, Ricks can be found in a number of fields to inspire a sporting son in your family. Tennis doubles player Rick Leach reached the world number one spot with forty-six titles and five Grand Slams, Canadian paraplegic athlete Rick Hansen took home six medals from Paralympic Games (half of them gold) in wheelchair racing events, and eight-time NBA All-Star and Hall of Fame small forward Rick Barry led the league in scoring and steals, was named Finals MVP, and won an NBA championship (along with an ABA championship with four ABA All-Star appearances).

Some Ricks prefer to go fast and ride their way to victory, either with horses (like two-time world champion chuckwagon driver and rodeo star Rick Fraser and horse racing jockey Rick Wilson, who won nearly five thousand races) or race cars (like multiple motorsport Hall of Famer Rick Mears, who won the Indianapolis 500 four times, as well as twenty-six races and three championships in Champ Car)!

If your little Rick likes to go fast, then let him check out horse riding or go-karts, otherwise he may find success in just about any other sport, from tennis to basketball.

Richard "Rick" Barry III, Basketball (Small Forward), Golden State Warriors, USA, 1965–1980

Rick Fraser, Rodeo (Chuckwagon Racing), Canada, 1976–2018

Richard "Rick" Hansen, Wheelchair Racing, Canada, 1980–1987

Rick Leach, Tennis, USA, 1987–2011

Rick Mears, Auto Racing (Champ Car), USA, 1976–1992

Rick Wilson, Horse Racing (Jockey), USA, 1972–2007

RICKEY/RICKY

The last of the main variations, nicknames, and diminutives of *Richard* is Rickey/Ricky, though they can be short for other names as well. We see winners with these names concentrated in a couple different sports, though there are outliers, like two-time Olympic (demonstration) gold-medalist water skier Ricky McCormick, who won tricks and jumping world championships and was inducted into the Water Skiing Hall of Fame. Meanwhile, the incomparable Ricky Carmichael has competed on two and four wheels in NASCAR and beyond, excelling in motocross with five X Games medals (three of them gold) and no fewer than 150 wins and sixteen championships across the different AMA series!

Over on the gridiron, running back Ricky Williams was the league's rushing yards leader and played in the Pro Bowl in 2002, while New Orleans Saints seven-time Pro Bowl linebacker Rickey Jackson led the NFL in forced fumbles four times and was inducted into the Pro Football Hall of Fame.

Among the best-of-the-best in their respective team sports have been MLB ten-time All-Star left fielder and Hall of Famer Rickey "Man of Steal" Henderson, who was the AL stolen base leader twelve times, won two World Series, and earned a Gold Glove and three Silver Slugger Awards while setting multiple records, and Australian cricket batting legend Ricky Ponting, who stands amongst the best batsmen of all time with multiple records, wins including three Cricket World Cups and two Champions Trophies, accolades like Cricketer of the Decade 2000, and induction into the ICC Hall of Fame.

Rickeys and Rickys are tremendous athletes, and a boy in your family with one of these names has wide-open possibilities. Let him discover where his talents lie and support him on his journey toward inevitable success!

Richard "Ricky" Carmichael, Motorcycle Racing (Motocross/Supercross)/Auto Racing (NASCAR), USA, 1997–2011

Rickey "Man of Steal" Henderson, Baseball (Left Fielder), Oakland Athletics, USA, 1979–2003

Rickey Jackson, Football (Linebacker), New Orleans Saints, USA, 1981–1995

Ricky McCormick, Water Skiing, USA, 1960–1982

Ricky Ponting, Cricket (Top-Order Batsman), Tasmanian Cricket Team, Australia, 1992–2013

Errick "Ricky" Miron (Williams Jr.), Football (Running Back), Miami Dolphins, USA, 1999–2011

RIDDICK

While the name Riddick has roots in an obscure Scottish and Northern Irish place name, in the world of boxing, it's synonymous with one of the great heavyweight champions. Riddick Bowe went pro in 1989, and only three years later achieved undisputed heavyweight champion of the world status by defeating Evander Holyfield! Bowe lost only one match in his career (a re-match against Holyfield); won forty-three fights; became the very first boxer to unify a title by winning all four major belts in the World Boxing Association, World Boxing Council, International Boxing Federation, and World Boxing Organization; and was inducted into the International Boxing Hall of Fame. Riddick is definitely a tough name that you can give to your little heavyweight, ensuring he'll be able to confront his opponents and stay standing no matter what.

Riddick Bowe, Boxing (Heavyweight), USA, 1989–2008

ROALD

Whether or not your family has Norwegian lineage, if you're looking for an interesting "R" name and hoping for a kid who likes ice skating, consider Roald, which comes from Old Norse roots that can mean "famous rulers." Norway has given the world two famous rulers of the speed skating world with this name, world champion Roald Larsen and Olympic gold-medalist Roald Aas.

Roald Aas, Speed Skating, Norway, 1951–1960

Roald Larsen, Speed Skating, Norway, 1921–1928

ROB

Rob, like *Robbie/Robby*, came about as a diminutive of the name *Robert*. There are fewer Robs who have made it into the "bright fame" promised by the Germanic name origin, but they've made quite an impact in a few different places. In gridiron football, two-time Pro Bowl wide receiver Rob Moore led the NFL in receiving yards, and five-time Pro Bowl tight end Rob "Gronk" Gronkowski ranks among the best players in his position, leading in receiving touchdowns, setting multiple NFL records, and winning four Super Bowls.

But that's not all. Champion Robs have also appeared in everything from rowing (with Australian world champion Rob Mitchell) to table tennis (with British Paralympic gold-medalist Rob Davies), rugby (with English World Rugby Hall of Fame fly-half Rob Andrew, who won a Premiership and Grand Slam), and long-distance running (with Australian marathon world champion and winner of multiple international marathons Rob de Castella)!

Whether he's called it as a nickname or given it on his birth certificate, a young Rob in your family has wide-open athletic potential!

Christopher Robert "Rob" Andrew, Rugby (Fly-Half), Newcastle Falcons, England, 1985–1999

Francois Robert "Rob" de Castella, Marathon, Australia, 1977–1993

Robert "Rob" Davies, Table Tennis, Wales, 2007–current

Robert "Rob" Gronkowski, Football (Tight End), New England Patriots, USA, 2010–2021

Rob Mitchell, Rowing, Australia, 1995–2003

Robert "Rob" Moore, Football (Wide Receiver), Arizona Cardinals, USA, 1990–2002

ROBBIE/ROBBY

As with *Rob*, Robbie and Robby are nearly always diminutives of *Robert*. Whether he uses it as a shortened form or is called Robbie or Robby straight out, a boy with this name will have a good chance to have a penchant for going fast in one way or another and love excitement . . . and even danger. There's no place they can't succeed, and they've popped up in everything from MMA (with UFC welterweight and EliteXC middleweight champion "Ruthless" Robbie Lawler) to rugby (with Australian hooker/halfback Robbie Farah, who won two Premierships, the 2005 NRL grand final, and the 2009 Rugby League Four Nations).

On the fields of international football (or soccer here in the US), English UEFA Fair Play Award-winner Robbie Fowler won an FA Cup, UEFA Cup, and UEFA Super Cup; and Irish MLS All-Star and MVP Robbie Keane scored nearly four hundred goals across his entire career while winning an MLS Cup and Nations Cup and being named MLS Cup MVP, and MLS Best XI four times.

Getting to the fastest Robbies and Robbys, first we hit the horse track with American thoroughbred jockeys Robbie Davis, who won nearly 3,400 races from 1981 to 2002, and Robby Albarado, who has survived all sorts of injuries, has a partially titanium skull, and has won over 5,200 races! Last but absolutely not least are the true daredevils: motorcycle stunt drivers. Australian Robbie Maddison's accomplishments include setting the world record for distance ridden on water by surfing with a dirt bike and setting the world record for motorcycle jump distance, while Robbie Knievel (son of Evel) broke and set multiple records by jumping all manner of obstacles and gaps all around the world.

Robby Albarado, Horse Racing (Jockey), USA, 1990–current

Robbie Davis, Horse Racing (Jockey), USA, 1981–2002

Robert "Robbie" Farah, Rugby (Hooker/Halfback), Wests Tigers, Australia, 2002–2019

Robert "Robbie" Fowler, Soccer (Striker), Liverpool Football Club, England, 1993–2012

Robert "Robbie" Keane, Soccer (Striker), LA Galaxy, Ireland, 1997–2018

Robert "Robbie" Knievel, Motorcycle Stunt Performing, USA, 1989–2011

Robert "Robbie" (Ruthless) Lawler, MMA (Welterweight/Middleweight), USA, 2001–current

Robert "Robbie" Maddison, Motorcycle Stunt Performing, Australia, 2004–2017

ROBERT

With Germanic roots for "bright" and "fame," Roberts around the world work and strive toward their name's glorious origins. With its immense and evergreen popularity, it should come as no surprise that the name Robert has achieved fame all across the sporting world, and in many cases, multiple times within the same discipline. We'll get to those, but first some singular examples, like Austrian Olympic gold-medalist weightlifter Robert Fein, who set twenty-three world records in the early 1900s; French four-time Paralympic gold-medalist and three-time world champion wheelchair fencer Robert Citerne; and Scottish Triple Crown–winning rugby star Robert Shaw, who was called the "greatest player of his generation."

Indoors on the hardwood court, clutch power forward/small forward Robert Horry set records for his seven NBA championships with three different teams, playoff three-pointers, and Finals steals, while Hall of Fame center Robert Parish played in nine All-Star games and won four championships, setting a record for 1,611 games played in the process.

In the water, freestyle swimmer Robert Welbourn of England collected two gold medals, two silvers, and a bronze from Paralympic Games; and American swimmer

Robert Finke has won gold and silver at World Championships and two Olympic gold medals. On skates, Canadian pairs figure skater Robert Paul took home four world championships and Olympic gold, and Dutch speed skater Robert Rintje Ritsma became a two-time World Single Distance and four-time World Allround champion.

Roberts love becoming world champions on the water, including rowers Robert Chambers of England in the late 1800s and Australian Robert Richards a hundred years later, British sprint canoeists Robert Joce and Robert Owen, and Brazilian sailing legend Robert Scheidt, who took home five medals from the Olympics (including two golds) and seventeen from World Championships (a dozen of them being wins)!

Interestingly, by far the largest concentration of famous athletic Roberts have found their success in track and field events. At the highest end are Canadian Olympic gold-medalist and two-time world champion sprinter Robert Esmie, German Olympic gold-medalist and three-time world champion discus thrower Robert Harting, Kenyan five-time world champion marathon runner and four-time Boston Marathon-winner Robert "Mwafrika" Cheruiyot, Canadian six-time Paralympic gold-medalist wheelchair racer Robert Easton, Polish four-time Olympic gold-medalist and three-time world champion racewalker Robert Korzeniowski, and blind British eight-time Paralympic gold-medalist runner Robert Matthews.

Even in such a crowded field, a couple of athletes stand out for their accomplishments, and perhaps for their ability to inspire a new generation of boys striving to succeed and make their marks upon the world, like top-ranked Polish soccer striker Robert Lewandowski who has scored more than 650 goals in over 930 senior and international appearances. His teams have won dozens of trophies, while on a personal level, Lewandowski has earned the Ballon d'Or Striker of the Year twice, European Golden Shoe twice, The Best FIFA Men's Player twice, FIFA Club World Cup Golden Ball, UEFA Men's Player of the Year, Golden Foot, World Soccer Player of the Year twice, four Guinness World Records, and much more.

And then there's Robert "The Runningman" Garside, whose claim-to-fame is nothing less than being the first person to run around the world! That almost unimaginable feat took over five-and-a-half years and covered thirty-five thousand miles traversing twenty-nine countries on six continents; the run has been confirmed by numerous witnesses, reenactors, the Guinness World Record organization, and more.

- **Robert Chambers**, Rowing, England, 1853–1868
- **Robert "Mwafrika" Cheruiyot**, Marathon, Kenya, 2002–2011
- **Robert Citerne**, Wheelchair Fencing (Foil/Épée/Sabre), France, 1987–2014
- **Robert Easton**, Para-Athletics, Canada, 1977–1988
- **Robert Esmie**, Track & Field (Sprinting), Canada, 1993–1997
- **Robert Fein**, Weightlifting, Austria, 1929–1937
- **Robert Finke**, Swimming (Freestyle), USA, 2017–current
- **Robert "The Runningman" Garside**, Long-Distance Running, England, 1996–2007
- **Robert Harting**, Track & Field (Discus), Germany, 2001–2018
- **Robert Horry**, Basketball (Power Forward/Small Forward), Los Angeles Lakers, USA, 1992–2008
- **Robert Joce**, Slalom Canoeing, England, 1981–1983
- **Robert Korzeniowski**, Track & Field (Racewalking), Poland, 1990–2004

- **Robert Lewandowski**, Soccer (Striker), Fußball-Club Bayern München e. V., Poland, 2005–current
- **Robert Matthews**, Track & Field (Middle-Distance Running), England/New Zealand, 1984–2004
- **Robert Owen**, Slalom Canoeing, England, 1981–1983
- **Robert Parish**, Basketball (Center), Boston Celtics, USA, 1976–1997
- **Robert Paul**, Figure Skating, Canada, 1955–1960
- **Robert Richards**, Rowing, Australia, 1997–2000
- **Robert Rintje Ritsma**, Speed Skating, Netherlands, 1988–2008
- **Robert Scheidt**, Sailing, Brazil, 1985–current
- **Robert Shaw**, Rugby (Fly-Half/Wing/Center), Cities District, Scotland, 1934–1939
- **Robert Welbourn**, Swimming (Freestyle), England, 2004–2014

ROBERTO

We've looked at multiple diminutives of the name *Robert*, but going internationally, we can also find variants in other languages, like the Italian, Portuguese, and Spanish Roberto. Even more than those other names, athletes named Roberto really congregate and succeed in certain events with only a handful of outliers like fencing; Roberto Ferrari is a two-time fencing world champion and Paralympian Roberto Marson won twenty-six medals (sixteen of them gold) across fencing, swimming, and throwing events!

You have to be careful getting in a ring or octagon with a Roberto, especially if they're anything like Brazilian Abu Dhabi Combat Club World Champion and seven-time World No-Gi Champion jiu-jitsu ultra-heavyweight Roberto "Cyborg" Abreu, Italian Olympic gold-medalist and two-time world champion super heavyweight boxer Roberto Cammarelle, or Panamanian boxing phenom Roberto "Manos de Piedra" (Hands of Stone) Durán, who collected world championships in four different weight classes across a record-tying five decades of bouts.

How about international football? Attacking midfielder Roberto Rivellino was on Brazil's 1970 FIFA World Cup-winning team and was named to the FIFA 100 Greatest Living Footballers in 2004, while much more recently, Roberto Carlos became one of the top-ranked left-backs of all time by playing in over 1,100 senior and international games; winning dozens of trophies including the 2002 FIFA World Cup; and being awarded a similar number of accolades. And from Italy came Roberto Baggio (the "Divine Ponytail"), who appears on many lists of top forwards and was awarded everything from World Soccer's World Player of the Year 1993 to the Ballon d'Or, FIFA World Player of the Year, Onze d'Or/de Bronze/d'Argent, Onze de Onze three times, FIFA World Club Silver Ball, FIFA World Cup All-Star Team, World Soccer's Greatest Players of the Twentieth Century, FIFA World Cup Dream Team, Golden Foot, and more.

Robertos have also made big plays on the baseball diamond. Two Puerto Rican two-time World Series champions and Hall of Famers are synonymous with America's pastime: twelve-time All-Star second baseman Roberto Alomar, who took home ten Gold Glove Awards and four Silver Sluggers, and Pittsburgh Pirates right fielder Roberto Clemente, who scored fifteen All-Star appearances, four NL batting championships, an NL MVP, twelve Gold Gloves, and more!

Consider the name Roberto for a son who will be a true team player, bringing glory and fame to himself and his team members—whether that's on or off the field.

- **Roberto "Cyborg" de Abreu Filho**, Brazilian Jiu-Jitsu, Brazil, 2001–current
- **Roberto Alomar Velázquez**, Baseball (Second Baseman), Toronto Blue Jays, Puerto Rico, 1988–2004

Roberto "Divine Ponytail" Baggio, Soccer (Forward/Attacking Midfielder), Juventus Football Club, Italy, 1982–2004

Roberto Cammarelle, Boxing (Super Heavyweight), Italy, 2002–2013

Roberto Carlos da Silva Rocha, Soccer (Left-Back/Defensive Midfielder), Real Madrid Club de Fútbol, Brazil, 1991–2016

Roberto Clemente Walker, Baseball (Right Fielder), Pittsburgh Pirates, Puerto Rico, 1955–1972

Roberto "Manos de Piedra" Durán Samaniego, Boxing (Lightweight/Welterweight/Light Middleweight/Middleweight), Panama, 1968–2001

Roberto Ferrari, Fencing (Sabre/Foil), Italy, 1950-1960

Roberto Marson, Wheelchair Fencing (Épée/Foil/Sabre)/Para-Athletics/Swimming (Freestyle/Breaststroke/Backstroke), Italy, 1964–1982

Roberto Rivellino, Soccer (Attacking Midfielder), Sport Club Corinthians Paulista, Brazil, 1965–1981

ROBIN/ROBYN

A unisex name with at least one notable variant in Robyn, Robin arose in medieval English as yet another diminutive of *Robert*. From examples in the wide world of sports, it's clear that Robins particularly excel at working and succeeding with others, dominating team sports in the United States and around the world. These include sports like soccer (with Dutch two-time Premier League Golden Boot striker Robin van Persie, who won a UEFA Cup, KNVB Cup, and FA Cup), and ice hockey (with defenseman Robyn Regehr, who won the Stanley Cup with the Los Angeles Kings and a World Cup with his native Canada team).

Cricket has seen numerous Robins reach the highest rankings. Indian all-rounder Robindra "Robin" Singh scored nearly seven thousand runs in first-class cricket and won the Ranji Trophy and Titan Cup, and Indian batsman/wicketkeeper Robin Uthappa was a top scorer and part of the 2007 ICC World Twenty20-winning team.

Over on the baseball diamond, two-time All-Star third baseman Robin Ventura won six Gold Gloves and an Olympic gold medal with Team USA, Robin Yount was a three-time All-Star and two-time AL MVP shortstop and center fielder with the Milwaukee Brewers and won a Gold Glove and three Silver Slugger Awards, and seven-time All-Star starting pitcher Robin Roberts led the MLB in wins four times and strikeouts twice; both Yount and Roberts were inducted into the Hall of Fame.

Robyn Regehr, Ice Hockey (Defense), Calgary Flames, Canada, 1999–2015

Robin Roberts, Baseball (Pitcher), Philadelphia Phillies, USA, 1948–1966

Robindra "Robin" Singh, Cricket (All-Rounder), Tamil Nadu Cricket Team, India, 1983–2001

Robin Uthappa, Cricket (Batsman/Wicketkeeper), Royal Challengers Bangalore, India, 2002–2023

Robin van Persie, Soccer (Striker), Arsenal Football Club, Netherlands, 2001–2019

Robin Ventura, Baseball (Third Baseman), Chicago White Sox, USA, 1989–2004

Robin Yount, Baseball (Shortstop/Center Fielder), Milwaukee Brewers, USA, 1974–1993

ROCCO/ROCKY

Rocco and its common diminutive (and general nickname) Rocky come from an old Germanic root that seems to mean "rook" or "crow." When it comes to sports, NFL running back Rocky Bleier won four Super Bowl championships with the Pittsburgh Steelers; Australian rugby star Rocky Elsom made it onto top flankers lists with a Premiership, European Cup, and two Heineken Cup wins; and German endurance race driver Rocky

Rockenfeller has won 24 Hours of Daytona, 24 Hours of Nürburgring, and 24 Hours of Le Mans races. Rockys love baseball, with outfielder Rocky Colavito, who played in nine All-Star games and led the American League in home runs and RBIs, hit four home runs in one game, and whose trade perhaps led to a curse on the Cleveland Indians . . .

Meanwhile, art imitates life and life imitates art with a huge number of Rockys in boxing! Rocky Balboa may have gotten the silver screen glory, but real-life accolades have gone to boxers like British WBA super-middleweight champion Rocky Fielding, who ended his career with a 30–3 record. In the 1940s, the world was introduced to two of the greatest Rockys of all time: world middleweight champion Rocky Graziano perfected the knockout punch with a 67–10–6 record, including fifty-two KOs, and Rocky Marciano was the only undefeated world heavyweight champion ever with a 49–0 career and numerous records!

A Rocco or Rocky in your family may not find everlasting glory in the sweet science of boxing, but wherever he ends up, he'll be a fighter and push towards his goals with all of his strength.

- **Thomas Rocco "Rocky Graziano" Barbella**, Boxing (Welterweight/Middleweight), USA, 1942–1952
- **Robert "Rocky" Bleier**, Football (Running Back), Pittsburgh Steelers, USA, 1968–1980
- **Rocco "Rocky" Colavito Jr.**, Baseball (Outfielder), Cleveland Indians, USA, 1955–1968
- **Rocky Elsom**, Rugby (Flanker), New South Wales Waratahs, Australia, 2008–2014
- **Michael "Rocky" Fielding**, Boxing (Super-Middleweight/Light-Heavyweight), England, 2010–2022
- **Rocco "Rocky" Marciano**, Boxing (Heavyweight), USA, 1947–1956
- **Mike "Rocky" Rockenfeller**, Auto Racing (24 Hours of Le Mans), Germany, 2001–current

ROD

If there's one thing that links *Roderic*s, *Roderick*s, *Rodney*s, *Rodrigo*s, and more, it's that they can also be called by the short yet powerful diminutive Rod! A longtime nickname for a multitude of names, Rod is an all-weather favorite of athletes and has been used by some very successful competitors. Ice hockey has witnessed the exploits of Canadians NHL All-Star center and Stanley Cup champion Rod Brind'Amour, who won a World Championship with his national team, and Hall of Fame New York Rangers right wing Rod Gilbert, who played in eight All-Star games; while on the gridiron, Denver Broncos three-time Pro Bowl wide receiver Rod Smith led the NFL in receptions and won two Super Bowls, and cornerback Rod Woodson's eleven Pro Bowl appearances, Super Bowl championship, two NFL interceptions leader titles, records, and more led to his induction into the Pro Football Hall of Fame.

One Rod is famous for his baseball achievements: eighteen-time MLB All-Star first and second baseman and Hall of Famer Rod Carew, who was the AL batting champion seven times.

If you appreciate the sporting history and competitive nature of these athletes, then consider giving this name to your son; you can put any of the variety of "Rod-" names on his birth certificate or cut out the middleman and name him Rod outright. Either way, you may have a champion baseball infielder or football or ice hockey player on your hands.

- **Roderic "Rod" Brind'Amour**, Ice Hockey (Center), Carolina Hurricanes, Canada, 2011–current
- **Rodney "Rod" Carew**, Baseball (First Baseman/Second Baseman), Minnesota Twins, Panama, 1967–1985
- **Rodrigue "Rod" Gilbert**, Ice Hockey (Right Wing), New York Rangers, Canada, 1960–1978

- **Roderick "Rod" Smith**, Football (Wide Receiver), Denver Broncos, USA, 1994–2007
- **Roderick "Rod" Woodson**, Football (Cornerback), Pittsburgh Steelers, USA, 1987–2003

RODGER/ROGER/ROGERS

Roger, and its various alternate forms like Rodger and Rogers, may come from old Germanic roots meaning "famous spear," but the name has spread to many different places around the world and is used by all sorts of people (not just warriors). The athletic accomplishments achieved by these men are very impressive and range from cycling's Roger Ilegems of Belgium and rowing's Roger Jackson of Canada both winning Olympic gold medals, to auto racing's Rodger Ward winning the Indianapolis 500 twice and seizing twenty-six checkered flags and two championships in Champ Car, and cricket's Indian all-rounder Roger Binny winning the 1983 Cricket World Cup and 1985 World Championship of Cricket!

On American football fields, running back Roger Craig played most of his ten-year career with the San Francisco 49ers and had four Pro Bowl appearances and three Super Bowl wins (and was the first player to score three touchdowns in a Super Bowl), and Dallas Cowboys six-time Pro Bowl quarterback Roger Staubach led his team to two Super Bowl championships while being named Super Bowl MVP and NFL Man of the Year, leading the league in passing touchdowns and passer rating four times, and being inducted into the Hall of Fame.

America's pastime has seen three legendary players with these names, starting with Hall of Fame second baseman Rogers "the Rajah" Hornsby, who is considered one of the greatest batters of all time with a World Series championship in 1926, two NL MVPs, two Triple Crowns, seven NL batting championships, and two NL home run leader and four NL RBI leader titles. Twenty years after Hornsby's career ended, right fielder Roger Maris stepped up to the plate, setting home run records, playing in seven All-Star games, winning three World Series championships with the Yankees and Cardinals, and earning a Gold Glove, two AL MVPs, an AL home run leader title, and the AL RBI leader ranking twice. Last but certainly not least is eleven-time All-Star pitcher Roger Clemens, who won two World Series championships and seven Cy Young Awards; led the MLB in wins five times, ERA seven times, and AL strikeouts five times; and set multiple records, including twice throwing twenty strikeouts in standard nine-inning games.

Other Rogers forge ahead on their own to set world records and achieve fame and fortune, like English middle-distance runner Roger Bannister, who ran the first recorded sub-four-minute mile, and, of course, Swiss tennis phenom Roger Federer, who won Olympic gold and silver, held the world number one singles rank for 310 weeks overall (with a record consecutive stretch of 237 weeks), and ranks second of all time in titles (with 103 and twenty majors).

As you can see, a little boy named Roger (or Rodger or Rogers) can have tremendous athletic potential and can find lots of inspiration from other Rogers who have come before him.

- **Roger Bannister**, Track & Field (Middle-Distance Running), England, 1948–1954
- **Roger Binny**, Cricket (All-Rounder), India Men's National Cricket Team, India, 1979–1987
- **William Roger Clemens**, Baseball (Pitcher), Boston Red Sox, USA, 1984–2007
- **Roger Craig**, Football (Running Back), San Francisco 49ers, USA, 1983–1993
- **Roger Federer**, Tennis, Switzerland, 1998–2022
- **Rogers "the Rajah" Hornsby**, Baseball (Second Baseman), St. Louis Cardinals, USA, 1915–1937

Roger Ilegems, Road/Track Cycling, Belgium, 1984–1991

Roger Jackson, Rowing, Canada, 1964–1972

Roger Maris, Baseball (Right Fielder), New York Yankees, USA, 1957–1968

Roger Staubach, Football (Quarterback), Dallas Cowboys, USA, 1969–1979

Rodger Ward, Auto Racing (Champ Car), USA, 1950–1966

RODRIGO

Rodrigo may have come about as an Italian, Portuguese, and Spanish variant of *Roderick* (from German roots for "fame" and "ruler"), but three champions with this name who have raised their fists to the sky in glory have all come from Brazil. Mixed martial artist Rodrigo Gracie, of the famed Gracie family, was an Abu Dhabi Combat Club Submission Fighting World Champion; equestrian show jumper Rodrigo Pessoa leapt to Olympic gold and bronze, a world championship, and over seventy Grand Prix wins; and beach soccer forward Rodrigo da Costa has won around the world with a trophy collection including the Euro Winners Cup twice, Intercontinental Cup three times, FIFA Beach Soccer World Cup 2017, and World Beach Games 2019!

You don't have to have Brazilian heritage to name a son Rodrigo, but if you do, he may enjoy combat sports, riding horses, and playing team sports on the beach.

Rodrigo da Costa, Beach Soccer (Forward), BSC Kristall, Brazil, 2014–current

Rodrigo Gracie, MMA (Middleweight/Light-Heavyweight), Brazil, 1998–2006

Rodrigo Pessoa, Equestrian (Jumping), Brazil, 1981–2014

ROMAN

As with so many other things from the Roman Empire, the name Roman has spread all around the world, so you can find champion Romans from many different countries and in many different sports and events. Just some of those include chess, with Israeli-American Grandmaster and theoretician Roman Dzindzichashvili; boxing, with Israeli former IBO heavyweight world champion Roman Greenberg; track and field, with Czech multi-talented Roman Šebrle, who solidified his position among the best-ever with Olympic and world championship gold and silver in decathlon and multiple world championships in heptathlon; and luge, with Russian three-time world champion and nine-time World Cup-winner Roman Repilov.

Some sports and positions seem particularly favored by Romans, starting with playing defense on the ice! That's proven by Czech Olympic gold-medalist and three-time NHL All-Star Roman Hamrlík and Swiss Nashville Predators four-time All-Star Roman Josi. On the gridiron, four-time Pro Bowl quarterback Roman Gabriel was NFL MVP and led the league in passing yards and passing touchdowns twice. Greco-Roman wrestling has long been a popular sport in Russia, as evidenced by Soviet Roman Rurua, who won Olympic gold and silver and four world championships, and Russian two-time Olympic gold-medalist, three-time world champion, and two-time World Cup-winner Roman Vlasov.

No matter where in the world your family comes from, you can consider the name Roman for a son who may enjoy wrestling, football, ice hockey, or any other mental or physical exercise!

Roman Dzindzichashvili, Chess, Israel/USA, 1966–current

Roman Gabriel Jr., Football (Quarterback), Los Angeles Rams, USA, 1962–1977

Roman Greenberg, Boxing (Heavyweight), Israel, 1999–2009

Roman Hamrlík, Ice Hockey (Defense), New York Islanders, Czech Republic, 1990–2013

Roman Josi, Ice Hockey (Defense), Nashville Predators, Switzerland, 2007–current

Roman Repilov, Luge, Russia, 2015–current

Roman Rurua, Greco-Roman Wrestling, USSR, 1964–1972

Roman Šebrle, Track & Field (Decathlon/Heptathlon), Czech Republic, 1991–2013

Roman Vlasov, Greco-Roman Wrestling, Russia, 2011–current

RON

Ronalds may compete and succeed on their own or as part of teams, but Rons are always at their best when they're working with others on or off the field, diamond, rink, or sand. This is proven by members of various Halls of Fame, including beach volleyball legend Ron Von Hagen, who won sixty-two Open Beach Tournaments; Canadian four-time NHL All-Star center and two-time Stanley Cup champion Ron Francis; and nine-time AFL All-Star offensive tackle Ron Mix, who won the AFL championship in 1963 with the San Diego Chargers.

Rons love baseball in particular, with four-time All-Star New York Yankees pitcher Ron Guidry, who won two World Series, five Gold Gloves, an AL Cy Young, and the Roberto Clemente award; and Hall of Fame Chicago Cubs third baseman Ron Santo, who played in nine All-Star games and took home five Gold Gloves.

Ronald "Ron" Francis Jr., Ice Hockey (Center), Pittsburgh Penguins, Canada, 1981–2004

Ronald "Ron" Guidry, Baseball (Pitcher), New York Yankees, USA, 1975–1988

Ronald "Ron" Mix, Football (Offensive Tackle), San Diego Chargers, USA, 1960–1971

Ronald "Ron" Santo, Baseball (Third Baseman), Chicago Cubs, USA, 1960–1974

Ronald "Ron" Von Hagen, Beach Volleyball, USA, 1962–1978

RONALD

The name Ronald is Scottish and comes from Old Norse roots meaning "advice/counsel," and "ruler." Ronalds in sports have included a slugger, and two rowers, with Venezuelan three-time MLB All-Star outfielder and hitter Ronald Acuña Jr., who has won two Silver Sluggers, the NL stolen base leader ranking, and membership in the 30-30 club while playing with the Atlanta Braves.

Ronalds seem particularly good at rowing and paddling events, as evidenced by a pair of two-time Olympic gold-medalists: Dutch rower Ronald Florijn and German sprint canoeist Ronald Rauhe, who has also won a breathtaking twenty-six medals at World Championships, including sixteen golds.

Ronald Acuña Jr., Baseball (Outfielder/Designated Hitter), Atlanta Braves, Venezuela, 2018–current

Ronald Florijn, Rowing, Netherlands, 1978–1996

Ronald Rauhe, Sprint Canoeing, Germany, 1997–current

RONALDO

In Portuguese, the name *Ronald* became Ronaldo, which seems to be particularly suited to playing soccer, or football as they call it in Brazil! That's where multiple football stars come from, with two major powerhouses who rank among the best all-time players in particular. Attacking midfielder/winger "Ronaldinho" (Ronaldo de Assis Moreira) had long stints with Barcelona and Milan, winning many trophies including FIFA Confederations Cup 2005 and FIFA World Cup 2002, and collecting awards and accolades that include FIFA World Cup All-Star Team, FIFA 100, FIFA World Player of the Year twice, World Player of the Year twice, Ballon d'Or, Onze d'Or, FIFPro World Player of the Year twice, Golden Foot, Ballon d'Or Dream Team, and more.

His career overlapped with another legendary Ronaldo, striker Ronaldo Nazário de Lima, whose trophy collection included nearly a dozen championships and not one but two FIFA World Cups (1994 and 2002). With multiple top-scorer titles, this Ronaldo had a long stint with Real Madrid and was awarded a staggering number of accolades, just some of which include FIFA World Player of the Year three times, Pichichi Trophy twice, World Player of the Year three times, FIFA World Cup Golden Ball, FIFA World Cup All-Star Team twice, FIFA 100, Ballon d'Or Dream Team, and Ballon d'Or twice!

If a young Ronaldo in your family is not interested in soccer, perhaps combat sports will be more to his liking. He may hone his skills and competitive edge like two-time black belt world champion and three-time World Jiu-Jitsu champion mixed martial artist Ronaldo "Jacare" Souza dos Santos, who has won an Abu Dhabi Combat Club Submission Fighting World Championship, two CBJJO World Jiu-Jitsu Cups, and the Strikeforce Middleweight Championship.

Ronaldo "Ronaldinho" de Assis Moreira, Soccer (Attacking Midfielder/Winger), Fútbol Club Barcelona, Brazil, 1998-2015

Ronaldo Nazário de Lima, Soccer (Striker), Real Madrid Club de Fútbol, Brazil, 1993-2011

Ronaldo "Jacare" Souza dos Santos, MMA (Light Heavyweight/Middleweight), Brazil, 2003-2021

RONNIE/RONNY

If you guessed that Ronnie is a diminutive of *Ronald*, then give yourself a gold star! Meanwhile, Ronny can have a bit more of a complicated origin and is used as a name all on its own more often. Both of these variants have an athletic pedigree, and together, they suggest a couple sports that a Ronnie or Ronny in your family might enjoy. If he's tough and likes to scrap, then he may find a career in the octagon, like Brazilian King of the Cage super heavyweight champion mixed martial artist Ronny Markes. If he has a need for speed, then he could be a champion behind the wheel, like Italian Super GT driver Ronnie Quintarelli, who has won eighteen races and two championships. Or if he likes to run around with his friends on the field, then he could find his place playing football, like Hall of Fame cornerback/safety Ronnie Lott, whose fourteen-season career included ten Pro Bowl appearances, four Super Bowl wins with the San Francisco 49ers, and leaderboard rankings in forced fumbles and interceptions (twice).

Ronnies and Ronnys aren't constrained just to those sports and can find their place anywhere, including on the slopes, like German four-time world champion Nordic combined skier Ronny Ackermann; in the gym, like eight-time (consecutive) Mr. Olympia-winner Ronnie Coleman, who's considered one of the top two bodybuilders of all time; or at the billiards table, like English snooker master Ronnie O'Sullivan, who has set multiple world records while winning seven World Snooker Championships, seven masters, twenty-one Triple Crowns, and more!

Ronny Ackermann, Nordic Combined Skiing, Germany, 1995-2010

Ronald "Ronnie" Coleman, Bodybuilding, USA, 1990-2007

Ronald "Ronnie" Lott, Football (Cornerback/Safety), San Francisco 49ers, USA, 1981-1995

Ronny Markes, MMA (Heavyweight), Brazil, 2007-current

Ronald "Ronnie" O'Sullivan, Snooker, England, 1992-current

Ronnie Quintarelli, Auto Racing (Super GT), Italy, 2000-current

RORY

Whether you're Irish, have red hair in your family, or really like rugby or golf, then the unisex name Rory (from Irish meaning "red king") might be a great choice for your kid! Irish rugby hooker Rory Best won a combined Pro12 championship, four Six Nations championships, two Grand Slams, and four Triple Crowns; and Irish golfer Rory McIlroy has won thirty-six professional events and four majors (US Open, Open Championship, and two PGA Championships).

Rory Best, Rugby (Hooker), Ulster Rugby, Ireland, 2004–2019

Rory McIlroy, Golf, Ireland, 2007–current

ROSS

The name Ross is Scottish and English, coming from a place name for an area in Northern Scotland and meaning "headland" or "promontory." Ross is a great name that has two very different historical exemplars. On the one hand, there are athletes with this name who find their skills lend themselves to the snowboard, like Olympic gold-medalists Ross Rebagliati of Canada on the giant slalom and world champion Ross Powers on the halfpipe. And on the other, there are team sports champions who have excelled at batting, like New Zealand cricket batsman Ross Taylor, who became the first-ever player to appear in one hundred matches in all three international cricket formats while winning the HRV Cup and 2019–2021 ICC World Test Championship, and 1800s fair-foul bunting baseball legend Ross Barnes, who won three batting championships and led the National Association and National League in stolen bases, triples twice, doubles three times, and hits and runs scored four times!

You should definitely be prepared for a Ross in your family—if he likes cold weather, introduce him to the snowboard; if not, teach him good batting fundamentals.

Charles Roscoe "Ross" Barnes, Baseball (Second Baseman/Shortstop), Rockford Forest Citys, USA, 1866–1881

Ross Powers, Snowboarding, USA, 1996–2011

Ross Rebagliati, Snowboarding, Canada, 1990–1998

Luteru Ross Taylor, Cricket (Middle-Order Batsman), Central Districts, New Zealand, 2002–2020

ROY

From the same Irish root meaning "red" as *Rory*, the name Roy has the added bonus of looking and sounding similar to "roi," the French word for "king." Outside of the United States, athletic royalty with this name has included Australian multi-sport champion Roy Fowler, who won three Paralympic gold medals each in lawn bowls and swimming, and Australian tennis singles world number one Roy Emerson, who won 110 titles and a record twenty-eight Grand Slam titles.

American Roys are most at home on the baseball diamond. Two Hall of Fame Roys stand at the heights of baseball: catcher Roy Campanella was a three-time All-Star and batting champion in the Negro leagues before his stellar MLB career with eight All-Star appearances, three National League MVP awards, and a World Series championship with the Brooklyn Dodgers in 1955, and eight-time All-Star pitcher Roy Halladay won two Cy Young awards, led the MLB twice in wins, and threw both a perfect game and a post-season no-hitter!

If you live in the United States then a basic understanding of baseball is definitely key for a boy you name Roy, though he may branch out and find another sport to his liking. He may follow in the footsteps of legendary boxer Roy Jones Jr., who stands among the best pound-for-pound fighters of all time and has multiple world championship titles in four different weight classes.

Roy Campanella, Baseball (Catcher), Brooklyn Dodgers, USA, 1937–1957

Roy Emerson, Tennis, Australia, 1968–1983

Roy Fowler, Para-Athletics, Australia, 1964–1988

Harry Leroy "Roy" Halladay III, Baseball (Pitcher), Toronto Blue Jays, USA, 1998–2013

Roy Jones Jr., Boxing (Middleweight/Heavyweight), USA, 1989–current

RUDI/RUDY

The names *Rudolf/Rudolph* and *Rodolfo* are great, but a lot of people with those names prefer to go by the short forms Rudi or Rudy. Athletes with these shortened names can have success in sports popular in their parts of the world, like German soccer forward and FIFA World Cup 1990 champion Rudi Völler; Indonesian badminton icon Rudy Hartono, who won a world championship and the Thomas Cup four times; and American seven-time MLB All-Star first baseman Rudy York, who won the 1945 World Series with the Detroit Tigers and led the American League in home runs and RBIs.

Uniquely, Rudys prove that any body type and size can succeed and achieve lasting fame! There have been tall basketball players, like French three-time NBA All-Star center and three-time Defensive Player of the Year Rudy Gobert, who has led the league in rebounds and blocks, and five-time All-Star power forward/center Rudy LaRusso. On the short end—but in no way lacking heart—Daniel "Rudy" Ruettiger's story of playing one game with the Notre Dame Fighting Irish football team was made into the iconic sports film *Rudy*, while Rudy Wanderone became one of the most well-known pool players of all time with the nickname "Minnesota Fats."

Rudy Gobert, Basketball (Center), Utah Jazz, France, 2011–current

Rudy Hartono, Badminton, Indonesia, 1967–1982

Rudolph "Rudy" LaRusso, Basketball (Power Forward/Center), Minneapolis Lakers, USA, 1959–1969

Daniel "Rudy" Ruettiger, Football (Defensive End), Notre Dame Fighting Irish Football Team, USA, 1974–1976

Rudolf "Rudi" Völler, Soccer (Forward), Associazione Sportiva Roma, Germany, 1977–1996

Rudolf "Rudy" (Minnesota Fats) Wanderone, Pool (Seven-Ball/Nine-Ball/Trick Shooting), USA, 1926–1984

Preston Rudolph "Rudy" York, Baseball (First Baseman), Detroit Tigers, USA, 1934–1948

RUDOLF/RUDOLPH

Rudolph and Rudolf come from Germanic roots for "fame" and "wolf," which is pretty awesome even if those names aren't exactly at the top of the baby name charts these days. Four athletes with these names from four different countries have succeeded in four different sports! Soviet weightlifter Rudolf Plyukfelder became an Olympic gold-medalist and three-time world champion in the late 1950s and early '60s, South African rugby lock Rudolph "RG" Snyman has won a United Rugby Championship with the Munster provincial team and a Rugby World Cup with the Springboks, German racing driver Rudolf Caracciola won eleven races and three championships in the 1930s in the European Drivers' Championship (predecessor to Formula 1), and Hungarian sabre fencer Rudolf Kárpáti is one of the most successful competitors of all time with six Olympic gold medals and seven world championship wins (plus three silvers and two bronzes).

A Rudolf or Rudolph in your family won't necessarily love hanging out in a gym, crashing into his opponents on the pitch, driving fast, or sword fighting, but whatever he chooses as his life's focus, he'll dominate and crush the competition!

Otto Wilhelm Rudolf Caracciola, Auto Racing (European Drivers' Championship), Germany, 1930–1952

Rudolf Kárpáti, Fencing (Sabre), Hungary, 1948–1977

Rudolf Plyukfelder, Weightlifting, USSR, 1959–1964

Rudolph "RG" Snyman, Rugby (Lock), Bulls, South Africa, 2015–current

RUSH

See *Georg/George/Georges* for Georges "Rush" St-Pierre.

RUSSELL

A perfect name for families with short people and red hair, Russell comes from Norman roots that mean "little red one." Athletic Russells are fond of achieving fame and glory as part of a team! On the gridiron, two Russells won Super Bowl XLVIII with the Seattle Seahawks in 2014: two-time Pro Bowl offensive tackle Russell Okung and nine-time Pro Bowl quarterback Russell Wilson, who has led the NFL in passer rating and passing touchdowns.

Not just great at playing football, Russells can succeed in any team environment, including baseball, like four-time All-Star catcher Russell Martin (who has taken home a Gold Glove and Silver Slugger), and basketball, like Olympic gold-medalist and world champion point guard Russell Westbrook (who played in nine NBA All-Star games, was named league MVP and All-Star MVP twice, and led the NBA in scoring twice and assists three times)!

Russell Martin Jr., Baseball (Catcher), Los Angeles Dodgers, Canada, 2006–2019

Russell Okung, Football (Offensive Tackle), Seattle Seahawks, USA, 2010–2020

Russell Westbrook III, Basketball (Point Guard), Oklahoma City Thunder, USA, 2008–current

Russell Wilson, Football (Quarterback), Seattle Seahawks, USA, 2012–current

RUSTY

A common nickname for *Russ* and *Russell*, Rusty originated as a familiar adjective for "red" and so works great for people with red hair. Way back in the 1960s, Rusty Staub joined the MLB, eventually playing right field, designated hitter, and first base and earning six All-Star appearances in his twenty-three seasons. More recent athletes with this name include world champion speed skater Rusty Smith, Hawaiian three-time longboard surfing champion Rusty Keaulana, and Motorsports Hall of Fame racing driver Rusty Wallace, who drove to fifty-five wins and a championship in NASCAR's top series!

Russ "Rusty" Keaulana, Surfing, USA, 1993–2010

Rusty Smith, Speed Skating, USA, 1998–2006

Daniel "Rusty" Staub, Baseball (Right Fielder/Designated Hitter/First Baseman), Houston Colt .45s, USA, 1963–1985

Russell "Rusty" Wallace Jr., Auto Racing (NASCAR), USA, 1980–2005

RUTH

See *Georg/George/Georges* for George "Babe" Ruth Jr.

RYAN/RYNE

The Emerald Isle is the source of the unisex name Ryan (and its lesser-known variant Ryne), which comes from an old Irish family name and roots that possibly mean "little king." With a high degree of popularity across English-speaking countries, it's no surprise to see that the name has had quite a bit of success on the athletic front in a ton of different events. A little king in your family could find his own winning sport in anything from auto racing, like Indianapolis 500-winner Ryan Hunter-Reay, who has won sixteen IndyCar races and a championship; to skateboarding, like pro Ryan Sheckler, who has won seven medals at X Games, including three golds; cycling, like Australian two-time Olympic gold-medalist and world champion track cyclist Ryan Bayley; and esports, like fighting games legend Ryan "Prodigal Son" Hart, who has won so many tournaments (including two Evos) that he holds four Guinness World Records!

Even beyond all of those, there are yet more events in which multiple Ryans have made big strides, starting with a pair of them in BMX riding (Ryan Nyquist, who has won sixteen medals at X Games, including four golds, and Australian five-time X Games gold-medalist and three-time Nitro World Games–winner Ryan Williams, who also won two Nitro World Games gold medals in best scooter tricks!).

Ryans have also appeared in ice hockey (with All-Star left wing Ryan Smyth, who won an Olympic gold medal, two world championships, and a World Cup with his national team; and two-time Olympic gold-medalist, three-time All-Star, and Stanley Cup champion center Ryan Getzlaf) and gridiron football (with four-time Washington Redskins Pro Bowl outside linebacker and defensive end Ryan Kerrigan, and five-time Carolina Panthers Pro Bowl center Ryan Kalil). Possibly the most winning trio of Ryans have been American swimmers Ryan Held (freestyle–Olympic gold medal and fourteen medals from World Championships, seven of them gold), Ryan Murphy (backstroke and medley–six Olympic medals, four of them gold and twenty-seven medals from World Championships, fourteen of them gold), and Ryan Lochte (multiple strokes–twelve Olympic medals, six of them golds, sixty-five medals from World Championships, thirty-nine of them gold, and multiple world records).

Last but decidedly not least are the Ryans and Rynes of Major League Baseball! Four-time All-Star and World Series champion pitcher Ryne Duren's fastball and power combined with his poor vision inspired the Ricky "Wild Thing" Vaughn character in *Major League*. At the top of their game were two NL home run leaders and NL MVPs in six-time All-Star Milwaukee Brewers left fielder Ryan Braun, who won five Silver Sluggers, and ten-time All-Star and Hall of Fame Chicago Cubs second baseman Ryne Sandberg, who won seven Silver Sluggers and nine Gold Gloves.

Name your little king Ryan or Ryne and he'll be ready for the big leagues before you know it!

Ryan Bayley, Track Cycling, Australia, 1997–2008

Ryan Braun, Baseball (Left Fielder), Milwaukee Brewers, USA, 2007–2020

Rinold "Ryne" Duren, Baseball (Pitcher), New York Yankees, USA, 1954–1965

Ryan Getzlaf, Ice Hockey (Center), Anaheim Ducks, Canada, 2005–2002

Ryan "Prodigal Son" Hart, Esports (Fighting Games), England, 1994–current

Ryan Held, Swimming (Freestyle), USA, 2016–current

Ryan Hunter-Reay, Auto Racing (IndyCar), USA, 1998–current

Ryan Kalil, Football (Center), Carolina Panthers, USA, 2007-2019

Patrick Ryan Kerrigan, Football (Outside Linebacker/Defensive End), Washington Redskins, USA, 2011-2021

Ryan Lochte, Swimming (Backstroke/Freestyle/Medley), USA, 2004–current

Ryan Murphy, Swimming (Backstroke/Freestyle), USA, 2011–current

Ryan Nyquist, BMX, USA, 1995–current

Ryne Sandberg, Baseball (Second Baseman), Chicago Cubs, USA, 1981–1997

Ryan Sheckler, Skateboarding, USA, 2003–2014

Ryan Smyth, Ice Hockey (Left Wing), Edmonton Oilers, Canada, 1994–2014

Ryan Williams, BMX, Australia, 2008–current

GIRLS

RACHAEL/RACHEL

The name Rachel, with its variant Rachael, dates back to biblical Hebrew and means "ewe." There's nothing docile and sheep-like about the athletes with these names, though! They've been all-stars and champions in a number of different sports, though one particularly seems to draw them in and provide a field for their glory: soccer. At the pinnacle of women's soccer are English winger/forward Rachel Yankey, who has won dozens of trophies; and forward/full-back Rachel Daly, whose honors include a WSL Golden Boot, NWSL Challenge Cup MVP, Best XI, Golden Boot, and being named WSL Player of the Season and FA Women's Super League Player of the Month twice!

While it would definitely be a good idea to introduce the soccer basics to a girl named Rachel or Rachael in your family, she could also go a different way and will succeed at any other sport or activity she chooses. She could even follow in the footsteps of greats like Australian Olympic gold-medalist field hockey player Rachel Imison, English World Triathlon Long Distance Champion Rachel Joyce, and Australian world champion, three-time World Team Champion, and three-time World Doubles Champion squash player Rachael Grinham. Or she could be a pioneer and achieve things first, like English cricket batter Rachael Heyhoe Flint, who dominated her time in the game with six straight Test series wins, winning the first Women's Cricket World Cup in 1973, and more.

Rachel Daly, Soccer (Forward/Full-Back), Houston Dash, England, 2008–current

Rachael Grinham, Squash, Australia, 1994–current

Rachael Heyhoe Flint, Cricket (Batter), West Midlands Women's Cricket Team, England, 1960–1985

Rachel Imison, Field Hockey (Goalkeeper), Australia, 2000–2006

Rachel Joyce, Triathlon, England, 2008–2017

Rachel Yankey, Soccer (Winger/Forward), Arsenal Women Football Club, England, 1996–2016

RAFAELA

The Portuguese/Spanish Rafaela may come from the biblical Hebrew *Raphael*, meaning "God heals," but women with this name are wholly focused on kicking butt! Hand-to-hand martial arts are the preferred outlet for Brazilian Rafaelas, including submission grappler Rafaela Guedes, who has won two gold medals each at World No-Gi Championships and Pan No-Gi Championships, as well as a gold and bronze on the Abu Dhabi Grand Slam Jiu-Jitsu World Tour, and judoka Rafaela Silva, whose accomplishments include an Olympic gold medal, seven medals from World Championships (two of them gold), sixteen from International Judo Federation (IJF) Grand Slam events, and seven golds, four silvers, and two bronzes from IJF Grand Prix.

Name your daughter Rafaela and she'll be tough, powerful, and independent.

Rafaela Guedes, MMA (Submission Grappling), Brazil, 2019–current

Rafaela Lopes Silva, Judo, Brazil, 2011–current

RAGNHILD

Names don't get much more Viking-sounding than Ragnhild, a Norwegian moniker that comes from mighty Old Norse roots meaning "counsel," "power of the gods," and "battle"! You don't have to come from the frozen northlands to give a really cool daughter this name; she may prefer indoor sports like handball and take after Olympic gold-medalist Ragnhild Aamodt, or she may find her fun and success on the slopes like two-time Olympic gold-medalist and four-time World Cup-winning cross-country skier Ragnhild Haga, and like Ragnhild Myklebust, who holds the record for medals at Winter Paralympic Games with two golds and a bronze in biathlon, eight medals in ice sledge speed racing (four golds), and sixteen golds in cross-country skiing!

Ragnhild Aamodt, Handball (Right Wing), Norway, 2002–current

Ragnhild Haga, Cross-Country Skiing, Norway, 2010–2023

Ragnhild Myklebust, Para-Skiing, Norway, 1988–2002

RAISA

Raisa is one of those names that have different origins and meanings depending on which culture or part of the world uses it. It can mean "leader" in Arabic, "rose" in Yiddish, or come from a reference to the goddess Hera in Greek! As flexible as the name is, so, too, will be a girl named Raisa in your family; she may prefer summer or indoor sports like volleyball and take after Cuban two-time Olympic gold-medalist Raisa O'Farrill Bolanos, or she may enjoy cold weather activities and hitting the slopes like Soviet four-time world champion cross-country skier Raisa Smetanina, whose four gold, five silver, and one bronze medal made her the first woman to win ten medals at Winter Olympics.

Raisa O'Farrill Bolanos, Volleyball (Opposite Hitter), Cuba, 1992–1996

Raisa Smetanina, Cross-Country Skiing, USSR, 1974–1992

RAMONA

From Germanic roots for "advice/counsel" and "protection" came the name *Raymond*, and then *Ramon*, and finally a feminine version in Ramona. Popular in disparate parts of the world, the name has reached athletic excellence primarily in Germany, though it's ready for a comeback here in the United States. A girl you name Ramona may be multi-talented, enjoy martial arts, or work well in lockstep with others, especially if she takes after some of the other amazing women who share her name. Ramona Neubert won the 1983 heptathlon world championship, the first such event, and broke the world record four times during her career; visually impaired judoka Ramona Brussig battled her way to two gold medals and two bronzes at Paralympic Games; and Ramona Balthasar rowed to victory as part of eight and quadruple sculls teams at the Olympics and World Championships, respectively!

Ramona Balthasar, Rowing, Germany, 1985–1990

Ramona Brussig, Judo, Germany, 1999–current

Ramona Neubert, Track & Field (Heptathlon), Germany, 1978–1983

RANDI

Another name with multiple origins like *Raisa*, the unisex Randi can be a diminutive of *Miranda* (from Latin meaning "wonderful") or an evolution of an Old Norse name with roots for "counsel" and "beautiful." Whatever the source, Randi is a fun name for a girl who will be a team player and work well with others to get things done, just like Norwegian world champion soccer forward Randi Leinan.

Randi Leinan, Soccer (Forward), Norway, 1995–1997

RAQUEL

Rachel is a great name, but if you're looking for something a little different, consider one of its variants, like Raquel. Athletes with these names have gone in various directions, with some succeeding individually and some as part of teams. The latter includes Brazilian volleyball outside hitter Raquel Silva, who won two World Grand Prix gold medals, a silver, and a bronze, and Costa Rican soccer forward Raquel Rodríguez, whose trophies thus far include an NWSL Challenge Cup, International Champions Cup, and NWSL Championship. And on their own, Spanish golfer Raquel Carriedo-Tomás won five professional events, and bantamweight mixed martial artist Raquel Pa'aluhi is a five-time No Gi World Champion.

The name Raquel brings with it flexibility and determination to succeed wherever it goes!

Raquel Carriedo-Tomás, Golf, Spain, 1995–2004

Raquel Pa'aluhi Canuto, MMA (Bantamweight), USA, 2010–2017

Raquel Rodríguez Cedeño, Soccer (Forward), Sky Blue FC, Costa Rica, 2016–current

Raquel Peluci Xavier Camargo da Silva, Volleyball (Outside Hitter), Brazil, 1998–2005

RATCHANOK

The story of Thai badminton world champion and former world number one singles player Ratchanok "May" Intanon is inspiring. She learned to play her favorite sport as a child on the badminton courts at the confectionary factory where her parents worked, and then set records for the youngest champion in various events while earning prize money that helped her family. From there she was destined for fame on the world stage, winning multiple medals in events like the Sudirman Cup, Uber Cup, Asian Games, SEA Games, and more, including, of course, her 2013 women singles world championship.

Ratchanok is definitely a unique name that can give a girl in your family an independent spirit, a champion's drive, and a dedication to her loved ones.

Ratchanok "May" Intanon, Badminton, Thailand, 2008–current

REANNE

The name Reanne has a couple of varied origins, either from a feminine variant of *Ryan* or from *Reanna*. Hand-eye coordination, spatial awareness, and the ability to focus under tremendous pressure are gifts you can bestow upon a daughter you name Reanne . . . at least if she takes after English snooker pro Reanne Evans! Reaching the top women's rank in the world, Evans won no fewer than twelve World Women's Snooker Championships, solidifying her spot as the most successful woman ever in the sport.

Reanne Evans, Snooker, England, 2002–current

REBECCA/REBEKAH/REBEKKAH

Popular across the English-speaking world, the name Rebecca (along with its variants like Rebekah) comes from biblical Hebrew and potentially a root meaning "tie" or "snare." Many Rebeccas have tied their fame and fortune to athletic endeavors and won big in many different fields on the world's stage. Some champions with these names succeed alongside their teammates, including flyhalf Rebecca Mahoney of New Zealand, who won two Rugby World Cups with the Black Ferns; New Zealand soccer defender Rebekah Stott, who has won five W-League Championships and two W-League Premierships; and Canadian three-time gold medalist and two-time world champion ice hockey forward Rebecca Johnston!

Meanwhile, there are several sports and events in which multiple Rebeccas have won big. These include track cycling, with Australian two-time world champion Rebecca Wiasak and Rebecca Twigg, who won six world championships. On the hardwood courts, wheelchair basketball player Rebecca Murray won two Paralympic gold medals, WNBA All-Star center Rebecca Lobo took home Olympic gold and was inducted into the Pro Basketball Hall of Fame, and forward Rebekkah Brunson had five WNBA All-Star selections and won a record five WNBA championships!

Many athletes with these names have found their competitive edge on or in the water. The largest collection has been in swimming, with Canadian three-time freestyle world champion Rebecca Smith, British two-time Olympic freestyle gold medalist and two-time world champion Rebecca Adlington, and American Rebecca Soni, who took home six medals from Olympic Games, including three golds, and ten medals from World Championships, including seven wins!

Also in the water, British diver Rebecca Gallantree won a team world championship in 2015. On the surface, Rebecca Giddens won a canoe slalom world championship, while in rowing, British Rebecca Shorten and Australian Rebecca Joyce won world championships, while Australian Rebecca Sattin and New Zealander Rebecca Scown won two!

Whether competing on her own or with a team, a little Rebecca (or Rebekkah or Rebekah) in your family is sure to find success of her own, and maybe more likely in things like basketball or anything to do with water.

Rebecca Adlington, Swimming (Freestyle), England, 2008–2012

Rebekkah Brunson, Basketball (Forward), Minnesota Lynx, USA, 2004–2018

Rebecca Gallantree, Diving, England, 2012–2016

Rebecca Giddens, Slalom Canoeing, USA, 1999–2004

Rebecca Johnston, Ice Hockey (Forward), Calgary Inferno, Canada, 2007–current

Rebecca Joyce, Rowing, Australia, 1988–1998

Rebecca Lobo, Basketball (Center), New York Liberty, USA, 1997–2003

Rebecca Mahoney, Rugby (Flyhalf), Wellington Rugby Football Union, New Zealand, 2000–2016

Rebecca Murray, Wheelchair Basketball, USA, 2008–current

Rebecca Sattin, Rowing, Australia, 1999–2004

Rebecca Scown, Rowing, New Zealand, 2005–current

Rebecca Shorten, Rowing, Northern Ireland, 2018–current

Rebecca Smith, Swimming (Freestyle), Canada, 2017–current

Rebecca Soni, Swimming (Breaststroke), USA, 2004–2012

Rebekah Stott, Soccer (Defender), SC Sand, New Zealand, 2010–current

Rebecca Twigg, Road/Track Cycling, USA, 1982–1997

Rebecca Wiasak, Track Cycling, Australia, 2014–current

REGINA

Regina is a perfect name for your little princess (it comes from Latin for "queen"), though she won't just be a damsel in distress. Instead, she'll be a fierce competitor her opponents will fear, just like German boxer Regina Halmich, who held world championship belts in light flyweight, flyweight, and super flyweight and ended her career with a staggering 54–1–1 record!

Regina Halmich, Boxing (Flyweight), Germany, 1994–2007

REGLA

If you're a fan of volleyball, you may want to consider for your daughter the Spanish name Regla, meaning "rule." During its absolutely dominant era from 1989 to 2000, the Cuban national volleyball team featured not one but two athletes named Regla, outside hitter/opposite Regla Bell and middle blocker Regla Torres! Together they won two World Grand Prix, three World Cups, two world championships, and three Olympic gold medals, while separately, Bell won another World Cup and Torres won a World Grand Champions Cup.

Regla Bell MacKenzie, Volleyball (Outside Hitter/Opposite), Cuba, 1991–2014

Regla Torres Herrera, Volleyball (Middle Blocker), Cuba, 1989–2002

RENATA/RENATE

Much more popular in Europe than the United States, Renata is a feminine variant of the Latin *Renatus* meaning "born again," with Renate being the preferred form in Germany, Netherlands, and Norway. Both of these names have solid athletic heritage and can inspire a little one in your family should you choose Renata or Renate. If she prefers winter sports, she can look to Dutch three-time world champion speed skater Renate Groenewold; Canadian CWHL All-Star defense player Renata Fast, who won an Olympic gold medal and two world championships; and Austrian three-time world champion alpine ski racer Renate Götschl, who stands among the greatest ever in her sport with a combined 110 medals from World Cup events, including forty-six golds.

On the other hand, your Renata or Renate may gravitate more toward fun in the sun and outdoor adventuring, like Austrian Hall of Fame water skier Renate Hansluvka, who won two world championships in jumping; and German three-time Olympic gold-medalist sprinter Renate Stecher.

Renata Fast, Ice Hockey (Defense), Toronto Furies, Canada, 2010–current

Renate Götschl, Alpine Skiing, Austria, 1993–2009

Renate Groenewold, Speed Skating, Netherlands, 1997–2010

Renate Hansluvka, Water Skiing, Austria, 1959–1966

Renate Stecher, Track & Field (Sprinting), Germany, 1969–1976

RENEE/RENÉE

With or without an accent, Renee comes from the same source as *Renata/Renate*: the Latin name *Renatus*, meaning "born again." Renees and Renées have had some outstanding athletic achievements, and a daughter you give one of those names to can absolutely continue that trend, whether she likes to play basketball, duel with swords, ski the tallest mountains, or even slide stones on ice! Past champions in those fields include Canadian world champion curling lead Renee Simons; Swiss Olympic gold-medalist alpine slalom skier Renée Colliard; and French foil fencer Renée Garilhe, who won thirteen medals (three of them gold) at World Championships in the 1940s and '50s. On the hardwood courts, Canadian wheelchair basketball player Renee del Colle won two Paralympic Games gold medals and two Wheelchair Basketball World Championships, while WNBA All-Star point guard Renee Montgomery won two WNBA championships with the Minnesota Lynx.

Renée Colliard, Alpine Skiing, Switzerland, 1956

Renee del Colle, Wheelchair Basketball, Canada, 1992–2000

Renée Garilhe, Fencing (Foil), France, 1947–1958

Renee Montgomery, Basketball (Point Guard), Minnesota Lynx, USA, 2009–2019

Renee Simons, Curling (Lead), Canada, 2004–current

RHONDA/RONDA

A relatively new name, Rhonda first appeared in the early 1900s. It may have come from a combination of existing names *Rhoda* and *Linda* or from a place name from the Rhondda Valley in South Wales. When it comes to sports, Rhondas with the "h" in their name are experts at crushing rubber balls on the court, like Australian world champion squash player Rhonda Thorne and American four-time world champion racquetball player Rhonda Rajsich; both were ranked number one in the world at the top of their careers.

Rondas, meanwhile, have walked two very different paths, with basketball center Ronda Jo Miller taking home gold with the USA team at the 1997 Deaflympics and MMA superstar (turned WWE wrestler) Ronda Rousey fighting her way to the Strikeforce Women's Bantamweight Championship, UFC Women's Bantamweight Championship, and later the UFC Hall of Fame.

Depending on the spelling of her name, her height, or her ferocity, a Ronda or Rhonda in your family may also enjoy racquet sports, play basketball, or get involved in martial arts!

Ronda Jo Miller, Basketball (Center), USA, 1997–2014

Rhonda Rajsich, Racquetball, USA, 2000–current

"Rowdy" Ronda Rousey, MMA (Featherweight/Bantamweight), USA, 2010–2016

Rhonda Thorne, Squash, Australia, 1977–1985

RICKI

A unisex name that can come from the *Ricky* family or as a diminutive of *Frederica*, Ricki is a fun moniker that can give a girl a love of video games, as well as ferociously taking down her opponents one-on-one. That's especially true if she takes after Ricki "HelloKittyRicki" Ortiz, an American esports champion specializing in the *Street Fighter* franchise and who has won and placed at major tournaments like Evo and Capcom Cup!

Ricki "HelloKittyRicki" Ortiz, Esports (Fighting Games), USA, 2001–current

RILEY

From either an Irish surname of unknown origin or an English place name meaning "rye clearing" comes the unisex name Riley, and with it the drive to compete along with a team and to cultivate a variety of very specific skills. A daughter you name Riley may even have the discipline and tenacity to become a world champion artistic gymnast like Riley McCusker, who achieved that feat with the United States women's national gymnastics team in 2018!

Riley McCusker, Artistic Gymnastics, USA, 2016–current

RINA

A truly international name, Rina has appeared in multiple languages and societies with very different origins and meanings. In Japanese, it can be written with characters that translate to "white jasmine," "village," and "vegetables"; it can come from a Sanskrit root for "melted"; it can mean "song" or "joy" in Hebrew; and it can be used as a short form for various names, including *Caterina* and *Catharina*.

The types of competitive events in which the name Rina has appeared on leaderboards and podiums are as varied as the name's origins. They range from the traditional Japanese strategy board game Go (with six dan-ranked prodigy Rina Fujisawa, who set multiple records because of her youth), to running events (with Australian/British Rina Hill, who won the 1992 Brisbane Marathon before embarking on a triathlon career that would include a Long Distance World Championship, Indoor Triathlon World Championship, two Aquathlon World Championships, and more), and kickboxing (with "Panchan" Rina Okamoto, who has held the Knock Out-Black Female Minimumweight Championship, Knock Out-Black Female Atomweight Championship, and Rebels-Black Women's 46kg Championship with a 14–2 record).

A Rina in your family may not embark upon a career at the board game table, trekking long distances, or in the ring, but she will be a girl of many talents and unlimited potential.

Rina Fujisawa, Go, Japan, 2010–current

Rina Hill, Marathon/Triathlon, Australia/England, 1992–2004

"Panchan" Rina Okamoto, Kickboxing (Atomweight/Minimumweight), Japan, 2017–current

RITA

A somewhat more modern take on its parent name, Rita began as a diminutive of the Italian *Margherita*. The name has spread to distant corners of the globe, with interesting examples in Hungarian water polo world champion and World Cup-winner Rita Drávucz and Kenyan long-distance runner Rita Jeptoo, who won major marathons in Stockholm, Milan, Chicago, and Boston twice!

Whether you use Rita as a name on its own or as a nickname for *Margherita* for your daughter, she, too, could reach international levels of success running, playing water polo, or participating in any other sport that she loves.

Rita Drávucz, Water Polo (Field Player), Hungary, 1995–2012

Rita Jeptoo, Marathon, Kenya, 2004–2014

ROBERTA

A feminine version of the name *Robert*, Roberta brings "bright fame" to athletes, especially in Brazil and Italy . . . and can do the same for a girl in your family! Sometimes this comes in more down-to-earth formats, like cricket (with Brazilian all-rounder and national team captain Roberta Moretti, who won the 2019 South American Cricket Championship), tennis (with Italian doubles player Roberta Vinci, who reached the world top spot with twenty-five titles and five majors), and volleyball (with Brazilian two-time World Grand Prix-winning setter Roberta Ratzke, who has won multiple Brazilian and South American titles). On the other hand, some Robertas find their place in more exotic and extreme sports, like Italian Roberta Pedranzini (who has won nine gold medals and four silvers in ski mountaineering World Championships).

Roberta de Melo Moretti Avery, Cricket (All-Rounder), Cricket Poços, Brazil, 2013–current

Roberta Pedranzini, Ski Mountaineering, Italy, 2003–2012

Roberta Ratzke, Volleyball (Setter), Brazil, 2007–current

Roberta Vinci, Tennis, Italy, 1999–2018

ROBIN/ROBYN

The name *Robert* has had a laundry list of associated diminutives and nicknames over the years, and that list includes the unisex Robin (and variant Robyn). A young Robin or Robyn in your family may love horses, play volleyball, or just grow up to be super strong if she takes after stellar athletes like strongwoman and bodybuilder Robin Coleman, who played "Hellga" on *American Gladiators*; world champion weightlifter Robin Goad; horse racing jockey Robyn Smith, who achieved numerous firsts on her way to winning 247 races; and Dutch two-time FIVB Volleyball Women's Club World Championship "Best Blocker" Robin de Kruijf, who has won more than a dozen trophies.

Robin "Hellga" Coleman, Strength Competition/Bodybuilding, USA, 1997–2006

Robin de Kruijf, Volleyball (Middle Blocker), Netherlands, 2006–current

Robin Goad, Weightlifting, USA, 1987–2000

Robyn Smith, Horse Racing (Jockey), USA, 1969–1980

ROSA

Similar to *Rose*, the name Rosa did not actually originate with the rose flower, but rather with a Germanic root meaning "fame" and can mean "dew" in Slavic languages. Name your daughter Rosa and she's sure to go the distance in any task, sport, or challenge she faces, just like Portuguese marathon runner Rosa Mota, who won Olympic gold and bronze, a world championship, and major city races in Chicago, Tokyo, London, Boston, and more!

Rosa Maria Correia dos Santos Mota, Marathon, Portugal, 1982–1992

ROSE

Most people assume the name Rose comes from the flower, and while it's become associated with it, its origins actually stretch back through Norman French to Germanic roots for "famous" and "type." The most famous types of Roses in sports are fast, tough, and never back down. Name your daughter Rose and she could go toe-to-toe with anyone, just like two-time UFC Strawweight Champion Rose Namajunas or soccer midfielder Rose Lavelle, who has won the 2019 FIFA Women's World Cup and numerous other events while being awarded the Best Player SheBelieves Cup, National Women's Soccer League Best XI, and CONCACAF W Championship Best XI!

Rosemary "Rose" Lavelle, Soccer (Midfielder), OL Reign, USA, 2014–current

Rose "Thug" Namajunas, MMA (Strawweight), USA, 2010–current

ROSEMARIE/ROSEMARY

Really like the names *Rose* and *Mary* and can't decide between them for your daughter? Combine them! Rosemarie and Rosemary have been popular all around the world, and either one of them can inspire a girl in your family to great feats in track and field events or swimming if they take after champions like German Olympic gold-medalist high jumper Rosemarie Ackermann; Kenyan long-distance runner Rosemary Wanjiru, who won the Tokyo Marathon and gold and silver at World Marathon Majors; Australian Paralympic breaststroke gold medalist Rosemary Eames, who broke twenty world records and won ten international gold medals in her too-brief career; and German Olympic gold-medalist and four-time butterfly and medley world champion Rosemarie Gabriel.

Of course, nothing can stop your Rosemarie or Rosemary from finding her own preferred field; she might love racing across the water, like Australian Olympic gold-medalist rower Rosemary Popa, or atop mighty thoroughbreds, like horse racing jockey Rosemary Homeister Jr., who won over 2,700 races!

Rosemarie Ackermann, Track & Field (High Jump), Germany, 1972–1980

Rosemary Eames, Swimming (Backstroke/Breaststroke/Butterfly/Freestyle), Australia, 1982–1986

Rosemarie Gabriel, Swimming (Butterfly/Medley), Germany, 1972–1976

Rosemary Homeister Jr., Horse Racing (Jockey), USA, 1992–2015

Rosemary Popa, Rowing, Australia, 2005–current

Rosemary Wanjiru, Long-Distance Running, Kenya, 2015–current

ROSI

The name Rosi has a number of possible origins, though most often it's a diminutive of any variety of "Ros-" names, including *Rosa* and *Rose*. A girl named Rosi can do just about anything, though there's a good chance she'll enjoy activities and sports in the cold; that's especially true if she takes after competitors like Swiss world champion curler Rosi Manger or German alpine skier Rosi Mittermaier, who won two gold medals and a silver at Olympic Games, three golds at World Championships, and stood on forty-one World Cup podiums with ten wins.

Rosi Manger, Curling (Lead), Switzerland, 1978–1980

Rosa "Rosi" Mittermaier, Alpine Skiing, Germany, 1967–1976

ROSIE

There's no shortage of diminutives and alternate forms of the classic name *Rose*, and one of the most popular over the years has been Rosie. Famous for its strength and longevity (just think of Rosie the Riveter), this name or nickname can provide your daughter with a long and successful career no matter what she likes to do, just like golfer Rosie Jones, who won twenty-five professional events, and horse racing jockey Rosie Napravnik, who rode to nearly 1,900 wins.

Rosie Jones, Golf, USA, 1982–2006

Anna Rose "Rosie" Napravnik, Horse Racing (Jockey), USA, 2005–2014

RUIXUE

Quite uncommon in North America, Ruixue is a Chinese name made up of sections that can be translated as "small," "breeze," or "snow." While winter sports are great, Ruixue seems a bit more at home inside the gym, the domain of Chinese wrestler Jing Ruixue, who won two world championship gold medals (along with a silver and a bronze).

Choose Ruixue for your daughter and she'll be a breath of fresh air, potentially preferring the snowy domain of her name or strengthening herself and taking down her opponents on the mat.

Jing Ruixue, Freestyle Wrestling, China, 2005–2012

RUMAY

While the name Rumay has ancient roots in Sanskrit, in international competition it couldn't be more modern and cutting edge. Rumay "Hafu" Wang is an esports pro and an expert at a list of different games. She won the *Bloodline Champions* DreamHack Summer 2011 championship and has competed at the highest levels in *World of Warcraft*, *Hearthstone*, and more.

Combine the classic with the new in your daughter with the name Rumay, giving her an appreciation for the past and the tools to succeed in the future.

Rumay "Hafu" Wang, Esports (*Bloodline Champions/Hearthstone*), USA, 2008–current

RUTH/RUTHIE

Popular with classmates, co-workers, and teammates and having a predisposition toward playing basketball and participating in track and field events can describe a girl (or boy!) you name Ruth, and whom you may call Ruthie. The name Ruth stretches back all the way to biblical Hebrew and meant "friend," though it was also later associated with an archaic English word meaning "pity" or "compassion" (as in "ruthless").

There are some clear trends we can see with athletes named Ruth or its diminutive, starting with those who have played hard and made big wins on the basketball court, including WNBA All-Star and Olympic gold-medalist forward/center Ruth Riley, who won two WNBA championships and was named finals MVP; and two-time All-Star, two-time Olympic gold-medalist, and world champion guard Ruthie Bolton. In the track and field world, you can find Olympic gold medalists like steeplechase runner Ruth Jebet of Bahrain and Spanish high jumper Ruth Beitia; German two-time Olympic gold-medalist Ruth Fuchs; and Kenyan long-distance runner Ruth Chepng'etich, who has won two gold medals and a bronze in World Marathon Majors and a marathon world championship.

On the other hand, your little Ruth may discover her skills and love of the game take her in a different direction, possibly into golf (like Ruth Jessen, who won thirteen professional events), baseball (like three-time All-American Girls Professional Baseball League All-Star catcher Ruth "Tex" Lessing, who won the 1947 championship with the Grand Rapids Chicks), or even pool (like Ruth McGinnis, who is considered one of the greatest women players of all time—she was named "Queen Billiard Player of the World" in 1934 by the World Billiards Association and was inducted into multiple Halls of Fame).

Ruth Beitia Vila, Track & Field (High Jump), Spain, 2000–2017

Alice Ruth "Ruthie" Bolton, Basketball (Guard), Sacramento Monarchs, USA, 1990–2004

Ruth Chepng'etich, Long-Distance Running, Kenya, 2016–current

Ruth Fuchs, Track & Field (Javelin), Germany, 1971–1978

Ruth Jebet, Track & Field (Steeplechase), Bahrain, 2013–current

Mary Ruth Jessen, Golf, USA, 1956–1985

Ruth "Tex" Lessing, Baseball (Catcher), Grand Rapids Chicks, USA, 1944–1949

Ruth McGinnis, Pool (Straight), USA, 1934–1964

Ruth Riley, Basketball (Forward/Center), Detroit Shock, USA, 2001–2014

RYAN

Some may say that "the best defense is a good offense," but good defense and helping out her team is the name of the game when it comes to a girl named Ryan! The unisex name has come to the forefront of women's soccer in the United States with defender/midfielder Ryan Williams, who has won the Women's International Champions Cup, NWSL Shield twice, and NWSL Championship twice.

Name a girl in your family Ryan to have a true team player and defender.

Ryan Williams, Soccer (Defender/Midfielder), North Carolina Courage, USA, 2018–current

S

BOYS

SACHIN

We begin the "S" section with Sachin, a name that comes from Sanskrit for "true" or "real." A real one if there ever was, Sachin Tendulkar is an absolute legend in cricket, ranked among the best of the best and considered a successor to Don Bradman. Sachin ranks at the top of run-scorers in both ODI and Test, with more than eighteen thousand and fifteen thousand, respectively; won major events like the 2002 ICC Champions Trophy (joint-winner) and 2011 Cricket World Cup; was given numerous awards; and was inducted into the ICC Cricket Hall of Fame.

Choose the name Sachin for your son and he'll be a powerful force on any team, scoring goals and elevating those around him to achieve true greatness.

Sachin Tendulkar, Cricket (Batsman), Mumbai Indians, India, 1988–2013

SAEED/SAÏD

From an Arabic root meaning "happy" or "lucky" comes the family of Sa'id names with lots of different spellings and variations, including Saeed and Saïd. Athletes with these names have made big impacts in several countries, with some of the foremost including Moroccan middle-distance runner Saïd Aouita, who won world championships in 3000 meters and 5000 meters, an Olympic gold medal in 5000 meters, and an Olympic bronze medal in 800 meters; and Pakistani cricket bowler Saeed Ajmal, who was ranked number one in his position in the world (twice!) on his way to setting multiple records and winning the 2005 ANB-AMRO Twenty-20 Cup, 2009 ICC World Twenty20, and more.

If you like these names, you have several choices when it comes to spellings, but any of them will give a son a love of competition, winning, and—more importantly—having fun and being happy.

Saeed Ajmal, Cricket (Bowler), Faisalabad Wolves, Pakistan, 1996–2017

Saïd Aouita, Track & Field (Middle-Distance Running), Morocco, 1980–1991

SAM

A highly versatile and unisex name, Sam can be a short form for numerous monikers, including *Samuel*, *Samson*, and more. Across the spectrum of sports, we see Sams congregating and winning in several specific fields.

Many athletes with this name are team players, like basketball greats NBA All-Star point guard Sam Cassell, who won two championships with the Houston Rockets and another with the Boston Celtics; and five-time All-Star shooting guard Hall of Famer Sam Jones, whose massive ten NBA championships put him second on the all-time record list. A singular Sam who was part of a truly iconic team, cricket all-rounder Sam Loxton played alongside Don Bradman on the Australian "Invincibles" team through their undefeated tour of England in 1948.

On the baseball diamond, the most successful Sams have mostly been pitchers, with two-time All-Star Sam "Toothpick" Jones throwing a no-hitter in 1955 and leading the National League in wins, ERA, and strikeouts three times; and "Sudden Sam" McDowell pitching in six All-Star games and leading the American League in ERA and strikeouts five times.

From America's pastime to the football field, we find multi-position player Sam Baker, who played in four Pro Bowls and led the NFL in scoring in 1957; and five-time Pro Bowl linebacker Sam Huff, who won the 1956 NFL championship with the New York Giants and was later inducted into the Pro Football Hall of Fame.

And last but not least is the golf course and American Sam Snead, who is credited with 142 wins, including a record-setting (later tied by Tiger Woods) eighty-two PGA wins and seven majors. His "perfect swing" led to his appearance on countless lists of top golfers of all time, a long list of records set and broken, and induction into the World Golf Hall of Fame and others.

Sam is a great name on its own or as a diminutive for a longer form like *Samuel* or *Samson*, and it can provide your son with a huge number of athletic inspirations. They might lead him to success playing with friends on basketball, football, or baseball teams; or even draw him to the links!

- **Loris "Sam" Baker**, Football (Kicker/Punter), Philadelphia Eagles, USA, 1953–1969
- **Samuel "Sam" Cassell Sr.**, Basketball (Point Guard), Houston Rockets, USA, 1993–2009
- **Robert "Sam" Huff**, Football (Linebacker), New York Giants, USA, 1956–1969
- **Samuel "Sam" (Toothpick) Jones**, Baseball (Pitcher), San Francisco Giants, USA, 1947–1964
- **Samuel "Sam" Jones**, Basketball (Shooting Guard), Boston Celtics, USA, 1957–1969
- **Samuel "Sam" Loxton**, Cricket (All-Rounder), Victoria Men's Cricket Team, Australia, 1946–1958
- **Samuel "Sudden Sam" McDowell**, Baseball (Pitcher), Cleveland Indians, USA, 1961–1975
- **Samuel "Sam" Snead**, Golf, USA, 1934–1973

SAMMIE/SAMMY

Just like *Sam*, the unisex Sammy and the rarer form Sammie are diminutives of many different names, including *Samuel*, *Samson*, and others. Unlike highly successful athletes named Sam who have tended to congregate in several sports, competitors with the names Sammie and Sammy are spread out across different events. These range from freestyle wrestling (like world champion Sammie Henson) to diving (like Olympic two-time platform gold medalist Sammy Lee), water skiing (like four-time men's world overall title-winner and world jump record breaker Sammy Duvall), and marathon running (like Kenyan runner Sammy Korir, who won major races in Florence, Cancún, Amsterdam (twice), Turin, San Diego, Rotterdam, and Seoul).

Some of the most famous Sammys have been team sports players. NFL Hall of Famer and six-time Pro Bowl quarterback, punter, and safety Sammy Baugh dominated the league in the 1940s, winning two NFL championships with the Washington Redskins and racking up leaderboard top spots, including passing yards four times, passing touchdowns twice, passer rating three times, and more. Last but certainly not least is Dominican-American MLB seven-time All-Star right fielder Sammy Sosa! The home run slugger was named National League MVP in 1998, took home six Silver Sluggers and the NL Hank Aaron award, and led the National League in RBIs and home runs twice each.

A Sammie or Sammy in your family will have unlimited options when it comes to a sport or athletic event, ranging anywhere from solo activities to team sports. Anywhere he lands, he'll have fun while also winning big!

Samuel "Sammy" Baugh, Football (Quarterback/Safety/Punter), Washington Redskins, USA, 1937–1952

Sammy Duvall, Water Skiing, USA, 1979–1998

Samuel "Sammie" Henson, Freestyle Wrestling, USA, 1990–2006

Sammy Korir, Marathon, Kenya, 1996-2012

Samuel "Sammy" Lee, Diving, USA, 1942–1951

Samuel "Sammy" Sosa, Baseball (Right Fielder), Chicago Cubs, Dominican Republic/USA, 1989–2007

SAMUEL

If you name your athletic and competitive son Samuel (from biblical Hebrew meaning "name of God" or "God has heard") but don't call him *Sam* or *Sammy*, there's a good chance he could be a jumper, an ice skater, or a soccer player! And that's especially true if he takes after 1904 Olympic gold-medalist high jumper Samuel Jones; Canadian ice hockey defenseman/left wing Samuel "Hamby" Shore, who won the Stanley Cup with the Ottawa Senators in 1905, 1910, and 1911; or not one but two soccer stars born in Cameroon. French center-back Samuel Umtiti won the FIFA World Cup in 2018, while Golden Foot and FIFA Club World Cup Golden Ball-winning Samuel Eto'o stands among the all-time great strikers, scoring over four hundred goals; winning an Olympic gold medal, and numerous championships; and being named African Player of the Year four times, FIFA FIFPro World XI twice, UEFA Club Forward of the Year, and more!

Samuel Eto'o Fils, Soccer (Striker), Fútbol Club Barcelona, Cameroon, 1997–2019

Samuel Jones, Track & Field (High Jump), USA, 1904

Samuel "Hamby" Shore, Ice Hockey (Defense/Left Wing), Ottawa Senators, Canada, 1904–1918

Samuel Umtiti, Soccer (Center-Back), Olympique Lyonnais, France, 2010–current

SANATH

Like *Sachin* and *Saeed*, Sanath is a name associated with great success in cricket, particularly as it relates to Sri Lankan all-rounder Sanath Jayasuriya. The Hindi name and epithet of Brahma can mean "eternal," and the fame Sanath won over two decades on the pitch will surely last forever. His many records and achievements include being the first and only player to score ten thousand runs and take three hundred wickets in a single format (ODI); solidifying his standing among the best of all time by winning the 1996 Cricket World Cup and being named its MVP; and earning forty-seven Man of the Match awards, eleven ODI Man of the Series, four Test Man of the Match, a Test Man of the Series, five T20I Man of the Match, and countless more.

A boy you name Sanath will be able to do it all in whatever sport he prefers, playing offense and defense and helping his team to victory and long-lasting fame!

Sanath Jayasuriya, Cricket (All-Rounder), Bloomfield Cricket and Athletic Club, Sri Lanka, 1989–2012

SANDER/SÁNDOR

With Alexander the Great's domination of the ancient world and the spread of Hellenism, it's little surprise that the name *Alexander* and its many variants appear all over the place. In Europe, it has led to the interesting short forms Sander and Sándor.

Athletes with these names have succeeded at the highest levels in a few different sports and events, and five of them are Olympic gold medalists! From Hungary, sprint canoeist Sándor Tótka won his gold in 2020, along with world championships in 2014 and 2015, and fencers Sándor Gombos and Sándor Erdős won team golds in 1928 and 1972, respectively. Team players who won their Olympic gold medals on grass include Dutch field hockey defender Sander van der Weide, who won a World Cup and four Champions Trophies, and Hungarian soccer striker Sándor Kocsis, who was awarded FIFA World Cup Golden Boot, FIFA World Cup All-Star Team, and a spot on the World Soccer 100 Greatest Footballers of All Time for his achievements, which include scoring over 450 goals.

If you name your son Sander or Sándor, he, too, could have Olympic aspirations, whether he prefers paddling in a canoe, gracefully sword fighting, or playing with his teammates in field hockey or soccer.

Sándor Erdős, Fencing (Épée), Hungary, 1972–1976

Sándor Gombos, Fencing (Sabre), Hungary, 1926–1937

Sándor Kocsis, Soccer (Striker), Budapest Honvéd Football Club, Hungary, 1946–1965

Sándor Tótka, Sprint Canoeing, Hungary, 2013–current

Sander van der Weide, Field Hockey (Defender), Netherlands, 1996–2006

SANDY

A highly flexible (and unisex) name, Sandy has appeared as a diminutive or nickname for *Alexander*, *Santos*, *Sanford*, and many others.

Here in the USA, it's been proven that a Sandy's place is on the baseball diamond! Name or call your son Sandy and teach him how to throw, catch, and hit as early as you can. He'll have iconic heroes to look up to, like the father and son Alomars, All-Star second baseman Sandy Alomar Sr. and six-time All-Star catcher Sandy Alomar Jr.; and, of course, famed Dodgers power pitcher Sandy Koufax! A seven-time All-Star, National League MVP, and two-time World Series MVP, Koufax won four Word Series championships, three Cy Young Awards, and three Major League Triple Crowns while leading the MLB in wins three times and strikeouts four times and pitching a perfect game and four no-hitters. He broke numerous records with his four-seam fastball and legendary curveball during his relatively short twelve-season career before retiring at only thirty years old, and subsequently was the youngest player ever inducted into the Baseball Hall of Fame.

Santos "Sandy" Alomar Velázquez Jr., Baseball (Catcher), Cleveland Indians, Puerto Rico, 1988–2007

Santos "Sandy" Alomar Conde Sr., Baseball (Second Baseman), California Angels, Puerto Rico, 1964–1978

Sanford "Sandy" Koufax, Baseball (Pitcher), Los Angeles Dodgers, USA, 1955–1966

SATCHEL

Satchel, a type of bag with a strap, might seem like an odd choice for a nickname . . . but not if you're a baseball fan! If you are, you'll be well familiar with Leroy "Satchel" Paige, the powerful pitcher who played in the Negro leagues and Major League Baseball primarily in the 1920s, '30s, and '40s. Nicknamed for the way he carried around bags (or possibly because he tried to steal one), Satchel was known for his incredible fastball and other unique pitches, like the tricky "hesitation" pitch, and accumulated numerous records, including six Negro league All-Star appearances (two in the MLB), a World Series championship in both leagues, and being the oldest player to get his start in the MLB!

Whether you name your son Leroy or not, consider the nickname Satchel for him and teach him baseball fundamentals as soon as possible; he may just find his signature pitches and embark on a long, storied career.

Leroy "Satchel" Paige, Baseball (Pitcher), Cleveland Indians, USA, 1926–1953

SATOSHI

A very *smart* name, the Japanese Satoshi can mean things like "intelligence," "intellect," "clever," and "wisdom" depending on the characters used to write it. Those qualities will surely manifest in a boy in your family with this name, giving him the acumen and skills to back it up to succeed in any endeavor, particularly when it comes to tough one-on-one confrontations. And he can look to iconic examples who share his name, like baseball pitcher Satoshi Komatsu, who won the World Baseball Classic; IBF bantamweight champion boxer Satoshi Shingaki; three-time Paralympic gold-medalist judoka Satoshi Fujimoto; and multi-talented martial artist Satoshi Ishii, who won Olympic gold in judo and held the HEAT MMA heavyweight championship.

Satoshi Fujimoto, Judo, Japan, 1996–2016

Satoshi Ishii, Judo/MMA/Kickboxing/Boxing (Heavyweight), Japan/Croatia, 2004–current

Satoshi Komatsu, Baseball (Pitcher), Orix Buffaloes, Japan, 2007–2016

Satoshi Shingaki, Boxing (Bantamweight), Japan, 1982–1990

SAWAO

Many possible translations of the Japanese name Sawao summon idyllic landscapes like "mountain stream," while in the gym it provides grace and strength. The best-known exemplar of this is artistic gymnast Katō Sawao, who ranks among the most successful Olympians of all time with eight gold medals, three silvers, and a bronze won in competitions from 1968 to 1976, including three successive Team golds; he also took home a world championship in 1974!

Katō Sawao, Artistic Gymnastics, Japan, 1968–1976

SCHALK

A traditional Dutch name that came about as a shortened form of *Godschalk* (from *Gottschalk* and Old German roots for "servant of God"), Schalk carries with it an intense strength and love of battling it out with teammates on the pitch! We can see that in two South African rugby champions, each of whom lifted the Webb Ellis trophy for winning a Rugby World Cup. Loose-forward Schalk Burger was a two-time SA Rugby Player of the Year and won the 2007 Rugby World Cup, while hooker Schalk Brits won four Premierships, the European Champions Cup twice, and the 2019 Rugby World Cup.

Schalk Brits, Rugby (Hooker), Saracens Rugby Club, South Africa, 2002–2019

Schalk Burger Jr., Rugby (Loose-Forward), Stormers, South Africa, 2003–2019

SCOTT

Not all Scotts are Scots, though the name did originate as a last name referring to someone from Scotland. People named Scott are awesome and great writers, but they also have a lot of athletic potential in different fields.

There are a few specific events that Scotts seem particularly good at, with pairs of them standing on top of podiums in swimming (American Olympic freestyle gold medalists Scott Goldblatt and Scott Tucker, who is also a four-time world champion) and ice skating (American Olympic gold-medalist and four-time world champion figure skater Scott Hamilton and Canadian ice dancer Scott Moir, who won five medals at the Olympics (three golds and two silvers), seven at World Championships (three golds), and six at Grand Prix Finals (one gold) and, along with his partner Tessa Virtue, is the most decorated pairs figure skater in the history of the Olympics).

The biggest concentrations of Scotts have occurred in two team sports, one on the ice and the other on the diamond. Top ice hockey players include two all-time defense greats and Hall of Fame inductees in five-time All-Star Scott Niedermayer (who won the Stanley Cup four times, two Olympic gold medals, a world championship, and a World Cup) and thirteen-time All-Star and three-time Stanley Cup champion Scott Stevens. In America's pastime, three-time All-Star pitcher Scott Kazmir was an AL strikeout leader, and seven-time All-Star third baseman Scott Rolen won the 2006 World Series, took home eight Gold Gloves and a Silver Slugger, and was inducted into the Hall of Fame.

A son you name Scott can achieve anything he sets out to do, and chances are he'll be a great help to his teammates and co-workers along the way. Give him the chance to try out baseball, ice hockey, swimming, or anything else he thinks of and let him lead the way!

Scott Goldblatt, Swimming (Freestyle), USA, 1995–2005

Scott Hamilton, Figure Skating, USA, 1976–2009

Scott Kazmir, Baseball (Pitcher), Tampa Bay Devil Rays, USA, 2004–2021

Scott Moir, Ice Dancing, Canada, 1990–2019

Scott Niedermayer, Ice Hockey (Defense), New Jersey Devils, Canada, 1991-2010

Scott Rolen, Baseball (Third Baseman), Philadelphia Phillies, USA, 1996–2012

Ronald Scott Stevens, Ice Hockey (Defense), New Jersey Devils, Canada, 1982–2004

Scott Tucker, Swimming (Freestyle), USA, 1995–2003

SCOTTIE/SCOTTY

Scotts are great, but sometimes they're just better with a more familiar diminutive like Scottie or Scotty. If you call your Scott one of these names, he may like shredding the slopes on a snowboard like X Games gold-medalist and 2004 World Quarterpipe Champion Scotty Lago or Australian three-time halfpipe world champion Scotty James, who won eight X Games SuperPipe medals (five of them gold), four golds and a bronze in halfpipe, and overall at Snowboard World Cup events.

If cold weather isn't his thing, then your son could find inspiration from nine-time X Games-medalist (three golds, three silvers, and three bronzes) BMX rider Scotty Cranmer; Vietnamese-American five-time World Series of Poker champion and World Poker Tour-winner Scotty Nguyễn; and, of course, legendary basketball small forward Scottie Pippen, who played in seven All-Star games, won six NBA championships with the Chicago Bulls and two Olympic gold medals on the "Dream Team," was named NBA All-Star Game MVP, led the league in steals, set numerous records, and was inducted into the Basketball Hall of Fame.

Scott "Scotty" Cranmer, BMX, USA, 2005–2016

Scott "Scotty" James, Snowboarding, Australia, 2008–current

Scott "Scotty" Lago, Snowboarding, USA, 1996–2012

Thuận "Scotty" Nguyễn, Card Gaming (Poker), Vietnam/USA, 1983–current

Scotty "Scottie" Pippen Sr., Basketball (Small Forward), Chicago Bulls, USA, 1987–2008

SEAN

The name *John* (from biblical Hebrew meaning "God is gracious") is massively popular around the world, and it has also been turned into many variant forms, including the Irish Sean. Sean hasn't been confined just to the Emerald Isle, and its prevalence across the English-speaking world is reflected in the range of champion athletes with this name who have graced the podiums and leaderboards of numerous events. Those in team sports include three-time MLB All-Star first baseman Sean "The Mayor" Casey; world champion basketball small forward Sean Elliott, who played in two NBA All-Star games and won the NBA championship in 1999 with the San Antonio Spurs; and MLS All-Star and MLS Cup MVP goalkeeper Sean Johnson, who has won an MLS Cup, and the CONCACAF Gold Cup three times.

Interestingly, many Seans seem to gravitate toward sports that are all about being tough and smashing into your opponents! Irish kickboxer Sean Clancy is the current WBC Muaythai Super Lightweight World Champion, while boxer Sean O'Grady held the WBA Lightweight Championship during his 81-5 career in the 1970s and '80s. On the rugby pitch, New Zealand hooker Sean Fitzpatrick cemented his spot on the all-time greats list with eight National Provincial Championships, two Super Rugby championships, nine Bledisloe Cups, two Tri Nations championships, winning the 1987 Rugby World Cup, and more.

If you name your son Sean, you should find some healthy sports and activities for him to channel his innate aggression and competitiveness.

Sean "The Mayor" Casey, Baseball (First Baseman), Cincinnati Reds, USA, 1997–2008

Sean Clancy, Kickboxing (Lightweight), Ireland, 2009–current

Sean Elliott, Basketball (Small Forward), San Antonio Spurs, USA, 1989–2001

Sean Fitzpatrick, Rugby (Hooker), Auckland Rugby Union, New Zealand, 1986–1997

Sean Johnson, Soccer (Goalkeeper), New York City Football Club, USA, 2009–current

Sean O'Grady, Boxing (Lightweight), USA, 1975–1983

SEBASTIAN/SÉBASTIEN

From humble roots including a Roman name for people from a town in Asia Minor and, further back, an Ancient Greek word for "venerable" comes the name Sebastian and its French variant Sébastien. In modern times, these names have been associated internationally with some team players like French esports *Dota 2* champion Sébastien "Ceb" Debs, who won two back-to-back The International tournaments with the OG team; and Italian soccer forward Sebastian Giovinco, whose career playing around the world has seen him win Supercoppa Italiana twice, an MLS Cup, an MLS Golden Boot, and a King Cup while being named MLS All-Star four times, MLS Best XI three times, and MLS MVP.

Beyond the team sports, though, Sebastians and Sébastiens just seem destined for racing! This can range from bobsledding (like German three-time world champion Sebastian "Wastl" Huber) to middle-distance running (like British two-time Olympic gold-medalist and World Cup-winner Sebastian "Seb" Coe), and sprint canoeing (like Sebastian Brendel of Germany, who has won three gold medals and a bronze at Olympic Games and twenty-four medals at World Championships, thirteen of them gold). But the trend is most noteworthy in auto racing. Swiss crossover driver Sébastien Buemi won twenty-three races and three championships in the FIA World Endurance Championship series before joining Formula E and winning thirteen races and a championship there, and German Sebastian Vettel is a Formula 1 legend with fifty-three wins and four championships. Finally, two French drivers have absolutely dominated the World Rally Championship series: Sébastien Ogier has won fifty-seven races and eight championships and Sébastien Loeb has won eighty races and nine championships!

Get ready to chase after your son if you name him Sebastian or Sébastien because he'll love going fast in any way he can!

- **Sebastian Brendel**, Sprint Canoeing, Germany, 2011–current
- **Sébastien Buemi**, Auto Racing (Formula E), Switzerland, 2004–current
- **Sebastian "Seb" Coe**, Track & Field (Middle-Distance Running), England, 1977–1990
- **Sébastien "Ceb" Debs**, Esports (*Dota 2*), France, 2011–2021
- **Sebastian Giovinco**, Soccer (Forward), Toronto Football Club, Italy, 2006–2022
- **Sebastian "Wastl" Huber**, Bobsleigh, Germany, 1928–1935
- **Sébastien Loeb**, Auto Racing (Rally), France, 1998–current
- **Sébastien Ogier**, Auto Racing (Rally), France, 2005–current
- **Sebastian Vettel**, Auto Racing (Formula 1), Germany, 2003–2022

SERGE

Serge is the first in a series of names that come to us from the ancient Roman family name *Sergius*, and potentially Etruscan roots before that. Serge is a French form of the name, though it appears around the world in various French and English-speaking countries. And despite the original translation of the name as "servant," athletes with it are beholden to no one and have gone out and done amazing things. Canadian ice hockey Hall of Fame defenseman Serge Savard played in four NHL All-Star games and pioneered the "Savardian Spin-o-rama" move, and French bodybuilder Serge Nubret conquered the competitive scene by being named World's Most Muscular Man and winning Mr. Universe, Mr. Olympus, Mr. World, and two world championships.

Teach your son named Serge how to swim early on and introduce him to paddling and he may take after Canadian marathon canoe racer Serge Corbin, who's considered among the all-time greatest in his sport, or French sailor Serge Maury, who won Olympic gold and a Finn Gold Cup.

- **Serge Corbin**, Marathon Canoe Racing, Canada, 1973–current
- **Serge Maury**, Sailing, France, 1971–1976
- **Serge Nubret**, Bodybuilding, France, 1960–2003
- **Serge Savard**, Ice Hockey (Defense), Montreal Canadiens, Canada, 1966–1983

SERGEI/SERGEY

From French *Serge* we move east to Belarus and Russia, which produced the Sergei and Sergey forms of the original Roman *Sergius*. Now, a young Sergei or Sergey can find inspirations in previous champions for everything from volleyball (like Russian Olympic gold-medalist, World League-winner, and two-time World Cup champion outside hitter Sergey Tetyukhin) to freestyle wrestling (like Soviet six-time world champion and two-time Olympic gold-medalist Sergei Beloglazov), artistic gymnastics (like three-time Olympic gold-medalist and world champion Sergey Kharkov, who has competed for the USSR, Russia, and Germany), and chess (like Russian Grandmaster Sergey Karjakin, who was the youngest person in the world to achieve that rank at the time)!

Finally, we head into the cold with a number of Russian athletes. Outdoors, biathlete

Sergei Tchepikov won six Olympic medals (two golds), fourteen medals at World Championships (two golds), and five individual wins and two overall titles at World Cups. The rest achieved their glory on the ice, including Olympic gold-medalist and three-time world champion ice dancer Sergei Ponomarenko, and two-time Olympic gold-medalist and four-time world champion figure skater Sergei Grinkov. Probably the most famous group of Russian Sergeis are the ice hockey players, Hockey Hall of Famers, right wing Sergei Makarov (two-time Olympic gold-medalist, eight-time world champion, and Challenge Cup-winner) and legendary center Sergei Fedorov (three-time world champion, six-time NHL All-Star, and three-time Stanley Cup champion).

You don't need Russian or Belarusian heritage to name a son Sergei or Sergey, but if you do, he could very well have an affinity for sports on the ice and snow. Get him ski and ice-skating lessons and he could one day hoist the Stanley Cup above his head!

Sergei Beloglazov, Freestyle Wrestling, USSR, 1979-1988

Sergei Fedorov, Ice Hockey (Center/Defense), Detroit Red Wings, USSR/Russia, 1986-2012

Sergei Grinkov, Figure Skating, USSR/Russia, 1986-1995

Sergey Karjakin, Chess, Ukraine/Russia, 2001-current

Sergey Kharkov, Artistic Gymnastics, Russia, 1988-2001

Sergei Makarov, Ice Hockey (Right Wing), Calgary Flames, USSR, 1976-1997

Sergei Ponomarenko, Ice Dancing, USSR, 1980-1996

Sergei Tchepikov, Biathlon, USSR/Russia, 1986-2007

Sergey Tetyukhin, Volleyball (Outside Hitter), Russia, 1992-2018

SERGI

The next descendent of the Latin *Sergius* is the name Sergi, originally a Catalan and Georgian variant that is not super popular in North America. Where it has seen a lot of action is in Spain with world champion track cyclist Sergi Escobar, Olympic gold- and silver-medalist and two-time world champion water polo player Sergi Pedrerol, and a couple of great defensive soccer players in Barcelona: stars left-back Sergi Barjuán (La Liga three times, Copa del Rey twice, Supercopa de España twice, UEFA Cup Winners' Cup, and UEFA Super Cup) and midfielder/full-back Sergi Roberto (La Liga seven times, Copa del Rey six times, Supercopa de España three times, UEFA Champions League twice, UEFA Super Cup, and FIFA Club World Cup)!

Name your son Sergi and get him out on the soccer (or "football" if you prefer) field!

Sergi Barjuán Esclusa, Soccer (Left-Back), Fútbol Club Barcelona, Spain, 1990-2005

Sergi Escobar Roure, Track Cycling, Spain, 2001-2008

Sergi Pedrerol Cavallé, Water Polo (Field Player), Spain, 1992-2001

Sergi Roberto Carnicer, Soccer (Midfielder/Full-Back), Fútbol Club Barcelona, Spain, 2008-current

SERGIO

Our final *Sergius*-based name is the Italian and Spanish Sergio, and like *Sergi*, the majority of the champion athletes with this name have risen through the ranks in soccer! The list is extensive, with classic greats like Argentinian 1986 FIFA World Cup-winning defensive midfielder Sergio "Checho" Batista, and forward Sergio Bertoni, who won an Olympic gold medal in 1936 and the FIFA World Cup in 1938 with the Italy team.

Two Spanish defenders have proven themselves among the best of the best, with FIFA

World Cup All-Star Team defensive midfielder Sergio Busquets winning FIFA World Cup 2010, and more, while FIFA World Cup Dream Team and FIFA World Cup All-Star Team center-back Sergio Ramos's trophy collection includes the 2010 FIFA World Cup and dozens more while being crowned La Liga Best Defender five times, winning the FIFA Club World Cup Golden Ball, and being named to FIFA FIFPro World 11 eleven times, UEFA Team of the Year nine times, FIFA Confederations Cup Dream Team, and UEFA Ultimate Team of the Year!

Sergios don't necessarily have to go into soccer, though, and some inspiring winners with this name have appeared in various sports and events. Some of them compete with teammates, like Italian two-time Olympic gold-medalist tandem cyclist Sergio Bianchetto, who also won two sprint world championships; and Brazilian volleyball libero Sérgio Dutra dos Santos, who ranks among the best ever with two gold and two silver medals from Olympic Games, two world championships, two World Grand Champions Cup wins, two World Cups, and seven World League championships.

Finally, there are Sergios who have made it all on their own, like Spanish golfer Sergio García, who has thirty-six professional wins and one major title; and Cuban-American bodybuilder Sergio "The Myth" Oliva, who is considered one of the all-time greats with an astounding list of championships, including a Mr. World, Mr. Universe, Mr. Olympia three times, Mr. Olympus three times, Mr. Galaxy twice and more!

- **Sergio "Checho" Batista**, Soccer (Defensive Midfielder), Tosu Futures, Argentina, 1981–1999
- **Sergio Bertoni**, Soccer (Forward), Pisa Sporting Club, Italy, 1935–1950
- **Sergio Bianchetto**, Track Cycling, Italy, 1960–1969
- **Sergio Busquets Burgos**, Soccer (Defensive Midfielder), Fútbol Club Barcelona, Spain, 2007–current
- **Sergio García Fernández**, Golf, Spain, 1999–current
- **Sergio "The Myth" Oliva**, Bodybuilding, Cuba/USA, 1962–1985
- **Sergio Ramos García**, Soccer (Center-Back), Real Madrid Club de Fútbol, Spain, 2003–2023
- **Sérgio Dutra dos Santos**, Volleyball (Libero), Brazil, 1992–2020

SETH

Seth is a biblical Hebrew name and comes from a word meaning "placed" or "appointed." Three very unique American athletes with this name have *placed* among the elites in their sports: NFL three-time Pro Bowl linebacker and Super Bowl champion Seth Joyner, two-time Olympic gold-medalist and world champion snowboarder Seth Wescott, and 2016 Esports Console Player of the Year Seth "scump" Abner, who's considered one of the world's greatest *Call of Duty* players having won over thirty tournaments, two Major League Gaming X Games gold medals, and a Call of Duty World Championship.

Name a boy Seth in your family and he could be way into football, snowboarding, or video games!

- **Seth "scump" Abner**, Esports (*Call of Duty*), USA, 2011–current
- **Seth Joyner**, Football (Linebacker), Philadelphia Eagles, USA, 1986–1998
- **Seth Wescott**, Snowboarding, USA, 2003–2011

SEUNG-

The unisex Korean name Seung can be used either on its own or as part of a two-syllable name, and it brings to a child very positive vibes with possible translations (based on the characters used to write it) like "rise/ascend" or "victory." Interestingly, South Korean athletes with Seung- names frequently appear at the top of sports or similar events in pairs!

Racquet sports have witnessed the excellence of badminton Sudirman Cup mixed team champion Seo Seung-jae and Olympic gold-medalist table tennis singles player Ryu Seung-min, while elite marksmen with these names include two-time world champion pistol sport shooter Han Seung-woo and archer Lee Seung-yun, who has won Olympic gold and an individual world championship.

A boy with a name starting with Seung- in your family may gravitate toward racquet or paddle sports, or sharpshooting, but he may also set out on his own and forge his own path in something unique, like speed skater Lee Seung-hoon, who has taken home six medals from Olympic Games, including two golds, four medals from World Single Distance Championships, and four medals from Short Track World Championships!

- **Han Seung-woo**, Sport Shooting (Pistol), South Korea, 2016–current
- **Lee Seung-hoon**, Speed Skating, South Korea, 2005–current
- **Lee Seung-yun**, Archery, South Korea, 2013–current
- **Ryu Seung-min**, Table Tennis, South Korea, 2001–2012
- **Seo Seung-jae**, Badminton, South Korea, 2018–current

SHANE

A variation on the name *Sean* (an Irish version of *John*), Shane has a history of popularity in the United States ever since the western film with the same name debuted in 1953. You may not find a lot of cowboys named Shane these days, but you will find a number of talented and successful athletes in quite a few different fields! These range from surfing (with Hawaiian Rip Curl Pro and O'Neill Surf Challenge champion big wave surfer Shane Dorian) to ice hockey (with Canadian two-time world champion and two-time NHL All-Star right wing Shane Doan).

Some Shanes find their place facing off against their opponents one-on-one in the ring, battling it out with fists and feet, like the iconic (and awesomely nicknamed) boxer "Sugar" Shane Mosley, who held multiple world championships in three different weight classes.

Outside North America, Shanes have made big impacts on rugby and cricket. On the pitch, Australian Brisbane Broncos prop Shane Webcke was named Daily M Prop of the Year three times, Rugby League Player of the Year, and NRL Team of the 1990s for his four Grand Final wins, 2004 Tri-Nations, and 2000 Rugby League World Cup championships; and Welsh 2008 IRB Player of the Year wing/scrum half Shane Williams stands on multiple leaderboards for his position and country with several Grand Slams to his name, two Six Nations championships, and more.

In cricket, Shanes in Oceania have really shined with a trio of Australians; the 1999 Cricket World Cup-winning team included both all-rounder Shane Lee and record-setting bowler Shane Warne, while all-rounder Shane Watson is one of the game's all-time greats, with a trophy collection of two Cricket World Cups, two ICC Champions Trophies, number one rankings among both all-rounders and batters, numerous awards, and more.

Wherever you live, a Shane in your family will have the drive to compete and win. He may be a fighter or team player or enjoy participating in international sports or the local favorite. Whatever his athletic destiny, you should strongly consider the nickname "Sugar" for him!

Shane Doan, Ice Hockey (Right Wing), Phoenix Coyotes, Canada, 1995–2017

Shane Dorian, Surfing, USA, 1992–current

Shane Lee, Cricket (All-Rounder), New South Wales Men's Cricket Team, Australia, 1992–2002

"Sugar" Shane Mosley, Boxing (Lightweight/Welterweight/Middleweight), USA, 1993–2016

Shane Warne, Cricket (Bowler), Victoria Men's Cricket Team, Australia, 1990–2013

Shane Watson, Cricket (All-Rounder), Rajasthan Royals, Australia, 2000–2020

Shane Webcke, Rugby (Prop), Brisbane Broncos Rugby League Football Club Ltd., Australia, 1995–2006

Shane Williams, Rugby (Wing/Scrum Half), Neath Rugby Football Club, Wales, 1998–2015

SHAOANG

Some names transcend nations, languages, and history while also bringing along athletic skill and a love of competition. Shaoang is just such a one, probably most famous for the mid-1990s Chinese flower-and-bird painter Zhao Shao'ang. Now, though, it belongs to Chinese-Hungarian short track speed skater Liu Shaoang, who has set world records and already amassed a collection of medals, including two Olympic golds and two bronzes and thirteen World Championship medals (six of them gold)!

Not only can the name Shaoang inspire your son to achievement and glory, but when paired with a sibling named *Shaolin*, it's absolutely unstoppable!

Liu Shaoang, Speed Skating, Hungary/China, 2015–current

SHAOLIN

Often associated with kung fu and the Chinese Buddhist monastery in the Shaoyang Valley—and coming from a place name for a forest on Mount Shaoshi—Shaolin is also the name of one half of the duo of Chinese-Hungarian Olympic gold-medalist short track speed skaters! Along with Shaoang and their 5000-meter relay teammates, Shaolin won Hungary's first-ever Winter Olympics gold medal in 2018, and his medal count also includes an Olympic bronze and ten podiums at World Championships (including two golds).

If you're looking for a unique name with an ancient pedigree and a recent history of athletic excellence, then Shaolin may be just the ticket—and it pairs perfectly with *Shaoang* for two brothers who will compete and win together.

Liu Shaolin, Speed Skating, Hungary/China, 2013–current

SHAQUILLE

Tall, powerful, and intimidating are aspects that come to mind with the modern name Shaquille that originates in *Shakil*, from an Arabic root for "handsome."

Towering over the competition is the big man himself, basketball center Shaquille O'Neal! An absolute icon of his sport, O'Neal won a World Cup and an Olympic gold medal with the Dream Team and was inducted into the Basketball Hall of Fame. In his nineteen years in the NBA, Shaquille was selected as an All-Star fifteen times; was named MVP, NBA All-Star Game MVP, and NBA Finals MVP; led the league in scoring twice; and won the NBA championship four times, three times with the Los Angeles Lakers and once with Miami Heat! Those are the major headlines, but his legacy is cemented for all time as one of the greatest players ever with numerous awards, records, and places held on multiple leaderboards.

A Shaquille in your family may not become a basketball legend at seven feet, one inch and

325 pounds, but he'll find a good balance in life between playing hard and working hard. And he'll love to go by the nickname Shaq.

Shaquille "Shaq" O'Neal, Basketball (Center), Los Angeles Lakers, USA, 1992–2011

SHAUN/SHAWN/SHAWNE

Just as *Sean* is a variation of the name *John*, so, too, does Sean have its own different versions like unisex Shaun and Shawne. No matter where they're from, Shauns, Shawns, and Shawnes are excellent athletes across the board (or field, rink, or pitch).

In cricket, Australian bowler Shaun Tait won the 2007 Cricket World Cup, and in the NBA, four-time All-Star small forward/power forward Shawn Marion won the 2011 NBA championship with the Dallas Mavericks, and power forward Shawn Kemp played in six All-Star games and won a world championship in 1994 with Team USA. Finally, on the gridiron, there are not one, not two, but three three-time Pro Bowlers with these names: defensive tackle Shaun Rogers, sacks leader linebacker Shawne Merriman, and Seattle Seahawks running back Shaun Alexander, who led the league in rushing yards, rushing touchdowns twice, and scoring to be named MVP and Offensive Player of the Year.

While so many Shauns, Shawns, and Shawnes have excelled in team settings, others have gone just as far on their own and give future athletes with these names even more inspiration in unique settings. These include two-time welterweight world champion boxer Shawn Porter, whose career ended with a 31-4-1 record; four-time world champion wakeboarder Shaun Murray; and multi-talented athlete Shaun White, who won two gold medals, two silvers, and a bronze from the X Games in vert skateboarding, as well as three Olympic gold medals and thirteen golds, three silvers, and two bronzes from X Games in snowboarding!

Shaun Alexander, Football (Running Back), Seattle Seahawks, USA, 2000–2008

Shawn Kemp Sr., Basketball (Power Forward), Seattle SuperSonics, USA, 1989–2003

Shawn Marion, Basketball (Small Forward/ Power Forward), Phoenix Suns, USA, 1999–2015

Shawne Merriman, Football (Linebacker), San Diego Chargers, USA, 2005–2012

Shaun Murray, Wakeboarding, USA, 1995–current

Shawn Porter, Boxing (Welterweight/ Middleweight), USA, 2008–2021

Shaun Rogers, Football (Defensive Tackle), Detroit Lions, USA, 2001–2013

Shaun Tait, Cricket (Bowler), South Australia Cricket Team, Australia, 2002–2016

Shaun White, Snowboarding/Skateboarding, USA, 2002–2022

SID/SIDNEY

Sidney and its iconic diminutive Sid come from Old English and a place name meaning "wide island" (the proposed origin coming from the Normandy town "Saint Denis" is not likely). You don't have to come from an island to give your son this somewhat old-fashioned name that has an interesting athletic heritage around the English and French-speaking world.

Sidneys have always been team players, and the name was represented on leaderboards across the better part of the twentieth century. In the NFL, Chicago Bears MVP and three-time Pro Bowl quarterback Sid Luckman racked up four NFL championships and led the league in completion percentage, passing yards three times, and passing touchdowns three times, and was later inducted into the Hall of Fame. Basketball would see a couple of its own Sidneys making it big with 1972 NBA Rookie of the Year power forward Sidney Wicks playing in four All-Star games in the 1970s, while in the '80s, five-time All-Star shooting guard Sidney Moncrief was named Defensive Player of the Year twice and earned induction into the Basketball Hall of Fame.

Up in Canada, the action is all on the ice! Sidney "The Next One" Crosby was drafted into the NHL in 2005, and since then, the Pittsburgh Penguins center has played in nine All-Star games, won the Stanley Cup three times, was named All-Star Game MVP, and amassed dozens of awards and other trophies, all of which has made him undisputedly one of the greatest players of all time. On the international scene, Crosby has also won a world championship, a World Cup, and two Olympic gold medals!

A Sidney in your family (whom you can absolutely nickname Sid) can stick to sports and events that are popular in his country or branch out and pick something more unique. Whatever he chooses, he'll have the skills and love of the game like the athletes who have come before him.

- **Sidney "The Next One" Crosby**, Ice Hockey (Center), Pittsburgh Penguins, Canada, 2005–current
- **Sidney "Sid" Luckman**, Football (Quarterback), Chicago Bears, USA, 1939–1950
- **Sidney Moncrief**, Basketball (Shooting Guard), Milwaukee Bucks, USA, 1979–1991
- **Sidney Wicks**, Basketball (Power Forward), Portland Trail Blazers, USA, 1971–1982

SIEGFRIED

Do you love rowing and Germanic heroic legends? Then Siegfried is the perfect name for your son! From Old German roots for "victory" and "peace," the name is historically most famous for the hero of the *Nibelungenlied*, but more recently it was borne to victory in the water by German three-time Olympic gold-medalist and three-time world champion rower Siegfried Brietzke.

- **Siegfried Brietzke**, Rowing, Germany, 1971–1980

SILVIO

The Italian and Spanish name Silvio may come from a Latin root for "woods" or "forest," but in modern times, elite athletes have brought it to the track and the soccer field. Cuban sprinter Silvio Leonard took home more than a dozen medals from international events in the 1970s and '80s, including two golds at World Cups. Over in international football, Portuguese full-back Sílvio Manuel Pereira recently wrapped up his career winning the Copa del Rey, Taça de Portugal, Taça da Liga three times, UEFA Europa League, and UEFA Super Cup, while in the 1930s, '40s, and '50s, Italian Silvio Piola's 350-plus goals in senior and international appearances and wins like the Central European International Cup and 1938 FIFA World Cup cemented his place on lists of the all-time great strikers.

Name your son Silvio and he'll be a fast runner; he may even enjoy hiking and camping in the woods too!

- **Silvio Leonard**, Track & Field (Sprinting), Cuba, 1973–1985
- **Sílvio Manuel de Azevedo Ferreira Sá Pereira**, Soccer (Full-Back), Rio Ave Futebol Clube, Portugal, 2006–2023
- **Silvio Piola**, Soccer (Striker), Società Sportiva Lazio, Italy, 1929–1954

SIMON/SZYMON

The name Simon comes to us via Greek from ancient Hebrew and a meaning of "hearing" or "listening," and it has spawned several alternate versions over the years, with a notable one being the Polish Szymon. Simons (and Szymons) from around the world have found their places on podiums and leaderboards for a large number of sports and events, with some singular champions reaching heights in archery (Australian world champion and

Olympic gold-medalist Simon Fairweather), hammer throwing (Szymon Ziółkowski of Poland, who also won a world championship and a gold medal from the Olympics), and even chess (English Grandmaster Simon Williams).

On wheels, British cyclist Simon Yates won a world championship and general classification at the Vuelta a España, and in the triathlon, Canadian Simon Whitfield won Olympic gold in 2000 and British Simon Lessing conquered the International Triathlon Union Long Distance World Championship and won the standard ITU World Championship four times. In one-on-one combat sports, British visually impaired judoka Simon Jackson won three Paralympic gold medals and Canadian martial artist and two-time Glory middleweight champion kickboxer Simon Marcus won a WCK Muay Thai World Light Heavyweight championship, International Federation of Muaythai Amateur World Championships gold and silver medals, the Lion Fight Light Heavyweight championship, a World Combat Games muay thai gold medal, and more.

The largest concentration of Simons competing at top levels is in winter sports like Canadian ice hockey left wing Simon Gagné, who won Olympic gold and a World Cup with his national team and played in two All-Star games and won the Stanley Cup in the NHL. Out on the slopes, American Simon Dumont won nine X Games medals (including four golds) and Swiss ski jumper Simon Ammann has won a staggering four Olympic gold medals, four medals at World Championships, a Ski Flying World Championship, twenty-three individual World Cup wins, and one overall title.

A young Simon (or Szymon!) in your family may not always listen to you, but he should definitely be fun to take out for a run, a bike ride, some sparring, or a day of skiing.

Simon "Simi" Ammann, Ski Jumping, Switzerland, 1998-current

Simon Dumont, Freestyle Skiing, USA, 2004-2013

Simon Fairweather, Archery, Australia, 1988-2004

Simon Gagné, Ice Hockey (Left Wing), Philadelphia Flyers, Canada, 1999-2015

Simon Jackson, Judo, England, 1988-2012

Simon Lessing, Triathlon, England, 1988-2008

Simon Marcus, Kickboxing (Light Heavyweight/Cruiserweight/Middleweight), Canada, 2006-current

Simon Whitfield, Triathlon, Canada, 1999-2013

Simon Williams, Chess, England, 1993-current

Simon Yates, Road/Track Cycling, England, 2010-current

Szymon Ziółkowski, Track & Field (Hammer Throw), Poland, 1995-2014

SIXTEN

While it may sound like a combination of two numbers to English speakers, Sixten is a Swedish name that comes from pretty tough Old Norse roots for "victory" and "stone." "Tough as rocks" and "a winner" are absolutely ways of describing Swedish skier Sixten Jernberg, who went from blacksmithing and lumberjacking to winning nine cross-country skiing medals at the Olympics (four of them gold) and six at World Championships (four of them gold)!

Sixten is a cool name that will almost certainly be unique among your son's classmates and friends, and it can give him a love of working hard and playing hard in the snow.

Edy Sixten Jernberg, Cross-Country Skiing, Sweden, 1952-1964

SOHAIL

The name Sohail may come from an Arabic root for "level" or "even," but there's nothing merely on the level about the skill of Pakistani athletes Sohail Abbas and Sohail Tanvir. The former became an international field hockey legend as the "king of the drag flick" by setting multiple scoring records and winning the Indian Premier Hockey League championship, 1999 Sultan Azlan Shah Cup, and 2010 Asian Games Hockey championship, while the latter is a world-renowned cricket bowler with impressive stats and the championship at the 2009 ICC World Twenty20!

Giving the name Sohail to your son will set him well above the level, whether he seeks success in sports, business, or any other competitive environment.

Sohail Abbas, Field Hockey (Full-Back), Pakistan, 1997–2012

Sohail Tanvir, Cricket (Bowler), Rawalpindi, Pakistan, 2004–current

SOREN/SØREN

Soren/Søren is a Danish name that comes from an ancient Roman family name and Latin meaning "stern," but a son you give it to will just want to compete and have fun! And if he's anything like famous athletes with his name who have come before, he may enjoy fencing, wrestling, or video games, like American world champion épée fencer Soren Thompson; two-time Intercalated Games gold-medalist Greco-Roman wrestler Søren Jensen; and four-time League Championship Series All-Star and three-time LCS MVP *League of Legends* esports icon Søren "Bjergsen" Bjerg, who won the 2015 Intel Extreme Masters, 2017 Rift Rivals championship, 2022 LCS Lock In championship, and six LCS championships.

Søren "Bjergsen" Bjerg, Esports (*League of Legends*), Denmark, 2012–2023

Søren Jensen, Greco-Roman Wrestling, Denmark, 1904–1912

Soren Thompson, Fencing (Épée), USA, 2003–current

SOSLAN

Ossetia may be a far-flung region in the Caucasus Mountains running from the Black Sea to the Caspian Sea, but the name Soslan that originated there (from a Turkic root meaning "menacing") has reached the world's stage thanks to two Russian freestyle wrestlers. In the 2010s, Soslan Ramonov won Olympic gold, a world championship, a gold medal at Military World Games, and two at World Military Championships. Ramonov followed in the footsteps of Soviet two-time Olympic gold-medalist, four-time world champion, and World Cup gold-medalist Soslan Andiyev!

A Soslan in your family may be a tough opponent and menacing on the mat, but he'll be a fair competitor and earn every accolade he achieves.

Soslan Andiyev, Freestyle Wrestling, USSR, 1973–1984

Soslan Ramonov, Freestyle Wrestling, Russia, 2011–2018

STAN/STANLEY

Stan is a good old-fashioned name that is most often a short form of *Stanislav* or Stanley, which comes from Old English words meaning "stone clearing." In tennis, Swiss doubles player Stan Wawrinka is an Olympic gold-medalist and Hall of Famer Stan Smith held world number one spots in both singles and doubles, with sixty-four and fifty-four titles, respectively! In soccer, legendary Stanley Matthews's long career lasted until he was fifty years old and saw him play in over 850 senior and international matches, be named FWA Footballer of the Year twice, be given the inaugural Ballon d'Or award in 1956, and so much more.

On the gridiron, Stan Jones played multiple positions for the Chicago bears, was selected for seven Pro Bowls, won the 1963 NFL championship, and earned induction into the Pro Football Hall of Fame. Over on the ice, Canadian Chicago Blackhawks center Stan Mikita would play in nine All-Star games and win the Stanley Cup in 1961, earning his place in hockey history with induction into the Hall of Fame.

Major League Baseball has also seen some champion Stans: Hall of Fame St. Louis Cardinals outfielder/first baseman Stan "the Man" Musial, who was selected as All-Star twenty times in his twenty-two seasons, led the National League in RBIs twice, won seven NL batting championships, was named National League MVP three times, and won three World Series championships! A legend in the sport, Musial set numerous records and still stands as one of the greatest batters and players of all time.

Name your son Stanley or call him Stan and he'll be a devoted team player, working best with his friends and teammates and maximizing his abilities and skills to win big!

Stanley "Stan" Jones, Football (Guard/ Offensive Tackle/Defensive Tackle), Chicago Bears, USA, 1954–1966

Stanley Matthews, Soccer (Outside Right), Blackpool Football Club, England, 1932–1965

Stanley "Stan" Mikita, Ice Hockey (Center), Chicago Blackhawks, Canada, 1958–1980

Stanley "Stan" (The Man) Musial, Baseball (Outfielder/First Baseman), St. Louis Cardinals, USA, 1941–1963

Stanley "Stan" Smith, Tennis, USA, 1969–1985

Stanley "Stan" Wawrinka, Tennis, Switzerland, 2002–current

STANISLAV

From Eastern Europe and Slavic roots for "stand/become" and "glory" comes the name Stanislav. Athletic history tells us that Stanislavs are really good at competing in modern events with ancient weapons!

Your son named Stanislav may prefer something that dates back to ancient times and follow in the footsteps of people like Ukrainian two-time world champion archer Stanislav Zabrodsky or Russian sabre fencer Stanislav Pozdnyakov, who won a mighty four Olympic gold medals and a bronze, as well as seventeen medals at World Championships (ten of them gold)!

Stanislav Pozdnyakov, Fencing (Sabre), Russia, 1992–2008

Stanislav Zabrodsky, Archery, USSR/Ukraine, 1989–2004

STEFAN

Beyond the most common *Stephen* and *Steven* forms, there are many other variants of the name around the world, including Stefan. Mostly from Europe, Stefans tend to congregate in certain types of athletic events, some of them surprising. A Stefan in your family should feel free to find his own unique path, as we can see with record-setting Swedish high jumper Stefan Holm, who took home Olympic gold and four world championships.

When it comes to water sports and tennis, athletes with this name have made big waves. These include Serbian two-time Olympic gold-medalist and two-time world champion water polo center back Stefan Mitrović, who also won a World Cup and nine World Leagues; and Swedish tennis star Stefan Edberg, who was ranked number one in the world in both singles and doubles (with forty-one and eighteen titles, respectively) and won a total of nine Grand Slams, a Masters

Grand Prix win, four Davis Cups, four Masters Series, and four Championship Series titles.

Ice and snow events are also quite popular with this name, as we can see with speed skating's Dutch Stefan Groothuis, who raced to gold at the Olympic Games in 2014 and two World Championships; ski jumping's Austrian Olympic gold-medalist and two-time world champion Stefan Kraft, who has won thirty individual World Cup events; and luge's Stefan Krauße of Germany, who dominated doubles and teams events in the 1980s and '90s with two Olympic gold medals, a silver, and a bronze; seven world championship golds and four silvers; and three golds, two silvers, and two bronzes at World Cup Championships!

Next up are the fastest Stefans on two wheels. Utilizing pedal power, German track cyclist Stefan Nimke raced to four Olympic medals, including a gold, and seven medals from World Championships, including two wins. Over on motorcycles, Belgian motocross legend Stefan Everts tops the charts with 101 race wins and a record ten championships.

As with many names that are popular in Europe, Stefan has been particularly momentous in football (soccer), especially two Germans with top-tier records: FIFA World Cup 1990-winning defender/midfielder Stefan Reuter, who won most of his major victories with Borussia Dortmund, and FIFA XI and UEFA Club Footballer of the Year midfielder Stefan Effenberg, who won the US Cup, Bundesliga three times, DFB-Pokal twice, DFL-Supercup, UEFA Champions League, and Intercontinental Cup.

If you name your son Stefan, you should absolutely introduce him to swimming, tennis, ice skating, skiing, bike riding, and soccer, though he may surprise you and find a niche sport that suits his particular set of skills!

Stefan Edberg, Tennis, Sweden, 1983–1996

Stefan Effenberg, Soccer (Midfielder), Borussia Mönchengladbach, Germany, 1987–2004

Stefan Everts, Motocross, Belgium, 1988–2006

Stefan Groothuis, Speed Skating, Netherlands, 2003–2016

Stefan Holm, Track & Field (High Jump), Sweden, 1997–2008

Stefan Kraft, Ski Jumping, Austria, 2012–current

Stefan Krauße, Luge, Germany, 1988–1998

Stefan Mitrović, Water Polo (Center Back), Serbia, 2006–current

Stefan Nimke, Track Cycling, Germany, 1997–2012

Stefan Reuter, Soccer (Center-Back/ Midfielder), Ballspielverein Borussia 09 e. V. Dortmund, Germany, 1984–2004

STEFF/STEPH

People with names like *Stefan* and *Stephen* often go by the diminutives Steff and Steph, and there's a definite power that they bring . . . especially when it comes to skiing and playing basketball! If you've got a young one who likes to go by these short forms, then you should absolutely teach him the fundamentals on the slopes and the hardwood court; if he works really hard, he could turn out like Austrian Olympic gold-medalist and three-time world champion ski racer Steff Eberharter, who claimed a staggering seventy-five World Cup podiums (with twenty-nine of them wins), or nine-time NBA All-Star point guard Steph Curry! The Golden State Warriors basketball legend has won four NBA championships, two scoring championships, and two Three-Point Contests; was named NBA Finals MVP and NBA MVP twice; led the league in steals; joined the 50-40-90 club; and set multiple league records. Curry has also won a World Championship and World Cup with the United States national team.

Wardell Stephen "Steph" Curry II, Basketball (Point Guard), Golden State Warriors, USA, 2009–current

Stephan "Steff" Eberharter, Alpine Skiing, Austria, 1990–2004

STÉPHANE

Like *Stefan*, Stéphane is another variant of *Stephen*. Similarly, there's a good chance a boy with one of these names may find ice hockey or racing exciting.

Some Stéphanes in particular like to go fast, like Stéphane Ortelli, who won the 24 Hours of Le Mans, Spa 24 Hours, and 12 Hours of Sebring (GT1), while the remaining Stéphanes could be found on the international football field. Some of the most feted athletes with this name have been Swiss striker Stéphane Chapuisat, who won the Bundesliga twice, DFB-Supercup twice, Swiss Super League, UEFA Champions League, and Intercontinental Cup; Belgian FIFA World Cup All-Star Team center-back Stéphane Demol, who won his local Belgian Cup and Belgian Supercup twice each; and French UEFA Cup Golden Boot striker Stéphane Guivarc'h, whose trophy collection includes a UEFA Intertoto Cup and FIFA World Cup 1998.

Stéphane Chapuisat, Soccer (Striker), Ballspielverein Borussia 09 e. V. Dortmund, Switzerland, 1986–2006

Stéphane Demol, Soccer (Center-Back), Royal Standard de Liège, Belgium, 1984–2000

Stéphane Guivarc'h, Soccer (Striker), En Avant Guingamp, France, 1989–2002

Stéphane Ortelli, Auto Racing (24 Hours of Le Mans), France, 1995–current

STEPHEN

Stephen is a modern version of an Ancient Greek name that came from a word meaning "that which surrounds," and which came to mean "crown" or "wreath." That makes Stephen a perfect name for a champion athlete who's crowned after a hard-won victory! Stephens fitting this description have succeeded in a number of different fields. In team sports, these include baseball, with Washington Nationals three-time All-Star and World Series champion pitcher Stephen Strasburg, who was named World Series MVP, led the National League in wins and strikeouts, and earned the Babe Ruth award, a Silver Slugger, and Golden Spikes; and football, with New England Patriots four-time Pro Bowl placekicker Stephen Gostkowski, who won four Super Bowls, led the NFL in scoring five times, and set multiple NFL records.

On the other hand, lots of Stephens make it all on their own, in events ranging from mixed martial arts (with World Association of Kickboxing Organizations amateur world champion Stephen Thompson, who had an undefeated fifty-eight wins and one no-contest kickboxing career) to artistic gymnastics (with pommel horse-world champion and World Cup gold-medalist Stephen Nedoroscik) and darts (with English two-time World Masters champion and 2014 BDL World Darts champion Stephen Bunting).

Then pairs of Stephens have appeared among the top echelons of two different categories. On two wheels, Irish road cyclist Stephen Roche became a Triple Crown winner in 1987 by winning the Tour de France, Giro d'Italia, and a World Championship, while more recently, Australian track cyclist Stephen Wooldridge took home an Olympic gold medal and four world championships. Last but certainly not least, the world of snooker has seen the exploits of two great Scots in six-time major tournament-winner Stephen Maguire and seven-time world champion Stephen Hendry, whose tremendous career, world number one ranking, and numerous records place him firmly on the all-time greats list.

Name your son Stephen and he'll be crowned for his accomplishments in whatever field he chooses; in particular, see if he enjoys track and field, bike riding, or billiards games!

- **Stephen Bunting**, Darts, England, 1997–current
- **Stephen Gostkowski**, Football (Placekicker), New England Patriots, USA, 2006–2020
- **Stephen Hendry**, Snooker, Scotland, 1985–current
- **Stephen Maguire**, Snooker, Scotland, 1998–current
- **Stephen Nedoroscik**, Artistic Gymnastics, USA, 2019–current
- **Stephen Roche**, Cycling (Road), Ireland, 1981–1993
- **Stephen Strasburg**, Baseball (Pitcher), Washington Nationals, USA, 2010–2022
- **Stephen Thomas**, Ice Sledge Hockey/Sailing/Skiing, Wales, 2002–current
- **Stephen Thompson**, Kickboxing/MMA (Welterweight), USA, 2010–current
- **Stephen Wooldridge**, Cycling (Track), Australia, 2002–2007

STEVE

A common diminutive for *Stephen* and *Steven*, Steve is a mainstay in lots of sports in the English-speaking world, and a boy you call Steve can do just about anything he can imagine. Best of all, he can take inspiration from champions with his name in everything from the most physical of events to the most cerebral! Athletes with this name include volleyball opposite Steve Timmons, whose medal collection includes two golds and a bronze from Olympic Games, as well as a gold each from a World Championship and World Cup; English six-time world champion snooker player Steve Davis; two-time World Series of Poker bracelet-winner Steve Billirakis; and *Magic: The Gathering* legend Steve O'Mahoney-Schwartz, who won four Grand Prix events and the Pro Tour.

Pairs of tremendous Steves have conquered their rivals in the pool, racing across the ice, and on the pitch. Freestyle swimming is a favorite of athletes with this name; Steve Clark won three Olympic gold medals in freestyle relay events in 1964, and Australian Steve Holland swam to a 1500-meter world championship and two world records in 1973. Two Steves were on Team USA's bobsleigh team that won America's first gold medal in sixty-two years: world champion Steve Mesler and Steve Holcomb, who also collected two Olympic silvers, five golds and five bronzes from World Championships, fourteen medals at World Cup Championships, and a staggering sixty-one medals at World Cup races. In the land down under, this name has reached the highest tier of cricket with two batters ranked among the all-time best with 1987 and 1999 Cricket World Cup champion Steve Waugh and Steve Smith, whose trophies include the 2015 Cricket World Cup, 2021 ICC T20 World Cup, and 2023 ICC World Test Championship final and awards like ICC Cricketer of the Year, ICC Test Player of the Year twice, and ICC Men's Test Player of the Decade.

On tracks, fields, and courses, multiple world record-setter Steve Williams sprinted to two world championships; Steve Hooker pole vaulted to Olympic gold, a World Cup, and two world championships for Australia; and American Steve "Pre" Prefontaine helped inspire a new generation of runners breaking numerous national records in the early 1970s.

Meanwhile, Canadians on the ice who have battled their way to hockey victory include Hall of Famer five-time Montreal Canadiens Stanley Cup champion left wing Steve Shutt; and Steve Yzerman, who was the Detroit Red Wings ten-time All-Star center and three-time Stanley Cup champion and won an Olympic gold medal.

America's pastime has seen two ten-time

All-Stars with National League MVP, four-time Gold Glove-winner, and World Series champion first baseman Steve Garvey and Hall of Fame pitcher Steve Carlton, who led the National League in wins four times and strikeouts five times, won a Gold Glove and the NY Cy Young four times, and became a two-time World Series champion.

How about basketball? All-Star shooting guard Steve Smith won an NBA championship, World Cup, and Olympic gold medal; three-point record-setting point guard Steve Kerr won a world championship and five NBA championships with the Chicago Bulls and San Antonio Spurs before becoming the highly successful head coach of the Golden State Warriors; and Canadian eight-time All-Star point guard Steve Nash was named NBA MVP twice, led the league in assists five times, reached the 50-40-90 club four times, and was inducted into the Basketball Hall of Fame.

Steves have also had a big impact on football, with these best-of-the-best seven-time Pro Bowl players and Hall of Famers: Seattle Seahawks NFL Man of the Year and two-time receiving yards leading wide receiver Steve Largent, and Offensive Player of the Year and two-time NFL MVP quarterback Steve Young, who led the NFL in completion percentage five times and passer rating six times and won the Super Bowl three times with the San Francisco 49ers!

Steven "Steve" Billirakis, Card Gaming (Poker), USA, 2004–current

Steven "Steve" Carlton, Baseball (Pitcher), Philadelphia Phillies, USA, 1965–1988

Stephen "Steve" Clark, Swimming (Freestyle), USA, 1960–1964

Steve Davis, Snooker, England, 1978–2016

Steven "Steve" Garvey, Baseball (First Baseman), Los Angeles Dodgers, USA, 1969–1987

Steven "Steve" Holcomb, Bobsleigh, USA, 1998–2017

Stephen "Steve" Holland, Swimming (Freestyle), Australia, 1973–1976

Steven "Steve" Hooker, Track & Field (Pole Vaulting), Australia, 2006–2010

Stephen "Steve" Kerr, Basketball (Point Guard), Chicago Bulls, USA, 1988–2003

Stephen "Steve" Largent, Football (Wide Receiver/Holder), Seattle Seahawks, USA, 1976–1989

Steven "Steve" Mesler, Bobsleigh, USA, 2004–2010

Stephen "Steve" Nash, Basketball (Point Guard), Phoenix Suns, Canada, 1996–2015

Steven "Steve" O'Mahoney-Schwartz, Card Gaming (*Magic: The Gathering*), USA, 1996–2007

Stephen "Steve" Owen, Football (Tackle/Guard), New York Giants, USA, 1924–1933

Steve "Pre" Prefontaine, Track & Field (Long-Distance Running), USA, 1973–1975

Stephen "Steve" Shutt, Ice Hockey (Left Wing), Montreal Canadiens, Canada, 1972–1985

Steven "Steve" Smith, Basketball (Shooting Guard), Miami Heat, USA, 1991–2005

Steven "Steve" Smith, Cricket (Batter), New South Wales Men's Cricket Team, Australia, 2007–current

Steve Timmons, Volleyball (Opposite), USA, 1984–1992

Stephen "Steve" Waugh, Cricket (Batter), New South Wales Men's Cricket Team, Australia, 1984–2002

Steve Williams, Track & Field (Sprinting), USA, 1972–1984

Jon Steven "Steve" Young, Football (Quarterback), San Francisco 49ers, USA, 1984–1999

Stephen "Steve" Yzerman, Ice Hockey (Center), Detroit Red Wings, Canada/USA, 1983–2006

STEVEN

The name Steven was a product of medieval English adapting *Stephen*, but it is also a variation of *Stefan*. And as with those other names, athletes with this one are not merely restricted to one sport, though as we'll see there is a preponderance of them in one event. Interestingly, Stevens are overwhelmingly partners or team players who succeed by maximizing their skills alongside others! We can see this in speed skating with Australian Steven Bradbury, who won Olympic gold on his own and a relay world championship; trampoline gymnastics with three-time Synchro World Cup-winner Steven Gluckstein; cricket with English World ODI XI and T20 XI bowler Steven Finn, who was on the team that won the 2010–2011 Ashes series; and ice hockey with Canadian Tampa Bay Lightning seven-time All-Star center and two-time Stanley Cup champion Steven Stamkos.

Stevens have been particularly successful in soccer. Around the world, Swiss winger/attacking midfielder Steven Zuber has conquered multiple countries' top leagues by winning the Swiss Cup, Russian Premier League, Russian Super Cup twice, Super League Greece, and Greek Cup; and UEFA Europa League–winning defensive midfielder Steven Nzonzi won the 2018 FIFA World Cup with France. Last but not least, Liverpool midfielder Steven Gerrard won numerous trophies on his way to being named UEFA Club Footballer of the Year, FIFA FIFPro World XI three times, UEFA Team of the Year three times, and UEFA Ultimate Team of the Year; given the Onze d'Argent and FIFA Club World Championship Silver Ball; and inducted into multiple Halls of Fame.

Teach your son Steven the value of working alongside others and there's no limit to how far he'll go!

Steven Bradbury, Speed Skating, Australia, 1991–2002

Steven Finn, Cricket (Bowler), Middlesex County Cricket Club, England, 2005–current

Steven Gerrard, Soccer (Midfielder), Liverpool Football Club, England, 1998–2016

Steven Gluckstein, Trampoline Gymnastics, USA, 2009–2016

Steven Nzonzi, Soccer (Defensive Midfielder), Stoke City Football Club, France, 2007–current

Steven Stamkos, Ice Hockey (Center), Tampa Bay Lightning, Canada, 2008–current

Steven Zuber, Soccer (Winger/Attacking Midfielder), Grasshopper Club Zürich, Switzerland, 2008–current

STIRLING

Depending on the tradition, Stirling can come from either a place name for a city in Scotland or from the name *Sterling*, which means "excellent" and comes from Old English for "little star." A Stirling in your family will be your little star, excelling at going fast and claiming victory! He'll follow in the footsteps of champions like Australian rugby multi-position 2002 Super Rugby Player of the Year Stirling Mortlock, who won the Bledisloe Cup and Tri Nations while reaching the leaderboards for scoring points in Super Rugby, and legendary British racing driver Stirling Moss, who sped to sixteen victories in Formula 1 and purportedly won 212 out of 529 races across various series!

Stirling Mortlock, Rugby (Center/Wing/Fullback), ACT Brumbles, Australia, 1998–2012

Stirling Moss, Auto Racing (Formula 1), England, 1948–1962

SUNG-

As with many Korean names, the unisex Sung can mean a variety of different things depending on the characters used to write it (including "finished" or "succeeded"), and it is combined with numerous secondary syllables to make a number of unique forms. Just as varied are the sports and competitive events that people with these names find great success in! These can range from badminton (like world champion and former singles and doubles world number one Ko Sung-hyun) to skeleton (like "Iron Man" Olympic gold-medalist Yun Sung-bin), and even esports (like Overwatch League and Overwatch World Cup MVP, three-time Overwatch League All-Star, and Overwatch World Cup champion Bang "JJoNak" Sung-hyeon).

Meanwhile, soccer is a favorite of athletes with these names, like two-time J.League Best XI goalkeeper Jung Sung-ryong, whose career in South Korea and Japan resulted in ten championships, and wing-back/midfielder Choi Sung-yong, who won the K League, Korean FA Cup, Korean League Cup twice, Korean Super Cup, Asian Club Championship, Asian Super Cup, and A3 Champions Cup!

Bang Sung-hyeon "JJonak", Esports (*Overwatch*), South Korea, 2017–2022

Choi Sung-yong, Soccer (Wing-Back/Midfielder), Suwon Samsung Bluewings, South Korea, 1997–2010

Jung Sung-ryong, Soccer (Goalkeeper), Kawasaki Frontale, South Korea, 2006–current

Ko Sung-hyun, Badminton, South Korea, 2007–current

Yun "Iron Man" Sung-bin, Skeleton, South Korea, 2012–current

SUNIL

If you love international team sports and the color blue, then the name Sunil might be a good choice for your son! From Sanskrit roots meaning "very dark blue," Sunil has a strong presence in India and the West Indies with athletes in cricket and soccer. Fans of the former will be familiar with Trinidadian 2012 T20 World Cup champion bowling all-rounder Sunil Narine and, of course, Indian ICC Cricket Hall of Fame opening batsman Sunil Gavaskar, whose long list of accolades includes winning the 1983 Cricket World Cup, 1984 Asia Cup, and 1985 Benson & Hedges World Championship of Cricket while racking up numerous awards and records to make him one of the greatest players of all time.

Meanwhile, on the football fields of India and beyond, forward Sunil Chhetri (seven-time AIFF Player of the Year, three-time FPAI Indian Player of the Year, Hero of the Intercontinental Cup, and Hero of the Indian Super League) has become the third-highest current international goal scorer while winning over a dozen championships and numerous awards, including the 2018 Indian Super Cup Golden Boot!

Sunil Chhetri, Soccer (Forward), Bengaluru Football Club, India, 2002–current

Sunil Gavaskar, Cricket (Opening Batsman), Bombay Cricket Team, India, 1967–1987

Sunil Narine, Cricket (Bowling All-Rounder), Kolkata Knight Riders, West Indies, 2008–current

SURESH

The name Suresh has ancient and powerful roots coming from Sanskrit meaning "ruler of the gods," and it brings with it strength, speed, and accuracy perfect for a batter (or batsman). That's especially true of Indian cricketer Suresh Raina, the first batsman from his country to hit a century in all three international cricket formats and the winner of both the 2011 Cricket World Cup and 2013 ICC Champions Trophy.

Suresh Raina, Cricket (Batsman), Uttar Pradesh Cricket Team, India, 2002–2022

SVEN

A name that's eminently appropriate for a son, Sven comes from an Old Norse word for "boy." A Sven in your family has a good chance of liking winter sports, if Svens around the world are any indication, but he could branch out into another field of competition too, like German super-middleweight world champion boxer Sven Ottke, who never lost a match in his 34–0 career; or Belgian cyclist Sven Nys, who has won dozens of cyclo-cross races and championships, including eleven medals from World Championships (four of them gold).

Finally, there are the cold weather Svens who have made a name for themselves on the ice and snow, including German Olympic gold-medalist and two-time world champion ski jumper Sven Hannawald, who also won two ski flying world championships; Dutch long track speed skater Sven Kramer, who took home nine medals from Olympic Games (four of them gold), nine golds and three bronzes at World Allround events, and twenty-one golds, three silvers, and two bronzes at World Single Distance Championships; and German four-time Olympic gold-medalist and seven-time world champion biathlete Sven Fischer, whose World Cup career included ninety podium standings and two overall titles!

Sven Fischer, Biathlon, Germany, 1991–2007

Sven Hannawald, Ski Jumping, Germany, 1993–2004

Sven Kramer, Speed Skating, Netherlands, 2003–2022

Sven Nys, Cyclo-Cross, Belgium, 1998–current

Sven Ottke, Boxing (Super-Middleweight/Light-Heavyweight), Germany, 1985–2004

GIRLS

SABINE

The Sabines were an ancient tribe of people living in modern-day Italy, and it's from them that we get the European name Sabine. Originally more common across Denmark, France, and the Netherlands, it has come to be most prominent in Germany, although it has the potential to lead a young girl to athletic excellence anywhere. Nearly across the board we see Sabines engaged in racing and sports that let them channel their inner need for speed. Some utilize vehicles, including the canoe (like Swiss two-time world champion sprint canoeist Sabine Eichenberger), race cars (like Veranstaltergemeinschaft Langstreckenpokal Nürburgring champion Sabine Schmitz, who won the 24 Hours of Nürburgring race twice), and bicycles (like German Olympic gold-medalist and two-time world champion cross-country and marathon racer Sabine Spitz).

Other Sabines prefer running, jumping, skating, or skiing on their own two feet, including team pursuit Olympic gold-medalist speed skater Sabine Völker; Sabine Busch, who is a three-time world champion sprinter and hurdler; Sabine Braun, who won two world champions in the pentathlon and one in the heptathlon; and six-time World Cup champion alpine skier Sabine Ginther.

Chances are excellent that a young Sabine in your family will also like to go fast—and find her own unique way of doing so.

Sabine Braun, Track & Field (Heptathlon/Pentathlon), Germany, 1984–2002

Sabine Busch, Track & Field (Sprinting/Hurdling), Germany, 1982–1991

Sabine Eichenberger, Sprint Canoeing, Switzerland, 1996

Sabine Ginther, Alpine Skiing, Austria, 1988–1993

Sabine Schmitz, Auto Racing (Veranstaltergemeinschaft Langstreckenpokal Nürburgring), Germany, 1996–2016

Sabine Spitz, Cycling (Cross-Country), Germany, 2001–current

Sabine Völker, Speed Skating, Germany, 2002–2006

SABRE

Sabre is an ancient word for a type of curved sword (and occasionally a variation of "sabra," which is Hebrew for "prickly pear"), and if you're particularly cool, it could be a name for your daughter! She may even approach the awesomeness level of Sabre Norris, the Australian skateboarding and surfing prodigy who was the youngest surfer ever to compete in Sydney International Women's Pro surfing competition, won the Bondi Bowl-A-Rama, and was the third woman to land a 540 and the first woman to land a McTwist at the X Games!

A Sabre in your family may not be an extreme sports phenom or world-famous YouTuber, but she'll have her own unique style and thrash any sport she enters.

Sabre Norris, Skateboarding/Surfing, Australia, 2016–current

SAINA

Coming potentially from an ancient root word meaning "princess," the name Saina has come to prominence in India and international badminton competition thanks to former world number one-ranked Saina Nehwal. A record-setter in her home country, Saina has won ten Superseries titles among her twenty-four international wins, as well as three gold medals from Commonwealth Games.

Choose the name Saina for your little princess, teach her the basics of racquet sports, and she'll turn out great too!

Saina Nehwal, Badminton, India, 2005–current

SAM

Athletes named *Samantha* may have gone out and conquered a number of different and varied sports, but those girls who go by the unisex short form Sam are one and all team players! Call your daughter Sam and she'll assuredly follow in their footsteps, working best alongside others and maximizing everyone's skills to win the day. She may find that success in sports such as ice hockey (like Premier Hockey Federation All-Star and world champion forward Sam Faber), or water polo (like world champion and Olympic gold-medalist goalkeeper Sam Hill).

Or she may join the multiple champion Sams in field hockey and soccer, including English Olympic gold-medalist field hockey defender Sam Quek; two-time Olympic gold-medalist and Champions Challenge champion field hockey forward/midfield Sam Harrison of New Zealand; 2020 US Soccer Female Player of the Year and NWSL Best XI midfielder Sam Mewis, who has won the FIFA Women's World Cup 2019; and Australian two-time W-League Player's Player of the Year and five-time PFA Australian Women's Footballer of the Year Sam Kerr, who is ranked among the best forwards of all time with a huge number of wins along with tons of awards, accolades, and records!

Samantha "Sam" Faber, Ice Hockey (Forward), Connecticut Whale, USA, 2005–current

Samantha "Sam" Harrison, Field Hockey (Forward/Midfield), New Zealand, 2009–current

Samantha "Sam" Hill, Water Polo (Goalkeeper), USA, 2015–current

Samantha "Sam" Kerr, Soccer (Forward), Chelsea Football Club Women, Australia, 2008–current

Samantha "Sam" Mewis, Soccer (Midfielder), North Carolina Courage, USA, 2013–current

Samantha "Sam" Quek, Field Hockey (Defender), England, 2008–2020

SAMANTHA

Samantha may be a great name, but its origins are obscure and generally lost to time. It may have come about as a feminine version of *Samuel* (from Hebrew for "name of God"), possibly with a suffix meaning "flower." Quite a few Samanthas have excelled in team sports and multi-person events, ranging from softball (like National Pro Fastpitch Cowles Cup champion first base Samantha Findlay) to artistic gymnastics (like team world champion Samantha Peszek), volleyball (like Mexican outside hitter Samantha Bricio, whose international career has included Italian and Russian championships), and tennis (like Australian doubles star Samantha Stosur, who was number one in the world with thirty-one titles and seven Grand Slams).

Samanthas also do quite well on their own conquering opponents, their own limitations, and even nature itself! In the pool, American swimmer Samantha Arsenault won Olympic gold in the 4x200-meter freestyle and Australian Samantha Riley was a five-time world champion in breaststroke and medley events. On the track, English modern pentathlete Samantha Murray won three world championships in team and individual events, as well as an individual World Cup. And on the waves, Australian surfer Samantha Cornish was ranked number one in the world and won the Billabong Pro Maui and Quiksilver Roxy Pro Gold Coast.

Naming a daughter Samantha will give her an indomitable will and the skills to match, as well as a drive to challenge herself and succeed, whether that's in the backyard or at competitions.

Samantha Arsenault, Swimming (Freestyle), USA, 2000

Samantha Bricio, Volleyball (Outside Hitter), Mexico, 2010–current

Samantha Cornish, Surfing, Australia, 1991–current

Samantha Findlay, Softball (First Base/Second Base), Chicago Bandits, USA, 2005–2011

Samantha Murray, Track & Field (Pentathlon), England, 2010–2016

Samantha Peszek, Artistic Gymnastics, USA, 2004–2015

Samantha Riley, Swimming (Breaststroke), Australia, 1991–1999

Samantha Stosur, Tennis, Australia, 1999–2023

SANA/SANAA

Sana and Sanaa are modern names descended from an Arabic word meaning "brilliance," "radiance," or "splendor." Athletes with these names who have shown their brilliance to the world include Pakistani two-time Asian Games gold-medalist cricketer Sana Mir, who has set multiple records in her home country, and Moroccan visually impaired sprinter and long jumper Sanaa Benhama, who won three gold medals at Paralympic Games and nine medals at IPC World Championships (including two more golds).

A Sana or Sanaa in your family is sure to have her own radiance that will shine brightly in whatever field she chooses!

Sanaa Benhama, Para-Athletics, Morocco, 2008–2016

Sana Mir, Cricket (All-Rounder), Zarai Taraqiati Bank Limited Women's Cricket Team, Pakistan, 2005–2019

SANDA

One of countless names that evolved from the Ancient Greek *Alexander* ("defender of men") is Sanda, a Croatian, Latvian, and Romanian form that came about as a diminutive of *Alexandra*. A rare jewel of a name in the United States, Sanda can drive your daughter to great deeds and potentially a powerful presence on the water, like Romanian Olympic gold-medalist and two-time world champion rower Sanda Toma, who was undefeated in three years of international competition at the highest levels!

Sanda Toma, Rowing, Romania, 1976–1981

SANDI/SANDY

Like *Sanda*, *Sandra*, and more, Sandi and Sandy are derivations of the classic Greek name *Alexander* and sometimes short forms of longer names like *Alexandra*. A young Sandi or Sandy in your family might enjoy such pursuits as field hockey, track and field events, or even competitive swimming. If she does, she can potentially take after Zimbabwean field hockey forward Sandy Chick, who won a gold medal alongside her identical twin sister in 1980; two-time world champion pole vaulter and record-setter Sandy Morris; or three-time Olympic gold-medalist freestyle swimmer Sandy Neilson, whose victories came when she was only sixteen years old!

Alexandra "Sandy" Chick, Field Hockey (Forward), Zimbabwe, 1980

Sandi Morris, Track & Field (Pole Vaulting), USA, 2015–current

Sandra "Sandy" Neilson, Swimming (Freestyle), USA, 1971–1996

SANDRA

Sandra, a name that comes to us via the Italian *Alessandra* and ultimately from the Greek *Alexander*, may not make a girl into a "protector of men," but it can instill within her a love of sports and competing both on her own and with teammates. That perfectly describes German equestrian Sandra Auffarth, who won an individual eventing world championship, and two world championships and two Olympic gold medals in team eventing!

Sandras can succeed all on their own, as evidenced by Romanian artistic gymnast Sandra Izbaşa, who won Olympic gold in floor exercise and on the vault; and Croatian two-time Olympic gold-medalist, two-time world champion, and six-time Diamond League-winning discus thrower Sandra Perković; or solely alongside others, like Canadian Olympic gold-medalist and three-time world champion curling skip Sandra Schmirler; Dutch Olympic gold-medalist and four-time world champion field hockey player Sandra Le Poole; and German bobsledder Sandra Kiriasis, whose medal collection includes a gold and a silver from Olympic Games; seven golds, five silvers, and a bronze from World Championships; and eight golds, four silvers, and a bronze from World Cup events.

There are certain sports in which Sandras particularly seem to excel, notably swimming and golf. In the pool, Australian Sandra Morgan won Olympic gold in the 4x100-meter freestyle while German Sandra Völker won world championships in that event and multiple backstroke distances. On the links, Sandra Palmer won twenty-eight times with two majors, and World Golf Hall of Famer Sandra Haynie racked up a massive forty-four professional wins and four majors!

If you name your daughter Sandra, then let her figure out which sport is her favorite . . . but it couldn't hurt to introduce her to swimming or golf just in case.

Sandra Auffarth, Equestrian (Eventing), Germany, 2011–current

Sandra Haynie, Golf, USA, 1961–1989

Sandra Izbaşa, Artistic Gymnastics, Romania, 2002-2013

Sandra Kiriasis, Bobsleigh, Germany, 2000–2014

Alexandra "Sandra" Le Poole, Field Hockey (Striker), Netherlands, 1978–1986

Sandra Morgan, Swimming (Freestyle), Australia, 1956–1960

Sandra Palmer, Golf, USA, 1964–1997

Sandra Perković, Track & Field (Discus), Croatia, 2009–current

Sandra Schmirler, Curling (Skip), Canada, 1981–1999

Sandra Völker, Swimming (Freestyle/Butterfly/Backstroke), Germany, 1991–2004

SANIA/SANJA/SANYA

This family of names has very interesting and varied origins, including an Arabic name meaning "brilliant" or "splendid," a Slavic root meaning "dream," or yet another variation of the Greek *Alexander*. A girl in your family with any of these names will find her brilliant athletic dream come true wherever her skills and talents may take her. She can find inspiration in Croatian record-setter and backstroke world champion Sanja Jovanović; Indian tennis player Sania Mirza, who reached the world doubles number one spot and won forty-three titles and six majors; or American four-time Olympic gold-medalist, six-time world champion, and three-time World Relays gold-medalist sprinter Sanya Richards-Ross!

Sanja Jovanović, Swimming (Backstroke), Croatia, 2001–2018

Sania Mirza, Tennis, India, 2003–2023

Sanya Richards-Ross, Track & Field (Sprinting), USA, 2003–2016

SAORI

The Japanese name Saori can mean a number of different things depending on which kanji characters are used to write it, including "sand," "now," and "weaving." It may not be in the sand, but athletes with this name have had great success on courts, fields, and mats, and so, too, may one in your family! She could follow in the footsteps of acclaimed two-time women's team Uber Cup-winning badminton player Saori Kondo; soccer defender Saori Ariyoshi, who has won gold and silver at Asian Games, an AFC Women's Club Championship, AFC Women's Asian Cup twice, Empress's Cup three times, and more; and Saori Yoshida, who cemented her place among the best freestyle wrestlers of all time with three golds and a silver from Olympic Games, thirteen golds from World Championships, and four golds each from Asian Games and Asian Championships.

Saori Ariyoshi, Soccer (Defender), Nippon TV Tokyo Verdy Beleza, Japan, 2008–current

Saori Kondo, Badminton, Japan, 1976–1981

Saori Yoshida, Freestyle Wrestling, Japan, 2002–2019

SARA

A slightly shorter variant of the biblical Hebrew *Sarah*, Sara is a great name for a physical girl who plays hard and likes to win, especially when it comes to going fast, wrestling, playing across a net, or running and jumping! This is clearly established when looking at Australian Olympic gold-medalist road cyclist Sara Carrigan; American submission wrestling world champion and freestyle wrestling World Cup-winner Sara McMann; and Japanese freestyle wrestling Olympic gold-medalist and world champion Sara Dosho.

When it comes to volleyball, Italian 2006 FIVB World Grand Prix Best Blocker Sana Anzanello won a world championship and two World Cup events. With racquets, Italian Sara Errani reached the world tennis doubles number one spot, winning twenty-seven titles and five Grand Slams. And in the world of track and field, Italian runner Sara Bottarelli won a World Mountain Running World Championship, Croatian javelin thrower Sara Kolak and Italian high jumper Sara Simeoni both took home Olympic gold, and Sara Mae Berman was the first unofficial female winner of the Boston Marathon in the 1969, 1970, and 1971 runnings (before women were officially allowed to enter in 1972).

Of course, your Sara isn't locked into these choices and can instead find her success in any field on her own, becoming a world champion like Egyptian weightlifter Sara Ahmed, Italian karateka Sara Battaglia, or rhythmic gymnast Sara Bayón, or winning with partners and teammates like Swedish two-time orienteering world champion Sara Hagström, or Colombian archer Sara López, who has won five world championships, seven World Cup Finals, two World Games, and an incredible twenty-five World Cup events!

- **Sara Ahmed**, Weightlifting, Egypt, 2013–current
- **Sara Anzanello**, Volleyball (Middle Hitter-Blocker), Italy, 1995–2013
- **Sara Battaglia**, Karate, Italy, 2006–2016
- **Sara Bayón**, Rhythmic Gymnastics, Spain, 1997–1999
- **Sara Mae Berman**, Marathon, USA, 1964–2000
- **Sara Bottarelli**, Long-Distance Running, Italy, 2011–current
- **Sara Carrigan**, Road Cycling, Australia, 1999–current
- **Sara Dosho**, Freestyle Wrestling, Japan, 2013–current
- **Sara Errani**, Tennis, Italy, 2002–current
- **Sara Hagström**, Orienteering, Sweden, 2014–current
- **Sara Kolak**, Track & Field (Javelin), Croatia, 2014–current
- **Sara López**, Archery, Colombia, 2011–current
- **Sara McMann**, Freestyle Wrestling/Submission Wrestling/MMA (Bantamweight), USA, 2003–current
- **Sara Simeoni**, Track & Field (High Jump), Italy, 1971–1986

SARAH

In Hebrew, the name Sarah means "lady," "noblewoman," or "princess," but when it comes to athletics and sports, the women with this name hardly just sit pretty and watch from the sidelines. On the contrary, Sarahs mix it up and get in the thick of things, with some of the toughest examples including British two-time taekwondo world champion Sarah Stevenson and New Zealand rugby forward Sarah Hirini, who led her teams to two Olympic gold medals, two Women's Rugby World Cups, and two Rugby World Cup Sevens trophies! Sarahs can also be precise and accurate, hitting or shooting to score like Belgian Archery World Cup gold-medalist Sarah Prieels and Canadian Sarah Pavan, who won world championships in both indoor and beach volleyball, as well as five Beach Volleyball World Tour championships.

Sarahs have shown propensities toward a number of sports and events. Starting with pairs who have been victorious on two wheels, and on the cricket field, we have BMX racer Sarah Walker of New Zealand (who raced to three gold medals, three silvers, and three bronzes at World Championships, as well as a Supercross World Cup) and American Sarah Hammer (who racked up eight track cycling world championships), and Australian bowler Sarah Coyte (who won the Women's National Cricket League seven times, ICC Women's World Twenty20 2014, and Women's Cricket World Cup 2013) and English wicketkeeper/batter Sarah Taylor (who set multiple records while being named ICC Women's ODI Cricketer of the Year and ICC Women's T20I Cricketer of the Year twice and winning the 2017 Women's Cricket World Cup)!

Next up are Sarahs on skis. Swiss skier Sarah Höfflin won a slopestyle Olympic gold medal and a big air X Games gold medal, Canadian Sarah Burke became a world champion on the halfpipe and dominated the X Games with five superpipe gold medals, and American paralympic skier Sarah Will set a Paralympic Games record with thirteen medals, twelve of them gold.

In the pool, Swedish swimmer Sarah Sjöström has set (and continues to hold!) world records on her way to winning three medals at Olympic Games, including a gold in butterfly, and thirty-one medals at World Championships (sixteen of them gold); and British athletic legend Sarah Storey has a dual career with sixteen Paralympic Games medals and sixteen World Championships medals in swimming and, in cycling, twelve Paralympic gold medals; fourteen golds, two silvers, and two bronzes in Para Track World Championships; and ten golds and two silvers in Para Road World Championships!

Not *in* the water but *on* it have been winning rowers, including American two-time world champion Sarah Garner, and British two-time women's quad World Rowing Championship gold-medalist Sarah Winckless. Under wind power instead of oars, English Yngling-class sailor Sarah Ayton won two Olympic gold medals and two world championships.

Last up are the Sarahs who have competed and excelled on ice! Sarah Hughes won Olympic gold in figure skating, while the rest have been ice hockey forwards like two-time world champion Sarah Parsons, Olympic gold-medalist and two-time world champion Sarah Nurse, and Sarah Vaillancourt, who won two Olympic gold medals, a world championship, a Women's 4 Nations Cup, two MLP Nations Cups, and the Clarkson Cup, giving her the rare Triple Gold Club ranking.

A Sarah in your family may be predisposed to one of these sports or she could embark on her own unique adventure in life, proving herself and succeeding wherever it takes her.

- **Sarah Ayton**, Sailing, England, 2004–2011
- **Sarah Burke**, Freestyle Skiing, Canada, 2001–2012
- **Sarah Coyte**, Cricket (Bowler), Adelaide Strikers, Australia, 2009–current
- **Sarah Garner**, Rowing, USA, 1997–2000
- **Sarah Hammer**, Track Cycling, USA, 2006–2017
- **Sarah Hirini**, Rugby (Forward), Manawatu Rugby Football Union, New Zealand, 2011–current
- **Sarah Höfflin**, Freestyle Skiing, Switzerland, 2012–current
- **Sarah Hughes**, Figure Skating, USA, 1999–2003
- **Sarah Nurse**, Ice Hockey (Forward), Toronto Furies, Canada, 2015–current
- **Sarah Parsons**, Ice Hockey (Forward), US National Team, USA, 2005–2010
- **Sarah Pavan**, Beach Volleyball, Canada, 2008–current
- **Sarah Prieels**, Archery, Belgium, 2010–current
- **Sarah Sjöström**, Swimming (Butterfly/Freestyle/Backstroke), Sweden, 2008–current
- **Sarah Stevenson**, Taekwondo, England, 1998–2013
- **Sarah Storey**, Swimming (Backstroke/Breaststroke/Freestyle)/Road Cycling, England, 1992–current
- **Sarah Taylor**, Cricket (Wicketkeeper-Batter), Sussex Women's Cricket Team, England, 2004–2021
- **Sarah Vaillancourt**, Ice Hockey (Forward), Montreal Stars, Canada, 2003–2013
- **Sarah Walker**, BMX, New Zealand, 2008–current
- **Sarah Will**, Para-Alpine Skiing, USA, 1992–2002
- **Sarah Winckless**, Rowing, England, 1998–2009

ŠÁRKA

Looking for a name that has a heroic lineage, will make your daughter stand out on the roll call, and can give her the skills and drive to compete in track and field or skiing? Then Šárka may be perfect for you! A character in Czech folk tales, Šárka led a revolt of women against overbearing men, using her intelligence and guile to get the upper hand. In modern times, the name has been lauded in athletics with Czech world champions in the triple jump (Šárka Kašpárková) and slalom skiing (Šárka Strachová).

Šárka Kašpárková, Track & Field (Triple Jump), Czech Republic, 1992-2006

Šárka Strachová, Alpine Skiing, Czech Republic, 2002-2017

SASHA

A diminutive of *Alexander*-family names like *Aleksandra* and *Alexandra* from Russia and Ukraine, the unisex Sasha is a name that embodies precision and grace, whether that's on the ice or under fire in video games! This is most apparent when looking at figure skater Sasha Cohen, who won gold and silver at Grand Prix Final events, and Canadian professional esports competitor Sasha "Scarlett" Hostyn, who became the first woman to win a major *StarCraft II* tournament at the Intel Extreme Masters.

Alexandra "Sasha" Cohen, Figure Skating, USA, 1992-2010

Sasha "Scarlett" Hostyn, Esports (*StarCraft II*), Canada, 2011-current

SATU

The Finnish name Satu is perfect for a girl who believes in fairy tales and who is an excellent shot! Meaning "fairy tale" or "fable," the name has garnered international fame in the sport shooting world thanks to Finnish trap shooter Satu Mäkelä-Nummela, who set an Olympic record on her way to winning a gold medal with her shotgun in 2008.

Satu Mäkelä-Nummela, Sport Shooting (Trap), Finland, 1995-current

SEIKO

"Holy/sacred" and "child" is one way to translate kanji symbols used to write the Japanese name Seiko. Consider giving it to your daughter to make her strong and unstoppable, taking after four-time World Wrestling Championships gold-medalist Seiko Yamamoto.

Seiko Yamamoto, Freestyle Wrestling, Japan, 1997-2013

SEIMONE/SIMONA/SIMONE

An alternate version of *Simon*, the name Simona and its different versions come from a Hebrew root related to "hearing." There are several accomplished athletes with variations on this name, including pro-basketball player and Olympic gold-medalist Seimone Augustus, and Romanian multiple gold-medalist gymnast Simona Amânar. Amânar is fantastic, but even she is overshadowed by the most-decorated-of-all-time gymnast: Simone Biles. In just over ten years, she's collected no fewer than forty-one Olympic and World Championship medals, including seven Olympic golds, and she's mastered multiple events with numerous skills named after her.

Pick a name like Seimone, Simona, or Simone for a powerhouse of a child who's a good listener.

Simona Amânar, Artistic Gymnastics, Romania, 1994-2000

Seimone Augustus, Basketball (Guard-Forward), Minnesota Lynx, USA, 2006-2020

Simone Biles, Artistic Gymnastics, USA, 2012-current

SERENA

The name Serena may be a descendant of the Latin adjective for "serene," but that's probably not a descriptor you think of when considering the tennis powerhouse known as Serena Williams. The US pro has racked up the most Grand Slam singles titles of any player in the Open Era, which is still just a part of her success story. Serena also has record wins in doubles alongside her sister Venus, and she's worked hard off the court to support women and minorities in sports and around the world. Let Williams's singular determination, strength, and success story inspire a Serena in your family to achieve anything she sets out to do and break records along the way. Consider pairing Serena with *Venus* for two (or twin) daughters.

Serena Williams, Tennis, USA, 1995–current

SEUNG-

"Rise/ascend" or "victory" are two possible translations based on the Hanja characters used to write the unisex Korean name Seung, which can be used on its own or as part of a two-syllable name with various suffix forms. South Korean athletes have taken these names to the highest levels of athletic victory in three very different events, with badminton Uber Cup champion Bae Seung-hee, two-time taekwondo world champion Lee Seung-min, and speed skater Park Seung-hi, who raced to two gold and three bronze medals at Olympic Games, as well as nine golds, six silvers, and a bronze at World Championships both on her own and with her team.

Choose a form of Seung that you like for your daughter and introduce her to racquet sports, martial arts, and especially ice skating!

Bae Seung-hee, Badminton, South Korea, 2001–2011

Lee Seung-min, Taekwondo, South Korea, 1990–1996

Park Seung-hi, Speed Skating, South Korea, 2010–2018

SHA'CARRI

A modern, invented name, Sha'Carri can be a variation on the name *Shakari* (from Zulu or Hebrew), the name *Carrie*, or something else entirely. No matter where it comes from, this name is going places . . . fast, and that's thanks to world champion and Olympic gold-medalist sprinter Sha'Carri Richardson! The sixth-fastest woman of all time, Sha'Carri posts wins and record times on her own in the 100 meter and with Team USA in the 4x100-meter relay, and is renowned for her speed as well as her flamboyant personality, hair, and nails. Take inspiration from Richardson in naming your daughter Sha'Carri and she'll be confident in competing . . . as well as correcting others on the pronunciation of her name.

Sha'Carri Richardson, Track & Field (Sprinting), USA, 2019–current

SHAN

Possibly coming from the Shan County, a member of the Zhou dynasty, or a Mandarin word for "mountain," Shan is often a surname, but when it's used as a first name, it can make a girl into a real go-getter with an explosive personality, a keen eye, and the ability to track down whatever she's aiming for. In those areas she can take after Chinese skeet shooter Zhang Shan, who won Olympic gold in 1992 by beating a crowded field of men and women in the final mixed event of its kind!

Zhang Shan, Sport Shooting (Skeet), China, 1989–2017

SHANNON

Shannon is an *old* name, coming from a river in Ireland and possibly a root meaning "ancient." Down under in Australia, the name is synonymous with the rough-and-tumble game of rugby, brought to the fore by prop Shannon Mato, who won the 2020 NRL Premiership with the Brisbane Broncos, and Olympic gold-medalist flanker Shannon Parry. In North America, Shannons have found success in a few different fields, including rowing (like Olympic gold-medalist Shannon Crawford), soccer (like two-time Women's Professional Soccer All-Star midfielder Shannon Boxx, who won three Olympic gold medals and the 2015 FIFA Women's World Cup with the USA team), and gymnastics (like "Magnificent Seven" member Shannon Miller, whose trophy collection includes five golds, three silvers, and a bronze from World Championships and two golds, two silvers, and three bronzes from the Olympics).

No matter where you live, Shannon could be a great name for your active and athletic little girl who may go all the way in rugby, rowing, soccer, gymnastics, or anything else she loves.

- **Shannon Boxx**, Soccer (Midfielder), San Diego Spirit, USA, 1994–2015
- **Shannon Crawford**, Rowing, Canada, 1992
- **Shannon Mato**, Rugby (Prop/Lock), Queensland Reds, Australia, 2018–current
- **Shannon Lee Miller**, Artistic Gymnastics, USA, 1989–1997
- **Shannon Parry**, Rugby (Flanker), Australia Women's National Rugby Union Team, Australia, 2010–2023

SHARON/SHARRON

Fancy footwork and phenomenal balance are hallmarks of Sharons and Sharrons, whose names come from a biblical Hebrew place name meaning "a plain" and a flowering shrub. American surfer Sharron Weber conquered two world championships in the early 1970s and has been inducted into the Surfing Walk of Fame, while English martial artist Sharon Rendle won Olympic gold and two world championships in judo in the 1980s.

A Sharon (or Sharron) in your family will be just as swift and skillful, whether on the water, on the mat, or anywhere else her travels take her.

- **Sharon Rendle**, Judo, England, 1985–1996
- **Sharron Weber**, Surfing, USA, 1968–1974

SHAWN

The unisex name Shawn came about as a variant of the Irish *Sean*. In the United States, the name reached its highest athletic fame and popularity with "America's Sweetheart" Shawn Johnson East. The artistic gymnast had many successes in US and Pan American Games, with her biggest accomplishments coming in 2007 with floor exercise, all-around, and team gold medals at World Championships, and in 2008 with a balance beam gold medal at the Olympics and silvers in team, all-around, and floor exercise!

Name your daughter Shawn and she, too, will be flexible, outgoing, and capable, achieving her dreams and making you proud.

- **Shawn Johnson East**, Artistic Gymnastics, USA, 2004–2012

SHEILA/SHEILLA

The origins of the name Sheila stretch back all the way to an ancient Roman family name by way of the Irish name *Cecilia*. A Sheila (or Sheilla) is a force of nature, able to focus through singular tasks or branch out in different directions and still come out on top! Just look at amazing and inspirational figures like Sheila Taormina, who won a World Triathlon Championships Series event (as well as an Olympic gold medal in freestyle swimming); speed skater Sheila Young, who won one of each medal at the Olympics (the first American to win three medals at one Winter Games) and three world championships (as well as three more world championships in cycling); or Brazilian volleyball opposite spiker/outside hitter Sheilla Castro, whose medal collection includes two Olympic golds, two golds and a silver at World Grand Champions Cups, seven golds and three silvers at World Grand Prix events, and more.

Sheilla Tavares de Castro, Volleyball (Opposite Spiker/Outside Hitter), Brazil, 2001–2021

Sheila Taormina, Swimming (Freestyle)/ Triathlon, USA, 1991–2008

Sheila Young, Speed Skating/Track Cycling, USA, 1973–1982

SHELLEY/SHELLY

"Clearing on a bank" may not seem like the most interesting origin for a name, but that's where the English place name Shelley/Shelly comes from. In modern times, the name has appeared in a couple of different fields, though nothing specifically on a bank of a river. British skeleton racer Shelley Rudman won the Skeleton World Cup in 2012 and the world championship in 2013, and in the mid-1990s, Australian field hockey midfielder Shelley Andrews racked up an Olympic gold medal, World Cup, and four Champions Trophy championships. Shellys really love to run, from long distances, like American World Cross Country Championships gold-medalist Shelly Steely, to sprinting, like Jamaican world-renowned athlete and record-breaker Shelly-Ann Fraser-Pryce, whose medal collection includes three golds, four silvers, and a bronze at Olympic Games; eleven golds and four silvers at World Championships; a gold and a silver at World Athletics Finals; and many more.

Guide a Shelley or Shelly in your family with proper training to hone her skills and favorite activities and she'll race to victory and success!

Michelle "Shelley" Andrews, Field Hockey (Midfielder), Australia, 1993–1999

Shelly Ann Fraser-Pryce, Track & Field (Sprinting), Jamaica, 2007–current

Shelley Rudman, Skeleton, England, 2004–2014

Anne Rochelle "Shelly" Steely Ramirez, Long-Distance Running, USA, 1985–2000

SHERYL

See *Cheryl/Sheryl*.

SHIRLEY

From the same origins as *Shelley/Shelly* comes Shirley, an old-fashioned name that still has a lot of life in it, especially for a girl who likes to hit golf balls or go as fast as she can! On the links, Shirley Spork was one of the co-founders of the LPGA Tour in 1950, and nine years later, Shirley Englehorn joined the Tour and ended up winning eleven events, including the 1970 LPGA Championship. Elite Shirleys who have felt the need for speed, and achieved it, include British two-time Olympic gold-medalist sailor Shirley Robertson; Australian track and field athlete Shirley Strickland, who won three golds, a silver, and three bronze medals at Olympic Games in sprinting and hurdling events; freestyle swimmer Shirley Babashoff, whose medal collection includes three golds and six silvers from Olympics and two golds, seven silvers, and a bronze from World Championships; and Shirley "Cha Cha" Muldowney, who was the first woman to become a Top Fuel dragster racer and went on to win eighteen races and three championships!

Shirley Babashoff, Swimming (Freestyle), USA, 1972–1976

Shirley Englehorn, Golf, USA, 1959–1979

Shirley "Cha Cha" Muldowney, Auto Racing (NHRA), USA, 1958–2003

Shirley Robertson, Sailing, Scotland, 1993–2007

Shirley Spork, Golf, USA, 1950–2017

Shirley Strickland, Track & Field (Sprinting/Hurdling), Australia, 1948–1956

SILKE/SYLKE

You may not hear the name Silke/Sylke very often here in the United States, but it's much more popular in Germany, with a long history coming from either a diminutive of *Celia* or *Cecilia* (in turn from a Latin root meaning "heaven"). It's shown up in a few different athletic spheres; starting with aquatic events, breaststroke swimmer Silke Hörner is a two-time Olympic gold-medalist and world champion.

On the track and field scene, javelin thrower Silke Renk won Olympic gold in 1992, and in the '80s, Silke Möller sprinted to three world championships. On the luge, Silke Kraushaar-Pielach has won one of each Olympic medal; four golds, four silvers, and two bronzes from World Championships; and five golds and six silvers at World Cup events, and Sylke Otto has won two Olympic golds; six golds, three silvers, and three bronzes from World Championships; and four golds, four silvers, and a bronze at World Cups. Wheelchair fencer Silke Schwarz fought her way to six medals at Paralympic Games, including a gold, and legendary soccer goalkeeper Silke Rottenberg was named German Female Footballer of the Year on her way to winning the UEFA Women's Championship three times and the FIFA Women's World Cup twice!

Let your daughter stand out from the crowd from the very first roll call and in her chosen sport, where she's sure to do great, by giving her the name Silke or Sylke.

Silke Hörner, Swimming (Breaststroke), Germany, 1985–1988

Silke Kraushaar-Pielach, Luge, Germany, 1995–2008

Silke Möller, Track & Field (Sprinting), Germany, 1983–1990

Sylke Otto, Luge, Germany, 1991–2007

Silke Renk, Track & Field (Javelin), Germany, 1988–1996

Silke Rottenberg, Soccer (Goalkeeper), 1. FFC Frankfurt, Germany, 1988–2008

Silke Schwarz, Wheelchair Fencing (Foil/Épée), Germany, 1996–2000

SILVIA/SYLVIA

Silvia and its more common variant Sylvia have been names for a very long time and come from Latin for "wood" or "forest." While a Silvia or Sylvia in your family may enjoy the outdoors, her athletic endeavors are likely to be of the indoor variety, especially if she takes after past icons with her name. Artistic gymnast Silvia Stroescu won Olympic team all-around gold in 2004 for Romania, two-time Woman Bowler of the Year Sylvia Wene became the first woman to roll a perfect game in official competition and then the first to do it three times, and eight-time WNBA All-Star center Sylvia Fowles had a stellar career with two championships and being named league MVP, Finals MVP twice, and Defensive Player of the Year four times; leading the league in blocks twice and rebounding three times; and winning a world championship and four Olympic gold medals with the USA Basketball team!

Sylvia Fowles, Basketball (Center), Minnesota Lynx, USA, 2008–2022

Silvia Stroescu, Artistic Gymnastics, Romania, 2001–2004

Sylvia Wene, Bowling, USA, 1950–1962

SIOBHAN

Yet another name that comes from the same Hebrew origin as *John* ("God is gracious"), the Irish Siobhan evolved by way of *Jeanne* and the Norman French *Jehanne*. You don't have to come from the Emerald Isle to name a girl in your family Siobhan, but if you do, she very well may enjoy playing soccer with her friends, swimming, or playing video games! Any of those would put her in good company with three-time freestyle world champion swimmer Siobhán Haughey of Hong Kong, Australian six-time Paralympic gold-medalist and six-time International Paralympic Committee Swimming World Championships gold-medalist Siobhan Paton, or esports champion Siobhan "HaganeNoTema" Bielamowicz, who took her domination of *Attack on Titan Tribute Game* to win the 2018 1v1 Damage Duel Championship. On the field, Irish midfielder Siobhán Killeen collected four FAI Women's Cups, three Women's National League championships, and two WNL Cups; and English goalkeeper Siobhan Chamberlain took home the Cyprus Cup twice, an FA Women's Cup, and an FA Women's Championship.

Siobhan "HaganeNoTema" Bielamowicz, Esports (*Attack on Titan Tribute Game*), Australia, 2014–2019

Siobhan Chamberlain, Soccer (Goalkeeper), Bristol Academy W.F.C., England, 1999–2020

Siobhán Haughey, Swimming (Freestyle), Hong Kong, 2013–current

Siobhán Killeen, Soccer (Midfielder), Shelbourne Ladies, Ireland, 2011–current

Siobhan Paton, Swimming (Freestyle/Backstroke/Breaststroke/Medley), Australia, 1997–2000

SJOUKJE

How cool is the Dutch name Sjoukje, embodying speed, power, and grace while coming from the Old Norse name Sigurd and roots meaning "victory" and "guardian"? Name your daughter Sjoukje and she could be a mighty warrior like the Sigurd of legend or even a champion figure skater like 1960s Dutch Olympic gold-medalist and three-time world champion Sjoukje Dijkstra!

Sjoukje Dijkstra, Figure Skating, Netherlands, 1953–1964

SKY

The world around us presents all sorts of features and concepts that can make great names, and one of the best has to be the sky itself, which comes from an Old Norse word meaning "cloud." Shoot for the top and give this lofty name to your daughter; she may have her head in the clouds sometimes, but she'll also be down-to-earth when it comes to playing sports and competing. She may even be a child phenom like British-Japanese Sky Brown, who became the youngest professional skateboarder in the world at eight years old and has thus far won a world championship, two X Games gold medals, a gold and a silver on the Dew Tour, and an Olympic bronze medal!

Sky Brown, Skateboarding, England/Japan, 2016–current

SKYLAR

A great name for a girl who's into books or basketball, the unisex Skylar comes from a Dutch root meaning "scholar." Here in the United States, it has reached the upper echelon of basketball players with the inspirational Skylar Diggins-Smith, a six-time WNBA All-Star point guard who has won an Olympic gold medal with USA Basketball. She has also won three Basketball 3x3 world championships and is a hero off the court thanks to her work with kids.

Skylar Diggins-Smith, Basketball (Point Guard), Tulsa Shock, USA, 2013–current

SOFIA/SOFIYA/SOPHIA

For a girl who will be wise beyond her years, and quite possibly enjoy water sports, consider the name Sophia (from Greek for "wisdom") or one of its variants Sofia or Sofiya. Hungarian-born chess Woman Grandmaster Polgar Sofia exemplifies the intelligence behind the name, while the physical prowess can be seen in Soviet artistic gymnast Sofia Muratova, who won eight medals at the Olympics (including two golds) and three golds and two silvers at World Championships; sabre fencer Sofiya Velikaya, who took home two Olympic golds and three silvers, along with eight world championship golds, five silvers, and three bronzes; and American NWSL Best XI soccer right back Sofia Huerta, whose trophy case includes a W-League Champ, NWSL Shield, The Women's Cup, CONCACAF Women's Championship, and three SheBelieves Cups.

Meanwhile, many athletes with these names seem to feel at home in or on the water! Sophia Herzog swam to two of each color medal at World Championships, Peruvian Surfers Hall of Famer Sofía Mulánovich has won three world championships and became the Absolute World Champion, and Greek sailor Sofia Bekatorou won Olympic gold and four world championships in various watercraft. Finally, frozen water makes snow, which is where Italian alpine skier Sofia Goggia has won Olympic gold and silver medals and a massive forty-eight medals at World Cup events, including twenty-two wins.

Sofia Bekatorou, Sailing, Greece, 1994–2019

Sofia Goggia, Alpine Skiing, Italy, 2012–current

Sophia Elizabeth Herzog, Swimming (Breaststroke), USA, 2015–current

Sofia Huerta, Soccer (Right Back), Chicago Red Stars, USA, 2015–current

Sofía Mulánovich, Surfing, Peru, 2002–current

Sofia Muratova, Artistic Gymnastics, USSR, 1949–1964

Polgar Sofia, Chess, Hungary/Israel, 1989–current

Sofiya Velikaya, Fencing (Sabre), Russia, 2003–current

SONIA/SONJA

So many popular names end up having diminutives, and *Sophia* got an interesting one in the Russian *Sonya*, which in turn has had variations in Sonia and Sonja. Athletes with these names have ranged far and wide, both in country of origin and in the sports they've conquered, everything from field hockey and Zimbabwean defender Sonia Robertson (who, alongside her twin sister, won Olympic gold in 1980) to curling and Canadian three-time Paralympic gold-medalist Sonja Gaudet; track and field and Irish middle-distance runner Sonia O'Sullivan, who won a world championship, two World Cross-Country Championships, and a World Cup; and figure skating and Norwegian three-time Olympic gold-medalist, ten-time world champion, and movie star Sonja Henie.

Similarly, a Sonia or Sonja in your family will accept no barriers, finding her own path in the world and letting nothing stand in her way.

Sonja Gaudet, Wheelchair Curling (Lead), Canada, 2006–2014

Sonja Henie, Figure Skating, Norway, 1922–1956

Sonia O'Sullivan, Track & Field (Middle-Distance Running), Ireland, 1990–2007

Sonia Robertson, Field Hockey (Defender), Zimbabwe, 1980

SOO-/SU-

Precision, accuracy, and focus are synonymous with athletes given Korean Soo- and Su- names that can have various meanings based on the characters used to write them. Martial artist Lim Su-jeong used expert moves to win an Olympic gold medal and world championship in taekwondo, and then there are pairs of champions in racquet sports, and marksmanship. Seo Su-yeon became a para table tennis world champion in 2018, and in the 1990s, badminton pro Bang

Soo-hyun won Olympic gold and silver and the Sudirman Cup twice. Sharpshooter Ahn Soo-kyeong took gold in air pistol at the 2003 ISSF World Cup and archer Kim Soo-nyung won four Olympic gold medals and four world championships. Meanwhile on the links, Kang Soo-yun has won a very impressive fifteen professional events!

Whether it's hitting bullseyes, shooting holes in one, or slamming precision serves, a daughter with a Soo- or Su- name is sure to hit the mark every time.

Ahn Soo-kyeong, Sport Shooting (Pistol), South Korea, 2004–2008

Bang Soo-hyun, Badminton, South Korea, 1988–1996

Kang Soo-yun, Golf, South Korea, 1997–current

Kim Soo-nyung, Archery, South Korea, 1988–2000

Lim Su-jeong, Taekwondo, South Korea, 2002–2011

Seo Su-yeon, Table Tennis, South Korea, 2013–current

SOPHIE

While the Russian version of *Sophia* gave us *Sonia* and *Sonja*, the French form Sophie is a very popular name on its own. The wisdom of this name has led many Sophies to excel at team sports, and so it's quite likely a young Sophie in your family will enjoy playing along with her friends and working together on projects (and the field) toward victory.

Cricket fans will recognize the name from Sophie Molineux of Australia, who has won numerous awards and helped her national team to wins at the 2018 ICC Women's World Twenty20, 2019 Women's Ashes, and 2020 ICC Women's T20 World Cup.

In other sports, stolen base legend Sophie Kurys earned four All-Star selections as second basewoman and won two championships in the All-American Girls Professional Baseball League while leading the league in runs scored six times and stolen bases seven times (and later being inducted into the National Women's Baseball Hall of Fame), and Canadian soccer midfielder Sophie Schmidt's trophy case includes an NWSL Challenge Cup, Algarve Cup, Four Nations Tournament championship, CONCACAF Women's Championship, and a gold and bronze medal from the Olympics!

Sophie Kurys, Baseball (Second Base), Racine Belles, USA, 1943–1952

Sophie Molineux, Cricket (All-Rounder), Melbourne Renegades, Australia, 2015–current

Sophie Schmidt, Soccer (Midfielder), Houston Dash, Canada, 2005–current

STACEY/STACY

The unisex name Stacy has multiple variations and origins, potentially arising as a diminutive of *Anastasia* (from Greek meaning "resurrection") or coming from the medieval name *Stace* (in turn from *Eustace* and ultimately Greek meaning "fruitful" or "well-built"). Staceys and Stacys have found their way to podiums and winners' circles in various English-speaking parts of the world, and in quite a few different fields. The solo competitors who have achieved lasting fame include English snooker player Stacey Hillyard, who won a world championship at the age of fifteen; Professional Darts Corporation world champion Stacy Bromberg; and Olympic gold-medalist and three-time world champion pole vaulter Stacy Dragila.

Then there are those who have won with teammates on courts, fields, water, and ice, including world champion rower Stacy Apfelbaum; two-time Olympic gold-medalist softball catcher Stacey Nuveman-Deniz; New Zealander rugby center Stacey Fluhler, who has won Olympic gold, a Rugby World Cup Sevens championship, and two Women's

Rugby World Cups; and Canadian 3 Nations Cup-winner and four-time world champion ice hockey forward Stacy Wilson.

A Stacey or Stacy in your family has endless opportunities when it comes to finding her unique talents and athletic preferences.

Stacy Apfelbaum, Rowing, USA, 1984

Stacy Bromberg, Darts, USA, 1979–2012

Stacy Dragila, Track & Field (Pole Vaulting), USA, 1996–2009

Stacey Fluhler, Rugby (Center), New Zealand, 2015–current

Stacey Hillyard, Snooker, England, 1991–1995

Stacey Nuveman-Deniz, Softball (Catcher), USA, 2000–2008

Stacy Wilson, Ice Hockey (Forward), Moncton Blades, Canada, 1986–1998

STAFANIE

If you like the name *Stephanie* but are looking for something a little different for your daughter, then consider the uncommon variation Stafanie! If you do, she'll always need to spell out her name for people she meets, but she'll also be a strong presence on any athletic field with multiple skills . . . just like Jamaican cricketer Stafanie Taylor, who has set multiple records in her home country and with the international West Indies team (including becoming the second women's T20I player to score three thousand runs) while winning the 2010 Women's T20 Challenge and being named ICC Women's Cricketer of the Year 2011, ICC Women's ODI Cricketer of the Year 2012, and ICC Women's T20I Cricketer of the Year 2015!

Stafanie Taylor, Cricket (All-Rounder), Sydney Thunder, Jamaica, 2002–current

STANKA

A girl will surely rise up and achieve fame through her strength and skill if she's named Stanka, an Eastern European name derived from *Stanislav* (itself from roots for "become" and "glory"). Anyone can look up to Bulgarian wrestler Stanka Zlateva, a two-time World Female Wrestler of the Year and winner of five world championships and more!

Stanka Zlateva, Freestyle Wrestling, Bulgaria, 2001–2012

STEFANIA/STEFANIYA

The popular name *Stephen* (from Greek meaning "crown" or "wreath") has spawned many variants around the world, including *Stephanie* and its own set of different versions. Among those are Stefania and Stefaniya! These are certainly interesting names, familiar and yet unique, and have a history of crowning achievement with Russian three-time world champion RS:X windsurfer Stefania Elfutina and Italian cross-country skier Stefania Belmondo, who collected ten medals from Olympic Games (two of them gold), thirteen medals from World Championships (four of them gold), and ninety-three podium results in World Cup events (twenty-seven of them wins).

Stefania Belmondo, Cross-Country Skiing, Italy, 1987–2002

Stefaniya Elfutina, Sailing, Russia, 2009–current

STEFFI

Stephanie may have become *Stefania* and *Stefaniya* in Eastern Europe, but in Germany, the name also got the diminutive Steffi. In turn, German athletes with this name have gone on to great deeds.

Some Steffis like going really fast over ice, like world champion skeleton racer Steffi Jacob and luger Steffi Martin, who swept her international events with two gold medals at Olympics and World Champions each and an overall Luge World Cup championship.

Meanwhile, the name is synonymous with

one athlete over all others, and of course that's tennis phenom Steffi Graf! Widely considered one of the greatest players of all time, Hall of Famer Graf broke numerous records during her career, including the longest length of time holding the world number one singles ranking and winning 107 titles, twenty-two majors, and a full set of medals at Olympic Games (and thus the first ever "Golden Slam").

Will a Steffi in your family love tennis, or another sport, and boost its popularity around the world like Graf? Maybe, so let her explore her interests and find her perfect match.

Stefanie "Steffi" Graf, Tennis, Germany, 1982–1999

Steffi Jacob, Skeleton, Germany, 1996–2002

Steffi Martin, Luge, Germany, 1982-1988

STEPHANIE

The most popular of the feminine variations of *Stephen*, Stephanie was among the top ten baby names in the United States for seventeen years between 1972 and 1993. It may have dropped a bit in the rankings since then, but it's still a solid name for a competitive girl, especially one who enjoys swimming or playing soccer! She'll be in good company with British Paralympic gold-medalist and world champion relay swimmer Stephanie Slater; Australian three-time Olympic gold-medalist swimmer (medley and freestyle) Stephanie Rice; British Stephanie Millward, who swam to ten medals at Paralympic Games (including two golds) and eleven at World Championships (four of them gold); and Canadian Stephanie Dixon, who swam to seven golds, eight silvers, and two bronzes at the Paralympics.

On football (soccer) fields around the world, Stephanies have made their marks as defenders, providing a solid defense while their teammates charge forward and score. Defender Stephanie Cox won Olympic gold in 2008 with the United States Women's National Team, and Canadian goalkeeper Stephanie Labbé got her Olympic gold medal in 2020 and won both an NWSL Shield and Championship.

Your Stephanie not interested in swimming or soccer? No problem! She can find inspirational figures in various other sports, including track cycling with world champion, Paralympic gold-medalist, and two-time Para-cycling Track world champion Stephanie Morton; esports with Canadian five-time *Counter-Strike* and *Counter-Strike: Global Offensive* world champion Stephanie "missharvey" Harvey; and surfing with Australian eight-time world champion Stephanie Gilmore, who has won thirty-four events on the World Surf League Championship Tour and been inducted into the Surfers' Hall of Fame.

Stephanie Cox, Soccer (Defender), Seattle Reign FC, USA, 2009–2021

Stephanie Dixon, Swimming (Backstroke/Freestyle/Medley), Canada, 2000–2010

Stephanie Gilmore, Surfing, Australia, 2005–current

Stephanie "missharvey" Harvey, Esports (*Counter-Strike*), Canada, 2003–2019

Stephanie Labbé, Soccer (Goalkeeper), KIF Örebro DFF, Canada, 2006-2022

Stephanie Millward, Swimming (Backstroke/Butterfly/Freestyle/Medley), England, 2000–2016

Stephanie Morton, Track Cycling, Australia, 2005–2020

Stephanie Rice, Swimming (Medley/Freestyle), Australia, 2006–2014

Stephanie Slater, Swimming (Butterfly/Freestyle/Medley), England, 2006–2018

STINA/STINE

While in the United States names like *Christina* and *Christine* can be shortened into *Chris* and *Tina*, Scandinavians have given the world unique short forms in Stina and Stine. Interestingly, athletes with these two "S" names have had great successes in three fields: soccer, handball, and skiing events! First up are two current soccer players, 2022 Danish Women's Football Player of the Year defender Stine Pedersen, who has won the Norwegian Women's Cup twice, and Swedish striker Stina Blackstenius, who has collected the Svenska Cupen three times, an FA Women's League Cup, and the Algarve Cup.

Handball may not be super popular here in the United States, but in Europe, it's big business, and that's where you'll find the best-of-the-best, like world champion right-back Stine Skogrand, who won the Danish Cup and EHF European League; and three-time world champion center-back Stine Oftedal, who has taken home the Hungarian Cup three times and the EHF Champions League win twice.

Last but certainly not least are the Stinas and Stines on skis! Some prefer ski orienteering, like Norwegian World Cup-winner and four-time world champion Stine Kirkevik, while others branch out into freestyle skiing, like Norwegian Olympic gold-medalist and world champion Stine Hattestad; or cross-country skiing and biathlon, like Stina Nilsson of Sweden, who has won Olympic gold, two silvers, and two bronzes, as well as two World Championship golds and five silvers, and has stood on fifty World Cup podiums, with twenty-six wins.

You can call your daughter Stina or Stine as a short form of a longer name or give her one of those directly, but either way you should strongly consider teaching her how to ski or play soccer.

Emma Stina Blackstenius, Soccer (Striker), Linköping Football Club, Sweden, 2011-current

Stine Hattestad, Freestyle Skiing, Norway, 1988-1994

Stine Kirkevik, Ski-Orienteering, Norway, 2001-2006

Stina Nilsson, Cross-Country Skiing/Biathlon, Sweden, 2012-current

Stine Oftedal, Handball (Center-Back), Norway, 2007-current

Stine Pedersen, Soccer (Defender), Vålerenga Fotball Damer, Denmark, 2012-current

Stine Skogrand, Handball (Right-Back), Norway, 2009-current

SUE

The first in a series of names descended from the biblical Hebrew *Shoshannah* and a root meaning "lily," Sue is generally seen as fairly old-fashioned here in the United States. However, it has a tradition of athletic excellence and is ready for a comeback! Sues can be strong and mighty, like Australian three-time Women's World Powerlifting champion Sue Roberts, or they can be quick and agile, like WNBA point guard Sue Bird, who was a dominating force in the WNBA (thirteen All-Star appearances, four championships, and leader rankings in peak performer twice and assists three times) and international competition (five Olympic gold medals and four world championships). And don't worry, even if your daughter you name Sue isn't super strong or tall, she can still accomplish amazing things and go on.

Suzanne "Sue" Bird, Basketball (Point Guard), Seattle Storm, USA, 2002-2022

Sue Roberts, Powerlifting, Australia, 1980-1987

SUNG-

With various meanings depending on the characters used to write it, as well as unique secondary syllables, the South Korean unisex name Sung- has lots of flexibility and a solid history lending it an air of agility and accuracy. Jung Sung-sook became a world champion judoka in 1995, while more recently, Park Sung-hyun has won eighteen professional golf events and two majors and has been ranked number one in the world on multiple occasions. Meanwhile, archers Lee Sung-jin and Park Sung-hyun have competed together and against each other, the former winning two Olympic gold medals and a silver along with two world championships and the latter setting records on her way to three Olympic golds and a silver and eight medals at World Championships (including four golds)!

Give your daughter a Sung- name and she'll have fantastic hand-eye coordination and the skills to win in her chosen field.

Jung Sung-sook, Judo, South Korea, 1993–2000

Lee Sung-jin, Archery, South Korea, 2004–2012

Park Sung-hyun, Archery, South Korea, 2001–2008

Park Sung-hyun, Golf, South Korea, 2012–current

SUSAN/SUSANN

Like *Sue*, Susan and Susann are names that ultimately come from Hebrew meaning "lily," via English and German/Scandinavian languages, respectively. Name your daughter Susan (or add the extra "n" for Susann) and she'll be able to compete anywhere and in any capacity. Just look at the incredible women who have come before, like Hungarian-American chess Grandmaster and Women's World Chess Champion Susan Polgar, who was raised from childhood to play the game; Norwegian World Women's Handball Championship-winner Susann Bjerkrheim; and dog sled racer Susan Butcher, who set multiple records on her way to winning the Iditarod Trail Sled Dog Race four times!

Susann Bjerkrheim, Handball (Center Back), Norway, 1993–2000

Susan Butcher, Sled Dog Racing, USA, 1978–1995

Polgar Zsuzsanna "Susan", Chess, Hungary/USA, 1984–current

SUSANNAH/SUZANNA/SUZANNE

Susannah and Suzanna are pretty straightforward variants on the classic Hebrew *Shoshannah* (which means "lily"), while in French, it evolved to Suzanne. Girls and women with these names have the potential for athletic success, as well as leading the pack and breaking through to set records or be the first to accomplish something! American wheelchair racer Susannah Scaroni has won gold and bronze at Paralympic Games in the 5000-meter and 800-meter events, respectively; Dutch volleyball setter Suzanne Freriks won gold at the World Grand Prix; and French tennis legend Suzanne Lenglen won twenty-one titles and eight Grand Slams and was the first women's singles world number one.

Suzanne Freriks, Volleyball (Setter), Netherlands, 2000–2011

Suzanne Lenglen, Tennis, France, 1912–1927

Susannah Scaroni, Wheelchair Racing, USA, 2012–current

SUSI/SUSIE/SUZIE/SUZY

The most casual of the *Sue/Shoshannah* family of names, Susi, Susie, Suzie, and Suzy are diminutives of *Susanne* and *Susan*.

Individual competitors winning and setting records have included Australian swimmer Susie "Madame Butterfly" O'Neill, who took home eight medals from Olympic Games (including two golds) and eighteen from World Championships (four of them golds); Indonesian Olympic gold-medalist, world champion, and five-time World Cup-winning badminton legend Susi Susanti; and Armenian-German boxer Susi Kentikian, who held multiple world flyweight titles, was the first-ever World Boxing Association female Super Champion, and retired with a 36-2-1 record.

Susis, Suzies, and Suzys also play well with partners and on teams! Center Suzy Shortland won two Rugby World Cups with the New Zealand team; guard Suzie McConnell-Serio helped the US women's basketball team win a world championship and gold and bronze at Olympic Games; German luger and bobsledder Susi Erdmann's medal count (in singles, two-woman, and team) includes nine golds, three silvers, and a bronze from World Championships and four golds and four bronzes from World Cup Championships; and New Zealand cricket all-rounder Suzie Bates has set multiple records and firsts (like being the first Twenty20 International cricketer ever to score three thousand runs) and was named T20I Cricketer of the Year and ICC Women's ODI Cricketer of the Year twice.

If you name your daughter something like *Susan* or *Susanne*, consider calling her Susi, Susie, Suzie, or Suzy to unlock her championship potential!

- **Suzannah "Suzie" Bates**, Cricket (All-Rounder), Otago Sparks, New Zealand, 2002–current
- **Suzy Batkovic**, Basketball (Center), Townsville Fire, Australia, 2003–2019
- **Susi-Lisa Erdmann**, Luge/Bobsleigh, Germany, 1977–2006
- **Suzannah "Suzie" Fraser**, Water Polo (Driver), Australia, 2006–2008
- **Susianna "Susi" Kentikian**, Boxing (Flyweight), Armenia/Germany, 2005–2016
- **Suzie McConnell-Serio**, Basketball (Guard), Cleveland Rockers, USA, 1985–2000
- **Susan "Susie" (Madame Butterfly) O'Neill**, Swimming (Butterfly/Freestyle), Australia, 1990–2000
- **Suzy Shortland, Rugby (Center)**, New Zealand Women's Rugby Union Team, New Zealand, 1997–2002
- **Lucia Francisca "Susi" Susanti Haditono**, Badminton, Indonesia, 1987–1997
- **Suzanne "Susie" Wolff**, Auto Racing (Deutsche Tourenwagen Masters), Scotland, 2002–2015

SVETLANA

You don't have to be Eastern European to name a daughter Svetlana. From a Slavic root for "light" or "shining," this name has been used by a host of champions from Russia and its surroundings and in several different sports. Svetlanas have conquered everything from handball (Bosnian-Serb Olympic gold- and silver-medalist center-back Svetlana Kitić) to weightlifting (Kazakhstani two-time world champion Svetlana Podobedova) and synchronized swimming (Svetlana Romashina, who stands among the best ever in her sport with a solid gold trophy collection of seven Olympic wins, twenty-one World Championships, and thirteen European Championships)!

Svetlanas do have some interesting preferences in their fields, starting with artistic gymnastics and chess. Svetlana Boginskaya won three gold medals at the Olympics on the vault for the USSR and Unified Teams, as well as five world championships (in team, all-around, floor exercise, and balance beam), while Svetlana Khorkina took home two Olympic gold medals on uneven bars (along with four silvers and a bronze) and, in World Championships, nine golds, eight silvers, and three bronzes. Meanwhile, the brainiest Svetlanas include Estonian Woman FIDE Master and Lady Grandmaster Svetlana Zainetdinova and Russian International Master and Woman Grandmaster Svetlana Matveeva.

The largest concentrations of athletes with this name have occurred in skiing sports (notably the biathlon) and track and field events! On the slopes, skiers/markswomen include Belarusian three-time world champion biathlete Svetlana Paramygina, Russian two-time Olympic gold-medalist and five-time world champion Svetlana Ishmouratova, and Soviet seven-time world champion Svetlana Petcherskaia. In warmer climes, Svetlana Ulmasova raced to two first-place finishes at World Cross Country Championships; Svetlana Zakharova won the Honolulu Marathon three times, as well as the Boston and Chicago races; Svetlana Feofanova pole-vaulted to two world championships; and Svetlana Masterkova won Olympic gold and a world championship in the 1500-meter and another Olympic gold in the 800-meter.

Svetlana is by no means a name locked to Eastern Europe, and it can inspire a girl in your family to athletic (and mental) feats of greatness, whether she likes chess, gymnastics, skiing, running, or anything else!

- **Svetlana Boginskaya**, Artistic Gymnastics, USSR/Belarus, 1987–1996
- **Svetlana Feofanova**, Track & Field (Pole Vaulting), Russia, 2000–2012
- **Svetlana Ishmouratova**, Biathlon, Russia, 1996–2006
- **Svetlana Khorkina**, Artistic Gymnastics, Russia, 1994–2004
- **Svetlana Kitić**, Handball (Center-Back), Yugoslavia, 1976–2006
- **Svetlana Masterkova**, Track & Field (Middle-Distance Running), Russia, 1991–2003
- **Svetlana Matveeva**, Chess, Russia, 1984–current
- **Svetlana Paramygina**, Biathlon, Belarus, 1983–2001
- **Svetlana Petcherskaia**, Biathlon, USSR, 1989–1992
- **Svetlana Podobedova**, Weightlifting, Kazakhstan, 2003–current
- **Svetlana Romashina**, Synchronized Swimming, Russia, 2005–2020
- **Svetlana Ulmasova**, Long-Distance Running, USSR, 1978–1983
- **Svetlana Zainetdinova**, Chess, Estonia, 1984–current
- **Svetlana Zakharova**, Long-Distance Running, Russia, 1997–2009

SYDNEY

A variant of *Sidney*, which comes from an English place name meaning "wide island," the name Sydney can be great for a defender or a goal scorer! Ice hockey goaltender Sydney Rossman was a National Women's Hockey League All-Star and won the Isobel Cup in the Premier Hockey Federation championship in 2019 with the Minnesota Whitecaps, while NWSL Best XI soccer forward Sydney Leroux has won a NWSL Shield with Seattle Reign and, with the United States Women's National Soccer Team, the Algarve Cup twice, CONCACAF Women's Championship, an Olympic gold medal, and the 2015 FIFA Women's World Cup.

- **Sydney Leroux**, Soccer (Forward), Orlando Pride, USA, 2005–current
- **Sydney Rossman**, Ice Hockey (Goaltender), Connecticut Whale, USA, 2013–2019

SYLVIE

Descended from a Latin word for "forest" like *Silvia* and *Sylvia*, the modern Czech and French form Sylvie has come to represent women who compete and win overwhelmingly in events that take place on or in water, ice, and snow! These include Canadian Olympic gold-medalist springboard diver Sylvie Bernier, French two-time world champion biathlete Sylvie Becaert, Canadian Olympic gold-medalist and five-time world champion short track speed skater Sylvie Daigle, and International Water Ski Federation Hall of Famers Sylvie Maurial of France, who was the 1973 slalom world champion and won a gold medal in jumping at the 1972 Olympic Games demonstration, and Sylvie Hülsemann of Luxembourg, who became a world champion at sixteen years old on her way to more than ninety international wins and two world championships.

Name your daughter Sylvie and introduce her to the wide world of activities on the water, ice, and snow and she's sure to find her favorite!

Sylvie Becaert, Biathlon, France, 2003–2010

Sylvie Bernier, Diving, Canada, 1982–1984

Sylvie Daigle, Short Track Speed Skating, Canada, 1979–1994

Sylvie Hülsemann, Water Skiing, Luxembourg, 1957–1979

Sylvie Maurial, Water Skiing, France, 1962–1973

T

BOYS

TADAHIRO

"Faithful" and "ocean" are just two of the many different meanings that the Japanese name Tadahiro can have depending on which kanji characters are used to write it, but don't assume a little boy with this name will seek out water sports. Tadahiro Nomura had a legendary judo career, winning not just a world championship, but also being the only person ever to win Olympic gold in the event at three successive Olympic Games (1996, 2000, and 2004)!

Naming your son Tadahiro will ensure that he'll be unstoppable!

Tadahiro Nomura, Judo, Japan, 1996–2015

TAKASHI

Takashi's potential translations (depending on the Japanese kanji characters used to write it) can include "prosperous," "noble," "gentleman," and "history." Give the noble name Takashi to a boy in your family and he'll make history, especially if he follows in the footsteps of gentlemen who have come before him. These include solo competitors (like 9-dan-ranked shogi player Takashi Abe, and Olympic gold-medalist freestyle swimmer Takashi Yokoyama) and men who have succeeded alongside others (like MLB All-Star pitcher and NPB four-time All-Star, two-time champion, and strikeout leader Takashi Saito; Yokohama Marinos soccer winger Takashi Mizunuma, who won the J1 League, Japan Soccer League twice, JSL Cup three times, and Emperor's Cup six times; and two-time world champion artistic gymnast Takashi Ono, whose individual and team Olympic medal tally was five golds, four silvers, and four bronzes!).

Takashi Abe, Shogi, Japan, 1985–current

Takashi Mizunuma, Soccer (Winger), Yokohama F. Marinos, Japan, 1983–1995

Takashi Ono, Artistic Gymnastics, Japan, 1952–1964

Takashi Saito, Baseball (Pitcher), Yokohama BayStars, Japan, 1992–2015

Takashi Yokoyama, Swimming (Freestyle), Japan, 1932

TAKERU

There are lots of cool translations for the Japanese name Takeru depending on the characters used to write it, including "warrior," "fierce," "health," "noble," and "mountain." Two fierce warriors with this name have made it to the top of the mountain to be ranked among the very best in their respective sports, and they are *very* different. Kickboxer Takeru Segawa has had an absolutely dominating career in K-1, achieving a 42-3 record while becoming the first fighter in the promotion to hold two weight championships at once and the only person ever to hold three. Meanwhile, Takeru "The Tsunami" Kobayashi is hailed as a driving force behind the popularization of international competitive eating; he won the world-famous Nathan's Hot Dog Eating Contest six times and has set dozens of world records eating everything from grilled cheese sandwiches to cow brains.

A young Takeru in your family will continue the trend of being a noble, fierce, and healthy warrior . . . just be prepared for him to like to fight and eat a lot!

Takeru "The Tsunami" Kobayashi, Competitive Eating, Japan, 2000-2017

Takeru Segawa, Kickboxing (Bantamweight), Japan, 2008-current

TAO

You may not have achieved universal harmony just yet, but don't let that stop you from considering the unisex name Tao (a Chinese concept unifying yin and yang) for your boy. If you do call him Tao, he may enjoy lifting weights, riding his bike, or kayaking, especially in rough waters! He can get inspiration in these activities from Chinese world champion weightlifter Tian Tao; British cyclist Tao Geoghegan Hart, who won General Classification in the 2020 Giro d'Italia; and record-setting kayaker Tao Berman, whose incredible feats include paddling down a 98.4-foot waterfall, surfing a thirty-seven-foot wave in a kayak, winning numerous freestyle and racing championships, and more.

Tao Berman, Kayaking, USA, 1999-2012

Tao Geoghegan Hart, Road/Track Cycling, England, 2010-current

Tian Tao, Weightlifting, China, 2013-current

TAOUFIK/TAUFIK/TEVFIK

From an Arabic root for "being successful" and the name *Tawfiq* meaning "good fortune" comes a whole family of variations, including Taoufik, Taufik, and Tevfik. Athletes with these names come from several countries and have manifested the success of their names in several different events, from track and field (Algerian Olympic gold-medalist and two-time silver-medalist middle-distance runner Taoufik Makhloufi) to badminton (Indonesian Olympic gold-medalist, world champion, and two-time Thomas Cup-winner Taufik Hidayat) and Greco-Roman wrestling (Turkish Olympic gold-medalist and two-time world champion Tevfik Kış).

Whether it's in wrestling, badminton, running, or another sport, an athletic son with one of these names is sure to have good fortune and great success!

Taufik Hidayat, Badminton, Indonesia, 1998-2013

Tevfik Kış, Greco-Roman Wrestling, Turkey, 1956-1968

Taoufik Makhloufi, Track & Field (Middle-Distance Running), Algeria, 2007-current

TAZIO

If you like uncommon Italian names and want a little boy who will love going fast (in any way he can), then Tazio might be a great pick. Descended from an ancient Roman name that may have come from the Sabine tribe in modern-day Italy, Tazio has an impeccable lineage in European auto racing's "Flying Mantuan" Tazio Nuvolari! Following a successful motorcycle racing career in the 1920s, Nuvolari began competing on four wheels and quickly racked up a huge (and varied) number of victories, including 150 wins across major racing series. Widely considered one of the greatest drivers of his era, Tazio is a fantastic role model for any future speedster who shares his name.

Tazio "Flying Mantuan" Nuvolari, Auto Racing (European Drivers' Championship), Italy, 1920–1950

TED

Ted and its more casual sibling *Teddy* are traditionally diminutives of *Edward* and *Theodore*, but of course they can be nicknames for other names or serve as names all on their own. Teds have made history in North America and the United Kingdom as consummate sportsmen, posting wins, championships, and records across several different sports, like American thoroughbred horse racing jockey Ted Atkinson, who won nearly 3,800 races and was inducted into the National Museum of Racing and Hall of Fame; and prolific English welterweight boxer Ted "Kid" Lewis, who dominated the scene in the 1910s and '20s with two stints as the World Welterweight Champion and an unofficial record of 232–46–23.

Two sports have witnessed the stellar accomplishments of two Teds, starting with a pair of ice hockey Hall of Famers: MVP center Ted "Teeder" Kennedy, who was part of the 1940s and '50s Toronto Maple Leafs dynasty, winning a record five Stanley Cup championships and establishing himself as a crucial goal-scorer, and Detroit Red Wings left wing "Terrible" Ted Lindsay, who was named All-Star eleven times and won four Stanley Cups on his way to a permanent spot on the list of best-ever players.

Last but certainly not least are the iconic sluggers in America's pastime! Catcher Ted Simmons played in eight All-Star games between 1972 and 1983, earning a Silver Slugger award and ranking on leaderboards for batting average, career hits and doubles, total bases, and more. And then there's Boston Red Sox left fielder Ted Williams, consistently ranked as one of the greatest hitters in MLB history! Williams was an All-Star every year of his nineteen-year career; was named American League MVP twice; led that league in batting six times, home runs four times, and RBIs four times; won the Triple Crown twice; and set numerous records, including the highest on-base percentage of .482, being the last player to hit over .400 in a season, and hitting the highest career batting average of any player primarily in the live-ball era!

A Ted in your family can accomplish anything he sets his mind to, including an athletic career that will make it into the record books! Definitely teach him the basics of baseball and ice hockey when he's little.

Theodore "Ted" Atkinson, Horse Racing (Jockey), USA, 1938–1959

Theodore "Ted" (Teeder) Kennedy, Ice Hockey (Center), Toronto Maple Leafs, Canada, 1942–1957

Robert Blake Theodore "Ted" (Terrible Ted) Lindsay, Ice Hockey (Left Wing), Detroit Red Wings, Canada, 1944–1965

Ted "Kid" Lewis, Boxing (Light Heavyweight/Middleweight/Welterweight), England, 1909–1929

Ted Simmons, Baseball (Catcher), St. Louis Cardinals, USA, 1968–1988

Theodore "Ted" Williams, Baseball (Left Fielder), Boston Red Sox, USA, 1939–1960

TEDDY

Like its shorter sibling *Ted*, Teddy is most commonly a diminutive of *Edward* or *Theodore*, but unlike the *Teds* who have concentrated in a few different sports, Teddys have spread out into numerous and varied events. In team sports, English soccer forward Teddy Sheringham won an FA Cup, UEFA Champions League, and Intercontinental Cup while being named Premier League

Golden Boot, Premier League Player of the Month twice, PFA Players' Player of the Year, FWA Footballer of the Year, and more.

In individual competitions, French triple jumper Teddy Tamgho won two world championships in the early 2010s, and French judoka Teddy Riner has set records on his way to collecting three gold and two bronze medals from the Olympics; twelve golds, a silver, and a bronze at World Championships; four golds at World Masters; eleven golds at International Judo Foundation Grand Slams; and six golds at International Judo Foundation Grand Prix!

Introduce a son you name (or call) Teddy to a wide variety of sports and let him find his perfect match.

Edward "Teddy" Sheringham, Soccer (Striker), Millwall Football Club, England, 1983–2008

Teddy Riner, Judo, France, 2007–current

Teddy Tamgho, Track & Field (Triple Jump), France, 2009–current

TELMO

A fast Spanish pronunciation of "Saint Elmo" resulted in the creation of the name Telmo, which, in the world of sports, will forever be associated with the soccer forward known as "Zarra." Pedro Telmo Zarraonandía Montoya was an early phenom, quickly rising to the professional leagues and joining Athletic Club in 1940, which led to a career that would see him score over three hundred senior and international goals; win a La Liga championship, the Copa del Rey five times, Copa Eva Duarte, six Pichici Trophies, and a Golden Pichichi Trophy; and set multiple scoring and championship records; his record for Spanish goal scoring lasted until Lionel Messi overtook it in 2014, but he still holds the record for Copa del Rey goals.

Telmo is a fun and unique name that deserves a comeback; give it to your son and teach him soccer fundamentals so he can draw inspiration from Zarra!

Pedro "Zarra" Telmo Zarraonandía Montoya, Soccer (Forward), Athletic Club, Spain, 1939–1957

TEÓFILO

You don't need to be religious to appreciate and even give your son the Portuguese and Spanish name Teófilo, from Ancient Greek meaning "friend of god." A boy named Teófilo will be competitive and patriotic, a champion with love of the game and country, just like Cuban heavyweight boxer Teófilo Stevenson, who won three Olympic gold medals and three world championships and was considered one of the greatest boxers of his time.

Meanwhile, Peruvian attacking midfielder Teófilo Cubillas set numerous scoring records on his way to being named South American Footballer of the Year, CONMEBOL All-Star, and Copa America Best Player; being given FIFA World Cup All-Star Team, World Soccer The 100 Greatest Footballers of All Time, and FIFA 100 honors; and winning a Taça de Portugal, Copa América, and the United Soccer League championship twice.

Teófilo Juan Cubillas Arizaga, Soccer (Attacking Midfielder), Club Alianza Lima, Peru, 1966–1989

Teófilo Stevenson Lawrence, Boxing (Heavyweight), Cuba, 1935–1988

TERENCE/TERRENCE

An ancient Roman name with an unknown origin traveled down the centuries to become Terence, which then split into an entire family of variants, including Terrence. When it comes to athletic and competitive people with these names, speed is the key, whether it's slashing through the water, flying over hurdles, or powering through the water! We can see all of this in action with

British Olympic gold-medalist rower Terence Sanders, two-time world champion hurdler Terrence Trammell, and South African deaf swimmer Terence Parkin, who has won an astonishing twenty-nine gold medals, three silvers, and a bronze at the Deaflympics; ten golds, eight silvers, and three bronzes at Swimming World Cup events; a silver medal at the Olympic Games; and, as a bonus, a gold and silver at the World Deaf Cycling Championships.

Terence Parkin, Swimming (Breaststroke/Medley)/Cycling, South Africa, 1997–2013

Terence Sanders, Rowing, England, 1924–1939

Terrence Trammell, Track & Field (Hurdling), USA, 2000–2010

TERRY

Terry is a versatile unisex name, serving as a diminutive for the entire family of *Terence* names, as well as being a variant of *Thierry*. Terrys in sporting events are just as versatile, running, racing, throwing, catching, kicking, goaltending, and more—sometimes even overcoming adversity in the most amazing and inspirational ways, like Australian para-athlete Terry Giddy, whose Paralympic Games medal count includes a gold in discus, three silvers in discus and racing, and two bronzes in shot put.

On the gridiron, iconic Pittsburg Steelers quarterback Terry Bradshaw guided the team through one of its greatest periods, winning four Super Bowl championships in six years (from 1974 to 1979), playing in three Pro Bowls, leading the league in touchdowns twice, being named Super Bowl MVP twice, and being inducted into the Pro Football Hall of Fame.

On the baseball diamond, St. Louis Cardinals center fielder Terry Moore played in three All-Star Games and won two World Series championships; on racetracks, Terry Labonte won twenty-two NASCAR Cup races and two championships, as well as an IROC championship, and was inducted into the Motorsports Hall of Fame of America; and on the ice, Canadian goaltender Terry Sawchuk played in eleven All-Star games, won four Stanley Cup championships, and set multiple records for players in the Original Six era and beyond to earn his place in the Hockey Hall of Fame.

Whether it's on his birth certificate or just something you call him, a Terry in your family has boundless potential to win and become a champion, but he can also inspire others through his hard work and accomplishments.

Terry Bradshaw, Football (Quarterback), Pittsburgh Steelers, USA, 1970–1983

Terence "Terry" Giddy, Para-Athletics, Australia, 1969–2006

Terrance "Terry" Labonte, Auto Racing (NASCAR), USA, 1975–2014

Terry Moore, Baseball (Center Fiedler), St. Louis Cardinals, USA, 1935–1948

Terrance "Terry" Sawchuk, Ice Hockey (Goaltender), Detroit Red Wings, Canada, 1949–1970

THIAGO

The Portuguese name Thiago has a very interesting origin; it's a diminutive of *Santiago*, which in turn came from "Saint James," which comes from *Jacob* meaning "supplanter" in Hebrew. Brazilian Thiagos have found athletic success leaping and hitting, including Olympic gold-medalist pole vaulter Thiago Braz, and volleyball outside spiker Thiago Alves, who has won two gold medals at the World Grand Champions Cup and three at World League. Clearly, then, if you name your son Thiago (whether you're Brazilian or not), he can find his perfect athletic match on a track or field, or on the court—but then again, he could follow in the fast footsteps of soccer players!

Thiagos winning the most trophies on the fields of international football include Spanish UEFA Team of the Year and FIFA FIFPro World11-ranked Thiago Alcântara, and center-back Thiago Silva, who is widely considered one of the best defenders in history and was named to the UEFA Team of the Year three times, FIFA FIFPro World11 three times, FIFA Confederations Cup Dream Team, FIFA World Cup All-Star Team twice, FIFA World Cup Dream Team twice, and more!

- **Thiago Alcântara do Nascimento**, Soccer (Midfielder), Fußball-Club Bayern München e. V., Spain, 2008–current
- **Thiago Soares Alves**, Volleyball (Outside Spiker), Brazil, 2000–current
- **Thiago Braz da Silva**, Track & Field (Pole Vaulting), Brazil, 2013–current
- **Thiago Emiliano da Silva**, Soccer (Center-Back), Paris Saint-Germain Football Club, Brazil, 2002–current

THIERRY

From Gothic roots meaning "ruler of the people" came the name *Theodoric*, which evolved in French to the modern Thierry. Athletes with this name (mostly from France) have become champions in some very interesting and unique fields.

Orienteer Thierry Gueorgiou set the record at World Orienteering Championships with fourteen gold medals (along with two more at World Cups and another at World Games); handball goalkeeper Thierry Omeyer was named World Championship MVP and Player of the Year while winning two Olympic gold medals and five world championships; and World Rugby Player of the Year Thierry Dusautoir set records for tackling (including the most in an international game) while winning five French Championships, a Heineken Cup, Six Nations Championships, and a Grand Slam.

Last but certainly not least is one of the greatest soccer strikers of all time. With over four hundred goals in over nine hundred appearances, Thierry Henry has a lengthy list of records, wins, and accolades, including the 1998 FIFA World Cup, two European Golden Shoes, two Onze d'Or awards; multiple Player of the Year, Team of the Year, and Team of the Century nominations; four MLS All-Star selections; inclusion in the FIFA 100; and inductions into multiple Halls of Fame.

The name Thierry can spur on your son to great deeds and world renown, whether that's in a team sport, embarking on solo adventures, or any other activity or focus he sets his mind to!

- **Thierry Dusautoir**, Rugby (Flanker), Stade Toulousain, France, 2001–2017
- **Thierry Gueorgiou**, Orienteering, France, 1997–2017
- **Thierry Henry**, Soccer (Striker), Arsenal Football Club, France, 1994–2014
- **Thierry Omeyer**, Handball (Goalkeeper), France, 1994–2019

THOMAS

A classic name that goes all the way back to the Founding Fathers in the United States (and well beyond), Thomas ultimately comes from an Aramaic word meaning "twin." While lots of athletes with this name go by a diminutive like *Tom* or *Tommy*, there are still plenty who have taken the full name to the top of leaderboards and championship rankings. Thomases have succeeded in a wide range of events and sports, from fencing (like German Olympic gold-medalist and world champion foil fencer Thomas Bach) to luge (like German two-time Olympic gold-medalist and three-time world champion Thomas Köhler) and soccer (like multi-talented German Bayern Munich player Thomas Müller, who earned a FIFA World Cup Golden Boot, two FIFA World Cup All-Star Team and a FIFA World

Cup Dream Team selections, a Silver Boot and Ball, and numerous scoring awards on his way to the 2014 FIFA World Cup!).

In swimming pools around the globe, Australian freestyle and medley swimmer Thomas Fraser-Holmes took home a set of medals from World Championships, while German para table tennis players Thomas Brüchle and Thomas Schmidberger won gold at World Championships and World Team Championships playing together, while Austrian tennis pro and "King of Clay" Thomas Muster reached the singles world number one spot in 1996 and won forty-four titles and a Grand Slam.

The greatest number of "twin"-named champion athletes have won their events on the slopes or in track and field events! The first group includes Thomas Oelsner of Germany, who won ten Paralympic medals (half of them gold) in biathlon and cross-country skiing; and two of the greatest skiing champions in recent history in Norwegian five-time Olympic gold-medalist and six-time world champion cross-country skier Thomas Alsgaard, who won fifty-four World Cup medals (including twenty-five golds), and Austrian three-time Olympic gold-medalist and eight-time world champion ski jumper Thomas Morgenstern, who won three Sky Flying World Championships and 107 medals at World Cup events, including thirty-nine golds.

Finally, we get to the jumpers, throwers, and runners in the world of track and field. German javelin thrower Thomas Röhler took home Olympic gold in 2016, American hurdler Thomas Curtis won the 110-meter event at the very first Olympics in 1896, Thomas Munkelt of Germany did the same eighty-four years later (and won a World Cup race), and, despite ingesting literal poison and drinking brandy on the way, Thomas Hicks won the marathon at the 1904 Olympic Games (even though he technically crossed the finish line after an athlete who cheated by taking a shortcut in a car!). Austrian wheelchair racer Thomas Geierspichler has won eight medals at Paralympic Games, including two golds; American sprinter Thomas Burke won the first Olympic 100- and 400-meter races in 1896; and Thomas Schönlebe of Germany sprinted to two world championships and a World Indoor Games gold medal.

You can't go wrong giving a kid the classic and respected name Thomas, which can inspire him to great athletic feats in running, skiing, tennis, or anywhere else he finds himself competing.

Thomas Alsgaard, Cross-Country Skiing, Norway, 1993–2003

Thomas Bach, Fencing (Foil), Germany, 1973–1980

Thomas Brüchle, Table Tennis, Germany, 2011–current

Thomas Burke, Track & Field (Sprinting), USA, 1896–1897

Thomas Curtis, Track & Field (Hurdling), USA, 1896

Thomas Fraser-Holmes, Swimming (Freestyle/Medley), Australia, 2010–current

Thomas Geierspichler, Wheelchair Racing, Austria, 2000–2016

Thomas Hicks, Marathon, USA, 1901–1909

Thomas Köhler, Luge, Germany, 1962–1968

Thomas Morgenstern, Ski Jumping, Austria, 2003–2014

Thomas Müller, Soccer (Attacking Midfielder/Forward), Fußball-Club Bayern München e. V., Germany, 2008–current

Thomas Munkelt, Track & Field (Hurdling), Germany, 1975–1984

Thomas "King of Clay" Muster, Tennis, Austria, 1985–2011

Thomas Oelsner, Nordic Combined Skiing, Germany, 1994–2010

Thomas Röhler, Track & Field (Javelin), Germany, 2012–current

Thomas Schmidberger, Table Tennis, Germany, 2011–current

Thomas Schönlebe, Track & Field (Sprinting), Germany, 1983–1993

THORSTEIN/THORSTEN/TORSTEIN/TORSTEN

"Thor's stone" in Old Norse is a pretty cool origin for a name to give your son, and that's exactly where the family of Thorstein/Thorsten/Torstein/Torsten names comes from! While these names are naturally most popular in Scandinavian countries and Germany, there's no geographic limit to where one of them can be given to a boy who, like a god throwing a stone, will have tremendous strength and accuracy.

That's definitely backed up by the athletes with these names who have come before, from marksmen like Olympic gold-medalists Thorstein Johansen of Norway (rifle) and Torsten Ullman of Sweden (pistol) to German three-time world champion pool player Thorsten Hohmann.

If shooting targets, balls, or goals don't appeal to a Thorstein, Thorsten, Torstein, or Torsten in your family, he may prefer cold weather sports like snowboarding and follow in the footsteps of three-time Norwegian X Games gold- and silver-medalist Torstein Horgmo, who also picked up gold and silver on the Winter Dew Tour!

Thorsten Hohmann, Pool (Nine-Ball/Straight), Germany, 1995–current

Torstein Horgmo, Snowboarding, Norway, 2007–2015

Thorstein Johansen, Sport Shooting (Rifle), Norway, 1907–1920

Torsten Ullman, Sport Shooting (Pistol), Sweden, 1933–1954

TIBOR

If you're looking for a unique-sounding "T" name that will inspire your son to be a great team player (especially in soccer or water polo), consider the Czech, Hungarian, and Slovak Tibor (from a place name in Italy)! He may follow in the footsteps of European Silver Boot soccer midfielder Nyilasi Tibor (who won the Hungarian Cup three times, Austrian Bundesliga three times, Austrian Cup, and top scorer awards in Hungary, Austria, and the UEFA) or three-time Olympic gold-medalist, world champion, and World Cup-winning water polo wing Benedek Tibor, who won multiple Hungarian, Italian, and European championships.

Benedek Tibor, Water Polo (Wing), Hungary, 1989–2012

Nyilasi Tibor, Soccer (Midfielder), Ferencvárosi Torna Club, Hungary, 1972–1988

TIGER

The fierce spirit, the tenacity, and the eye of the tiger can all be your son's; just name him Tiger! This iconic animal name has shown up in a few different sports over the years, and primarily by the toughest of the tough. Australian rugby hooker Tiger Black helped the St. George Dragons win their first premiership; in boxing, Tiger Flowers became the very first African-American World Middleweight Boxing Champion in 1926 and had a 135–17–8 record; more than seventy years later, Tiger Smalls won the WBO Inter-Continental Featherweight and Universal Boxing Association World Featherweight titles; and NHL All-Star forward Tiger Williams became infamous as an enforcer and set multiple records for penalty minutes that he still holds.

Of course, the most famous athlete with this big cat name is Tiger Woods, one of the greatest golfers of all time. His accomplishments and records are numerous, including a tied record for PGA wins (eighty-two) among his incredible 110 professional events and fifteen majors. Tiger held the world number one spot for a record length of time and was inducted into the World Golf Hall of Fame the same year he took a step back from active competitive play. For long stretches of his career, Woods was considered unstoppable, and his skills and longevity have changed the game and even led to the evolution of professional golf courses.

- **Ernest "Tiger" Black**, Rugby (Hooker), St. George Dragons, Australia, 1937–1940
- **Theodore "Tiger" Flowers**, Boxing (Middleweight), USA, 1918–1927
- **Tiger Smalls**, Boxing (Featherweight), USA, 1993–2007
- **David "Tiger" Williams**, Ice Hockey (Forward), Toronto Maple Leafs, Canada, 1974–1988
- **Eldrick "Tiger" Woods**, Golf, USA, 1996–2021

TIM

From an Ancient Greek name meaning "honoring god" comes *Timothy*, and of course its two signature diminutives in Tim and *Timmy*. When it comes to athletics, the majority can be found with this shortest form, and together, they have accumulated a mind-boggling number of awards, wins, championships, trophies, medals, and more. They've succeeded by striving on their own and alongside partners and teammates, around the world, and in all manner of events that range from figure skating, like American two-time world champion pairs skater Tim Wood, to competitive eating, like Tim "Eater X" Janus, who won numerous events and still holds records in nigiri sushi, ramen noodles, and tiramisu; mixed martial arts, like two-time UFC Heavyweight Champion Tim Sylvia; and auto racing, like Tim Flock, who won thirty-nine NASCAR Grand National Series races and two championships in the 1950s.

Cricket fans from the Southern Hemisphere will be familiar with Tim May, whose bowling helped the Australia team win its first Cricket World Cup in 1987; New Zealand 2019–2021 ICC World Test Championship-winning bowling all-rounder Tim Southee; and Australian wicketkeeper-batter Tim Paine, who won the 2009 ICC Champions Trophy and the 2017–2018 and 2019 Ashes. The NHL has seen the exploits of American four-time All-Star and Stanley Cup champion goaltender Tim Thomas and Canadian seven-time All-Star, four-time Stanley Cup champion, and Hall of Fame defenseman Tim Horton.

On soccer fields in the US and beyond, American MLS Best XI goalkeeper and 2017 MLS Goalkeeper of the Year Tim Melia has won two US Open Cups, and American three-time MLS All-Star and two-time MLS Best XI goalkeeper Tim Howard won multiple trophies while being named MLS Goalkeeper of the Year, MLS MVP, US Soccer Athlete of the Year, FIFA Confederations Cup Golden Glove, CONCACAF Men's Goalkeeper of the Year three times, and more. In the NBA, point guard Tim Hardaway played in five All-Star games (and won an Olympic gold medal with the United States national basketball team) and San Antonio power forward/center Tim Duncan established himself as one of the greatest of all time with fifteen All-Star appearances and five championships; being named MVP twice, Finals MVP three times, Teammate of the Year, and All-Defensive First Team eight times; being inducted into the Hall of Fame; and more!

Tim Brown, who ranks among the greatest wide receivers of all time as the first player in that position to win the Heisman Trophy and, with the Raiders, played in nine Pro Bowls, led the league in kickoff return yards and co-led in receptions, and set multiple records on his way to being inducted into the Pro Football Hall of Fame.

Tims on the baseball diamond range from Hall of Fame pitcher "Smiling" Tim Keefe, who led the National League in wins in 1886 and wins and strikeouts in 1888, to 2000s San Francisco Giants pitcher Tim "The Freak" Lincecum, who played in four All-Star games, won three World Series championships, led the National League in strikeouts three times, earned two NL Cy Young awards, and pitched two no-hitters! The top baseball Tims are five-time All-Star third baseman Tim Wallach, who collected two Silver Sluggers and three Gold Glove awards; and Hall of Fame left fielder Tim "Rock" Raines, who played in seven All-Star games, won three World Series championships (two with the New York Yankees and one with the Chicago White Sox), won the National League batting championship, and led the National League in stolen bases four times.

A little Tim in your family may have a slightly better-than-average chance to excel at team sports, but whatever path he embarks upon, he'll have plenty of great role models with this name to inspire him.

- **Timothy "Tim" Brown**, Football (Wide Receiver), Los Angeles Raiders, USA, 1988–2004
- **Timothy "Tim" Duncan**, Basketball (Power Forward/Center), San Antonio Spurs, USA, 1997–2016
- **Julius Timothy "Tim" Flock**, Auto Racing (NASCAR), USA, 1949–1966
- **Timothy "Tim" Hardaway Sr.**, Basketball (Point Guard), Golden State Warriors, USA, 1989–2003
- **Miles Gilbert "Tim" Horton**, Ice Hockey (Defense), Toronto Maple Leafs, Canada, 1949–1974
- **Timothy "Tim" Howard**, Soccer (Goalkeeper), Everton Football Club, USA, 1997–2021
- **Tim "Eater X" Janus**, Competitive Eating, USA, 2005–2016
- **Timothy "Tim" (Smiling Tim) Keefe**, Baseball (Pitcher), New York Giants, USA, 1880–1893
- **Timothy "Tim" (The Freak) Lincecum**, Baseball (Pitcher), San Francisco Giants, USA, 2007–2016
- **Timothy "Tim" May**, Cricket (Bowler), South Australia Men's Cricket Team, Australia, 1984–1996
- **Timothy "Tim" Melia**, Soccer (Goalkeeper), Sporting Kansas City, USA, 2007–current
- **Timothy "Tim" Paine**, Cricket (Wicketkeeper-Batter), Tasmania Men's Cricket Team, Australia, 2005–current
- **Timothy "Tim" (Rock) Raines Sr.**, Baseball (Left Fielder), Montreal Expos, USA, 1979–2002
- **Timothy "Tim" Southee**, Cricket (All-Rounder), Northern Districts Men's Cricket Team, New Zealand, 2006–current
- **Timothy "Tim" Sylvia**, MMA (Heavyweight), USA, 2001–2015
- **Timothy "Tim" Thomas Jr.**, Ice Hockey (Goaltender), Boston Bruins, USA, 1997–2014
- **Timothy "Tim" Wallach**, Baseball (Third Baseman), Montreal Expos, USA, 1980–1996
- **Timothy "Tim" Wood**, Figure Skating, USA, 1965–1970

TIMMY

Prefer Timmy to *Tim* or *Timothy*? Then get your kid into soccer or racing and he could take after Swedish World Rallycross driver Timmy Hansen, who has won thirteen races and a championship, or Belgian Golden Shoe defensive midfielder Timmy Simons, whose trophy collection includes three Belgian Cups, four Belgian Supercups, two Bruges Matins, and the Jules Pappaert Cup!

- **Kenneth Timmy Hansen**, Auto Racing (Rallycross), Sweden, 2011–current
- **Timothy "Timmy" Simons**, Soccer (Defensive Midfielder), Club Brugge Koninklijke Voetbalvereniging, Belgium, 1994–2018

TIMO

The European name Timo is most often derived from the same origin as *Timothy*, though it can also come from a variation of the name *Dietmar*, but ultimately it comes from Gothic roots meaning "famous people." Either way, Timo sounds cool and is a great option for a son who will enjoy things like racquet sports, field hockey, soccer, or driving really, really fast! In these endeavors he can look up to people like German two-time World Cup table tennis champion Timo Boll; field hockey defender Timo Weß, who won two Olympic gold medals, two World Cup gold medals, a Champions Trophy, and an Indoor World Cup with the Germany team; and German soccer players like goalkeeper Timo Hildebrand (who won a Copa del Rey, Bundesliga, and UEFA Intertoto Cup twice, and FIFA Confederations Cup Golden Boot) and forward Timo Werner (whose trophy collection includes a DFB-Pokal championship, UEFA Champions League, UEFA Super Cup, FIFA Club World Cup, and FIFA Confederations Cup).

When it comes to racing, Timos don't get much faster than Finns in World Rally Championships (eleven-time winner and 1985 champion Timo Salonen and co-driver Timo Rautiainen, who participated in thirty wins and two championships) and Germans in endurance racing (legendary Timo Bernhard won the 24 Hours of Le Mans twice, 12 Hours of Sebring, 24 Hours of Daytona, and 24 Hours of Nürburgring five times; collected the "triple crown of endurance racing"; and broke the Nürburgring Nordschleife lap time speed record–the first time it's been broken in thirty-five years!).

Timo Bernhard, Auto Racing (24 Hours of Le Mans), Germany, 1998–2019

Timo Boll, Table Tennis, Germany, 2002–current

Timo Hildebrand, Soccer (Goalkeeper), Verein für Bewegungsspiele Stuttgart 1893 e. V., Germany, 1999–2015

Timo Rautiainen, Auto Racing (Rally), Finland, 1990–2019

Timo Salonen, Auto Racing (Rally), Finland, 1974–2002

Timo Werner, Soccer (Forward), RasenBallsport Leipzig e.V., Germany, 2013–current

Timo Weß, Field Hockey (Defender), Germany, 2000–2012

TIMOTHY

Tim and *Timmy* are fun, but Timothy (from Greek roots meaning "honoring god") is the original and still holds up today. The name has appeared on podiums for swimming and middle-distance running in international competitions, with Australian swimmers like Paralympic freestyle gold-medalist Timothy Disken and two-time World Para Swimming Championship medley winner Timothy Hodge, and Kenyan 1500-meter world champion runner Timothy Cheruiyot. A Timothy in your family may enjoy running or swimming fast, but he could also be incredibly well-rounded in athletics and performance, like three-time NFL Pro Bowl running back and kick returner Timothy Brown, who won two NFL championships and led the league in kickoff return yards twice . . . and also had successful stints as a singer and an actor in Hollywood!

Thomas "Timothy" Brown, Football (Running Back/Kick Returner), Philadelphia Eagles, USA, 1959–1968

Timothy Cheruiyot, Track & Field (Middle-Distance Running), Kenya, 2014–current

Timothy Disken, Swimming (Freestyle/Breaststroke/Medley), Australia, 2014–current

Timothy Hodge, Swimming (Backstroke/Breaststroke/Butterfly/Medley), Australia, 2015–current

TJ/T.J.

Not typically a name all on its own, TJ or T.J. is usually an abbreviation for first and middle names or a "T" first name and the Junior suffix. Interestingly, T.J.s in sports are predominantly super tough and hard hitting! Gridiron football is the main playground of T.J.s, with three two-time Pro Bowlers in tight end T.J. Hockenson, Green Bay Packers Super Bowl champion guard T.J. Lang, and Denver Broncos Super Bowl champion strong safety T.J. Ward; and 2021 NFL Defensive Player of the Year linebacker T.J. Watt, whose career with the Pittsburgh Steelers has included five Pro Bowl appearances, a forced fumbles co-leader ranking, awards, and multiple sacks records!

While there's a good chance a T.J. or TJ in your family will be a rough-and-tumble kid, he might also end up working with animals or enjoying going fast like Brazilian horse racing jockey T.J. Pereira, who has won more than 1,750 races.

- **Thomas James "T.J." Hockenson**, Football (Tight End), Detroit Lions, USA, 2019–current
- **Thomas John "T.J." Lang**, Football (Guard), Green Bay Packers, USA, 2009–2018
- **Tiago Josué "T.J." Pereira**, Horse Racing (Jockey), Brazil, 1994–current
- **Terrell Ray "T.J." Ward Jr.**, Football (Strong Safety), Cleveland Browns, USA, 2010–2020
- **Trent Jordan "T.J." Watt**, Football (Linebacker), Pittsburgh Steelers, USA, 2017–current

TOBIAS

Like countless others, Tobias was originally a religious name, in this case coming from a biblical Hebrew name meaning "God is good." If athletic history is any indication, a son you name Tobias will be good at either soccer or luge! International football has seen the exploits of two-time Swedish Midfielder of the Year Tobias Linderoth, who won the Danish Superliga twice, Royal League twice, Süper Lig, and Turkish Super Cup; and Alisvenskan two-time Player of the Season, Top Scorer, and Forward of the Season Tobias Hysén, who won the Alisvenskan twice, Svenska Cupen four times, and a Football League Championship.

Meanwhile, racing over the ice to victory has been Austrian five-time world champion Tobias Schiegl, six-time Olympic gold-medalist and nine-time world champion Tobias Arlt, and Tobias Wendl, whose incredible medal collection includes six Olympic golds; nine golds, seven silvers, and two bronzes from World Championships; and eighty-two golds, forty-eight silvers, and twenty-six bronzes from World Cup events!

- **Tobias Arlt**, Luge, Germany, 2006–current
- **Glenn Tobias Hysén**, Soccer (Forward/Winger), Idrottsföreningen Kamraterna Göteborg, Sweden, 1998–2022
- **Tobias Linderoth**, Soccer (Defensive Midfielder), Football Club Copenhagen, Sweden, 1995–2010
- **Tobias Schiegl**, Luge, Austria, 1993–2010
- **Tobias Wendl**, Luge, Germany, 1993–current

TOBY

In medieval times, the name *Tobias* got a more "modern" variant in Toby, a name that can give your son a love of soccer or rowing. This is especially true if he takes after athletes like British two-time world champion rower Toby Garbett or Belgian soccer defender Toby Alderweireld, who won a KNVB Cup, La Liga, Emir of Qatar Cup, Belgian Pro League, Belgian Cup, and Belgian Super Cup!

- **Toby Alderweireld**, Soccer (Defender), Tottenham Hotspur Football Club, Belgium, 2008–current
- **Toby Garbett**, Rowing, England, 1997–2008

TODD

The English name Todd comes from a Middle English surname with a root meaning "fox," and being primarily used in the United States, it's unsurprisingly found most often among athletes playing baseball and football. However, if you name your son Todd, he's not necessarily locked in to one or both of those. Todds have made big strides in lots of different events, with singular competitions ranging from track and field (like Australian Paralympic gold-medalist and International Paralympic Committee World Championships gold-medalist shot putter Todd Hodgetts) to golf (like Todd Hamilton, who won seventeen professional events and one major).

Todds have also succeeded with partners and teams in cricket, like Australian bowler Todd Murphy on the winning 2021–2023 ICC World Test Championship team; beach volleyball, like Olympic gold-medalist and world champion Todd Rogers; and tennis, like Australian former world doubles number one Todd Woodbridge, who won eighty-three titles, twenty-two grand slams, and Olympic gold and silver medals. On the ice, sledge hockey forward Todd Nicholson won a Paralympic gold medal and two medals from World Championships.

Fans of America's pastime are sure to be familiar with the likes of pitcher Todd Worrell, who went from being named the National League Rookie of the Year to playing in three All-Star games and leading the National League in saves twice; and Colorado Rockies five-time All-Star first baseman Todd Helton, who, in 2000, was the MLB batting champion and RBI leader and won three Gold Gloves, four Silver Sluggers, and a National League Hank Aaron award!

Last but not least are the Todds of the NFL: Rams three-time Pro Bowl running back Todd Gurley, who led the league in rushing touchdowns twice and was named Offensive Player of the Year in 2017, and Raiders five-time Pro Bowl tight end Todd Christensen, who led the league in receptions twice and won the Super Bowl twice!

- **Todd Christensen**, Football (Tight End), Oakland Raiders, USA, 1978–1988
- **Todd Gurley II**, Football (Running Back), St. Louis Rams, USA, 2015–2020
- **William Todd Hamilton**, Golf, USA, 1987–2010
- **Todd Helton**, Baseball (First Baseman), Colorado Rockies, USA, 1997–2013
- **Todd Hodgetts**, Track & Field (Shot Put), Australia, 2012–current
- **Todd Murphy**, Cricket (Bowler), Sydney Sixers, Australia, 2020–current
- **Todd Nicholson**, Ice Sledge Hockey (Forward), Canada, 1999–2010
- **Todd Rogers**, Beach Volleyball, USA, 1996–current
- **Todd Woodbridge**, Tennis, Australia, 1988–2005
- **Todd Worrell**, Baseball (Pitcher), St. Louis Cardinals, USA, 1985–1997

TOM

Most often a diminutive of *Thomas*, the name Tom has enjoyed massive popularity in the United States and beyond. With so many people named or nicknamed Tom out there, it should come as no surprise that Toms are very well represented in sports, specifically American favorites like football and baseball. However, don't feel like a son named Tom in your family is limited to these, as Toms have had success all over! In individual events, these have ranged from bowling (like ten-time PBA Tour-winner Tom Baker, who won a major and played sixty-five perfect games) to freestyle skiing (like world champion, four-time Winter Dew Tour gold-medalist, and X Games gold-medalist SlopeStyle legend Tom Wallisch).

Toms have conquered things like cricket (with batsman "Long" Tom Moody, who won the 1987 and 1999 Cricket World Cups) and skateboarding (American Tom Schaar, who was the first person to land a 1080 while winning ten medals at the X Games, including two golds). Riding the waves were surfing innovator Tom Blake, who won the inaugural Pacific Coast Surfriding Championship and a Hawaiian Surfboard Paddling Championship, and three-time world champion Tom Curren, who racked up thirty-three championship event wins. In first-person shooter esports competitions, Tom "Tsquared" Taylor led the highly successful Major League Gaming team Str8 Rippin and won the *Halo 3* event at the 2008 MLG Las Vegas Championship while Tom "Ogre 2" Ryan is considered the greatest *Halo* player of all time, with more than forty championships at major events.

Danish endurance racer Tom Kristensen sped into the record books by winning the 24 Hours of Le Mans nine times (as well as races and championships across multiple other series), while bodybuilder Tom Platz won the 1980 Mr. Universe competition, and Tom "The Albatross" Stoltman of Scotland won the World's Strongest Man competition two years in a row.

When it comes to golf, Scottish father and son duo "Old Tom" and "Young Tom" Morris (each of whom won The Open Championship four times) were some of the sport's earliest professional players. Then there are Basketball Hall of Famers in five-time All-Star small forward/shooting guard and NBA champion Tom Gola and six-time All-Star power forward Tom Heinsohn, who won eight championships with the Boston Celtics.

If your kid's name is Tom Murray then there's a decent chance he'll enjoy rowing, just like the American world champion and Olympic gold-medalist from New Zealand with the same name. Other Toms who have found success on the water include British Paralympic gold-medalist rower and four-time world champion Tom Aggar; two-time Olympic gold-medalist rower, world champion, and World Cup-winner Tom James; and German two-time Olympic gold-medalist and six-time world champion sprint canoeist Tom Liebscher. Not *on* the water but *in* it have been Canadian three-time Paralympic gold-medalist Tom Hainey, and American two-time medley Olympic gold-medalists Tom Dolan, who also won two world championships, and Tom Shields, who also won four world championships.

America's pastime is full of Toms who have excelled, and at the top of that list are a couple of National Baseball Hall of Fame pitchers: ten-time All-Star, World Series champion, and World Series MVP Tom Glavine, who won two National League Cy Young awards and four Silver Sluggers and led the National League in wins five times, and twelve-time All-Star "Tom Terrific" Seaver, who won three National League Cy Young awards; led the National League in wins three times, ERA three times, and strikeouts five times; and threw a no-hitter in 1978.

Reaching the highest echelon of football players, we find Los Angeles Rams Pro Football Hall of Famers, like three-time NFL champion split end Tom Fears, who led the league in receptions twice, receiving yards, and receiving touchdowns, and eleven-time Pro Bowl offensive guard Tom Mack. Of course, one Tom stands as the pinnacle when it comes to football, and that's quarterback Tom Brady. With fifteen Pro Bowl appearances in twenty-three seasons in the NFL, Brady won six Super Bowls with the New England Patriots and another with the Tampa Bay Buccaneers; was named NFL MVP three times, Super Bowl MVP five times, and NFL Offensive Player of the Year twice; led the NFL in passing touchdowns five times, passing yards four times, passer rating twice, and completion percentage; and set numerous records that securely place him among the list of best quarterbacks of all time (and possibly *the* best).

Truly, a young athlete named Tom has unlimited potential, able to hone his skills in any sport he enjoys and become a legend for those who follow him.

Tom Aggar, Para-Rowing, England, 2006–2016

Tom Baker, Bowling, USA, 1976–2009

Thomas "Tom" Blake, Surfing, USA, 1927–1955

Thomas "Tom" Brady Jr., Football (Quarterback), New England Patriots, USA, 2000–2022

Tom Curren, Surfing, USA, 1983–1993

Thomas "Tom" Dolan, Swimming (Medley), USA, 1993–2000

Thomas "Tom" Fears, Football (Split End), St. Louis Rams, Mexico/USA, 1948–1956

Thomas "Tom" Glavine, Baseball (Pitcher), Atlanta Braves, USA, 1987–2008

Thomas "Tom" Gola, Basketball (Small Forward/Shooting Guard), Philadelphia Warriors, USA, 1955–1966

Thomas "Tom" Hainey Jr., Swimming (Breaststroke/Butterfly/Freestyle/Medley), Canada, 1984–1988

Thomas "Tom" Heinsohn, Basketball (Power Forward), Boston Celtics, USA, 1956–1965

Thomas "Tom" James, Rowing, Wales, 2004–2012

Tom Kristensen, Auto Racing (24 Hours of Le Mans), Denmark, 1991–2014

Tom Liebscher, Sprint Canoeing, Germany, 2013–current

Thomas "Tom" Mack, Football (Offensive Guard), Los Angeles Rams, USA, 1966–1978

Thomas "Tom" (Long Tom) Moody, Cricket (Batsman), Worcestershire County Cricket Club, Australia, 1985–1999

Thomas "Tom" (Old Tom) Morris, Golf, Scotland, 1860–1896

Thomas "Tom" (Young Tom) Morris, Golf, Scotland, 1865–1875

Thomas "Tom" Murray, Rowing, New Zealand, 2011–current

Thomas "Tom" Murray, Rowing, USA, 1993–1999

Thomas "Tom" Platz, Bodybuilding, USA, 1973–1987

Tom "Ogre 2" Ryan, Esports (First-Person Shooters), USA, 2003–2016

Tom Schaar, Skateboarding, USA, 2012–current

George Thomas "Tom" Seaver, Baseball (Pitcher), New York Mets, USA, 1967–1986

Thomas "Tom" Shields, Swimming (Butterfly/Freestyle/Backstroke), USA, 2008–current

Tom "The Albatross" Stoltman, Strength Athletics, Scotland, 2012–current

Tom "Tsquared" Taylor, Esports (First-Person Shooters), USA, 2005–2015

Tom Wallisch, Freestyle Skiing, USA, 2009–2013

TOMAS/TOMÁS/TOMÁŠ/TOMASZ

With its strong history and popularity around the world, the name *Thomas* was inevitably adapted into numerous localized variants, four of which are grouped here. Athletes with these names have accomplished incredible things in many different fields, including rugby (like Irish 2009 Six Nations Champion and Grand Slam–winning scrum half Tomás O'Leary), tennis (like Czechoslovakian world doubles number one Tomáš Šmíd, who won fifty-six titles and two Grand Slams), and speed skating (like Swedish three-time Olympic gold-medalist Tomas Gustafson).

"Twins" with these names have made it big in international track and field events, with Polish two-time Olympic gold-medalist shot putter Tomasz Majewski and Czech three-time world champion decathlete Tomáš Dvořák, as well as sprint canoeing, with Lithuanian three-time world champion Tomas Gadeikis and German Olympic gold-medalist and five-time world champion Tomasz Wylenzek.

Ice hockey goaltender Tomáš Vokoun won two world championships with the Czech team, Swedish left wing Tomas Holmström took home an Olympic gold medal with his national team and won four NHL Stanley Cup championships with the Detroit Red Wings, and Czech five-time NHL All-Star defenseman and All-Star Game Accuracy Competition champion Tomáš Kaberle won the Stanley Cup with the Boston Bruins, as well as a world championship.

Your specific choice of spelling and accent usage will most likely depend on your lineage and cultural/national background, but whichever version of Tomas you choose for your son will give him a love of competition and winning. Support his interests and skills, and let him try out for ice hockey, canoeing, or track and field!

Tomáš Dvořák, Track & Field (Decathlon/Heptathlon), Czech Republic, 1990–2006

Tomas Gadeikis, Sprint Canoeing, Lithuania, 2005–2014

Sven Tomas Gustafson, Speed Skating, Sweden, 1979–1992

Bengt Tomas Holmström, Ice Hockey (Left Wing), Detroit Red Wings, Sweden, 1990–2012

Tomáš Kaberle, Ice Hockey (Defense), Toronto Maple Leafs, Czech Republic, 1994–2016

Tomasz Majewski, Track & Field (Shot Put), Poland, 1999–2016

Tomás O'Leary, Rugby (Scrum Half), Munster Rugby, Ireland, 2005–2017

Tomáš Šmíd, Tennis, Czechoslovakia, 1976–1992

Tomáš Vokoun, Ice Hockey (Goaltender), Nashville Predators, Czech Republic, 1995–2014

Tomasz Wylenzek, Sprint Canoeing, Germany, 2002–2010

TOMMI/TOMMIE/TOMMY

Tom may be the most popular diminutive of *Thomas*, but Tommi, Tommie, and Tommy may be the most fun. The first is a traditional Finnish form of the name, while the last is used all over the English-speaking world. There's a general trend among competitors with these names toward driving fast, running, throwing baseballs, and playing football. Starting with speed lovers, we have Tommy Milton, who won the Indianapolis 500 twice despite being blind in one eye, and Finnish rally legend Tommi Mäkinen, who won twenty-four races and four World Rally Championships. On the baseball diamond, Tommys are pitchers through and through, like All-Star Tommy Byrne, who won the 1949 and 1956 World Series with the New York Yankees, and four-time All-Star Tommy John, who earned the nickname "The Bionic Man" for playing a staggering twenty-six seasons in Major League Baseball.

Racing for the win have been track and field stars like American sprinter Tommie Smith, who won the 200-meter event at the 1968 Olympic Games by being the first person to run that event in under twenty seconds; and English runner Tommy Hampson, whose Olympic gold medal in 1932 came with the first 800-meter run quicker than one minute and fifty seconds. Meanwhile, on the fields of gridiron football, Atlanta Falcons linebacker Tommy Nobis played in five Pro Bowls, and Hall of Fame flanker/halfback Tommy McDonald earned six Pro Bowl selections, won an NFL championship with the Philadelphia Eagles, and led the league in receiving touchdowns twice and receiving yards.

Tommis and Tommys have quite varied tastes outside of those sports as well, including boxing (like American World Boxing

Organization heavyweight champion Tommy Morrison, who ended his career with a 48-3-1 record and an MMA win), collectible card games (like Finnish two-time *Magic: The Gathering* Pro Tour champion—the first player to achieve that distinction—and Hall of Famer Tommi Hovi), golf (like Tommy Bolt, who won twenty professional events and one major), table tennis (like British Paralympian Tommy Taylor, who won eight gold medals and a bronze in that sport, in addition to a gold and a bronze in snooker and a gold and two bronzes in lawn bowls), and bowling (like American Tommy Jones, who has won twenty PBA Tour events and two majors while scoring thirty-seven perfect games).

Whether it's in a common sport or event (like racing, baseball, football, or running) or something more unique (like card games, bowling, table tennis, and the like), a Tommi, Tommie, or Tommy will have unlimited potential and a fair and competitive spirit.

- **Thomas "Tommy" Bolt**, Golf, USA, 1946–1971
- **Thomas "Tommy" Byrne**, Baseball (Pitcher), New York Yankees, USA, 1943–1957
- **Thomas "Tommy" Hampson**, Track & Field (Sprinting), England, 1930–1932
- **Tommi Hovi**, Card Gaming (*Magic: The Gathering*), Finland, 1996–2004
- **Thomas "Tommy" (The Bionic Man) John Jr.**, Baseball (Pitcher), Chicago White Sox, USA, 1963–1989
- **Tommy Jones**, Bowling, USA, 2000–current
- **Tommi Mäkinen**, Auto Racing (World Rally Championship), Finland, 1987–2003
- **Thomas "Tommy" McDonald**, Football (Flanker/Halfback), Philadelphia Eagles, USA, 1957–1968
- **Thomas "Tommy" Milton**, Auto Racing (Indianapolis 500), USA, 1914–1957
- **Tommy Morrison**, Boxing (Heavyweight)/ MMA (Cruiserweight), USA, 1988–2009
- **Thomas "Tommy" Nobis Jr.**, Football (Linebacker), Atlanta Falcons, USA, 1966–1976
- **Tommie Smith**, Track & Field (Sprinting)/ Football (Wide Receiver), Cincinnati Bengals, USA, 1967–1969
- **Tommy Taylor**, Para-Athletics, England, 1960–1984

TONY

Tony is not just for Italians and cartoon tigers—it's a highly versatile name that came about as a nickname for *Anthony*, *Antonio*, and others. While it still serves in that respect, it is also popular as a name all on its own. While some truly stand-out Tonys have conquered their individual sports, broken records, and become synonymous with their specialties, most champion athletes with this name have excelled in pairs and team events. They include Indonesian-American badminton pairs and team player Tony Gunawan, who won an Olympic gold medal, two world championships, and the Thomas Cup twice; and French six-time NBA San Antonio Spurs All-Star point guard Tony Parker, who won four NBA championships and was named NBA Finals MVP.

Baseball has featured several top-notch Tonys with Dominican five-time All-Star shortstop Tony Fernández, who won four Gold Gloves and the 1993 World Series with the Toronto Blue Jays, and San Diego Padres fifteen-time All-Star right fielder, legendary consistent hitter, and National Baseball Hall of Famer Tony "Mr. Padre" Gwynn, who took home five Gold Glove and seven Silver Slugger awards and scored eight National League batting championships.

On the fields of gridiron football, Dallas Cowboys four-time Pro Bowl quarterback Tony Romo led the league in passer rating and completion percentage in 2014, and Tony Gonzalez established himself as one of the greatest tight ends of all time, earning induction into the Pro Football Hall of Fame with fourteen Pro Bowl selections, leading the league in receptions in 2004, and setting tight end records for most career receiving yards and most career receptions.

A boy you name (or give the nickname) Tony can become the pinnacle of his particular skill, like race driver Tony Bettenhausen, who won twenty-two races and two Indy car championships; bodybuilder, powerlifter, and popular professional wrestler Tony Atlas, who won the Mr. USA and Mr. Universe competitions; and Northern Irish horse racing jockey Tony McCoy, who holds records for his 4,358 wins and twenty consecutive Champion Jockey classifications.

Last but certainly not least is Tony Hawk, widely considered the most famous and influential skateboarder of all time; his accomplishments include pioneering the "900"; winning ten gold medals, three silvers, and three bronzes at the X Games; holding the title of National Skateboard Association World Champion twelve years in a row; and winning seventy-three out of 103 events he entered. Hawk has also parlayed his fame into other ventures, including philanthropic work, and continues to be an icon in his sport.

Tony Atlas (Anthony White), Bodybuilding/Powerlifting, USA, 1979–1985

Melvin Eugene "Tony" Bettenhausen, Auto Racing (Champ Car), USA, 1941–1961

Octavio Antionio "Tony" Fernández Castro, Baseball (Shortstop), Toronto Blue Jays, Dominican Republic, 1983–2001

Anthony "Tony" Gonzalez, Football (Tight End), Kansas City Chiefs, USA, 1997–2013

Tony Gunawan, Badminton, Indonesia/USA, 1996–2012

Anthony "Tony" (Mr. Padre) Gwynn Sr., Baseball (Right Fielder), San Diego Padres, USA, 1982–2001

Anthony "Tony" Hawk, Skateboarding, USA, 1981–2003

Anthony "Tony" McCoy, Horse Racing (Jockey), Ireland, 1992–2015

William Anthony "Tony" Parker Jr., Basketball (Point Guard), San Antonio Spurs, France, 1999–2019

Antonio "Tony" Romo, Football (Quarterback), Dallas Cowboys, USA, 2003–2016

TRACY

In modern times, the unisex name Tracy (from an ancient place name for the Thracian region in southeast Europe) has been used more for girls, but that hasn't stopped a couple of men from bringing it to the forefront of their sports. NBA shooting guard/small forward Tracy McGrady played in seven All-Star games, was named Most Improved Player, and led the league in scoring twice, while in the boxing ring, Tracy Patterson held world championships in two weight classes (super bantamweight and super featherweight) and, along with his dad, Floyd Patterson, became the first father and son duo to have won world boxing titles!

Tracy remains an excellent name for a dedicated athlete who will be fast and tough (perhaps finding his skills match up well in basketball or boxing) and who may choose to follow in his father's footsteps to achieve success.

Tracy McGrady Jr., Basketball (Shooting Guard/Small Forward), Orlando Magic, USA, 1997–2013

Tracy Patterson, Boxing (Super Bantamweight/Super Featherweight), USA, 1985–2001

TRAVIS

From the same root as the word "traverse" and an old English place name given to people living near fords or bridges comes the name Travis. In modern days, this moniker has become closely associated with team sports and, in turn, can inspire a boy in your family to work hard alongside his friends and teammates to win and succeed on or off the field. He'll be in good company with football players like Kansas City Chiefs ten-time Pro Bowl tight end Travis Kelce, who has won three Super Bowl championships and set multiple records, including total receiving yards in a season by a tight end (1,416), games with one hundred-plus yards receiving by a tight end (thirty-five), seasons with one thousand-plus receiving yards by a tight end (seven), and more. There's also cricket middle-order batsman Travis Head, who led Australia to victory in the 2021–2023 ICC World Test Championship.

While it's clear that most athletes named Travis excel with teams, there are some who find their home driving or piloting and accomplish amazing things on their own! Travis Pastrana has raced and won on two wheels and four (and even on the water in powerboats); his lengthy list of accomplishments includes five Moto X gold medals at Gravity Games; eleven golds, four silvers, and two bronzes from X Games in Moto X and Rally Car events; two event wins and a championship in Nitro Rallycross; four championships in Rally America; an incredible stunt career; and multiple world records in stunts and races.

Travis Head, Cricket (Middle-Order Batsman), Adelaide Strikers, Australia, 2011–current

Travis Kelce, Football (Tight End), Kansas City Chiefs, USA, 2013–current

Travis Pastrana, Motocross/Auto Racing (Rally America), USA, 1999–current

TRISTAN/TRISTRAM

While it later became associated with a French word meaning "sad," the unisex name Tristan actually comes from a Celtic root meaning "noise" or "tumult" and led to variants like Tristram. It's quite likely that a boy you give one of these names to will be noisy and boisterous, but also an athletic child eager to play and win in sports like ice hockey, football, or baseball. These favorites can be seen with Canadian two-time NHL All-Star goaltender Tristan Jarry and Tampa Bay Buccaneers two-time NFL Pro Bowl offensive tackle and Super Bowl champion Tristan Wirfs. With these names you can also nickname your son *Tris*, especially if he plays baseball so he can take after early-1900s batting legend Tristram "Tris" Speaker, who won three World Series championships and a batting championship, was named American League MVP, led the American League in home runs and RBIs, set multiple records (including career doubles and outfield assists), and was inducted into the National Baseball Hall of Fame!

Tristan Jarry, Ice Hockey (Goaltender), Pittsburgh Penguins, Canada, 2015–current

Tristram "Tris" Speaker, Baseball (Center Fielder), Boston Americans, USA, 1907–1928

Tristan Wirfs, Football (Offensive Tackle), Tampa Bay Buccaneers, USA, 2020–current

TY

If you're hoping for a son who enjoys playing football or baseball, or who likes to ride things with a lot of power, consider giving him a name that begins with "Ty-" and calling him Ty! Traditionally a diminutive of *Tyler*, *Tyrone*, *Tyson*, and *Tyrus*, Ty is a very American name and one that has seen a lot of successes in athletic competitions and sports. ProRodeo Hall of Fame rodeo cowboy Ty Murray won nine world championships riding horses and bulls while in the NFL, Indianapolis Colts wide receiver T.Y. Hilton played in four Pro Bowls and led the league in receiving yards, and five-time Pro Bowl cornerback Ty Law led in interceptions and won three Super Bowls with the New England Patriots, which led to his induction into the Pro Football Hall of Fame.

Center fielder and legendary hitter (as well as

a complex and controversial figure) Ty Cobb played nearly the entirety of his career with the Detroit Tigers and amassed an incredible record, including twelve American League batting championships and a Triple Crown; being named AL MVP; leading his league in home runs, RBIs four times, and stolen bases six times; and setting almost one hundred MLB records, including combined runs scored and batted in, career batting average, and career batting titles. For his achievements, Cobb was inducted into the inaugural National Baseball Hall of Fame class in 1936.

- **Tyrus "Ty" (the Georgia Peach) Cobb**, Baseball (Center Fielder), Detroit Tigers, USA, 1905–1928
- **Eugene "T.Y." Hilton**, Football (Wide Receiver), Minneapolis Colts, USA, 2012–current
- **Tajuan "Ty" Law**, Football (Cornerback), New England Patriots, USA, 1995–2009
- **Ty Murray**, Rodeo, USA, 1987–2002

TYLER

The unisex name Tyler may have its roots as an occupational surname meaning "roof tiler" from an Old English word for "tile," but a boy you name Tyler will never be pigeon-holed into one thing and will have the chance to discover where his talents and enjoyment lie, even if that leads him into something very unique. Tylers before him have won and conquered challenges in everything from kayaking (like Tyler Bradt, who did a record 189-foot drop over Palouse Falls) to powerlifting (like multiple international bench press champion Tyler Moore) and esports (like battle royale pro gamer and streamer Tyler "Ninja" Blevins, who won the 2018 E3 Fortnite Pro-Am tournament).

Both American swimmers Tyler Reed and Tyler Clary have won freestyle world championships, while the latter also took home an Olympic gold medal in butterfly, and three Tylers have excelled in soccer. Tyler Bennett won Paralympic gold in men's seven-a-side football, MLS All-Star Goalkeeper Tyler Miller won the 2016 MLS Cup with the Seattle Sounders, and 2022 US Soccer Player of the Year midfielder Tyler Adams has won domestically and abroad with a USL Cup, MLS Supporters Shield, DFB-Pokal championship, and CONCACAF Nations League championship.

Some of the toughest Tylers have taken to the ice hockey rink. American NHL All-Star center and two-time Tampa Bay Lightning Stanley Cup champion Tyler Johnson is in good company with a number of Canadians: All-Star right wing and world champion Tyler Ennis; ice sledge hockey player Tyler McGregor, who has won two gold medals and four silvers at world championships; two-time world champion right wing Tyler Toffoli, who won the Stanley Cup in 2014 with the Los Angeles Kings; and world champion center Tyler Seguin, who played in six NHL All-Star games and won the 2011 Stanley Cup with the Boston Bruins.

- **Tyler Adams**, Soccer (Midfielder), RasenBallsport Leipzig e.V., USA, 2015–current
- **Tyler Bennett**, Para-Athletics (Soccer), USA, 2010–current
- **Richard Tyler "Ninja" Blevins**, Esports (*Fortnite/PUBG/Halo/Call of Duty*), USA, 2011–current
- **Tyler Bradt**, Whitewater Kayaking, USA, 2001–2012
- **Tyler Clary**, Swimming (Backstroke/Butterfly/Medley), USA, 2007–2016
- **Tyler Ennis**, Ice Hockey (Right Wing), Buffalo Sabres, Canada, 2009–current
- **Tyler Johnson**, Ice Hockey (Center), Tampa Bay Lightning, USA, 2011–current
- **Tyler McGregor**, Ice Sledge Hockey (Forward), Canada, 2011–current
- **Tyler Miller**, Soccer (Goalkeeper), Los Angeles Football Club, USA, 2012–current

Tyler Moore, Powerlifting, USA, 2011–current

Tyler Reed, Swimming (Freestyle), USA, 2012–2013

Tyler Seguin, Ice Hockey (Center), Dallas Stars, Canada, 2010–current

Tyler Toffoli, Ice Hockey (Right Wing), Los Angeles Kings, Canada, 2011–current

TYRONE

Coming from a Gaelic place name in Northern Ireland, the name Tyrone might be built on Old Irish roots meaning "born from yew tree" or Latin meaning "well born." Tyrones come in all shapes and sizes, and they can surprise you with success where you might not expect it! That's nowhere truer than with NBA legendary point guard Tyrone "Muggsy" Bogues, who ranked on many leaderboards during his long fourteen-year career and had nearly 150 double-doubles (not to mention winning a world championship with the USA Basketball Men's National Team) despite being the league's shortest player ever at five feet three inches. Other awesome athletes with this name include Australian rugby player Tyrone Peachey, who has played in multiple positions on his way to winning an NSW Cup Grand Final, multiple Rugby League All-Stars Matches, and more; and Jamaican soccer defender Tyrone Marshall, whose trophy collection features two MLS Cups, two Supporters' Shields, and three US Open Cups.

Tyrone "Muggsy" Bogues, Basketball (Point Guard), Charlotte Hornets, USA, 1987–2001

Tyrone Marshall, Soccer (Defender), Los Angeles Galaxy, Jamaica, 1998–2012

Tyrone Peachey, Rugby (Lock), Penrith Panthers, Australia, 2013–current

TYSON

From an Old French word meaning "firebrand" and then a classic English nickname meaning "quarrelsome person" comes the name Tyson, and while a son you give this name to may not be quarrelsome, he can definitely take his fiery spirit into any competition and win big! Some Tysons do their best work alongside teammates, like basketball center Tyson Chandler, who earned an All-Star selection, received a Defensive Player of the Year award, and won the 2011 NBA championship with the Dallas Mavericks, in addition to winning a world championship and an Olympic gold medal with the USA team!

Bridging the team players and the solo acts is American sprinter Tyson Gay, who won world championships in the 100-meter, 200-meter, and 4x100-meter relay, as well as two World Cup gold medals and another at World Relays; he also tied for the second fastest athlete ever (tied with Yohan Blake and just behind Usain Bolt).

Onto the solo athletes, Australian artistic gymnast Tyson Bull won the horizontal bar event at the 2022 World Challenge Cup, American Rubik's Cube speedsolver Tyson Mao has won nearly fifty medals at major events and set the world record for blindfolded 3x3x3, and Irish Traveller heavyweight boxer Tyson Fury has achieved lineal world champion status after collecting world championships on his way to his current 34-2-1 record.

Tyson Bull, Artistic Gymnastics, Australia, 2010–current

Tyson Chandler, Basketball (Center), Chicago Bulls, USA, 2001–2020

Tyson Fury, Boxing (Heavyweight), England, 2008–current

Tyson Gay, Track & Field (Sprinting), USA, 2005–2016

Tyson Mao, Rubik's Cube Speedsolving, USA, 2006–current

GIRLS

TAE/TAI

Tae and Tai can be related, because sometimes the former is a variant of the latter, though they do have different origins, with the first being Japanese (written with characters meaning "many"/"much" and "crystal") and the second being Chinese (meaning "very" or "extreme"). Both of these names have reached the highest heights in winter sports, with American world champion pairs figure skater Tai Babilonia and Japanese Olympic gold-medalist mogul freestyle skier Tae Satoya.

Name your daughter Tae or Tai and she, too, may find herself at home on the snow or ice!

Tai Babilonia, Figure Skating, USA, 1973–1980

Tae Satoya, Freestyle Skiing, Japan, 1998–2010

TAJ

A unisex name fit for royalty, Taj comes from an Arabic word meaning "crown" . . . and it's perfect for a family that loves basketball and produces tall children! Your Taj will surely look up to iconic six-time WNBA All-Star power forward/center Taj McWilliams-Franklin, who won two WNBA championships with the Detroit Shock and Minnesota Lynx and still stands as the league's all-time offensive rebounding leader. Outside of the WNBA, McWilliams-Franklin has won big all around the world with multiple championships in Australia and across Europe, as well as a world championship!

Taj McWilliams-Franklin, Basketball (Power Forward/Center), Orlando Miracle, USA, 1993–2012

TAMARA

Tamara has an interesting history, being a Russian form of *Tamar*, which is an ancient name that comes from Hebrew and means "date palm." It's been a little while since the name has stood on the podiums of international athletic competitions, but it's sure ready for a comeback with a little girl who can play and compete hard! She can succeed at anything she tries, though she may gravitate toward alpine skiing, like American combined skier world champion Tamara McKinney, who won a massive forty-five medals at World Cup events (eighteen of them gold); or artistic gymnastics, like Soviet Tamara Manina, who won two team Olympic gold medals (and three silvers and a bronze in vault and balance beam) and five world championships in team, vault, and floor exercise (plus a silver and two bronzes in vault and all-round).

Tamara Manina, Artistic Gymnastics, USSR, 1953–1964

Tamara McKinney, Alpine Skiing, USA, 1978–1990

TAMIKA

While Tamika has amassed popularity in the United States, it has two usual origins from very different parts of the world. Sometimes Tamika is a variant of the Japanese name *Tamiko* (which can be written with characters meaning "beautiful child"), while other times it comes from Swahili. Whether you align with either of those lineages or not, Tamika is another name like *Taj* that is particularly great for girls who will enjoy playing basketball, specifically in forward positions! Power forward Tamika Whitmore set the stage with a Jones Cup win in 1998 with USA Basketball and a WNBA All-Star selection in 2006, while small forward Tamika Catchings took the world by storm at the beginning of the twenty-first century. Considered one of the greatest WNBA players ever, Catchings earned ten All-Star selections in her fifteen-year career; won the WNBA championship in 2012 with the Indiana Fever; was named WNBA MVP, WNBA Finals MVP, and Defensive Player of the Year five times; led the league in steals eight times; and set multiple records, including all-time steals, playoffs all-time leading scorer, playoffs all-time rebounds, playoffs all-time steals, and more. She also collected four Olympic gold medals and two world championships.

Tamika Catchings, Basketball (Small Forward), Indiana Fever, USA, 2002–2016

Tamika Whitmore, Basketball (Power Forward), New York Liberty, USA, 1999–2009

TAMMY

What began as a diminutive for *Tamara* and other "Tam-" names, Tammy has become a full-fledged name in and of itself. On the hardwood, Tammys playing center have had a big impact on basketball with Tammy Jackson, who won a world championship with the United States women's national basketball team and no fewer than four WNBA championships (including the very first one!) with the Houston Comets, and Canadian two-time WNBA All-Star Tammy Sutton-Brown, who won a WNBA championship with the Indiana Fever.

Beyond the court, synchronized swimmer Tammy Cleland won a gold medal at the Olympics and another at the World Aquatic Championships, and English cricket batter/wicketkeeper Tammy Beaumont won the 2017 Women's Cricket World Cup and has smashed records to score the highest of any English woman in Test cricket, become one of only two women to score a century in all three international cricket formats, and more. Whether it's playing basketball, swimming, or playing something more exotic (like cricket), a Tammy in your family will have a competitive spirit and a love of the game.

Tamsin "Tammy" Beaumont, Cricket (Batter/Wicketkeeper), Kent Women Cricket Team, England, 2007–current

Tammy Cleland-McGregor, Synchronized Swimming, USA, 1994–1996

Tammy Jackson, Basketball (Center), Houston Comets, USA, 1990–2002

Tamara "Tammy" Sutton-Brown, Basketball (Center), Indiana Fever, Canada, 2001–2012

TAMYRA

An uncommon name that likely shares an origin with *Tamara*, Tamyra can give your daughter both inner and physical strength, along with the courage to take her opponents to the mat and defeat them. That's especially true if she takes after freestyle wrestler (and current WWE pro wrestler) Tamyra Mensah-Stock, who has won an Olympic gold medal, two gold medals and two bronzes at World Championships, three gold medals from Golden Grand Prix Ivan Yarygin events, three gold medals at Pan American Championships, another gold medal at Pan American Games, and more!

Tamyra Mensah-Stock, Freestyle Wrestling, USA, 2016–current

TANIA/TANJA

The family of Tania, Tanja, and similar names has an interesting history, coming about as variants of *Tanya*, which was originally a diminutive of the Russian *Tatiana*, which in turn came from the Roman name *Tatius* (of uncertain meaning). Regardless of the convoluted path it took to have these names in the modern world, Tanias and Tanjas in competition have proven themselves on snow, in water, at track and field events, and over the chess table! These include Swiss Olympic gold-medalist snowboarder Tanja Frieden; Italians world champion diver Tania Cagnotto and water polo forward Tania Di Mario, who won Olympic gold and a world championship; Serbian Paralympic gold-medalist and World Para Athletics Championship-winning javelin thrower Tanja Dragić; and Indian chess prodigy Tania Sachdev, who achieved the ranks of International Master and Woman Grandmaster.

Name your daughter Tania or Tanja and introduce her to a wide world of sports so she, too, can find her favorite event.

Tania Cagnotto, Diving, Italy, 2000–2016

Tania Di Mario, Water Polo (Forward), Italy, 1997–2016

Tanja Dragić, Track & Field (Javelin), Serbia, 2011–2012

Tanja Frieden, Snowboarding, Switzerland, 1997–2010

Tania Sachdev, Chess, India, 2005–current

TARA

Whether your inspiration is the Irish origin in a place name that may have meant "elevated place" or the Sanskrit root meaning "star," Tara can be the perfect choice for naming a daughter who will be more than just a jock, able to confront and overcome major challenges and really make a difference in life. Nowhere is that more evident than with icons like swimmer Tara Kirk, who set a world record in the 100-meter breaststroke on her way to winning thirteen medals at World Championships, and Tara Llanes, who won multiple BMX and mountain biking championships before suffering a spinal injury in a crash, but she continues to push herself and compete in wheelchair tennis and basketball!

Other remarkable Taras include dual Olympic gold-medalist ice hockey defense players Tara Mounsey of the USA (1998) and Tara Watchorn of Canada (2014); Olympic gold-medalist weightlifter Tara Cunningham; Canadian three-time world champion track cyclist Tara Whitten; snowboarder Tara Dakides, who won multiple X Games slopestyle and big air events; and Olympic gold-medalist, world champion, and two-time Grand Prix of Figure Skating Final-winning figure skater Tara Lipinski, who broke records for being the youngest Olympic and world champion and the first to hit the triple loop-triple loop jump combination in competition.

Tara Cunningham, Weightlifter, USA, 1997–2004

Tara Dakides, Snowboarding, USA, 1999–2011

Tara Kirk, Swimming (Breaststroke/Medley), USA, 2000–2007

Tara Lipinski, Figure Skating, USA, 1993–2002

Tara Llanes, BMX/Mountain Bike Racing/ Wheelchair Basketball, USA, 1989–current

Tara Mounsey, Ice Hockey (Defense), Brown Bears, USA, 1996–2002

Tara Watchorn, Ice Hockey (Defense), Boston Blades, Canada, 2008–current

Tara Whitten, Track Cycling, Canada, 2008–2016

TATIANA/TATJANA/TATYANA

While we don't know exactly what the ancient Roman name *Tatius* meant, we do know that it was the origin of the Russian Tatiana, which in turn has multiple variants, including the predominantly Russian Tatjana and Bulgarian and Russian Tatyana. Most of the champion athletes with these names come from Russia and surrounding countries, and a lot of them have succeeded in sports that are typically associated with those areas—but not all! They have the capacity to enjoy and excel in a wide range of activities, with solo sports ranging from swimming (like South African breaststroke Olympic gold-medalist and world champion Tatjana Schoenmaker) to speed skating (like Soviet two-time Olympic gold-medalist and world champion Tatyana Averina) and weightlifting (like Russian five-time world champion Tatiana Kashirina). German luger Tatjana Hüfner has won a set of Olympic medals in singles and eight world championships in solo and team events, while women winning with partners and teams exclusively include Olympic gold-medalist cross-country relay skier Tatiana Sorina and record-breaking Ukrainian-Russian pairs figure skater Tatiana Volosozhar, who won two Olympic gold medals, a world championship, a Grand Prix Final championship, and more.

Women with these names really can do it all, honing their bodies and minds to perfection. In track and field events, Russian 400-meter sprinter Tatyana Alekseyeva raced to Olympic gold and a world record with her relay team in 1997, and Tatyana Lebedeva leapt to a full set of Olympic medals and six golds and two silvers from World Championships in long jump and triple jump. Estonian Woman Grandmaster Tatjana Fomina won numerous chess championships in her home country, and Russian two-time Women's Chess Olympiad gold-medalist and FIDE Women's Grand Prix-winner Tatiana Kosintseva reached the rank of Grandmaster.

Of course, no discussion of athletes with Russian names would be complete without talking about gymnastics. Two Ukrainian Tatianas made history by winning team gold medals at the 1991 World Championships for the Soviet Union and the 1992 Olympic Games for the ex-Soviet Unified Team! Tatiana Gutsu and Tatiana Lysenko also each won an individual gold medal at the 1992 Olympics, Gatsu's in the all-around and Lysenko's on the balance beam. Lysenko also had a great showing at the World Cup Final in 1990, with gold medals in all-around and uneven bars and a bronze in floor exercise.

Tatyana Alekseyeva, Track & Field (Sprinting), Russia, 1985–1998

Tatyana Averina, Speed Skating, USSR, 1970–1980

Tatjana Fomina, Chess, Estonia, 1971–2014

Tatiana Gutsu, Artistic Gymnastics, Ukraine, 1988–1992

Tatjana Hüfner, Luge, Germany, 2003–current

Tatiana Kashirina, Weightlifting, Russia, 2006–current

Tatiana Kosintseva, Chess, Russia, 2002–current

Tatyana Lebedeva, Track & Field (Long Jump/Triple Jump), Russia, 1998–current

Tatiana Lysenko, Artistic Gymnastics, Ukraine, 1990–1994

Tatjana Schoenmaker, Swimming (Breaststroke), South Africa, 2015–current

Tatiana Sorina, Cross-Country Skiing, Russia, 2017–current

Tatiana Volosozhar, Figure Skating, Ukraine/Russia, 2004–2016

TAWN

A word that means "to make something tan/golden-brown" or "tawny," Tawn is also a name used by an incredible American water skier! Tawn Larsen-Hahn made huge waves in the 1980s and '90s with her twin sister, Britt, by becoming the first female trick skiers and collecting many wins, awards, and championships. Tawn alone would set four world records on her way to winning seven Masters' championships and four Women's World Tricks championships, earning herself a spot in the Water Ski Hall of Fame.

Whether or not golden-brown hair (or having twins) runs in your family, Tawn could be a very fun name for a girl who loves water sports and high flying, and it pairs perfectly with a sister named Britt.

Tawn Larsen-Hahn, Water Skiing, USA, 1985–1999

TEGLA

Tegla is truly a name that can imbue a person with a great purpose in life, lifting them from humble beginnings to great feats of skill and inspiring them to share their heart and spirit with the world. A member of the Pokot tribe in Kenya, Tegla Loroupe found her love of running in her youth but was deemed too small and thin to be a runner by Athletics Kenya. How wrong they were, because Loroupe went on to an amazing career as a long-distance runner, as well as an international voice for peace and diplomacy! Her numerous wins include five World Half Marathon Championship gold medals, the New York Marathon twice (including her very first marathon run), Rotterdam Marathon three times, Berlin Marathon, Leipzig Marathon, London Marathon, Rome Marathon, and more. Outside of competition, Tegla has worked with multiple countries, institutions, and celebrities to foster peace around the world, particularly in her native Kenya and Africa.

Tegla Loroupe, Long-Distance Running, Kenya, 1989–2011

TENEALE

A name from down under, and possibly a feminine variant of *Neal*, Teneale is ideal for a girl at home on the water . . . and who likes to go fast. She'll have the perfect role model to look up to in New Zealand two-time world champion sprint canoeist Teneale Hatton, who has also competed (and won) in ocean canoe racing and surf lifesaving!

Teneale Hatton, Sprint Canoeing, New Zealand, 2009–2015

TENLEY

A name with a modest origin but big possibilities, Tenley comes from an English surname that might have its roots in Old English words meaning "point" and "woodland" or "clearing." It was brought to international fame in the 1950s by the inspirational American figure skater Tenley Albright. After suffering from polio, Albright focused on her skating, eventually winning gold and silver medals at the Olympics, two golds and two silvers at World Championships, and more. But that wasn't the end of her story; after skating, Tenley dove into her medical career, graduating from Harvard Medical School and becoming a surgeon, professor, and member of multiple elite schools and institutions!

A daughter you name Tenley will have the intelligence, ability, and drive to succeed at her goals no matter what they are, winning at sports and academics and making a real difference in the world.

Tenley Albright, Figure Skating, USA, 1951–1956

TERESA/TEREZA/THERESA

Most likely from Ancient Greek roots either for "summer" or "harvest," the Teresa/Tereza/Theresa family of names became popular in Portugal and Spain before spreading out into the wider world. The reach they've attained can be seen through the uniqueness and variety of the athletes with them who have made it onto the world's stage, who include Spanish two-time 470 class Olympic gold-medalist sailor Theresa Zabell; New Zealand rugby center Theresa Fitzpatrick, who has won Olympic gold and silver medals, a Rugby World Cup Sevens championship, and two Women's Rugby World Cups; and Czech record-breaking deaf alpine skier Tereza Kmochová, who won eight gold medals, six silvers, and a bronze at Deaflympics in various events.

In the pool, American Theresa Andrews won Olympic gold medals in backstroke and medley, while Spanish disabled swimmer Teresa Perales has set multiple records on her way to winning a gold medal, two silvers, and two bronzes from World Championships, as well as a monumental seven golds, ten silvers, and ten bronzes at Paralympic Games. American Teresas have also posted big numbers on the basketball court with two Hall of Famers in five-time WNBA All-Star guard and two-time Defensive Player of the Year Teresa Weatherspoon, who led the league in assists and steals twice and won an Olympic gold medal and world championship, and point guard Teresa Edwards, who won the Jones Cup twice, two world championships, and a record-breaking four Olympic gold medals and a bronze!

Pick a spelling you like and name your daughter Teresa, Tereza, or Theresa to give her athletic prowess and the drive to overcome obstacles and break records.

Theresa Andrews, Swimming (Backstroke), USA, 1984

Teresa Edwards, Basketball (Point Guard), Atlanta Glory, USA, 1984–2004

Theresa Fitzpatrick, Rugby (Center), Blues Women, New Zealand, 2016–current

Tereza Kmochová, Alpine Skiing, Czech Republic, 2007–2019

Teresa Perales Fernández, Swimming (Freestyle/Butterfly), Spain, 1997–2020

Teresa Weatherspoon, Basketball (Guard), New York Liberty, USA, 1988–2004

Theresa Zabell Lucas, Sailing, Spain, 1992–1996

TERRI

A fighter in any competition is what you'll get by naming a girl in your family Terri, a unisex name that comes either from Gothic roots for "ruler of the people" (by way of the medieval name *Thierry*) or from a diminutive of *Theresa*! Australian vision-impaired track cyclist Terri Poole set five tandem cycling world records on her way to winning two gold medals at Paralympic Games and four gold medals at IPC Track and Road World Championships, while British boxer Terri Harper has won two world championship titles in two weight classes and currently holds a 14–1–1 record.

Terri Harper, Boxing (Super-Featherweight/Lightweight/Super-Welterweight), England, 2017–current

Teresa "Terri" Poole, Track Cycling, Australia, 1994–2001

TESSA

Theresa can be the source of *Terri*, but it's also the parent name of the contracted form Tessa. Belgian Professional Footballer of the Year soccer forward Tessa Wullaert has been a dominant force in European soccer, amassing championships that include the Belgian Women's Cup three times, Belgian Women's Super League twice, DFB-Pokal three times, Bundesliga twice, FA Cup, and FA Women's Cup, as well as winning the Belgian Golden Shoe three times. Olympic gold medals have been won by Australian 470 class sailor Tessa Parkinson and British javelin thrower Tessa Sanderson, while two Canadian athletes with this name have been hugely successful on the ice. Ice hockey defensewoman Tessa Bonhomme helped her teams win five 4 Nations Cups, two world championships, and an Olympic gold medal, and ice dancer Tessa Virtue skated to three Olympic gold medals and two silvers, seven medals at World Championships (including three golds), seven medals at Four Continents Championships, and another gold at a Grand Prix Final event, giving her a record number of wins in Olympic Games and overall.

If you give the name Tessa to your daughter, then introduce her to ice skating early; she may find it's the perfect place to show off her toughness or her agility and grace!

Tessa Bonhomme, Ice Hockey (Defense), Toronto Furies, Canada, 2004–2013

Tessa Parkinson, Sailing, Australia, 1997–2008

Theresa "Tessa" Sanderson, Track & Field (Javelin), England, 1976–1997

Tessa Virtue, Ice Dancing, Canada, 1994–2019

Tessa Wullaert, Soccer (Forward), RSC Anderlecht Féminin, Belgium, 2008–current

TIA

Tia is many things to many people; it is a diminutive of names that end in "-tia," means "aunt" in Portuguese and Spanish, and is a goddess of peaceful death for the North American Pacific Northwest Haida indigenous people. It's also the name of an exemplary Belgian track and field athlete! Tia Hellebaut set national records as she won a gold medal in the pentathlon at World Indoor Championships and an Olympic gold medal in the high jump.

Let her be an inspiration to a little girl you name Tia, who will be multitalented and highly competitive.

Tia Hellebaut, Track & Field (High Jump/ Pentathlon), Belgium, 2001-2013

TINA

A fully individual name on its own now, Tina came about as a diminutive form of a number of different names, including *Catharina*, *Christina*, *Katarina*, *Martina*, and others. Competitive Tinas from the United States and Slovenia have achieved some really impressive things, with the latter including Olympic gold-medalist and world champion judoka Tina Trstenjak (who took home seven gold medals, five silvers, and five bronzes from International Judo Foundation (IJF) Grand Slams, and seven golds, two silvers, and two bronzes from IJF Grand Prix events) and two-time Olympic gold-medalist and four-time world champion alpine ski racer Tina Maze (who collected no fewer than eighty-one medals from World Cup races, twenty-six of them gold).

American Tinas have very specific skills, with *Fortnite* esports pro Tina "TINARAES" Perez winning the Twitch Rivals: TwitchCon Fortnite Showdown and placing in the top five in numerous tournaments. On the basketball court, WNBA center Tina Charles has played in eight All-Star games, been named league MVP and Peak Performer four times, led in rebounding four times and scoring twice in the WNBA, and taken home three Olympic gold medals and three world championships with USA Basketball, while Basketball Hall of Fame small forward/power forward Tina Thompson was selected as All-Star nine times, won four WNBA championships with the Houston Comets, was named WNBA All-Star Game MVP, and won Russian and Euro championships, two Olympic gold medals, and a World Cup.

You don't have to have Slovenian or American heritage to name your daughter Tina, but if you do, you should definitely teach her the fundamentals of basketball . . . but also let her try out judo, skiing, and video games!

Tina Charles, Basketball (Center), New York Liberty, USA, 2010–current

Tina Maze, Alpine Skiing, Slovenia, 1999–2015

Tina "TINARAES" Perez, Esports (*Fortnite*), USA, 2018–2021

Tina Thompson, Basketball (Small Forward/ Power Forward), Houston Comets, USA, 1997–2014

Tina Trstenjak, Judo, Slovenia, 2006–2022

TIRIL

A name inspired by nineteenth-century Norwegian poetry, Tiril is a cool moniker that's ready for worldwide fame and can bring your daughter a love of skiing and playing in the cold. That's especially true if she follows in the tracks of athletes from Norway like freestyle skier Tiril Christiansen, who won gold and silver Winter X Games medals in slopestyle and a full trio of medal colors in big air and slopestyle from Winter X Games Europe; two-time world champion cross-country skier Tiril Weng, who won three World Cup races and one overall title; and biathlete Tiril Eckhoff, whose medal collection includes two golds, three silvers, and three bronzes from the Olympics; ten golds, two silvers, and three bronzes from World Championships; and, from World Cup events, eighty-seven total medals with fifty golds, three discipline titles, and one overall!

Tiril Sjåstad Christiansen, Freestyle Skiing, Norway, 2013–current

Tiril Eckhoff, Biathlon, Norway, 2008–2023

Tiril Weng, Cross-Country Skiing, Norway, 2015–current

TIRUNESH

Chances are good that you're not familiar with the name Tirunesh, but you definitely should be. It has a beautiful origin, coming from the Amharic language in Ethiopia and meaning "I am/you are good." Not just good but great is Ethiopian long-distance runner Tirunesh Dibaba, who has raced to three Olympic gold medals and three bronzes, nine golds and three silvers from World Championship events, and a suite of a gold, a silver, and two bronzes at World Marathon Majors!

Consider the name Tirunesh for a daughter who will be inherently good and who will definitely like to run and feel the wind on her face.

Tirunesh Dibaba, Long-Distance Running, Ethiopia, 2003–current

TONI

Another name that came about as a short form or diminutive (in this case from names like *Antonia*, *Antoinette*, and others), Toni has become a name used all on its own. Tonis have been doing remarkable things in sports since at least the 1950s, when Toni Stone pioneered women playing baseball as the first to play regularly on a professional team; due to segregation, she wasn't allowed in the All-American Girls Professional Baseball League, so she played in the Negro American League and became an almost mythical figure with tales of hitting a single off of a Satchel Paige fastball in an exhibition game. More recently, Australian water skier Toni Neville solidified her place among the top jumpers of all time by becoming the first woman to jump further than two hundred feet, winning four medals at World Championships, setting four World Jump Records, and being inducted into the Water Ski & Wake Sports Hall of Fame.

A Toni in your family will definitely be unstoppable once she finds her perfect sport or activity, so make sure to let her learn about everything out there—and don't be surprised if she bucks traditions or plays competitively with men too.

Toni Neville, Water Skiing, Australia, 1991–2002

Marcenia "Toni" Stone, Baseball (Second Base), Indianapolis Clowns, USA, 1949–1954

TONYA

Antonia, *Antonina*, and other names descended from the Roman *Antonius* have given us the name Tonya. It's an ideal moniker for a tough and strong girl, with role models like WNBA All-Star guard Tonya Edwards, who won the Jones Cup with USA Basketball and went on to a successful coaching career; MMA fighter Tonya Evinger, who held the Invicta Bantamweight Championship; and bodybuilder Tonya Knight, who won an IFBB Grand Prix and Ms. International and was inducted into the International Federation of BodyBuilding and Fitness Hall of Fame!

Tonya Edwards, Basketball (Guard), Columbus Quest, USA, 1999–2002

Tonya Evinger, MMA (Bantamweight/ Featherweight), USA, 2006–current

Tonya Knight, Bodybuilding, USA, 1984–1993

TORA/TORAH

Two similar-sounding names with two very different religious origins, Tora is a Scandinavian feminine form of *Thor* (which means "thunder" in Old Norse) while the uncommon name Torah is the name of the Hebrew Bible. Both names (especially combined with a last name that begins with "B") can inspire a girl to love winter sports and playing in the snow, just like Australia's top Winter Olympian Torah Bright, who won Olympic gold and silver in snowboard halfpipe along with two gold medals, two silvers, and a bronze in superpipe at the X Games, and Norwegian two-time Olympic gold-medalist biathlete Tora Berger, who won eight gold medals, five silvers, and five bronzes from World Championships and stood on sixty-three World Cup podiums with twenty-eight wins and two discipline titles!

Tora Berger, Biathlon, Norway, 1999–2014

Torah Bright, Snowboarding, Australia, 2003–2020

TORI

A name that means "victory" is perfect for a competitive and athletic girl, and that's exactly what you'll get with a Tori in your family! She may enjoy volleyball, boxing, or track and field, like Best Blocker of Nations League Tori Dixon, who won a volleyball world championship and two Nations League events; boxer Tori Nelson, who held world championship belts in three different weight classes and has a professional record of 20–2–3; or sprinter Tori Bowie, who raced to a full set of Olympic medals and two golds and a bronze from World Championships. And if "regular" sporting activities aren't for her, a daughter named Tori may head out onto more extreme paths, like adventurer Tori Murden, who holds multiple records as the first woman to climb Lewis Nunatak in the Antarctic, first woman and American to row solo across the Atlantic, and first woman and American to ski to the geographic South Pole!

Frentorish "Tori" Bowie, Track & Field (Sprinting), USA, 2013–2019

TeTori "Tori" Dixon, Volleyball (Middle Blocker), USA, 2014–current

Victoria "Tori" Murden, Rowing/Skiing/ Mountain Climbing, USA, 1988–1999

Tori Nelson, Boxing (Middleweight/ Welterweight), USA, 2010–current

TRACEY/TRACIE/TRACY

The unisex name Tracy (from an ancient place name for the Thracian region in southeast Europe) is another name that has spread around the world and has evolved into a whole family of variants, including Tracey and Tracie. Just as varied as the forms of the name are the sports in which athletes with them have excelled, with solo acts like Australian quadriplegic athletics competitor Tracey Freeman, who won six gold medals and four silvers in discus, javelin, shot put, and more at Paralympic Games, and American tennis pro Tracy Austin, who set records for championships at a young age, reached the world number one spot in singles, and won thirty titles, three Grand Slams, and two US Opens. In team events, rugby loosehead prop Tracey Waters won the 1998 Rugby World Cup with the New Zealand team, Australian field hockey defensewoman Tracey Belbin took home an Olympic gold medal and a gold and two silvers from World Championships, and Canadian wheelchair basketball player Tracey Ferguson won three Paralympic gold medals and four world championships.

Meanwhile, the biggest collection of champion Traceys, Tracies, and Tracys have made their mark in the pool! American Hall of Fame synchronized swimmer Tracie Ruiz took home two Olympic gold medals and a silver, along with a gold and silver at World Championships; Tracy Wiscombe of Scotland won five Paralympic medals, including two golds, and nine medals at World Championships, including three golds (mostly in freestyle events); Australian Tracey Cross accumulated ten freestyle and butterfly medals from Paralympics, three from World Championships, and two from World Championships and Games for the Disabled; and International Swimming Hall of Famer Tracy Caulkins set three world records on her way to winning three Olympic gold medals and five golds, a silver, and two bronzes across various World Championship events.

There's a good chance a daughter you name Tracey, Tracie, or Tracy will love to be in the water, but whether she chooses swimming as her main sport or branches out into something else, she'll be a force to be reckoned with.

- **Tracy Austin**, Tennis, USA, 1977–1994
- **Tracey Belbin**, Field Hockey (Defense), Australia, 1987–1992
- **Tracy Caulkins**, Swimming (Butterfly/Freestyle/Medley), USA, 1978–1984
- **Tracey Cross**, Swimming (Freestyle/Butterfly/Medley), Australia, 1990–2000
- **Tracey Ferguson**, Wheelchair Basketball, Canada, 1991–2015
- **Tracey Freeman**, Para-Athletics, Australia, 1972–1996
- **Tracie Ruiz**, Synchronized Swimming, USA, 1982–1988
- **Tracey Waters**, Rugby (Loosehead Prop), Canterbury Rugby Football Union, New Zealand, 1995–1998
- **Tracy Wiscombe**, Swimming (Freestyle), Scotland, 1996–2002

TRICIA/TRISCHA

The noble bearing of *Patricia* (from a Latin name meaning "nobleman") is no less apparent in women who go by the short form Tricia or variants like Trischa. And athletes with these names are capable of truly astounding feats! Ice hockey forward Tricia Dunn-Luoma won a full set of Olympic medals in successive games from 1998 to 2006, wrestler Tricia Saunders became the first American woman to win a world championship and the only one to win more than two on her way to collecting four world championships and being inducted into the National Wrestling Hall of Fame, and blind swimmer Trischa Zorn holds the record for most medals at Paralympic Games (in addition to multiple other records) at fifty-five with forty-one golds, nine silvers, and five bronzes!

No matter what stands in her way, a Tricia or Trischa in your family will not only find a way to succeed, but she will leave her mark on the world and challenge those who come after her. Definitely introduce her to swimming, wrestling, and ice hockey!

- **Patricia "Tricia" Dunn-Luoma**, Ice Hockey (Forward), Minnesota Whitecaps, USA, 1996–2006
- **Patricia "Tricia" Saunders**, Freestyle Wrestling, USA, 1992–2001
- **Trischa Zorn**, Swimming (Backstroke/Breaststroke/Butterfly/Freestyle/Medley), USA, 1980–2004

TRINE

Unless your family comes from Scandinavia, you may not be familiar with Trine (from *Katrine* and, ultimately, the same root as *Katherine*), but it's a solid name for a girl who will be nimble and accurate, especially when it comes to sports and activities involving throwing! She'll be in good company with Danish Olympic gold-medalist right-back Trine Nielsen; Norwegian world champion

Trine Haltvik, whose career lasted from age sixteen to forty-one and included 834 goals scored in 241 international games; and Norwegian two-time world record-breaking javelin thrower Trine Hattestad, who won Olympic gold and bronze medals and two golds and a bronze at World Championships.

Trine Haltvik, Handball (Center Back), Norway, 1981–2006

Elsa Katrine "Trine" Hattestad, Track & Field (Javelin), Norway, 1982–2000

Trine Nielsen, Handball (Right-Back), Denmark, 1998–2013

TRISTAN

The unisex name Tristan (from a Celtic root meaning "noise" or "tumult") is not just for boys; it works great for anyone who loves to go fast, play in cold weather, and perfectly accessorize for any occasion. This describes American skeleton racer Tristan Gale, who dyed her hair red, white, and blue for the 2002 Olympic Games . . . and then won the gold medal in the inaugural women's event!

Tristan Gale, Skeleton, USA, 2001–2006

TSVETANKA

An uncommon name outside of its native Bulgaria, Tsvetanka has a very pretty origin coming from a word for "flower" or "blossom." Let a girl you name Tsvetanka blossom into a skilled and competitive woman, perhaps finding her talent in throwing sports like Bulgarian world champion discus thrower Tsvetanka Khristova!

Tsvetanka Khristova, Track & Field (Discus), Bulgaria, 1982–2004

TYLER

You need good balance, tenacity, and accuracy to tile roofs, which are all qualities that come along with the unisex name that stems from that profession: Tyler. Tylers are equally good on land and water, too, with successful soccer players in the US and Great Britain like forward Tyler Lussi (who has won a National Women's Soccer League Championship, Shield, and Challenge Cup) and Irish midfielder Tyler Toland (who won a Women's Challenge Cup in North Ireland, the Scottish Women's Premier League Cup, and the Scottish Women's Cup). Meanwhile, Australian surfer Tyler Wright set the record for the youngest Championship Tour event-winner at only fourteen years old on her way to collecting fourteen wins at World Tour events and two back-to-back World Surf League championships!

Tyler Lussi, Soccer (Forward), Portland Thorns, USA, 2017–current

Tyler Toland, Soccer (Midfielder), Celtic Football Club Women, Ireland, 2017–current

Tyler Wright, Surfing, Australia, 2008–current

U

BOYS

UDHAM

Ideal for a boy who will do his absolute best at whatever he tries (especially team sports), Udham is an Indian Sikh and Punjabi name that means "effort" or "one who makes effort." The name was catapulted to stardom by Indian field hockey center-forward Udham Singh, who collected three gold medals and a silver from Olympic Games between 1952 and 1964.

Udham Singh, Field Hockey (Center-Forward), India, 1947–1964

UDO

Some say that your name dictates the success you'll achieve in life, and for people named Udo (from an Old Frankish/Old High German root meaning "wealth" or "fortune" or a West African Igbo word meaning "peace"), that's pretty neat. Germany has given the world a number of winning athletes with this name in a variety of events, from bobsleigh with world champion Udo Lehmann; to track cycling and fencing with Udo Hempel and Udo Wagner (respectively), who each won a gold and silver medal at Olympic Games; soccer with Bayern Munich defender Udo Horsmann, who won the Bundesliga twice, DFB-Pokal, European Cup, and Intercontinental Cup; and judo with Olympic gold- and bronze-medalist and two-time world champion Udo "Quelle" Quellmalz.

Put your son on the path to fortune, peace, and athletic victory with the name Udo!

Udo Hempel, Track Cycling, Germany, 1968–1983

Udo Horsmann, Soccer (Defender), Fußball-Club Bayern München e. V., Germany, 1973–1986

Udo Lehmann, Bobsleigh, Germany, 1994–2004

Udo "Quelle" Quellmalz, Judo, Germany, 1987–1996

Udo Wagner, Fencing (Foil), Germany, 1988–1992

ULF

If Ulf sounds like "wolf," it's for a good reason, as it comes from an Old Norse word for the ferocious canine. Naming your son Ulf will give him some competitive traits associated with the noble wolf, perhaps working together successfully in a pack, like Swedish ice hockey players Ulf Dahlén (world champion left wing) and Ulf Samuelsson (two-time

Stanley Cup champion defenseman who is known for his hard hits), or the German soccer striker Ulf Kirsten, who won multiple top-scorer awards and many trophies (DDR-Oberliga twice, FDGB-Pokal twice, and DFB-Pokal). Or maybe your Ulf will branch out and take down the competition as a lone wolf, like Swedish chess International Master and Grandmaster Ulf Andersson and German Olympic gold-medalist and two-time world champion shot putter Ulf Timmermann, who broke the world record on multiple occasions and was the first (of only four people ever) to perform a shot put over twenty-three meters!

Ulf Andersson, Chess, Sweden, 1967–2018

Ulf Dahlén, Ice Hockey (Left Wing), San Jose Sharks, Sweden, 1985–2003

Ulf Kirsten, Soccer (Striker), Bayer 04 Leverkusen Fußball GmbH, Germany, 1983–2003

Ulf Samuelsson, Ice Hockey (Defense), Pittsburgh Penguins, Sweden, 1981–2000

Ulf Timmermann, Track & Field (Shot Put), Germany, 1981–1992

URI

From a root meaning "my light" in biblical Hebrew comes the name Uri, which has risen to fame with some highly successful Israeli athletes. On the soccer field, right-back Uri Benjamin won the Liga Leumit Premier League twice and the Israel Super Cup with Hapoel Be'er Sheva, and two-time Israeli Player of the Year and Top Scorer of the League midfielder Uri Malmilian played most of his career with Beitar Jerusalem and, in total, won the Israel State Cup five times, Israeli Championship twice, and Israel Super Cup twice. Meanwhile, infant polio victim Uri Bergman became an eleven-time Paralympic gold-medalist swimmer across a number of different strokes and events!

Let your son be the light of your family with the name Uri, and definitely teach him how to swim and play soccer.

Uri Benjamin, Soccer (Right-Back), Hapoel Be'er Sheva Football Club, Israel, 1973–1980

Uri Bergman, Swimming (Breaststroke/Butterfly/Freestyle/Medley), Israel, 1976–1988

Uri Malmilian, Soccer (Midfielder), Beitar Jerusalem Football Club, Israel, 1973–1993

USAIN

A Caribbean name that has connections to an Arabic root meaning "handsome," Usain is quite literally the fastest name in the world thanks to Jamaican sprinter Usain "Lightning" Bolt. The athlete's list of accomplishments is extraordinary, with eight Olympic gold medals; eleven golds, two silvers, and a bronze from World Championships; a host of records at those events; and three current world records in the 100-meters, 200-meters, and 4x100-meters relay, firmly placing him atop the list of the greatest sprinters of all time!

Whether it's in track and field competition or just thinking on his feet, an Usain in your family is sure to be fast as well and deserving of the nickname "Lightning."

Usain "Lightning" Bolt, Track & Field (Sprinting), Jamaica, 2004–2017

UWE

Uncommon in North America, Uwe is a German name with a long lineage, though ultimately an uncertain origin; it may come from Old Norse roots meaning "edge of a sword," "awe," or "fear." Uwes work best on teams, particularly on the water like eight-time world champion lightweight rower Uwe Maerz and rower Uwe Heppner, whose Olympic gold medal and four golds and three bronzes from World Championships were won in quadruple and double sculls events. Three-time German Footballer of the Year and German Football Champion striker Uwe Seeler was selected to the FIFA World Cup All-Star Team and FIFA 100 and two-time NHL All-Star defenseman Uwe Krupp won Stanley Cup championships with the Colorado Avalanche and Detroit Red Wings.

Naming your son Uwe will guarantee that he's *awe*some and that he'll be a valuable and successful member of a team in the boardroom, on the field, or wherever else he applies himself.

Uwe Heppner, Rowing, Germany, 1979–1989

Uwe Krupp, Ice Hockey (Defense), Buffalo Sabres, Germany, 1982–2003

Uwe Maerz, Rowing, Germany, 1992–1996

Uwe Seeler, Soccer (Striker), Hamburger Sport-Verein e.V., Germany, 1953–1978

GIRLS

ULIANA/ULJANA

Juliana and other names that come from the Roman *Julius* are great, and from Russia and Ukraine we get "U" variants like Uliana and Uljana. These names are perfect for girls who are graceful and agile or tall and powerful, but highly competitive either way! You can see this in Russian athletes like Olympic gold-medalist, four-time world champion, and three-time World Cup Final-winning rhythmic gymnast Uliana Donskova and basketball center Uljana Semjonova, who never lost an international event as she won two Olympic gold medals and three world championships and was inducted into the Basketball Hall of Fame. Semjonova also holds the record for the largest feet ever in women's basketball at size 21 (EU 58)!

Uliana Donskova, Rhythmic Gymnastics, Russia, 2007–2012

Uljana Semjonova, Basketball (Center), TTT Riga, USSR, 1968–1989

ULLA

Names that have arisen as diminutives from different sources are always really interesting, and that's the case with Ulla, which has been used as a short form of the German *Ursula* and Scandinavian *Ulrika* and *Hulda*! Ullas are strong and tough, always know where they are and where they're going, and good with animals, as proven by Belgian Olympic gold-medalist judoka Ulla Werbrouck; Swedish orienteering competitor Ulla Lindkvist, who became the first solo woman world champion on her way to winning three gold medals and three silvers from World Championships; and German equestrian Ulla Salzgeber, whose dressage medals include two golds, a silver, and a bronze from Olympic Games; two golds and two bronzes from World Championships; and two golds and a bronze from World Cup events.

Ulla Lindkvist, Orienteering, Sweden, 1962–1972

Ulla Salzgeber, Equestrian (Dressage), Germany, 1997–current

Ulla Werbrouck, Judo, Belgium, 1990–2001

ULRIKA/ULRIKE

Two of many alternate feminine variants of the name *Ulrich* (which comes from Old German roots meaning "heritage" and "ruler"), the Swedish Ulrika and German Ulrike have almost always appeared on the leaderboards of sports that have to do with water, ice, and snow. Swedish diver Ulrika Knape won three medals each at Olympic Games and World Championships, with golds in both on the platform, and German sprint canoeist Ulrike Deppe raced across the water to three world championship gold medals and four silvers. Ulrika Bergman won Olympic gold and two world championships on the ice with the Sweden curling team, and Austrian alpine skier Ulrike Maier won five World Cup events and two Super-G world championships.

If your daughter whom you name Ulrika or Ulrike somehow does not like water or winter sports, that's okay; she can have success in something else, like track and field, following in the footsteps of German two-time Olympic gold-medalist high-jumper Ulrike Meyfarth!

Ulrika Bergman, Curling (Alternate), Sweden, 1997–2006

Ulrike Deppe, Slalom Canoeing, Germany, 1969–1983

Ulrika Knape, Diving, Sweden, 1972–1976

Ulrike Maier, Alpine Skiing, Austrian, 1984–1994

Ulrike Meyfarth, Track & Field (High Jump), Germany, 1971–1984

URŠA/URŠKA

Slovene short forms for *Ursula* (which comes from Latin for "little bear"), Urša and Urška are real "bears" of names that can give your daughter a high-flying career or hobby or a ferocity to take down her opponents face-to-face. She'll definitely look up to ski jumper Urša Bogataj, who has won three individual and three team events in World Cup and two gold medals at the 2022 Olympic Games, or judoka Urška Žolnir, who fought her way to three International Judo Federation Grand Slam gold medals; a gold, two silvers, and a bronze at IJF Grand Prix events; and Olympic gold and bronze medals!

Urša Bogataj, Ski Jumping, Slovenia, 2012–current

Urška Žolnir, Judo, Slovenia, 2003–2012

URSULA

Ursula is a diminutive of the Latin word for a feminine bear, ultimately meaning "little bear." There's a good chance that a daughter you name Ursula will enjoy paddle and rowing sports, just like two-time World Rowing Championships coxed quad sculls winner Ursula Unger and Ursula Gläser, who won four gold medals and a bronze in various canoe events at World Championships. Ursulas who prefer colder climes can take inspiration from biathlete Ursula "Uschi" Disl, who racked up thirty individual wins in World Cup events, nine medals (including two golds) from Olympic Games, and nearly twenty medals from World Championships (including eight wins)!

Ursula "Uschi" Disl, Biathlon, Germany, 1990–2006

Ursula Gläser, Canoeing, Germany, 1959–1965

Ursula Unger, Rowing, Germany, 1973–1975

UTA

"Wealth" and "fortune" are sure to follow an Uta in your family, as those are the original meanings of the Old High German root that led to the name *Otto*, then *Udo*, and then the feminine Uta. She might find her fame in track and field events, like German long-distance runner Uta Pippig, who was the first woman to win the Boston Marathon three times consecutively (according to official results) and won multiple other major events; mountain climbing, like activist and philanthropist Flutura "Uta" Ibrahimi of Albania, who was the first woman from her country to summit Mount Everest and the first woman from the Balkans to climb seven 8000-meter peaks; or judo, like Japanese Olympic gold-medalist, four-time world champion, seven-time International Judo Federation Grand Slam-winner, and four-time IJF Grand Prix-winner Uta Abe!

Uta Abe, Judo, Japan, 2017–current

Flutura "Uta" Ibrahimi, Mountaineering, Albania, 2014–current

Uta Pippig, Marathon, Germany, 1986–1996

V

BOYS

VADIM/VADYM

Vadim and its rarer variant Vadym have a convoluted and uncertain origin; they appear most often in Eastern Europe (namely Belarus, Russia, and Slovenia) and might come from the older name *Bademus*, from *Vladimir*, or from roots including "accuse," "peace," "world," and "rule." Athletes with these names have succeeded in a few different events, including track and field, like Belarusian world champion hammer thrower Vadim Devyatovskiy; fencing, like Ukrainian Olympic gold-medalist sabre champion Vadym Gutzeit; ice hockey, like center Vadim Shipachyov, who won Olympic gold and silver and world championship gold, silver, and two bronzes; and biathlon, like Belarusian three-time world champion Vadim Sashurin, who stood on twenty-nine World Cup event podiums with six wins.

Name your son Vadim (or Vadym) and raise him to respect competition and sportsmanship; he'll have the potential to succeed in athletics wherever his skills take him!

- **Vadim Devyatovskiy**, Track & Field (Hammer Throw), Belarus, 2003–2008
- **Vadym Gutzeit**, Fencing (Sabre), Ukraine, 1991–2005
- **Vadim Sashurin**, Biathlon, Belarus, 1989–2006
- **Vadim Shipachyov**, Ice Hockey (Center), Severstal Cherepovets, Russia, 2005–current

VAKHTANG

If you're looking for a unique "V" name to give to your son that will make him ferocious, flexible, and powerful on the mat, then consider Vakhtang, a Georgian name that has possible roots meaning "wolf-bodied" in Old Persian! He can look up to athletes like two Georgian two-time world champion wrestlers, Vakhtang Balavadze, who competed in freestyle, and Vakhtang Blagidze, who wrestled Greco-Roman and won an Olympic gold medal.

- **Vakhtang Balavadze**, Freestyle Wrestling, Georgia, 1952–1960
- **Vakhtang Blagidze**, Greco-Roman Wrestling, Georgia, 1978–1981

VALENTIN

The Roman name *Valentinus* (from a Latin word meaning "strong" or "healthy") has led to numerous different versions and variations around the world, with Valentin frequently appearing in Eastern Europe, as well as parts of Western Europe. That's where we find soccer players with this name scoring goals and winning trophies, like Torpedo Moscow midfielder Valentin Ivanov who won the Soviet Top League twice, the Soviet Cup, 1960 UEFA European Football Championship, and the 1956 Olympic gold medal while earning a UEFA European Championship Golden Boot and FIFA World Cup Top Scorer award.

Soviet athletes were also known for their prowess on the wrestling mat, as proven by Greco-Roman world champions Valentin Olenik and Valentin Nikolayev, the latter winning Olympic gold as well. Bulgaria got into the action, too, with freestyle wrestler Valentin Yordanov, who won Olympic gold and bronze medals and seven golds, two silvers, and a bronze from World Championships in the 1980s and '90s.

A young Valentin in your family may feel the lineage of his name and go into soccer or wrestling, or he may branch out and put his skills to good use in events that combine lots of different talents, such as the pentathlon, like French four-time world champion Valentin Prades, or artistic gymnastics, like Soviet four-time Olympic gold-medalist and five-time world champion Valentin Muratov!

Valentin Ivanov, Soccer (Midfielder), Football Club Torpedo Moscow, USSR, 1952–1966

Valentin Muratov, Artistic Gymnastics, USSR, 1948–1958

Valentin Nikolayev, Greco-Roman Wrestling, USSR, 1951–1960

Valentin Olenik, Greco-Roman Wrestling, USSR, 1964–1968

Valentin Prades, Track & Field (Pentathlon), France, 2013–current

Valentin Yordanov, Freestyle Wrestling, Bulgaria, 1980–1996

VALERI/VALERY

The Belarusian, Georgian, Russian, and Ukrainian family of Valeri/Valery names traces its origin back to another Roman family name (*Valerius*) and Latin word, in this case meaning "to be strong." That sense of strength is ubiquitous across the generations of athletes with these names. Starting with artistic gymnasts in the 1980s and '90s, Azerbaijani Olympic gold-medalist Valery Belenky is a two-time world champion, and Valeri Liukin won two gold and two silver medals from the Olympics, as well as two golds and a bronze from World Championships, while pioneering the triple back flip on floor and other unique skills.

Strength goes best when it's supporting and being supported by a team; this is illustrated by Soviet Hall of Fame ice hockey left wing Valeri Kharlamov, who won two gold medals and a silver at Olympic Games; eight golds, two silvers, and a bronze at World Championships; and three selections to the World Ice Hockey Championships All-Star Team.

On the other hand, strength is crucially important when competing (and winning!) all on your own, especially in BASE jumping (like Russian Valery Rozov, who broke multiple records and performed the highest BASE jump in the world), speed skating (like two-time World Sprint Championships-winner Valery Muratov), weightlifting (like Olympic gold-medalist and two-time world champion Valery Shary), and Greco-Roman wrestling (like Valery Rezantsev, who won two Olympic gold medals and five world championships in the 1970s).

Name your son Valeri or Valery to instill in him the strength to compete and succeed in just about any sport or profession.

Valery Belenky, Artistic Gymnastics, Azerbaijan/Germany, 1989–1997

Valeri Kharlamov, Ice Hockey (Left Wing), CSKA Moscow, USSR, 1967–1981

Valeri Liukin, Artistic Gymnastics, USSR, 1987–1994

Valery Muratov, Speed Skating, USSR, 1968–1976

Valery Rezantsev, Greco-Roman Wrestling, USSR, 1970–1976

Valery Rozov, BASE Jumping, Russia, 1998–2017

Valery Shary, Weightlifting, USSR, 1975–1976

VALTTERI

From the same Germanic roots for "ruler of the army" that *Walter* shares comes the powerful Finnish name Valtteri. On the soccer fields of Finland, center-back Valtteri Moren has won the Finnish championship six times, Finnish Cup three times, and the Finnish League Cup. On the ice, hockey defenseman Valtteri Kemiläinen earned an Olympic gold medal in 2022, and center Valtteri Filppula has won Olympic gold and silver, a world championship, and a Stanley Cup with the Detroit Red Wings. On Formula 1 racetracks, driver Valtteri Bottas has charged to the lead and won ten races.

Valtteri is a cool and unique name here in the United States, perfect for a boy who will focus his energies on either defense or offense and will likely enjoy team sports and going fast.

Valtteri Bottas, Auto Racing (Formula 1), Finland, 2008–current

Valtteri Filppula, Ice Hockey (Center), Detroit Red Wings, Finland, 2003–current

Valtteri Kemiläinen, Ice Hockey (Defense), Tappara, Finland, 2012–current

Valtteri Moren, Soccer (Center-Back), Helsingin Jalkapalloklubi, Finland, 2009–current

VANGIPURAPU

If you're looking to give your son the name of a true champion, as well as one that's on the more complex side, consider naming him after Indian cricket legend Vangipurapu Venkata Sai Laxman! VVS for short, Laxman was one of his country's "Fab Four" of cricket and racked up several records as a batsman, including being one of only ten players from his country to appear in over one hundred Test matches and scoring the most runs in a single domestic season (1,415). Nicknamed "Very Very Special" and the "God of Fourth Innings," VVS had particular success against Australia and shares the record for highest run partnership (376) in third innings of a Test match with Rahul Dravid.

Vangipurapu Venkata Sai "VVS" Laxman, Cricket (Batsman), Hyderabad Cricket Team, India, 1992–2011

VIC

The full name *Victor* may mean "winner," but some champions work best with the sleeker short form Vic! These have included Russian two-time Olympic gold-medalist snowboarder Vic Wild, and Australian multi-talented para-athlete Vic Renalson, who won three Paralympic gold medals and a silver in weightlifting, plus six more medals (two of them gold) in throwing events. Meanwhile, a pair of Vics made their name on the baseball diamond: Venezuelan two-time MLB All-Star outfielder Vic Davalillo, who won a Gold Glove and World Series championships with the Pittsburgh Pirates and Oakland Athletics, and New York Yankees pitcher Vic Raschi, who played in four All-Star games, won six World Series (five of them consecutively), and led the American League in strikeouts in 1951.

Whether it's a short form for something longer or his full name, call your son Vic and get him a baseball glove as soon as he can hold it!

- **Víctor "Vic" José Davalillo Romero**, Baseball (Outfielder), Cleveland Indians, Venezuela, 1963–1980
- **Victor "Vic" Raschi**, Baseball (Pitcher), New York Yankees, USA, 1946–1955
- **Victor "Vic" Renalson**, Para-Athletics/ Weightlifting, Australia, 1964–1976
- **Victor "Vic" Wild**, Snowboarding, Russia, 2013–current

VICTOR/VIKTOR

It doesn't get much better for an athlete or competitor to have a name that means "victor" or "conqueror," which is the Latin origin of the name Victor and its variant Viktor! It's no surprise, then, that tons of Victors have become victors in a huge number of sports and events, starting in common team sports like baseball, with Venezuelan five-time All-Star designated hitter/catcher Víctor Martínez, who won two Silver Slugger Awards; ice hockey, with Swedish world champion and four-time NHL All-Star defenseman Victor Hedman, who won two Stanley Cup championships with the Tampa Bay Lightning; and rugby, with South African Victor Matfield, who solidified his place among the sport's greatest locks with three Currie Cups, three Super Rugby championships, two Tri-Nations championships, and the 2007 Rugby World Cup.

Victors and Viktors have also succeeded in more individual and unique sports, including swimming (with Olympic gold- and two-time silver-medalist and two-time world champion Victor Davis), track and field (with Soviet three-time Olympic gold-medalist triple jumper Viktor Saneyev), badminton (with Danish Olympic gold-medalist and two-time world champion Viktor Axelsen, who won the Thomas Cup), and gymnastics (with Soviet legend Viktor Chukarin, who won seven gold, three silvers, and a bronze medal at the Olympics and three world championships). Soviets excelled in one-on-one physical and mental events, including Greco-Roman wrestling (with five-time world champion Viktor Igumenov), sabre fencing (with four-time Olympic gold-medalist Viktor Sidyak, who also took home a silver and a bronze), and chess (with Grandmaster Viktor Korchnoi, who began his career in Soviet Russia before defecting to Switzerland).

Athletes with these names have popped up at the top of leaderboards in very different sports too! Some of the strongest of the Victors and Viktors include Soviet Olympic gold-medalist weightlifter Viktor Mazin and Dominican bodybuilder Víctor Martínez, who won multiple International Federation of BodyBuilders events, including the 2007 Arnold Classic. Quick reflexes and reaction time are crucial to many competitive events, as we can see with Victors in esports (like French *Rocket League* pro Victor "Fairy Peak" Locquet, who won the Season 7 World Series championship, and American 2017 ELEAGUE Street Fighter V Invitational-winner Victor "Punk" Woodley, who has won eight Capcom Pro Tour events) and speed skating (like South Korean-born Russian Viktor An, who many consider to be the greatest of all time with his six gold medals and two bronzes from Olympic Games; twenty golds, ten silvers, and five bronzes from World Championships; six medals from World Team Championships; two World Cup overalls; and multiple event and world records).

Last but certainly not least are the numerous Victors and Viktors who have been playmakers on the soccer fields of the world. Among the top goalkeepers of the twenty-first century have been Brazilian Bola de Prata-winner Victor Bagy (whose defense led his teams to winning the Copa do Brasil twice, Campeonato Gaúcho, Copa Libertadores, Recopa Sudamericana, Campeonato Mineiro five times, and a FIFA Confederations Cup) and Spanish two-time La Liga Best Goalkeeper Víctor Valdés (who has won a

Belgian Cup, La Liga six times, Copa del Rey twice, Supercopa de España six times, UEFA Champions League three times, UEFA European Championship, UEFA Super Cup twice, FIFA Club World Cup twice, the 2010 FIFA World Cup, and the Zamora Trophy five times!).

Name your son Victor or Viktor to make him a true victor, whether that's on the soccer field, on the speed skating track, or even playing video games!

- **Viktor An**, Short Track Speed Skating, South Korea/Russia, 2002–2020
- **Viktor Axelsen**, Badminton, Denmark, 2010–current
- **Victor Leandro Bagy**, Soccer (Goalkeeper), Clube Atlético Mineiro, Brazil, 2002–2021
- **Viktor Chukarin**, Artistic Gymnastics, USSR, 1946–1956
- **Victor Davis**, Swimming (Breaststroke), Canada, 1982–1989
- **Victor Hedman**, Ice Hockey (Defense), Tampa Bay Lightning, Sweden, 2007–current
- **Viktor Igumenov**, Greco-Roman Wrestling, USSR, 1966–1972
- **Viktor Korchnoi**, Chess, USSR/Switzerland, 1951–2014
- **Victor "Fairy Peak" Locquet**, Esports (*Rocket League*), France, 2016–current
- **Víctor Martínez**, Baseball (Designated Hitter/Catcher), Cleveland Indians, Venezuela, 2002–2018
- **Víctor Martínez**, Bodybuilding, Dominican Republic, 1997–2020
- **Victor Matfield**, Rugby (Lock), Bulls, South Africa, 1998–2016
- **Viktor Mazin**, Weightlifting, USSR, 1979–1982
- **Viktor Saneyev**, Track & Field (Triple Jump), USSR, 1968–1980
- **Viktor Sidyak**, Fencing (Sabre), USSR, 1968–1980
- **Víctor Valdés Arribas**, Soccer (Goalkeeper), Fútbol Club Barcelona, Spain, 2000–2017
- **Victor "Punk" Woodley**, Esports (*Street Fighter*), USA, 2016–current

VIJAY

Like *Victor* and its Latin origin, the Indian name Vijay comes from a Sanskrit word for "victory" and is highly recommended for a competitive boy who likes to play hard and win. Winning is exactly what some very notable Indian cricketers did, including Vijay Bharadwaj, who won the Irani Trophy twice and Ranji Trophy four times in the 1990s and 2000s; Vijay Hazare, who captained the national team to its very first Test win and set records like being the first Indian first-class batsman to score a triple century, the first Indian to score two triple centuries, and the first Indian to reach one thousand Test runs; and legendary batsman Vijay Merchant, who still holds the second-highest first-class batting average in history (after Don Bradman, of course) after more than seventy years.

The most notable athlete with this name in recent history has been Fijian golfer Vijay Singh, who has won sixty-five professional events (including three major championships), been ranked number one in the world, and been inducted into the World Golf Hall of Fame!

- **Raghvendrarao Vijay Bharadwaj**, Cricket (Batsman), Karnataka, India, 1994–2005
- **Vijay Hazare**, Cricket (Batsman/Medium-Pace Bowler), Maharashtra Cricket Team, India, 1934–1958
- **Vijay Merchant**, Cricket (Batsman), Bombay Cricket Team, India, 1929–1951
- **Vijay Singh**, Golf, Fiji, 1982–current

VINCE

The name *Vincent* has a great pedigree and a common familiar nickname in *Vinnie/Vinny*, but don't sleep on the shortest form Vince! And while athletes going by those other names show up in more varied sports, it seems all Vinces excel when competing alongside others (even if they succeed on their own as well), like American sprinter Vince Matthews, who won two Olympic gold medals, one in the 400-meter and one in the 4x400-meter relay, and Australian sprint canoeist Vince Fehérvári, who took home seven gold medals, three silvers, and two bronzes from World Championships (and set a world record) in kayaks with one, two, and four athletes.

The other top Vinces are all team sports stars. On the hardwood court, legendary dunker Vince Carter was selected for eight NBA All-Star teams and won the Slam Dunk Contest in 2000, a Sportsmanship Award, Teammate of the Year, and an Olympic gold medal. On gridiron football fields, five-time Pro Bowl nose tackle Vince Wilfork won two Super Bowls with the New England Patriots.

Vincent "Vince" Carter Jr., Basketball (Shooting Guard/Small Forward), Toronto Raptors, USA, 1998–2020

Vince Fehérvári, Sprint Canoeing, Australia, 1993–2003

Vincent "Vince" Matthews, Track & Field (Sprinting), USA, 1967–1972

Vincent "Vince" Wilfork, Football (Nose Tackle), New England Patriots, USA, 2004–2016

VINCENT

Thousands of years ago, noble Romans named their children *Vicentius*, based on a Latin word meaning "to conquer," and you can carry on that tradition today with its descendant Vincent! This is another name that has spread around the world, and so athletes with it can be found scoring goals, winning races, and hitting shots in a number of different events. Inspirational Vincents run the gamut, from rugby (like French wing Vincent Clerc, who won the Heineken Cup three times, Top 14 championship three times, Six Nations Championship three times, and two Grand Slams) to sport shooting (like American three-time Olympic gold-medalist, five-time world champion, and World Cup Final–winning skeet shooter Vincent Hancock), biathlon (like French Olympic gold-medalist, two-time world champion, and seven-time World Cup event-winner Vincent Defrasne), and BASE jumping and free-flying (like Frenchman Vincent Reffet, who set multiple world records in the air and won six championships at major international free-fly events).

Vincents appear somewhat more likely to excel in certain sports. Starting with racquet and paddle events, American Vincent Richards reached the world number one tennis singles spot and won forty-six titles, four Grand Slams, and two gold medals and a silver at the 1924 Olympic Games. On the slopes, para-alpine skier Vincent Gauthier-Manuel took home one of each color medal from the Paralympics, as well as four golds from World Championships in various events, while cross-country skier Vincent Vittoz won the 2005 30-kilometer skiathlon world championship and nine World Cup events.

On two wheels, French track cyclist Vincent Le Quellec became a two-time world champion in the late 1990s, and French mountain biker Vincent Hermance collected eight gold medals, eight silvers, and four bronzes from World Championships in the 2000s and 2010s.

Vincents have made big moves all over the soccer field, like Belgian scoring center-back Vincent Kompany! His wins include the Belgian First Division championship twice, UEFA Intertoto Cup, Premier League four times, FA Cup twice, and EFL Cup four times, and his many accolades feature two Belgian First Division Man of the Season awards, a Belgian Golden Shoe, Belgian Professional Footballer of the Year, two Belgian Ebony

Shoes, multiple Manchester City and Premier League awards, and more!

Vincent Clerc, Rugby (Wing), Stade Toulousain, France, 1998–2018

Vincent Defrasne, Biathlon, France, 1999–2010

Vincent Gauthier-Manuel, Para-Alpine Skiing, France, 2010–2014

Vincent Hancock, Sport Shooting (Skeet), USA, 2005–current

Vincent Hermance, Mountain Bike Cycling, France, 2001–2016

Vincent Kompany, Soccer (Center-Back), Manchester City Football Club, Belgium, 2003–2020

Vincent Le Quellec, Track Cycling, France, 1995–2001

Vincent Reffet, BASE Jumping, France, 2002–2020

Vincent Richards, Tennis, USA, 1926–1951

Vincent Vittoz, Cross-Country Skiing, France, 1996–2011

VINCENZO

In addition to its diminutives *Vince* and *Vinnie/Vinny*, *Vincent* has multiple variations around the world, including the Italian Vincenzo. You don't have to be Italian to give this name to your son, but if you do, you should introduce him to a wide range of sports and activities to see which ones he prefers. He just might find his favorite in rowing, fencing, wrestling, or cycling, just like coxed pair world champion Vincenzo Capelli, Olympic gold-medalist sabre fencer Vincenzo Cuccia, two-time Olympic gold-medalist Greco-Roman wrestler Vincenzo Maenza, or road cyclist Vincenzo Nibali, who stands among the top seven racers in his sport with wins at all three major Grand Tours; he won the Tour de France, Vuelta a España, and the Giro d'Italia twice!

Vincenzo Capelli, Rowing, Italy, 2011–2016

Vincenzo Cuccia, Fencing (Sabre/Épée), Italy, 1924

Vincenzo Maenza, Greco-Roman Wrestling, Italy, 1978–1992

Vincenzo Nibali, Road Cycling, Italy, 2005–2022

VINNY

Vinny is a common diminutive of *Vincent*, but it can also be short for other names, including *Vinicio*, *Vinicius*, and *Vincenzo*. Like the Vinces, the most highly successful athletes with this name have made their marks in team sports, though with some exceptions when it comes to combat sports! Brazilian mixed martial artist Vinny Magalhães won a World Jiu-Jitsu Championship and a gold medal at the 2011 Abu Dhabi Combat Club and held the Titan FC Light Heavyweight and M-1 Global Light Heavyweight championships.

Mexican two-time MLB All-Star third baseman Vinny Castilla won three Silver Slugger awards and led the National League in RBIs, and two-time NFL Pro Bowl quarterback Vinny Testaverde led the AFC in passing touchdowns twice and passer rating once during his epic twenty-one-season career. On the ice, left wing/center Vinny Prospal won two world championships with his native Czech Republic ice hockey team and Canadian center Vinny Lecavalier won a World Cup on the international stage and played in four NHL All-Star games and won the Stanley Cup with the Tampa Bay Lightning.

A Vinny in your family should definitely be introduced to team sports that he can play with his friends, but he may gravitate more toward martial arts and scrapping!

Vinicio "Vinny" Castilla Soria, Baseball (Third Baseman), Colorado Rockies, Mexico, 1991–2006

Vincent "Vinny" Lecavalier, Ice Hockey (Center), Tampa Bay Lightning, Canada, 1998–2016

Vinicius "Vinny" de Magalhães, MMA (Light Heavyweight), Brazil, 2006–current

Václav "Vinny" Prospal, Ice Hockey (Left Wing/Center), Tampa Bay Lightning, Czech Republic, 1993–2013

Vincent "Vinny" Testaverde Sr., Football (Quarterback), Tampa Bay Buccaneers, USA, 1987–2007

VIRAT

While it may not be a common name in the United States, Virat (from the Sanskrit for "majestic" or "brilliant") is due for a surge in popularity thanks to its connection to one of the most skilled and beloved cricketers of all time. Virat Kohli, top-order batsman for India's national team and the domestic Delhi and Royal Challengers Bangalore, has consistently smashed records and garnered high acclaim in his sport since his professional debut in 2008. Just a few of his accomplishments include being the only cricketer named Player of the Tournament twice in T20 World Cup, having the second most centuries in ODI and third most in international cricket, and being the fastest batsman to eight thousand, nine thousand, ten thousand, eleven thousand, and twelve thousand runs in ODI!

If you're a cricket fan, Virat might be just the name you're looking for; give it to a child who will play hard and gain the respect of his teammates.

Virat "Cheeku" Kohli, Cricket (Top-Order Batsman), Delhi Cricket Team, India, 2008–current

VIRENDER

A heroic name combining a root meaning "brave man" with Indra, the Hindu sky god and king of the devas, Virender has twice made an impact on the world's stage in athletics. Deaf freestyle wrestler Virender Singh won a set of medals at World Deaf Wrestling Championships and three golds and a bronze at Deaflympics and even inspired a feature film based on his life and career.

On the cricket pitch, meanwhile, Virender Sehwag became known as one of the greatest opening batsmen of all time by becoming the first Indian named Wisden Leading Cricketer in the World; winning the 2002 ICC Champions Trophy, 2007 T20 World Cup, and 2011 Cricket World Cup; and setting multiple domestic and international records!

Consider the name Virender for your son and he'll overcome any challenges life throws at him to become an inspirational character and a true champion.

Virender Sehwag, Cricket (Opening Batsman), Delhi Cricket Team, India, 1997–2021

Virender Singh, Freestyle Wrestling, India, 2002–2017

VITALI/VITALY

Despite having names that come from a Latin root meaning "vital" or "full of life," athletes named Vitali and Vitaly are almost all about knocking down, and out, their opponents! They range from Russian mixed martial artist Vitaly Minakov, who won four sambo world championships and held the Bellator MMA Heavyweight World Championship, to Ukrainian boxer Vitali Klitschko, who has defeated fifteen opponents in title fights to win his multiple world heavyweight championships (and successfully defended those titles twelve times) and share the world's stage with his brother and fellow heavyweight champion, Wladimir.

Obviously, a young Vitali or Vitaly in your family will be strong and tough, a fierce competitor and a defender of his people. He may also combine his strength with agility, like legendary artistic gymnast Vitaly Scherbo of Belarus, who set multiple world records on his way to collect six gold medals and four bronzes from Olympic Games and twelve golds, seven silvers, and four bronzes from World Championships!

Vitali Klitschko, Boxing (Heavyweight), Ukraine, 1996–2013

Vitaly Minakov, MMA (Heavyweight), Russia, 2010–current

Vitaly Scherbo, Artistic Gymnastics, Belarus, 1990–1997

VITOR

Victors and *Viktors* are all over the world, but Portuguese has given us the alternate form of Vitor. No less "victorious" than the rest, athletes with this name can inspire a Vitor in the next generation to be unstoppable in the ring or octagon! This is exemplified by Brazilian mixed martial artists like UFC 12 Heavyweight Tournament Champion, UFC Light Heavyweight Champion, and Cage Rage World Light Heavyweight Champion Vitor Belfort, and Vítor Ribeiro, who held the Cage Rage World Lightweight and Shooto World Lightweight Championships and won four gold medals and a silver at World Jiu-Jitsu Championships.

Vitor Belfort, MMA/Boxing (Heavyweight/Middleweight), Brazil, 1996–current

Vítor Ribeiro, MMA (Lightweight), Brazil, 2001–2013

VIVIAN

While generally considered a feminine name these days, the unisex Vivian (from a Latin word meaning "alive") has long been considered a strong masculine moniker! In that usage, it stretches back to the turn of the twentieth century with English soccer forward Vivian Woodward, who scored a record number of goals in Great Britain's 1908 and 1912 Olympic gold medal wins; decades later, English defender Vivian Anderson won a First Division championship, League Cup three times, European Cup twice, European Super Cup, and Anglo Scottish Cup.

Vivians have ranged from Antiguan Hall of Fame cricket batsman Viv Richards, who won the 1975 and 1979 Cricket World Cups with the West Indies team, was named one of Wisden's Five Cricketers of the Century, and set numerous records on the pitch to become known as one of the greatest batsmen of all time, to English explorer Vivian Fuchs, who led the very first overland Antarctica expedition in 1958.

Bring back the name Vivian for your boy who will truly live a life of excitement and achievement, whether that's in a team sport, competing on his own, or even traveling to the ends of the Earth.

Vivian "Viv" Anderson, Soccer (Defender), Nottingham Forest Football Club, England, 1974–1995

Vivian Fuchs, Exploration, England, 1953–1958

Isaac Vivian "Viv" Richards, Cricket (Batsman), Leeward Islands Cricket Team, Antigua and Barbuda, 1971–1993

Vivian Woodward, Soccer (Forward), Tottenham Hotspur Football Club, England, 1895–1920

VLADIMIR/VOLODYMYR

The classic Eastern European name Vladimir, and its Ukrainian variant Volodymyr, come from Slavic roots for "rule" and "great" or "famous." There have been lots of great athletes and competitors with these names who have become famous, with many of them concentrated in a few different events, although they have also spread out into a variety of sports, including cycling (like Ukrainian track world champion Volodymyr Rybin), racewalking (like Volodymyr Holubnychy, who won two gold medals, a silver, and a bronze from Olympic Games in the 20-kilometer walk events), and gymnastics (like

Soviet four-time Olympic gold-medalist and six-time world champion artistic gymnast Vladimir Artemov).

Russian rifle sport shooter Vladimir Maslennikov took home one of each color medal from World Championships, Bulgarian biathlete Vladimir Iliev won gold and bronze medals at Summer World Championships events (and a silver in the winter), and Kazakh Vladimir Smirnov won a gold, four silvers, and two bronzes at the Olympics; eleven world championship medals (including four golds); thirty-two World Cup events; and two overall titles in cross-country skiing.

The pairs of highly successful Vladimirs who have succeeded in the same events are very interesting, starting with those in America's pastime. Dominican right fielder/designated hitter Vladimir Guerrero Sr. played in nine All-Star games from 1999 to 2010, earning an American League MVP, eight Silver Slugger awards, and induction into the National Baseball Hall of Fame, and then his son Vladimir Guerrero Jr. made his debut in the MLB in 2019 and has already accumulated four All-Star selections, a Gold Glove and Silver Slugger, the AL Hank Aaron award, and the MLB home run leader spot in 2021!

Next up are the Vladimirs and Volodymyrs who have been experts on the ice, wielding swords, and wrestling. Ice hockey defenseman Vladimir Lutchenko won two Olympic gold medals for the USSR in the 1970s, current Russian right wing Vladimir Tarasenko has played in four NHL All-Star games and won the Stanley Cup with the St. Louis Blues, and Soviet defenseman Vladimir Konstantinov had success domestically and internationally, with three gold medals and a bronze at World Championships, as well as a Stanley Cup championship with the Detroit Red Wings (and an honorary second one posthumously). Facing off in fencing, Ukrainian sabre fencer Volodymyr Lukashenko took home a set of world championship medals in the early 2000s, and Soviet Vladimir Nazlymov won three Olympic gold medals, two silvers, and a bronze in sabre fencing. Greco-Roman wrestling was the domain of Soviet four-time world champion Vladimir Zubkov, while Vladimir Yumin won four world championships and an Olympic gold medal for the USSR in freestyle wrestling.

You don't have to be Russian or Ukrainian to name your son Vladimir or Volodymyr, but if you do, you should teach him to play ice hockey, wrestle, and practice with swords, though he may also take after his dad (especially if your family enjoys baseball).

- **Vladimir Artemov**, Artistic Gymnastics, USSR, 1983–1989
- **Vladimir Guerrero Jr.**, Baseball (First Baseman/Designated Hitter/Third Baseman), Toronto Blue Jays, Canada, 2019–current
- **Vladimir Guerrero Sr.**, Baseball (Right Fielder/Designated Hitter), Montreal Expos, Dominican Republic, 1996–2011
- **Volodymyr Holubnychy**, Track & Field (Racewalking), USSR, 1960–1976
- **Vladimir Iliev**, Biathlon, Bulgaria, 2006–current
- **Vladimir Konstantinov**, Ice Hockey (Defense), Detroit Red Wings, USSR, 1984–1997
- **Volodymyr Lukashenko**, Fencing (Sabre), Ukraine, 2000–2009
- **Vladimir Lutchenko**, Ice Hockey (Defense), HC CSKA Moscow, USSR, 1967–1981
- **Vladimir Maslennikov**, Sport Shooting (Rifle), Russia, 2016–current
- **Vladimir Nazlymov**, Fencing (Sabre), USSR, 1968–1980
- **Volodymyr Rybin**, Track Cycling, Ukraine, 2003–2010
- **Vladimir Smirnov**, Cross-Country Skiing, Kazakhstan, 1983–1998
- **Vladimir Tarasenko**, Ice Hockey (Right Wing), St. Louis Blues, Russia, 2010–current
- **Vladimir Yumin**, Freestyle Wrestling, USSR, 1973–1980

Vladimir Zubkov, Greco-Roman Wrestling, USSR, 1970–1975

VLADISLAV

Like *Vladimir/Volodymyr* and *Vyacheslav*, Vladislav is a traditional Slavic name, in this case from noble roots meaning "rule" and "glory." A boy you give this name to can find glory in defending his team from their opponents, like Soviet ice hockey goaltender Vladislav Tretiak, who claimed his spot on the list of all-time greats in his position by winning three gold medals and a silver from Olympic Games; ten golds, two silvers, and a bronze at World Championships; the 1979 NHL Challenge Cup; and the 1981 Canada Cup, as well as being inducted into the inaugural class of the International Ice Hockey Federation Hall of Fame.

On the other hand, if your son's pursuits are more cerebral and aggressive, you could introduce him to chess, just like Russian child prodigy Vladislav Artemiev, who became a Grandmaster at sixteen and has won multiple gold medals at World Team Chess Championships.

Vladislav Artemiev, Chess, Russia, 2015–current

Vladislav Tretiak, Ice Hockey (Goaltender), CSKA Moscow, USSR, 1968–1984

VYACHESLAV

Another powerful Russian and Ukrainian "V" name, Vyacheslav comes from Slavic roots for "more glory" and has achieved exactly that for a number of Olympians, world champions, winners, record breakers, and more. They've ranged from Soviet two-time Olympic gold-medalist and two-time world champion cross-country skier Vyacheslav Vedenin to Russian mixed martial artist Vyacheslav Vasilevsky, who held the M-1 Global Light Heavyweight World Champion title and won six sambo world championships; and Soviet volleyball setter Vyacheslav Zaytsev, who won a gold medal and two silvers from the Olympics; two golds and two silvers from World Championships; and two golds and a silver at World Cup events!

In the boxing ring, Soviets Vyacheslav Lemeshev and Vyacheslav Yanovskiy won an Olympic gold medal each in 1972 and 1988, respectively. A trio of Soviet Vyacheslavs proved their worth on the water with sprint canoeists Olympic gold-medalist and world champion Vyacheslav Ionov, two-time world champion Vyacheslav Kononov, and three-time Olympic gold-medalist and world champion rower Vyacheslav Ivanov, who set records for race times and medal counts.

Of course, we couldn't talk about an Eastern European name without addressing the athletes with it who played ice hockey! There are four iconic Russians who have found their glory on the ice: Olympic gold-medalist and world champion center Vyacheslav Butsayev; two-time Stanley Cup and two-time Gagarin champion left wing Vyacheslav "Slava" Kozlov; two-time KHL All-Star defenseman Vyacheslav "Slava" Voynov, who won the Gagarin Cup, two Stanley Cups, and an Olympic gold medal; and two-time Olympic gold-medalist and two-time world champion center Vyacheslav "Slava" Bykov.

Let your son seek and attain as much glory as possible by giving him the name Vyacheslav (and attendant nickname Slava) and teaching him to be a fair competitor and a supportive team player.

Vyacheslav Butsayev, Ice Hockey (Center), CSKA Moscow, Russia, 1987–2007

Vyacheslav "Slava" Bykov, Ice Hockey (Center), CSKA Moscow, Russia, 1979–2000

Vyacheslav Ionov, Sprint Canoeing, USSR, 1964–1967

Vyacheslav Ivanov, Rowing, USSR, 1956–1969

Vyacheslav Kononov, Sprint Canoeing, USSR, 1970–1974

Vyacheslav "Slava" Kozlov, Ice Hockey (Left Wing), Detroit Red Wings, Russia, 1987–2015

Vyacheslav Lemeshev, Boxing (Middleweight), USSR, 1972–1975

Vyacheslav Vasilevsky, MMA (Light Heavyweight/Middleweight/Welterweight), Russia, 2008–current

Vyacheslav Vedenin, Cross-Country Skiing, USSR, 1968–1972

Vyacheslav "Slava" Voynov, Ice Hockey (Defense), Los Angeles Kings, Russia, 2006–current

Vyacheslav Yanovskiy, Boxing (Light Welterweight), USSR, 1984–1997

Vyacheslav Zaytsev, Volleyball (Setter), USSR, 1975–1988

GIRLS

VALENTINA

From the same origin in a Roman name and Latin root for "strong" and "healthy" as *Valentin*, Valentina is used most often in Italy and Eastern Europe, but it can be great anywhere! Sometimes athletes with this name compete (and win) on their own, like Italian world champion mountain runner Valentina Belotti; Ukrainian bodybuilder Valentina Chepiga, who won multiple international competitions, including the 2000 Jan Tana Classic, 2002 GNC Show of Strength, and 2000 Ms. Olympia (heavyweight class); and Kyrgyzstani/Peruvian mixed martial artist Valentina "Bullet" Shevchenko, who held the UFC Women's Flyweight Championship and won eight world championships and two World Combat Games events in Muay Thai.

Other women have succeeded by striving alongside partners and teammates in events such as rowing, like Italian double sculls Olympic gold-medalist Valentina Rodini, and road cycling, like Russian two-time team time trial world champion and winner of the Tour de France Féminin Valentina Polkhanova.

Other notable Valentinas include two foil fencers: Russian Valentina Sidorova, who is an Olympic gold-medalist, and Italian record-breaking six-time Olympic gold-medalist and sixteen-time world champion Valentina Vezzali, who won sixty-five medals in international competitions. And Russian chess Grandmaster Valentina Gunina has won Women European Individual Chess Championships three times, three gold medals at Women's Chess Olympiads, a Women's World Team Chess Championship, and the

2016 London Chess Classic Super Rapidplay Open!

Naming a daughter Valentina can give her a healthy love of competition and the strength to win, whether that's on her own or with a team.

- **Valentina Belotti**, Mountain Running, Italy, 2002–2017
- **Valentina Chepiga**, Bodybuilding, Ukraine, 1993–current
- **Valentina Gunina**, Chess, Russia, 2006–current
- **Valentina Polkhanova**, Road Cycling, Russia, 1990–1994
- **Valentina Rodini**, Rowing, Italy, 2013–current
- **Valentina "Bullet" Shevchenko**, MMA (Bantamweight/Flyweight/Lightweight), Kyrgyzstan/Peru, 2003–current
- **Valentina Sidorova**, Fencing (Foil), USSR, 1976–1980
- **Maria Valentina Vezzali**, Fencing (Foil), Italy, 1993–2016

VALERIE

Descended from a Roman family name and a root meaning "to be strong," Valerie is a powerful name sure to give a girl the drive and determination to hone her body and skills to win. She will have incredible figures who share her name to look to for inspiration, including French two-time kickboxing world champion and WIBF Welterweight World Champion Valérie Hénin and New Zealander shot putter Valerie Adams who set numerous records on her path to winning two gold medals, a silver, and a bronze from the Olympics, as well as eight world championships!

- **Valerie Adams**, Track & Field (Shot Put), New Zealand, 2002–2022
- **Valérie Hénin**, Kickboxing/Boxing (Lightweight/Welterweight), France, 1987–2001

VANESSA

Some names have ancient origins and have been around for thousands of years . . . and others were invented by writers a few hundred years ago! Such is the case with Vanessa, created by Jonathan Swift in his poem "Cadenus and Vanessa" (written in 1713 and published in 1726). From there, the name gained popularity in the English-speaking world and has appeared in some pretty interesting sports and competitions. While Vanessas can play well on teams (as proven by New Zealander two-time Rugby World Cup-winning wing Vanessa Cootes and Canadian CONCACAF W Championship Best XI soccer center-back Vanessa Gilles, who has won an Olympic gold medal), many more of them seem to prefer striking out on their own.

Italian artistic gymnast Vanessa Ferrari became an all-around world champion in 2006 (with four other medals from World Championships in her collection); skateboarder Vanessa Torres became the first woman to win a gold medal at the X Games with a Park win in 2003; esports fighting game pro and Championship Gaming Series (CGS) first draft pick Vanessa Arteaga won the 2007 CGS Season *Dead or Alive 4* Female Individual championship; Australian para-athlete Vanessa Low has won a pair of gold medals in the long jump at Paralympic Games and World Championships, as well as other medals in sprinting; and Portuguese triathlete Vanessa Fernandes collected one of each color medal from International Triathlon Union (ITU) World Championships, two golds from ITU World Cup events, and another two golds from ITU Duathlon World Championships.

A Vanessa can do anything she puts her mind to and can conquer any challenge that gets in her way!

- **Vanessa "Vanessa" Arteaga**, Esports (Fighting Games), USA, 2007–2008

Vanessa Cootes, Rugby (Wing), Waikato Rugby Union, New Zealand, 1995–2002

Vanessa Ferrari, Artistic Gymnastics, Italy, 2002–current

Vanessa Fernandes, Triathlon, Portugal, 2002–2016

Vanessa Gilles, Soccer (Center-Back), Football Club des Girondins de Bordeaux, Canada, 2017–current

Vanessa Low, Para-Athletics, Australia, 2009–current

Vanessa Torres, Skateboarding, USA, 2003–current

VANINA

A highly flexible name that can be a diminutive of various names, including *Evangelina* and *Ghjuvannina*, Vanina is a unique moniker for a fun and cool girl who will enjoy playing with her friends out in the sun. In that, she'll take after Argentinian field hockey forward Vanina Oneto, who won gold and silver medals at World Cup events and a full set of medals at Champions Trophy tournaments!

Vanina Oneto, Field Hockey (Forward), Argentina, 1991–2004

VASHTI

From biblical Hebrew (and the first wife to King Ahasuerus in the Book of Esther), Vashti has uncertain origins but may come from a Hebrew word for "thread" or a Persian root meaning "best" or "excellent." Excellence is exactly what American high-jumper Vashti Cunningham has exhibited, rising to prominence in the 2010s and winning gold and silver medals at World Indoor Championships!

Give your daughter the chance to reach untold heights with this classic and beautiful name.

Vashti Cunningham, Track & Field (High Jump), USA, 2016–current

VENUS

In the past, the name Venus was synonymous with the Roman goddess of beauty and love (analogous to the Greek Aphrodite). But that all changed in the 1990s and now the name brings with it a sense of power and speed thanks to the massive success of tennis phenom Venus Williams! One of the greatest players of all time, Venus has an incredible record, including being ranked number one in the world in both singles and doubles (forty-nine singles titles and seven Grand Slams, and twenty-four doubles titles and fourteen majors), holding an unbeaten record in Grand Slam doubles finals with her sister Serena, winning four gold medals and a silver from Olympic Games, earning countless awards, and smashing numerous records. She's been just as impressive off the court as well, fighting for equal pay for female athletes and starting and running successful business ventures.

Combining beauty and inner strength, speed, and power, the name Venus will make your daughter an absolute force of nature. It pairs well with a sister named *Serena*.

Venus Williams, Tennis, USA, 1994–current

VERA/VIRA

While it later came to be associated with a Latin word meaning "true," the name Vera comes from a Russian root for "faith" (and, totally separately, an Albanian word for "summer"). There are also variants like the accented Czech form Věra and Ukrainian Vira. Multiple Veras have proven to be masters of track and field events, chess, volleyball, gymnastics, and more, but many Veras tend to prefer winning with partners and teams. These range from Soviet equestrian Vira Misevych, who won an Olympic team dressage gold medal, to Russian Olympic gold- and silver-medalist and synchronized diver Vera Ilyina, and Czech table tennis player Věra Votrubcová, whose six gold medals, three silvers, and four bronzes from World Championships came mostly in doubles, mixed doubles, and team events

In winter sports, there have been Soviets like world allround champion speed skater Vera Bryndzei and Olympic gold-medalist and world champion luger Vera Zozulya, while in summer track and field events, hurdler Vera Komisova and long-jumper Vera Krepkina won gold at the Olympics. Just as fierce, competitors across the chess board have been Russian Woman Grandmaster Vera Nebolsina and Czech eight-time world champion Vera Menchik, who was the first and longest-reigning Women's World Chess Champion (1927–1944) and for whom the Women's Chess Olympiad trophy is named.

Veras are very flexible on the volleyball court, able to excel in any position, like Russian world champion setter Vera Ulyakina, Soviet Olympic gold-medalist middle blocker and world champion Vera Lantratova, and Soviet two-time Olympic gold-medalist outside hitter, world champion, and World Cup-winner Vera Galushka-Duyunova.

The most numerous successful Veras (who are overwhelmingly Czech and Russian) have shown off their grace and skill in international gymnastics! These include Czech Olympic team gold-medalist Věra Růžičková; Russian Olympic rhythmic gymnastics group all-around gold medalist Vera Shimanskaya; Czech seven-time Olympic gold-medalist and four-time world champion Věra Čáslavská, who set multiple records during her career; and Russian rhythmic gymnast Vera Sessina, who collected an incredible medal count of six golds, two silvers, and a bronze from World Championships; four golds, a silver, and two bronzes from World Cup Finals; eleven golds, twelve silvers, and a bronze from Grand Prix Final; and a set of each color from World Games!

True grace, skill, and determination will be the gifts you give a daughter along with her name Vera, as well as faith in her abilities to succeed in her chosen field, profession, or sport.

Vera Bryndzei, Speed Skating, USSR, 1975–1978

Věra Čáslavská, Artistic Gymnastics, Czechoslovakia, 1958–1968

Vera Galushka-Duyunova, Volleyball (Outside Hitter), USSR, 1968–1974

Vera Ilyina, Diving, Russia, 1991–2004

Vera Komisova, Track & Field (Hurdling/Sprinting), USSR, 1980

Vera Krepkina, Track & Field (Long Jump/Sprinting), USSR, 1952–1960

Vera Lantratova, Volleyball (Middle Blocker), USSR, 1960–1971

Vera Menchik, Chess, Czechoslovakia/England, 1923–1944

Vira Misevych, Equestrian (Dressage), USSR, 1977–1981

Vera Nebolsina, Chess, Russia, 2001–current

Věra Růžičková, Artistic Gymnastics, Czechoslovakia, 1948

Vera Sessina, Rhythmic Gymnastics, Russia, 2002–2009

Vera Shimanskaya, Rhythmic Gymnastics, Russia, 2000

Vera Ulyakina, Volleyball (Setter), Russia, 2002–current

Věra Votrubcová, Table Tennis, Czechoslovakia, 1936–1947

Vera Zozulya, Luge, USSR, 1976–1982

VERENA/VRENI

Possibly related to a Latin root for "true," Verena (with the fun diminutive Vreni) is a great name for a girl in your family who may enjoy playing soccer but will almost definitely like skiing! Of course, that's if she follows in the footsteps of German soccer defender Verena Schweers, who has won the Bundesliga twice, DFB-Pokal three times, and UEFA Women's Champions League twice; German para-athlete Verena Bentele, who has won five Paralympic gold medals in biathlon and seven in cross-country skiing; and Swiss alpine ski racer Verena "Vreni" Schneider, who stands among the winningest women ever in her sport with three gold medals, a silver, and a bronze from Olympic Games; three golds, two silvers, and a bronze from World Championships; and a staggering fifty-five golds, twenty-eight silvers, and eighteen bronzes from World Cup events, as well as three overall titles.

Verena Bentele, Biathlon/Cross-Country Skiing, Germany, 1998–2010

Verena "Vreni" Schneider, Alpine Skiing, Switzerland, 1984–1995

Verena Schweers, Soccer (Defender), Verein für Leibesübungen Wolfsburg e. V., Germany, 2006–2020

VERONICA/VERONIKA

Through a complicated series of events, the name Veronica/Veronika actually comes from the Latin name *Berenice* by way of an epithet applied to a saint with that name. Regardless of its origins, one of these names can instill in your daughter a love of sports and competing, whether that's in track and field events, in the snow, rowing, or even using her brain to claim victory! She'll follow in the footsteps of some notable women, like Czech discus throw and shot put Paralympic gold-medalist Veronika Foltová; Jamaican record-breaking sprinter Veronica Campbell-Brown, whose medal count includes three golds, three silvers, and two bronzes from the Olympics and five golds, seven silvers, and a bronze from World Championships; German Olympic gold-medalist and world champion cross-country skier Veronika Schmidt; Romanian two-time Olympic gold-medalist and four-time world champion rower Veronica Cochela; and Austrian Woman International Master chess phenom Veronika Exler.

Veronica Campbell-Brown, Track & Field (Sprinting), Jamaica, 2000–2016

Veronica Cochela, Rowing, Romania, 1985–2000

Veronika Exler, Chess, Austria, 2008–current

Veronika Foltová, Para-Athletics, Czech Republic, 2004

Veronika Schmidt, Cross-Country Skiing, Germany, 1974–1982

VICKI/VICKIE/VICKY

Victoria and *Viktoria* are great names, but for some, they're a little long. Thankfully, they had natural diminutive forms in Vicki, Vickie, and Vicky, which have been used by iconic winners and record-breakers in curling, squash, basketball, and a number of other sports and events. Scottish curlers Vicki Chalmers and Vicky Wright won a world championship and an Olympic gold medal, respectively, while on the squash court, Australian former world number one singles player Vicki Cardwell won a set of medals from world championships in the 1980s. Then there are the hardwood court players, like center Vickie Orr, who won a world championship with USA Basketball in 1992; two-time WNBA All-Star shooting guard Vickie Johnson, who won the Kim Perrot Sportsmanship Award; and WNBA All-Star forward Vicky Bullett, who won a world championship, and both gold and bronze medals at Olympic Games.

Outside of those sports where women with these names have appeared together, they've found success all over the map with single competitors winning in synchronized swimming (Canadian World Aquatics Champion Vicky Vilagos) and sprint canoeing (Austrian K-2 500-meter world champion Vicki Schwarz). British triathlete Vicky Holland has won alone and on teams with gold at World Triathlon Championship Series Overall, ten medals (five of them gold) at World Triathlon Series events, and two gold medals, a silver, and a bronze at Mixed Relays, while solo champions include golfer Vicky Hurst, who has won eight professional tournaments, and bodybuilder Vickie Gates, who won three Ms. International competitions in a row (1999–2001).

Whether you're coming up with a nickname for your daughter named *Victoria* or *Viktoria*, or just looking for a short name all on its own, the family of Vicki, Vickie, and Vicky can give you a name perfectly suited for your little winner who can succeed at any task, whether she's on her own or alongside partners and teammates.

Victoria "Vicky" Bullett, Basketball (Forward), Charlotte Sting, USA, 2009-current

Vicki Cardwell, Squash, Australia, 1978–1997

Victoria "Vicki" Chalmers, Curling (Second), Scotland, 2011-current

Ondrea "Vickie" Gates, Bodybuilding, USA, 1993–2003

Vicky Holland, Triathlon, England, 2010–current

Vicky Hurst, Golf, USA, 2008–current

Vickie Johnson, Basketball (Shooting Guard), New York Liberty, USA, 1997–2009

Victoria "Vickie" Orr, Basketball (Center), USA Basketball, USA, 1987–1992

Viktoria "Vicki" Schwarz, Sprint Canoeing, Austria, 2005–2012

Vicky Vilagos, Synchronized Swimming, Canada, 1980–1992

Victoria "Vicky" Wright, Curling (Second/Third), Scotland, 2013-2022

VICTORIA/VIKTORIA

Victoria and its variant Viktoria have long been popular names around the world, and for good reason; they come from Latin and mean "victory"! You can't find a better name choice for an athletic and competitive daughter, and one who just might prefer something like chess, tennis, cycling, skiing, or gymnastics if she takes after such people as Russian artistic gymnasts two-time uneven bars world champion Viktoria Komova and Olympic team gold-medalist and World Cup-winner Viktoria Listunova; Estonian chess Woman International Master Viktoria Baškite; Belarusian former world number one singles tennis player Victoria Azarenka, who has won twenty-one titles and two majors, as well as Olympic gold and bronze medals; British two-time Olympic gold-medalist and sixteen-time world champion-medalist (nine of them gold) track cyclist Victoria Pendleton; and German alpine ski racer Viktoria Rebensburg, who won giant slalom gold and bronze medals at the Olympics and nineteen gold, eighteen silver, and twelve bronze medals from World Cup events.

Victoria Azarenka, Tennis, Belarus, 2003–current

Viktoria Baškite, Chess, Estonia, 2000–current

Viktoria Komova, Artistic Gymnastics, Russia, 2008–2018

Viktoria Listunova, Artistic Gymnastics, Russia, 2018–current

Victoria Pendleton, Track Cycling, England, 2006–2012

Viktoria Rebensburg, Alpine Skiing, Germany, 2006–2020

VIOLA

While a viola is a stringed musical instrument, the name Viola stretches back to ancient Rome and a Latin word meaning "violet." Whether she's into violet the color or violets the flower, a girl named Viola in your family has a lot of potential when it comes to competition, particularly rowing, skiing, and swimming, as proven by her predecessors

German rowers Viola Goretzki and Viola Poley, who each won an Olympic gold medal in 1976 (but in different events!) and a world championship; German cross-country skier Viola Bauer, who collected one of each color medal from Olympics and world championships, as well as five World Cup team wins; and Italian eight-time world champion open water swimmer Viola Valli. On the other hand, if she's more the head-in-the-clouds type, she could fly high like Viola Gentry, the first woman pilot from North Carolina and the first woman to set a non-refueled endurance flight record!

Viola Bauer, Cross-Country Skiing, Germany, 1999–2007

Viola Gentry, Aviation, USA, 1928–1954

Viola Goretzki, Rowing, Germany, 1975–1976

Viola Poley, Rowing, Germany, 1976–1978

Viola Valli, Swimming (Long-Distance), Italy, 1997–2002

VIOLET/VIOLETA/VIOLETTA/VIOLETTE

It doesn't take a degree in classics with an emphasis in Latin to figure out where the names Violet, Violeta, Violetta, and Violette come from; if you guessed the purple flower, you'd be right! The Latin word "viola" became the name Violet, and as it spread around the world, the name picked up numerous variant forms in different places and different languages, including the Hungarian, Italian, and Russian Violetta and the French Violette. A girl with one of these flowery names can excel at any sport, like Russian two-time world champion épée fencer Violetta Kolobova, but it's more than likely she'll enjoy pushing herself to be the fastest, whether that's on foot, on the water, or on wheels.

Bulgarian rower Violeta Ninova raced to a double sculls world championship, while the 1920s saw two incredible pioneers in English long-distance runner Violet Piercy, who set the first women's world record in the marathon in 1926, and British race driver Violette Cordery, who set a long-distance driving record the same year and became the first woman to win the Dewar Trophy from the Royal Automobile Club!

Violette Cordery, Auto Racing (Long Distance), England, 1920–1930

Violetta Kolobova, Fencing (Épée), Russia, 2010–current

Violeta Ninova, Rowing, Bulgaria, 1983–1988

Violet Piercy, Long-Distance Running, England, 1926–1936

VIORICA

A floral name from Romania, Viorica comes from the same Latin word for "violet" as *Viola* and *Violet/Violeta/Violetta/Violette* and can refer to the alpine squill flower or sweet violet. Interestingly, while those flowers thrive in woods and mountain grasslands, athletes with this name have almost exclusively excelled at rowing on the water! These include two-time eight world champion Viorica Neculai, Olympic gold-medalist and world champion coxed four rower Viorica Ioja, and Viorica Susanu, whose races in eight, coxless pair, and doubles culls events yielded four Olympic gold medals and a bronze, as well as five golds, three silvers, and three bronzes from World Championships.

Clearly this name is ideal for a girl who will like flowers and watercraft, but if she prefers sports on land, she can get inspiration from Olympic gold-medalist long jumper Viorica Viscopoleanu!

Viorica Ioja, Rowing, Romania, 1983–1986

Viorica Neculai, Rowing, Romania, 1989–1993

Viorica Susanu, Rowing, Romania, 1997–2008

Viorica Viscopoleanu, Track & Field (Long Jump), Romania, 1964–1972

VIRGINIA

While many high-level athletes named Virginia go by the diminutive *Ginny*, the full form (from a Roman family name attributed to a related Latin word meaning "young woman") is still a solid choice. The name hit the world stage in the 1960s, '70s, and '80s with British tennis pro Virgina Wade, who reached the world number one doubles rank (and number two in singles) with dozens of titles, four doubles majors, and a slew of records, including the most times played at Wimbledon (twenty-six).

Give a girl in your family the name Virginia to make her a fantastic all-around competitor and a true master of her preferred event!

Sarah Virginia Wade, Tennis, England, 1968–1986

VIVIAN/VIVIANE/VIVIANNE

"Run, fight, and score" could be the mantra of athletes named the unisex Vivian, Viviane, or Vivianne, all of which descend from an Ancient Latin root meaning "alive." Brazilian mixed martial artist Viviane Araújo held the Pancrase strawweight championship before moving up to flyweight in the UFC; Kenyan long-distance runner Vivian Cheruiyot won four medals (including one gold) at Olympic Games, as well as four golds and two silvers from World Championships and three Diamond League championships; and Dutch soccer player Vivianne Miedema's two Bundesliga championships, FA Women's Super League championship, FA WSL Cup, and UEFA Women's Championship, numerous records, and dozens of player and top-scorer awards place her among the best strikers and goal scorers of all time!

Give your daughter one of the Vivian name variations to inspire her to run fast, fight hard, and bring her team to victory.

Viviane Araújo, MMA (Flyweight/Strawweight), Brazil, 2015–current

Vivian Cheruiyot, Long-Distance Running, Kenya, 1999–current

Anna Margaretha Marina Astrid "Vivianne" Miedema, Soccer (Forward), Arsenal Women Football Club, Netherlands, 2011–current

VOLHA

From far off Belarus comes the name Volha, a variant of *Olga*, which in turn comes from an Old Norse root meaning "blessed." Two athletes have combined the blessings of their physical prowess with hard work and dedication to achieve greatness: visually impaired track and field athlete Volha Zinkevich, who won two gold medals, three silvers, and a bronze in sprinting and long jump events at Paralympic Games, and sprint canoeist Volha Khudzenka, who has collected five golds, three silvers, and five bronzes at World Championships!

Volha Khudzenka, Sprint Canoeing, Belarus, 2011–current

Volha Zinkevich, Para-Athletics, Belarus, 2000–2012

VONETTA

The modern name Vonetta can be a feminine variant of *Vaughn* or *Von* and gained popularity in the United States in the 1970s (alongside the career of Hollywood actress Vonetta McGee). Born in 1973, Vonetta Flowers was a natural athlete who first participated in track and field events before discovering bobsledding. Flowers joined Jill Bakken to compete in the two-woman bobsleigh event at the 2002 Olympic Games in Salt Lake City and returned home with the gold medal, becoming the first Black athlete to win gold at Winter Olympics!

Vonetta is a perfect name for a talented girl with a drive to compete and succeed, who will find her perfect event, sport, or profession in which to shine.

Vonetta Flowers, Bobsleigh, USA, 2002–2006

W

BOYS

WADE

A classic English name, Wade comes from Old English roots for either "ford" or "to go." Wades overwhelmingly are team players, working best alongside their teammates to achieve victory, like NFL Pro Bowl offensive lineman Wade Smith or Canadian ice hockey defenseman Wade Redden, who was selected for two NHL All-Star games and won a World Cup of Hockey with his national team.

But there's one sport you absolutely *must* introduce a boy named Wade in your family to, and that's baseball! He may take after pitchers like All-Star Wade Miley, who threw a no-hitter in 2021; three-time All-Star Wade Davis, who led the National League in saves and won the World Series with the Kansas City Royals; and, of course, legendary Hall of Fame third baseman and slugger Wade Boggs, who played in twelve consecutive All-Star games and won the 1996 World Series with the New York Yankees, five American League batting championships, two Gold Gloves, and eight Silver Sluggers! Boggs was also famously superstitious about specific rituals that ensured his and his team's success, so don't be concerned if your Wade has to have everything just right before he's ready to hit the field.

- **Wade Boggs**, Baseball (Third Baseman), Boston Red Sox, USA, 1982–1999
- **Wade Davis**, Baseball (Pitcher), Tampa Bay Rays, USA, 2009–2021
- **Wade Miley**, Baseball (Pitcher), Arizona Diamondbacks, USA, 2011–current
- **Wade Redden**, Ice Hockey (Defense), Ottawa Senators, Canada, 1996–2013
- **Wade Smith**, Football (Offensive Lineman), Houston Texans, USA, 2003-2014

WALKER

Walker is an uncommon first name, but it comes from a medieval occupational surname for people known as "walkers" or fullers; they would step on or otherwise press wet, unprocessed wool to clean and thicken it. Many Walkers, like Wades, have proven themselves as team players, like Los Angeles Dodgers two-time All-Star pitcher and World Series champion Walker Buehler, who participated in a combined no-hitter in 2018; eight-time All-Star catcher Walker Cooper, who won two World Series championships with the St. Louis Cardinals in the 1940s; and four-time MLS All-Star soccer center-back and two-time MLS Defender of the Year Walker Zimmerman, who has won the US Open Cup,

Supporter's Shield twice, CONCACAF Gold Cup, and CONCACAF Nations League and was named to the MLS Best XI four times.

Outside of the team sports, there has been one competitor with this name who definitely became known for "stepping" on it: off-road and short-course race driver Walker "The Legend" Evans! A member of the Off-Road Motorsports Hall of Fame, Motorsports Hall of Fame of America, and West Coast Stock Car Hall of Fame, Evans racked up over 140 wins in desert and short-course races (including nine wins at the Baja 1000) and twenty-one championships.

A Walker in your family may find his place striving and winning with a team or become legendary on his own by chasing his dreams.

Walker Buehler, Baseball (Pitcher), Los Angeles Dodgers, USA, 2017–current

William Walker Cooper, Baseball (Catcher), St. Louis Cardinals, USA, 1940–1957

Roger Walker "The Legend" Evans, Auto Racing (Short-Course Off-Road Drivers Association), USA, 1969–2000

Walker Zimmerman, Soccer (Center-Back), Nashville Soccer Club, USA, 2013–current

WALLACE

They may have a name that originally meant "outsider" (from Norman French for "foreigner"), but Wallaces are mostly team players in professional and international sports. These include basketball power forward Wallace "Wah Wah" Jones, who won an Olympic gold medal for the United States in 1948; Brazilian Olympic gold-medalist volleyball opposite Wallace de Souza, who took home two gold medals from World Grand Champions Cups and one from the Nations League; and Brazilian soccer center-back Wallace da Silva, who won Campeonato Baiano three times, Copa Libertadores, Copa do Brasil, Campeonato Carioca, and FIFA Club World Cup.

A son you name Wallace (and who doesn't utilize a diminutive like *Wally*) might also succeed at track and field events, like Brazilian Paralympic gold-medalist shot putter Wallace Santos or American sprinter Wallace Spearmon Jr., who won two world championships in the 4x100-meter relay!

Wallace "Wah Wah" Jones, Basketball (Power Forward), Indianapolis Olympians, USA, 1949–1952

Wallace Santos, Para-Athletics, Brazil, 2020

Wallace Reis da Silva, Soccer (Center-Back), Clube de Regatas do Flamengo, Brazil, 2008–current

Wallace de Souza, Volleyball (Opposite), Brazil, 2006–2022

Wallace Spearmon Jr., Track & Field (Sprinting), USA, 2005–2015

WALLY

Wally has traditionally been a diminutive for *Wallace* and *Walter*, though it can appear on its own as well. Wallys seem to prefer rugby, swimming, and baseball (based on the icons of those sports who have come before), but they're not strictly limited to those sports, as you can see with NFL Chicago Bears defensive tackle/end Wally Chambers, who played in three Pro Bowls, and Canadian multiple Hall of Fame inductee harness racing driver Wally Hennessey, who led horses to win over eleven thousand races during his long career.

Australian Rugby League Hall of Famer Wally Prigg revolutionized the position of lock and captained the national team during the 1930s, while Wally "The King" Lewis would continue those trends forty years later by winning three Premierships, two Kangaroo Tours, a Golden Boot, numerous player awards, the rank of "Immortal," and induction into multiple Halls of Fame.

American Wallys have had particular success in the pool and on the baseball diamond.

The 4x200-meter was definitely the key event at Olympic Games, with Wally O'Connor winning the gold medal in the freestyle version in 1948 and the 1924 gold-winning team relay including both Wally Wolf and Wally Ris, the latter who also won a second gold medal that same year in the 100-meter freestyle event. In America's pastime, Wallys are outfielders and sluggers through and through, with two-time All-Star and three-time World Series champion Wally Moses, who is the only player to make two walk off steals of home; three-time All-Star and three-time World Series champ Wally Moon, who won a Gold Glove; and four-time All-Star Wally Berger, who led the National League in home runs and RBIs in 1935.

Walter "Wally" Berger, Baseball (Outfielder), Boston Braves, USA, 1930–1940

Wallace "Wally" Chambers, Football (Defensive Tackle/End), Chicago Bears, USA, 1973–1979

Walter "Wally" Hennessey, Horse Racing (Harness Driver), Canada, 1975–2005

Walter "Wally" (The King) Lewis, Rugby (Five-Eighth/Lock), Fortitude Valley Diehards, Australia, 1978–1992

Wallace "Wally" Moon, Baseball (Outfielder), Los Angeles Dodgers, USA, 1954–1965

Wallace "Wally" Moses, Baseball (Right Fielder), Philadelphia Athletics, USA, 1935–1951

James Wallace "Wally" O'Connor, Swimming (Freestyle)/Water Polo (Field Player), USA, 1924–1936

Walter "Wally" Prigg, Rugby (Lock), Central Charlestown, Australia, 1927–1939

Walter "Wally" Ris, Swimming (Freestyle), USA, 1948

Wallace "Wally" Wolf Jr., Swimming (Freestyle/Medley), USA, 1948–1964

WALT

While *Walters* are quite varied in the competitive events they enjoy and dominate, Walts are a bit more focused, notably in baseball, football, and basketball! Under the lights, fans have cheered on MLB All-Stars like American League RBI leader first baseman Walt "Moose" Dropo and World Series champion shortstop Walt Weiss; on the gridiron, Dallas Texans/Kansas City Chiefs linebacker Walt Corey was an AFL All-Star in 1963 and a two-time AFL champion; and on the hardwood, four-time All-Star center and Hall of Famer Walt Bellamy won Olympic gold, and Hall of Fame point guard Walt "Clyde" Frazier played in seven All-Star games, earned an NBA All-Star Game MVP, and won two NBA championships with the New York Knicks.

Name your son Walt, or *Walter* and call him Walt for short, and teach him the fundamentals of baseball, football, and basketball while also imparting to him the importance of playing with others and good sportsmanship. However, if he seems like he likes going fast rather than playing on a team, then encourage that too; he may feel the need for speed like drag racer and land speed record-breaker Walt Arfons, who was part of the first drag racing team to top 150 miles per hour in the quarter mile, the first to pilot a dragster with a jet engine, and more!

Walter "Walt" Arfons, Auto Racing (Dragsters), USA, 1952–1965

Walter "Walt" Bellamy, Basketball (Center), Chicago Packers, USA, 1961–1974

Walter "Walt" Corey, Football (Linebacker), Dallas Texans, USA, 1960–1966

Walter "Walt" (Moose) Dropo, Baseball (First Baseman), Boston Red Sox, USA, 1949–1961

Walter "Walt" Frazier, Basketball (Point Guard), New York Knicks, USA, 1967–1979

Walter "Walt" Weiss, Baseball (Shortstop), Oakland Athletics, USA, 1987–2000

WALTER

A militant name invoking strength, Walter comes from Germanic roots for "power" or "authority" and "army." Walters have spread out across many different sports and competitions, with one rising to the top in each field. Walters who have become champions alongside teams include sport shooter Walter Stokes, who won the 1924 Olympic gold medal with the USA free rifle team.

Hall of Fame Washington Senators pitcher Walter Johnson dominated Major League Baseball during his career from 1907 to 1927, during which time he won two World Series championships, two American League MVPs, and three Triple Crowns; led the American League in wins six times, ERA five times, and strikeouts a massive twelve times; pitched a no-hitter; and set the record for career shutouts (110) that he still holds today.

Last but certainly not least in team sports is football Hall of Fame Walter "Sweetness" Payton, one of the greatest running backs (and overall football players) of all time! During his thirteen seasons with the Chicago Bears, Payton played in nine Pro Bowls; won Super Bowl XX; was named NFL MVP, Offensive Player of the Year, and Man of the Year; led in rushing yards and rushing touchdowns; and set numerous records and still has the most starts of any running back.

Onto the individual sports, American track and field athlete Walter Tewksbury headed to Paris for the 1900 Olympic Games, where he took home two gold medals, two silvers, and a bronze in sprinting and hurdling events. Indoors, Walter Williams Jr. has won a record forty-seven Professional Bowlers Association Tour titles, been named PBA Player of the Year a co-record seven times, and bowled more than 110 perfect games; outside, he's also a nine-time horseshoes world champion. And then there's World Golf Hall of Famer Walter Hagen, who won fifty-eight events and eleven majors (third most of all-time after Nicklaus and Woods).

Walter is a name that will bring your son an open vista of possibilities, with the underlying power and authority to conquer whatever field, sport, or profession he chooses!

- **Walter Hagen**, Golf, USA, 1912–1942
- **Walter Johnson**, Baseball (Pitcher), Washington Senators, USA, 1907–1927
- **Walter "Sweetness" Payton**, Football (Running Back), Chicago Bears, USA, 1975–1987
- **Walter Stokes**, Sport Shooting (Rifle), USA, 1924
- **Walter Tewksbury**, Track & Field (Sprinting/Hurdling), USA, 1899–1913
- **Walter Williams Jr.**, Bowling/Horseshoes, USA, 1970–current

WARREN

Whether it's triumphing on the field or overcoming adversities to reach untold heights, a Warren will be the shining jewel in your family with a name that comes from Norman French and either a root meaning "animal enclosure" or a place name in Normandy.

Two incredible Warrens have been inducted into the Pro Football Hall of Fame, starting with seven-time Pro Bowl defensive tackle Warren Sapp, who won Super Bowl XXXVII with the Tampa Bay Buccaneers and was named NFL Defensive Player of the Year. He's in good company with quarterback Warren Moon, who began his professional career racking up accomplishments in Canadian football before joining the NFL; there he would play in nine Pro Bowls, be named NFL Offensive Player of the Year and Man of the Year, and lead the league in passing yards twice and passing touchdowns.

Last but not least is Major League Baseball pitcher Warren Spahn, who played most of his twenty-one seasons with the Boston (then

Milwaukee) Braves. The Hall of Fame inductee played in seventeen All-Star games; won the 1957 World Series and a Cy Young award; led the National League in wins eight times, ERA three times, and strikeouts four times; and threw two no-hitters.

Harold Warren Moon, Football (Quarterback), Houston Oilers, USA, 1978–2000

Warren Sapp, Football (Defensive Tackle), Tampa Bay Buccaneers, USA, 1995–2007

Warren Spahn, Baseball (Pitcher), Boston Braves, USA, 1942–1965

WAYNE

Even if your family has never featured any wagon-makers, you can still consider the name Wayne (from Old English for "wagon") for an upcoming child. Notable athletes with this name have included 1970s water skier Wayne Grimditch and, more recently, European football's Wayne Rooney, but there's one Wayne who will always stand above the rest. That, of course, is Wayne Gretzky, the "Great One" and one of ice hockey's top players of all time. His long career stretched from 1978 to 1999 and included a string of major accomplishments, including leading goal scorer in NHL history and the only player to score more than two hundred points in a season (which he did *four* times) and over one hundred points scored in sixteen seasons. Gretzky famously played for four different NHL teams, starting with a dazzling stint winning four championships with the Edmonton Oilers.

Wayne may be perfect for a child in your family, especially if you enjoy the cold and indoor sports, and he'll be a "great one" in whatever field he chooses to pursue.

Wayne "the Great One" Gretzky, Ice Hockey (Center), Edmonton Oilers, Canada, 1978–1999

Wayne Grimditch, Water Skiing, USA, 1969–1978

Wayne Rooney, Soccer (Forward/Midfielder), Manchester United, England, 2002–2021

WERNER

A boy you name Werner won't necessarily be part of a "protecting army" (with a name that comes from Old German roots for "aware/cautious" and "army"), but he might find his temperament and skills lead him to long bike rides, throwing sports, or playing soccer with his friends. In those respects, he'll follow in the footsteps (or foot pedals) of athletes like German two-time world champion 2000-meter tandem cyclist Werner Otto, Swiss four-time world champion shot putter Werner Günthör, or teammates full back Werner Kohlmeyer and defender Werner Liebrich, who were both on the German soccer team that won the 1954 FIFA World Cup!

Werner Günthör, Track & Field (Shot Put), Switzerland, 1986–1993

Werner Kohlmeyer, Soccer (Full Back), 1. Fußball-Club Kaiserslautern e. V., Germany, 1941–1960

Werner Liebrich, Soccer (Defender), 1. Fußball-Club Kaiserslautern e. V., Germany, 1943–1962

Werner Otto, Track Cycling, Germany, 1968–1973

WES

A natural diminutive of *Wesley* and *Westley*, Wes is a cool short name that's quite versatile. Champion athletes going by Wes have played on offense and defense, outside and indoors, setting records and playing perfect games. Manchester United soccer defender Wes Brown collected a number of trophies during his career, including the Premier League championship five times, FA Cup twice, Football League Cup twice, FA Community Shield, and UEFA Champions League twice, while NBA center Wes Unseld earned five All-Star selections, an NBA MVP, and Finals MVP; won an NBA championship; led the league in rebounds during his 984 games with the Bullets; and was inducted into the Basketball Hall of Fame.

On the football field, athletes named Wes are fast and agile, making them ideal wide receivers like four-time Pro Bowler and Hall of Famer Wes Chandler, who led the league in receiving yards and touchdowns, and Wes Welker, who played in five Pro Bowls, led the NFL in receptions three times, and shares the record for the longest receiving touchdown at ninety-nine yards.

Indoors, professional bowler Wes Malott has won ten Professional Bowlers Association titles and one major and rolled over forty perfect games!

- **Wesley "Wes" Brown**, Soccer (Defender), Manchester United Football Club, England, 1996–2018
- **Wesley "Wes" Chandler**, Football (Wide Receiver), San Diego Chargers, USA, 1978–1988
- **Wesley "Wes" Malott**, Bowling, USA, 2005–current
- **Westley "Wes" Unseld Sr.**, Basketball (Center), Baltimore Bullets, USA, 1968–1981
- **Wesley "Wes" Welker**, Football (Wide Receiver), New England Patriots, USA, 2004–2015

WESLEY

With a name that originated as a place name in Old English meaning "west meadow" or "clearing," it just makes sense that Dutch attacking midfielder Wesley Sneijder reached the top ranks of his position with numerous European and Middle Eastern championships, a UEFA Champions League, and FIFA Club World Cup as well as player awards like UEFA Club Midfielder of the Year, FIFA World Cup Silver Ball, FIFA World Cup Bronze Boot, FIFA World Cup All-Star Team, FIFA World Cup Dream Team, and FIFA FIFPro World XI.

Not in a meadow but on long racecourses, Kenyan runner Wesley Korir won the Boston Marathon and the Los Angeles Marathon twice, while somewhat far from meadows, Wesley So earned his chess Grandmaster status and won the 2019 FIDE World Fischer Random Chess Championship, two Grand Chess Tour titles, and individual and team gold medals at the Forty-Second Chess Olympiad.

Name your son Wesley to give him a love of playing outside and be sure to teach him how to play soccer, but also be open to his indoor hobbies.

- **Wesley Korir**, Long-Distance Running, Kenya, 2008–2017
- **Wesley Sneijder**, Soccer (Attacking Midfielder), Amsterdamsche Football Club Ajax, Netherlands, 2002–2019
- **Wesley So**, Chess, USA, 2005–current

WHITEY

See *Edoardo/Eduardo/Edward* for Edward "Whitey" Ford and *Georg/George/Georges* for George "Whitey" Kurowski.

WIL/WILL

Another set of very versatile names like *Wes*, Wil and Will are typically short for *William* but can also be diminutives for other "Wil-" names or used as full names on their own. Wils and Wills can be good at anything, from swimming, like American breaststroke and medley expert Will Licon, who took home a set of each color medal from World Championships, to table tennis, like English Paralympic gold-medalist and three-time silver medalist Will Bayley, and wheelchair rugby and para-cycling, like multi-talented Paralympic athlete Will Groulx, who won multiple gold medals in different competitions in both events.

How about a Wil and a Will in track and field?

Both Wilbert "Wil" London and Will Claye won two world championships in mixed relay/4x400-meter relay and triple jump, respectively.

Meanwhile, the biggest category of successful athletes with these names are the baseball players! In the All-Star category are not one but two Will Smiths: the Los Angeles Dodgers World Series champion catcher, and the relief pitcher who set MLB records by winning back-to-back-to-back World Series championships from 2021 to 2023 with the Atlanta Braves, Houston Astros, and Texas Rangers. Way back in the late 1800s, American Association pennant-winner and two-time American Association wins champion pitcher Will "Whoop-La" White dazzled crowds with his incredible curveballs as he set multiple records (some of which he still holds, like complete games, games started, innings pitched, and batters faced), and more than one hundred years later, six-time All-Star first baseman Will Clark would lead the National League in RBIs and win a National League Championship Series MVP, a Gold Glove, two Silver Sluggers, and a Golden Spikes award!

Naming your son *William*, *Wilfredo*, *Wilbert*, or something similar? Call him Will (or Wil) and get that kid in T-ball as soon as he's ready.

- **William "Will" Bayley**, Table Tennis, England, 2008–current
- **William "Will" Clark Jr.**, Baseball (First Baseman), San Francisco Giants, USA, 1986–2000
- **Will Claye**, Track & Field (Triple Jump), USA, 2011–current
- **William "Will" Groulx**, Wheelchair Rugby/Para-Cycling, USA, 2004–2016
- **William "Will" Licon**, Swimming (Breaststroke/Medley), USA, 2014–current
- **Wilbert "Wil" London III**, Track & Field (Sprinting), USA, 2017–current
- **William "Will" Smith**, Baseball (Catcher), Los Angeles Dodgers, USA, 2019–current
- **William "Will" Smith**, Baseball (Relief Pitcher), Atlanta Braves, USA, 2012–current
- **William "Will" (Whoop-La) White**, Baseball (Pitcher), Cincinnati Red Stockings, USA, 1877–1886

WILBUR

Alternatively claimed as coming from Germanic roots meaning "resolute" or "willful" or from "wild boar" in Middle English, Wilbur is definitely seen as an old-fashioned name these days. However, it's ready for a comeback and would be a great pick for a family who loves baseball or auto racing! Get inspiration for a Wilbur in your family from three-time MLB All-Star pitcher Wilbur Wood, who twice led the American League in wins, and racing driver Wilbur Shaw, whose love affair with the Indianapolis Motor Speedway saw him win the Indianapolis 500 three times, become the first person to win it twice in a row, and head up efforts to restore the track after its disuse during World War II.

- **Warren Wilbur Shaw**, Auto Racing (Indianapolis 500), USA, 1927–1954
- **Wilbur Wood Jr.**, Baseball (Pitcher), Chicago White Sox, USA, 1961–1978

WILFRED/WILFRIED

Like *Wilbur*, Wilfred (from Old English roots meaning "desiring peace") isn't exactly topping the charts of baby names in the United States in the twenty-first century, although it does retain a certain popularity in other places around the world—Germany even has its own form in Wilfried. Athletes with these names who have competed on their own have proven to be fast and strong, like Kenyan Olympic gold-medalist and world champion 800-meter medium-distance runner Wilfred Bungei; German wrestler Wilfried Dietrich, who won a gold medal, two silvers, and two bronzes at both Olympic Games and World Championships in both freestyle and Greco-Roman events; and Puerto Rican Hall of Fame boxer Wilfred Benítez, who became the youngest world champion at only seventeen, on his way to becoming a triple world champion in three different weight classes.

More Wilfreds and Wilfrieds have competed and won as part of teams, such as biathletes like five-time world champion (relay and team) Wilfried Pallhuber. Luger Wilfried Huber raced to an Olympic gold medal in 1994 with the Italian team and English cricket all-rounder Wilfred Rhodes dazzled audiences with his slow bowling as he set records that still hold today for the most appearances in first-class cricket (1,110) and most wickets taken (4,204) and earned induction into the ICC Cricket Hall of Fame.

Bring the name Wilfred (or Wilfried) back into prominence by giving it to your son and encouraging him on his athletic and competitive endeavors!

- **Wilfred "Wilfredo" Benítez**, Boxing (Welterweight/Light Middleweight), Puerto Rico, 1973–1990
- **Wilfred Bungei**, Track & Field (Middle-Distance Running), Kenya, 1998–2010
- **Wilfried Dietrich**, Greco-Roman/Freestyle Wrestling, Germany, 1956–1972
- **Wilfried Huber**, Luge, Italy, 1985–2010
- **Wilfried "Willi the Kid" Pallhuber**, Biathlon, Italy, 1985–2007
- **Wilfred Rhodes**, Cricket (All-Rounder), Yorkshire County Cricket Club, England, 1898–1930

WILLIAM

A very popular name in English-speaking countries, William comes from Germanic roots for "will" and "helmet" or "protection." Protecting one's brain is crucial for competing in something like chess, the preferred game of 1800s expert William Lewis, who may have been the first player called "Grandmaster," and William Watson, who was bestowed the official rank of Grandmaster in 1990. Other Williams are famous for rifle sport shooting (American William Leushner and English William Pimm, who competed against each other in the 1908 and 1912 Olympic Games and won a gold, silver, and two bronzes and two golds and a bronze, respectively) and swimming (French 4x100-meter freestyle world champion William Meynard and Australian three-time Paralympic gold-medalist William Martin).

American gridiron football has witnessed the excellence of Williams, too, with four-time Pro Bowlers in Atlanta Falcons running back William Andrews and defensive end William Fuller.

Meanwhile, many Williams have thrown, run, vaulted, rolled, and leapt to victory in track and field events, ranging from pole vaulting (like American William Hoyt, who won the gold medal at the first modern Olympics in 1896) to long jump (like Swedish Olympic gold- and bronze-medalist William Petersson), 4x400-meter relay (like American Olympic gold-medalist and world record-breaker William Stevenson), and para-athletics and lawn bowls (like William McLeod of Scotland, who won Paralympic gold medals in the 60-meter dash and singles lawn bowls).

Williams have succeeded in other sports, too, like American William Larned, who reached the world number one spot in tennis singles in 1901 and won forty-eight titles and seven Grand Slams around the turn of the twentieth century. There are not one, not two, but three Olympic gold-medalists named William Smith, with the English field hockey player (1920), South African boxer (1924), and American freestyle wrestler (1952). They're in good company with American middleweight boxer William "Gorilla" Jones, who won the National Boxing Association Middleweight Boxing Championship of the World title in 1932 and ended his career with 122 wins, and Uruguayan soccer defender William Martínez, whose long list of wins include the Torneo de Honor three times, Copa Libertadores twice, Intercontinental Cup, the 1956 South American Championship, and the 1950 FIFA World Cup.

With training, dedication, and lots of hard work, a William in your family could become a world champion or Olympic gold-medalist too! Support him by teaching him about fair play and sportsmanship and helping him to find the best place to focus his talents.

- **William Andrews**, Football (Running Back), Atlanta Falcons, USA, 1979–1986
- **William Fuller Jr.**, Football (Defensive End), Houston Oilers, USA, 1984–1998
- **William Hoyt**, Track & Field (Pole Vaulting), USA, 1896
- **William "Gorilla" Jones**, Boxing (Middleweight), USA, 1924–1940
- **William Larned**, Tennis, USA, 1890–1911
- **William Leushner**, Sport Shooting (Rifle), USA, 1901–1920
- **William Lewis**, Chess, England, 1822–1870
- **William Martin**, Swimming (Freestyle/Butterfly), Australia, 2019–current
- **William Martínez Carreras**, Soccer (Defender), Club Atlético Peñarol, Uruguay, 1943–1970
- **William McLeod**, Para-Athletics/Lawn Bowls, Scotland, 1976–1980
- **William Meynard**, Swimming (Freestyle), France, 2009–2016
- **Reinhold William Petersson**, Track & Field (Sprinting/Long Jump), Sweden, 1918–1924
- **William Pimm**, Sport Shooting (Rifle), England, 1908–1912
- **William Smith**, Field Hockey (Outside Right), England, 1920
- **William Smith**, Boxing (Bantamweight), South Africa, 1924–1936
- **William Smith**, Freestyle Wrestling, USA, 1952
- **William Stevenson**, Track & Field (Sprinting), USA, 1924
- **William Watson**, Chess, England, 1990–current

WILLIE/WILLY

The longer, and some would say more casual, diminutive of *William* is Willie, a name that has appeared on leaderboards and trophies from Scottish golfers to American football and baseball players. Wherever Willies show up, though, they have the capacity to succeed, even in such varied sports as ice hockey (like Canadian world champion defenseman Willie Mitchell, who won two Stanley Cups with the Los Angeles Kings), horse racing (like jockey Willie Martinez, who has won over 3,300 races), figure skating (like Austrian four-time world champion Willy Böckl), basketball (like four-time NBA All-Star small forward Willie Naulls, who won three NBA championships with the Boston Celtics), lawn bowls (like Willie Wood of Scotland, who won eight gold medals, four silvers, and four bronzes from World Outdoor Championships), and pool (like nineteen-time World Straight Pool Champion Willie Mosconi, who set numerous records, invented multiple trick shots, and is ranked among the greatest billiards players of all time).

Up next are Willies on the links! Scottish Willie Anderson had nine wins, four majors, the record for winning three consecutive titles, and induction into the World Golf Hall of Fame; and Scottish Willie Macfarlane won twenty-two events and one major in the first half of the twentieth century.

The history of track and field events at Olympic Games is rife with Willies on podiums, with some of the most successful including American gold medalist long jumper Willie Steele (1948), gold medalist hurdler Willie Davenport (1968), and sprinter Willie Smith, who won a gold medal in the 1984 4x400-meter relay, as well as two gold medals in the same event at Athletics World Cup events!

Getting into the biggest collections of Willies takes us to the football field first. The Pro Football Hall of Fame is full of highly successful men with this name, including Green Bay Packers five-time Pro Bowl defensive end Willie Davis, who won five NFL championships and two Super Bowls; Kansas City Chiefs two-time AFL All-Star and six-time Pro Bowl middle linebacker Willie Lanier, who won the Super Bowl in 1970 and was named NFL Man of the Year in 1972; Green Bay Packers eight-time Pro Bowl safety and 1962 interceptions leader Willie Wood, who won five NFL championships and two Super Bowl championships; and five-time AFL All-Star and four-time Pro Bowl cornerback Willie Brown, who is tied for the most passes intercepted in an AFL game (four) and who won the 1967 AFL championship and Super Bowl XI with the Oakland Raiders.

As with the *Will*s, many Willies have an innate love of the game of baseball—and a phenomenal track record to show it!

There are National Baseball Hall of Famers like six-time All-Star first baseman Willie McCovey, who led the National League in home runs three times and RBIs twice and was named National League MVP, and Pittsburgh Pirates seven-time All-Star left fielder/first baseman Willie Stargell, who led the National League in home runs twice and RBIs; was named National League MVP, World Series MVP, and National League Championship Series MVP; and won two World Series championships and the Roberto Clemente Award. Of course, the number one Willie in all of our hearts is "the Say Hey Kid," Willie Mays. With twenty-four All-Star appearances (tied for second of all time), two National League MVPs, a National League batting championship, twelve Gold Gloves, the Commissioner's Award, the 1954 World Series championship; leading the National League in home runs four times and stolen bases four times; and earning numerous records and accomplishments (including hitting four home runs in one game), the center fielder is cemented for all-time as one of the greatest ball players the world has ever seen!

Call your son Willie to instill in him the competitive spirit and excellence of athletes before him. You never know where his sporting adventures will take him, but he'll always rise to the occasion and try his very best.

- **William "Willie" Anderson**, Golf, Scotland, 1896–1910
- **Willy Böckl**, Figure Skating, Austria, 1913–1928
- **William "Willie" Brown**, Football (Cornerback), Denver Broncos, USA, 1963–1978
- **William "Willie" Davenport**, Track & Field (Hurdling), USA, 1964–1976
- **Willie Davis**, Football (Defensive End), Green Bay Packers, USA, 1958–1969
- **Willie Lanier**, Football (Middle Linebacker), Kansas City Chiefs, USA, 1967–1977
- **William "Willie" Macfarlane**, Golf, Scotland, 1912–1946
- **Willie Martinez**, Horse Racing (Jockey), USA, 1989–current
- **Willie "the Say Hey Kid" Mays Jr.**, Baseball (Center Fielder), San Francisco Giants, USA, 1951–1973
- **Willie McCovey**, Baseball (First Baseman), San Francisco Giants, USA, 1959–1980
- **William "Willie" Mitchell**, Ice Hockey (Defense), Minnesota Wild, Canada, 2000–2016
- **William "Willie" Mosconi**, Pool (Straight), USA, 1933–1982
- **William "Willie" Naulls**, Basketball (Small Forward), New York Knicks, USA, 1956–1966
- **Willie Smith III**, Track & Field (Sprinting), USA, 1979–1996

Wilver "Willie" Stargell, Baseball (Left Fielder/First Baseman), Pittsburgh Pirates, USA, 1962–1982

William "Willie" Steele, Track & Field (Long Jump), USA, 1948

William "Willie" Wood, Bowls, Scotland, 1974–2011

William "Willie" Wood Sr., Football (Safety), Green Bay Packers, USA, 1960–1971

WILLIS

An evolution of an English surname based on the name *Will*, Willis as a first name brings with it precision accuracy that can be applied to shooting, passing, or catching. NFL running back Willis McGahee earned two Pro Bowl selections during his stint with the Baltimore Ravens; Willis Lee headed to the Antwerp Olympic Games in 1920 to win five gold medals, a silver, and a bronze in various sport shooting events; and New York Knicks seven-time All-Star center Willis Reed Jr. won two NBA championships, was named NBA Finals MVP twice and All-Star Game MVP, and was inducted into the Basketball Hall of Fame!

Willis Augustus Lee Jr., Sport Shooting (Rifle), USA, 1920

Willis McGahee III, Football (Running Back), Baltimore Ravens, USA, 2003–2013

Willis Reed Jr., Basketball (Center), New York Knicks, USA, 1964–1974

WILT

Wilton, typically an English surname that came from towns in England whose names meant "willow town," "well town," and "town on the river Wylye," is a pretty rare given name these days, but it has a huge legacy when it comes to sports. And if your family loves basketball and tends to have tall children, then *Wilton* (and its diminutive Wilt) may be a perfect choice for you! It's the name shared by basketball legend Wilt Chamberlain, the seven-foot, one-inch NBA center whose outstanding career (not to mention off-the-court exploits and personality) has placed him among not only the greatest basketball players ever, but also the greatest American athletes overall. During his fourteen seasons, Chamberlain played in thirteen All-Star Games; won NBA championships with the Philadelphia 76ers and Los Angeles Lakers, seven scoring championships, and eleven rebounding championships; was named NBA Finals MVP and All-Star Game MVP; and led the league in assists. He set more than seventy records, including the most points in one game (one hundred) and the most rebounds in one game (fifty-five), led the NBA to change multiple rules based on his dominance of the game, and was inducted into the Naismith Memorial Basketball Hall of Fame.

Wilton "Wilt" Chamberlain, Basketball (Center), Los Angeles Lakers, USA, 1958–1973

WLADIMIR

A typically Russian variant of the Eastern European name *Vladimir*, Wladimir has become known predominantly in combat sports, whether it's elegant swordplay or brutal knockouts in the ring. Olympic gold medals tie together the two most famous Wladimirs, with German épée fencer Wladimir Resnitschenko, who won gold in 1992, and Ukrainian boxer Wladimir Klitschko, who took home the super-heavyweight win in 1996. Together with his brother Vitali, Klitschko dominated the heavyweight boxing scene for over ten years, from 2004 to 2015; during this "Klitschko Era," he was a two-time world champion and set multiple records, including longest cumulative heavyweight title reign of all time, most fighters beaten for the heavyweight championship, most wins and title defenses of the unified championship, and more.

Consider the name Wladimir for your son who will grow up to be a powerful physical presence and unbeatable in one-on-one confrontations.

- **Wladimir Klitschko**, Boxing (Heavyweight), Ukraine, 1996–2017
- **Wladimir Resnitschenko**, Fencing (Épée), USSR/Germany, 1988–1992

WOLFGANG

Wolfgangs don't necessarily travel with wild canines, though their name does come from Old German roots for "wolf" and "path" or "travel." Instead, notable competitors with this name (mainly from Germany) have harnessed their hunger for victory into things like equestrian events, chess, soccer, and sled and sleigh winter sports! Equestrian Wolfgang Brinkmann won Olympic gold with the German show jumping team and Wolfgang Uhlmann earned chess Grandmaster status in 1959 and played well into the 2010s. The West German 1974 FIFA World Cup championship team included not one but two Wolfgangs, with goalkeeper Kleff (who also won the Bundesliga five times, DFB-Pokal, UEFA Cup twice, and UEFA European Championship) and attacking midfielder Overath (who was named to the FIFA XI and FIFA World Cup All-Star Team). Racing down icy tracks, Austrian luger Wolfgang Linger won two gold medals and a silver at three successive Olympic Games; three golds and two bronzes at World Championships; and a gold, silver, and three bronzes at World Cup Championships, while German bobsleigh pilot Wolfgang Hoppe collected two golds, three silvers, and a bronze at Olympics; six golds, a silver, and seven bronzes at World Championships; and four golds, three silvers, and four bronzes at World Cup Championships!

Give your son the spirit of a wolf and the dedication of these champion athletes with the name Wolfgang.

- **Wolfgang Brinkmann**, Equestrian (Show Jumping), Germany, 1988
- **Wolfgang Hoppe**, Bobsleigh, Germany, 1983–1998
- **Wolfgang Kleff**, Soccer (Goalkeeper), Borussia Mönchengladbach, Germany, 1968–2008
- **Wolfgang Linger**, Luge, Austria, 2000–2014
- **Wolfgang Overath**, Soccer (Attacking Midfielder), 1. Fußball-Club Köln 01/07 e. V., Germany, 1962–1977
- **Wolfgang Uhlmann**, Chess, Germany, 1954–2012

GIRLS

WEI/WEI-

As is the Chinese tradition, the unisex name Wei (sometimes with a secondary name attached) can mean a variety of different things based on the characters used to write it; in this case, it can mean "power," "high" or "towering," "great" or "extraordinary," and more. "Power" is a particularly apt translation because two women with this name have shown their immense strength in international weightlifting and powerlifting events! Taiwanese Chen Wei-ling won an Olympic gold medal in weightlifting and a gold, silver, and two bronze medals in powerlifting at World Games and set multiple records for the 44- and 47-kilogram weight classes, while weightlifter Deng Wei of China also won Olympic gold, as well as five world championships and multiple world records.

Name your daughter Wei and let her develop her powerful inner strength into a winning form, whether that's in the gym, the classroom, or any other place she channels her competitive nature.

Chen Wei-ling, Weightlifting/Powerlifting, Taiwan, 2003–2016

Deng Wei, Weightlifting, China, 2010–2019

WEILI

Typically based on *Wei*, Weili takes the strength of that name and adds a ferocity and tenacity that will serve someone well in the ring or cage (or anywhere else for that matter). A Weili in your family can look up to the Chinese two-time UFC Women's Strawweight champion and former Kunlun Fight Women's Strawweight Champion mixed martial artist Zhang Weili, who has studied sanda, kickboxing, muay thai, and shuai jiao and currently holds a 24–3 MMA record!

Zhang Weili "Magnum," MMA (Flyweight/Strawweight), China, 2013–current

WENDIE/WENDY

Considered a very "friendly" name and popularized by James Barrie in *Peter Pan*, Wendy is related to the Welsh *Gwendolen* (from a root meaning "white" or "blessed") and has a variant in Wendie. In the wide world of sports have been several world champion Wendys, like sprinter Wendy Vereen, platform diver Wendy Wyland, and Australian four-time world champion surfer and Surfing Walk of Fame inductee Wendy Botha. Some of the biggest winners with these names include Swiss alpine ski racer Wendy Holdener, whose medal collection includes a gold, two silvers, and three bronzes from Olympic Games; three golds and three silvers from World Championships; and five wins, twenty second places, and twenty-three third places in World Cup races, while French soccer center-back Wendie Renard's incredible career has seen her win the Division 1 Féminine championship sixteen times, Coupe de France ten times, UEFA Women's Champions League eight times, Trophée des Championnes twice, Cyprus Cup twice, and a SheBelieves Cup while being named to FIFA Women's World Cup All-Star Team, FIFA Women's World Cup Dream Team, FIFA FIFPro World XI seven times, and more!

Name your daughter Wendy (or Wendie) and she'll be a fierce—and friendly—competitor and winner, whether she enjoys playing soccer, skiing, surfing, diving, running, or anything else.

Wendy Botha, Surfing, South Africa/Australia, 1987–1992

Wendy Holdener, Alpine Skiing, Switzerland, 2010–current

Wendie Renard, Soccer (Center-Back), Olympique Lyonnais Féminin, France, 2006–current

Wenda "Wendy" Vereen, Track & Field (Sprinting), USA, 1984–1996

Janna Wendy Wyland, Diving, USA, 1982–1986

WENMEI

Do you hope for a girl who will love racquet sports but also be whimsical and have her head in the clouds? Consider the Chinese name Wenmei, which can be written with characters meaning "cloud patterns" or "rose"! Starting early with World Junior Championships wins, Li Wenmei has had a powerful badminton career with team wins at both Sudirman Cup and Uber Cup events and can be a source of inspiration for a girl who shares her name.

Li Wenmei, Badminton, China, 2010–current

WHITNEY

From an Old English place name meaning "white island," the name Whitney has long been a staple in the United States and thus has appeared on several podiums and leaderboards. Freestyle wrestler Whitney Conder won twice at Pan American Games; soccer defender Whitney Engen's time on the United States women's national team saw it win a W-League championship, WPS championship, FA Women's Super League, three Algarve Cups, a CONCACAF Women's Championship, SheBelieves Cup, and the 2015 FIFA Women's World Cup; and world champion swimmer Whitney Hedgepeth is an Olympic gold-medalist.

Name your daughter Whitney and introduce her to wrestling, soccer, and swimming and she may find her lifelong favorite event!

Whitney Conder, Freestyle Wrestling, USA, 2015–current

Whitney Engen, Soccer (Defender), Chicago Red Stars, USA, 2009–2016

Whitney Hedgepeth, Swimming (Backstroke/Freestyle/Medley), USA, 1987–1996

WILLA

While the name Willa may be a feminine variant of *William* (meaning "will" and "helmet" or "protection"), American water-skiing legend Willa Cook wore no helmet during her daring acrobatics racing across the water! Cook won dozens of national events, five world events, and the overall world title three times while revolutionizing the sport by adding ballet moves to create swivel skiing and the beginnings of freestyle.

A young Willa in your family will make her mark on a sport she chooses, finding victory and the opportunity to express her own unique style!

Willa Cook, Water Skiing, USA, 1945–1959

WILMA

An old-fashioned name that also descends from *William* by way of *Wilhelm* and *Wilhelmina*, Wilma is all about speed and dedication. This is an ideal name for a girl whom you'll have to chase around the house, but who will have a love of running and competing while overcoming whatever gets in her way. Dutch long-distance runner Wilma Rusman won both the Rotterdam and Reykjavik Marathons, while closer to home, sprinter Wilma Rudolph made history. Suffering polio as a child and forced to wear a leg brace for most of her youth, Rudolph became a world-class athlete; at sixteen years old, she won a bronze medal at the 1956 Olympics, and then at the 1960 Games, she took home three gold medals while setting multiple world records! A true inspiration, Wilma Rudolph continued her hard work after her sprinting career was over, fighting for equal rights and working with athletes and children.

Wilma Rudolph, Track & Field (Sprinting), USA, 1956–1962

Wilma Rusman, Long-Distance Running, Netherlands, 1983–1989

WINIFRED

The name Winifred has uncertain origins, from the Latin *Winifreda*, and possibly a Welsh name meaning "blessed" and "stream" or "pacify," or from a variant of the Old English *Winfred*, which might have meant "friend of peace." Whatever the true source, Winifreds had some interesting accomplishments in England in the early 1900s. Tennis player Winifred McNair won the 1913 Wimbledon doubles title and a doubles gold medal at the 1920 Olympic Games, while aviation pioneer Winifred Spooner flew to the Siddeley and Harmon Trophies in the 1928 and 1929 King's Cup air races!

Bring the name Winifred into the twenty-first century with a girl in your family who will fly high and work really well with partners.

Winifred McNair, Tennis, England, 1906–1925

Winifred Spooner, Aviation, England, 1927–1933

WYOMIA

The name Wyomia can come from a Native American Algonquian-Wakashan word for "wide plain," which sounds like a perfect practice location for runners like Wyomia Tyus. She won gold in the 100-meter and silver in the 4x100-meter relay in her first Olympic Games in 1964, and then in 1968 took home two more gold medals in the same two events to become the first Olympian ever to retain the 100-meter title!

Consider the iconic name Wyomia for your daughter and give her the gift of quickness and repeated success through hard work and practice.

Wyomia Tyus, Track & Field (Sprinting), USA, 1964–1982

X

BOYS

XABIER/XAVIER

Having a child is always the start of a new part of your life, and while it doesn't always come with a new home, you can choose for your son the name Xavier (or its variant form Xabier), which comes from a Basque place name meaning "new house." Such a boy could grow up to enjoy racing across waterways or playing team sports with his friends, especially if he follows in the footsteps of tremendous Xabiers and Xaviers who have come before him. These include Olympic gold-medalists like Spanish sailor Xabier Fernández, who also took home three gold medals from World Championships. In the United States, NFL cornerback Xavier Rhodes played in three Pro Bowls during his time with the Minnesota Vikings, while in Australia, cricket bowler Xavier Doherty helped his national team win the 2015 Cricket World Cup.

Spanish football (soccer) has seen the ascendancy of two athletes with these names going by the diminutives Xabi and Xavi, two incredible midfielders who led their national team to victory in the 2010 FIFA World Cup! Spanish Player of the Year and La Liga Best Midfielder Xabier "Xabi" Alonso won multiple European championships and was named FIFA FIFPro World XI twice. Meanwhile, in more than one thousand appearances, Xavier "Xavi" Hernández won a FIFA Club World Cup, UEFA European Championship twice, and dozens of regional titles; was named World Soccer Player of the Year 2010, UEFA Club Midfielder of the Year, and La Liga Midfielder of the Year three times; and was given numerous honors, including FIFA World Cup Dream Team, FIFA FIFPro World XI six times, and Ballon d'Or Dream Team.

- **Xabier "Xabi" Alonso Olano**, Soccer (Midfielder), Real Madrid Club de Fútbol, Spain, 1999–2017
- **Xavier Doherty**, Cricket (Bowler), Tasmania Men's Cricket Team, Australia, 2001–2017
- **Xabier Fernández Gaztañaga**, Sailing, Spain, 2001–2010
- **Xavier "Xavi" Hernández Creus**, Soccer (Midfielder), Fútbol Club Barcelona, Spain, 1997–2019
- **Xavier Rhodes**, Football (Cornerback), Minnesota Vikings, USA, 2013–2022

XIAOJUN

Typical for Chinese names, the unisex Xiaojun has many different possible translations depending on which characters are used to write it, some of which include "small" and "daybreak," "valiant" and "army," "king" or "ruler," and "good horse" or "fast." The fastest athlete with this name has been Lin Xiaojun, whose short track speed skating career for South Korea and then China has seen him win a gold and bronze medal from Olympic Games and six golds and three silvers from World Championships, while the strongest athlete has arguably been two-time Olympic gold-medalist and five-time world champion weightlifter Lü Xiaojun. Combining speed, strength, and toughness is WBC Silver Super Bantamweight Champion boxer Qiu Xiaojun, who currently holds a 21-4 professional record.

Lin Xiaojun, Short Track Speed Skating, South Korea/China, 2017-current

Lü Xiaojun, Weightlifting, China, 2008-current

Qiu Xiaojun, Boxing (Super Bantamweight), China, 2010-current

XIAOPENG

With both high and low meanings that can form the unisex name depending on the Chinese characters used to write it, Xiaopeng can reflect things and concepts like "dwarf bamboo," "daybreak/sky/heaven," "clouds/mist," and "friend." Xiaopengs have conquered events at both types of Olympics and beyond, like world champion freestyle skier Han Xiaopeng, who was also the first Chinese man to win a gold medal at Winter Olympics; Shandong Luneng soccer midfielder Li Xiaopeng, who won a Chinese Jia-A League championship, the Chinese FA Cup three times, and the Chinese Super League Cup; and another Li Xiaopeng, who won four Olympic gold medals and eight world championships in artistic gymnastics.

Consider this unique name with its many interesting translations for a child who will play hard and win no matter what season it is!

Han Xiaopeng, Freestyle Skiing, China, 2006-2007

Li Xiaopeng, Artistic Gymnastics, China, 1997-2009

Li Xiaopeng, Soccer (Midfielder), Shandong Taishan Football Club, China, 1994-2005

XIAOPING

The same initial segment "Xiao" (see *Xiaojun* and *Xiaopeng*) combines with a second syllable that can be translated as "level," "even," and "peaceful" to create the Chinese name Xiaoping. Inner peace can be balanced with physical aggression in sports, as perfected by boxer Zhang Xiaoping, who won a gold medal in the light heavyweight class at the 2008 Olympic Games and became the second Chinese boxing gold medalist only hours after the first!

Name your son Xiaoping and he, too, can find his focus and peace through the sweet science or another martial art.

Zhang Xiaoping, Boxing (Light Heavyweight), China, 2007-2008

XIN

If you're looking for a cool name starting with "X" that can inspire a son to be fast and accurate, consider the unisex Xin, which has a wide variety of possible meanings depending on the Chinese characters used to write it, including "heart/mind/soul," "trust/believe," "happy/joyous/delighted," "dawn/morning," "prosperous/wealthy," and "fresh/new." On the world's stage, a couple of Xins with the same family name have made big moves in recent years. Soccer defensive midfielder Xu Xin has won the Chinese Super League four times, Chinese FA Cup twice, and Chinese FA Super Cup three times, while former world singles number one table tennis player Xu Xin has won seventeen World Tour Singles titles, two gold medals, and a bronze from

Olympic Games; ten golds, a silver, and two bronzes from World Championships; and seven golds and a silver from World Cup events!

Xu Xin, Soccer (Defensive Midfielder), Guangzhou Football Club, China, 2013–current

Xu Xin, Table Tennis, China, 2009–current

XUANZE

While a boy you name *Xin* may be the master of table tennis, a Xuanze can follow in the footsteps of Xia Xuanze and become a champion badminton player! A singles world champion whose career straddled the twentieth and twenty-first centuries, Xia won two gold medals, a silver, and a bronze with the Chinese team at the Thomas Cup from 2000 to 2006, as well as many more medals in Asian competitions.

Xia Xuanze, Badminton, China, 1997–2006

GIRLS

XIA

With potential translations like "great/grand," "summer," and the poetic "rosy clouds" (depending on the Chinese characters used to write it), the name Xia is pretty and powerful. It has been elevated to the top of podiums by Olympic gold-medalist weightlifter Yang Xia and sprinter Zhou Xia, who has won four gold medals at Paralympic Games and two golds and two silvers at World Championships.

Name your daughter Xia to give her a love of summer, a rosy disposition, and a drive to compete with strength or speed!

Yang Xia, Weightlifting, China, 1993–2001

Zhou Xia, Para-Athletics, China, 2016–current

XIAOJUN

Xiaojun is a Chinese unisex moniker that can be written with a number of different characters that give it different meanings, including "small" and "daybreak," "valiant" and "army," "king" or "ruler," and "good horse" or "fast." Speed is definitely an asset when it comes to playing volleyball, getting that perfect locked shrug, and housing the hitter on the other side, which is exactly what Chinese middle blocker Yang Xiaojun did to help her teams win gold and bronze at Olympic Games, a gold medal at the FIVB Volleyball Women's World Championship, and a gold at the FIVB World Cup.

Give the name Xiaojun to your daughter and she'll be valiant and fast, able to get into position and defend the line wherever she competes or works!

Yang Xiaojun, Volleyball (Middle Blocker), China, 1984–1988

XIAOLING

Another "Xiao-" based name like *Xiaojun*, Xiaoling has possible meanings by combining "small," "dawn/daybreak," or "know/understand" with "tinkling of jade," "spirit/soul," and more. This name has reached international podiums in two very different sports, but with two similarly triumphant athletes. Geng Xiaoling of Hong Kong helped popularize the martial art of wushu taolu, winning five world championships, as well as a gold medal at the 2008 Beijing Wushu Tournament. Overlapping her career was that of Zhang Xiaoling. Despite a foot injury requiring amputation in her youth, Zhang grew up to become a table tennis world champion and won nine gold medals at Paralympic Games (twelve medals in total across a ten-year span)!

A Xiaoling in your family will be quick and agile, perfectly suited to martial arts and racquet sports, and hard-working, despite obstacles in her way.

Geng Xiaoling, Wushu Taolu, Hong Kong, 2005–2018

Zhang Xiaoling, Table Tennis, China, 1988–2008

XIAOMENG

A Chinese name that be written with characters that mean "dawn/daybreak," "dwarf bamboo," "the sound of wind and rain," "night/dark/moon," and "dream," Xiaoming is the perfect combination of fantastical and technological, whimsy and determination. This is exemplified in esports champion Li Xiaomeng, better known as "Liooon," who became the first woman to win a BlizzCon Esports tournament when she triumphed over the international competition to take home the Hearthstone Grandmasters Global Finals championship in 2019!

Name your daughter Xiaomeng and she's likely to enjoy playing video games and immersing herself in worlds of fantasy . . . but also working hard and beating the competition.

Li Xiaomeng "Liooon," Esports (*Hearthstone*), China, 2017–2020

XIN

The unisex name Xin has a variety of possible meanings depending on the Chinese characters used to write it, including "heart/mind/soul," "trust/believe," "happy/joyous/delighted," "dawn/morning," "prosperous/wealthy," and "fresh/new." While men named Xin have triumphed in soccer and table tennis, Wang Xin took things to a new height . . . specifically ten meters up, where the Chinese diver won Olympic gold and bronze and two world championships in platform and synchro!

A girl in your family will also love water sports and won't be afraid of heights if you give her the name Xin.

Wang Xin, Diving, China, 2007–2011

XINGFANG

A multi-part Chinese name with translations that could include "rise/flourish/prosper," "execute/perform," "star/planet," "clever/intelligent," or "apricot" plus "fragrant," "virtuous," or "beautiful," Xingfang can inspire a daughter to be clever and virtuous in her execution on the badminton court, just like Chinese former world number one-ranked Xie Xingfang, who won two world championships, a World Cup, and three gold medals each at the Sudirman Cup and Uber Cup!

Xie Xingfang, Badminton, China, 2000–2009

XINMEI

A *plum* name for a *happy* kid, Xinmei can be written with characters meaning–you guessed it–"happy/joyous" and "plum." While a daughter you give this name to may not enjoy eating plums, she might like throwing round objects, just like Chinese world champion shot putter Sui Xinmei!

Sui Xinmei, Track & Field (Shot Put), China, 1990–1998

XUAN

As with many Chinese names, there are numerous ways of translating the characters that can be used to write the name Xuan, though perhaps the most applicable are "profound" or "high/lofty." A Xuan in your family may be poised and comfortable in high or lofty situations, especially if she takes after Chinese artistic gymnast and balance beam specialist Liu Xuan, who won gold and bronze medals from both Olympics and World Cup Finals!

Liu Xuan, Artistic Gymnastics, China, 1994–2000

XUE

While the Chinese unisex name Xue can be written in characters that mean "snow" or "study/learning," athletes named Xue have become winners and champions in sports and events not specifically related to snow. The closest they come is figure skater Shen Xue, who, together with her husband, amassed a stellar medal count, including a gold medal and two bronzes at Olympic Games; three golds, three silvers, and a bronze at World Championships; three golds and a silver at Four Continents Championships; and six golds, a silver, and two bronzes at Grand Prix Finals! Fencer Tan Xue won a sabre world championship; long-distance runner Bai Xue won the Beijing Marathon in 2008 and a marathon world championship a year later; and, channeling her name's "study" ideal, Zhao Xue achieved the rank of chess Grandmaster and won three gold medals at both the Women's Chess Olympiad and Women's World Team Chess Championships.

Whether her talents and proclivities draw her more toward winter sports, book learning, or anything else, a Xue in your family will be passionate about her hobbies and profession, ready and willing to go the distance and excel by herself or with a beloved partner!

Bai Xue, Long-Distance Running, China, 2005–2010

Shen Xue, Figure Skating, China, 1996–2010

Tan Xue, Fencing (Sabre), China, 2001–2011

Zhao Xue, Chess, China, 2004–current

XUERUI

Will the name Xuerui ensure that your daughter is short or that she loves to play in the snow? Or how about a love of competitive sports involving racquets and the skills to win big? Maybe! The name can be written in Chinese characters with elements that mean "snow" and "small/tiny," and it has been made famous on the badminton scene by Olympic singles gold medalist Li Xuerui, who won two gold medals and a silver at the Sudirman Cup and three golds and a bronze at the Uber Cup.

Li Xuerui, Badminton, China, 2010–2019

XUEYING

With the same "snow" initial character as *Xue* and *Xuerui*, the name Xueying adds a second syllable that can be written with characters meaning everything from "flower/petal" to "brave/hero," "clever/talented," and even "lustrous/luster of gems!" World Championships and Olympic Games have seen the talents of brave athletes with this name, including world champion weightlifter Li Xueying, who set Olympic records on her way to winning gold, and Olympic gold-medalist and four-time world champion trampoline gymnast Zhu Xueying.

Choose the characters and translations that fit your family best when naming a daughter Xueying and she, too, will be prepared to work out, get strong, and fly high!

Li Xueying, Weightlifting, China, 2009–2012

Zhu Xueying, Trampoline Gymnastics, China, 2017–current

Y

BOYS

YANG

A highly versatile name, the unisex Yang can be a given name or a surname and can be written with Chinese characters translated as "ocean," "light/sun," and more. Chinese athletes with this name can inspire a young Yang to great heights in gymnastics (like Olympic gold-medalist and two-time world champion artistic gymnast and rings expert Liu Yang), track and field (like two-time Paralympic gold-medalist and four-time world champion wheelchair racer Liu Yang), table tennis (like six-time Paralympic gold-medalist and five-time world champion Ge Yang), badminton (like former world number one singles player Yang Yang, who won two world championships, two World Cups, three Thomas Cups, and more), and swimming (like four-time Paralympic gold-medalist and two-time International Paralympic Committee world champion Yang Yang, and Sun Yang, who has cemented his place among the best freestyle swimmers of all time with a medal count of three golds, two silvers, and a bronze from Olympic Games; eleven golds, two silvers, and four bronzes from World Championships; multiple records; and more!).

- **Ge Yang**, Table Tennis, China, 2001–2016
- **Liu Yang**, Artistic Gymnastics, China, 2013–current
- **Liu Yang**, Wheelchair Racing, China, 2006–2016
- **Sun Yang**, Swimming (Freestyle), China, 2007–2019
- **Yang Yang**, Badminton, China, 1983–1991
- **Yang Yang**, Swimming (Freestyle/Backstroke), China, 2012–2015

YAO

See *Ming* for Yao Ming.

YEVGENI/YEVGENY

You don't need to have a wealthy family to name your son Yevgeni or Yevgeny, which are Russian names that come from Ancient Greek roots meaning "well born" (the same origin as the name *Eugene*). A boy so-named will have plenty of highly successful sports figures to look up to, both in traditional Russian specialties, like ice hockey, and events you may not typically associate with the country, like swimming. They've conquered everything from water polo (with Olympic gold-medalist and world champion defender Yevgeny

Grishin) to tennis (with Olympic gold-medalist and former world number one singles player Yevgeny Kafelnikov, who won twenty-six singles titles and twenty-seven doubles titles in the 1990s and 2000s), weightlifting (with Olympic gold- and silver-medalist and two-time world champion Yevgeny Minayev), and speed skating (with seven-time world record setter Yevgeny Grishin, who won four gold medals and a silver at Olympic Games between 1956 and 1964).

Russians like Yevgeny Lagunov and Yevgeny Korotyshkin have made waves in modern international swimming competitions, winning a gold, five silvers, and four bronzes and three golds, three silvers, and three bronzes (respectively) at World Championships. Last but not least are the three Yevgenis who were part of the Soviet ice hockey dominance of the 1960s and '70s: forward Yevgeni Mayorov won the 1963 world championship and 1964 Olympic gold medal, while left wings Yevgeni Mishakov and Yevgeni Zimin were on the national teams that won Olympic gold in both 1968 and 1972!

A Yevgeni or Yevgeny in your family will be a strong competitor in any sport or event he chooses, though he may prefer swimming (and a Yevgeni, specifically, should definitely be introduced to ice hockey).

Yevgeny Grishin, Speed Skating, USSR, 1954–1964

Yevgeny Grishin, Water Polo (Defender), USSR, 1980–1988

Yevgeny Kafelnikov, Tennis, Russian, 1992–2010

Yevgeny Korotyshkin, Swimming (Butterfly), Russia, 2003–2012

Yevgeny Lagunov, Swimming (Freestyle), Russia, 2004–2015

Yevgeni Mayorov, Ice Hockey (Forward), HC Spartak Moscow, USSR, 1956–1969

Yevgeny Minayev, Weightlifting, USSR, 1956–1966

Yevgeni Mishakov, Ice Hockey (Left Wing), HK Lokomotiv Moscow, USSR, 1965–1972

Yevgeni Zimin, Ice Hockey (Left Wing), HC Spartak Moscow, USSR, 1964–1977

YIFU

Accuracy and longevity are two qualities you can pass on to a son by giving him the Chinese name Yifu, which can be written with characters meaning "clothing," "attach to," "foster/different father," and more. On the international sporting scene, pistol marksman Wang Yifu become one of the most successful Olympic Games sport shooters by winning two gold medals, three silvers, and a bronze between 1984 and 2000 with several firsts and records along the way!

Wang Yifu, Sport Shooting (Pistol), China, 1984–2004

YOGI

See *Laurence/Lawrence* for Lawrence "Yogi" Berra.

YO-HAN/YO-HWAN

Korean names built on a "Yo-" base can be translated into a variety of things depending on the characters used to write them (including "shine/sparkle/dazzle," "glory/glorious," and "writing brush"). In the case of FC Seoul soccer right-back Go Yo-han, who has won the K League 1 championship three times, the FA Cup, League Cup twice, and EAFF East Asian Cup, his name is actually a direct translation of the name *John*.

From the soccer field to the computer screen, we come to esports *StarCraft* legend Lim Yo-hwan, better known in some circles as "BoxeR," whose dominance at tournaments included numerous individual and team championships as he innovated new game play strategies and helped propel esports onto the global stage!

Whether it's based on a traditional Korean naming convention or a translation from another language, choose Yo-han or Yo-hwan for a boy who will be quick and nimble, whether he's kicking the ball down the soccer field or battling aliens in a video game.

Go Yo-han, Soccer (Right-Back/Midfielder), FC Seoul, South Korea, 2004–current

Lim Yo-hwan "BoxeR," Esports (*StarCraft*), South Korea, 1999–2013

YOHAN

A French variant of *Johann* (from Hebrew meaning "God is gracious"), Yohan appears to be a name that can give a boy speed and power . . . especially in his legs! This is borne out by three incredible athletes in three different sports, starting with French soccer midfielder Yohan Cabaye, who won the Ligue 1 championship three times, Coupe de France twice, and Coupe de la Ligue twice, and super middleweight kickboxer Yohan Lidon, who has won three world championships. But the fastest of all Yohans is Jamaican sprinter Yohan Blake, winner of two gold medals and two silvers from Olympic Games, two gold medals from World Championship, and two golds and a bronze from World Relay events.

Yohan Blake, Track & Field (Sprinting), Jamaica, 2006–current

Yohan Cabaye, Soccer (Midfielder), Lille Olympique Sporting Club, France, 2004–2020

Yohan Lidon, Kickboxing (Super Middleweight), France, 1998–current

YOUNG-

"Flower," "petal," "brave," and "hero" are just some of the ways the unisex "Young-" name can be translated, depending on the Korean characters used to write it. On soccer fields in South Korea, K League 1 Best XI midfielder Lee Young-jin was named K League All-Star Game MVP and K League '90s All-Star Team; his list of trophies includes the K League 1 championship, Korean National Championship, and Dynasty Cup.

In other sports and events, sharpshooter Kim Young-min became a pistol world champion in 2018, and there's a trio of Olympic gold-medalists: baseball second baseman Ko Young-min, Greco-Roman wrestler Kim Young-nam, and foil fencer Kim Young-ho.

These are all great physical athletes and inspiring figures for a boy given a "Young-" name in your family, but what if he's really into video games? Then he can aspire to the dedication, skill, and success of Lee Young-ho, better known as "Flash," who is considered one of the best *StarCraft* players of all time, with major wins including the GOMTV Star Invitational, Bacchus OSL (as its youngest champion), four Afreeca Starleague Season championships, World Cyber Games championship, Intel Extreme Masters championship, and signature comeback wins!

Kim Young-ho, Fencing (Foil), South Korea, 1997–2000

Kim Young-min, Sport Shooting (Pistol), South Korea, 2014–2018

Kim Young-nam, Greco-Roman Wrestling, South Korea, 1984–1988

Ko Young-min, Baseball (Second Baseman), Doosan Bears, South Korea, 2002–2016

Lee Young-jin, Soccer (Midfielder), LG Cheetahs, South Korea, 1986–1997

Lee Young-ho "Flash," Esports (*StarCraft*), South Korea, 2007–current

YOUNIS/YUNUS

The biblical story of Jonah is pretty famous, so it shouldn't come as a big surprise that the name (meaning "dove" in Hebrew) has spread and been adapted across the globe. Arabic and Turkish forms include Younis and Yunus, each of which has a triumphant athlete who has brought his name to glory. American soccer midfielder Yunus Musah has won two CONCACAF Nations League championships and was named CONCACAF Nations League Finals Best XI, while Pakistani cricket middle-order batsman Mohammad Younis Khan ranks among the best players ever in his position with an Asia Cup and T20 World Cup wins and multiple records set and held, including being the only Test cricketer to score a century in all eleven countries that play that style!

Naming your son Younis or Yunus may not lead him to be a world-famous soccer or cricket player, but he'll enjoy team sports and excel at his specific position when working with others.

Mohammad Younis Khan, Cricket (Middle-Order Batsman), Habib Bank Limited Cricket Team, Pakistan, 1998–2017

Yunus Musah, Soccer (Midfielder), Valencia Club de Fútbol, USA, 2019–current

YUJI

With potential translations including "divine intervention/protection," "hero," and "manly," it's no wonder that the Japanese name Yuji has gone on to do great things, and it will continue to do so with a boy with that name in your family! He may follow in the footsteps of those who have come before and find his place on the wrestling mat, on the soccer field, or clambering up rocks and mountains, or he may go his own way and find his specific place in the world. Either way, he'll be in good company with Olympic gold-medalist and four-time world champion freestyle wrestler Yuji Takada; sport climber Yuji Hirayama, who has won at Rock Master and twice at Lead World Cup events while setting records (including multiple El Capitan speed records, being the first climber ever to onsight an 8c/5.14b, multiple first ascents, and more); and Japanese Footballer of the Year defender Yuji Nakazawa, who won the J1 League championship twice, Emperor's Cup, and AFC Asian Cup twice and was named AFC Asian Cup Best XI, J.League MVP/Best XI five times, and AFC Asian Cup All-Time Dream XI.

Yuji Hirayama, Rock Climbing, Japan, 1999–2012

Yuji Nakazawa, Soccer (Defender), Yokohama F. Marinos, Japan, 1999–2018

Yuji Takada, Freestyle Wrestling, Japan, 1974–1984

YUKIO

Give your son the gift of being happy (and potentially heroic) in life (and possibly have an interest in baseball, pool, skiing, or gymnastics) with the Japanese name Yukio, which can be written with characters translated as "happiness," "hero," and more! He can look up to sports success stories like Olympic gold-medalist baseball outfielder Yukio Arai, nine-ball world champion Yukio Akakariyama, Olympic gold-medalist ski jumper Yukio Kasaya (who was the first athlete from his country to win at Winter Games), and artistic gymnast Yukio Endō, who collected five gold medals and two silvers from Olympic Games and three golds, five silvers, and a bronze from World Championships.

Yukio Akakariyama, Pool (Nine-Ball), Japan, 2008–current

Yukio Arai, Baseball (Outfielder), Yakult Swallows, Japan, 1984–2000

Yukio Endō, Artistic Gymnastics, Japan, 1960–1968

Yukio Kasaya, Ski Jumping, Japan, 1964–1976

YUN/YUN-

The name Yun may have possible translations in "cloud" and "allow" or "consent" when it's written with different characters, but when it comes to elite competitions, it's clear that the name (on its own or with a secondary syllable, per Korean tradition) can inspire excellent hand-eye coordination, quick reflexes, and the drive to become the very best. Audiences have witnessed these qualities in esports legend Lee Yun-yeol, better known as "NaDa," who became one of the top ranked *StarCraft* players in the world with three consecutive KPGA Tour championships, three OnGameNet StarLeagues championships, and more, and in the fast play of former badminton world number one doubles player Cai Yun, who won Olympic gold and silver, four golds and two bronzes at World Championships, a gold and a bronze at the World Cup, five gold medals at the Thomas Cup, six gold medals at the Sudirman Cup, and more!

Expect a son with a "Yun-" name to have quick hands and excellent reaction times; introduce him to fast-paced sports and he could become world-famous.

Cai Yun, Badminton, China, 2003–2015

Lee Yun-yeol "NaDa," Esports (*StarCraft*), South Korea, 2002–2012

YURI/YURIY/YURY

A mighty family of Belarusian, Russian, and Ukrainian names, the unisex Yuri, Yuriy, and Yury descend from the same origin as the name *George*, which comes from Ancient Greek meaning "farmer" or "earthworker." From those humble beginnings, these names have reached the heights of multiple sports with trophies, medals, records, and more thanks to a series of Soviet and Russian athletes. Two-time Olympic gold-medalist and world champion hammer thrower Yuriy Sedykh set the world record in 1986 that he still holds; freestyle swimmer Yury Prilukov has won six gold medals, three silvers, and two bronzes at World Championships; and Russian Footballer of the Year left-back/left-winger Yuri Zhirkov's trophy collection includes the Russian Premier League championship five times, Russian Cup six times, Russian Super Cup six times, Premier League championship, UEFA Cup, and FA Cup.

Meanwhile, not one but two Yuris are ranked among the greatest gymnasts! Between 1956 and 1964, Yuri Titov won Olympic gold, five silvers, and three bronzes, as well as four gold medals, a silver, and four bronzes from World Artistic Gymnastics Championships. A couple decades later, Yuri Korolyov came onto the scene and became one of the most successful non-Olympian gymnasts of all-time with nine gold medals, three silvers, and a bronze from World Championships and five golds, four silvers, and three bronzes from World Cup events.

Whether or not your family has Eastern European roots, you can empower your son with the name Yuri, Yuriy, or Yury and give him the strength and agility to succeed in any field he chooses, including any athletic competition.

Yuri Korolyov, Artistic Gymnastics, USSR, 1981–1989

Yury Prilukov, Swimming (Freestyle), Russia, 2002–2008

Yuriy Sedykh, Track & Field (Hammer Throw), USSR, 1976–1995

Yuri Titov, Artistic Gymnastics, USSR, 1956–1964

Yuri Zhirkov, Soccer (Left-Back/Left-Winger), Professional Football Club CSKA, Russia, 2001–2022

YURIK

While athletes with the *Yuri/Yuriy/Yury* family of names have branched out into several different events, those with the similarly "farmer"-based name Yurik have been a bit more focused. If your son follows in their footsteps, he'll be strong . . . like, really strong. Armenian weightlifters have topped the charts with two-time world champion Yurik Sarkisyan, who won a total of eight medals, and Olympic gold-medalist Yurik Vardanyan, who won seven golds and a bronze from World Championships and set multiple records, including being the first 82.5-kilogram competitor to achieve a four hundred kilogram total!

If you name your son Yurik, be sure to get him a set of weights.

Yurik Sarkisyan, Weightlifting, Armenia, 1979–2002

Yurik Vardanyan, Weightlifting, Armenia, 1977–1985

YUSUKE

While some of the possible translations of the Japanese name Yusuke can include elements like "help," "friend," and "assistance" (depending on the characters used to write it), only one notable Yusuke-named athlete has succeeded with his team; artistic gymnast Yusuke Tanaka has an Olympic gold and silver, as well as a gold, two silvers, and two bronzes from World Championships.

Meanwhile, boxer Yusuke Kobori held the WBA lightweight championship with a record of 23-3-1, vert skater Yusuke Aihara won four major events with twelve total podium appearances, and esports fighting game professional Yusuke Momochi battled his way to the 2014 Capcom Cup, 2015 EVO, and 2019 EVO Japan championships.

There's nothing preventing a son you name Yusuke from being a good team player, but he's more likely to rely on his skills and participate in solo activities; teach him to believe in himself and never stop fighting!

Yusuke Aihara, Skateboarding, Japan, 2008–current

Yusuke Kobori, Boxing (Lightweight), Japan, 2000–2009

Yusuke "Momochi" Momochi, Esports (Fighting Games), Japan, 2008–current

Yusuke Tanaka, Artistic Gymnastics, Japan, 2012–2018

YUTAKA

"Luxuriant," "bountiful," "abundant," and "plentiful" are just some of the translations of characters you can use to write the Japanese name Yutaka, which are appropriate because the accomplishments of the athletes with this name have been numerous. Four-time J1 League Best XI soccer defender Yutaka Akita helped his teams win the J1 League championship four times, the J.League Cup three times, and the Emperor's Cup twice; and legendary horse racing jockey Yutaka Take has set numerous records during his lengthy career, with over two hundred wins outside of Japan and more than 4,300 in his home country! On the baseball field, Hanshin Tigers seven-time Nippon Professional Baseball All-Star infielder Yutaka Wada won two Central League Best Nine awards, three Central League Golden Gloves, and an Olympic gold medal.

Name your son Yutaka to give him abundant skills and the chance to win plentiful awards and trophies!

Yutaka Akita, Soccer (Defender), Kashima Antlers, Japan, 1993–2007

Yutaka Take, Horse Racing (Jockey), Japan, 1987–current

Yutaka Wada, Baseball (Infielder), Hanshin Tigers, Japan, 1985–2001

YUVRAJ

Royalty is the theme of the name Yuvraj, coming from Sanskrit roots meaning "heir apparent" or "crown prince." A little prince with this name in your family can look up to a royal figure in sports, cricket icon Yuvraj Singh! The Indian all-rounder led his team to win the 2002 Champions Trophy, 2007 T20 World Cup, and 2011 World Cup; accumulated dozens of awards, including seven ODI Player of the Series selections; and set multiple records, including hitting the first six sixes in one over during an international match between two Test teams and reaching the fastest fifty in Twenty20 Internationals and in all T20 cricket. He has also been a hero off the pitch, creating a charity to help cancer patients.

Whether he chooses to play cricket or any other sport, a little Yuvraj in your family will be a princely competitor, just like Singh.

Yuvraj Singh, Cricket (All-Rounder), Punjab Cricket Team, India, 1996–2019

YUZURU

Are you hoping for a son who will have skill and grace matched with dedication and ambition, as well as a winning career and a strong drive to support those in need? Then consider giving him the name Yuzuru! It can be written with characters translated as "allow," "permit," "yield," or "concede," but in the case of figure skater Yuzuru Hanyu, it means "tie the bowstring" because his parents wanted for him a dignified life, straight and narrow, with confidence and strength. Ranked among the greatest skaters of all time, Hanyu's exemplary record includes two Olympic gold medals; two golds, three silvers, and two bronzes from World Championships; a gold and three silvers from Four Continents Championships; four golds and two silvers from Grand Prix Finals; and more. He also pioneered more complex and daring moves and set nearly two dozen records.

Yuzuru Hanyu, Figure Skating, Japan, 2004–current

GIRLS

YAJUN

While the Chinese name Yajun can be written with characters meaning "elegant" or "refined" and "beautiful jade," a girl you give this name to will be no shrinking violet. Encourage her to get in shape and be strong and she just may surprise you with her dedication to building up her body, following in the footsteps of Chinese two-time world champion weightlifter Li Yajun!

Li Yajun, Weightlifting, China, 2014–2018

YAMILÉ/YAMILET

The Spanish accented Yamilé and its variant Yamilet come from an Arabic word meaning "beautiful" by way of *Jamil* and *Jamilah*, and a trio of athletes with these names have had beautiful successes on international stages in three different kinds of events. Basketball center Yamilé Martínez helped the Cuban team to victory at the Pan American Games, Dominican artistic gymnast Yamilet Peña has won gold on the vault at Pan American Championships and Central and Caribbean Games, and triple jumper Yamilé Aldama leapt to victory at World Championships, Pan American Games, All-Africa Games, African Championships, Central American and Caribbean Games, and Ibero-American Championships while competing for Cuba, Sudan, Great Britain, England, and Scotland.

Choose this unique name for a girl who will run fast and jump high and far!

Yamilé Aldama, Track & Field (Triple Jump), Cuba/Sudan/Scotland, 1996–2014

Yamilé Martínez Calderón, Basketball (Center), Cuba, 1992-2007

Yamilet Peña Abreu, Artistic Gymnastics, Dominican Republic, 2001-current

YANA

From Eastern Europe comes the name Yana, which is a descendant of the same biblical Hebrew name as *John* (and many others) that means "God is gracious." Fierce competitors have propelled the name (or nickname) Yana to international fame in a few different categories, including fencing, with Russian two-time Olympic gold-medalist and two-time world champion sabre fencer Yana Egorian, and swimming, with record-breaking Ukrainian medley master Yana Klochkova, who won four Olympic gold medals and a silver, as well as ten golds and four silvers at World Championships. Meanwhile, Russian Yanas have dominated rhythmic gymnastics, first in the 1990s with four-time world champion and five-time Grand Prix Final-winner Yana Batyrshina and then in the 2000s and 2010s with thirteen-time world champion and eight-time World Cup Final-winner Yana Kudryavtseva!

Name your daughter Yana and she'll be graceful and powerful, putting her skills to good use in the water, with swords, or performing on the mat.

Yanina "Yana" Batyrshina, Rhythmic Gymnastics, Russia, 1995-1998

Yana Egorian, Fencing (Sabre), Russia, 2011-current

Yana Klochkova, Swimming (Medley), Ukraine, 1997-2009

Yana Kudryavtseva, Rhythmic Gymnastics, Russia, 2007-2017

YANG

"Ocean," "light," and "sun" are a few of the translations you can make with the Chinese characters you use to write the unisex name Yang, which can be both a given name and a surname. Athletes with this name have racked up an absolutely massive medal count, and if you name your daughter Yang, you should introduce her to badminton and definitely ice skating! Yu Yang held the world number one rank in badminton doubles and won gold and bronze at Olympics; three golds, two silvers, and two bronzes at World Championships; four golds at the Sudirman Cup; three golds at the Uber Cup; and lots more. Meanwhile, Chinese short track speed skating teams have included not one, not two, but three champion Yangs in modern times, most recently with three-time Olympic gold-medalist and fourteen-time World Championships-medalist Zhou Yang. In the 1990s, two Yang Yangs competed in the sport and were given the nicknames "A" and "S" (for their birth months of April and September); S won six golds, five silvers, and six bronzes at World Championships and four golds and a silver at World Team Championships, while A took home two golds, two silvers, and a bronze from Olympic Games; twenty-eight golds, including six overalls, nine silvers, and five bronzes from World Championships; four golds and four silvers at World Team Championships; and more!

Yang Yang "A," Short Track Speed Skating, China, 1994-2005

Yang Yang "S," Short Track Speed Skating, China, 1995-2002

Yu Yang, Badminton, China, 2002-2014

Zhou Yang, Short Track Speed Skating, China, 2007-2015

YANI

Variations of the name Yani have appeared in multiple cultures and languages around the world, and a Yani in your family may really like to run fast or prefer to spend her time on the links. She can find inspiration from

Argentinian Paralympic gold- and bronze-medalist sprinter Yani Martínez, who also stood on six World Championship podiums, or Taiwanese two-time LPGA Tour Player of the Year Tseng Yani, who has won seventy-seven professional golf events and five majors, becoming the youngest player ever to achieve that second feat!

Yanina "Yani" Martínez, Para-Athletics (Sprinting), Argentina, 2011–current

Yani Tseng, Golf, Taiwan, 2007–current

YANQING

The Chinese feminine name Yanqing has the typical wide range of possible translations based on the characters used to write it, just some of which include "elegant/handsome," "beautiful/gorgeous," "swallow (the bird)," "high officer/noble," "clear/pure/clean," and "blue/green." However, none of those quite do justice to Chinese weightlifter Chen Yanqing, who came from a very humble childhood in a poor fishing village to international fame as a two-time Olympic gold-medalist and two-time world champion!

Choose the name Yanqing for your daughter if you like any of the proposed translations or if you'd like her to beat the odds and become known for her strength and tenacity.

Chen Yanqing, Weightlifting, China, 1997–2008

YAPING

Do short people and a love of racquet sports run in your family? Then Yaping might be an interesting option for your daughter! While it can be written in Chinese characters that can be translated as "second," "Asia," "level/even," "peaceful," or "wander/travel," the name was made famous in the sports world by four-time Olympic gold-medalist and nine-time world champion table tennis player Deng Yaping! A true giant in the game, Deng was initially discounted from eligibility to play because of her four-foot, eleven-inch height.

Deng Yaping, Table Tennis, China, 1986–1997

YARGELIS

The uncommon Spanish name Yargelis can be traced back to a feminine form of a combination of *Jorge* and *Luis* and can be given to an athletic girl who will enjoy complex activities with multiple steps. If she gravitates toward track and field events, she can look up to Cuban three-time world champion triple jumper Yargelis Savigne!

Yargelis Savigne, Track & Field (Triple Jump), Cuba, 2003–2012

YEKATERINA

See *Ecaterina/Ekaterina/Yekaterina*.

YELENA

In Greek mythology, Helen (whose name has an uncertain origin possibly meaning "torch" or related to the moon) may have launched a thousand ships, but in modern days, her name has inspired interesting and unique variants around the world, including the Russian Yelena. Women with this name have proven to be incredible competitors, with multiple winners and champions in several sports and events, though they're not just restricted to things like rowing, volleyball, gymnastics, swimming, and track and field. Yelenas can be found in just about any sport, from handball (Russian two-time world champion Yelena Dmitriyeva) to fencing (Azerbaijani two-time sabre world champion Yelena Jemayeva), equestrian events (Soviet dressage Olympic gold-medalist, and two-time world champion Yelena Petushkova), sport shooting (Azerbaijani three-time International Paralympic Committee World

Cup pistol champion Yelena Taranova), and cross-country skiing (Russian Yelena Välbe, who won three gold medals and four bronzes at Olympic Games, a record fourteen golds and three silvers at World Championships, and twenty-four team and forty-five individual wins at World Cup events, with five overall titles and one discipline title).

Moving into the sports in which multiple Yelenas have succeeded, we first hit the water with the rowers! They include two-time world champions Yelena Antonova and Yelena Khloptseva, who also won a gold and a bronze medal at the Olympics. Yelenas have also propelled their national volleyball teams to international glory with two middle blockers on the Soviet 1980 Olympic gold-medalist team (Yelena Akhaminova and Yelena Andreyuk), followed eight years later by opposite Yelena Volkova on the 1988 gold medalist team, and in the 1990s and 2000s by outside hitter Yelena Godina, who anchored the Russian team on their way to winning a world championship and a World Grand Champions Cup while being named 1999 FIVB World Grand Prix Best Blocker and 2006 World Championship Best Server.

Gymnastics, a traditional favorite of Russians, is another sport that has seen Yelenas standing atop world podiums. In recent times, that's been in rhythmic gymnastics with Yelena Posevina, who swept two Olympic gold medals, six world championships, two World Cup Final gold medals, and seven European Championships between 2003 and 2008. In the 1980s, it was all about the Soviet artistic gymnasts with highly successful Yelena Shushunova, who won medals across all events at World Championships and collected two golds, a silver, and a bronze at Olympics; five golds, four silvers, and two bronzes at World Championships; four golds and a bronze at World Cup Finals; and more!

In the pool, Yelena Antonova and Yelena Soya were on the Russian gold medal-winning synchronized swimming team in 2000, while Yelena Ovchinnikova won the same eight years later. From the USSR, breaststroke expert Yelena Volkova won gold and bronze at the 1991 World Championships, and Belarusian breaststroke and medley swimmer Yelena Rudkovskaya won gold and bronze at the 1992 Olympic Games.

The largest concentration of champions with this name have been Russians in track and field events held around the world! They range from Olympic gold-medalists like 3000-meter runner Yelena Romanova and high jumper Yelena Yelesina to world champion and Olympic gold-medalists like sprinter Yelena Ruzina, racewalker Yelena Nikolayeva, and pole vaulter Yelena Isinbayeva, who won two Olympic gold medals and a bronze; seven golds, a silver, and a bronze from World Championships; and a gold at the World Cup.

Yelenas have done it all, and a girl you give this name to will have every opportunity to find her favorite sport or event and give it all she's got.

Yelena Akhaminova, Volleyball (Middle Blocker), USSR/Ukraine, 1979–1995

Yelena Andreyuk, Volleyball (Middle Blocker), USSR, 1980

Yelena Antonova, Rowing, USSR, 1973–1976

Yelena Antonova, Synchronized Swimming, Russia, 1994–2000

Yelena Dmitriyeva, Handball (Left Wing), Russia, 2007–2009

Yelena Godina, Volleyball (Outside Hitter), Russia, 1991–2011

Yelena Isinbayeva, Track & Field (Pole Vaulting), Russia, 2002–2016

Yelena Jemayeva, Fencing (Sabre), Azerbaijan, 1999–2008

Yelena Khloptseva, Rowing, Russia, 1978–1992

Yelena Nikolayeva, Track & Field (Racewalking), Russia, 1987–2004

Yelena Ovchinnikova, Synchronized Swimming, Russia, 2008

Yelena Petushkova, Equestrian (Dressage), USSR, 1964–1987

Yelena Posevina, Rhythmic Gymnastics, Russia, 2000–2008

Yelena Romanova, Track & Field (Middle-Distance Running), USSR, 1987–1996

Yelena Rudkovskaya, Swimming (Breaststroke), USSR/Belarus, 1991–1993

Yelena Ruzina, Track & Field (Sprinting), Russia, 1992–1995

Yelena Shushunova, Artistic Gymnastics, USSR, 1981–1988

Yelena Soya, Synchronized Swimming, Russia, 1999–2000

Yelena Taranova, Sport Shooting (Pistol), Azerbaijan, 2000–2012

Yelena Välbe, Cross-Country Skiing, Russia, 1987–1998

Yelena Volkova, Swimming (Breaststroke), USSR, 1988–1992

Yelena Volkova, Volleyball (Opposite), USSR, 1981–1988

Yelena Yelesina, Track & Field (High Jump), Russia, 1990–2003

YELIZAVETA

If you like the name *Elizabeth* but are looking for one of its rarer variants, consider the Russian Yelizaveta! It's cool and has lots of potential for nicknames and diminutives, and your daughter will always know her place in an alphabetical list. She may also take a liking to water sports like canoeing and kayaking, even finding inspiration for competition in those sports from Russian Olympic gold-medalist and world champion sprint canoeist Yelizaveta Dementyeva.

Yelizaveta Dementyeva, Sprint Canoeing, USSR, 1956–1958

YEON-/YUN-

With possible translations of "govern" and "allow/consent" for the first syllable, Korean Yeon- and Yun- names are super versatile when written with different characters and combined with select second syllables. Just as varied are the sports in which athletes with these names have triumphed! These range from badminton (with Uber Cup champion Bae Yeon-ju) to bodybuilding (with Jhi Yeon-woo, who won the 2013 Arnold Classic Europe Physique), soccer (with two-time WK League MVP forward Cha Yun-hee, who has won the WK League championship twice and the EAFF Women's Football Championship), rhythmic gymnastics (with Asian Games gold-medalist and eleven-time Asian Championship-winner Son Yeon-jae), and volleyball (with outside hitter Kim Yeon-koung, whose huge medal haul includes multiple championships in domestic leagues, and more, plus dozens of player awards for most valuable player and best spiker, scorer, and server!).

Choose a Yeon- or Yun- name for your daughter and she'll have unique possibilities and the skills and drive to capitalize on them.

Bae Yeon-ju, Badminton, South Korea, 2008–2016

Cha Yun-hee, Soccer (Forward), Goyang Daekyo Noonnoppi, South Korea, 2006–2017

Jhi Yeon-woo, Bodybuilding, South Korea, 2010–2017

Kim Yeon-koung, Volleyball (Outside Hitter), South Korea, 2005–current

Son Yeon-jae, Rhythmic Gymnastics, South Korea, 2010–2017

YIHAN

"Ceremonies/rites," "grand/elegant," "tolerate," and "contain" are just some of the translations for the elements that make up the Chinese name Yihan, depending on the different characters you can use to write it.

Elegant ceremonies are certainly on the horizon to celebrate a daughter to whom you give this name because she's sure to achieve great successes. She may enjoy sports on ice, like world champion short track speed skater Guo Yihan, or even racquet sports, like former world number one badminton player Wang Yihan, who won a world championship, a World Cup, four golds at the Sudirman Cup, three golds at the Uber Cup, and more!

Guo Yihan, Short Track Speed Skating, China, 2012–2017

Wang Yihan, Badminton, China, 2006–2016

YINING

A city and county in China, Yining is also a feminine name that may be translated as "easy peace" or "harmony" depending on the characters used to write it. The name has reached the heights of athletic achievement in table tennis with Zhang Yining, who is considered one of the greatest players of all time; she held the number one spot in the world for almost seven straight years, was the first-ever player to complete a Double Grand Slam, and won four Olympic gold medals; ten golds, two silvers, and four bronzes at World Championships; and four golds, two silvers, and a bronze at World Cup events.

Name your daughter Yining to give her a strong sense of history, as well as athletic prowess and agility that will serve her well in table tennis or any other event she chooses to pursue.

Zhang Yining, Table Tennis, China, 1999–2008

YOLANDA

Jumping, whether for distance or for grabbing a ball, seems to be the common thread among Yolandas, whose name comes through medieval French and, ultimately, a Latin root meaning "violet." A girl with this name in your family is sure to love jumping on her bed and may take a liking to track and field events or basketball if she follows in the footsteps of Russian world champion triple-jumper Yolanda Chen or eight-time WNBA All-Star center Yolanda Griffith, who is considered one of the greatest rebounders and defenders (and players in general), winning a WNBA championship, two rebounding championships, and two Olympic gold medals; being named WNBA MVP, WNBA Finals MVP, and Defensive Player of the Year; and being inducted into the Basketball Hall of Fame!

Yolanda Chen, Track & Field (Long Jump/ Triple Jump), Russia, 1983–1995

Yolanda Griffith, Basketball (Center), Sacramento Monarchs, USA, 1993–2009

YONG-/YOUNG/YOUNG-

Another unisex family of names, Yong- and Young- are primarily Korean and have the usual distinctiveness in that they can be combined with different secondary syllables and vary greatly in translations depending on which characters are used to write them; "brave," "perpetual/eternal," and "flower/ petal," are just some of these translations. Examples of athletes who have brought these names to international podiums and leaderboards include world champions like weightlifter Son Young-hee and épée fencer Kang Young-mi; golfer Kim Young, who won eight professional events; and Olympic gold-medalist archer Yun Young-sook. Table tennis is a particular favorite of athletes with these names, with dual world champions Pak Yong-ok and Yang Young-ja, who is also an Olympic gold-medalist!

Choose from the long list of options when it comes to naming your daughter Yong, Young, or a combination of one of those with a second part.

Kang Young-mi, Fencing (Épée), South Korea, 2015–current

Kim Young, Golf, South Korea, 1998–2009

Pak Yong-ok, Table Tennis, North Korea, 1976–1980

Son Young-hee, Weightlifting, South Korea, 2020–current

Yang Young-ja, Table Tennis, South Korea, 1982–1988

Yun Young-sook, Archery, South Korea, 1988

YU/YU-

A very short name that crosses over nations and languages, Yu and Yu- with a second syllable appear in Chinese, Japanese, and Korean. Naturally it has different translations in each, with Chinese characters including "jade/precious stone," "pleasant," or "rain" and Japanese characters including "excellence/superiority," "permanence," and "brave." You can research all of these origins and find one that really speaks to you; giving your daughter the name Yu or a combination Yu- name can result in her being good at scoring and shooting, like Japanese Tokyo Verdy Beleza soccer midfielder Yu Nakasato (who won the Nadeshiko League championship four times, Nadeshiko League Cup three times, Empress' Cup three times, and a gold medal at the Asian Games), and Chinese world champion rifle sport shooter Zhang Yu.

Alternatively, she may be focused on speed and racing on ice, like South Korean Olympic gold- and silver-medalist and world champion short track speed skater Lee Yu-bin, or in the water, like Chinese freestyle swimmer Yang Yu, who collected five gold medals, four silvers, and seven bronzes from World Championships!

Lee Yu-bin, Short Track Speed Skating, South Korea, 2018–current

Yu Nakasato, Soccer (Midfielder), Nippon TV Tokyo Verdy Beleza, Japan, 2011–current

Yang Yu, Swimming (Freestyle), China, 2000–2009

Zhang Yu, Sport Shooting (Rifle), China, 2021–current

YUE

It's common to jump for joy at the fertile blessing of having a daughter, and the name Yue combines those feelings with a predilection toward competition, getting strong, and battling to victory over opponents! A unisex name, Yue can be written in Chinese characters meaning "moon," "jump/leap," "joy," "pearl," and others, and in Japanese characters meaning "fertile" and "blessing." On the international stage, this name has been represented by Chinese world champion weightlifter Kang Yue, table tennis world champion and five-time Pro Tour-winner Wang Yue Gu of Singapore, and table tennis player Guo Yue of China, who won two gold medals and two silvers at Olympic Games, as well as ten golds, five silvers, and two bronzes at World Championships.

Guo Yue, Table Tennis, China, 2004–2015

Kang Yue, Weightlifting, China, 2009–current

Wang Yue Gu, Table Tennis, Singapore, 2005–2012

YUKI/YŪKI

A popular Japanese name, Yuki can have different meanings whether or not it includes an accent over the "u." Without, it can be written with characters that translate to "happiness," "snow," "reason" and "valuable," or "chronicle," while the inclusion of the accent offers the choice of "excellence/superiority," "permanence," "hope," "brightness," or "living." Yukis have proven formidable competitors in many different sports and events, both individually and on teams. Solo athletes include judokas like Asian Championships gold-medalist Yuki Yokosawa, and Yuki Hashimoto, who has won a gold, two silvers, and a bronze at Grand Prix events and four golds and two bronzes at Grand Slams.

On the snowy slopes, Yukis tend to work well alone or on teams, like ski jumper Yuki Ito (who won a mixed team world championship (and two bronzes), as well as two individual silver medals).

Striving best alongside others, former badminton doubles number one Yuki Fukushima collected a medal of each color at the Uber Cup, two golds and two bronzes at Asian Championships, and two golds at Asia Team Championships; Girl's Professional Baseball League infielder and designated hitter Yuki Kawabata was a three-time batting champion, three-time on-base percentage leader, MVP, and Golden Glove–winner; and soccer striker Yūki Nagasato was the first woman to play for a Japanese men's club and won three L.League championships, the Empress' Cup four times, and the 2011 FIFA Women's World Cup, in addition to numerous league goal-scoring awards!

Name your daughter Yuki or Yūki and teach her about all sorts of different sports so she can discover where she'll have the most fun (and success).

Yuki Fukushima, Badminton, Japan, 2018–current

Yuki Hashimoto, Judo, Japan, 2011–current

Yuki Ito, Ski Jumping, Japan, 2012–current

Yuki Kawabata, Baseball (Infielder/Designated Hitter), Saitama Astraia, Japan, 2009–2018

Yūki Nagasato, Soccer (Striker), Nippon TV Tokyo Verdy Beleza, Japan, 2001–current

Yuki Yokosawa, Judo, Japan, 2001–2007

YULIA/YULIYA

Eastern Europe has produced a couple of its own variants of the name *Julia*, which comes from the Latin *Julius*. In Belarusian, Bulgarian, Russian, and Ukrainian, there are Yulias and Yuliyas whose athletic exploits have been legendary. While most of them can be put in three categories (water-related, cold weather, and combat sports), women with these names can't always be put in specific boxes, like four-time track and field world champion (sprinting and hurdling) Yuliya Pechonkina and rhythmic gymnast Yulia Barsukova, who won Olympic gold as well as a gold medal and two bronzes from World Championships!

On the ice and snow, figure skater Yulia Lipnitskaya became the youngest woman to win Olympic gold (under the modern rules) in 2014, ski orienteer Yuliya Tarasenko became a two-time world champion in the mid-2010s, and cross-country skier Yuliya Chepalova collected three golds, two silvers, and a bronze from Winter Olympics; two golds, silvers, and bronzes at World Championships; and thirteen team and eighteen individual wins at World Cup events, with one overall and one discipline title.

In and on the water, meanwhile, Belarusian rower Yuliya Bichyk won three world championships (along with three silver medals and two bronzes); synchro and springboard diver Yuliya Pakhalina took home Olympic gold, three silvers, and a bronze, and three golds, three silvers, and two bronzes from World Championships; and breaststroke and medley swimmer Yuliya Yefimova set and broke several world records on her way to becoming a six-time world champion with seven silver medals and five bronzes.

Finally, there are the Yulias and Yuliyas who compete one-on-one and dominate their opponents on the mat, in the ring, and on the piste! These include world champion wrestlers like Ukrainian Yuliya Tkach and Azerbaijani Yuliya Ratkevich, Israeli World Kickboxing Champion Yulia Sachkov, and Russian sabre fencer Yuliya Gavrilova, who won Olympic gold and four world championships.

Set your daughter on the path to glory and gold with the name Yulia or Yuliya—and make sure to introduce her to martial arts and water and winter sports.

Yulia Barsukova, Rhythmic Gymnastics, Russia, 1996–2000

Yuliya Bichyk, Rowing, Belarus, 1999–2014

Yuliya Chepalova, Cross-Country Skiing, Russia, 1995–2009

Yuliya Gavrilova, Fencing (Sabre), Russia, 2009–2016

Yulia Lipnitskaya, Figure Skating, Russia, 2002–2017

Yuliya Pakhalina, Diving, Russia, 1995–2009

Yuliya Pechonkina, Track & Field (Sprinting/Hurdling), Russia, 2000–2007

Yuliya Ratkevich, Freestyle Wrestling, Azerbaijan, 2005–2016

Yulia Sachkov, Kickboxing (Strawweight), Israel, 2016–current

Yuliya Tarasenko, Ski Orienteering, Russia, 2013–2015

Yuliya Tkach, Freestyle Wrestling, Ukraine, 2008–current

Yuliya Yefimova, Swimming (Breaststroke), Russia, 2007–current

YULIMAR

A perfect name for a bold girl who will love to jump and fly through the air, Yulimar is considered a Spanish-Caribbean name built from a combination of *Yuli* and the popular "-mar" suffix. It was launched into world-renown by Venezuelan triple-jumper Yulimar Rojas, who has a phenomenal medal collection featuring gold and silver from the Olympics, seven world championships, two Diamond League wins, and more, as well as multiple world records!

Yulimar Rojas Rodríguez, Track & Field (Triple Jump), Venezuela, 2014–current

YUMILKA

Like *Yulimar*, Yumilka is a unique Spanish-Caribbean name, this time gaining massive prominence from an athlete from Cuba. Yumilka Ruíz played volleyball as an outside hitter from 1996 to 2014, during which time she won national and regional trophies in different leagues, multiple MVP and best scorer/spiker awards, two gold medals and a bronze at Olympic Games, a World Championship gold, a World Cup gold, and a World Grand Prix gold, two silvers, and a bronze!

A Yumilka in your family may not be inducted into the International Volleyball Hall of Fame like Ruíz, but she'll love playing with friends and leading her teams to victory.

Yumilka Daysi Ruíz Luaces, Volleyball (Outside Hitter), Cuba, 1996–2014

YUNLEI

Combining name elements *Yun* and *Lei* gets you Yunlei, which can give a daughter keen coordination, quick moves, a great choice in partners, and a winning personality. That's especially true if she takes after Zhao Yunlei, one of the greatest doubles and team badminton players of all time! Zhao's list of accomplishments is lengthy, including two gold medals and a bronze at Olympic Games; five golds, two silvers, and three bronzes at World Championships; three gold medals each at the Sudirman Cup and Uber Cup; world number one rankings; and more.

Zhao Yunlei, Badminton, China, 2009–2016

YUNXIA

The Chinese name Yunxia has the usual variety of translations depending on which characters are used to write it, including the very pretty "rosy clouds." It's definitely a fast name, as proven by middle-distance runner Qu Yunxia, who set the world record in the 3000-meter event, and Olympic gold-medalist and two-time world champion quadruple sculls rower Chen Yunxia!

Name your daughter Yunxia to inspire her to work hard and go fast, whether she's running, rowing, or just charging ahead in her own way.

Chen Yunxia, Rowing, China, 2019–current

Qu Yunxia, Track & Field (Middle-Distance Running), China, 1992–1993

YURI

A name that has evolved independently in different cultures and parts of the world, the Japanese unisex name Yuri is most famously written with characters meaning "lily" (but it can also be written to mean "reason," "village," "logic," "profit," "friend," and more). Choose this name for a girl in your family if you like flowers and golf, and hopefully she'll take after LPGA of Japan Tour star Yuri Fudoh, who won fifty professional events during her storied career!

Yuri Fudoh, Golf, Japan, 1996–2011

YURIKO

Combining *Yuri* and a unique third syllable, the Japanese name Yuriko can include additional translations, including "child." Naming a daughter Yuriko can produce a child who likes lilies or is an excellent team player and a defensive bulwark for her friends, compatriots, and teammates. That will make her just like famed Japanese volleyball middle blocker Yuriko Handa, who helped her team win the 1962 World Championship and the 1964 Olympic gold medal!

Yuriko Handa, Volleyball (Middle Blocker), Japan, 1959–1964

YVETTE

The French name Yvette (a feminine version of *Yves* and, ultimately, from a Germanic or possibly Celtic root for the yew tree) can inspire a daughter to achieve her athletic and competitive potential very early, whether that's finding her way through the big world, jumping over obstacles and using her strength in throwing, or even diving into troubled waters with teammates to score goals. British orienteer Yvette Baker became the youngest competitor in the World Orienteering Championships, events in which she's won a gold medal, two silvers, and a bronze. New Zealander track and field legend Yvette Williams would also achieve glory as the first woman from her country to win Olympic gold when she won the long jump in Helsinki in 1952. And Yvette Higgins was a key player in the Australia women's water polo team on their journey to winning the 1995 World Cup and the 2000 Olympic gold medal, for which she scored the winning goal!

Yvette Baker, Orienteering, England, 1983–2001

Yvette Higgins, Water Polo (Field Player), Australia, 1995–2002

Yvette Williams, Track & Field (Long Jump/Discus/Shot Put/Javelin), New Zealand, 1947–1954

YVONNE

Another French name descended from the same "yew tree" source as *Yvette*, Yvonne has come to be known in athletics as a name that likes to go fast, seeking victory through speed in a number of different events. These range from duathlon, like Dutch Long Distance Duathlon World Champion Yvonne van Vlerken, to sprint canoeing, like Austrian world champion Yvonne Schuring; running, like Scottish 3000-meter World Indoor Champion and two-time World Cup-winner Yvonne Murray; and speed skating, like Dutch three-time Olympic gold-medalist and record-setter Yvonne van Gennip.

Yvonnes particularly enjoy and are successful at cycling, like English 3000-meter pursuit world champion Yvonne McGregor and versatile Yvonne Reynders, who raced to four gold medals, two silvers, and a bronze at Road World Championships and three golds and three silvers at Track World Championships.

If you name your daughter Yvonne don't be surprised if she really likes to go fast, maybe even in unique ways! But if she doesn't, maybe martial arts will be more her style, like German Olympic gold-medalist judoka Yvonne Bönisch.

Yvonne Bönisch, Judo, Germany, 2003-2009

Yvonne McGregor, Road/Track Cycling, England, 1994-2001

Yvonne Murray, Track & Field (Middle-Distance Running), Scotland, 1981-1995

Yvonne Reynders, Road/Track Cycling, Belgium, 1958-1976

Yvonne Schuring, Sprint Canoeing, Austria, 2008-2015

Yvonne van Gennip, Speed Skating, Netherlands, 1983-1992

Yvonne van Vlerken, Triathlon, Netherlands, 2007-2009

Z

BOYS

ZAC/ZACH/ZACK

Typically short forms for names like *Zachary* and *Zackary* (or more unique things like *Zachariah*), Zac, Zach, and Zack are names that show up on a lot of teams, winning races, pennants, and more by being a strong part of a greater whole. We can find athletes with these names on the hardwood, in the pool, and on the baseball diamond with two-time NBA All-Star two-time Slam Dunk Contest-winning small forward/shooting guard Zach LaVine, who won Olympic gold with Team USA; freestyle relay gold medalist Zach Apple (2020 4x100-meter freestyle and 4x100-meter medley), who also won four world championships; and six-time All-Star pitcher Zach Greinke, who was the MLB ERA leader twice and won the AL Cy Young, six Gold Gloves, and two Silver Sluggers.

Football fans have cheered on three-time Pro Bowl tight end Zach Ertz, who won Super Bowl LII with the Philadelphia Eagles and holds the record for most receptions by a tight end in a single season (116); Dallas Cowboys eight-time Pro Bowl guard Zack Martin; and Miami Dolphins seven-time Pro Bowl middle linebacker Zach Thomas, who led the league in tackles twice, was named NFL Alumni Linebacker of the Year twice, and was inducted into the Pro Football Hall of Fame. Even international football fans have cheered on a Zack: MLS Goalkeeper of the Year, MLS All-Star, and MLS Best XI goalkeeper Zack Steffen, who won the Premier League championship twice, EFL Cup, and CONCACAF Nations League championships.

These are great sports to introduce to a little Zac, Zach, or Zack if he is a natural team player and works well with others.

- **Zachary "Zach" Apple**, Swimming (Freestyle), USA, 2017–2022
- **Zachary "Zach" Ertz**, Football (Tight End), Philadelphia Eagles, USA, 2013–current
- **Donald Zackary "Zack" Greinke**, Baseball (Pitcher), Kansas City Royals, USA, 2004–current
- **Zachary "Zach" LaVine**, Basketball (Small Forward/Shooting Guard), Chicago Bulls, USA, 2014–current
- **Zachary "Zack" Martin**, Football (Guard), Dallas Cowboys, USA, 2014–current
- **Zackary "Zack" Steffen**, Soccer (Goalkeeper), Columbus Crew, USA, 2015–current
- **Zachary "Zach" Thomas**, Football (Middle Linebacker), Miami Dolphins, USA, 1996–2009

ZBIGNIEW

The best athletes are those who can manage their emotions and stay calm in the face of adversity, which is a perfect ideal for a competitive boy named Zbigniew! You may not have heard that name before, but it's quite popular in Poland and comes from Slavic roots meaning "to dispel anger." Multiple people have elevated this name to glory in everything from speed skating (like Olympic gold- and bronze-medalist Zbigniew Bródka) to weightlifting (like two-time lightweight world champion Zbigniew Kaczmarek), glider piloting (like two-time 18-meter Class world champion Zbigniew Nieradka), and chess (like Grandmaster Zbigniew Pakleza).

The 1976 Olympic Games gold-medalist volleyball team from Poland included not one but two members with this name, outside hitter Zbigniew Lubiejewski, who won three Polish Cups and three Polish Championships closer to home, and middle blocker Zbigniew Zarzycki, who won a world championship, the CEV European Champions Cup, and two Polish Championships.

Give your son a competitive prowess applicable to any sport or event—as well as an innate ability to manage his anger—with the name Zbigniew!

Zbigniew Bródka, Speed Skating, Poland, 2006–current

Zbigniew Kaczmarek, Weightlifting, Poland, 1970–1980

Zbigniew Lubiejewski, Volleyball (Outside Hitter), Poland, 1969–1978

Zbigniew Nieradka, Aviation, Poland, 2006–2012

Zbigniew Pakleza, Chess, Poland, 2006–current

Zbigniew Zarzycki, Volleyball (Middle Blocker), Poland, 1968–1979

ZDENĚK/ZDENKO/ZDENO

Zdenko stands at the head of a family of names built off a Slavic root meaning "build" or "create," with variations like the Czech Zdeněk and Slovak Zdeno. Athletes with these names have had particular successes in canoeing events and soccer. Czech slalom canoeists Zdeněk Měšťan and Zdeněk Valenta both won world championship gold and several other medals in the 1960s, while sprint canoeist Zdeněk Škrland became an Olympic gold-medalist all the way back in 1936. Another Olympic gold medal was won by soccer defender Zdeněk Rygel in the 1980 Games.

Outside of the water and soccer fields, these names have been made famous in cycling with Czech three-time cyclo-cross world champion Zdeněk Štybar, chess with Croatian Grandmaster and 2006 European champion Zdenko Kožul, and ice hockey with Slovak six-time NHL All-Star defenseman (and—at six feet, nine inches—the tallest player ever in the NHL) Zdeno "Big Z" Chára, who won the Stanley Cup with the Boston Bruins and five All-Star Game SuperSkills Competition Hardest Shot contests and set multiple records, including the hardest shot in the NHL!

Any of these sports and competitive endeavors could be the favorite of a Zdeněk, Zdenko, or Zdeno in your family too; he'll find the best event to put his skills to good use and build a great future for himself.

Zdeno "Big Z" Chára, Ice Hockey (Defense), Boston Bruins, Slovakia, 1996–2022

Zdenko Kožul, Chess, Croatia, 1989–current

Zdeněk Měšťan, Slalom Canoeing, Czechoslovakia, 1965–1972

Zdeněk Rygel, Soccer (Defender), FC Baník Ostrava, Czechoslovakia, 1972–1986

Zdeněk Škrland, Sprint Canoeing, Czechoslovakia, 1936–1938

Zdeněk Štybar, Road Cycling/Cyclo-Cross, Czech Republic, 2006–current

Zdeněk Valenta, Slalom Canoeing, Czechoslovakia, 1961–1969

ZHIHAO/ZIHAO

Similar Chinese names, Zhihao and Zihao share some potential common elements depending on which characters are used to write them and can mean things like "will" or "ambition," "son," and "brave/heroic" or "chivalrous." What can you expect from a son who is given one of these names? Apparently excellent hand-eye coordination, good aim, and quick reflexes! This is borne out by competitors like world champion table tennis player Shi Zhihao, two-time Paralympic gold-medalist archer He Zihao, and esports legends like *Dota 2* player Chen Zhihao "Hao," whose 2014 The International championship with the Newbee eSports Club team set the record for the highest money prize ever in video games, and *League of Legends* mainstay Jian Zihao "Uzi," who won the 2018 Mid-Season Invitational championship and MVP, 2018 Rift Rivals championship, and two Pro League championships!

Chen Zhihao "Hao," Esports (*Dota 2*), China, 2011–2018

He Zihao, Archery, China, 2020–current

Jian Zihao "Uzi," Esports (*League of Legends*), China, 2012–2020

Shi Zhihao, Table Tennis, China, 1980–1981

ZHIYONG

The name Zhiyong can be written with characters meaning "wisdom/intellect," "extreme," "will/ambition" and "brave" or "perpetual/eternal." In the 2000s, Chinese weightlifter Shi Zhiyong had a great career, winning a gold medal at the 2004 Olympic Games and one at the 2005 World Championships. When Shi Lei appeared on the weightlifting scene a few years later, his coach recognized his potential and changed his name to Shi Zhiyong (after the former Olympic champion). The name change worked wonders and the second Shi Zhiyong has won two Olympic gold medals and three world championships while setting multiple world records!

The name Zhiyong will definitely imbue a son you give it to with strength and tenacity.

Shi Zhiyong, Weightlifting, China, 1999–2008

Shi Zhiyong, Weightlifting, China, 2012–current

ZINEDINE

From Arabic root words meaning "beauty of religion/faith" comes the traditional name *Zayn ad-Din* and its modern variant Zinedine.

Standing alone at the top of the charts, is iconic French attacking midfielder Zinedine Zidane, better known as "Zizou." Zizou established himself as one of all-time greats with dozens of trophies and nearly countless player awards. The multiple Hall of Famer's big wins include the La Liga championship, Supercoppa Italiana, Supercopa de España twice, UEFA Champions League, UEFA Super Cup twice, UEFA Intertoto Cup twice, Intercontinental Cup twice, UEFA European Championship, and, of course, the 1998 FIFA World Cup; his personal accolades include many regional awards, the FIFA World Cup Golden Ball, Onze de Bronze, Onze d'Argent three times, Onze d'Or three times, the coveted Ballon d'Or and being named FIFA XI four times, UEFA Club Midfielder of the Year, FIFA World Cup All-Star Team twice, World Soccer Awards Player of the Year, FIFA World Player of the Year three times, UEFA Club Footballer of the Year, FIFA World Cup Dream Team, and FIFA 100.

Name your son Zinedine and he's sure to enjoy running around and kicking balls with his friends on the field. You've even got a built-in nickname for him with "Zizou"!

Zinedine "Zizou" Zidane, Soccer (Attacking Midfielder), Real Madrid Club de Fútbol, France, 1989–2006

ZLATAN

The future is very bright for a boy in your family you name Zlatan, a name popular in Eastern Europe and which comes from a Slavic root for "gold" or "golden." He may also take a liking to sports that are more famous outside the United States, like handball and soccer! In that case, he can look up to people like Serbian Olympic gold-medalist and world champion handball goalkeeper Zlatan Arnautović.

Any boy named Zlatan who is the least bit interested in soccer will definitely learn about Swedish striker Zlatan Ibrahimović! Almost as infamous for his numerous altercations with other players and officials as he is famous for his skills and accomplishments on the field, Ibrahimović made history as one of the top strikers of all time with over 570 total goals scored in his career and a huge list of trophies, medals, and awards. These include the Supercopa de España twice, Ligue 1 championship four times, Coupe de France twice, Coupe de la Ligue three times, Trophée des Champions three times, UEFA Europa League, EFL Cup, FIFA Club World Cup, and UEFA Super Cup. His extensive list of awards is too long to include here, but features a Golden Foot and being named FIFA FIFPro World XI, UEFA Team of the Year four times, Serie A Footballer of the Year three times, Ligue 1 Player of the Year three times, Ligue 1 Top Scorer three times, Coupe de la Ligue Top Scorer, Coupe de France Top Scorer twice, MLS All-Star twice, and MLS Best XI twice.

Zlatan Arnautović, Handball (Goalkeeper), Yugoslavia, 1978–1989

Zlatan Ibrahimović, Soccer (Striker), Paris Saint-Germain Football Club, Sweden, 1999–2023

ZLATKO

If you're not sure about the name *Zlatan*, consider Zlatko! A diminutive of the above, Zlatko also means "golden" and carries with it the same predisposition for team sports, especially handball. Handball defenders like Serbian world champion center-back Zlatko Portner and Croatian Olympic gold-medalist and world champion right-back Zlatko Saračević each won a multitude of regional trophies to go along with their medals.

Zlatko Portner, Handball (Center-Back), Serbia, 1982–2003

Zlatan "Zlatko" Saračević, Handball (Right-Back), Croatia, 1977–2003

ZOLTAN/ZOLTÁN

A royal name for your little prince, Zoltan (with or without the accent over the "a") is a Hungarian and Slovak moniker that comes from a Turkish word meaning "king" or "sultan." Zoltans have many different skills, both mental and physical, as we can see in chess Grandmaster Varga Zoltán; swimmer Halmay Zoltán, who won three gold medals, five silvers, and a bronze in Olympic and Intercalated Games between 1900 and 1908; two-time Olympic gold-medalist and three-time world champion pommel horse gymnast Magyar Zoltán; and sprint canoeist Kammerer Zoltán, who won three gold medals each at Olympics and World Championships (as well as an Olympic silver and six World Championship silvers and six bronzes).

Which sport has seen more Zoltans reach the highest levels than others? Fencing has Ozoray Schenker Zoltán winning one medal of each color at the Olympics with sabre and foil, and sabre expert Horváth Zoltán collecting Olympic gold and silver and four golds, two silvers, and three bronzes from World Championships.

Set your son on a path to athletic victory and a princely future with the name Zoltan, and definitely introduce him to fencing (and maybe also gymnastics, canoeing, and chess)!

Halmay Zoltán, Swimming (Freestyle), Hungary, 1900–1908

Horváth Zoltán, Fencing (Sabre), Hungary, 1957–1966

Kammerer Zoltán, Sprint Canoeing, Hungary, 1997–2017

Magyar Zoltán, Artistic Gymnastics, Hungary, 1972–1980

Ozoray Schenker Zoltán, Fencing (Sabre/Foil), Hungary, 1912–1928

Varga Zoltán, Chess, Hungary, 1990–current

ZVONIMIR

If you want to ensure your son will always be last when lining up alphabetically, will be competitive but also seek world peace, and will undoubtedly enjoy playing soccer with his friends, then go with Zvonimir! The Slavic name is built from roots for "sound" or "chime" and "peace" or "world," and has been celebrated by fans of Serbian attacking midfielder Zvonimir Vukić (who won the First League of FR Yugoslavia championship twice, FR Yugoslavia Cup, Serbian SuperLiga twice, Serbian Cup, Ukrainian Premier League twice, Ukrainian Cup twice, and Ukrainian Super Cup), as well as two-time Croatian Footballer of the Year midfielder Zvonimir "Zvone" Boban (whose trophy collection includes the Serie A championship four times, Supercoppa Italiana three times, UEFA Champions League, and UEFA Super Cup).

Zvonimir "Zvone" Boban, Soccer (Midfielder), Associazione Calcio Milan, Croatia, 1985–2001

Zvonimir Vukić, Soccer (Attacking Midfielder), Fudbalski klub Partizan, Serbia and Montenegro, 1996–2015

GIRLS

ZAINAB

An Arabic name that most likely comes from a root word meaning "beauty" (or possibly a reference to a flowering tree or a variant on the name *Zenobia* meaning "life of Zeus"), Zainab can inspire a young girl in your family to play hard, run fast, and take out her opponents one by one until she achieves victory! In these respects, she can take after inspirational figures like Nigerian African Games gold-medalist mixed team badminton player Zainab Alabi; Syrian long-distance runner Zainab Bakkour, who raced to eight gold medals, five silvers, and a bronze at Arab Championships; and Swedish first-person shooter esports professional Zainab "zAAz" Turkie, who has won numerous major tournaments, including fifteen titles in *Counter-Strike: Global Offensive* alone!

Zainab Alabi, Badminton, Nigeria, 2019–current

Zainab Bakkour, Long-Distance Running, Syria, 1993–2004

Zainab "zAAz" Turkie, Esports (First-Person Shooters), Sweden, 2002–current

ZARA

Zara is an interesting name with a tangled knot of possible origins. There are multiple similar versions of it from around the world, including a Bulgarian diminutive of *Zaharina* (ultimately from the same Hebrew root meaning "God remembers" as *Zachariah*); the Arabic *Zahra*, meaning "shining," "brilliant," or "bright"; and *Zahrah*, which means "blooming flower." Whichever origin story you prefer, you can be confident in naming a daughter Zara to give her a love of traveling and making her mark on the world in interesting ways!

While the English bowler Zara Glover won three World Bowling Championship gold medals and two at World Tenpin Team Cup events, the other bearers of this name have ridden, surfed, and flown into the history books. British equestrian Zara Tindall won a gold medal in eventing and two silvers at World Championships, Belgian-British pilot Zara Rutherford became the youngest woman to fly a solo circumnavigation of the globe (and the first person ever to do it in a microlight aircraft), and English windsurfer Zara Davis set world speed records for the nautical mile and 500-meter, in addition to winning multiple speed world championships.

Zara Davis, Windsurfing, England, 1999–current

Zara Glover, Bowling, England, 2001–2007

Zara Rutherford, Aviation, Belgium/England, 2020–current

Zara Tindall, Equestrian (Eventing), England, 2003–current

ZDEŇKA

Grace, balance, and dedication to her team are qualities you can give to your daughter by naming her Zdeňka, a name that can come from Slavic roots for "build" and "glory." She'll build her own glory in any field or sport she chooses and will have a great source of inspiration in Czech artistic gymnast and balance beam specialist Zdeňka Veřmiřovská, who won Olympic gold and silver, and two golds and two silver medals at World Championships, including the team win at the very first women's event in 1934!

Zdeňka Veřmiřovská, Artistic Gymnastics, Czechoslovakia, 1934–1948

ZINAIDA

Some of the greatest names have origins that stretch back into antiquity, and such is the case with the traditionally Belarusian, Russian, and Ukrainian Zinaida, which ultimately comes from a reference to the Greek god Zeus. In modern times, Russians have elevated this name to international fame in athletics, specifically in the gymnasium, on the slopes, on city streets converted into racecourses, and on handball courts. Artistic gymnast Zinaida Voronina won a gold medal at Olympics and World Championships while setting a new bar for scoring over 9.900; cross-country skier Zinaida Amosova raced to Olympic gold and two world championships; Zinaida Semenova won the Dublin Marathon, Grandma's Marathon in Duluth, and the Twin Cities Marathon three times; and Zinaida Turchyna's long handball career included her winning two gold medals and a bronze at Olympic Games and two golds, two silvers, and a bronze at World Championships.

Give your daughter a name that draws power from the gods (and potentially a liking for skiing, running, gymnastics, or team sports) with the name Zinaida.

Zinaida Amosova, Cross-Country Skiing, USSR, 1976–1983

Zinaida Semenova, Long-Distance Running, Russia, 1998–2005

Zinaida Turchyna, Handball, USSR, 1973–1988

Zinaida Voronina, Artistic Gymnastics, USSR, 1966–1972

ZOE/ZOI

From an Ancient Greek root meaning "life" comes the name Zoe and its many variant forms, which have spread around the world but are most popular in English-speaking countries. Women with these names have achieved athletic glory in a few different places, with British Paralympic gold-medalist boccia player Zoe Robinson; Australian cricket all-rounder Zoe Goss, who won two World Cups with her national team; British-American freestyle skier Zoe Atkin, who won X Games gold on the superpipe; and snowboarder Zoi Sadowski-Synnott of New Zealand, who collected one medal of each color from the Olympics, two golds and three silvers at World Championships, and five golds, three silvers, and a bronze at X Games!

A Zoe or Zoi in your family will have a cool life, as well as a competitive nature that will draw her to find victory in her chosen field (which will likely be in winter sports).

Zoe Atkin, Freestyle Skiing, England, 2021-current

Zoe Goss, Cricket (All-Rounder), Western Australia Women Cricket Team, Australia, 1984-2006

Zoe Robinson, Boccia, England, 2008-2012

Zoi Sadowski-Synnott, Snowboarding, New Zealand, 2017-current

ZOLA

Runners often describe a state of serenity they find when going long distances. That's exactly where South African runner Zola Budd (whose name comes from a root meaning "calm" or "peaceful" in the Zulu Xhosa language) found her success! Budd won two World Cross Country Championships in the mid-1980s and set multiple world records, including the fastest mile that stood for thirty-eight years.

Give your daughter the gift of peace and the ability to go the distance with the name Zola.

Zola Budd, Long-Distance Running, South Africa, 1984-2015

ZSUZSANNA

The name Zsuzsanna (a Hungarian variant of *Susanna*, which comes from ancient roots and either Hebrew for "lily" or Egyptian for "lotus") is perfect for a little girl who will be strong, fast, and multi-talented. Hungarian elite athletes with this name have proven those qualities with Zsuzsanna "Zsu" Jakabos (who won more than twenty medals at European Championships in various swimming events, as well as two World Games gold medals in lifesaving) and modern pentathlete Zsuzsanna Vörös (who excelled at shooting, fencing, swimming, riding, and running, and won an Olympic gold medal and six golds, four silvers, and six bronzes at World Championships!).

Zsuzsanna "Zsu" Jakabos, Swimming (Freestyle/Butterfly/Medley)/Lifesaving, Hungary, 2004-current

Zsuzsanna Vörös, Track & Field (Pentathlon), Hungary, 1997-2009

ZULFIYA

Looking for a name that will give your daughter great strength and endurance, as well as a perfect head of hair? Then take a look at the Eastern European name Zulfiya that comes from a Perian root meaning "lock of hair," "tress," or "curl"! Though hair was probably the last thing on the minds of elite competitors like Russian Olympic gold-medalist and world champion road cyclist Zulfiya Zabirova and Kazakh three-time world champion weightlifter Zulfiya Chinshanlo.

Zulfiya Chinshanlo, Weightlifting, Kazakhstan, 2010-current

Zulfiya Zabirova, Road Cycling, Russia, 1995-2008

NON-BINARY

ALANA

Traditionally a feminine variant of *Alan*, Alana is a super cool name used by a pioneer in professional skateboarding. Non-binary athlete Alana Smith exploded onto the international scene in 2013, becoming the youngest person to medal in the X Games when they landed a 540 McTwist in the park event at only twelve years old! They've gone on to win at the World Cup of Skateboarding and participate in the 2020 Summer Olympics, becoming the first-ever openly non-binary competitor on that world stage.

Instill the same skill, grace, and drive to succeed in your child with the name Alana.

Alana Smith, Skateboarding, USA, 2013–current

DOMINIQUE

The unisex name Dominique is pretty prevalent among athletes, showing up with men and women (see their respective "D" sections), but it's also made a big splash in esports with the non-binary champion Dominique "SonicFox" McLean! A fighting game competitor, they have wins in multiple game franchises, in five Evolution Championship Series, and more. SonicFox is a dynamic and unique character (an openly gay, non-binary furry), whose incredible playing ability combined with their openness and willingness to stand up for themselves has earned them the Game Awards 2018 Esports Player of the Year, as well as a huge online following.

Dominique "SonicFox" McLean, Esports (Fighting Games), USA, 2012–current

MARIA

Most often used as a feminine name, Maria comes from the biblical Hebrew *Miryam* that may have originated from roots meaning "sea of bitterness," "rebelliousness," or "wished for child," or an Egyptian source meaning "love" or "beloved." Para-athlete Maria "Maz" Strong of Australia has really taken their last name to heart, overcoming adversity to become a successful athlete specializing in running and throwing sports; they won the inaugural 100-meter frame running event and a silver medal in shot put at the World Para Athletics Championships, as well as a bronze medal in shot put at the Paralympic Games!

The name Maria (and its awesome nickname Maz) can give a young athlete the strength not only to compete and win, but also to discover their innate skills and where best to apply them.

Maria "Maz" Strong, Para-Athletics, Australia, 2017–current

QUINN

The unisex name Quinn, from Old Irish and a root for either "sense"/"reason" or "chief," is perfect for anyone, especially a strong team player and someone brave enough to be who they truly are. That perfectly defines professional soccer player Quinn, the first openly trans and non-binary athlete to compete in and win a gold at the Olympics! They play on the Canada women's national soccer team, as well as in the National Women's Soccer League, and their trophy collection includes a NWSL Shield, The Women's Cup, Four Nations Tournament, Algarve Cup, Olympic bronze and gold medals, and a CONCACAF Awards Best XI selection.

Quinn can be an inspiring athletic hero for anyone sharing their name, of any gender or age!

Quinn, Soccer (Midfielder), OL Reign, Canada, 2013–current

ROBYN

The unisex name Robyn (from Germanic roots meaning "bright fame") is great for anyone who wants to improve themselves, work hard, and compete and is perfect for someone who will stand out from the crowd and make a mark on the world. In 2020, Australian wheelchair racer Robyn Lambird became the first openly non-binary athlete to win a medal at Paralympic Games when they scored bronze in an intense 100-meter sprint.

Robyn Lambird, Para-Athletics, Australia, 2016–current

TIMOTHY

Timothy is a name that stretches all the way back to Ancient Greek and comes from root words meaning "honoring god." Alongside their partner Ashley Cain, American pairs skater Timothy LeDuc won gold and bronze medals at World Team Trophy events. In their career, they became the first openly gay skater to become the US pairs champion and the first openly non-binary athlete in any sport to qualify for the Winter Olympics!

The name Timothy can impart agility, artistry, and athleticism to any child and future champion.

Timothy LeDuc, Figure Skating, USA, 2002–2022

AUTHOR BIO

Scott Rubin is a geek, toy collector/reviewer, husband, and father. He's been to Dodgers and Angels games in his native Los Angeles, watched the Orioles play in spring training in Sarasota, and played in the UCLA marching band, which gave him an appreciation for football at the Rose Bowl and on the road. Scott's interests have varied, and at times he's been a fan of NASCAR, MMA, and more.

At UCLA, Scott fell in love with everything Ancient Greek and Roman, and he went from a Classics major to a graduate degree focusing on Latin from UCSB. That education gave him an appreciation of etymology and the study of names, which was a big help in writing this book and its predecessor, *Naming Your Little Geek*. He strongly believes baby-naming books should be fun and thematic!

When he isn't researching names and athletes, Scott can typically be found streaming on Twitch or attending a geek convention near you. He lives in Southern California with his wife, two sons, and two cats.

ACKNOWLEDGMENTS

This book is the culmination of years of work, and I couldn't be prouder to put it out into the world. I haven't always been the biggest sports fan, but I sure love research and tackled this project with all of my energy. I learned a whole lot about many different sports and events along the way too!

Huge thanks go out to my family, my friends, and everyone who supports me in any way. And I have to give a special shout out to my parents who patiently watched me struggle at T-ball, taught me good sportsmanship even when you're losing, and showed me that the best part of attending sports events is the array of food and snacks!

I am forever grateful to Elaine Spencer at the Knight Agency and Christopher Robbins at Familius who helped put this book together, as well as the whole team at Familius for all of their hard work, especially my rock-star editor, Peg Sandkam.

Last but not least, this book could not exist without the talent, skill, and determination of athletes all around the world!

ABOUT FAMILIUS

VISIT OUR WEBSITE: WWW.FAMILIUS.COM

Familius is a global trade publishing company that publishes books and other content to help families be happy. We believe that happy families are key to a better society and the foundation of a happy life. The greatest work anyone will ever do will be within the walls of his or her own home. And we don't mean vacuuming! We recognize that every family looks different and passionately believe in helping all families find greater joy, whatever their situation. To that end, we publish beautiful books that help families live our 10 Habits of Happy Family Life: *love together, play together, learn together, work together, talk together, heal together, read together, eat together, give together,* and *laugh together*. Further, Familius does not discriminate on the basis of race, color, religion, gender, age, nationality, disability, caste, or sexual orientation in any of its activities or operations. Founded in 2012, Familius is located in Sanger, California.

CONNECT

Facebook: www.facebook.com/familiusbooks

Pinterest: www.pinterest.com/familiusbooks

Instagram: @FamiliusBooks

TikTok: @FamiliusBooks

THE MOST IMPORTANT WORK YOU EVER DO WILL BE WITHIN THE WALLS OF YOUR OWN HOME.